VIRGINIA WOOLF

A BIOGRAPHY

Also by Quentin Bell

On Human Finery
1947

The Schools of Design
1963

Ruskin
1963

Victorian Artists
1967

Bloomsbury
1968

The Brandon Papers
1985

Quentin Bell is a painter, sculptor, potter, writer, art critic, and teacher. He has been a lecturer in art education at King's College, Newcastle, and Professor of Fine Art at the University of Leeds and Oxford University. He has held the Chair of History and Theory of Art at the University of Sussex since 1967.

Mr. Bell once recalled: "Virginia Woolf was my aunt and as a child I illustrated and to some extent inspired some rather fanciful biographies of her friends and relations, hence the fact that I am mentioned in the preface of *Orlando* as 'an old and valued collaborator in fiction.'"

VIRGINIA WOOLF
A BIOGRAPHY

BY QUENTIN BELL

QUALITY PAPERBACK BOOK CLUB
NEW YORK

For
OLIVIER

CONTENTS

Volume I

Foreword	xv
Family Tree	xviii–xix
ONE 1882	1
TWO 1882–1895	22
THREE 1895–1897	40
FOUR 1897–1904	58
FIVE 1904–1906	87
SIX 1906–1908	112
SEVEN 1908–1909	128
EIGHT 1909	141
NINE 1910–June 1912	157
APPENDIX A Chronology	189
APPENDIX B Report on Teaching at Morley College	202
APPENDIX C Virginia Woolf and the Authors of *Euphrosyne*	205
APPENDIX D Clive Bell and the Writing of *The Voyage Out*	207
APPENDIX E The Dreadnought Hoax	213

Volume II

ONE
1912–1915   1

TWO
1915–1918   28

THREE
November 1918–December 1922   63

FOUR
1923–1925   89

FIVE
June 1925–December 1928   109

SIX
1929–1931   141

SEVEN
1932–1934   165

EIGHT
1934–1936   180

NINE
November 1936–September 1939   197

TEN
1939–1941   211

APPENDIX A
Chronology   227

APPENDIX B
Fantasy upon a Gentleman . . .   253

APPENDIX C
Virginia Woolf and Julian Bell   255

A Note on Sources and References   260

References   262

A Short Bibliography   282

Index   285

xii

LIST OF ILLUSTRATIONS

Pen-and-ink drawings in Volume I

Virginia and Vanessa skating by Vanessa, 1897, p. 49
Virginia by Duncan Grant, 1910, p. 156

Virginia Stephen, 1903
Mrs Leslie Stephen with Virginia, 1884
Sir Leslie Stephen, 1902
Virginia and Vanessa, 1894
Vanessa, Stella, and Virginia, c. 1896
Vanessa Stephen
Thoby Stephen
George Duckworth
Stella Duckworth
Adrian and Virginia, 1900
Violet Dickinson and Virginia, 1902
Clive Bell, c. 1906
The Emperor of Abyssinia and his suite
Virginia with Clive and Julian Bell, 1910
Virginia Woolf by Stephen Tomlin, 1931
Adrian Stephen
Virginia Stephen by Vanessa Stephen
Virginia and Leonard Woolf, 1914
Vanessa, 1914
Virginia walking in Cornwall, 1916
Duncan Grant, Maynard Keynes, and Clive Bell, 1919
Virginia, c. 1925
V. Sackville-West, 1900
Katherine Mansfield, 1920
Lady Ottoline Morrell by Simon Bussy

Lytton Strachey and Virginia
Julian Bell, 1932
Leonard and Virginia, 1928
Roger Fry, Desmond MacCarthy, and Clive Bell, 1933
Carrington, Ralph Partridge, and Lytton Strachey, 1930
Virginia with John Lehmann, c. 1931
Virginia with Ethel Smyth, 1932
Virginia with Angelica Bell, 1934
Virginia Woolf

FOREWORD

The purpose of the present volume is purely historical; and although I hope that I may assist those who attempt to explain and to assess the writing of Virginia Woolf, I can do so only by presenting facts which hitherto have not been generally known and by providing what will, I hope, be a clear and truthful account of the character and personal development of my subject. In no other way can I contribute to literary criticism. Even if I had the equipment for such a task I should not have the inclination; I have found the work of the biographer sufficiently difficult without adventuring in other directions and indeed the business of gathering and presenting the facts would hardly have been completed without help.

In the next volume I thank all my benefactors, but at the outset there are a few who must be mentioned.

The late Leonard Woolf persuaded me to attempt this work and helped me greatly when I was preparing the first draft of the present volume. The University of Leeds was willing to give me a sabbatical year in which to start my research, the University of Sussex actually gave it. A Leverhulme Research Award enabled me to use my time profitably. Mrs Ian Parsons has been most helpful and kind in every way; my wife has undertaken the arduous task of research assistant and the thankless role of critic. I wish that this book were worthy of their generosity.

❍   ❍   ❍

In writing this volume I have drawn to a very large extent upon unpublished material. I list here the most important collections, giving an indication of their content and of the abbreviations I have used. I have provided footnotes only when they seem to be of general interest; detailed references to sources will be given in Volume II together with a selective bibliography.

BERG COLLECTION. The New York Public Library, Astor, Lenox and Tilden Foundations; the Henry W. and Albert A. Berg Collection of English and American Literature.

In 1957 Leonard Woolf made an arrangement whereby the 27 manuscript volumes of Virginia Woolf's diaries (1915–1941) would become the property of the Berg Collection after his death. (These diaries are referred to as *AWD(Berg)*; the selection from them published by Leonard Woolf in 1953 as *A Writer's Diary* is abbreviated to *AWD*). The Berg Collection was thus able to become the nucleus of a Virginia Woolf archive and could acquire, both from Leonard Woolf and from other sources, a very considerable quantity of material of biographical and of literary interest. It includes eight early notebook diaries (which are referred to by short descriptive titles followed by *(Berg)*); and, among its collection of autograph letters, four important series from Virginia Stephen/Woolf: to her sister Vanessa Bell, to Violet Dickinson, to Vita Sackville-West, and to Ethel Smyth. For reference purposes I have abbreviated these names to initials, using always the married surnames of Virginia and Vanessa Stephen, viz: *VW* and *VB*.

The building of the Virginia Woolf archive in the Berg Collection was the particular care of the late Dr John Gordan, to whom I owe a debt of gratitude; my correspondence and my meetings with his successor Mrs Lola Szladits has been the most agreeable of necessities.

CHARLESTON PAPERS. King's College, Cambridge.

Letters and other papers of Clive Bell, Vanessa Bell and Duncan Grant, on deposit in the College Library, including the correspondence between Vanessa Bell and Roger Fry. I have used the initials *CB*, *VB*, *DG* and *RF* and the abbreviation *CH* (Charleston Papers) where appropriate.

The care of these documents has I fear added to the heavy burdens carried with such enviable competence, wisdom and good humour by Dr A. N. L. Munby, the Librarian.

MONK'S HOUSE PAPERS. The Estate of the late Leonard Woolf.

The papers which Leonard Woolf made available to me for the purposes of this biography comprise not only a great number of letters to and from his wife and himself, but also a considerable quantity of manuscripts. These I have loosely divided into manuscripts with a biographical interest (MH/A) and manuscripts of mainly literary interest (MH/B), and numbered.

I have also been able, through the kindness of his executrix, to make use of Leonard Woolf's own laconic but trustworthy diaries.

FOREWORD

There remain in the possession of the heirs and descendants of Sir Leslie Stephen the following sources of information which relate to Virginia Woolf and her family:

The 'Mausoleum Book' (*MBk*), written by Leslie Stephen after the death of his wife Julia in 1895.

Old family letters chiefly to or from Mrs Leslie Stephen and her children.

Two binders containing copies of the *Hyde Park Gate News* (*HPGN*) for 1891, 1892 and 1895.

Six manuscript memoirs by Vanessa Bell (*VB/MS I–VI*).

Letters from Virginia Woolf to Clive, Julian and Quentin Bell.

Minutes of the Play Reading Society, 1908–9 and 1914–15.

I am grateful to my sister Mrs David Garnett and my cousins Mrs Richard Synge and Mrs Nigel Henderson for their willingness to allow me to quote from these documents.

In addition I have consulted material in the possession of Mr Mark Arnold-Forster, Mrs Barbara Bagenal, the Marquess of Bath, the British Broadcasting Corporation, Mr Duncan Grant, Harvard University (the Houghton Library), Lord Kennet, Mr Nigel Nicolson, Mrs James Strachey, Professor John Waterlow and Mr David Garnett, whose copy of Adrian Stephen's diary I have been able to use; I cannot trace the original. To all these I am indebted for their help and consideration and for permission to quote where I have wished to do so.

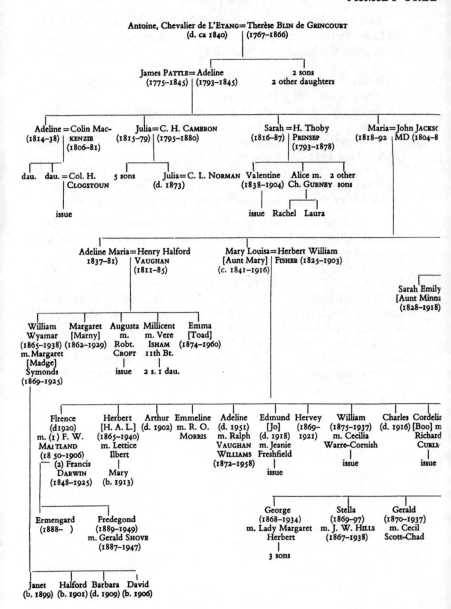

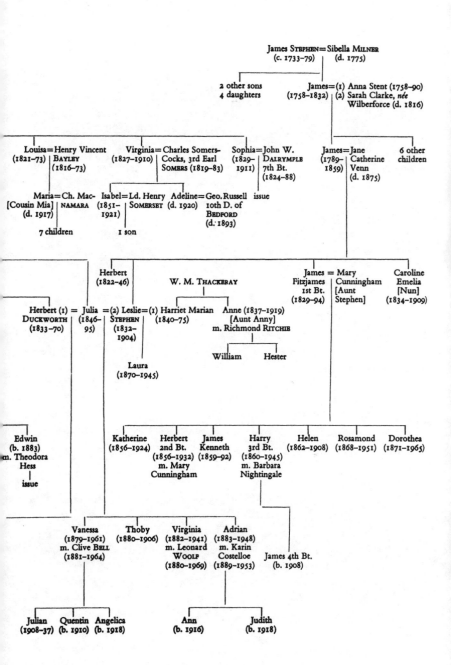

VOLUME I

Virginia Stephen

1882-1912

Chapter One

1882

VIRGINIA Woolf was a Miss Stephen. The Stephens emerge from obscurity in the middle of the eighteenth century. They were farmers, merchants and receivers of contraband goods in Aberdeenshire. Of James Stephen of Ardenbraught practically nothing is known save that he died about 1750, leaving seven sons and two daughters. Following the tradition of their race most of the sons wandered abroad to seek their fortunes. One, William Stephen, settled in the West Indies and prospered in the unpleasant trade of buying sickly slaves and then curing them sufficiently to make them fit for the market. Another, James, trained as a lawyer, became a merchant and was shipwrecked on the Dorset coast. A man of Herculean stature, he saved himself and four companions by the aid of his own exertions and a keg of brandy. It was dark, a tempest was raging; but they scaled a seemingly impossible precipice where "a cat could hardly have been expected to get up" and found themselves upon the Isle of Purbeck. Here James was first succoured and then entertained by Mr Milner, the Collector of Customs; he managed matters so well that he was able to secure not only much of the cargo of the vessel, but also the heart of Miss Sibella Milner, whom he secretly married.

The married life of Mr and Mrs James Stephen was not fortunate. He failed in business, fell into debt and presently found himself in the King's Bench Prison. In this predicament James Stephen reacted in a manner which was to set an example to his descendants. He took up his pen and argued his case. He was (so far as I know) the first of the Stephens to write a book and from that time on there was scarcely a one who did not publish and never, certainly, a generation which did not add something to the literary achievements of the family.

James Stephen also started a family tradition by carrying his argument to the courts. In fact, he went further and organised an agitation in the prison which nearly ended in an insurrection.

Imprisonment for debt was, he declared, a barbarous thing and moreover a thing repugnant to the spirit of the common law, to

I

Magna Carta, to statute law, justice, humanity and policy. These were things worth saying, but so far as he was concerned they had no practical effect and, in the end, he owed his release to his creditor. Stephen's legal and political battles had convinced him that his talents lay in the direction of advocacy rather than of commerce. He entered the Middle Temple, but the British Themis, who was to welcome so many of his descendants, rejected him. His protests had made him too many enemies and he was debarred by reason of his "want of birth, want of fortune, want of education and want of temper."

But there was a back door to the legal profession and by this Stephen made his entry. He became the partner of a solicitor under whose name he could carry on his business. It was not, however, a business which could bring him much credit. His clients were of a dubious kind. His work was done in public houses; it brought him little reputation and less money. His poor wife. who believed that these misfortunes were sent by the Almighty to punish her for having consented to a secret marriage, died in 1775. He followed her four years later. He was only forty-six; he left six children and about enough money to pay his debts.

James, the second of these six children, whom we may for convenience call "Master James," is the one who most concerns us. Brought up in an atmosphere of penury and litigation, he proved very much his father's son. He too was a writer of pamphlets and a pleader of causes; but whereas his father had been concerned with his own affairs, Master James used his argumentative talents for greater purposes. In the interests of patriotism and humanity he was to champion the cause of freedom and to start a war between two great nations.

His first campaign, however, was very much in the parental tradition. With little formal education James made his way to, entered, and despite ill-health pursued his studies at the Marischal College, Aberdeen. He read what was then called Natural Philosophy (i.e. science) and not without success; but he then found his way barred by an examination which was conducted in Latin. In this he knew that he would inevitably be failed and, what was even worse, be made to look ridiculous (he was a very sensitive man).

> What then was to be done? It may be thought an extraordinary thing that a youth of seventeen should have the boldness to conceive, and the dexterity to accomplish, a plan for covering his own defects, and saving his credit, by innovating on the established practice of an antient University. Yet this I conceived and effected.

In other words he had the regulations changed to suit his needs.

The passage here quoted is from the *Memoirs of James Stephen* written by himself for the use of his children. It is an interesting document made more entertaining by a certain vein of complacency in the author. Stephen felt able to congratulate himself on this and other triumphs, on the exertions which enabled him to surmount very serious disabilities and yet become a Member of Parliament, a Master in Chancery and a very respected member of society, because he could ascribe the glory of the business to a Higher Power.

God answered his prayers, God watched over his interests, God guided his footsteps. There are moments when the relationship between James Stephen and his Maker seems almost conspiratorial. He put his trust in Providence with such perfect simplicity that, while paying his addresses to one young woman, he got another with child. Nor was this confidence misplaced. Between them they managed matters in the most satisfactory way. He married the one and the other found a husband. Their bastard son became a most respectable clergyman.

As a public man Master James became identified with two great causes. Both resulted from a sojourn in the West Indies. Here there was already a family connection begun by his uncle William; here Stephen practised as a lawyer and here he saw how easily the British blockade was being broken by French and American traders. He who, in his youth, had been a zealous partisan of George Washington, was indignant. He was moved to write a pamphlet entitled *War in Disguise*, a pamphlet which resulted in the Orders in Council, the Continental Blockade and, much to Stephen's chagrin and astonishment, the War of 1812.

But from his first arrival in the Western Hemisphere, James had been dedicated to another and nobler cause. He first realised the infamy of slavery when he saw how monstrously a Negro might be treated by the West Indian Courts. Having once perceived the iniquity of the thing he made himself a restless and consistent friend of the oppressed. On his return to England he became the trusted ally of Wilberforce, whose sister he married after his first wife's death. In the House of Commons, when he was not defending the Orders in Council, he was attacking slavery; it was the refusal of the Government to act on this question which led to his withdrawal from Parliament.

There was, in the neighbourhood of Clapham, a group of friends: prosperous and worthy men marked by a certain decent godliness, a fair degree of wealth, an ardent concern for the enlightenment of the heathen and the liberation of the slave. Amongst them were Charles Grant and Zachary Macaulay, John and Henry Thornton, John Shore (later Lord Teignmouth), Granville Sharp, William Wilberforce, John and Henry Venn–respectively rector and curate of Clapham; these were the so-called 'saints' of the Clapham Sect. James was drawn to this evangelical society not so much by his religious views–although he certainly took the spiritual colour of his surroundings–as by his political opinions. But in general the Clapham Sect was concerned with works rather than with faith, with policies rather than with parties. The abolition, first of the slave trade, and then of slavery itself, was its grand motive. It was therefore compelled to fight for its beliefs at the hustings and in the House of Commons. Its leaders were not divines but politically conscious members of the middle classes, men therefore who knew that, to attain their ends, they must collaborate with persons whose humanitarianism had a different origin from theirs. Tories and Anglicans, they found themselves allied to Radicals, to Quakers and to the followers of Bentham–men who in other connections were their antagonists–while Pitt, the intimate friend and political ally of Wilberforce, had sometimes to be their enemy. In the great work of committee-making, pamphlet-writing and public agitation these sincere, eloquent and influential men had, therefore, to learn the political lessons of tolerance and compromise. Thus the Christianity of Stephen and his Clapham friends, ardent though it was, never attained the dogmatic certainty, the super-mundane, persecuting passion of some other sects.

The Clapham Evangelicals must have felt themselves to be, as indeed they were, the conscience of the British middle classes and therefore an enormous political power. For this reason, if for no other, they were concerned above all with moral questions and when, in later generations, the eschatological superstructure of their faith collapsed, the moral fabric remained. This persistence of the moral, as opposed to the theological, element in the beliefs of their great-grandparents was to have a very important effect upon a later generation.

Master James died in 1832, just before the final abolition of slavery in the British Empire. His legitimate sons all became lawyers; it was indeed a decidedly forensic family. The third son, yet another James, must have shown considerable talent at the Bar (they all did), for he was soon earning £3,000 a year–a very handsome income in those days. He moved, sacrificing much of his income, to a permanent position in the Colonial Office. His reason for doing this was clear enough. It was as an administrator that he could best carry on the great family campaign against slavery. He was known in Whitehall as 'Mr Over-Secretary Stephen,' for he was not simply one of those civil servants who gently but firmly override the wishes of those ministers who, nominally, are set above them. He was a civil servant with a policy; in fact it was more than a policy, it was a mission, which had to be imposed, willy-nilly, upon the Colonial Office, the Colonies themselves and whatever Government happened to be in power.

That policy was, of course, the policy of Emancipation, for although other matters, such as the grant of self-government to Canada, occupied some of his time, the protection of the Negro was the grand business of his administration. To oppose, to delay, to nullify and to thwart that policy was the aim of the Colonies themselves, by which, of course, I mean the ruling white minority in the Colonies. The colonists, as always, were ably assisted by influential friends in London. These had to be outwitted, argued down, browbeaten, and Mr Over-Secretary Stephen was the man to do it.

Sir James Stephen, as he eventually became, was a courageous, intelligent and capable administrator. He was also, as he himself admitted, anything but a simple man. He inherited all the boldness of his father and his grandfather; he was formidable and implacable, driving others almost as hard as he drove himself, working long hours in the Colonial Office and making others work equally hard, still finding time for numerous contributions to the *Edinburgh Review*, dictating 3,000 words before breakfast. A monster of industry and learning, he was also a vulnerable and an unhappy man. His achievement fell far short of his ideals. He was blamed for measures that he had opposed as well as for those which he had favoured; he felt such criticism deeply, all the more so because, as a civil servant, he could not reply to it. He was desperately shy, he was intensely pessimistic. He was so convinced of his own personal ugliness that he would not have a mirror in his room. He would shut his eyes rather than face an interlocutor. He wished he had been a clergyman, a recluse, anything but what he was. He was terrified of being comfortable and although he would not deny pleasure to others he was anxious to deny himself. Once he tasted a cigar and liked it so much that he resolved never to taste another. It occurred to him that he liked taking snuff–immediately he emptied his snuff box out of the window.

"Did you ever know your father do a thing because it was pleasant?" asked Lady Stephen of her son Fitzjames. "Yes, once, when he married you" was the prompt reply of yet another brilliantly argumentative Stephen.

But James Stephen's marriage was not simply pleasant—it was in the highest degree prudent. In marrying Jane Catherine Venn, Stephen allied himself completely with Clapham, for the Venns were, so to speak, at the very heart of the Sect. The Venns had always been clergymen; they receded in an unbroken succession of pastors to that time at which it first became respectable to have a priest as an ancestor; their connection with Clapham Rectory was a long one, and it was Jane Venn's grandfather's *Compleat Duty of Man* which provided the Clapham doctrine, if one may here speak of a doctrine.

It might be supposed that the daughter of an evangelical parsonage would hardly be the person to discourage Stephen's natural inclination to gloom and to self-mortification. But the Saints of Clapham were not in favour of immoderate austerities and the Venns, in particular, were a cheerful commonsensical race who loved to crack a joke and saw no harm in innocent pleasures. There was something a little mad in Stephen's self-mortification; Jane Catherine Venn was as sane a woman as ever breathed. She was also a handsome, amiable person with a strong disposition to look always on the happiest side of any matter. She provided her husband with a home in which he could forget the agonies of public life. It was, by modern standards, rigidly puritanical; their children were to go neither to balls nor to theatres—but neither might they condemn those who enjoyed such amusements; it was for them a sober but a happy place, lightened by the benevolence of their father and by their mother's laughter.

One thing more must be said about the household of Sir James Stephen. It respected art, by which I mean literary art (painting and music were, I surmise, neglected). Lady Stephen admired Cowper and Wordsworth, Scott and Campbell. Sir James turned to more serious and more edifying writers, but he could also appreciate Voltaire and Montaigne; his friends, who were not numerous, included J. S. Mill, the Venns, the Diceys, the Garratts, a serious and enlightened company.

Sir James had five children—one died in infancy, one in early manhood; but the other three survived and were to be of importance to the children of the next generation. They were: James Fitzjames, Caroline Emelia and Leslie, the father of Virginia.

Caroline Emelia will reappear in this story; she was an intelligent woman who fell, nevertheless, into the role of the imbecile Victorian

6

female. She fell in love with a student and had some reason to suppose that her affection was returned; but the young man never declared his feelings. He went to India and nothing more was heard of him. Her heart was broken and her health was ruined; at the age of twenty-three she settled down to become an invalid and an old maid. She lost her faith and set herself with great diligence to find another; after a number of experiments she discovered a congenial spiritual home in the Society of Friends.

Fitzjames, one may guess, smiled grimly at his sister's life of passive suffering and equable gentleness; but he would probably have allowed that a life devoted to religion and philanthropy was not unsuitable for a woman. He himself was, most emphatically, a man. His life had therefore to be more positive, more aggressive, more brutal. When he and Leslie went as day boys to Eton they were horribly bullied. He was ashamed of this always, for he felt that he had not resisted persecution stoutly enough. However, this humiliating acknowledgement of the superior strength of others came to an end at last. Fitzjames grew to be a big broad-shouldered fellow known to his playmates as 'Giant Grim' and well able to give blow for blow with anyone. He had, he said, learnt that: "to be weak is to be wretched, that the state of nature is a state of War and *Vae Victis* the great law of Nature."

His younger brother, Leslie, was a nervous, delicate boy, his mother's darling, fond of and over-excited by poetry, too sensitive to be able to endure an unhappy ending to a story. At school he needed all the protection that Fitzjames could give him and thus I see them: the tough, self-reliant, no-nonsense Fitzjames, shouldering his way through the horrors of a British public school with a frightened, delicate junior in tow. At Cambridge too, it was Fitzjames who led the way, who became known in the Union as the 'British Lion,' a roaring, crushing, rampageous debater, packing a cruel punch in argument, chosen for the brightness of his intellect and his manifest intellectual integrity as a member of that arch-intellectual society, the 'Apostles,' while Leslie, altogether gentler, more diffident, less brilliant, was never an Apostle and never emerged from the main rank of undergraduates.

It must have been clear to everyone that the elder brother would make a name for himself, would be called to the Bar, would become a judge and a baronet—as indeed he did; while Leslie would become a clergyman and sink gently into decent obscurity—as he might have done. All his life Leslie was, I think, matching himself against his all too admirable sibling. Fitzjames was physically strong; he too would make himself strong. Like Fitzjames he would walk for miles; but he would do more, he would run, he would row, he would scale mountains, and in fact he became, as he, in his self-deprecating way, put it, "wiry." He was in fact a famous walker, an oarsman, a coach of oarsmen, one of the great mountaineers of the nineteenth century. In the same way he adopted, I think, some of Fitzjames's robust habits of thought. He became half a philistine, almost anti-intellectual. He followed Bentham and J. S. Mill; he was "Broad Church," unsentimental and manly.

His nephews and nieces remembered Fitzjames in his later years as a powerful, bulky figure sternly buttoned into a frock coat conducting Lady Stephen to church every Sunday morning, there to pay his respects to a being in whom he had ceased to believe. "He has lost all hope of Paradise," declared the irreverent young, "but he clings to the wider hope of eternal damnation."

This was unjust; but it was true that, to him, evil seems to have been a much more real thing than goodness. His constant pre-occupation was with the vices that menaced society; he had no use for optimism, cant, gush, enthusiasm or–as it sometimes appears–for compassion. The engines of repression were to be ruthlessly employed; justice, though it must be administered with scrupulous fairness, demanded that punishments should be inflicted in a spirit of righteous vengeance. For all his scepticism he accepted the morality of his age with few reservations. He is as far from the genial libertinism of the eighteenth century as he is from its frivolity.

The same could be said of Leslie; the younger brother had the milder temper and the warmer heart; but this did not prevent him from sharing the same inhibitions and the same indignations or, it should be added, from displaying the same courageous intellectual integrity.

While Fitzjames went to London, the Bar and journalism, Leslie gained a Fellowship at Trinity Hall. At that time it was still necessary for a Fellow of Oxford or Cambridge to take Holy Orders. Leslie was ordained in 1859 and thereby committed to a set of propositions in which he did not really believe. It is indeed hard, in this sort of context, to know what we are to understand by the word 'belief.' It is difficult to imagine Leslie, at any period of his adult life, praying for rain in a drought or for fine weather during a wet spell, solemnly uttering the words:

> O Almighty Lord God, who for the sin of man didst once drown all the world, except eight persons, and afterwards of thy great mercy didst promise never to destroy it so again. . . .

It was in fact at this point that Leslie stuck. The year was 1862, he was thirty, he had become convinced that "Noah's Flood was a fiction" and that it was wrong for him to read the story as if it were sacred truth.

He had never been a zealot; he had preached the gospels as they were understood by F. D. Maurice and the Broad Church party, that is, in a spirit of reverential scepticism, and it would have been easy for him, as for so many others, to have paddled around Noah's Flood and never to have taken the plunge. Leslie had the courage to act resolutely in accordance with his convictions. He had a comfortable job at Cambridge but it involved telling what he now saw to be lies and this he refused to do.

At the same time it is possible that his loss of faith may have had unconscious motives. He had originally become a university teacher in order not to be a burden on his father; this involved, not only a profession of faith, but–for some years at all events–a celibate existence. After his father's death in 1859 he slowly realised, firstly that he was the most irreligious, then that he was the most uxorious of men. Gradually he discovered how much he longed for the outer world, how little he really had believed and how glad he was, now that his father could no longer be hurt by the avowal, to make his disbeliefs public.

To leave the security of Cambridge was a hazardous thing and he was, as he himself said, of a rather anxious temperament (this was an understatement), but he took the risk with an untroubled gaiety which, in later life, astonished him and came to London without money or prospects.*

In London, however, Fitzjames was ready to help him. Leslie was soon making a small but reputable name for himself in the Republic of Letters. He began as a journalist and an apologist for the Federal Cause in America, a cause which had few friends in this country. His sympathy for the Union led to a visit to the United States, to an interview with Lincoln and, more importantly, to a life-long friendship with James Russell Lowell, Charles Eliot Norton and Oliver Wendell Holmes. His politics were radical, very much inspired by his friend Fawcett; they were not, however, his main interest. He tended more and more towards philosophical speculation and literary criticism.

---

* MBk, p. 4. There is a passage in this work which can be construed in such a way as to suggest that an adventure of the heart altered the course of his life and diverted him from the celibacy and religion of Cambridge, to London, matrimony and agnosticism. But this is guesswork.

In 1882 he began, at the invitation of George Smith the publisher, to make one of the world's greatest instruments of scholarship: the *Dictionary of National Biography*; it is as the editor of that dictionary, as a literary critic and as an historian, that he is most gratefully remembered. He himself would rather have been remembered as a philosopher. His views were, to some extent, distorted by a morality which, though not as fierce as that of Fitzjames, was as narrow and as intolerant. It did not prevent him, however, from saying true, wise and amusing things about books and writers, or from taking a view of the world which is essentially honest, responsible and sane. Leslie Stephen's reputation has endured. Like Fitzjames he knew how to write a good forceful English, but there is more of intimacy, of delicacy, of humour and even of fantasy in the work of Leslie. In short he was more of an artist.

In the twenty years that followed Leslie's loss of faith he found himself as a writer and a thinker; he also found himself in another way. As we have seen, the escape from Cambridge was also an escape from the cloister; and although it took him some years to find a wife, when he at length did so he discovered that he was, in truth, a very domestic character. The wife whom he found was Harriet Marian, the younger daughter of Thackeray. She and Leslie fell in love and, after a rather awkward moment of hesitation and hanging back on his part, they were married.

We do not know much about the first Mrs Leslie Stephen. Her husband describes her as being neither very beautiful nor very clever; her nature was one of "quiet love"; she was amiable, gentle, simple with the simplicity of a child. Almost, one might guess from his account, a little dull, or at all events too childlike. And yet some of her letters have been preserved and from these it is evident that she had a sense of fun and was by no means deficient either in character or in intellectual curiosity. She seems, in fact, to have been a very proper wife for a highly intelligent man.

Certainly they were happy together, although their marriage encountered difficulties of a rather unusual kind. Until she found a husband the person whom Minny Thackeray loved best in the world was her sister Anny. In marrying the one sister Leslie discovered that he had, in a sense, married them both.

Now Anny was a more formidable, a more arresting personality than Minny. She was a novelist; her novels were tenuous, charming productions in which the narrative tended to get lost and in which something of her own vague, erratic, engaging personality is preserved. Minny considered that her sister was a genius; in this I suspect that she was mistaken, but she was a very talented person and one of her talents was for teasing. When Samuel Butler was at work upon *Shakespeare's Sonnets Rediscovered*, Anny bewildered him by remarking: "Oh Mr Butler, do you know my theory about the Sonnets–that they were written by Anne Hathaway?" Butler never realised that the joke was at his expense; he used to tell the story sadly shaking his head and exclaiming: "Poor lady, poor lady, that *was* a silly thing to say."★

At the age of seventy Aunt Anny, as she was called by all Leslie's children, could impress a child by her extraordinarily youthful, vigorous and resilient optimism; when she was young, not only in spirit but in years, her ebullience must have been overwhelming. It is not hard to believe that such cheerful impetuosity could sometimes be exasperating. Leslie found it so; he loved silence and she was for ever talking; he loved order, and she rejoiced in chaos; he prided himself on his realism, she was unashamedly sentimental; he worried about money, she was recklessly extravagant; he prized facts, she was hardly aware of them.†

> She and I had our little contentions. I had a perhaps rather pedantic mania for correcting her flights of imagination and checking her exuberant impulses. A[nny] and M[inny] used to call me the cold bath from my habit of drenching Anny's little schemes and fancies with chilling criticism.

But they were more seriously divided by the fact that between them there was a kind of undeclared war for possession of Minny. War is perhaps too strong a word, for the three were bound by strong ties of affection, and yet it was a sort of contest, a contest which lasted for several years until it began to turn decisively in Leslie's favour. For in time Minny came to the conclusion that her husband meant more to her than even her beloved sister. Perhaps she felt, as other women were to feel, how greatly Leslie depended upon her. At all events the marriage was eminently successful; it had been enriched by a daughter, Laura, born in 1870, and presently Minny was again pregnant. On the evening of 27 November 1875 she went to bed feeling slightly unwell. During the night Leslie was called to her.

★ Samuel Butler published *The Authoress of the Odyssey* in 1897. The story is recalled in *Night and Day* (p. 322); Mrs Hilbery in this novel is a pretty straight portrait of Aunt Anny. See also: Mary MacCarthy, *A Nineteenth-Century Childhood*, 1924, p. 89; and Hester Thackeray Fuller and Violet Hammersley, *Thackeray's Daughter*, Dublin, 1951, p. 7.

† "There are 40,000,000 unmarried women in London alone!" she once informed him. "Oh Anny, Anny!" See VW, *Collected Essays*, vol. IV, p. 77 ("Leslie Stephen").

I got up and found my darling in a convulsion. I fetched the doctor. I remember only too clearly the details of what followed; but I will not set them down. My darling never regained consciousness. She died about the middle of the day, 28 November, my 43^d birthday.

Leslie was shattered, heartbroken, and desolated. Anny, it is true, remained to take care of him and his daughter, but here a further blow was preparing. Laura was no longer a baby and it had already been evident to her mother that she was a backward child. In this period of bereavement it became increasingly obvious that she was not simply backward; there was something seriously wrong. Leslie began to suspect that Mrs Thackeray's madness had been inherited by her granddaughter. How bad her case might be it was too soon to tell; but clearly she would require special treatment. This domestic agony served to increase the tension between Leslie and Anny; Louise, the nurse, set herself against Anny's authority and Leslie took her side. The scenes which, while Minny was alive, had been held in check became more frequent and more painful.

And then, rather surprisingly, Anny fell in love with young Richmond Ritchie, her cousin, her godson and her junior by seventeen years. He returned her affection and the flirtation, which had been treated as nonsense, suddenly became the real thing. Leslie found Anny and Richmond kissing each other in the drawing room and insisted that they should either marry or part. Although the marriage turned out well, Leslie hated the whole business; he was, as he realised, jealous; the quasi-maternal situation of the bride also aroused feelings in him the nature of which he may not have understood, and of course he lost his housekeeper.

Anny's place was for a time taken by Leslie's sister; but if Anny had been too resilient a companion Caroline Emelia was altogether too flaccid.

> Now Milly has loved me all her life; she has been much more like a twin than a younger sister; . . . Yet, as I found myself saying at this time, she was too like me to be helpful. If I put an argument in order to have it contradicted, she took it so seriously that I thought there must be something in it; if I was in doubt, she fell into utter perplexity; if I was sad, she began to weep–a performance which always came too easily to her. Consequently though a most affectionate she was a most depressing companion. And then, the society which suited me would have struck her as worldly; while her friends, though very worthy & some of them very clever people, struck me as intolerably dull.

The plan was tried and needless to say it failed. Milly's health broke down almost at once and Leslie began to look for a professional housekeeper. The Huxleys recommended a Fraülein Klappert who had been a governess in their household. But there was another solution, one that Leslie had had in mind for some time and which was considerably more to his taste.

On the evening of 27 November, 1875, a few hours before Minny fell into those convulsions which were the prelude to her death, the Stephens had been visited by a close friend of the Thackeray sisters, Mrs Herbert Duckworth, a young widow. Feeling her own chronic grief as a kind of intrusion upon their happiness–for they still had a few hours of happiness–she had soon withdrawn to her own sad home. For her, after her husband's death in 1870, "all life seemed a shipwreck." Though left with three children, George, Stella and Gerald (a posthumous son), her despair was complete. But if she could no longer be happy she could at least be useful: she might comfort the afflicted and nurse the sick (in the 1870s her own relations seemed to sicken and to die in rather large numbers). She had, one might say, renounced the world, or at least she had renounced the happiness of the world, although this renunciation could hardly be called mystical, one of the consequences of her bereavement being a permanent loss of faith. It was this perhaps which enabled her to moderate her awe of Leslie Stephen the intellectual with a sympathetic interest in him as a man. After Minny's death it was almost a matter of course that she should comfort him, mediate between him and her own friend Anny, reproach him when he was unreasonable, and listen to his grievances with the affectionate patience of a sister. Between them there grew up a close friendship, but it was at once understood that it was to remain fraternal; each had a requiem candle to burn before the altar of the dead.

It is unnecessary to describe the process which led to Leslie's sudden *éclaircissement*, a revelation vouchsafed to him just outside Knightsbridge Barracks when he said to himself "I am in love with Julia!" and knew that he might again be happy, nor yet his gradual passage from the consciousness to the declaration of passion and hers from a kind, sad, but completely unqualified rejection, not so much of him, as of marriage, love, and happiness itself, to the faint adumbration of a tentative surrender. For at last, after much debate, she did find herself in a situation in which she was at least ready to contemplate the proposition that life might yet offer certain possibilities of felicity.

In the end it was Fraülein Klappert who settled the business. Both Leslie and Julia felt that her installation would bring about a definitive arrangement, setting the seal, as it were, upon their separation. There was, at all events, enough finality in the proposal to make Julia Duckworth aware of her own feelings; she realised that she could not break with Leslie. They were married on 26 March 1878.

O   O   O

I must now attempt to say something about Virginia's mother's family. Here there is a good deal of uncertainty, of legend, and of scandal.

According to Virginia's cousin H. A. L. Fisher, the historian, there was at the Court of Versailles during the last years of the old régime a certain Chevalier Antoine de l'Etang; his person was pleasing, his manners courtly, his tastes extravagant and his horsemanship admirable. He was attached to the household of Marie Antoinette—too much attached it is said, and for this he was exiled to Pondicherry where, in 1788, he married a Mlle Blin de Grincourt.

M de l'Etang entered and died in the service of the Nawab of Oudh; he left three daughters. Adeline, the one with whom we are concerned, married a James Pattle who was, we are told, a quite extravagantly wicked man. He was known as the greatest liar in India; he drank himself to death; he was packed off home in a cask of spirits, which cask, exploding, ejected his unbottled corpse before his widow's eyes, drove her out of her wits, set the ship on fire and left it stranded in the Hooghly.

The story has been told many times. Some parts of it may be true. It is certainly true that Mrs Pattle came to London in 1840 with a bevy of daughters and that these ladies had a reputation for beauty. Four of them should be mentioned in these pages: Virginia, Sarah, Julia and Maria.

Virginia Pattle, the most beautiful of the sisters, married Charles Somers-Cocks and became Countess Somers; she was a dashing, worldly woman, impulsive, rather eccentric, who lived in great style. Of her daughters, one became Duchess of Bedford; the other, Isabel, married Lord Henry Somerset. This alliance, though grand, was by no means happy. Lord Henry, a charming man it seems, delighted Victorian drawing rooms with his ballads. He was, I believe, the author of *One More Passionate Kiss;* this embrace was reserved, however, not for his beautiful wife but for the second footman. Lady Henry endured his infidelities for a time but presently she could stand no more. She confided in her mother who, allowing her indignation to master her prudence, made a public scandal. The sequel is interesting in as much as it gives a notion of the ethos of the Victorian age and of a system of morality which Virginia Woolf and her contemporaries were to encounter and to oppose.

Lord Henry fled to Italy and there, in that land of Michelangelesque young men, lived happily ever after. His wife discovered that she had been guilty of an unformulated, but very heinous, crime: her name was connected with a scandal. Good society would have nothing more to do with her. She was obliged to retire from the world and decided to devote herself to the reclamation of inebriate women, a task which she undertook with so much good sense and good humour that she won the affection and admiration, not only of men of charity and good will, but even of the women she assisted.

Sarah Pattle made her empire in a less fashionable but more interesting part of the world. She married Thoby Prinsep, an Anglo-Indian administrator of some eminence who was, until its dissolution, a member of the Council of the East India Company. The Prinseps settled outside London in an old farm house, Little Holland House, in what is now Melbury Road, Kensington; it was a pretty, rambling, comfortable sort of place and here, while her sister collected the aristocracy of birth, she entertained the aristocracy of intellect. Tennyson, Sir Henry Taylor, Thackeray and his daughters, William Allingham, Tom Hughes, Mr Gladstone, and Disraeli were *habitués*. They were able, at Little Holland House, to enjoy a respite from the formality, the regularity and the stuffiness of mid-Victorian society. Their hostess was both charming and eccentric. Meals were oddly timed and oddly disposed. There was something outlandishly charming, something free and easy about Little Holland House and to this ambience the painters must have made an important contribution. Chief amongst them was G. F. Watts; he was, for many years, a resident, Mrs Prinsep having 'taken him up' and established him in a studio. Holman Hunt, Burne-Jones and Woolner were very frequent visitors and so, it would seem, was Ruskin.*

But perhaps the most remarkable of the artists who frequented Little Holland House was Julia Margaret Cameron, the second of the Pattle sisters, the least beautiful but the most gifted. Like Sarah,

---

* Ruskin refers to Mrs Prinsep and her sister (probably Countess Somers) as "two, certainly, of the most beautiful women in a grand sense—(Elgin marbles with dark eyes)—that you could find in modern life . . ." The former he regarded as an old friend. See *The Winnington Letters of John Ruskin*, ed. Van Akin Burd, London, 1969, p. 149 (Ruskin to Margaret Bell, 3–4 April 1859; this letter contains a lively picture of an evening at Little Holland House).

Julia had married an Indian Civilian, like her she had a passion for artists and men of letters. It has been said of her that "she doubled the generosity of the most generous of her sisters, and the impulsiveness of the most impulsive. If they were enthusiastic, she was so twice over; if they were persuasive, she was invincible."

The inhabitants of Putney saw her–and we may justly envy them –talking and walking in flowing red velvet towards the Railway Station; in one hand a cup of tea, in the other a teaspoon, by her side an embarrassed friend who attempts, vainly, to decline the gift of a priceless Cashmere shawl. They saw in her an eccentric; we see in her an immortal, not one of the great immortals, but still an artist who has survived and will survive.

Not that she would ever have achieved immortality if, when she was fifty, her daughter had not given her a camera. She began at once to take photographs. It became her passion, her vocation. Beautiful women and distinguished men were obliged, for she was of an imperious nature, to sit for the long poses that were then necessary. Her friends and servants were disguised as angels and Arthurian heroes; they were draped, garlanded, muffled and photographed. A family legend persisted according to which Tennyson and Mr Gladstone were posed under a tree and forbidden to move while she sought some necessary implement of her mystery. While searching she was distracted by some other project and left the poet and the statesman immobile for two hours beneath a shower of rain.

Vague, silly and sentimental, Mrs Cameron had, nevertheless, a streak of pure genius. She needed a curb or a brake, something that would restrain her sentimentality. In her letters and, no doubt, in her unfinished novel she was unbridled–it was Sir Henry Taylor's nightmare that he would one day have to read that novel. But the nature of her art, an art which after all deals with facts, supplied a check; there were indeed occasions when she could find her way past fact to fancy with disastrous results but, when called upon to give the likeness of a sitter her disposition of forms, her choice of pose, her Venetian understanding of chiaroscuro, are miraculously subtle and strong and she does the kind of thing that Watts might have done had he been a greater artist. She is the best of the Victorian portraitists and has given us a worthy monument of the society in which she lived–a milieu, to quote Ellen Terry, "where only beautiful things were allowed to come."

Hither Maria Jackson, the fourth of the Pattle sisters, brought her three daughters, Adeline, Mary and Julia. Maria had married yet another Anglo-Indian, Dr Jackson; he had a flourishing practice in

Calcutta but he does not seem to have been a person of any distinction. In his wife's letters, at all events, he cuts practically no figure at all. It was her daughters who interested her; she loved them all, but principally, I think, Julia; or at least Julia, because she was so unhappy and because she devoted herself so much to her mother, became in the end her mother's dearest child. To her she wrote, once, twice, sometimes three times a day and often there would be an additional telegram to her "dear heart," her "lamb." Her grand topic was health, or rather maladies; she was not a doctor's wife for nothing. When, after her first husband's death, Julia became a kind of unofficial nurse, she reported symptoms to her mother who, with great assurance, diagnosed and recommended treatment. When there was not a sister, a niece, a cousin, a grandchild to fill her page with medical details, she had an unfailing store of her own afflictions: she suffered from headaches, rheumatism, giddiness and indigestion, which she treated with morphia and chloral. Second only to the question of how to preserve health was the question of beauty, and here too she was full of excellent advice. Only very rarely is one reminded, in all the voluminous correspondence between Mrs Jackson and her daughter, of the aesthetic and intellectual interests of Little Holland House. Reading her one feels as though one were struggling through a wilderness of treacle. Mrs Jackson was as good as gold; but there is not one original thought, very little commonsense and not the slightest dexterity in the use of language in all her hundreds and hundreds of letters.

Mrs Jackson's letters display the dull side of the Pattles; their silliness, their gush, their cloying sweetness, their continual demands for affection and with it a mawkish vein, a kind of tender gloating over disease and death. Of the recipient I have already said a little. Julia was perhaps the most beautiful of Mrs Jackson's daughters, the one most intimately connected with the Little Holland House circle. Her effect upon the Pre-Raphaelites was notable; it was said that she could have married either Holman Hunt or Woolner: in an age of crinoline she was 'aesthetically' draped; Burne-Jones used her as a model, and I think that the 'Burne-Jones type' owes something to her profile.

Mrs Jackson used to say that every man who met her fell in love with her. Mrs Jackson was a goose; but there may be a certain measure of truth in this and it is perhaps because everyone was in love with her that she is so elusive a subject. Both her husband and her daughter attempted to describe her. Leslie Stephen has drawn the portrait of a saint and because she is a saint one cannot quite believe in her. He speaks of her beauty and here his accuracy is attested by her aunt Cameron's many photographs; he speaks of her goodness and certainly she was a good woman; he admits that some people found her stern and noticed that sorrow had left something of gravity in her which time could not eradicate, but it is from other sources that we know that although she could be playful and gay with her children she could also be severe and that, although she looked like a saint, her wit could be almost shocking. Mrs Ramsay in *To the Lighthouse*, although she is drawn only from a child's memories, seems to me more real and more convincing than Leslie's portrait. All the loveliness, the tenderness is there; but Mrs Ramsay is not perfect; neither she, nor the woman in the Cameron photographs, was so 'pure' as the lady whom Leslie imagined to be unaware of her own beauty. Mrs Ramsay's relationship with her husband is not entirely saintly; she is ever so slightly critical; she is capable of mockery. She is, as Leslie himself noticed, a matchmaker but, as he did not notice, not always a wise one; there is a trace of self-assurance, a little blindness in her management of other people's affairs. In short Virginia's portrait of her mother is more human, more fallible, perhaps more likeable than that painted by Leslie.

Julia certainly did not lack courage. When she married Leslie he was a middle-aged widower without much money; between them they had four children and one of the children was insane. To this family they added a fifth in 1879, a girl, whom, since she had a half-sister named Stella, they called Vanessa.* In the following year a son was born who was named after his great-uncle Thoby. Here they decided to bring their family to a halt.

But contraception was a very imperfect art in the nineteenth century; less than eighteen months later, another daughter was born. She was named Adeline Virginia.

○ ○ ○

As soon as she was able to consider such things, Virginia believed that she was the heiress to two very different and in fact opposed traditions; indeed she went further and held that these two rival streams dashed together and flowed confused but not harmonised in her blood. The Stephens she saw as a very definable race. In the nursery it was believed that all Stephens were born with little tails seven inches long, but discounting this tradition (which was, I

---

* Leslie's study of Swift was published in 1882; he may already have been at work on it when he gave what was then a very unusual name to his daughter.

believe, invented to annoy Virginia's Stephen cousins) it will I hope be clear that they had a very marked pattern of behaviour. They were all writers; they all had some gift, some pleasure in the use of the English language. But they wrote like men who are used to presenting an argument, who want to make that argument plain but forcible; seeing in literature a means rather than an end.

Their minds are formed to receive facts and when once they have a fact so clearly stated that they can take it in their hands, turn it this way and that, and scrutinise it, they are content; with facts, facts of this kind, they can make useful constructions, political, juridical or theological. But for intuitions, for the melody of a song, the mood of a picture, they have little use. There is therefore a whole part of human experience of which they fight shy, in which they confess themselves frankly at a loss, as Leslie did at Little Holland House, or which they dismiss as sentimental humbug.

The Stephens were bold, as advocates have to be bold. They had plenty of moral, physical and mental audacity. James the debtor insulting Lord Mansfield or scaling the rocks of the Dorset coast in a tempest, James the Master remaking the regulations of an ancient university, Sir James browbeating ministers, Leslie defying God upon the escarpments of the Matterhorn, are bold figures and, like most bold figures, they are capable of brutality; but they were not insensitive—no, certainly they were not insensitive. James the Master in Chancery was a troubled and compassionate man deeply worried by his inability to speak Latin; Sir James, his son, was very obviously neurotic; Leslie, like Fitzjames, built a façade of stern commonsensicality and behind it sheltered a quivering bundle of vulnerable feelings. The very strength of the Stephens was rooted in weakness; the prodigious capacity for hard work, the ability to take risks, the athletic feats were but the sorties of a garrison that has no walls.

The Pattles were an altogether less intellectual race than the Stephens; they had no aptitude for words, they are chiefly remembered for their faces. So far as the records go—and we can now look at five generations—it seems that a certain kind of beauty appears and reappears, sometimes vaguely, sometimes strikingly reincarnated from avatar to avatar. This type lies dormant in the men of the family to re-emerge in their daughters, those daughters who have delighted successive generations of artists. It is the painters who have most admired these women. It is hard to look at their features without admiration; they were magnificently formed, grave, noble, majestic, but neither vivacious nor very approachable. Their beauty suggests, and is sometimes associated with, a certain moral grandeur, a certain monumentality of character. They were not bluestockings; we shall not find amongst them the great pioneers of female emancipation, and in this they differ from families which in other respects were close to them, as for instance the Stracheys and the Darwins.

But even the vague benevolence, the woolly-minded silliness, the poetic gush, the cloying, infuriating sentimentality that one finds in Maria Jackson can somehow be lifted out of folly into poetry and to something like genius in the case of Mrs Cameron.

Here then were the two sides of Virginia's inheritance, an inheritance which was, at all events, real enough in her imagination. It is not hard to find labels for the paternal and maternal sides: sense and sensibility, prose and poetry, literature and art, or, more simply, masculine and feminine. All such labels are unsatisfactory but they suggest something that is true.

To this it is necessary to add a further distinction. Julia and her family were, socially, a little better than the Stephens. Both Julia and Leslie belonged to the upper middle classes but within those classes there were many fine shades of difference. Julia's first husband was certainly a much better *parti* than Leslie; he came from a family in Somerset so long established that, despite its commercial origin, it counted as landed gentry; their children were given the name de l'Etang; Julia herself had aristocratic connections which were sufficiently impressive; the Duchess of Bedford was her first cousin. Among her sisters, cousins, uncles, and aunts family feeling was strong; they relied, in a very aristocratic fashion, upon influence and patronage. When one of Julia's relations did make a really disastrous *mésalliance* the young couple were firmly but kindly removed to the Colonies.

The Stephens on the other hand had but recently escaped from the lower middle class. James the debtor was an unsuccessful foreign adventurer; his son, although not a political hack, had done political hackwork and was socially insecure. Sir James was the first to establish them securely in the professional classes; but his children had neither the money nor the influence of the Prinseps, the Camerons or the Duckworths. Their achievements had been founded upon intellect and initiative, their dignities had been won in courts of law and their family pride was the pride of the *noblesse de robe*.

Considered collectively Mr and Mrs Leslie Stephen belonged to what one might call the lower division of the upper middle class. (Speaking academically I should place them on the margin between an upper and a lower second.) They kept seven maid-servants but no man-servant. They might sometimes travel in a cab but kept no carriage; when they went by rail they travelled third class. The ladies had their clothes made by a reasonably good dressmaker. Leslie was a member of the Athenaeum and of course of the Alpine Club. Despite their grand relations they did not venture into what was called 'high society;' in fact they lived very quietly, although Julia had her 'Sunday Afternoons' when a visitor might encounter a part of the intellectual society of London. Their house was in a respectable part of town.

It was taken for granted that the boys would go to public schools and then to Cambridge. As for the girls, they would, in a decorous way, become accomplished and then marry.

Chapter Two

1882-1895

VIRGINIA was born on 25 January 1882, at No 22 Hyde Park Gate. The house still stands and bears her father's name. It had five storeys and to these the Stephens added two further storeys of atrocious design. It is a tall dark house with a fairly large back garden.

At the top of this house were two nurseries inhabited by the children of Leslie's second marriage. Laura, Minny's child, lived apart until she was sent to a "Home" and eventually to an asylum in York.* George, Gerald and Stella were well past the nursery stage when Virginia first knew them; thus the nursery was a unit of four members: Vanessa, Thoby and Virginia being joined by Adrian, who was born in 1883, and they were not divided by any great difference in age.

In one respect Virginia was an unusual child; it took her a very long time to learn to talk properly; she did not do so until she was three years old. Her sister and no doubt her parents were very worried. In appearance she was, like Vanessa, remarkably pretty; a plump, round-faced child with the eyelids and the mouth of a Buddhist carving, deeply sculpted but exquisitely smooth. She had rosy cheeks and green eyes—thus her sister remembered her, impatiently drumming on the nursery table for a breakfast that she had not yet learnt to call for in words.

Words, when they came, were to be then, and for the rest of her life, her chosen weapons. I say weapons, for in that nursery there was both love and conflict. Vanessa, although but a year older than Thoby, was almost maternal in her care of him, shielding him from harm, sacrificing herself for his benefit and loving him tenderly. He, from the first, learnt to take such ministrations for granted and to be, if not spoiled, outrageously favoured. Already, when he was quite small, he was described as a stalwart, determined, masterful little boy; he would be yet another Stephen, not a delicate nervous Stephen like his father but a jolly rumbustious extrovert like his uncle Fitzjames, while Vanessa, it seemed, would be a thorough

* Where she died in 1945.

22

Pattle. Thus these two made an excellent pair in the nursery; the girl delighted to give, the boy to receive.

Virginia, inevitably, turned this symmetrical pattern of reciprocal affection into a triangle. The arrival of Adrian did not result in a re-formation of the original pattern; for Virginia tended to cling to the older children and was in fact as much devoted to Thoby as was Vanessa. Thoby was so much more obviously admirable, whereas Adrian was delicate and doleful and tiny. Thus the two girls must in some measure have competed for Thoby's favour.

Despite this latent and, it would appear, unconscious rivalry, the two sisters were from the first, and for as long as they lived, passionately fond of each other. But their mutual admiration was felt, or at least expressed, in rather different and very characteristic ways. Vanessa, while perceiving Virginia's precocious brilliance, her cleverness and her command of language, was bowled over, above all, by her sheer beauty. "She reminded me always of a sweet pea of a special flame colour." Virginia, while conscious of Vanessa's loveliness, valued above all her sister's calm honesty, her grave assumption of responsibility for the younger ones, her quiet unceasing benevolence, her practicality and her good sense. Also, from a very early age, she understood something of the magic of friendship, the peculiar intimacy which comes to those who have had private languages and private jokes, who have played in the twilight amidst the grown-up legs and skirts under the table. She not only loved her sister but, it would seem, loved the affectionate relationship between them. Thus, for the elder, appearances were always the most fascinating things in the world, or at least, when she loved, love presented itself to her in a visible form. For the younger, the charm of sisterly love lay simply in the intimate communication with another being, the enjoyment of character. From the first it was settled between them that Vanessa was to be a painter and Virginia a writer.

There was of course a good deal of skirmishing in the nursery; it is of interest, not so much because it happened–no nursery, surely, is complete without it–but because of the manner in which hostilities were conducted. Vanessa and Thoby were unoriginal in their tactics; they yelled and hurled abuse and on occasion, no doubt, came to blows; sometimes, when the provocation was gross enough, they would 'tell tales.' Virginia used her nails* and, at a very early

* "Miss Virginia, aged 2½, scratches her brother, aged 4. I insist upon and ultimately obtain an apology or kiss. She looks very thoughtful for some time and then says, Papa, why have we got nails? There is a bit of infantile teleology

age, discovered that she could torment her sister by scratching a distempered wall—a thing which set poor Vanessa's teeth dreadfully on edge; but later on she learnt to use her tongue and this was far worse; she called Vanessa 'The Saint'; it was the *mot injuste*, it stuck and even the grown-ups smiled and joined in the sarcasm, to which no adequate retort seemed possible.

But it was not by words alone that Virginia could vent her displeasure. Then, as always, she knew how to "create an atmosphere," an atmosphere of thunderous and oppressive gloom, a winter of discontent. It was done without words; somehow her brothers and sisters were made to feel that she had raised a cloud above their heads from which, at any moment, the fires of heaven might burst, and here again it was hard to find any reply.

And yet, there was a reply. Those who can thrust a rapier into their adversary's psyche know how it is done because they themselves are vulnerable. This at all events was true of Virginia. There was some technique for making her turn 'purple with rage.' What it was we do not know; but Thoby and Vanessa knew and there were terrible occasions when she did turn a colour which her sister described as "the most lovely flaming red." It would be interesting to know how this was done, still more interesting to know whether, as Vanessa surmised, these paroxysms were not wholly painful to Virginia herself.

From the first she was felt to be incalculable, eccentric and prone to accidents. She could say things that made the grown-ups laugh with her; she did things which made the nursery laugh at her. Is it to this, or to a rather later period, that we can ascribe an incident in Kensington Gardens when, not for the last time by any means, she lost, or at least lost control of, her knickers? She retired into a bush and there, in order to divert public attention, she sang *The Last Rose of Summer* at the top of her voice. It was this and similar misadventures which earned her, in the nursery, the title of "The Goat" or more simply "Goat," a name which stuck to her for many years.

None of the children were baptised. Leslie would have considered such a performance ridiculous and indeed profane, but they had godparents of a kind: "persons in a quasi-sponsorial relationship." Vanessa, Thoby and Adrian appear to have been provided with prosaic and unrewarding sponsors. But Virginia's godfather was James Russell Lowell, who celebrated her birth with the gift of a

---

for you. I replied: To scratch Froudes (not exactly in those terms)." Leslie Stephen to C. E. Norton, 23 December 1884. (I am indebted to Professor John Bicknell for calling my attention to this letter.)

silver cup and some indifferent verses and to whom she wrote a letter when she was six years old. It is the earliest document in her hand.

MY DEAR GODPAPA HAVE YOU BEEN TO THE ADIRONDACKS AND HAVE YOU SEEN LOTS OF WILD BEASTS AND A LOT OF BIRDS IN THEIR NESTS YOU ARE A NAUGHTY MAN NOT TO COME HERE GOOD BYE YOUR AFFECT^E VIRGINIA.

Naturally amiable and, as the children later came to believe, more than half in love with their mother, Lowell was open to such persuasions. When he was minister to the Court of St. James's he frequently visited 22 Hyde Park Gate and, when he was replaced by President Cleveland's nominee, he continued to pay summer visits to England. From a ring chain purse he would produce threepenny bits for each child; but for Virginia there was always a sixpence. This was distinction enough, but nursery jealousy knew no bounds when he gave her a real live bird in a cage. Undoubtedly, in the competition for godparents, Virginia had won hands down.

The children slept in the night nursery at the top of the house and there, from quite an early age, Virginia became the family story-teller. When the lights had been extinguished, all save that which came from the dying coal fire, she would begin her tale. There was one involving the Dilke family next door which continued from night to night beginning always with Vanessa's invocation: "Clementé, dear child . . . ," this said in a very affected drawl and then Virginia becoming Clementé would begin: gold would be discovered beneath the nursery floor and this treasure trove would purchase enormous meals of bacon and eggs, the favourite diet of the young at 22 Hyde Park Gate; and so it went on, a mounting fantasy becoming grander and vaguer, until Clementé slept and her audience had to wait until the following night for her next adventure.

In this cosy propinquity, not only stories but diseases were shared by all. In the Spring of 1888 the children were attacked by whooping cough. They were very ill, lost a lot of weight and were sent off to Bath to convalesce. Soon they all made a complete recovery–all save Virginia. When they returned she was no longer so round and so rosy as she had been. She was marked, very gently but still perceptibly, by that thin, fine, angular elegance which she kept all her life. Nor was this all; at the age of six she had become a rather different kind of person, more thoughtful and more speculative.

One evening, jumping about naked in the bathroom, she shocked and startled her elder sister by asking her which of her parents she liked best. Vanessa was appalled that such a question could be put; but she replied at once, for she was a very honest and forthright girl, that she thought she loved her mother best. Virginia, after much delay and deliberation, decided that she preferred her father. This odd little exchange seemed, to Vanessa, to mark the transformation in her. From now on conversations between the sisters became more thoughtful and more serious.

Whether this intellectual revolution resulted from her illness it is impossible to say. But one may fairly guess that it had nothing to do with Virginia's formal education. Leslie and Julia had decided, whether from motives of economy or from a belief in their own pedagogic attainments, to educate their children themselves. That is to say that the boys would have their elementary teaching and the girls the main part of their schooling at home. There were indeed governesses, both Swiss and French (including one who was thrown under a table by Vanessa and Thoby), but the main part of the teaching seems to have been done by Julia and Leslie.

Before Virginia was seven, Julia was trying to teach her Latin, history and French, while Leslie took the children in mathematics; he had previously taught George and Gerald and certainly believed that he had some gift for instruction; he had even attempted, pathetically enough, to make an intelligence for his poor mad Laura. But, a wrangler himself, he was quite unable to perceive the difficulties that a small child encounters when faced by a simple calculation; naturally he lost his temper. The only one of his children who had aptitude enough to learn any mathematics from him was Thoby. Vanessa's arithmetic was always rudimentary and Virginia continued throughout her life to count on her fingers. Neither was Julia a good teacher. In dealing with her own children she had a hasty temper. Virginia may have learnt some Latin from her, but she was never fluent in any modern language and her history, like her sister's spoken French, was learnt later in life. The foreign nurses and governesses invariably learnt English from the children and gave no language in return.

The best lessons were probably given out of school hours. When he was not teaching, Leslie could be an enchanting father; he had a talent for drawing with which he delighted his children; he could cover sheets with pencilled animals or cut creatures out of paper with magical precision. He could tell stories of dizzy alpine adventures, sometimes he would recite poetry and in the evenings he might read aloud, often from the novels of Sir Walter Scott, and call on his children to discuss what they had heard.*

There were other sources of enlightenment. Thoby returned home from his first school – Evelyns – and in an odd shy way – walking up and down stairs as he talked – told Virginia about the Greeks, about Troy and Hector and a whole new world which captured her imagination. Perhaps it was then that she decided that one day, like Thoby, she would learn Greek; and perhaps it was then that she realised that the Greeks belonged to Thoby in a way that they didn't belong to her, that they formed a part of the great male province of education – this I think was how she saw it – from which she and Vanessa were to be excluded.

The acquisition of female accomplishments was not much compensation. Drawing, dancing, music and graceful deportment had to be learnt – or at least they had to be taught. Drawing was a success: Mr Ebenezer Cook, who taught Vanessa, was a remarkable man; but the other teachers were unsympathetic. Neither of the girls was musical, neither loved the music teacher who expected her pupils to attain such deftness that they could play a scale with a sixpence on their knuckles – the sixpence would be a reward for this feat and was once contemptuously, humiliatingly, given to Vanessa when she had failed.†

Singing was better; but here Virginia disgraced herself. She discovered that the music mistress, Miss Mills, a well-known practitioner of the tonic sol-fa system, was intensely religious; in answer to a question about the meaning of Christmas, Virginia replied that it was to celebrate the Crucifixion, and then exploded in such peals of laughter that she had to be removed from the room. They were taught riding and 'graceful deportment' and there were dancing classes; these were conducted by the then celebrated Mrs Wordsworth. She wore black satin and a glass eye and she carried a stick. At her command all the little girls jumped up and down, as though in a frenzy; the Miss Stephens voted the thing a bore and retired whenever they dared to long sessions in the lavatory. But the piano lessons were the worst; they were a torment second only to that final horror, the visits to the dentist, on which occasions the

* "At the end of a volume my father always gravely asked our opinion as to its merits, and we were required to say which of the characters we liked best and why. I can remember his indignation when one of us preferred the hero to the far more life-like villain." VW in F. W. Maitland, *The Life and Letters of Leslie Stephen*, 1906, p. 474.
† The incident is remembered in *The Waves*, p. 47.

girls tossed up to decide which should go in first; the loser would have a further hour of dreadful anticipation in the waiting-room.

But, when their interests were engaged, the sisters were ready to undertake their own education. Vanessa, having obtained a copy of *The Elements of Drawing*, set herself painfully to perform the tasks which Ruskin enjoins, and Virginia remembered her slowly and carefully filling rectangles with perfectly regular hatching in the manner prescribed in *Exercise Number Seven*. Virginia produced a newspaper. It was not, at first, a single-handed venture, for Thoby was a partner in the enterprise; but much of the time he was at a boarding school, and gradually the thing fell into her hands almost entirely. It is perhaps significant that the paper carried very few illustrations; they would have been Vanessa's concern; but she was too shy to exhibit her work. Virginia also had her diffidence, but it was weaker than her longing for publication. The *Hyde Park Gate News* started in 1891* and, so far as we can tell, it appeared weekly until April 1895. Thus, when the first number appeared Virginia was just nine years old. Like other children she enjoyed playing at being grown up, but whereas they usually do so with the aid of hats, skirts, trousers and umbrellas, she played the game with words and phrases; half giggling at her own audacity, half seriously, she apes the grandest journalistic style. When a son returns home and meets his brother she celebrates the occasion thus:

> How sweet it was to see him bend down with eyes expressing worlds of joy! (O how much can eyes express!) and kiss the rosy frontispiece turned up to him.

Or again, the Stephen children adopted a stray dog which, having fouled the carpets beyond bearing, was sent to the Lost Dogs' Home and there refused admittance:

> So the boy turned him lose to wander at his own sweet will "Like a drop searching for it's fellow traveller in the vast ocean". Nothing more has as yet been heard of him.

The *Hyde Park Gate News* was read by the grown-ups, certainly by Leslie and Julia and perhaps by others; Mrs Jackson took an interest in it. Virginia was able to watch her public reacting to her prose. This was made possible by the position of a cheerful little room at the back of the house at Hyde Park Gate; this room was made almost

---

* The first number that we have is dated 6 April 1891, and as this is the 9th in a weekly series we may assume that the first issue was on 9 February 1891. The series continues with gaps until 19 December 1892 after which no more files exist until 7 January 1895.

entirely of glass, it had a skylight and big glass windows facing the garden. Here the sisters would sit together and Virginia would read aloud from Charlotte M. Yonge–they kept a score of the number of deaths in those very necrological novels–and later, Thackeray, George Eliot and indeed most of the Victorian novelists. And from this room the girls could see into the large double drawing-room. Vanessa would put the latest number of the *News* on her mother's sofa while her parents were at dinner. Then there was an interval of suspense.

Virginia was always enormously sensitive to criticism and, when her parents came into the drawing-room, her excitement became almost unbearable. For a time the paper would lie unnoticed; then at last Julia would pick it up and begin to read. Would there be any spoken comment? That was the awful question; and when, calmly but distinctly, Julia observed to Leslie: "Rather clever, I think," the authoress was, for a time, in heaven.

With such a public it is not surprising that the policy of the journal was, from a parental point of view, impeccable. *An Article on Cheekiness* roundly declares that:

> Young children should be nipped in the bud of cheekiness otherwise impertinance which when the child increases in years it grows into audacity. It is then indeed a great hinderance to mankind. . . .

But this, I suspect, was written by Thoby. Virginia's devotion to the cause of discipline was qualified. It does not prevent her from being, in her own way, audacious.

> Miss Millicent Vaughan [Virginia's cousin] has honoured the family of Stephen with her company. Miss Vaughan has like a dutiful sister been to Canada to see her long absent sister who is residing there. We hope that no pangs of jealousy crossed her mind when she saw her sister so comfortably settled with a husband when she herself is searching the wide world in quest of matrimony. But we are wandering from our point like so many old people. She came on Monday and is still at 22 Hyde Park Gate.

Did she, one would like to know, read the family newspaper?

Then there was General Beadle, "the prince of talkers." Enough is preserved of his sovereign talk to show that, at the age of nine, Virginia knew a bore when she met one.

The *Hyde Park Gate News* also contains some first efforts at fiction; but they are not as amusing as the news items. *The Midnight Ride* (signed A. V. S.) is her first extant story. In 1927 she noted that she could make up situations but, she adds: "I cannot make up plots." This is certainly true of *The Midnight Ride*. Here she contrives a situation in which a boy will have to ride at midnight through a dangerous North American bog to see his brother, who lies ill at school. Having sent him off she loses interest in the adventure and the story folds up in the tamest fashion. A series of letters from imaginary people is more successful. They are love letters written in the belief that all adult love-making is, in itself, funny. ". . . you have jilted me most shamefully," writes Mr John Harley to Miss Clara Dimsdale; who replies: "As I never kept your love-letters you can't have them back. I therefore return the stamps which you sent."

There is also some fun in *A Cockney's Farming Experiences*, a serial inspired by the adventures of Mr Briggs in *Punch*; *Punch* was a strong influence on these early productions.

One returns to the news and tries to deduce a picture of the Stephen family. The first thing that strikes the modern reader is the great number of people who made up a household in those days. In addition to the eight children there were seven servants, of whom the chief was always Sophy, the cook and the family treasure. Dogs play an important part in their lives and seem to have been far more ferocious then than now; there are also rats, bugs and relations, in particular the Fishers, the Duckworths, the Vaughans, the Stephens, Mrs Jackson, Countess Somers, the Duchess of Bedford. There are a few distinguished names: Meredith, Burne-Jones, Walter Headlam–but these are rather distant figures.

The usual joys and calamities of family life are recorded: lamps flare, pipes burst, children fall ill, brothers go off to school, there are visits to the circus and the zoo; but the grand event of the year is the summer exodus to Cornwall. It was in 1881, the year before Virginia's birth, that Leslie, on one of his many walking tours, discovered St Ives, "at the very toenail," as he put it, "of England." In the following year he took a house, Talland House, on the high ground above the bay, and thither the family went every summer. St Ives must, therefore, have been one of Virginia's earliest memories.

That day [Wednesday, 11 May 1892] is stamped deeply in the minds of the juveniles for two things. The first was ices and the second was that Madame Mao who we may as well inform our readers is the Stephens' instructress in the art of music was to come twice a week!!! But this blow was very much softened by the fact that the Stephens were going to St Ives very much earlier than usual. This is a heavenly prospect to the minds of the juveniles who adore St Ives and revel in its numerous delights. . . .

The annual promise and recollection of St Ives made London, by comparison, a poor place and the excursions to Brighton to see Mrs Jackson (she died in April 1892) or the Vaughans and the Fisher cousins (who were not popular) were no substitute. It was better to wander in Kensington Gardens, which had then a certain wildness; here Vanessa and Virginia would lie in the grass and consume three-penny worth of Fry's chocolate and a copy of *Tit-Bits*, their favourite journal, to which Virginia sent an early effort at fiction which, needless to say, was not published. At some earlier period, wandering in the long grass which lay between the Round Pond and the Flower Walk, the children were delighted to discover the abandoned corpse of a small black dog. But even this was small compensation for seeing the Spring and the Summer go by in London streets. St Ives was the only real country and the children longed for it.

I have a lively image, although it is based upon very slender evidence, of that family exodus: Mr and Mrs Stephen, the girls, Adrian (Thoby might come later from school), Stella and perhaps her brothers, Sophy the cook, Ellen the parlour maid, a Swiss governess and all their luggage in surely no fewer than two four-wheelers, the children bubbling with excitement as they made their way to Paddington Station to catch, let us say, the 10.15 (the 9 o'clock train was impossibly bad, stopping at every conceivable little station). And then the long journey, starting in high spirits as the *Cornish Express* bustled from Paddington to Bristol, reaching Temple Meads at 12.45; here there was an opportunity to get a luncheon basket unless, of course, they had their own sandwiches; then followed the long, hot, sticky and increasingly quarrelsome journey, nature relieved into a chamber pot, papers, books, the *Strand Magazine* crumpled and discarded on seats, an interminable hot afternoon. It was nearly 4 o'clock when the train drew into Plymouth and thereafter its conduct was hesitant and dilatory. They went by way of Truro, arriving at St Erth at a quarter to seven, which gave the travellers exactly six minutes to get themselves and their belongings onto the little branch-line train to St Ives. By now, however, lassitude would have been replaced by excitement; the children had seen the ocean at Hayle, after which the train travels along the coast, skirting Carbis Bay until it reaches the terminus at St Ives just after seven.

It was a summer evening, and there were still hours of daylight. Talland House was not far from the Station; one might almost run there. There stood the hedge of escalonia by the gate and beyond it was the garden, all up and down the slope with a galaxy of little lawns and shrubberies and private places; there was the cricket pitch where 'small cricket' was played all through the afternoon and so late into the evening that the ball had to be covered with luminous paint that they might continue, and beyond it the sea. And that first night of the holiday, they would hear the sound of the waves breaking on the shore and know that for weeks and weeks it would be theirs.

On Saturday morning Master Hilary Hunt and Master Basil Smith came up to Talland House and asked Master Thoby and Miss Virginia Stephen to accompany them to the light-house as Freeman the boatman said that there was a perfect tide and wind for going there. Master Adrian Stephen was much disappointed at not being allowed to go.

Thus the *Hyde Park Gate News* for 12 September 1892, and the literary historian may, if he so wishes, find in this report what Henry James calls the *donné* of one of Virginia's most celebrated works. The point is not one that can be proved; but certainly St Ives provided a treasury of reminiscent gold from which Virginia drew again and again; we find it not only in *To the Lighthouse*, but in *Jacob's Room* and, I think, in *The Waves*. For her, Cornwall was the Eden of her youth, an unforgettable paradise, and she was always grateful to her parents for having fixed on that spot. She was to love other places, but for Cornish people and Cornish things she had a kind of patriotic emotion; they seemed to be made of some particularly fine matter which made them more romantic and more distinguished than the products of any other soil.

Family life at St Ives was rather shabby and casual; Talland House was untidy and overrun with people. For in addition to the family there were guests: cousins, uncles, nephews and nieces in great quantities; Meredith, who used to sit under a tree reading his poetry to Julia and Mrs Jackson, Lowell, Henry James, and a number of obscurer characters who had failed or had yet to make a name for themselves, as, for instance, Mr Wolstenholme, known to the children as 'The Woolly One.' He had been a brilliant mathematician but his opinions and his life had made Cambridge impossible; he had married disastrously and came to Talland House to get away from his wife; he spiced his mathematics with opium.*

And there were younger people, those whom Virginia described as the tyrants and demi-gods of their childish world: their half-brothers Gerald and George who went to Eton and Cambridge; their

---

* It seems probable that Virginia had him in mind when she described Mr Carmichael in *To the Lighthouse*.

half-sister Stella, who grew up to a world where one 'came out'; Jack Hills, a young solicitor who came in pursuit of Stella, Kitty Lushington, an old friend and the daughter of an old friend–it was under the jackmanii in the garden of Talland House that she agreed to marry another of the younger guests, Leo Maxse. All of these were to play an important part in Virginia's life; more important, perhaps, than the friends of her own age, for although they met a good many other children–there were tea-parties and picnics and such like junketings–in retrospect it seemed to Virginia that "us four," as they called themselves, formed a rather isolated group. We may suppose that their more private and more juvenile amusements, as for instance their funeral ceremonies for birds and mice, were family affairs. Cricket, on the other hand, was more adult, more public and more social. Indeed it was on the cricket ground during the summer of 1893 that Virginia first knew a boy who was later to become interesting to her–though he was then only six–for Dick and Rupert Brooke were zealous participants in the daily games at Talland House. Cricket was played with enthusiasm, and Virginia was considered a formidable bowler.* Leslie's favourite exercise was walking; he would sometimes go for what he called "a potter," covering thirty miles or so. His children were also expected to be pedestrians and their father encouraged them to botanise as they walked; but botany never went very far; they preferred what they called "bug hunting." This was an occupation that was begun unofficially and then, with the help of Jack Hills, put on a regular footing with all the proper apparatus of nets, collecting boxes, setting boards, killing bottles, cabinets and works of reference. The Stephen children collected butterflies and moths for many years, in fact until they were quite grown up.

As blood sports go, the killing of lepidoptera has a good deal to recommend it: it can offend only the most squeamish of humanitarians; it involves all the passion and skill of the naturalist, the charm of summer excursions and sudden exhilarating pursuits, the satisfaction of filling gaps in the collection, the careful study of text books, and, above all, the mysterious pleasure of staying up late, and walking softly through the night to where a rag, soaked in rum and treacle, has attracted dozens of slugs, crawly-bobs and, perhaps, some great lamp-eyed, tipsy, extravagantly gaudy moth. This again was

---

* "Gin can bowl a good deal better than some of the chaps who came this term." Thoby to Adrian and Virginia c. 1891. " . . . the demon bowler as she was called by her brothers in the nursery . . ." George Rylands in *Portrait of Virginia Woolf*, BBC Home Service, 29 August 1956.

something that Virginia never forgot and to which she returns affectionately in her writings.

But it was the sea that made the splendour of their holidays. The sea invited them to sailing, to fishing and to bathing. Bathing indeed was something in which the whole family was involved. William Fisher, their cousin, who taught the children to make a paddle boat and was known as 'The Admiral'–which indeed he was in all seriousness to become, remembered his aunt Julia bobbing about in the water in a large black hat. The most dramatic sport and the grandest event that the sea could offer was the taking of the pilchards; but this was something for which the children and indeed a great part of the population of St Ives longed in vain. Day after day the Huer waited in his little white watch house on the cliff for that darkening of the ocean that would bring out boats to draw the fish, not by the thousand but by the million, from the silver commotion of the waves. One year they were sighted and the Huer's horn was sounded; but the shoal passed out of the bay and was lost. And so the pilchards became a kind of dream, a Cornish myth that was anticipated but never realised from summer to summer.*

But there was much else that the sea could give: the annual regatta, the sands, the rock pools with sea anemones blooming below the darting fishes, the great bay with its sails and its steamers hull down on their way up to Bristol, or to Cardiff or perhaps to Brazil. And there was Cornish cream and the Town Crier with his muffin bell–not that these came directly from the sea–and the general richness and happiness of life.

This was the season of the year when a basket lowered from the window on a string might, if Sophy were in a good mood, come up again heavy with fine things from the grown-up dinner table. If she were in a bad mood, nothing came up but a severed string. This was the time when Virginia could walk out with her father to the Loggan rock of Tren Crom and the fairyland of great ferns which stood high above a child's head, or to Halestown Bog where the osmunda grew; when Mrs Latham brought live blue lobsters in a bucket into the kitchen and the great storms of autumn sent

---

* There is a mystery here: "It was only in 1905, when, after Father's death, us four took a little lodging house at Carbis Bay that the pilchards came . . . All the years that we were at St Ives the pilchards never came; and the pilchard boats drowsed in the bay. . . ." MH/A 5c. See also *Cornwall Diary*.

But: "How nice it is that you have seen the great event of the St Ives Year the taking of pilchards. How pretty of Adrian it was to say it was a fleet 'of light' I am so glad for all your sakes . . ." Mrs Jackson to Mrs Leslie Stephen, 12 October 1889.

waves and sea birds screaming towards the Gurnard's Head.

It was the happiest time of a happy childhood. For certainly they were fortunate, and would have been so if they had only had one week at Margate. Julia could have created what Virginia called "The felicious family of Stephen" in most situations. But in St Ives, feeling the beatitudes of life as keenly as she did, Virginia was allowed a taste of paradise.

Like any other earthly paradise it was menaced. From the outset, Virginia's life was threatened by madness, death and disaster. Whether there was, in those early years, any seed of madness within her, if those "purple rages" were the symptom of some psychic malady, we do not know; neither probably did she; but madness walked the streets. I write advisedly; the scene in *The Years* where the child Rose sees a man exposing himself by a lamp-post is based on experience; there was such a man who hung around Hyde Park Gate and was seen by both Vanessa and Virginia. And of course there was madness in the home; Laura, 'Her Ladyship of the Lake,' was still with the Stephens in 1891 and was a considerable burden upon poor Julia. So far as I can make out she was regarded as a joke by her half-sisters. They wrote her letters, they treated her, I suppose, more or less as an equal; but she could do disconcerting things–calmly throw a pair of scissors into the fire–and there must, as they grew up, have been something disquieting about her. Something much more disquieting was to follow.

Fate struck Fitzjames. He had achieved a great deal: he was a judge, a baronet; he had finished his great work on the history of the criminal law. Then in 1889 his handling of the Maybrick case led to attacks in the press; in 1891 he was advised to retire and did so. Meanwhile his second son, J. K. Stephen, had met disaster.

J. K. Stephen* stands with a red flower in his buttonhole, gazing serenely at the dons of King's in their Combination Room, a massive, powerful, genial figure. Having made a tremendous success at Eton as a scholar and an athlete he became a Fellow of his College; he was the author of light ingenious verses which, in their day, took the town by storm and *Lapsus Calami* is not quite forgotten even now. Fitzjames must have been enormously proud of him.

In 1886, while paying a visit to Felixstowe, the young man had an accident†; he damaged his head, and although the hurt did not appear to be serious it was, in fact, fatal and he began to go mad.

---

* Painted by Charles Furse.

† The nature of the accident is not certainly known; in the Stephen family it was said that he was struck by some projection from a moving train.

One day he rushed upstairs to the nursery at 22 Hyde Park Gate, drew the blade from a sword stick and plunged it into the bread. On another occasion he carried Virginia and her mother off to his room in De Vere Gardens; Virginia was to pose for him. He had decided that he was a painter–a painter of genius. He was in a state of high euphoria and painted away like a man possessed, as indeed he was. He would drive up in a hansom cab to Hyde Park Gate–a hansom in which he had been driving about all day in a state of insane excitement. On another occasion he appeared at breakfast and announced, as though it were an amusing incident, that the doctors had told him that he would either die or go completely mad.

But the most difficult and painful thing about his insanity was that it led him to desire Stella and violently to pursue her. The children were told to say that Stella was away, staying with relations in the country, whenever their cousin appeared. Fitzjames refused to admit that his son was mad; if he were troublesome then no allowances were to be made for him and Leslie should refuse to receive him.

"I cannot shut my door upon Jem," answered Julia.* She had the power to command him, even in his wildest moods, and she did all that she could for him until his death in February 1892. His father died two years later, broken-hearted.

Stella, the object of this unhappy passion, was a most important figure in the lives of her half-sisters. She was her mother's lieutenant, though by no means her favourite. Not very clever, but with a certain feminine wisdom, kind, gentle, quiet and beautiful; less strictly beautiful than her mother but with a more approachable loveliness than Julia's.† She had a number of eligible suitors, of whom the most determined was Jack Hills, a clever, bright, self-reliant young man. He proposed at St Ives during the summer of 1894 and, for one reason or another, she rejected him. It was, as events were to prove, an unwise decision and perhaps she felt a little of its unwisdom, for that night the children heard her crying in the next room. It must have been a rather disturbing incident and that summer they had other things to disturb them.

*Thus, Leslie Stephen (MBk, p. 60). But, through the kindness of Lady Hills, I have been able to see letters from Julia to Stella which show that this was precisely what she had to do, on one occasion at least.

† She was noticed by Holman Hunt, who had an eye for a pretty girl, and sat to him for the head of the Lady of Shalott (Manchester City Art Gallery). A study exists (Coll. Mrs Elizabeth Burt) but it was not used in the final picture. See Mary Bennett, William Holman Hunt (Exhibition Catalogue), 1969, p. 57, and W. Holman Hunt, Pre-Raphaelitism and the Pre-Raphaelite Brotherhood, 1913, II, p. 310.

Somebody had bought the land in front of Talland House and now a big oatmeal-coloured hotel rose up and turned its back on them, blotting out the view of the sea. Was it worth staying on? It was cumbersome and expensive having a house so far from London; expense always worried Leslie and expenses were growing. Thoby was going to Clifton and Adrian had also to be educated. A notice announcing that Talland House was to let made its appearance; there were no takers, but this was only a reprieve. The doors of paradise were closing.

That was in 1894; in January 1895, after an interval of three years, we are able to consult the *Hyde Park Gate News* and discover that Virginia, now about to celebrate her 13th birthday, has ceased to be a child. The hand in which these pages are written is much more adult, though not always easy to read.* Her spelling is orthodox, her language is on the whole correct. Her essays and her attempts at fiction are serious exercises based upon approved models.†

As might be expected, the charm and fun of the earlier numbers has evaporated. Occasionally a phrase, a joke, a turn of speech anticipates her adult style; but the general impression is rather flat. She is still writing for an adult audience; but now she has reached a self-conscious age and plays for safety. She attempts a novel of manners; she writes an article describing a dream in which she was God. These are both in their way interesting, but they are also very clearly the work of a girl making a deadly serious study of English literature.

The news is also of a more adult kind than in the previous series. There is an account of a performance at the Lyceum and a report of the wedding of Virginia's cousin Millicent Vaughan, whose search through "the wide world in quest of matrimony" was now safely concluded by an excellent match. There are many references to the exceptionally severe weather, and a long and competent report of a meeting held at the Mansion House with the object of rescuing Carlyle's house in Chelsea "from the tooth of time."

"For the last fortnight Mrs Leslie Stephen has been in bed with

---

* Some fluent and regular pages are clearly in Vanessa's hand; since she always denied making any contribution to the text of the paper, presumably she acted as an amanuensis.

† The following quotation from a letter written to his mother by Adrian in February 1894 gives a notion of what Virginia was reading, or at least of what she thought that he ought to be reading when he was eleven and she was twelve. ". . . tell Ginia that I have not taken any books by Tenyson or Wordsworth or any of the authors she mentioned but I've taken a book called The World of Adventure. . . ."

the influenza"–this was on March 4th. On the 18th we are told that she continues to improve, and on April 8th that George, Gerald and Stella are to go abroad in three days' time. This, almost certainly, was the last number of the *Hyde Park Gate News*.

Five years earlier, Mrs Jackson had written to her grandchildren begging them not to cause their mother any anxiety. It was a wise appeal for, even in that age of cheap domestic labour, a family of ten posed fearful problems for a very devoted mother. And there were so many other burdens upon her. Everyone who wanted help turned to her knowing that it would not be denied. After her death Virginia found in her mother's travelling desk all the letters received one morning at Talland House and brought to London to be answered. There was a letter from a woman whose daughter had been betrayed, a letter from her son George, one from her sister Mary Fisher, one from a nurse who was out of work; there were begging letters, there were many pages from a girl who had quarrelled with her parents. Everyone demanded some kind of help or sympathy, everyone knew that, from her, they would get it. Somehow she would find the time and the means to give aid and comfort. "Ah, thank Heaven, there is no post tonight!" she would exclaim on Saturday evening, and Leslie would protest: "There must be an end of this, Julia." But, as he knew too well, such protests were futile and, worse still, he himself was the heaviest of her burdens.

Essentially the happiness of the Stephen home derived from the fact that the children knew their parents to be deeply and happily in love. This, surely, was the genial fire from which they all drew comfort. But it was also the means whereby the whole edifice might be reduced to ashes. Despite her charities and her maternal commitments, Julia lived chiefly for her husband; everyone needed her but he needed her most. With his temperament and his necessities this was too great a task for even the most heroic of wives; his health and his happiness had to be secured; she had to listen to and to partake in his worries about money, about his work and his reputation, about the management of the household; he had to be fortified and protected from the world. He was, as he himself said, a skinless man, so nothing was to touch him save her soothing and healing hand.

His health was, necessarily, linked to hers and in the seventeen years of their marriage it had not been very good. The labours involved in the making of the *Dictionary of National Biography* were arduous; Virginia believed that she and Adrian had been crushed and cramped in the womb by those important volumes. In 1888 Leslie suddenly collapsed; there was another attack in 1890 and again he was ill in 1891. He suffered from insomnia and what he called "fits of the horrors"; Julia had to wake him up and comfort him. In 1891 she persuaded him to give up his work on the *Dictionary*; it was ruining his life. But still there was this incessant, and often quite fantastic worry about finance,* and here too Julia had to comfort, to reassure, and indeed to administer for him.

Beautiful still, but increasingly worn and harassed, Julia became more and more obsessed by time. She was always in a hurry, ever more anxious to save time by doing things herself, ever more anxious that others should be spared. And so she exhausted herself. Still young in years, she had raced through a lifetime in altruistic work and at length her physical resistance burnt out.

The attack of influenza mentioned in the *Hyde Park Gate News* was at length shaken off, but the *sequelae* were not. Towards the end of April Stella hastened back from the Continent, for clearly her mother's condition had taken a drastic turn for the worse. The doctor said something ominous about rheumatic fever; the relations gathered. On 5 May 1895 Julia died.

* It is said that Leslie told Edmund Gosse that he was completely ruined; there was only £1,000 left. Gosse and other men of letters decided that something must be done; but first it was necessary to know more about the financial situation of the Stephen family. Further enquiries revealed that what Leslie meant was that his favourable balance at the bank was reduced to £1,000; his income and his capital were unchanged.

Chapter Three

1895-1897

"HER death," said Virginia, "was the greatest disaster that could happen."

And yet, if Virginia's loss had simply been a shattering bereavement the situation would not have been so bad as to be unendurable. The real horror of Julia's death came in the mourning of her. Naturally, inevitably, the chief mourner was Leslie; he, a man of sixty-three, had every expectation of being nursed out of the world by a wife almost fifteen years his junior (and she would have done it so well). He had done his stint of widowerhood and had endured it with as much fortitude as any man could reasonably display. How then could fate do this to him? For a long time he abandoned himself to grief; his life, like his writing paper, was confined within a deep black border. His working hours he gave up to a panegyric on 'My Julia.' He wrote sentimentally and without restraint and yet he was, as he himself said, so much a professional author that he could not help making the thing readable and even amusing; it was, I suspect, his only consolation at this time.

But, outside the study, the sedative of work was gone. He resolved to teach those lessons which Julia had previously taken with the girls and gave up half the morning to this purpose. It was a large sacrifice and a sacrifice made with the very best intentions; but it did not make him a more cheerful or a less irascible teacher. In fact, it was an arrangement which brought no comfort to anyone.

At meals he sat miserable and bewildered, too unhappy and too deaf to know what was being said, until at length, in one scene after another all through that dreadful summer, he broke down utterly and, while his embarrassed children sat in awkward silence, groaned, wept and wished that he were dead.

In the accounts that Vanessa and Virginia have left of this period in their lives the image that recurs is one of darkness; dark houses, dark walls, darkened rooms, 'Oriental gloom.' And by this I think that they meant, not only physical darkness, but a deliberate shutting out of spiritual light. It was, for the children, not only tragic but chaotic and unreal. They were called upon to feel, not simply their

40

natural grief, but a false, a melodramatic, an impossibly histrionic emotion which they could not encompass.

Leslie now resembled one who, through long years of infirmity, has taught his body to move with the aid of a crutch and who then, suddenly, finds that his support has gone. In such an emergency stoicism, reserve, philosophy are all beside the point; you fall and, falling, clutch at whatever may save you from disaster. Leslie, snatching at the nearest support, found Stella.

Stella was, indeed, his legitimate prop. She accepted her position without question. She was ready to comfort, to console, to order dinner, to buy coal or underclothes, to chaperone the girls, to keep the house running without alarming expense, to make all social arrangements and in particular to marshal the long procession of sympathising females who came to be closeted with Leslie, to listen, to condole and then, emerging red-eyed and garrulous from his room, came with more comfort, more tears and more advice for Stella. All this was given to her as a duty and tacitly accepted; but in that household and at that season far more was required of her; she had to listen to her stepfather's confessions and to absolve him.

There had been differences between him and Julia—"trifles," but also "things that were not quite trifles"; he had not always been kind, not always considerate; and at the memory of such faults he groaned and cried aloud. If he had had a burden on his conscience like that which had tortured poor Carlyle he would be tempted to commit suicide, but that, he hoped, was not possible. Stella could bear witness; he had not, surely he had not, been as bad as Carlyle? And Stella, who didn't know much about the married life of Mr and Mrs Carlyle, bravely concurred, gallantly attempted to set his uneasy mind at rest.

All this was particularly hard on her because Leslie, after all, was not her father. They had never been very close, and indeed it is more than likely that she regarded him with a kind of resentment. Her passion had been all for her mother: to save *her* trouble and pain, to preserve *her* health, sometimes boldly to steal a part of her mother's load, these had been Stella's cares. And Julia, loving her less than she did the others, and loving Leslie more, had been willing to sacrifice her and the rest to his convenience, and—what was far worse from Stella's point of view—had sacrificed herself, so that at length, in the great campaign to save her mother from exhaustion, she had been defeated both by Leslie and by Julia.

In those last weeks when she was sent abroad, white, desperate, reluctant, knowing that Julia needed her, she was not recalled, but rather recalled herself, suspecting that her mother's letters concealed, as indeed they did conceal, the true gravity of her state. She arrived home so late that she seemed almost to have been cheated not only of her mother's life but of her very death.

Nevertheless, patient, reliable, uncomplaining, bowing to the inevitable yoke of her sex, she accepted her tasks. Pale as a plant that has been denied the sun, concealing the tears that often fell, she could nevertheless find the strength to help her mother's husband and his children; more particularly Adrian and Virginia. It was she who got Adrian off to school in the mornings and coped with his maddening habit of losing gloves, books and coats; it was she who had to look after Virginia, a care, which, as we shall see, now became urgent, heartbreaking and terrible.

Her half-brothers and sisters, who loved her, understood enough of all this to try as best they might to take something of her burden. Vanessa, at fifteen, had earned a reputation for good sense and practicality. She could be, no doubt she was, a comfort and Leslie himself made touching, heroic efforts at cheerfulness, and indeed not just at cheerfulness but at a real and emotionally genuine contact with his children, in which happiness could be regained without any unfaithfulness to his wife's memory and in which something constructive could be built out of their common sorrow. So there were moments when, with a supreme effort, he could again be a delightful parent. But such moments were brief and few. For most of the time the children had to live with a father who was in such a state of despairing, oppressive, guilt-ridden gloom that their own sharp, uncomplicated unhappiness seemed by contrast a relief.

Friends and relations observing the Stephen household at this time could discover two bright luminaries in what would otherwise have been a prospect of unrelieved gloom. Stella was, clearly, a model daughter. George Duckworth was the model brother. The eldest of the Duckworth children, he was now twenty-seven, very handsome, comfortably well-off, pleasant, urbane and generous. His devotion to his half-sisters was exemplary. He made them presents, he took endless trouble to arrange treats, parties, excursions; he would even go off butterfly-hunting with them, and this for a fashionable young man represents a considerable sacrifice.

After their mother's death his kindness knew no bounds; his was an emotional, a demonstrative nature; his shoulder was there for them to weep on; his arms were open for their relief.

At what point this comfortably fraternal embrace developed into something which to George no doubt seemed even more comfortable although not nearly so fraternal, it would be hard to say. Vanessa came to believe that George himself was more than half unaware of the fact that what had started with pure sympathy ended by becoming a nasty erotic skirmish. There were fondlings and fumblings in public when Virginia was at her lessons and these were carried to greater lengths–indeed I know not to what lengths–when, with the easy assurance of a fond and privileged brother, George carried his affections from the schoolroom into the night nursery.*

To the sisters it simply appeared that their loving brother was transformed before their eyes into a monster, a tyrant against whom they had no defence, for how could they speak out or take any action against a treachery so covert that it was half unknown even to the traitor? Trained as they were to preserve a condition of ignorant purity they must at first have been unaware that affection was turning to concupiscence, and were warned only by their growing sense of disgust. To this, and to their intense shyness, we may ascribe Vanessa's and Virginia's long reticence on the subject. George was always demonstratively emotional, lavish and irresponsible in his endearments and his embraces; it would have taken a very knowing eye to perceive that his caresses went perhaps further than was proper in even the most loving of brothers, and the bedtime pettings may have seemed no more than a normal extension of his daytime devotion. It would have been hard for his half-sisters to know at what point to draw a line, to voice objections, to risk evoking a painful and embarrassing scandal: harder still to find someone to whom they could speak at all. Stella, Leslie, the aunts–all would have been bewildered, horrified, indignant and incredulous.

Their only course seemed to be one of silent evasion; but even this was denied them; they must join in praising their persecutor, for his advances were conducted to an accompaniment of enthusiastic applause in which the girls could hear the repeated hope that 'dear George' would not find them ungrateful.

* "... this led us to the revelation of all George's malefactions. To my surprise, she [Janet Case] has always had an intense dislike of him; & used to say 'Whew-you nasty creature,' when he came in & began fondling me over my Greek. When I got to the bedroom scenes, she dropped her lace, & gasped like a benevolent gudgeon. By bedtime she said she was feeling quite sick, & did go to the W. C. which, needless to say, had no water in it." VW to Vanessa Bell, [25th July] 1911. However, Virginia also recorded Jack Hill's assurance that George had "lived in complete chastity until his marriage"; it depends on what one means by complete chastity. MH/A 15.

In later years Virginia's and Vanessa's friends were a little aston-ished at the unkind mockery, the downright virulence with which the sisters referred to their half-brother. He seemed to be a slightly ridiculous but on the whole an inoffensive old buffer, and so, in a sense, he was. His public face was amiable. But to his half-sisters he stood for something horrible and obscene, the final element of foulness in what was already an appalling situation. More than that, he came to pollute the most sacred of springs, to defile their very dreams. A first experience of loving or being loved may be enchant-ing, desolating, embarrassing or even boring; but it should not be disgusting. Eros came with a commotion of leathern wings, a figure of mawkish incestuous sexuality. Virginia felt that George had spoilt her life before it had fairly begun. Naturally shy in sexual matters, she was from this time terrified back into a posture of frozen and defensive panic.

I do not know enough about Virginia's mental illnesses to say whether this adolescent trauma was in any way connected with them. It is probable that George made himself disagreeable to her in this way at a later date, when fate struck again at the Stephen family,* whereas the first 'breakdown' or whatever we are to call it, must have come very soon after her mother's death.

And here we come to a great interval of nothingness, a kind of positive death which cannot be described and of which Virginia herself probably knew little – that is to say could recall little – and yet which is vitally important to her story. From now on she knew that she had been mad and might be mad again.

To know that you have had cancer in your body and to know that it may return must be very horrible; but a cancer of the mind, a corruption of the spirit striking one at the age of thirteen and for the rest of one's life always working away somewhere, always in suspense, a Dionysian sword above one's head – this must be almost unendurable. So unendurable that in the end, when the voices of insanity spoke to her in 1941, she took the only remedy that remained, the cure of death. But her mind could make a scar that would serve,

---

* Statements by Leonard Woolf and the late Dr Noel Richards suggest that George's advances were made shortly after his mother's death; on the other hand unpublished memoirs (MH/A 14, 15 and 16) by Virginia make it almost certain that his activities began at, or were continued to, a much later date, i.e. 1903 or 1904. It was not only George's attentions which disturbed Virginia: "I still shiver with shame at the memory of my half-brother, standing me on a ledge, aged about 6 or so, exploring my private parts." (VW to Ethel Smyth, 12 January 1941). A document (MH/A 5a) which came to light after the first publication of this vol-ume makes it clear that the half-brother here referred to was Gerald, not George.

in some measure, to heal and to conceal her lasting wound. She did not, could not, admit all the memories of her madness. What she did recall were the physical symptoms; in her memoir of this period she hardly mentions the commotions of her mind and although we know that she had already heard what she was later to call "those horrible voices," she speaks of other symptoms, usually physiological symptoms. Her pulse raced–it raced so fast as to be almost unbearable. She became painfully excitable and nervous and then intolerably depressed. She became terrified of people, blushed scarlet if spoken to and was unable to face a stranger in the street.

Dr Seton, the Stephens' family doctor,* put a stop to all lessons, ordered a simple life and prescribed outdoor exercise; she was to be out of doors four hours a day and it was one of Stella's self-imposed duties to take her for walks or for rides on the tops of buses.

The *Hyde Park Gate News* came to an end; for the first and only time Virginia lost the desire to write, although in 1896 she did keep a diary for a short time. But she read feverishly and continually. She went through a period of morbid self-criticism, blamed herself for being vain and egotistical, compared herself unfavourably to Vanessa and was at the same time intensely irritable.

St Ives was given up. Leslie could not bear the idea of going there without Julia and so, perhaps a month after her death, Gerald took a train to Cornwall, saw someone and settled the business. Each year now the Stephens looked for a summer residence. In 1895 they went to Freshwater in the Isle of Wight. That was almost their blackest period of mourning; in 1896 they took a house belonging to Mrs Tyndall, the scientist's widow, at Hindhead on the top of the North Downs, and this house became the setting for what should, in conventional terms, have been the last act in the romance of Stella Duckworth and Jack Hills.

John Waller Hills was an Etonian; he came of a very respectable family handsomely established in Cumberland but not, apparently, able to do much for Jack. His father had been a judge and something of a wit. His mother collected Chelsea enamel boxes and minor literary men. He himself was to be a solicitor; he had political ambitions and was an enthusiastic fisherman. He was an honest,

---

* Dr Seton–"my dear Dr Seton" as Virginia calls him in her diary for 1897– was much loved by all the children; he was a favourite also of the Woolf family in Lexham Gardens. Years later he met his two former patients Leonard and Virginia, now Mr and Mrs Woolf and his neighbours in Richmond, where he died in February 1917, aged ninety. (VW/VB, [Feb. 11] 1917.) "He was," said Leonard Woolf, "a doddering old man, but awfully nice."

tenacious fellow with a bad stutter; he had to wrestle with each sentence and yet in that conflict managed always to have his say in the end. He had refused to accept Stella's rejection of his suit and, in his refusal, he had a powerful ally in Julia. Julia was always a matchmaker and a friend to young lovers; she had been largely instrumental in carrying matters so far. After the first rupture, she had determined to mend matters and succeeded so well that, by the time of her death, the young man was again a frequent guest at Hyde Park Gate.

He proposed again and was again rejected. We can only guess at the reasons for this second refusal but, in view of what followed, it is likely that Stella was deterred, not by her feelings for Jack, but by a sense of duty to her step-father. She might not love Leslie or might love him only in a very tepid fashion; but he had laid a claim upon her conscience; he and his children were dependent upon her, he relied on her for the few scraps of comfort that he could now enjoy. To desert him would be inhuman. And so, following her conscience rather than her inclination, Stella refused Jack for a second time.

But he would no more accept the second refusal than the first; nor is it hard to see how the very situation which made Stella reject him could, from another point of view, be represented as the strongest argument in favour of marriage. That a girl of Stella's kindness and beauty, so obviously formed for matrimony and motherhood, should devote herself to a man who, after all, might live another twenty years was monstrous. Stella, at twenty-seven, was neither so young nor yet so old that she could easily sacrifice her time.

If she heard such arguments, she must, howsoever strong her moral rectitude, have allowed some inward sigh of assent to contradict her overt resolve to continue in that tedious and heart-breaking course of duty to which she found herself committed. And then, as the young lawyer could not have failed to point out, there was a further consideration: Vanessa was now seventeen; she had already shown an admirable degree of calm, of judgment, of practicality. She alone of the household was not dependent upon Stella and she, far more than Stella, was bound by natural claims. As Leslie's daughter she would find it easier to minister to and to sympathise with him. That these arguments, or something like them, were debated between Jack Hills and Stella Duckworth is made probable by the circumstances of Jack's third proposal.

This event left a profound, though confused, impression upon Virginia. On 22 August 1896, Jack Hills bicycled to Hindhead and lingered all the afternoon with the Stephens. It was a warm summer day followed by a hot summer night. Jack and Stella went into the garden after dinner and did not return. The children had business in the garden too–they had moths to catch–but Jack and Stella evaded them. The place seemed full of the rustle of skirts and the whisper of voices. There was some little drama–a tramp or other trespasser suspected and hailed by Thoby. When they came in Leslie sent the children upstairs; clearly he was perturbed. Everyone felt uneasy, frightened; there was a sense of expectancy, of fatality almost, in the house; the children collected in Adrian's room and waited to see what would happen. And then at last Stella came in; she was radiant, blushing. She was, she said, very happy. . . .

Adrian, feeling perhaps that he was losing a mother once more, wept; Leslie rebuked him. They must all be happy, for Stella was happy and besides, his Julia had always wished it.

My Julia [he wrote] . . . would have been more delighted than any of us: the thought of her approval would have reconciled me if reconciliation had been needed. . . . I cannot imagine that I could contemplate Stella's marriage with more perfect confidence and satisfaction under any conceivable circumstances. If any thing could make me happier, this ought to: but [he adds ominously] my happiness is a matter of rapidly diminishing importance.

Yes, they ought to, they must, rejoice, Adrian must dry his eyes. But how could Leslie obey his own injunctions? It was an irreparable blow; only one thing could reconcile him to it–the fact that Stella would not leave his house.

How this proviso was reached we do not know–perhaps Stella exacted it from her lover, perhaps Leslie made it the condition of his blessing. At all events matters were fixed in this manner in August and, so far as Leslie was concerned, that was the end of it.

But, having gained his first point the young man went on to gain his second. How would they live? Where would they live? Who would be the master of the house? The difficulties grew ever more formidable; the arrangement began to look less and less realistic. In the end Stella went to see her step-father and told him that she must, after all, have a house of her own. We do not know what passed between them; certainly there was an explosion, but she got her way. Even so there had to be a compromise. Stella would not go far; there was another house available, No 24 Hyde Park Gate, just across the street. They would live there. It was no distance.

But from now on Leslie spoke in increasingly despondent tones about the whole business. He groaned and sighed, "he has picked my pocket"; how could Stella marry such a man? The name Jack was "like the smack of a whip."

A painful transaction was made more painful by the discretions of the dying century. Leslie could not altogether scrutinise his own emotions and realise the extent and character of his jealousy. Had he done so a man of his high moral character could surely have come to terms with the situation. But he had to see matters through his own distorting glass: he, a lonely old widower, a man broken and distracted by grief, had been betrayed. This was his version of the matter and it was a version which was accepted by the host of female supporters who had once seen in Stella the model daughter and now discovered her to be disgracefully selfish. But Stella was not greatly troubled; she had the strength of one who is happily in love and forms part of a strong alliance.

Virginia did not much care for Jack Hills and, in a way, she detested the marriage. The loss of a sister was for her almost as important as was the loss of a daughter to Leslie; and yet she rejoiced. Her slow recovery was assisted by a newly discovered source of happiness–the spectacle of Stella coming to life again. For Stella, who had been pale, numb and desolate, bloomed, smiled, and radiated joy. Virginia had never before been in the presence of such happiness; in later years she used her memory of Stella's love as a measuring rod. If a couple were said to be in love she would consider whether their affection would bear comparison with Stella's love for Jack or Jack's for Stella; *that* had been the real thing. She had not imagined that human beings could know such joy; she supposed that this was some special, some quite unusual manifestation of love. Shyly she confided this belief to Stella who, hardly less shy, laughed, thought that it was nothing out of the common but something that her sisters would also discover. Vanessa was beautiful; she would be 'coming out' now; she too would know love and so would Virginia.

Things were in this posture, half exquisitely happy, half painfully sad, at the beginning of 1897. On 1 January the children decided to start keeping diaries. Virginia's diary was kept, regularly for the first six months, intermittently for a year and a day; from it we can get a fairly exact picture of what was to be a momentous period.

Beginning in the middle of the Christmas holidays the diary begins also by recording a number of entertainments–visits to the theatre and the pantomime, to the zoo twice, to the National Portrait Gallery and the National Gallery, a first glimpse of those new curiosities of science the 'Animatograph' and 'Röntgens Rays,'

Decorations by Vanessa at the foot of a letter from
Virginia to Thoby Stephen, 1 February 1897.
(King's College Library, Charleston Papers, VWTS 23.)

IN VIRGINIA'S HAND:

A libel I protest–my skating is
particularly graceful, and I never
once have come to grief this
winter–Maria shall not
ornament *my* letters
again in a hurry.

IN VANESSA'S HAND:

V. Stephen fecit.

threepenny seats at the Albert Hall. There was also an entertainment of a different kind: *Clementina's Lovers*, written by Thoby and acted by all the children for the benefit of the maids. Such performances were always advertised by means of a handbill which began thus:

DENIZENS OF THE KITCHEN
COME IN YOUR THOUSANDS!!

The audience usually consisted of one housemaid but on this occasion there were two: Elizabeth and Florrie, together with the French maid, Pauline. They applauded loudly, but although Thoby killed every one of his characters in the last act, Pauline remained under the impression that it was a performance of *Aladdin*. In the evenings, Leslie continued to read aloud to his children; in January 1897 he was reading *Esmond*; sometimes he would recite poetry. Presently Thoby returned to Clifton, where he was a thoroughly successful schoolboy, playing games with forceful enthusiasm and construing Latin roughly but on the whole efficiently. It was at this time that the children were amused to hear 'Aunt' Anny exclaim: "O Leslie, what a noble boy Thoby is!"

Adrian was following a less glorious and less happy career at Westminster, and Vanessa, while preparing for the Royal Academy at Mr Cope's School of Art, resumed lessons with her father.

Virginia, it would seem, had not had any lessons since November 1896. "I hope, though I still hope with trembling, that she is a bit better," wrote her father to her aunt Mary Fisher a year later. Clearly she was still in a very nervous condition. But in February Dr Seton allowed her to do some lessons; we find her on the 22nd learning history and German; in March she was studying Livy and records "I did some Greek."

Meanwhile she was reading a great deal. In her diary she keeps a careful record, noting the beginning and ending of each book. Between 1 January and 30 June 1897 she read the following: *Three Generations of English Women* (volumes 2 and 3); Froude's *Carlyle*—here she makes the following notes: "1st volume of Froude which is to be read slowly and then I'm to re-read all the books that he [Leslie] has lent me"; Creighton's *Queen Elizabeth*; Lockhart's *Life of Sir Walter Scott*; *The Newcomes*; Carlyle's *Reminiscences*; *The Old Curiosity Shop*; *Essays in Ecclesiastical Biography* by Sir James Stephen; *Felix Holt*; *John Halifax, Gentleman*; *Among My Books* and *My Study Windows* by J. R. Lowell; *A Tale of Two Cities*; *Silas Marner*; *The Life of Coleridge* by James Dykes Campbell; *The Heart of Princess Osra* by Anthony Hope; three volumes of Pepys; Macaulay's *History*;

Barchester Towers; a novel by Henry James; Carlyle's *French Revolution*, his *Cromwell* and his *Life of Sterling*; a work by Lady Barlow; *Shirley*; Thomas Arnold's *History of Rome*; *A Deplorable Affair* by W. E. Norris.

"Gracious, child, how you gobble," Leslie would say as he got up from his seat to take down the sixth or seventh volume of Gibbon, or Spedding's *Bacon* or Cowper's Letters. "But my dear, if it's worth reading, it's worth reading twice," he would go on and, to himself: "Ginia is devouring books, almost faster than I like."

It was about this time, however, that the system of issuing books came to an end and Virginia was granted the freedom of her father's library. There were certain books on his shelves, he managed shyly to convey, which were not, in his opinion, entirely suitable for young ladies and amongst them, it would appear, was *Trilby*. But his daughter must decide for herself what she ought to read; clearly literature was her great passion and literature had to be accepted with all its risks. She must learn to read with discrimination, to make unaffected judgments, never admiring because the world admires or blaming at the orders of a critic. She must learn to express herself in as few words as possible. Such were his precepts and such was the educational opportunity that he gave. Leslie might be a disastrous teacher of mathematics; but he made up for it as a teacher of English literature.

Apart from the *Hyde Park Gate News* and one essay, I do not think that Leslie ever saw any of her early attempts at writing. But there was plenty to see. Before she was thirteen Virginia was trying to imitate the novels or at all events the style of Hawthorne. Then about the year 1897 Leslie brought her Hakluyt's *Voyages* from the London Library. Thereafter she modelled herself upon the Elizabethans, wrote a long essay entitled *Religio Laici* and another, seemingly a more characteristic effort, *A History of Women*. Of these early manuscripts nothing remains.

We may think of Virginia at this period as a rather tall, rather thin overgrown girl reading or writing in a back room at Hyde Park Gate. Until the time of Stella's marriage, she had no room of her own; her reading and writing were done either in the glazed room at the back of the house or in an armchair in the day nursery. But wherever she might settle, she made a fortress from which she was not easily driven. This reluctance to leave the sober, but to her important, comforts of her work place appears more than once in her diary.

In January Jack Hills had an operation—it was a very slight affair;

but it led to the postponement of the wedding. After it he and Stella planned to go to Bognor for his convalescence and it was suggested that Virginia should go there too, presumably as a chaperone. This, she told her diary on 1 February, was "a terrible idea"; on 2 February she told her family the same thing. She would on no account go alone with Jack and Stella on such an expedition. She was pressed to change her mind; the pressure came, not from her father, but from her half-sister. Leslie in fact took a gloomy view of the proposed holiday. Bognor, he guessed, was "rather nasty, and somebody has told us that the drains are bad. . . . Perhaps I shall go for a night or two." In the end Virginia got Vanessa to come with her. It was a depressing excursion; they did not like the place and the weather was atrocious. Even Jack and Stella had to admit that it might lack charm for others. Leslie, when he arrived, observed with gloomy satisfaction that he never saw such ugly country or such bad weather in his life; the sea, he declared, was made chiefly of mud. Virginia had no doubt of the derivation of the name Bognor. Leslie's determination to hate the whole business is easily explicable, for he was in a mood to hate anything and to find fault with any plan that Jack and Stella might advance.* Virginia's reluctance to join the excursion is harder to explain. I will advert to it later. But in part her irritation was caused by the general bother and stress of a ceremonial wedding.

> Sunday 28 March '97. In the morning we three [Vanessa, Virginia and Adrian] went to Church at St Mary Abbots! This was the last Sunday on which the banns were to be read, so that we had resolved to go. It began at 11.30, and finished at 1.15. We had rummaged the house for prayer books and hymn books; our search produced two hymn books (tonic sol fa) and one prayer book. This last however was left behind. A little black gentleman showed us into seats at the top of the church. Soon music and singing began, the row in front of us rose, and behind a wheezy old lady began to follow the choristers in a toothless, tuneless whistle–So on for the rest of the performance–At certain parts we stood, then sat, and finally knelt–this I refused to do–My neighbour looked so miserable and uncomfortable–In the middle the banns of John Waller Hills and Stella Duckworth along with several others were

* A letter from Leslie to Thoby written in January gives a clear enough indication of his state of mind: "It is a regular thaw, though Stella wants to take V[anessa] and V[irginia] to a skating place at the Botanical Gardens. I said that it was not safe as a lot of people fell into the round pond on friday and the thaw will have made the ice worse. She said that Jack said it was safe. I said that Jack was a —— no, I did not say that because I have been told that she is to marry him on the 1st of April: a very proper day, I think " (30 January 1897).

read, and no one pronounced any reason why etc. etc. Our prayers and psalms were rather guess work–but the hymns were splendid. We had a sermon from a new pastor–he said "we shall never hear the beloved voice again" alluding to the departed vicar. The old ladies snuffled and sobbed.

Then there were dresses to be made; for the first time in her life, Virginia found herself obliged to wear stays, things which she found herself unable to name in her diary. There was the question of Stella's wedding and going-away dresses, the "dreadful idea" that Vanessa and Virginia ought to be bridesmaids, Stella writing to Thoby at Clifton and sending him a cheque so that he might make a presentable appearance at the wedding, Leslie protesting that he need not buy new clothes–"Do you think that I . . . may be allowed to go in my ordinary costume? I don't see why I should not; but am half afraid that Gerald may bully me." Apparently he did. Then there was Stella's present from the Stephen children to be discussed, the money to be found, the thing to be purchased and so on. And there were other presents; soon the place was crammed with lace, engravings, plate etc.–"about as amusing to me," said Leslie, "as the dry plants at Kew."

Friday 9th April '97. We did nothing all day but arrange presents and write cards etc.–All the morning was spent like this. In the afternoon Stella and Father went to Highgate [to visit Julia's grave]–At last about 11 o'clock at night things were more or less finished, Mrs Jones arrived with a supply of underclothing. We went to bed–but Stella and Georgie & Gerald stayed up till 2 packing in her room. Jack stayed away all day long–Too much to do to be dismal, though the last evening was in danger of ending unhappily. Remembered however (Nessa and I) our resolve to be calm and collected.

Saturday 10th April '97.
Stella & Jack's Wedding Day.
The morning was still rather a hurly-burly–The finishing touches to everything had to be given–Eustace [Hills*] came often to arrange things with Stella–Huge boxes of flowers arrived throughout the morning and had to be arranged. . . Adrian did not go to school. At about 12 the Fishers came–and Stella went up to dress. M. Emile the hairdresser did her hair and also Nessa's–goodness knows how we got through it all–Certainly it was half a dream, or a nightmare. Stella was almost dreaming I think; but probably hers was a happy one. We went to the church at 2. Jack was there looking quite well and happy. Then at about 2.15 or 30, Stella and father came in–Stella walking in her sleep–

* Jack's brother and best man.

her eyes fixed straight in front of her – very white and beautiful – There was a long service – then it was all over – Stella and Jack were married – We went up and saw her change her dress – and said goodbye to her – So they went – Mr and Mrs Hills! These are some sentimental tokens of the day – white rose leaves from S's bouquet and red tulips from ours that Jack gave us.

After three days, largely spent in discussing the late festivities with Kitty Maxse and Margaret Massingberd, recognised authorities on all mundanities, the Stephen family left for Brighton. It was far from being their favourite resort; moreover the whole business of the wedding had left Virginia in a state of nervous exasperation. On 13 April she went to bed "very furious and tantrumical," on the 15th she regrets her "beloved armchair" at Hyde Park Gate; then she observes of their rented house in Hove that "truly such a dismal place was never seen." Brighton itself was full of "third rate actresses turned out in gorgeous clothes – tremendous hats, powder and rouge; and dreadful young men to escort them." And on 21 April:

Father took Nessa and me for a walk along the Parade to the Steine or some place of that kind – near the Pagoda at the other end of Brighton – I regret to say that various circumstances conspiring to irritate me, I broke my umbrella in half.. . .

But in retrospect it appeared to be a season of hope. Stella's letters from Florence seemed to promise a new kind of life in Hyde Park Gate; there had been much talk of loneliness and separation but, now that the thing was done, all this seemed nonsense. Stella would be so close to them, in a young household, a home which would almost be theirs but which would be uncurtained by the gloom of age and mourning. Better still, Leslie was making an effort to adapt himself to the new situation. The last seven or eight months of the engagement had, he admitted, brought him "a good many selfish pangs: but – well I should be a brute if I really complained." Vanessa was old enough now to take Stella's place at home; she would soon be 'coming out'; such an emergence could not fail to be momentous and might be salutary; and there was Virginia, clearly destined for his own profession. He set himself to know her better; he began telling her about the distinguished literary figures of the past whom he had known when he was young. It seemed to be the beginning of a new and happier epoch in all their lives.

On the afternoon of 28 April, the day of their return to London, they were met at Victoria by George; he told them that Jack and Stella had returned and that Stella was in bed with a gastric chill. At Hyde Park Gate they discovered that she was very bad indeed.

On the 29th Dr Seton decided that it was not a chill; he looked very grave and diagnosed peritonitis. By that evening they were all living in a nightmare.

Stella was worse in the afternoon–the pain was bad–After tea Nessa went back again [to relieve the nurse] & I sat again over those eternal old Graphics and my Macaulay which is the only calm and un-anxious thing in this most agitating time–Dr Seton came after dinner, and was rather frightening. It is Peritonitis–she is to be kept quite quiet–there is to be another nurse, & straw put down on the road. Poor Jack very unhappy. This is one of the most terrible nights so far. No getting rid of the thought–all these ghastly preparations add to it–The people jar at every possible occasion. I slept with Nessa, as I was unhappy. News that she is better at about 11 o'clock–what shall I write tomorrow?

That was written on the night of the 29th; on the next day Stella was much better; the improvement was maintained; by 2 May she was believed to be out of danger and by 17 May she was able to take carriage exercise. Much to her horror Virginia was told that she must accompany her half-sister on these expeditions. It seemed to her that the streets had become murderous. On 25 February she had been in a carriage accident; on 26 March she saw a lady cyclist run over by a cart; on 8 May she had witnessed two accidents in Piccadilly; on the 12th a cart horse fell down in front of her; on the 13th there was a collision between a runaway carriage horse and a waggon. Did these accidents really occur? Her state of health since the wedding and, even more, since Stella's illness had been deteriorating. On 9 May she was examined by Dr Seton and lessons were stopped, she was ordered to have milk, outdoor exercise, and medicine. She was certainly in a nervous condition and I think that she imagined or greatly exaggerated some of the accidents; but one of them–the accident with the lady cyclist, certainly did happen.★ It was a particularly agitating business because the lady, who ran straight into a cart in Gloucester Road, came from the direction and at an hour which Vanessa would have taken on her way back from her art school. Leslie, who was there, thought for a moment that it was indeed she.

At all events, it is clear from her diary that she really had become terrified of the simplest journey through the streets; she makes fun

★ ". . . Ginia saw the whole thing. . . . The poor old Goat was in a dreadful state as you may think and now she wants me to give up riding altogether, which of course I shan't do. Its very unlucky that it should always be the goat who sees accidents." Vanessa Bell to Thoby Stephen, 28 March [1897].

of her own terror but it was real enough. Thus, a part of her reluctance to go out with Stella can be explained by her reluctance to go out with anyone anywhere in the streets of London. But I think there is something else here, a strange ambivalence about Stella herself. Virginia was equally reluctant to go with her to Bognor in February and when, later, it was proposed that Stella should go to convalesce in the country:

> She . . . irritated me extremely by saying that I should have to go with her when she goes away, which I with great vehemence, declared to be *impossible*.

Why was it impossible? Virginia might reasonably anticipate that Bognor in February would be unrewarding; but in a very hot, sticky London summer the idea of a country holiday need not have distressed her, unless it was Stella herself whom she wished to avoid.

Certain diary entries make me think that this was the case. There can be no question of Virginia's distress when, in the last days of April, she feared that Stella would die; but a week later when Vanessa reported that their half-sister was looking fatter and decidedly better than after the wedding, Virginia notes that, although this was most satisfactory she was "unreasonable enough" to be irritated; and, five days later:

> This Sunday a most distinct improvement upon last—Then we were not out of the wood (as [Dr] Broadbent said) Vaguely unhappy. Cousin Mia a fixture—melancholy and large, in the drawing room, and sympathetic enquirers dropping in every now & then—Now that old cow is most ridiculously well & cheerful—hopping about out of bed etc: Thank goodness, nevertheless—

That "nevertheless" certainly gives one cause for speculation. Without attempting to probe very deeply we can, at least, note that between a good, kind, not very clever woman standing in a position of vague authority—half elder sister, half surrogate mother—and a very nervous, irritable, intelligent girl of fifteen, there can be plenty of causes for friction and some kind of friction there surely was. During that summer of 1897 Virginia's health and Stella's were in some way connected; they were bound, not only by feelings of affection on both sides, but, on Virginia's, by a sentiment of guilt.

In late May, however, tensions relaxed a little. It was known that Stella was going to have a baby; it was believed that she was cured and this belief persisted, despite a relapse at the beginning of June. It seemed possible to try to enjoy the events of the summer; they were of two kinds: public and private. The Queen celebrated her

Diamond Jubilee; Vanessa 'came out.' She went to various parties and Virginia thought that she looked exceedingly beautiful; but her account of the great world was not encouraging; it was, she declared, uncommonly dull. As for the Jubilee, they saw troops and horses and the old lady who had come to the throne when Leslie was a boy; but it aroused no deep emotion. There was no pleasure to be got out of anything that summer.

I growl at every thing—the effect of nerves doubtless!... hot, hot, hot.

It was indeed a summer of "relentless, thundery, sunless heat." At night she continued reading long after her light was supposed to have been put out; Hawthorne, Miss Mitford and Cowper's letters were her night books; she also read Macaulay and Henry James because she found that they soothed her nerves, and clearly her nerves needed a sedative.

Years later Vanessa was to describe that summer as "three months of... horrible suspense, muddle, mismanagement, hopeless fighting against the stupidity of those in power." From this it would appear that she knew more of what was going on than did Virginia. But Virginia must have become aware that, although the doctors continued to be reassuring, Stella was not getting well and as this gradually became more and more apparent Virginia's health deteriorated, her psychological illness was accompanied by physical symptoms. She complained of rheumatic pains and presently had a temperature.

On 13 July Virginia found herself so ill at Stella's house that Dr Seton sent her to bed there. The next night Virginia had what she called "the fidgets," and Stella sat by her stroking and soothing her until it was almost midnight. Three nights later Virginia was taken back to Number 22; George carried her wrapped in Stella's fur cape. The nurse told her that Stella was better and Stella herself called out "goodbye" as Virginia passed her door. But on the following evening Stella was operated on and at three in the morning of 19 July George and Vanessa came to Virginia's room and told her that Stella was dead.

Chapter Four

1897-1904

IT will have been noticed that the tragedies of the Stephen family were enacted with the assistance of a chorus composed mainly of female friends and relatives. When Stella died, this body proved itself fully equal to the occasion: there had never, they wailed, been so perfect a creature–except her mother–it was indeed a tragedy, nobody deserved happiness more. Sorrow and despair became a universal theme, almost a duty; Helen Holland, a Duckworth cousin, insisted upon praying in the room in which Stella had died; Cousin Mia, Aunt Minna and Aunt Mary were in constant, lachrymose attendance. The horror of the occasion, already in the children's view substantial enough, was by every means magnified and funereally enriched. Virginia suffered intensely from what she called "the ghastly mourners." She and Vanessa were glad enough to escape to Painswick, to the Vicarage which, although it overlooked a celebrated churchyard shaded by no fewer than ninety-nine yew trees, seemed to them decidedly more cheerful than the darkness and lamentation of Hyde Park Gate.

Before following them thither it may be helpful to look more closely at this tragic chorus, or at least at some of its constituents, and also at the younger generation in which Virginia was beginning to make some friends.

Cousin Mia was a grumpy, massive specimen of the Victorian age; she was Julia's first cousin and was celebrated as a model of the domestic virtues. She never let a birthday pass without making a suitable present and she expected others to be equally punctilious; if any child should forget her kindness Cousin Mia would be elaborately and pointedly hurt. Being hurt was one of her talents. She collected and disseminated bad news; she loved to report illness or death; she would enter lovingly into every circumstance of mortality; she loved to mourn, to weep, to prophesy disaster.

Aunt Minna Duckworth, Julia's sister-in-law, painted watercolours; she was a rich, fat old lady and entirely commonplace, and in all these respects very unlike Aunt Mary, Julia's elder sister, the wife of Herbert Fisher and the mother of seven sons and four daughters. "My mother was a saint," declared her eldest son, H. A. L. Fisher. "A more selfless, unworldly being never drew breath. Her life was a perpetual surrender of ease and comfort to the service of others." Her nieces would have agreed, but they would have made certain qualifications. Their mother also, they felt, was a kind of saint; but she was a little less emphatically saintly. In the same way, they would have agreed with their distinguished cousin that Aunt Mary had great beauty, a beauty equal to but different from that of her sister. Julia's face is generous, intelligent and humorous; Mary has a Burne-Jones melancholy, her features are a little sharper, her cast of countenance is drooping, dyspeptic, almost bitter. Like Julia, Mary was heroic; Virginia noted the courage with which, exhausted and washed-out, she carried the weight of the family trials – and they were heavy – upon her back. But the warmth, the gaiety, the smiling philosophy of Julia's bravery is lacking. Moreover her feelings were a shade less pure; her magnanimity could be displayed in a way that punished the beneficiary.

> My dear Virginia *you* must have the last piece of cake; yes, I *am* particularly fond of it and there will be nothing left for tomorrow's tea; but it would give me particular pleasure to sacrifice it to you.

Such, according to Vanessa and Virginia, was the Fisher style, and, as Virginia said: "The Fishers would have made Eden un-inhabitable."

This overwhelming sweetness made their frequent family visits to Brighton, where the Fishers lived, a great trial and led the sisters to dislike that charming town for many years. And, of course, Aunt Mary was a constant visitor at Hyde Park Gate; she had to enquire, to observe, to interrogate; she had to know how her motherless nieces were behaving and if, in her opinion, they were behaving badly, she must exert the authority of a mother. Her curiosity was insatiable, her censure vigorous. Virginia felt that she was continually prying and making comments, continually extending long, soft, tough, elastic tentacles to try and bring her and Vanessa into the family embrace, to suck them in and assimilate them to the Fisher pattern of conduct, belief and manners.

The Stephen side of the family was hardly more popular with Virginia and Vanessa than were the Fishers. Aunt Caroline Emelia was kindly but dull; the family of Fitzjames Stephen was formidable but unsympathetic. Lady Stephen, his widow, was a distant though uncongenial figure; so too was Katherine, the eldest daughter – already Vice-Principal of Newnham. The sons Herbert and Harry, though generally censorious, were reasonably remote. But of the three other daughters they saw more than they liked. Dorothea, the youngest (who was rather a favourite with Leslie), was in particular a frequent and unwelcome visitor to Hyde Park Gate. She was an ardent and aggressive High Church Anglican, and lost no opportunity of asserting the dogmas of Christianity before her benighted cousins. "She talks," wrote Virginia, "every minute of the day, wants no encouragement but a yes or no, & will only be stopped by your going out of the room." These Stephen sisters were not stupid, but pompous, absurd, and opinionated: "the most ungainly creatures in the world," said Vanessa, "who insisted upon forgiving us however badly we behaved"; and to Virginia it seemed that they were ugly and sweated and were altogether hateful.

Virginia could get some entertainment but little else from her Fisher and Stephen cousins. Her relationship with the orphaned children of her mother's sister Adeline and Henry Halford Vaughan was altogether happier. Of these five, Emma, the youngest, who studied music, seems to have been Virginia's chief friend and correspondent. A good many of her letters to Emma have been preserved; they are lively productions full of private jokes and family gossip and certainly not dull, though they portray a fairly humdrum existence: Greek lessons, social encounters, bookbinding (a hobby pursued by both)–such were the topics that Virginia discussed with Emma. She wrote also to Emma's sister Margaret; but Margaret devoted her life to good work amongst the poor and was much less of an intimate. The only son in this family was William Wyamar; his importance lay in the fact that he was to marry Madge, a daughter of John Addington Symonds, who had once spent a winter at Hyde Park Gate when Virginia was seven years old and was known thereafter to the children as The Chief.

Madge must have seemed to Virginia a romantic figure. She had grown up among the Swiss mountains in an atmosphere of freedom, she was a writer, she was passionately interested in the arts–and there was something melancholy about her. Her father's death in 1893 had hit her very hard and she had an intense capacity for suffering. But there was also something childlike, wondering and fresh about her attitude to life. She was modern, adventurous, 'aesthetic'– very much a girl of the 'nineties, and this inevitably was attractive; and then she was herself attractive.

Virginia was in fact in love with her. She was the first woman– and in those early years Virginia fled altogether from anything male– the first to capture her heart, to make it beat faster, indeed to make it almost stand still as, her hand gripping the handle of the water-jug in the top room at Hyde Park Gate, she exclaimed to herself: "Madge is here; at this moment she is actually under this roof." Virginia once declared that she had never felt a more poignant emotion for anyone than she did at that moment for Madge.* Certainly it was a very pure and very intense passion–pure in almost every sense of the word; Virginia at sixteen, for all George's kissings and fumblings, was by modern standards almost unbelievably ignorant. It was pure also in its sincerity, in its lack of jealous feeling. It was the passion of a girl in a junior form for a dashing senior, not a passion based upon intimacy.

The friendship with Emma and the passion for Madge were valuable; they provided some measure of relief and refuge in the domestic storms of the period, those afflictions to which we must now return.

Stella's death did not produce a complete breakdown in Virginia's health; as will be seen she was more capable of meeting than of anticipating disaster. She seems in fact to have made a fairly good recovery, to have been well enough, at all events, to join in the business which occupied her and Vanessa very much at this time, that of comforting Jack. Virginia now beheld what was for her a new form of grief–the grief of a man whose future is entirely desolated and who suffers, along with everything else, the deprivation of physical love. He came to Painswick every week-end and when they left there they went, to please him, to spend a week at his parents' home, Corby Castle, near Carlisle. The house was splendid and gorgeously appointed, the river Eden where Jack fished for salmon was beautiful, the situation romantic, and, in her diary, Virginia noted:

Terrible long dinner. Everything grand & strange. Jack unhappy. Old Hills silly. Mrs Hills talkative & rather unpleasant, Susan [Lushington] talkative and very pleasant. VS and AVS silent & miserable. . . Everything is miserable and lonely. Why did we ever come?

The fact was that they didn't like Mrs Hills at all and she, evidently, didn't like them. There was an atmosphere of hard calculating snobbery which they found detestable. Worse still, their sacrifice, which was supposed to bring aid and comfort to Jack, was failing in its purpose and he seemed unaware of what they were doing for him. They returned to London with a sigh of relief. They could

* "V[irginia] told me the history of her early loves–Madge Symonds who is Sally in Mrs Dalloway." V. Sackville West, *Journal of Travel with VW*, 29 September 1928.

help him better there; and in fact he came to stay at 22 Hyde Park Gate that autumn while a new house was being prepared for him and was, indeed, a member of the family. As such he must have been a witness of the curious transactions which now took place.

It must be remembered, in considering what follows, that Leslie during these years of miserable bereavement was becoming more and more solitary. He was cut off from society by his deafness and by the loss of his friends.* He had good reasons for being sorry for himself. Nevertheless Jack was the chief mourner on this occasion and Leslie came very near the end of the funeral procession. He was of course afflicted, but his tread was elastic, his eyes were dry. Stella had been a nice, good, dear girl, but she had not actually been his daughter. She had been his prop; and already, before her death, she had ceased to serve him in that capacity. She had been snatched from him and he, like a sensible man, a philosopher, had reconciled himself to the situation. Stella's death was of course a very bad business; "poor boy," he muttered, blandly unconscious of the pain that he inflicted, "poor boy, he looks very bad," and Jack, hearing himself thus described, was miserably embarrassed and turned the conversation. But for himself, well, he could bear it, he had a new prop–his eldest daughter.

Virginia said that Leslie actually told Vanessa that, "when he was sad, she should be sad; when he was angry, as he was periodically when she asked him for a cheque, she should weep." But Leslie had bred a daughter who possessed just those qualities which he would have prized in a son: honesty, courage, firmness and tenacity; but in a girl, who, after all, should descend to some little sweet artifice in favour of the men she is appointed to serve, who should make a grace of weakness and display a certain charming, yielding timidity, these virtues became a wholly unwomanly boldness and obstinacy. One incident of those years which Virginia remembered tells us a good deal about the family and about Vanessa. One summer evening when she and Virginia and Adrian were walking in the garden enjoying themselves, their father called them in to play whist with him. They did not want to do so, nor did they join him until a long remorseful interval had elapsed. They found Leslie disconsolate and lonely. "Did you hear me call?" he asked. The younger ones remained silent but Vanessa admitted that she had. There was then,

* The final pages of the *Mausoleum Book* are largely a necrology: John Ormsby, James Dykes Campbell, Thomas Hughes, George Du Maurier, Mrs Gurney, Mrs Brookfield, F. W. Gibbs, James Payn, Henry Sidgwick, George Smith, Herbert Fisher–one by one they die and Leslie is left increasingly lonely.

as there always was, a certain devastating frankness about her which Virginia found at times appalling and at times comic. Thus she came better armed than Stella to meet the demands and the assaults of her father.

'Assaults' is not, I think, too strong an expression. It is at all events hard to find any other word for the Wednesday afternoon interviews when the weekly accounts were examined. Vanessa was responsible for these reckonings, everything had to be made out in a very detailed and elaborate way and Vanessa, whose arithmetic was shaky, found the technical side of the business hard enough. But the real trouble came if the weekly books exceeded a certain sum; and this, Sophy being inflexible in her adherence to a tradition of decent extravagance, they nearly always did. Then Leslie would be overcome by a terrible feeling of financial insecurity. He felt hurt by the world, he felt terrified and aggrieved; he insisted that his misery should be appreciated and shared and so he made a scene.

The scene would begin with groans and sighs, then expressions of rage, then really terrible outbursts of bellowing fury in which Leslie would quite literally beat his breast, sob, and declare that he, a poor, broken, bereaved old man was being callously hounded to ruin. They were shooting Niagara; they would have to go to the house in Wimbledon. "And you stand there like a block of stone. Don't you pity me? Haven't you a word to say to me?" For all this was heard in silence by Vanessa. "What an aggravating young woman I must have been," she reflected in later years. "I simply waited till the cheque was signed." There were occasions when, with the connivance of Sophy, the accounts could be cooked so as to be made palatable to Leslie, but such occasions were very rare. The row was, almost, a weekly event. It ended when Leslie, with a piteously trembling hand, signed the cheque, all the time acting, and acting superbly, the part of the ruined and injured father.

Virginia, who witnessed it all, was consumed with silent indignation. How could her father behave with such brutality and why was it that he reserved these bellowings and screamings for his women? With men his conduct was invariably gentle, considerate and rational, so much so that, when Virginia and her aunt Caroline Emelia Stephen suggested to Maitland, his biographer, that Leslie was sometimes rather difficult, Maitland simply wouldn't believe it. Leslie, he objected, was the most modest, the most reasonable of men—and so he was with his own sex. But he needed and expected feminine sympathy. Vanessa's fault, which exacerbated the situation, making it far worse than it had been with Julia or with Stella, was that she would not sympathise. She would do her duty; but that was all, and her notion of her duty by no means corresponded with his. A complete and self-effacing devotion was what he demanded and this she was not ready to provide.

The uncomfortable fact was that Vanessa's childhood statement that she preferred her mother to her father had now hardened into something more positive. She, being the eldest, had observed the manner in which first Julia and then Stella had immolated themselves in order to make Leslie comfortable. She had seen them wear themselves out and die; she did not feel inclined to follow their example. Moreover Vanessa was not only more intelligent and more resolute than Stella, she was more selfish; she was fortified by the unyielding egotism of the artist. In the Life Room, in that blessed peace which is broken only by the gentle scrape of charcoal upon paper, in that pleasant atmosphere of hard work and turpentine, she could for a time enjoy an existence which must have seemed utterly remote from Hyde Park Gate. For she could then inhabit a world in which certain questions of shape and colour, of tone and contour, of the behaviour of objects under different circumstances of illumination and disposition, were of supreme importance–matters which never bothered the heads of the other inhabitants of Hyde Park Gate. Leslie could certainly know nothing of such things. He, who had so often looked far over the plains of Lombardy from the summits of the High Alps, never once went down into Italy. Painting meant nothing to him at all. Virginia had a wider vision, but all her life she was intrigued, mystified and perplexed by her sister's art; it was something odd and alien, and because she was a writer she was in fact far closer to her father than was Vanessa. They had a common mystery, a common shop and, as she felt her vocation ever more loudly evident, there was a real bond of sympathy between them.

But Vanessa's art was her shield; she met adversity–and during these years her distresses were many–with the fortitude of a hard pressed but well-armed soldier. Moreover she had an ally. Jack Hills had no great reason to like his father-in-law, a father-in-law who had done all that he could to stop the match and had in the end only acquiesced with a groan. Now, so it must have appeared to him, Leslie, while remaining callously indifferent to Stella's death, was calmly setting out to exploit the next victim. At Painswick Jack Hills had confided equally in both sisters and both had been equally devoted to the task of comforting him; but he turned increasingly to Vanessa. She was only too ready to join with him in lamenting

Stella's death and, when it came to criticising Leslie, they had a common theme.

Virginia's diary tails away towards the end of 1897 and she finally makes an end of it in January 1898. Thereafter the evidence is scanty. The family went to Ringwood in the New Forest in the summer of 1898 but there are no substantial records of this holiday. In the following year they went to the Rectory at Warboys, within reach of Godmanchester and their Stephen cousins. Here Virginia decided again to keep a diary. It is in many ways an exasperating document. She had, at this time, taken to using a very fine pen and this led her to cultivate a minute, spidery, often virtually illegible hand, which she made more difficult to read by gluing her pages on to or between those of Dr Isaac Watts's *Right Use of Reason*.* The whole thing is now an admirable exercise in patience and decipherment.

This Warboys journal is very different from the diary of 1897. It is more grown-up, more reticent, more impersonal. The other occupants of the house, her father, Vanessa, Thoby, Adrian, and their guests, are barely mentioned. She describes people only when they are outside her immediate circle; as for instance the local curate or her Stephen cousins; an account of a perfectly horrible picnic with them is one of the best things in the diary. But her main purpose is to practise the art of writing.

> ... the edge of this ... [cloud] glistened with fire–vivid & glowing in the east like some sword of judgment or vengeance–& yet the intensity of its light melted & faded as it touched the gray sky behind so that there was no clearly defined outline. This is one observation that I have made from my observation of many sunsets–that no shape of cloud has one line that is the least sharp or hard–nowhere can you draw a straight line with your pencil & say "this line goes so" Everything is done by different shades and degrees of light–melting & mixing infinitely–Well may an Artist despair!
>
> This was the central point of the sunset but ... there was another glory, reflected indeed but no less glorious and perfect of its kind than the original. ... The afternoon had scattered gray clouds pall mall about the sky–some of these were now conglomerated into one vast cloud field in the east & south–others were sailing like solitary icebergs. All bore on them the imprint of the dying kiss of the sun. The icebergs

---

* *Logick/or/the right use of Reason/with a variety of rules to guard against error in the affairs of religion and human life as well as in the sciences /by* Isaac Watts, D.D., London/mdcclxxxvi. Virginia bought this in St Ives for its binding and its format: "Any other book, almost, would have been too sacred to undergo the desecration that I planned."

shone glowing pale crimson; the icefields [?] were broken up into exquisite blocks of crimson but a crimson which looked all the more delicate & exquisite that its background was soft cold gray.

This was all over in 10 minutes – When we got back home the east & west were rapidly taking on the darkness of night – No gleams of crimson lived to tell that the sun had sunk.

It is interesting to compare this Ruskinian exercise in descriptive writing with a letter written in the same spidery hand to her cousin Emma Vaughan.

12 August 1899   Warboys Rectory
                                                Warboys
                                                        Huntingdonshire
                                                (this is all the address necessary)

Dearly beloved Toad,

This morning we heard from Susan Lushington that she arrives on Monday at Huntingdon about 12.30. Some of us must, I expect meet her there, which means that we shall not be back here till 1.30 – I do not know when you will arrive (if at all) but we *expect* you for luncheon; therefore to be brief and at the same time explicit; if we are not <u>all</u>

here to greet you on your arrival shd. your arrival take place much before 1.30: we beg that you will in no way feel slighted, but that you will make yourself at Home – go on the Punt – feed the sea gull – visit the stables – examine the photographs – & take possession of our bedrooms & their appurtenances. I fear that Susan Lushington may in some way interrupt our afternoon, but she is sure to be unpacking, resting, & letter writing; besides she is a charming animal, & can play the Spinet to perfection. *Some* other people – toads I should say – nasty slimy crawling things – *think* they can play – ahem!

You see – my dear toad, that the terrible depression of this climate has not yet affected my spirits. I suspect you & Marny [Margaret Vaughan] of ulterior motives in thus blackening our minds. Or perhaps you are too unimaginative & soulless to feel the beauty of the place. Take my word for it Todkins, I have never been in a House, garden, or country that I liked half so well – leaving St Ives out of account. Yesterday we bicycled to Huntingdon – & paid a visit to our relatives [Lady Stephen and her family]. Coming back we forgot all our cares – (& they were many – Nessa & I each had a large string bag full of melons which bumped against our knees at every moment) in gazing – absorbing – sinking into – the Sky. You dont see the sky until you live here. We have ceased to be dwellers on the earth. We are really made of clouds. We are mystical & dreamy & perform Fugues on the Harmonium. Have you ever read your sister in law's Doges Farm?* Well

* *Days Spent on a Doge's Farm* by Margaret Symonds (Mrs W. W. Vaughan), 1893.

that describes much the same sort of country that this is; & you see how she, a person of true artistic soul, revels in the land. I shall think it a test of friends for the future whether they can appreciate the Fen country. I want to read books about it, & to write sonnets about it all day long. It is the only place for rest of mind & body, & for contentment & creamy potatoes and all the joys of life. I am growing like a meditative Alderney cow. And there are people who think it dull & uninteresting!!!!

This all flowed from my lips without my desire or knowledge. I meant only to be short & businesslike. Poor Toad—when you come I shall say to you—Have you read my letter and you will confess that you did try a bit of it on the road, & you really do mean to have another shot on the way back. And you are only waiting for a rainy day to finish it altogether. Augusta* thinks it bad for your eyesight, & Marny has telegraphed "Forbid you to read Virginia's letters" I am a little cracky this afternoon. It is the hottest day I have yet lived thro'; I have read a whole long novel through; beginning at breakfast this morning & ending at 4 P.M.

It is now tea time. ([Two words illegible] Toadus inquit)

I am very sorry to have written such a long letter, but I will write a digest in very black ink so as to make up.

Love to dear Marny & all my Nieces and nephew.

Yrs always Goatus.

Do find some News to tell us. We long for some.

Oh October October

I wish you were *ober*

[in a large legible hand] This letter only to say that we have to meet Susan Lushington on Monday morning so that we may be late for you, but shall be in for luncheon 1.30 anyhow; & beg that you will Make Yourselves at Home—& not think yourselves slighted! The rest all the better for keeping.

News of a certain person & another *unknown* urgently required.

Do you see how much superior this paper is to yours?

This letter, with its pace, its mockery, its exaggeration, its flights of fancy, is already, despite some schoolgirlish remarks, not unlike the kind of letter that she was to write in later years. And those who remember her conversation will recognise certain turns of phrase, a certain impetuosity of address, which shows that at the age of seventeen she was already very like the person whom they knew. In a sense then she was precocious and old for her years, but in another way she was still very much a child and a very timid child at that. Peering out from the edge of the nest she observed the drop

---

* Emma's elder sister, Mrs Croft.

below with terror, a terror that was increased by her sister's unlucky attempts to fly.

Vanessa was 'out' and the business of bringing her out was undertaken by George; Vanessa was not enjoying it at all and Virginia feared that she would enjoy it even less. It was an alarming prospect and she felt that she would be very much happier in the schoolroom. Here, with increasing health, she was fairly active learning both Greek and Latin. Greek was taught her by Miss Clara Pater,* the sister of Walter Pater–"very white and shrivelled" she called her–and then by Miss Case. Janet Case was "thorough"; she observed that Virginia had a tendency to rush for the sense of a passage leaving grammar and accents to look after themselves, and that with Miss Pater she had got away with a very slovenly approach to the language. She had now to go back to the beginning and learn her grammar anew. But despite, or because of, these severities she knew how to hold Virginia's attention, and indeed her regard. She argued and took her pupil's arguments seriously; she herself was intensely interested not only in the language but in the ideas of the Greeks; she had a passion for Aeschylus and for Euripides and saw their relevance to her own time; so the lessons became discussions in which Virginia must have learnt a good deal. In July 1901, writing to Thoby, she says that she is reading the *Trachiniae* and has gone through the *Antigone* and *Oedipus Coloneus*. There was some sparring between her and her teacher; she tried, but did not succeed in making Miss Case lose her temper. But the lessons were the beginning of a lifelong friendship.

Thoby, now at Cambridge, was also to some extent her teacher, or at all events an intellectual sparring partner; and the following extract from a letter which Virginia wrote to him on 5 November 1901 gives some idea of their discussions:

My real object in writing is to make a confession–which is to take back a whole cartload of *goatisms* which I used at Fritham & elsewhere in speaking of a certain great English writer–the greatest– I have been reading Marlow, & I was so much more impressed by him than I thought I should be, that I read Cymbeline just to see if there mightn't be more in the great William than I supposed. And I was quite upset! Really & truly I am now let in to [the] company of worshippers–though I still feel a little oppressed by his–greatness I suppose. I shall want a lecture when I see you; to clear up some points about the Plays. I mean about the characters. Why aren't they more human? Imogen & Posthumous

---

* Miss Pater is probably the origin of Miss Craye in "Slater's Pins Have No Points" in *A Haunted House*, 1943.

– & Cymbeline–I find them beyond me. Is this my feminine weakness in the upper region? But really they might have been cut out with a pair of scissors–as far as mere humanity goes. Of course they talk divinely. I have spotted the best lines in the play–almost in any play I should think–

Imogen says–Think that you are upon a rock, & now throw me again! & Posthumous answers–Hang there like fruit, my soul, till the tree die! Now if that doesn't send a shiver down your spine, even if you are in the middle of cold grouse & coffee–you are no true Shakespearian! Oh dear oh dear–just as I feel in the mood to talk about these things, you go & plant yourself in Cambridge.

Tomorrow I go on to Ben Jonson, but I shant like him as much as Marlow. I read Dr Faustus, & Edward II–& I thought them very near the great man–with more humanity I should say–not all on such a grand tragic scale. Of course Shakespeares smaller characters are human; what I say is that superhuman ones *are* superhuman. Just explain this to me–& also why his plots are just cracky things–Marlow's are flimsier; the whole thing is flimsier, but there are some very "booming" (Strachey's word) lines & speeches & whole scenes–When Edward dies for instance–...

The Strachey to whom she refers was one of Thoby's new friends; he had, it appeared, met some tremendously interesting fellows at Trinity: Strachey was a wit, a man of undoubted genius; there was also Sydney-Turner, another genius, who slept all day and sat up reading all night, browsing through Menander as you or I might glance through a newspaper; Woolf, a strange wild man of powerful intellect; Bell, who wrote poetry and knew about pictures and had a capital seat on a horse. Thoby found Bell's horsemanship almost as interesting as Sydney-Turner's erudition, for he took a hearty commonsense view of the world; just as his father had been a muscular Christian, so he was a muscular atheist. The intellectuals liked him and he liked them; but between him and them there was a tenuous but perceptible frontier–his nickname 'The Goth' conveyed a shade of affectionate disapproval; he was a little more conventional, a little more conservative than they, and while for them Cambridge was exhilarating because it was a place buzzing with ideas, for him it was also a theatre for the traditional delights of privileged youth. And so, when the intellectuals considered whether to invite him to join that arch-intellectual semi-secret society– the 'Apostles'–they concluded, not without heart-searching and hesitation, that he was not really 'apostolic'; his sympathies placed him closer to Bell than to the 'Bretheren'–Bell, who had Edna May to lunch in his rooms at Trinity, rode out to Newmarket and studied the works, not only of G. E. Moore, but of Surtees.

That Cambridge was then a place reserved for men and one in which their sisters could hardly enter save as rare shy intruders was undeniable; but Cambridge as reported by so heartily masculine an observer as Thoby would have appeared quite aggressively and unbearably anti-feminist. In Virginia this must have provoked a great deal of serious reflection. She and her sister might spend the mornings studying Greek or drawing from the cast; but their afternoons and their evenings were given up to those occupations which the men of the family thought suitable: looking after the house, presiding at the teatable, making conversation, being agreeable to George and Gerald and to *their* friends, being polite to Aunt Minna, Aunt Mary, Aunt Anny, Cousin Mia, Lady Stephen and all Leslie's friends and admirers. The grand intellectual adventures and liberties were kept for Thoby and would, later on, be available to Adrian, and if this cost money, as it did, then they, the daughters, would be sacrificed for the benefit of the sons. Clearly it was the sons who were to have the lion's share of life.

> I dont get anybody to argue with me now, & feel the want. I have to delve from books, painfully & all alone, what you get every evening sitting over your fire & smoking your pipe with Strachey, etc. No wonder my knowledge is but scant. Theres nothing like talk as an educator I'm sure. Still I try my best with Shakespeare. I read Sidney Lee's Life . . .

But Sidney Lee's life of Shakespeare, as Virginia understood very well, was no substitute for Lytton Strachey's conversation. For the rest of her life she considered herself to be ill-educated and felt that this was an injury inflicted on her by reason of her sex. This radical inequity in the arrangement of the world was to be revealed in quite another fashion, and one which hit Virginia and Vanessa hard.

At the end of Thoby's first year at Cambridge the family had spent the summer at Fritham in the New Forest, and it was here that George, taking Virginia aside one evening in the garden, had a serious talk about Vanessa. Vanessa, he explained, was behaving unwisely. She was seeing altogether too much of Jack Hills. It was, of course, most imprudent and people were beginning to talk. Could not Virginia use her influence?

Virginia had been more or less unaware of what was happening. She had indeed noticed that Jack was more with her sister than with her. But she had not realised that Vanessa's feelings of sympathy had turned to something more passionate. She was in fact falling seriously in love with Jack and he was, at all events, not unwilling to be loved.

Did George perceive the irony of the situation? Probably not; he must have been engrossed by a very understandable alarm, to which no doubt was added a certain jealousy. Under the law as it then stood—it was altered in 1907—a man was forbidden to marry his deceased wife's sister. Numerous attempts had been made to legalise such marriages. The Commons frequently passed bills which would have had this effect, but the Lords, inspired by the bishops, resisted the will of the elected House until 1896. A motion was then set before their Lordships which was so drafted as to placate a large section of the clergy, and was passed. But Lord Salisbury, the Prime Minister, voted against it and it was no doubt through his agency that it never reached the Commons. If it had, this story would have been very different; also it would have been told by someone else.

A love affair between Vanessa Stephen and Jack Hills was there-fore, of necessity, something guilty. The best issue that could be hoped for was a foreign marriage such as that of the Holman Hunts—not, perhaps, quite the marriage for a rising young solicitor with political ambitions. The more probable outcome would be scandalous. That an insufficiency of Parliamentary time or the political calculations of a Prime Minister should be able to convert an innocent affection into a sinful attachment seems a *reductio ad absurdum* of official morality. The fact that Parliament could make her an honest woman led Vanessa, who always had her doubts about Parliament, to question whether, in this usage of the word, 'honesty' had very much meaning. She came by her own hard and private road to conclusions very similar to those of Thoby's friends who maintained that virtue lay, not in the mere fact of obedience to rules or in a reverential attitude towards received traditions, but in a state of mind; her own state of mind, she decided, had nothing to do with the strength of the Unionist Party in Westminster.

None of this, one may imagine, ever occurred to George, nor, if it had done so, would he have given it a moment's attention. All that he knew, and all that he needed to know, was that "people would talk." His interests would be touched, his career would be jeopardised. The half-sister whom he had hoped to present as a social asset—and with her looks she might have captured the younger son of a duke—would become a disastrous social liability. But George certainly went beyond self-interested calculations. An affair of this kind was 'not the thing' and he most sincerely and ardently worshipped 'the thing' without ever wondering what in fact it might be. When he took Virginia aside that evening at Fritham he was, doubtless, convinced that he was acting in the interests of morality, the family, and, naturally, of Vanessa herself.

Virginia, taken unawares, hardly knew what to say, felt that it was very shocking, went guilelessly to her sister and, stammeringly, presented George's views. "So you take their side too," was Vanessa's reply: a reply so touching, so bitter, and at the same time so effective that Virginia at once discovered that she was, as always in all their struggles, at one with her sister.

The party against them was strong: George had many allies. But it must be noted that it had one signal weakness; Leslie, with a greatness of spirit which deserves to be remembered to his credit, refused, despite George's entreaties, to join the forces of public morality. In his view Vanessa had to decide this matter for herself. But, for the rest, the outlook was dark indeed. To Virginia, who may have been prejudiced, it seemed that Jack himself bore a heavy responsibility; he had encouraged Vanessa, drawn comfort from her kindness, without ever considering what price she might have to pay for it. He was thoughtless, he was selfish, he behaved with masculine egotism. But, of course, the chief tormentors belonged to George's faction and consisted largely of the usual regiment of female relations. Mary Fisher–again according to Virginia–was particularly vicious. So much so that Vanessa avoided her aunt and cut the Fishers when they met in the street. This conduct drew a reproof from Thoby. How much he understood of the business is unclear–in general he seems to have known very little of what was happening to his sisters–but at all events he knew what respect was due to his aunt and he announced with Olympian calm, but also with a hint of Olympian fire power, that he thought it not right that his aunt Mary should be treated so. Thoby was on the side of authority–masculine authority; if George wanted the girls to go to parties then they should go; if Leslie demanded sympathy, then the girls should be sympathetic. This attitude was made possible by the fact that there was never an explanation between Thoby and his sisters. Sex was taboo, the dead were taboo, half their most important emotions were taboo; they were all too shy to come out into the open. Vanessa, devoted as she was to her brother, and far too reserved to argue a point involving her own emotional life, must then have reached the nadir of her despair.

All this must be imagined against a background of small engagements and steady routine. During the years 1897–1904 life at 22 Hyde Park Gate must have been something like this: Vanessa would start the day with a ride up and down the Ladies' Mile on a horse given her by George. Breakfast at 8.30, first Vanessa and Gerald, then Leslie and Adrian, the latter usually late – half his gear forgotten – for school, the former groaning because there were no letters for him (Everyone has forgotten me) or growling over a bill from Barkers (We shall be ruined). Then Vanessa would descend to the basement, which was almost totally dark, interview Sophy and order the day's meals. Then she would bicycle off in a long dress and a large floppy hat to Mr Cope's School of Art or, later on, to the Academy Schools (she passed ahead of her friends from the Antique to the Life Room in 1902). Gerald might offer her a lift eastwards in his hansom – he had a regular hansom – on his way to the publishing business which he founded in 1898. George and Virginia would come down later, George completely armed for the gentilities of London life, shining, immaculate, impeccable; he would engage Virginia, if he could, with an account of his social triumphs of the previous night, before going off to his work as unpaid secretary to Charles Booth or Austen Chamberlain. Leslie would retire to his study and remain there all the morning. When George stopped chattering and left, Virginia too would go upstairs with Liddell and Scott to tackle Sophocles or Euripides or to write letters and essays. This she did in the old nursery at the top of the house. Here she accumulated a great many books and here she sometimes received friends or teachers – Janet Case or one of the Vaughan girls. The room had white walls and bright blue curtains. Her manner of working was unusual. She had a desk standing about 3 feet 6 inches high with a sloping top; it was so high that she had to stand to her work. For this peculiar method of operation she advanced various reasons but it would seem that her principal motive was the fact that Vanessa, like many painters, stood to work in order to be able to move away from and look at her canvas. This led Virginia to feel that her own pursuit might appear less arduous than that of her sister unless she set matters on a footing of equality, and so for many years she stood at this strange desk and, in a quite unnecessary way, tired herself.*

Like Vanessa, Virginia would be dressed with little regard for fashion and of the two Virginia would be the more untidy; from ten till one the great world could be ignored. After lunch – Leslie's lunch always consisted of a mutton chop – social claims might become more urgent and by 4.30 they were important, for there

* "For the rest of her life," says Holroyd, *Lytton Strachey*, vol. I, p. 404; this is certainly an exaggeration – possibly until 1912.

was tea to be taken in the front room which at Hyde Park Gate was separated from the back by folding doors. In this room, the Stephen girls might entertain Mrs Humphry Ward, Mr C. B. Clarke, Mr F. W. Gibbs and, to represent the younger generation, Mrs Maxse and her sister Miss Susan Lushington, the Miss Massingberds, the Miss Stillmans, Mr Ronald Norman–all those whom Adrian was later to call the 'Hyde Park Gaters': Freshfields, Booths, Protheroes, Pollocks, Creightons, Ritchies. These families, socially and intellectually respectable representatives of the middle class, many of them eminent or connected with eminence, many of them neighbours of the Stephens in Kensington, had been friends of Leslie and Julia; it was assumed that, in their generation, the children would also be friends. There might also be aunts and cousins and they all had to be arranged socially. The right person had to be found to shout the right things into Leslie's ear trumpet and the young ladies, who now had to appear as such, had to make the right kind of small talk. This art they learnt and never entirely lost–the art of being agreeable, of watching the happiness of guests, of providing suitable social mixtures– the art, in fact, of pleasing. In later life Virginia thought that something of it had leaked into her ink–not when she was writing her novels, but in her reviewing. Here she was, she felt, too polite, too much the young lady, altogether too deferential.

The task was not an easy one. Leslie was a social problem. He could be amusing and sometimes he enjoyed being reminiscent; but he was easily bored and when he was bored he would groan to himself. Leslie's groans were, indeed, one of the more disheartening phenomena of Hyde Park Gate. He would groan in despair at his bereavement; he would groan over his bank balance; it was also said that he was heard one night slowly ascending the stairs, groaning at each step and loudly exclaiming: "Why won't my whiskers grow? Why won't my whiskers grow?"

But Leslie's teatime groans were, only too often, the prelude to something far worse. Leslie was deaf enough not to hear, or to pretend not to hear, his own conversations with himself.

"Why won't that young man go?" he would suddenly demand in a dreadfully audible voice. Or again, when his old friend Frederick Waymouth Gibbs had, for a space of twenty minutes or so, imparted a great mass of information concerning the Dominion of Canada, Leslie would produce an enormous groan and remark, in a deafening whisper: "Oh Gibbs, what a bore you are." Then some young woman–Kitty Maxse very likely, for she had every social accom-

plishment at her finger tips, would have to coax and flatter the indignant (but undeniably boring) Mr Gibbs back into a good humour
again.

The day was always full of social arrangements; arrangements to
spare Leslie unwelcome visitors, to see that someone would be in
when someone else called, to cope with various horrors, such as
Aunt Mary, Cousin Mia and so on. And when the social difficulties
of tea had been negotiated the far more perilous business of the
evening had to be managed. Before dinner the family retired to dress,
no matter how quiet the evening that lay before them. The Duckworth brothers were, of course, impeccably got up; but, despite the
presents that they received, the young ladies were hard put to it
to make an acceptable toilette. Acceptable that is to George, who
would examine his half-sisters with the keen and pitiless eye of a
sergeant major inspecting a recruit. If he detected the least contra-
vention of decorum as he understood it, as for instance when
Virginia had the bright idea of making her evening dress out of
cheap green furnishing material, he would express his displeasure
with curt and brutal acerbity. And then, later in the evening, when
Leslie, who had spent the interval between tea and dinner in his
study, returned thither to read Hobbes or Bentham, to smoke
innumerable clay pipes–each a virgin used but once,* so that his
fender was littered with their shattered debris the next morning–
George would carry his sisters out into the great world.

George was bitterly disappointed in Vanessa; she seemed determined to spoil her own chances in life. She fell in love with the wrong
person and when he, George, poured gifts into her lap she was so
unreasonable as to protest. How could any girl in her senses
(particularly one with an allowance of fifty pounds a year) complain
at being given fans, necklaces, dresses, flowers, an Arab mare for
the Row and invitations to half the great houses in London? But
Vanessa did complain, although at first her protests were probably
silent. Indeed, to begin with she did enjoy being taken to dances,
even though she was still wearing mourning–very beautifully
confected mourning–for Stella; but soon her feelings changed and
although she loved pretty clothes a time came when she began to
look upon her evening dresses as a penitent looks upon her sheet.
She was shy, she was awkward, she was naturally silent; she danced

---

* Tobacco was a male prerogative. Vanessa and Virginia were forbidden to
smoke in their father's presence. Once, when a lady guest lit a cigarette, she was
roughly told by Leslie that his drawing-room was not a bar parlour. MH/A 5.
See also: VW, Collected Essays, Vol. IV, p. 79.

badly; but even if she had talked and danced with ease she would have found George's friends excruciatingly boring. George moved in stuffy, upper-class society; but it was not only that Vanessa could find nothing to say to these people; it was worse than that: she found George himself a bore. He could spoil a party by his mere presence: when Vanessa dined with old friends whom she liked he could and did damage the evening by turning up uninvited after the meal and making polite conversation until it was time to escort his sister home. For him, indeed, parties were not designed for pleasure; his sisters were taken out, not to enjoy themselves but to practise their profession, the great profession of getting husbands; he was there as an arbiter of elegance, a censor and a chaperon; every entertainment was to be considered an examination, and their performance would be judged with ruthless severity. The people whom they met might not please them, that did not matter; these were the 'right' people and to meet them was a duty.

Presently Vanessa began to resist. Each new invitation brought a struggle. George would implore and entreat, sometimes he would actually burst into tears, if still thwarted he would sulk; he would mobilise the family – Aunt Mary Fisher was always a sure ally – and the family would, loudly, angrily and repeatedly, fail to understand how Vanessa could be so foolish, so obstinate, so unwomanly, so downright ungrateful, as to reject George's generosity. And even when Vanessa thought that she had escaped she would find that George had secretly accepted an invitation in her name and that she was condemned to another evening or another week-end of misery and exasperation.

A time came, about the year 1900, when Vanessa's opposition became so troublesome that George decided he had better see whether he might not have better luck with Virginia. He gave her a brooch and told her that Vanessa's unkindness was such that it would drive him from home and – this was emotionally implied rather than said – he would find consolation in the arms of whores. It was for Virginia to rescue him from this awful fate by being a good sister and venturing into high society. Virginia, who had been to the Trinity Ball and had found it sufficiently amusing (it was made more so by the presence of Thoby's friend Bell), thought that perhaps Vanessa's complaints were exaggerated and agreed without too much difficulty.

She soon discovered her mistake: Vanessa had been bored; *she* was terrified. After all it was not so very long since she had been unable to endure the company of any stranger; now, faced by all the apparatus of a very dull section of 'good society' she found that, despite Stella's lessons, she was unable to dance at all gracefully, nor could she converse with the slightest ease in a ballroom. She went through agonies of embarrassment, miserable humiliating evenings when she couldn't find a partner, ghastly meaningless conversations which got bogged down and left her blushing and wordless.*

> ... the truth of it is, as we frequently tell each other, we are failures. Really, we cant shine in Society. I don't know how it's done. We aint popular – we sit in corners & look like mutes who are longing for a funeral. However, there are more important things in this life – from all I hear I shant be asked to dance in the next. ...

Things were made a little worse by the fact that George, for all his social ambitions, was, in practice, rather ham-handed. When he made Vanessa go with him to stay for the week-end at the Chamberlains they arrived at the wrong time and at the servants' entrance. Virginia remembered one evening when an even more ghastly mistake occurred.

On this occasion George took Virginia by herself to dine with the Dowager Countess of Carnarvon and her sister Mrs Popham of Littlecote, the dinner to be followed by a visit to the theatre. The evening began well enough; the two ladies seemed kind and Virginia felt encouraged to talk. In fact she began to speak with confidence and abandon. It was necessary, she said, that one should understand the need for expressing one's emotions. Had Lady Carnarvon read Plato? If so she would remember ...

Here Virginia said something awful, something appalling. We shall never know what it was, and perhaps she was simply talking too much; but she always had a terrifying way of forgetting her audience and, in the first years of the twentieth century, Plato could easily lead to topics which might appal Lady Carnarvon or Mrs Popham, topics entirely unsuitable for a young woman. Indeed, as George explained later, in the course of his reprimand: "they're not used to young women saying *anything*." Whatever it was that she said Virginia only became aware of her mistake when she observed that George was crimson with embarrassment. At once a new topic was started and Virginia knew that she had failed again.

---

* A quarter of a century later she wrote: "The heat has come, bringing with it the inexplicably disagreeable memories of parties, and George Duckworth; a fear haunts me even now, as I drive past Park Lane on top of a bus and think of Lady Arthur Russell and so on. I become out of love with everything ..." AWD (Berg), 25 May 1926.

But that was not the end of this disastrous evening. They had tickets for the French Actors. They put on their cloaks and left, Virginia still burning with shame but able to notice, despite the agitated efforts of Mrs Popham, that George gave his hostess a passionate kiss behind one of the pillars of the hall. And then there was the play. At first Virginia's misery was such that she hardly noticed what was going on upon the stage; moreover the French dialogue was too rapid for her ears; but presently the action became so dramatic that it compelled her attention. A gentleman was chasing a lady around the room, he gained upon her, she fell upon a sofa, he leapt upon her, at the same time unfastening his buttons and–the curtain fell.

Lady Carnarvon, Mrs Popham and George rose in consternation; together they beat a hurried retreat, shepherding Virginia before them out into the street, where the ladies departed in a brougham.

George, vexed with Virginia, and no doubt by his own social folly in taking his sister to such an entertainment, insisted nevertheless that the social duties of the evening were not over. They drove off in a hansom cab to Melbury Road to an evening party at the Holman Hunts where they found the Master with a large company explaining the sublimities of *The Light of the World*, which had recently returned to his studio after touring the principal cities of the Empire. There at least Virginia might feel safe from impropriety; but not for long. That night, in her bedroom she had once more to withstand the ardent embraces of George.

The incident may help to qualify the picture which Virginia drew of her relations with George at this time. She saw herself as the defenceless victim of George's social ambitions; she was snubbed, bullied, and compelled to jump like a lame dog through whatever circus hoops he might place before her. The picture, I fancy, is true enough as far as it goes; but this was not the whole picture. Virginia respected George's sex, she quailed before his authority, she was aware of her own poverty and of his affluence; but she was never guilty of weak submission.

As a child of I know not what age, she wrote a History of the Duckworths. It has been lost but the opening passage was something like this:

> One day when William Rufus was hunting in the New Forest he shot a duck. It fell into the middle of a pond and could not be recovered; but an active little page boy waded out into the water and recovered the bird. The king drew his sword and dubbed the lad saying: "Arise Sir Duckworth, for surely thou art worth many ducks."

George and Gerald were not amused and one may surmise that this little *jeu d'esprit* was meant to pain them. It expresses lightly, but not without malice, Virginia's estimate of the Duckworths. She was from an early age convinced that although the pattern of inheritance might give them beauty it did not give them intelligence. For that, the sharp wits of the Stephens were more to the purpose. George and Gerald could easily be mocked and Virginia was not the person to neglect such an opportunity; her social gaffes were painful to her, but she probably drew some satisfaction from her realisation that they were even more painful to George. On one occasion, when she was at a party, her drawers fell down while she was in the very act of saying goodbye to her hostess; she gathered everything up in a bundle and shuffled away as best she could; but on returning to Hyde Park Gate and finding George at home she came into the drawing-room and flourished the errant garments in his face. George was speechless with indignation.

And yet, her miseries were real enough. She could make a joke of them and tease George with them; but the fact remained that she and Vanessa were, as she said, "failures." In an essay written at this time she discussed her lack of success and then goes on to consider the merits of the man or woman who shines at dances. She is at some pains to be fair. She rejects the common view that the artificiality, the downright insincerity of the socially successful person is reprehensible. It represents the desire to please and to be pleased and that after all is not a bad thing: rather there is a certain gallantry, a certain philanthropy in this cultivation of the graces. The grapes, she seems to be saying, are not sour. And again, writing to an intimate friend:

> I went to *Two Dances* last week, but I think Providence inscrutably decreed some other destiny for me. Adrian and I waltzed (to a Polka!), and Adrian says he can't conceive how anyone can be idiotic enough to find amusement in dancing – and I see how they do it but feel all the really young Ladies far removed into another sphere – which is so pathetic – and I would give all my profound Greek to dance really well – and so would Adrian give anything he had.

But she did not always fail socially; the desire to succeed, though not quite in the way that George envisaged, was there. Few girls, conscious that they had more than their fair share of wits and beauty, could altogether renounce the *beau monde* at whose doors Virginia found herself. She could see clearly enough that most of its inhabitants were stupid; she could see that success, as George understood success, was a pretty dismal thing. There was much in Good

Society that she found hateful and frightening; but there was always something in it that she loved. To be at the centre of things, to know people who disposed of enormous power, who could take certain graces and prerogatives for granted, to mingle with the decorative and decorated world, to hear the butler announce a name that was old when Shakespeare was alive, these were things to which she could never be wholly indifferent. She was in fact a romantic snob. It was something which she never allowed to distort other values but it did play a part—quite an important part—in her life. In her youth she was ready to look at the world of rank and fashion, if only it could be sympathetically presented to her, and so was Vanessa. What they needed was a guide, not a tyrant but a friend, not a man but a woman—a woman with the tact, the imagination, the kindliness that could rob Mayfair of its terrors and make Kensington delightful. Living in and for society such a person would no doubt be at some points limited but the limitations would be so nearly transcended that, to a shy, intelligent girl, they would hardly be apparent; such a person might act as an evangelist of good society and be able, almost, to make one believe that it is possible to be at once worldly and unworldly. Virginia attempted to draw such a woman when she wrote *The Voyage Out*; she made a deeper, a more extensive examination in *Mrs Dalloway*. In real life she and Vanessa found her in Kitty Maxse.

Kitty Maxse had been a Miss Lushington; the Lushingtons were connected at a great many points with the Stephens, with Julia's family, with India, Clapham, the Bar and the Pre-Raphaelites. Mrs Vernon Lushington had been Julia's greatest friend, and had known the Stephen children for many years. Julia it was who had made the match between Kitty and Leopold Maxse which, it may be remembered, was settled under the jackmanii at Talland House. Leo Maxse was an invalid, enough of an invalid to be unable to take the active part in politics that he would have enjoyed; he was, nevertheless, the editor of the *National Review*. He was a difficult husband; there were no children. She was smart, with a tight, neat pretty smartness; her blue eyes looked at the world through half-closed lashes; she had a lovely mocking voice; she stood very upright.*

In some measure she inherited the Stephen girls. She was grateful

---

* Mrs Maxse was certainly the original of Mrs Dalloway, but I do not think that novel provides, or was meant to provide, an exact portrait. Lord David Cecil, who knew Mrs Maxse, does not see any close resemblance. Virginia comes closest to exact portraiture when she loves her model. She did not love Kitty Maxse.

to and had been deeply attached to Julia; she adopted a quasi-maternal attitude towards her daughters. Vanessa, as the eldest, most needed her help in dealing with the great world and she was quite sharp enough, quite sensible enough to perceive, even if Vanessa did not tell her, that George was not the perfect Cicerone for a tour of London Society. Guided as she was by excellent feelings and good principles, she proved really sympathetic and really helpful when Stella died; thereafter she became one of Vanessa's two most intimate friends. (The other, Margery Snowden, was a dowdy, desperately serious art student.)

Thus, with Kitty's assistance and in her own manner, Vanessa went into society.

Virginia was rather left behind on this excursion. She found Kitty far less sympathetic than did Vanessa; perhaps she was a little jealous; but also she detected a certain worldly brilliance, a kind of enamelled glitter that she did not like. She was continually telling herself that Kitty *was* a very good woman and yet, when she met her, recoiling. But she certainly had the entrée to a feminine aristocratic circle which was easier, less pretentious and quite as glamorous as that which George frequented. Lady Bath and her daughters Beatrice and Katherine Thynne (who married Lord Cromer), and their friend Lady Robert Cecil, these seemed to Virginia to have, not only rank, beauty and easy, pleasant good manners but a kind of lazy pagan majesty, a natural grace which fascinated her; she saw a good deal of them and enjoyed their society enormously; her guide thither was not Kitty but a friend of her own.

Before coming to this important friendship let us note that the years 1900, 1901 and 1902 progressed, so far as the Stephen family were concerned, sadly but without any very remarkable events. 1900 had been a year of crisis in the relationship between Vanessa and Jack Hills; thereafter it would seem that Jack gradually disengaged himself; at all events the affair died down, not, one may imagine, without pain to the principals and to Virginia. George must have been pleased but his own affairs were not progressing very well. He fell in love with Lady Flora Russell and, having learnt *Love in the Valley* by heart in order to impress her, went off to propose. This mnemonic feat succeeded in its object and he was able to write home announcing his engagement. The news, as may be imagined, was greeted with enthusiasm. Virginia telegraphed her congratulations. "She is," she wrote, "an Angel," and signed with her usual nickname. The telegram reached Islay thus: SHE IS AN AGED GOAT. It did not help matters but was not, it seems, the reason why the match was almost immediately broken off. George returned crestfallen and miserable and retired to bed, suffering, it was said, from shock.

That year 1902 saw the Coronation and a large distribution of honours. Leslie was offered a KCB. He seems to have felt some reluctance to accept such an honour but was apparently pressed to do so by his children, and notably by Thoby. Earlier in the same year he had an illness and consulted Sir Frederick Treves, who recommended an operation; just what he said we cannot tell, but Leslie wrote: "I consider this to be equivalent to a warning that my journey is coming to an end." In fact he probably knew that he had cancer. At the end of the year he wrote to his eldest son: "They have, I suppose, explained my state to you. I do not think that they have quite taken in the fact–it *is* a fact–that the trouble is now steadily increasing."

That summer the family was at Fritham again. It was their third stay there. The young people enjoyed riding in the New Forest and Sir Leslie, although his illness kept him pretty close to the house, liked the place. Amongst their visitors were Clive Bell and, more important from Virginia's point of view, Violet Dickinson.

Violet Dickinson was a friend of the Duckworths, and had been intimate with Stella; she became a Quaker but one with aristocratic connections: she was related to the Edens. Leslie noted that "her only fault is that she is 6 feet high." She had, he observed, "taken a great fancy to the girls, who went about with her all day & discoursed upon literary & other matters continuously–Miss D. told me many pleasant things about the two and admires Ginia's intelligence greatly." The admiration was mutual, though why Virginia was so bowled over by Violet it is not altogether easy to say. At the time of this visit to Fritham, when the friendship was still fairly new, Virginia attempted to describe Violet in words:

We . . . showed her to her room & left her to dust her long travel-stained limbs. She came down to dinner in flowing & picturesque garments–for all her height, & a certain comicality of face, she treats her body with dignity. She always wore suitable & harmonious clothes –though she made no secret of the fact that they had lived through more seasons than one. Indeed she was singularly unreserved in many ways; always talking & laughing & entering into whatever was going on with a most youthful zeal. It was only after a time that one came to a true estimate of her character–that one saw that all was not cheerfulness & high spirits by any means–She had her times of depression, & her sudden reserves; but it is true that she was always quick to follow a cheerful voice. In that lies much of her charm– . . .* To a casual observer she would appear, I think, a very high spirited, rather crazy, harum scarum sort of person–whose part in life was [to] be slightly ridiculous, warmhearted & calculated to make the success of any kind of party. She has a very wide circle of acquaintances mostly of the landed & titled variety in whose country houses she is for ever staying– & with whom she seems to be invariably popular. She is 37– & without any pretence to good looks,–which she knows quite well herself, & lets you know too–even going out of her way to allude laughingly to her gray hairs, & screw her face into the most comical grimaces. But an observer who would stop here, putting her down as one of those cleverish adaptable ladies of middle age who are welcome everywhere, & not indispensable anywhere–such an observer would be superficial indeed.

At which point the MS comes to an end, or rather, the page on which it is written is cut away.

Virginia's numerous letters to Violet have been preserved and from this it is clear to the modern reader, though it was not at all clear to Virginia, that she was in love and that her love was returned. For they are passionate letters, enchanting, amusing, embarrassing letters full of private jokes and endearments, letters in which Virginia invents nicknames for herself, imagines herself as some shy half-wild animal, a pet to be fondled and cherished; and from which one tries to conjure up a picture of the recipient.

She was certainly a very good woman, a woman gifted with humour, intelligence and patience. "You remind me," said Virginia, "of Mrs Carlyle" and then warned her not to risk that lady's fate and go rushing with too warm a heart after her pets. She attracted Virginia, I surmise, because she was so very unlike her; she had a breezy masculine assurance, a cheerful imperturbable balance, she was a lofty and reassuring tower of strength. But she must have had something more than strength, a certain real greatness of mind and character. She could take mockery, give sympathy, understanding and love with immense generosity. The other Stephen children, none of whom was stupid, all of whom were inclined to be critical, liked her. I would guess that they found her reactions to their taste. She would always have been on the side of decency and kindliness and good sense.

Like Madge Vaughan, Violet Dickinson fulfilled a need. She provided sympathy and stability at a time when it was badly needed. I do not think that she made any very great contribution to Virginia's

* Passage excised in the original

intellectual development. Virginia did indeed send her manuscripts for criticism (she also wrote a kind of joke biography of her friend) but I doubt whether Violet's criticism as distinct from her encouragement was very important to her. Her gifts were chiefly moral and, when other and more remarkable people came into Virginia's life, passion slowly faded into kindness. One must think of this friendship as an affair of the heart, where I think that in fact it remained; while the affair was at its height, that is to say from about 1902 to 1907, it was intense.

Violet Dickinson's sympathies were to be put to the test. When she came to stay at Fritham in 1902 Sir Leslie was anticipating an operation. In December it could be no further postponed; it seemed doubtful whether he would survive but in fact he made a good recovery, good enough to allow his children to celebrate Christmas boisterously, and was back at home in January. But in April 1903 it became clear to Dr Seton and the nurse that the disease was spreading and that the patient must soon die. This news was communicated to Vanessa, who told her brothers and sister and thought it best that Sir Leslie should, if possible, be kept in ignorance.

The word "soon" in Seton's report was given a more precise meaning by Treves, who saw the invalid in May and gave him six months to live. There was nothing that they could do but try and make his dissolution as easy as possible. It was a melancholy and unpleasant time for everyone, but of the children none, I think, suffered so much as Virginia. They all felt some affection and some guilt. Vanessa, who, more than any of them, was relieved—glad even–to be orphaned, dreamed after her father's death that she had committed a murder and although she had never heard of Freud, realised the connection and promptly stopped such dreaming. Thoby no doubt was upset; but with his sanguine character, his abundant and optimistic plans for the future, the thing was not too great a blow, while Adrian had very little affection for his father. But Virginia, although she had felt hatred, rage and indignation at Leslie's conduct to Vanessa, felt also very deep love for him. She saw that he was reluctant to die because his children had at last got to an age at which he could know them and, knowing, love them. He wanted to see what would become of them. In his present state he could no longer be a tyrant and his tyranny might be forgotten. Between him and Virginia a special bond had been established. She loved him and he, for his part, had for some time felt a special tenderness towards her. "Ginia," he wrote, "continues to be good to me and is a great comfort," and again: "She can be most fascinating." Thus, for her, the conflict of feelings was most acute and most miserable.

That summer they went to Netherhampton House, near Salisbury. Sir Leslie was still able to walk a little and Virginia took him to Wilton and Stonehenge. In the autumn, the usual chorus of female sympathisers came wailing down Hyde Park Gate. The dying man was apt to consider them with some impatience:

> The amiable ladies who come to see me are not many & I fear are rather apt to bore me. One has been here just now, talking very fast till I had to look as tired as I could to get her to go.

Caroline Emelia came to see him and could think of nothing to say. He groaned in manifest boredom and she descended, blowing her nose hard, the tears pouring down her pendulous cheeks. Kitty Maxse turned up and asked briskly why Leslie hadn't been to call on her for so long. "Rather too fashionable" was Virginia's comment. Aunt Anny was a constant visitor; she was in excellent spirits and had no doubt at all that Leslie would be himself again in no time; to at least one observer her cheerful optimism seemed positively cruel. Caught in the perpetual stream of interviews a gentleman and a lady sat in the drawing-room silent and unintroduced. At last the gentleman said: "I am Henry James." "I am Violet Dickinson," replied the lady and that was the end of their conversation.

But many, far too many, having bid adieu to the deaf and dying man upstairs had then to unburden themselves upon his daughters. They wept and insisted that the Stephen girls should weep with them. The relations seemed more numerous and more lachrymose than ever before. "Three mornings have I spent," declared Virginia, "having my hand held–and my emotions pumped out of me–quite unsuccessfully. They are good people I know but it would be merciful if they could keep their virtues and their affections and all the rest of it to themselves." "This illness," she observed, "is a revelation of what human nature can be–in the way of sentimentality and uselessness." Nor could Virginia keep these rebellious sentiments to herself. There was a break with Aunt Adeline (the Duchess of Bedford) and a row with Aunt Mary, who considered that Virginia failed in her duty to her relations. Altogether it was a time of mounting and almost unendurable distress. "Why must he die? And if he must why can't he?" Such, roughly, were Virginia's sentiments. Death was no stranger in that house but never before had he come with so deliberate a tread.

Leslie was clearly dying and, after a time he clearly wished to die, but still death would not come. The six months allowed by Sir Frederick Treves was at an end. A sad Christmas was followed by a gloomy New Year. On Christmas Eve Sir Leslie had attempted his yearly performance, a recital of Milton's *Ode on the Nativity*. He still knew the poem by heart but was too weak to utter the words.

In January there was a crisis, but even the crisis was prolonged and it was not until 22 February that death came at last.

Chapter Five

1904-1906

EVEN before their father's death, the Stephen children had agreed on the need to get away from Hyde Park Gate. A complete and permanent removal was already contemplated; but the immediate need, when once the decencies had been observed, was to escape from that dark and all too accessible house of mourning. They went with George to Manorbier on the Pembroke coast, a wild desolate place which clearly they all liked, for they were to return. Indeed Virginia's return in later years is no small tribute to the therapeutic power of the neighbourhood, for she was not happy, or, at least, much of her was unhappy. While the others set off in pursuit of birds or landscape subjects she began to write and it was here that she first got an inkling of the kind of thing that she wanted to write about.*

But now the writing did not go well; nothing went well; how could it? She had lost her father, and the event, which seemed terrible in anticipation, now appeared more heart-breakingly tragic. She was more than ever convinced that he had wanted to live and that the true and happy relationship between him and his children was only just beginning. She had never done enough for him; he had been lonely and she had never told him how much she valued him. At night she dreamed that he was alive again and that she could say all the things that she had meant to say. When they went for walks she kept thinking that they would find him waiting for them when they got home. His faults were forgotten, his kindness, his quickness, his intelligence were not.

All this produced a sadness which was natural enough and a feeling of guilt which is not uncommon when those we love are dead; but there was also something else—a feeling of profound irritation. She was irritated by the letters of condolence, by the obituaries—they missed the point; they gave no true idea of what her father had been

* "[At sixteen] . . . I was for knowing all that was to be known, and for writing a book—a book—but what book? That vision came to me more clearly at Manorbier aged 21, walking the down on the edge of the sea." AWD (Berg), 3 September 1922.

like. She was irritated also by her brothers and sister and indeed with herself. "I wonder how we go on as we do," she wrote, "as merry as grigs all day long." In her exasperation she could write only to Violet Dickinson and to Janet Case and tell them something – not much – of what she felt. Her grief, as she later realised, was something feverish, something morbid, something which made her feel isolated and afraid. In her attempts at writing she was, as she put it later, trying "to prove to myself that there was nothing wrong with me – which I was already beginning to fear there was."

Perhaps it was because of her condition that the Stephens decided on a more radical change. Manorbier was beautiful, but it lacked diversions. Gerald was going to Venice; Violet Dickinson was going to Florence; they decided that they too would go to Italy. They sailed on Good Friday; their train passed through the St Gotthard in a snowstorm; but at Como there was brilliant sunshine and at the end of two days' travelling they stepped into a gondola.

There were fatigues and annoyances; the Humphry Wards were on the train; Gerald was sometimes cross; he was not the perfect companion for such a journey.* And then, they had failed to book rooms and must hunt all through Venice at midnight looking for somewhere to sleep. But Virginia, who had hardly been further afield than Boulogne, was amazed and delighted. For a day or two she, and indeed all of them, were in a state of childlike astonishment and joy; they could hardly believe that the place was real.

This interval of delight was short lived; foreign travel distracts the mind, but it also tries the temper. Vanessa, to be sure, was having a fine time, discovering Tintoretto, finding fault with Ruskin and generally taking a professional interest in the scene which Virginia could not share, but, after ten days, even she was ready to leave Venice; they felt caged in the city, they longed to see some green country. They went to Florence; there they found some old friends – the Rasponis, whom they liked – but also Lytteltons, Humphry Wards, Carnarvons, Prinseps and even Aunt Minna. By this time Virginia, who had been delighted by her first sight of the Italians, was becoming disenchanted.† Also there were far too many Germans and "a strange race that haunts Hotels – Gnome like

* "Somehow Gerald's figure never did make part of the Venetian foreground I have in my mind." VW to Violet Dickinson, [March 1904].

† ". . . our travelling is not so delightful that we wish more than is necessary. There never was a *beastlier* nation than this in its railways, its streets, its shops, its beggars, & many of its habits. My dear Toad, where is a decent woman to look sometimes?" VW to Emma Vaughan, 25 April 1904.

women, who are like creatures that come out in the dark. An hotel is a sort of black Cave." There were of course compensations; but, comparing Vanessa's letters with those from Virginia, it seems that there was practically nothing that the elder sister did not like and very little to please the younger.

Violet Dickinson, who met them in Florence and who accompanied Virginia and Vanessa for some time, clearly had a good deal to put up with, and so did they all; Virginia had what she called "her tantrums." By the end of April they were all on their way home. They stopped a week in Paris where they found Beatrice Thynne. They sat in cafés, smoked cigarettes with a sense of great daring and talked to two young men: Thoby's friend Clive Bell and *his* friend Mr Kelly (later Sir Gerald Kelly P.R.A.). These were admirable guides to Paris: they went to the Salon, they went to the *Chat Blanc*, they went to Rodin's studio. In fact they had a very satisfying taste of Parisian life; but once again the real treat was for Vanessa.

This I think was an element in the storm that was now brewing. Vanessa had got what she wanted–her freedom. Now she could paint as she chose, see whom she chose, live as she chose and would no doubt marry as she chose. Her happiness in being delivered from the care and the ill-temper of her father was shockingly evident. She was clearly and unequivocally delighted, and Virginia, emotionally strained, exhausted and exasperated by the long months of Sir Leslie's last illness, still guilty and still inconsolable, found this more than she could bear.

We do not know, although we may fairly guess, that there were headaches, sudden nervous leapings of the heart and a growing awareness that there was something very wrong with her mind. In May she felt desperately anxious to be at work on something, something big and solid that would keep her restless thoughts occupied and, on the day after their return to London when Emma Vaughan came to borrow some letters, Virginia hardly knew what she was saying or doing.

In the breakdown that followed she entered into a period of nightmare in which the symptoms of the preceding months attained frantic intensity. Her mistrust of Vanessa, her grief for her father became maniacal, her nurses–she had three–became fiends. She heard voices urging her to acts of folly; she believed that they came from overeating and that she must starve herself. In this emergency the main burden fell upon Vanessa; but Vanessa was enormously helped by Violet Dickinson. She took Virginia to her house at Burnham Wood and it was there that she made her first attempt to commit suicide. She threw herself from a window, which, however, was not high enough from the ground to cause her serious harm.* It was here too that she lay in bed, listening to the birds singing in Greek and imagining that King Edward VII lurked in the azaleas using the foulest possible language.

All that summer she was mad. It was not until early September that she was able to leave Burnham Wood, thin and shaken, but sane enough to be able to live at peace with Vanessa. The Stephen family stayed that summer at Teversal in Nottinghamshire. Here Virginia was able to write short letters, to play a little tennis and to walk. Nurse Traill, who had looked after Sir Leslie, cared for her and presently she was able to do some Latin with Thoby. Her sanity had returned but she felt physical pains—headaches and neuralgia.

> Oh, my Violet, if there were a God I should bless him for having de-livered me safe and sound from the miseries of the last six months! You can't think what an exquisite joy every minute of my life is to me now, and my only prayer is that I may live to be 70. I do think I may emerge less selfish and cocksure than I went in and with greater understanding of the troubles of others. Sorrow, such as I feel now for father, is soothing and natural and makes life more worth having, if sadder. I can never tell you what you have been to me all this time—for one thing you wouldn't believe it—but if affection is worth anything you have, and always will have mine.

Her letters to Violet Dickinson are optimistic—over-optimistic; she was impatient to start writing again and believed herself to be more completely cured than she in fact was. Dr Savage, her specialist and an old friend of the family, insisted that she should live very quietly and, if possible, away from London. When, in October, the Stephens returned to Hyde Park Gate and began to make preparations for leaving it, it was felt that Virginia should not be involved in the turmoil of house-moving. She went therefore to stay with her aunt Caroline Emelia in Cambridge. Here she could see Adrian who was still at Trinity (Thoby had come down that summer), and the milieu was sufficiently quiet, for 'The Quaker' or 'Nun,' as Virginia called her aunt, led a life of tranquil benevolence in her small house, The Porch.

Moreover in Cambridge Virginia could find a useful and sedative

---

* It has been suggested that Virginia attempted to kill herself at the time of her first breakdown (i.e. in 1895). I can find no evidence of this; but that she was interested in the idea of self-destruction before the year 1904 seems likely enough, witness a remark made to Jack Hills at Queen Victoria's funeral: "Jack, do you think I shall ever commit suicide?" (p. i., Lady Hills).

employment for which she was well fitted. F. W. Maitland, the historian, had been one of the young men who used to stay with the Stephens at St Ives; he had married Florence Fisher, Virginia's cousin; Sir Leslie liked him and had asked, if there should be a "Life," that Maitland should write it. He was already working on this biography when Virginia went to Cambridge; there were letters which he felt should be read by her before he could see them—chiefly love letters between her parents—and she was to select and copy them. In addition he asked her for a few pages describing Leslie's relationship with his children: it was the first thing of hers that ever found its way into print. She was also almost certainly the source of some passages which followed this, passages in which Maitland touches, tenderly and discreetly, on Leslie's faults in matters of education and housekeeping and which conclude with a statement —it certainly expresses Virginia's belief—that at the end he felt and expressed nothing save affection for his children.

Jack Hills offered his advice on this occasion; he was afraid that Virginia might be injudicious in her choice of material; he wrote with all the prudent authority of a brother-in-law and a solicitor. Virginia's reply was fierce. She "cared 10,000 times more for delicacy and reserve where her parents were concerned than he could"; he had never really known or understood Leslie and if he wanted to offer criticism and advice he should offer it to Maitland; he was—but this she kept for Violet Dickinson—"a poor little red-tape-tied parchment Solicitor" and "had no more thought of what a book ought to be than the fat cow in the field opposite." Vanessa really agreed with her, but of course Vanessa was weak where Jack was concerned and therefore took his part. This was not her only quarrel with Vanessa, for Virginia after a fortnight was becoming restive at Cambridge; why could she not return to her own room in her own house? The doctors might forbid it but doctors, in her experience, were always wrong; they could guess at your disease but they could not cure you. Here, in Cambridge, she was sleeping badly; the Quaker got on her nerves and her nerves were things that her family understood and could allow for, whereas a Quaker aunt could not. But Vanessa took the exasperating view that doctor's orders were doctor's orders and must be obeyed; unfortunately she added, or Virginia persuaded herself that she added, something to the effect that it didn't much matter to anyone whether Virginia was in Cambridge or London. And this, of course, did not mend matters.

In the end a compromise was made: Virginia returned for ten

days to the new house in Gordon Square and then went to Giggles-wick School in Yorkshire where her cousin Will Vaughan was now Headmaster. Vanessa wrote to Madge Vaughan:

> She is really quite well now–except that she does not sleep very well–& is inclined to do too much in some ways. . . . She ought not to walk very far or for a very long time alone. . . . Now she goes out before beginning to write in the morning for ½ an hour alone . . . then she walks alone again before luncheon for ½ an hour–but in the after-noon she is rather dependent on someone else for a walk. Of course if she could go out with the children sometimes it would do perfectly. She goes to bed very early as I think you do & she is in all other ways absolutely normal in her doings.

Virginia surveyed the Vaughan household with some curiosity. Her first impression was that Will was by no means worthy of Madge. He was dominecring and thoroughly conventional. He was always afraid that Virginia would entertain Madge with "morbid" subjects; also she told the children stories which, if not precisely "morbid," were held to be unsuitable to the Sabbath, a day devoted to 'Sunday Books' of exemplary dullness. Madge had to perform all the chores, not only of a mother but of a headmaster's wife; it was taken for granted that her own work as an author would take second place. Virginia revised this opinion for a time–this was always to be her way–and discovered unsuspected moral and conjugal qualities in Will; but her first impression became her final opinion: Madge was yet another of the women whose lives and talents were to be sacrificed to their husbands.

Madge, who liked Virginia and "believed in her genius," was nevertheless sensible of Virginia's scrutiny and rather alarmed by it. After the visit we find Vanessa writing to reassure her:

> Don't be afraid that I shall quote what you say as "comic"–I know you think us all very critical–but really I dont think we criticise un-fairly– & we certainly dont laugh at people behind their backs & treat them affectionately to their faces. So dont ever be afraid that we shall talk of your "fads"! Ginia has talked to me of you & Will only in the most appreciative way– & I do think that the safeguard with her is that she always does see the real good in people. She is too clever not to find a great many people bores–& I think she often enjoys giving vigorous expression to feelings which though true are quite temporary –but when one knows her ways one can always tell how much is per-manent & how much will change–& I think I can honestly say that I have never heard her say a really unkind thing about anyone. So I dont think the criticism matters. Everyone who has brains must be critical

when they are young. She is sure to get more tolerant, & even now it does come partly from having a high standard in most things.

It is possible that Madge did not find this letter entirely reassuring. The visit to Giggleswick was memorable, not only because Virginia was able to learn something more about a person whom she had once adored and still liked, but because it provided her with a subject for her first published article.* While she was in Yorkshire she visited Haworth Parsonage and wrote an account of it which she sent to *The Guardian*, a London weekly newspaper catering for a clerical public; Mrs Lyttelton, the editor of the Women's Supplement, was a friend of Violet Dickinson. Virginia felt that she ought to earn some money, if only to recoup some of the expenses of her illness, and she was pretty sure that she could do as well as most of *The Guardian*'s reviewers, although she allowed that there was a certain knack of writing for the newspapers which she had still to learn.

Thanks to Violet Dickinson's initial introduction and continued encouragement, Virginia found in *The Guardian* a fairly regular outlet for her early attempts at journalism. She had been training herself to be a writer for a long time. That is to say she had been reading voraciously and writing assiduously. Her journals during these years consist, almost always, of careful essays written as though for publication: attempts to describe a day in the country, a visit to Earl's Court, a night spent listening to the music of a neighbour's dance, attempts to do very much the kind of thing that she achieves in the Haworth article. About this time she was also writing comic lives of Caroline Stephen, Aunt Mary Fisher and George Duckworth, all of which have alas perished; it is difficult not to suppose that they would have been more amusing than the essays in her journals. For these essays are not of biographic interest except in so far as they attest to the high seriousness and immense thoroughness with which Virginia prepared herself for the profession of letters. Her constant, almost compulsive reading and writing were intended to compensate for the fact that she had not had what she called "a real education," by which she meant a University education. Her practice in writing gave her a certain fluency, an ease of address unusual in a very young journalist; her indefatigable reading makes her appear, to modern

* Her review of *The Son of Royal Langbrith* by W. D. Howells was published by *The Guardian* on 14 December 1904; the Haworth article appeared a week later; but in fact the review was written after the article. See VW/VD, 26 November 1904.

eyes, by no means an ignoramus but a quite affectedly literate person. We live in a society which has less time for books and which is less dependent on the written word; we no longer take it for granted that all educated people are perfectly at home in English and French literature and will at once recognise a quotation from Johnson or La Rochefoucauld; it was a natural enough assumption for the daughter of Sir Leslie Stephen.

From now on, Virginia was regularly employed as a writer of short articles and reviews. She would turn her hand to almost anything.

From Giggleswick she returned to London and again to Cambridge and then went with the other Stephens to Aunt Minna's cottage in the New Forest (Aunt Minna was away). This Christmas holiday was to some extent marred for Virginia by *The Cornhill*, which had curtly rejected an article on Boswell's letters, and by Mr Haldane, the Liberal statesman, who wrote unenthusiastically to Violet Dickinson about Virginia's Haworth article.* It was Virginia's first taste of literary adversity and she did not like it. Nevertheless there was fun; Thoby and Adrian went out hunting; in the evening there was much eating, drinking and jollity. They sought out the silliest novels that they could find in Aunt Minna's bookcase and read them aloud roaring with laughter; they were young, irreverent and unrestrained. One curious occupation of Virginia's leisure during that holiday—her working time was mainly given to the writing of her contribution to Maitland's *Life of Leslie Stephen*—was drawing, and a few weak but not insensitive copies of Blake and Rossetti were the result.

Early in the new year, Virginia had an interview with Dr Savage; to her delight, he told her that she was completely cured and could now lead a normal life. This meant that she could return to London and join the household that had been established in her absence at No 46 Gordon Square, Bloomsbury.

When the Stephen children planned this move their friends and relations had been astonished and a little shocked. Kensington was a good address; Bloomsbury was not. "Kitty," wrote Virginia,

* "Also Haldane isn't exactly warm in his praise, and altogether I feel, as you read in the Bible, despised and rejected by men." (VW/VD, January 1905). What Haldane actually said was:

"Dear Miss Dickinson,

Thank you for showing me Miss S[tephen]'s article on Haworth—a place, as you know, of deep interest to me. What merits—but I think the writer can get still more inside her subject. This is a beginning however, and it shows talent . . ."
R. B. Haldane to Violet Dickinson, 27 December 1904.

"already screams against Bloomsbury" (this was in March 1904), and probably she was the first to do so. But it was precisely the virtue of the place that it lay so far from that dark house of many tragedies in which they had grown up. It was far from the favoured haunts of Aunt Minna, Cousin Mia, Aunt Mary and the rest. Also, it was cheap. Sir Leslie's children had not inherited much capital and they were rather vague about their income–a topic which shall be discussed upon a later page–but certainly they had every inducement to go to a district where rents were far lower than in Kensington. Vanessa had the additional motive of wishing to be close to the Slade School which, for a time, she attended.

No 46 Gordon Square was more spacious and much better lit than No 22 Hyde Park Gate, and Vanessa, when she took it over in the autumn of 1904, emphasised its qualities. Her ideas of interior decoration had been very much influenced by Charles and Katharine Furse,* in whose house she had admired big bare surfaces of white distemper on which pictures could stand in bold, emphatic isolation. It was part of a larger redirection in her ideas about art, and she told Clive Bell that she had succeeded in persuading Virginia that "there was nothing to be said" for that family idol, G. F. Watts. Watts belonged to the dark Victorian past; the new generation wanted air, simplicity and light. The move to Bloomsbury was to be an escape from the past and all its horrors.

There was, however, one fatal, one appalling drawback. Gerald was glad to part company with the Stephen children and to set up a bachelor establishment of his own; but George, always affectionate and kind, could not bear the idea of leaving his sisters with nobody but Thoby and Adrian, who from a social point of view were worse than useless, to look after them. He must be included in the party; he regretted no doubt that they should insist on going so far from the fashionable part of town, but, after all, it is not impossible to reach the West End from Gordon Square and go with them he ought and must. This resolution was received with dismay by the rest; but they hardly knew how to oppose so much well-intentioned fraternal feeling. They were in fact weak to the point of pusillanimity: for the long story of George's attentions had at length been made so far public that he could surely have been called to account. When Virginia went mad in the summer of 1904 Vanessa told Savage of

* Charles Furse, a member of the New English Art Club very much influenced by Whistler, had married Katharine, the youngest daughter of J. A. Symonds, and was therefore the brother-in-law of Madge Vaughan. He died just at this time (16 October 1904).

what had been happening and Savage, it seems, taxed George with his conduct.★ Even George might then have felt that his presence under the same roof as his half-sisters was no longer desirable. But he was invulnerably dense and incapable of pursuing a course that ran counter to his feelings and so, faced by his amiable insistence, they weakly acquiesced. Gone then were all their hopes of flying from the past: the past was coming to live with them.

And then, like a Goddess from a Machine, came Lady Margaret Herbert. George proposed; she accepted him and they were married "with immense pomp" while Virginia was still convalescing at Teversal in the autumn of 1904. Vanessa was a bridesmaid, and Adrian distinguished himself by losing all her luggage. The Bloomsbury ménage was saved from disaster.

The household to which Virginia returned in January of 1905 consisted therefore of the Stephen children and no one else.

I often wonder [wrote Vanessa to Madge Vaughan] how our doings now would strike someone who had known & lived with us years ago . . . it is really very ideal to have to arrange for a household all of much the same age. It makes most things very easy & all the difficulties of trying to meet opposite claims & of different generations are done away with. . . I only wish we could always go on like this–but after all we may for a long time yet. I dread every day to hear that Thoby is in love!

In a young establishment, unsupervised, unchaperoned, tired of the conventions that made Hyde Park Gate so tedious and so painful, all kinds of possibilities began to present themselves. Why dress for dinner? Why tolerate bores? Why bother about 'Society'? Why not make friends with people who would talk about art and literature, religion and love without humbug? Everything seemed possible. Or so it appeared; but in fact the liberties that the Miss Stephens now sought were, even by the standards of their own age, modest. Their immediate aims were of a negative kind; they wanted to be released from the continual and galling interference of their relations; they claimed liberty; but they certainly did not shout for licence. They scarcely in fact detached themselves from the conventions of a society which was still restrained by very strict

★ "George would fling himself on my bed, cuddling and kissing and otherwise embracing me in order, as he told Dr Savage later, to comfort me for the fatal illness of my Father–who was dying three or four storeys lower down of cancer." (MH/A 16). I infer that the only people who could have told Savage of this were Vanessa or Virginia; the occasion must have been Virginia's madness in 1904. The only witness on whose evidence Savage would have spoken to George would have been Vanessa.

rules. Virginia's innocence at this time was of a kind that would hardly be credible today; for all her reading she could not suppose that people of her acquaintance could be unchaste, and although she had met Corydon in the pages of Virgil she would have been horrified to learn that he was a friend of Thoby's and a visitor in Gordon Square. Leonard Woolf recalled that the first time he ever saw Virginia and Vanessa they were chaperoned by their cousin the Vice-Principal of Newnham, although they had only come to Trinity to call upon their brother. Leslie, who was old enough at the time of Virginia's birth to be her grandfather, belonged to the generation which came to maturity in the 'sixties; he was in fact 'early Victorian' and his agnosticism made him not less, but more, anxious to observe the proprieties. In this he was supported by the female relatives and of course by George. Thoby also was on the whole a guardian of established usages and his sisters were shy – Virginia desperately so. One can see how hard it must have been to break with the conventions and in fact Virginia lacked not only the courage but the desire to do so at that time.

That break may be dated from 16 February 1905, when Thoby, who was now reading for the Bar but wanted to see his Cambridge friends and had for this purpose announced that he would be At Home on Thursday evenings, entertained Saxon Sydney-Turner at 46 Gordon Square. On this first occasion he and his host and the dog Gurth formed the entire company. It must have been a quiet evening, for Saxon Sydney-Turner was not a lively companion. Indeed most of Thoby's friends seemed extremely silent and when the Miss Stephens began to put in an appearance on Thursday evenings Virginia, at all events, found their silence disconcerting. Two of them, Sydney-Turner and possibly R. G. Hawtrey, came to stay in Cornwall with the Stephen children that summer and Virginia observed them with amazement. They were, she declared:

> . . . a great trial; they sit silent, absolutely silent, all the time. Occasionally they creep to a corner and chuckle over a Latin joke. Perhaps they are falling in love with Nessa; who knows? It would be a silent and very learned process. However I don't think they are robust enough to feel very much. Oh women are my line and not these inanimate creatures. The worst of it is that they have not the energy to go . . .

What had they done with this vast privilege of University education that had been denied to her, Virginia? It seemed to have struck them dumb and made them dismal. They had a tremendous opinion of themselves and were more than a little affected, and their superior airs hardly seemed justified when from the mountain of their pretensions they extracted a somewhat ridiculous mouse–it was called *Euphrosyne*. This was a volume of poems, published privately in 1905, to which Clive Bell, Lytton Strachey, Walter Lamb, Saxon Sydney-Turner, Leonard Woolf and some others contributed and to which they seldom alluded in later life, so that the book would have been forgotten if Virginia had not been careful to keep its memory green. It was certainly an anti-climax; none of the contributors were true poets. Virginia laughed at it and began a scathing essay upon it and its contributors. (See Appendix C.)

So these were Thoby's remarkable friends. Here was Clive Bell who was supposed to be a mixture of Shelley and a country squire, and Sydney-Turner who was credited with–of all things–brilliance.

"If you mean wit," replied Thoby, "then no, he is not witty; but he is truthful, and if he is silent it is because he is careful to speak the truth," and, after a time, Virginia began to admit that there was something in what Thoby said. The reserve of these odd young men was not like that of the young men at the parties to which George had taken her; theirs were not the silences of men who are seeking for an appropriate banality. And when they did speak Virginia found that she was listening to a kind of conversation that had never come her way before. A chance remark, a discussable statement, something, let us say, about beauty in pictures, would suddenly breed loquacity. The question would be discussed at a higher and higher level and by fewer and fewer people.

> It filled me with wonder to watch those who were finally left in the argument, piling stone upon stone, cautiously, accurately, long after it had completely soared above my sight . . . One had glimpses of something miraculous happening high up in the air. Often we would still be sitting in a circle at two or three in the morning. Still Saxon would be taking his pipe from his mouth as if to speak, and putting it back again without having spoken. At last, rumpling his hair back he wd. pronounce very shortly some absolutely final summing up. The marvellous edifice was complete, one could stumble off to bed feeling that something very important had happened. It had been proved that beauty was–or beauty was not–for I have never been quite sure which–part of a picture.

Now this was rather different from those parties at which an exquisitely dressed young man might content himself with the simple phrase 'sort of' repeated with slight changes of emphasis throughout the evening. At these gatherings in Gordon Square no one was exquisitely dressed; certainly not the Miss Stephens. Here they were being asked to do something that had not been required of them before–to use their brains. The rest of them didn't much matter. For whereas the tacit purpose of a party in Belgravia was the pursuit of matrimony, the purpose of a party in Bloomsbury was to exchange ideas. It was this, the purely cerebral attitude of Thoby's Cambridge friends, or at least of most of them, which made them interesting to Virginia, and she was glad to be free of the marriage market.

In June 1906, rather less than a year after Virginia had written to Violet Dickinson describing Sydney-Turner and his friend as "inanimate creatures," Virginia wrote a short story in which she describes the life of two young women, Phyllis and Rosamund. They are the daughters of a high official, and live an entirely social life: "They seem indigenous to the drawing room." It is their place of business, the market-place in which they are to sell themselves for as much as they will fetch. Virginia considers them with sympathy, they have their decencies and their loyalties, they are neither insensitive nor stupid; nevertheless, drilled by their mother, they are destined to pass through a joyless courtship to a loveless marriage. Virginia sends them to a Thursday Evening at Gordon Square–it is as though the Miss Stephens of 1903 were to call upon the Miss Stephens of 1905. Phyllis and Rosamund are disconcerted by the indifference of these people to the mundanities of life, by the frank brutality of the conversation. Love is discussed, but for these people love was not the delicate game of adornment and enticement that Phyllis and Rosamund understood so well; it was "a robust, ingenuous thing which stood out in the daylight, naked and solid, to be tapped or scrutinised as you thought best." The visitors are unable to cope with this kind of frankness; they return home half attracted but on the whole displeased by what they have seen; such is not, they decide, the life for them.

And certainly, as it developed, Bloomsbury became more and more disconcerting. George, sweeping in proudly with his aristocratic bride upon his arm, with a bow and a flourish presented Sydney-Turner to her. Sydney-Turner was, as usual, lighting a pipe, nor would he stop doing so; he made a slight and slovenly pretence of rising from his chair, half nodded and kept his match alight. Their behaviour was no worse than their clothes. "Oh darling, how awful they do look!" wailed Kitty Maxse. "Deplorable, deplorable! How could Vanessa and Virginia have picked up such friends?" groaned Henry James.

And so, almost at once, the Stephen children were in trouble. Thoby's friends were 'unsuitable' and that they should remain talking, unchaperoned, with Thoby's sisters until three in the morning was even more 'unsuitable.' Inevitably a choice would in the end have to be made between the old friends and the new, but in 1905 Virginia could hardly imagine that such a choice was possible.

> I have been splashing about in racing society since I saw you, that is dined with George at Lady Carnarvon's—*young* Lady C. this time, thank God. It was the night of the Kemptown races, and we talked about horses all night, which are probably more interesting than books. Then I have seen Margaret [Lady Margaret Duckworth] who is a nice woman, and our acquaintance begins to grow promising. We shall have to know each other all our lives, so we can take time about it.

"All our lives," that was the term imposed by so close a relationship. Vanessa, I surmise, was already half-minded—if this were to imply dinner parties wholly devoted to the turf—that the sentence might be commuted, or indeed set aside. But even she, in her most wildly optimistic moments, could not then have supposed that when, many years later, an urbane gentleman enquired after "that delightful person your sister-in-law," she, Vanessa, would be at some pains to frame an answer that would not reveal the fact that she did not know whether the lady was alive or dead. For this was how the matter ended; Bloomsbury grew not only by the making, but by the breaking, of friendships.

Between the 'good society' and the 'bad company' that they entertained there could be no real choice, although it was many years before this became apparent. George and his smart friends presented no problem. Kitty Maxse and Violet Dickinson had superior claims to friendship and in 1905 a break with *them* must have seemed unthinkable; but already it was becoming clear that these "deplorable" young men represented the kind of values that Vanessa and Virginia most respected and, as they began to speak, they revealed characters which were not unattractive.

Virginia exaggerated (and perhaps I also have exaggerated) their silence; they can perhaps be divided into a central core, the mute circle of seekers after truth who sat puffing their pipes around the discreet shrine of G. E. Moore—Saxon Sydney-Turner, Leonard Woolf and Lytton Strachey—and an outer circle, more worldly and more garrulous, which, on the Thursday Evenings of 1905 and 1906, would include Thoby himself, Clive Bell, and Desmond MacCarthy who, though a thorough Mooreist, was never taciturn. Here it should be noted that these particular young men who were later to become Virginia's most intimate friends were not, at that time, separable as a group from the others–such as Ralph Hawtrey, Hilton Young, Jack Pollock, Walter Lamb or Robin Mayor–who had also been Thoby's friends at Cambridge and were welcomed by him on Thursday Evenings. It would be wrong I think to imagine an inner coterie distinguished from the rest.

One of the first of Thoby's friends to be invited to Gordon Square was Leonard Woolf, though he came only to say farewell on the eve of his departure for Ceylon. He dined with the Stephens on 17 November 1904; Virginia, in London for a week between her visits to Cambridge and Giggleswick, was present. He remembered her as being perfectly silent throughout dinner and noticed how ill she looked. But she observed him and collected stories about him. Lytton Strachey said that he was like Swift and would murder his wife. He despised the whole human race. He trembled all over, he was so violent, so savage; he had pulled his thumb out of joint in a dream; he was, in short, a serious and powerful figure; but he had gone off to live in a jungle and no one knew whether he would ever return.

Leonard Woolf was a mysterious figure in the distance; Saxon Sydney-Turner was an enigma in the foreground. He, undoubtedly, had a gift for silence and sometimes when he spoke he would endlessly and most eruditely discuss subjects of no conceivable interest, or he might be entirely cryptic. And yet he could also be illuminating; he was, obviously, extremely intelligent and extremely gifted; he wrote poems, he painted pictures; he was intensely musical, a fanatical concert and opera-goer who regularly made the pilgrimage to Bayreuth and could tell you who sang what part in which opera ever since Bayreuth began. He was also a composer and in a rare moment of expansion disclosed to Clive Bell:

> . . . my last Sonata [is] unique among my works for the appreciation it has found and containing passages that rank among the most beautiful ever written: my wish is to have it printed when I have polished certain parts of it but I don't know how to set about doing this.

This was in March 1906. Was it already apparent to Sydney-Turner's friends that he would never find out how to finish his Sonata, that it would remain unperformed and perish along with all his other compositions? I don't know. After the publication of *Euphrosyne* Virginia can hardly have supposed that he was to be a great poet, but he might be a musician; certainly it appeared that so astonishing a mind must one day achieve some spectacular feat.

"His friends," wrote Virginia when she attempted to write about him,

> continued to believe in him. He was going to be one of the great men of his time. Probably he was working at a poem, after office hours, when he came back to that dreary London lodging in a back street. "When is it coming out?" they pressed him. "Anyhow, show us what you've written." Or was it a history? Or was it a philosophy? . . . He was studying counterpoint. Also he was teaching himself to paint. He was studying Chinese . . . Nothing was actually published. But "wait a little" his friends said. They waited. . . .

That Lytton Strachey would also make a name for himself one day seemed equally clear. In so far as these young men had a leader it was he. Like Saxon Sydney-Turner he was a very silent man; but his silences were of an even more alarming kind; for whereas Sydney-Turner, when he surfaced, might bring with him a pearl of wisdom, Strachey showed sometimes a rakish fin and sometimes a row of wicked teeth. With one pungent, economical sentence he could reduce a party to helpless laughter or a fool to spluttering rage – and you might be the fool. Strachey was, perhaps, one of the reasons why Virginia was herself very silent at these Thursday evening meetings. She found him, I suspect, very frightening (almost any man was in some degree frightening); it was not until later that she was to discover how kind and sympathetic he could be. The Stracheys were always on the margin of her life and Lytton's sisters were what one might call her natural friends, for they belonged to very much the same world as the Stephens – the educated upper middle class of London. They were all of them formidable and they had a way of speaking that could strike terror. They could apply a verbal stress which gave their irony, their incredulity, their sudden shocked amazement at ignorance, dishonesty or inhumanity, a memorable quality. Their family jokes were numerous and arcane; they were far more of a clan than the Stephens, tied as they were to the older generation by a happier relationship and happier circumstances. It was only by degrees that Lytton became, for Virginia, the most important member of his family.

Desmond MacCarthy seemed even more certain of success than Lytton Strachey. He was of a slightly older generation at Cambridge – he came down as Thoby arrived there – and he was the most worldly of the younger Apostles. He went into London Society where he had seen the Miss Stephens looking, as he put it, "like slaves." He had the world at his feet; he was handsome, brilliant and talented. He had not much money but he had, I surmise, an easy chair, a cheerful fire, a desk, a ream of smooth writing paper, virgin save perhaps for three magnificent arresting words–the title of a novel. For when those virgin sheets were violated he was to be the great English novelist of the twentieth century. His shoulders were ready to accommodate the mantle of Henry James and, hearing him talk–for *he* certainly was not silent–you could not but conclude that he had so charmed and domesticated that intractable creature the English Language that it would do anything for him, give him a force, a range of subtlety that would take him anywhere–into the empyrean if he so wished, and with that, so much native genius and so much good nature. Even in those bright years of his early manhood Desmond MacCarthy was, no doubt, a trifle dilatory, a shade unreliable in the performance of tasks or the keeping of appointments, just a little exasperating. But did anyone, then or at any other time, dislike him? It is impossible to believe. He had, I suspect, a good deal to do with the genial social climate of Bloomsbury, with the reconciliation of difficult and angular characters and with the general spirit of tolerance and compromise which triumphed over the disputes and acerbities which were also a part of that environment.

Clive Bell also undoubtedly helped to temper the austerities of that society. He was, in a way, the strangest of the group. George noted with approval that he was different from the others in that he was better dressed, had a good seat on a horse and was an excellent wing shot; for while all the rest were pretty obviously intellectual, he came from a society which hunted birds, animals, and, in his case, girls. His family had made its way by means of coal to a sham gothic country house and a decent position in the County of Wiltshire. Clive, the younger son, went from Marlborough to Cambridge, where fate placed him on the same staircase at Trinity as Saxon Sydney-Turner, and where Thoby Stephen became his closest friend. At Cambridge he was, I think, underrated by his friends; they did not look in the one direction in which he was, intellectually, more alert than they. In his rooms hung a reproduction of a painting by Degas, someone of whom most of them had probably never heard, for Cambridge at the turn of the century was aesthetically blind. After he left Cambridge in 1902 he went to Paris and there made friends with Roderick O'Conor, Gerald Kelly and James Morrice. This eye for painting was a bond between him and

Vanessa, strengthened by the fact that he was able to show Thoby and his sisters something of Paris on their way back from Italy in May 1904. He had stayed for a few days with the Stephens at Teversal in September when Virginia was convalescing, and was thereafter, I think, a constant visitor to their house. In the summer of 1905 he proposed to Vanessa and was rejected; but not in such a manner as to leave him with no hope. Virginia soon became aware of this attachment and, I suspect, disapproved of it.

In 1905 Virginia began a connection with *The Times Literary Supplement* which was to last almost to the end of her life. Bruce Richmond, the editor, had invited Sir Leslie to contribute when the paper first started in 1902, but he had been able to do little. Now, a year after his death, Richmond approached his daughter, and on 10 March appeared her first article for him, a book review entitled *Literary Geography*. Bruce Richmond thought it "admirable" and sent her "another great fat book—which I don't much want as I know *nothing* of the subject."

In April Virginia and Adrian made a short trip to the Peninsula. They visited Oporto, Lisbon, Granada, Seville, saw the usual sights and had the usual experience of dirty inns, goat's milk, natural beauty and dilatory railways; the week-long journey out by sea in fine weather, the ship with its odd temporary life, its laziness, its bores, its places of refuge, made, I think, a more permanent impression upon the authoress of *The Voyage Out*. But it was clearly a satisfactory trip; they were glad to return but glad also to have made the journey. Back in London, Virginia found that Bruce Richmond had rejected her review of the "great fat book"—Edith Sichel's *Catherine de' Medici & The French Reformation*—on the grounds that it was not serious criticism from an historical point of view; but to make up for it he sent her three books about Spain. "You will be surprised to hear that I am an authority upon Spain," she wrote to Violet Dickinson, "but so it is."

There was another and more important excursion in that year; for now that it seemed that the good years had come back the four Stephen children decided, perhaps with a kind of symbolic intention, to return to St Ives. For Virginia, certainly, it was a deliberate exercise in nostalgia; the train that took them from Paddington was to carry them back into the past. They arrived at night, strolled up to Talland House as though they were still children returning from a day's outing, boldly opened the gate, mounted the familiar steps and reached the escalonia hedge through which they could see the stone urns, the bank of tall flowers, the lighted windows. The house seemed to have been waiting for them. Without breaking the spell the revenants returned in ghostly silence.

Broad daylight offered less equivocal delights. There had been changes in the town–new houses and new roads; but not enough to spoil their pleasure; here there were many remembered details to be verified with delight and many people who still remembered their parents with affection. The country, the sea, the inhabitants were all charming. They stayed until October and had the pleasure of seeing pilchards taken in the bay.

In October, Vanessa, on returning to town, realised a long meditated project–the Friday Club. This was a society which was to meet every week and to be concerned with the fine arts.* Virginia, who was not deeply interested but did attend some of the proceedings of this club, was amused by its factional disputes: "One half of the Committee," she wrote, "shriek Whistler and French impressionists, and the other are stalwart British." It was the first sign that Bloomsbury was going to be interested in the visual arts.

But Virginia herself was more involved in an activity of a rather different nature. Soon after her return to full health she had been approached by Miss Sheepshanks, a daughter of the Bishop of Norwich, who as effective Principal was anxious to recruit helpers at Morley College. This was an evening institute for working men and women which had been set up as an adjunct to the Old Vic in the Waterloo Road. Miss Sheepshanks' suggestion was that Virginia might "combine amusement and instruction–a little gossip and sympathy–and then 'talks' about books and pictures." "I'm sure I don't mind how much I talk, and I really don't see any limit to the things I might talk about," wrote Virginia to Violet Dickinson. "However as she is sure–the good Sheepshanks–that I shall be of the greatest use–I don't mind trying." Miss Sheepshanks's energy was such that she was able at one time or another to rope in the other Stephens too–Vanessa to teach Drawing, Thoby (and Clive Bell) Latin, and Adrian Greek; but, unlike Virginia, they soon lost interest.

Miss Stephen's students must sometimes have been puzzled, sometimes exhilarated, by her "talks," over the preparation of which she seems to have taken considerable thought.

---

* Clive Bell was on the original committee and so of course was Vanessa; Henry Lamb, Neville Lytton, E. M. O'R. Dickie, Pernel Strachey and Saxon Sydney-Turner were among the members. There were exhibitions and discussions; the discussions were not confined to questions of art. This club seems to have lasted until about 1912 or 1913.

Tomorrow also is my working women, for whom I have been making out a vivid account of the battle of Hastings. I hope to make their flesh creep!

Virginia believed that it was her task to fire the imagination of her students so that they might see "the flesh and blood in the shadows." But was she perhaps a little too imaginative? Was her version of English History rather too close to that which was later to fill the pages of *Orlando*? It appears from a later passage in the letter quoted above that the Ancient Britons were to perform at Hastings and one can understand the point of view of the authorities who persuaded her to turn to English Literature.

Then on Wednesdays I have my English Composition; 10 people: 4 men, 6 women. It is, I suppose, the most useless class in the College; and so Sheepshanks thinks. She sat through the whole lesson last night; and almost stamped with impatience. But what can I do? I have an old Socialist of 50, who thinks he must bring the Parasite (the Aristocrat)... into an Essay upon Autumn; and a Dutchman who thinks—at the end of the class too—that I have been teaching him Arithmetic; and anaemic shop girls who say they would write more but they only get an hour for their dinner, and there doesn't seem much time for writing. . . .

Or again:

I gave a lecture to four working men yesterday—one stutters on his m's and another is an Italian and reads English as though it were mediaeval Latin, and another is my degenerate poet, who rants and blushes and almost seizes my hand when we happen to like the same lines. . . . I can tell you the first sentence of my lecture: "The poet Keats died when he was 25; and he wrote all his work before that." Indeed—how very interesting, Miss Stephen.

Virginia taught at Morley until the end of 1907 and what her students got from her we cannot tell; we may however guess a little at what she got from them. Never before had she attempted to hold an intellectual discussion with her social inferiors. She felt that she must make it her business to get to know them; she got them to write essays about themselves, and there was one, a Miss Williams, who confided in her. These confidences gave her a first view of Grub Street; she found—and the discovery, though it cannot have been surprising, must have been impressive—a place almost without standards and entirely without integrity. Hacks laboured here to manufacture literary shoddy by the yard; Virginia could not but admire the intelligent industry of the particular hack who described these things to her and the frankness with which they were described; she must also have felt a kind of revolted curiosity, the feelings of a lady for a pavement drab. These revelations helped her to form a picture of what she was later to call "the Underworld," the demi-monde of letters, a region that was to loom large in her imagination.

But her main impression–for most of her students were consumers not producers of literature–was of hungry sheep that are not fed. She found them more intelligent than she had expected, but suffering terribly from being half-educated. Morley College could do something really useful for them; it failed and "those in authority" set her and her students to useless tasks–this at least was her view of the matter. Nevertheless she felt the need and the opportunity strongly enough to continue working at the College for three years.*

Virginia's commitment to Morley College obliged her to be in London during term time, and from the fact that she was able to fulfil it we may assume that her health remained stable. She did leave London from time to time–visiting her aunt at Cambridge, the Fishers at Oxford, the Cecils in Sussex, and Violet at Welwyn–and in 1906 she returned to Giggleswick for the Easter holiday, this time staying not with Madge Vaughan but in lodgings near her, and going for long walks on the moors alone with her dog Gurth. In August Vanessa and Virginia rented a decaying and beautiful moated house, Blo' Norton Hall, in a remote part of Norfolk, where they enjoyed what Virginia called "a sort of honeymoon–interrupted it is true with horrible guests."

But a really grand and important excursion had been planned for this year. The Stephens had decided they must see Greece. This undertaking involved the most tremendous preparations: Thoby and Adrian made their wills; boxes and stores, green veils, blue spectacles, white boots, grey felt hats, green-lined umbrellas, paintboxes and easels, medicaments and the help of Messrs Cook had all to be obtained; going to Greece was not so much a holiday as an expedition. Thoby and Adrian–after seeing their sisters settled in Norfolk–set off. They had a month's start, and rode on horseback from Trieste by way of Montenegro and Albania. Then the ladies– Vanessa, Virginia and Violet Dickinson–travelled by train to Brindisi and thence by boat to Patras. At Olympia on 13 September the two parties were reunited.

They had seen Marathon and Salamis and Athens would have been theirs too had not a cloud caressed it; at any rate they felt themselves

* See Appendix B.

charged on each side by tremendous presences. And to prove themselves duly inspired, they not only shared their wine flask with the escort of dirty Greek peasant boys but condescended so far as to address them in their own tongue as Plato would have spoken it had Plato learnt Greek at Harrow.

They were descending Mount Pentelicus and Virginia, as usual, was writing landscape:

> But the descent of Pentelicus is stayed by a flat green ledge where nature seems to stand upright for a moment before she plunges down the hill again. There are great plane trees spreading benevolent hands, and there are comfortable little bushes ranged in close domestic order, and there is a stream which may be thought to sing their praises and the delights of wine and song. You might have heard the voice of Theocritus in the plaint that it made on the stones, and certain of the English did so hear it, albeit the text was dusty on their shelves at home. Here at any rate nature and the chant of the classic spirit prompted the six friends to dismount and rest themselves.

Then they conversed and of course their main topic was Greece and the Greeks; they were eloquent and argumentative and perhaps a little too conscious of their surroundings and then, suddenly, the little bushes creaked and bent, and a great brown form surged out of them. It was only a monk carrying a load of wood; he was dirty and probably illiterate; but there was such a force in the eye with which he fixed them that Virginia was moved to emotions which, in their intensity if not in their nature, might have been inspired by Pan himself.

At the beginning of this century an English traveller with a classical education might find much to delight and much to distress him in modern Greece. He came in pursuit of an idea and found instead a reality which was at times disconcerting. Thoby, it would seem, was such a traveller and Virginia observed his enthusiasms and his perplexities with amusement and sympathy. But in fact her feelings agreed with his. Her reaction to Greece was very much what might have been expected of any cultivated young Englishwoman in the year 1906. She was wholly unaware of Byzantine art and uncritical of that of the fifth century; for the modern Greeks she did not care; she preferred the uncivilised Wallachians on the Noels' estate at Achmetaga. She was, as always, fascinated by her fellow guests in hotels and made up stories about them.

Vanessa's views might have been different—the thing that most impressed her was the way in which the Greeks situated their buildings–but Vanessa had not much opportunity to observe Greek art. When they landed at Patras she was feeling unwell; the train journey from Olympia to Corinth upset her further, but after a day or two she was able to go on to Athens. They then set off by boat for the Peloponnese to see Epidaurus, Tiryns and Mycenae; the return railway journey made Vanessa ill again and the party had to stop at Corinth for her to rest. Leaving her there with Violet and, as it seemed, recovering, Virginia, Thoby and Adrian made their pre-arranged excursion to Euboea to visit the Noels; on their return to Athens a few days later they found Vanessa once again in bed, and this time alarmingly ill.

It was an odd, anxious, unhappy view of Greece. Virginia spent much of her time in an Athens hotel bedroom reading Merimée and heating saucepans of goat's milk, which of course boiled over when the *Lettres à une Inconnue* proved too interesting. Downstairs, Thoby and Adrian fell into a violent dispute concerning the Portsmouth Road: was it macadamised beyond Hindhead or was it not? This occupied them for some days,* though Thoby was sufficiently sanguine–or social–to return once more to the Noels.

After about a fortnight Vanessa improved and they were able to revert to their original plan; Thoby returned to London, the rest of the party went on by sea to Constantinople. Vanessa was still very unwell; she had to be carried and nearly fainted when she was put on board at the Piraeus, and again when she reached Constantinople; but here the doctor said that she was well enough to return to England by train. They left Constantinople, of which Virginia saw but little, on 29 October and reached Dover on 1 November. Here George was waiting with a nurse for Vanessa. He told them that Thoby was in bed at 46 Gordon Square with a high temperature. Vanessa was made to go to bed at once but she couldn't sleep; she was worried about Thoby. On the following day he seemed better, his temperature had gone down. The doctor clearly didn't know what was wrong with him; it had been a sharp attack of "something or other" but there was no reason to think that it was anything serious or that it would not get better; for the time being both he and Vanessa were to stay in bed.

Thus Virginia and Adrian found themselves in control of a house containing two invalids while Violet, who would have been Virginia's great standby, was herself lying ill at her own house in Manchester Street. Virginia described herself as living in the midst of nurses, bedpans, carbolic and doctors and, she might have added,

* See *The Voyage Out*, p. 417.

in an atmosphere of deepening gloom; for although Vanessa was said to be getting better and Savage, called in to consider various nervous symptoms, pooh-poohed them–or at least said that they were not at all serious–Thoby was not responding to treatment. This was hardly surprising since the doctors had decided that he was suffering from malaria and it was only discovered after ten days, through the discreet but desperate intervention of the nurse, to be typhoid fever. It was found that Violet Dickinson also had typhoid.

Whether this mistake by the doctors was the cause of what followed I do not know. Certainly the Stephen family seems to have been unfortunate in its physicians; as in 1895 and 1897 there seems to have been a helpless, muddled drifting towards death. Thoby passed from crisis to crisis; he became listless, weary and weak; all he had left at the end was the courage to die bravely.

For Virginia the disaster which prostrated them all and which seemed to take the meaning out of their lives was made a little more horrible by the fact that Violet, herself lying desperately ill, was according to her doctors, in a condition to be profoundly affected by Thoby's death. Virginia was told that it must, at all costs, be kept from her. And so Virginia, who wrote to her daily, had to keep up the pretence that her brother was still alive. "We are going on well through the stages," she writes on 20 November, the day of Thoby's death. "Thoby is going on splendidly. He is very cross with his nurses, because they won't give him mutton chops and beer, and he asks why he can't go for a ride with Bell and look for wild geese." Thus she wrote three days after the funeral. This grim exercise in fiction continued day after day for almost a month, until the truth came out by accident and Virginia had to write to explain.

There was now another piece of news to be discussed. Two days after Thoby's death Vanessa in her despair had turned to Clive Bell for comfort and had agreed to marry him.

In a way this was a consolation; "There will be all Nessa's life to look forward to," she wrote to Violet. But might there not be some treachery in becoming as happy as Vanessa now was, even though her happiness, like that of Bernard in *The Waves*, was so strangely divided? And Clive–Virginia's feelings about him were mixed but they were often extremely critical. Was he worthy to marry a Stephen? And was she, Virginia, who had lost her favourite brother, who might yet lose her Violet, now also to lose her sister? She would have to leave Gordon Square where she had been so happy. The good years had been very brief and the Stephens were devoted to catastrophe. All this she may have thought, some of it she did think; but she seems on the whole to have behaved extraordinarily well, to have risen to an occasion which might have broken a stouter constitution than hers and to have kept her head and her temper when she might fairly have been expected to lose them.

Chapter Six

1906-1908

THOBY'S death was a disaster from which Virginia could not easily recover. Two years later she still felt her loss acutely; it was odd to be living in a world that did not contain him, and even after twenty years it still seemed to her that her own continuing life was no more than an excursion without him, and that death would be no more than a return to his company.

Her immediate desire was to know more of him. There was so much that she did not know, for Thoby did not repay his sisters' love with open affection or confidences–they were all too reserved for that and there were, of course, things that a fellow does not discuss with his sisters. There was therefore much of his private and intellectual life which remained mysterious and could now never be discovered unless, perhaps, one of his Cambridge friends would write something. She addressed herself to Lytton Strachey who, after a year, had to confess that he found the task too difficult. Clive refused it also and she talked to Saxon Sydney-Turner, who applied to Leonard Woolf in Ceylon, but he too was unable to help.

That unknown part of Thoby was important to her partly because she loved him and she sought, as we all seek, for that which our dead have taken from us for ever, partly for a more complex reason–an amused yet resentful curiosity about the privileged masculine society of Cambridge. Twice she returns to a kind of bittersweet speculation concerning the vanished being whom we reconstruct in our mind's eye–*ex pede Herculem*–deducing Jacob from his room, Percival from the sensations of his circumambient friends.

In a manuscript written at the end of her life she wonders what he might have become. "Mr Justice Stephen . . . with several books to his credit . . ." She begins to draw the picture of a successful Stephen, typical of his country and class and then, almost correcting herself, she decides that he was not that: there was something melancholy and original about him, the ordinary ambitions of life would not have mattered much to him.

One is inclined to wonder what role this masterful and persuasive young man, together with his wife–for he would surely have married–would have played in the life of his sisters; how would he have regarded Vanessa's increasing libertinism and Virginia's grow-ing tendency to flirtation? Would he have had what is called 'a steadying influence'? How would he have reacted to the Post-Impressionists, to the war and to his sister's novels? I suspect that, if he had lived, he would have tended to strengthen rather than to weaken those barriers of speech and thought and custom which were soon to be overthrown amongst his friends. It was his death which began to work their destruction: Mr Sydney-Turner and Mr Strachey became Saxon and Lytton, they were at Gordon Square continually and in her distress Virginia wanted to see no one save them and Clive–Thoby's Cambridge friends. It was then that Virginia discovered that these young men had not only brains but hearts, and that their sympathy was something different from the dreadful condolences of relations. As a result of Thoby's death Bloomsbury was refounded upon the solid base of deep mutual understanding; his death was also the proximate cause of Vanessa's marriage.

On New Year's Eve 1906 Virginia and Adrian joined Vanessa and Clive at Cleeve House. the home of the Bells, near Devizes. Virginia sat and wrote at a table which was furnished with an inkpot fashioned out of the hoof of a favourite hunter. The animal's name and the date of its death were inscribed upon a silver cartouche. She often adverted to that inkpot in later life: never, in her experience, had there been an inkpot like it; it seemed a note of the entire house. The place was populated by stuffed animals and to a large extent by living ones; animals dominated the conversation, yielding only occasionally to lawn tennis, hockey and the weather. The human inhabitants had something of the bucolic health of brutes, something of their ferocity, something of their niceness and a good deal of their intellectual limitations. It was all new to Virginia, quite different from Kensington or the world of Kitty Maxse or the Duckworths; this in fact was Philistia and for Vanessa, as a multitude of despon-dent letters bear witness, it was Tomi, a desolate place inhabited by Scythians to which she was periodically banished by the exigencies of marriage.

The two Miss Bells came down to dinner in pale blue satin with satin bows in their hair. Mr Bell presided, bluff, gruff and cordial at one end of the table, Mrs Bell, an attenuated rabbit-faced woman with strong religious principles, sat opposite him. What they made of Virginia, who seems to have been in one of her more fantastic moods and who on the following day exploded at lunch, lost her temper, strode out of the house and returned in the evening with the settled wish to be as charming as possible–heaven knows. They only saw her once again and the only member of the family, save her brother-in-law, to whom she was to become at all attached was Clive's brother Cory and he, it would seem, was not then present. In the 1920s, when she had become celebrated, they would refer to her with a diffidence, a kind of bewildered curiosity, as though she had two heads but was, nevertheless, a duchess–not the kind of thing to which they were accustomed.

Virginia's volatile behaviour probably had more to do with Vanessa than with Vanessa's new relations. Certainly, having seen the Bell family, she regarded the alliance with dismay; but her objections to the match had a deeper origin.

Vanessa was lost to her, ravished away and ecstatically, monstrously happy. It was intolerable, unbearable. And Clive was simply not good enough. He was pompous, polished and slight; how her sister–Thoby's sister and Sir Leslie's daughter–could match herself to such an absurd little creature was more than she could understand. And then, seeing them together, she allowed that Clive had after all very considerable good qualities; he was kind and clever and sensitive; he did understand Vanessa very well and made her beautifully happy. To be sure he was no genius, but then neither was Vanessa and Vanessa, it was apparent, was made for marriage. It would be intolerably, odiously egotistical to find fault with an arrangement that seemed so perfectly designed to bring felicity to two–at least two–amiable human beings. And yet . . .

So it went on; she was at war with herself: divided between an agonised perception of her sister's happiness and her own jealousy, a state of delight and of rage which endured for months and years and was to be qualified only by another sentiment which heightened, rather than relaxed, the tensions within her.

The immediate problem was the actual ceremony. It was fixed for 7 February. Henry James came to see Vanessa not long before; his views of the bridegroom were even more unfavourable than those of Virginia in her most hostile moods.

However, I suppose she knows what she is about, and seemed very happy and eager and almost boisterously in love (in that house of all the Deaths, ah me!) and I took her an old silver box ("for hairpins"), and she spoke of having got "a beautiful Florentine teaset" from you. She was evidently happy in the latter, but I winced and ground my teeth when I heard of it. She and Clive are to keep the Bloomsbury house, and Virginia and Adrian to forage for some flat somewhere–

Virginia having, by the way, grown quite elegantly and charmingly and almost "smartly" handsome. I liked being with them, but it was all strange and terrible (with the hungry *futurity* of youth;) and all I could mainly see was the *ghosts*, even Thoby and Stella, let alone dear old Leslie and beautiful, pale, tragic Julia – on all of whom these young backs were, and quite naturally, so gaily turned.

The night before the wedding they all went to *Fidelio*. "I hate her going away," wrote Virginia, "but I really have been quite good tempered." The marriage took place at St Pancras Registry Office. George lent his smart car for the occasion; the chauffeur, having never before been in such a plebeian quarter of the town, lost his way, causing Vanessa and Virginia to be late for the ceremony and the young couple, who had been persuaded by Virginia to go to Manorbier for a honeymoon, to miss their train at Paddington; the delay gave Vanessa time to write an affectionate note to her sister from the station. On the following day Virginia described herself as being "numb and dumb."

Virginia and Adrian planned to move into a new home before Clive and Vanessa returned from Manorbier, taking Sophia Farrell, the family cook, with them.* Virginia found a pleasant house (which had been Bernard Shaw's) at 29 Fitzroy Square; Adrian and Sophy both approved of it but there were others who did not. "Beatrice [Thynne] comes round, inarticulate with meaning, & begs me not to take the house because of the neighbourhood," she wrote to Violet, and Violet herself was wary. Virginia was not yet brave enough to defy her relations: "If I hint at any question of respectability to George, Gerald and Jack," she complained, "they will refuse to let me take it." She sought the advice of the Police and they, it seems, were reassuring; for late in March 1907, she and Adrian moved in.

To them the situation was entirely eligible: it was an agreeable house and not so close to Gordon Square that the Stephens became a mere annexe of the Bells, nor yet so far that the two households could not meet whenever they chose. It was ideally placed for the purposes of those friends who got into the habit of visiting one of the houses and then strolling over to the other. Bloomsbury now had two centres separated by a very convenient distance.

It had been Virginia's purpose in taking this new house to make

---

* Sophy, who was very stout, declared: "I ought to be able to cut myself up among the lot of you," adding more gravely: "but it must be Miss [Virginia]; she's such a harum scarum thing she wouldn't know if they sold her. She don't know what she has on her plate." MH/A 13e.

a home for Adrian. Adrian has not played a very large part in this story but now he was to be Virginia's chief companion. She had described him in 1903 as being "fifteen years younger than all the rest of us" although he was then nearly twenty and her junior by only eighteen months. Like so many of Virginia's hyperboles it contained a good deal of truth. In a family of slow developers he was the slowest. As the youngest he tried very hard to keep his end up; while the others were enthusiastic butterfly hunters he held aloof ostentatiously; when Thoby and Virginia started the *Hyde Park Gate News* he began a rival journal. He made two attempts, but the competition was too cruel; the editors of the *News* were condescending and advised him to become one of their contributors.*Leslie gave the same advice; but it was not taken; the *Pelican News* and its successor, *The Corkscrew Gazette*, soon petered out. His mother had been his great ally and advocate; he had been her favourite and he looked to her for love and protection. His father's heavy-handed attempts to teach him were frightening and bewildering; his record at Evelyn's and Westminster was undistinguished and he was compared, unfairly but inevitably, with Thoby.

He had inherited something of his father's moral and physical characteristics; he was sensitive and rather nervous, a thin, bony, almost stunted little boy known in the family as The Dwarf and very unlike his robust elder brother. This, oddly enough, was a reproach he was able to rebut. At the age of sixteen he began to sprout, at the age of eighteen he was six feet two inches high and he attained six feet five inches. The 'dwarf' had become a giant; but this beanstalk effort seemed almost a repetition of *The Corkscrew Gazette*: he had made himself taller than any of them, but to no purpose, and indeed he seemed physically exhausted by the effort. At Cambridge he appeared no more than the evening shadow of his brother, less brilliant, less charming. Embarking, as usual, on an independent line, he refused to follow current intellectual fashions; he did not believe in G. E. Moore who was, he declared, a fraud. Moore's followers, and Lytton Strachey in particular, resented his attitude and were snubbing.

Cambridge gave him a third and he went down in 1905 with no very clear idea of what he wanted to do. Gifted with an acute mind

* When Adrian was being analysed, in 1923, his analyst is reported to have said that he was "a tragedy"; "and this tragedy consists in the fact that he cant enjoy life with zest. I [Virginia] am probably responsible. I should have paired with him, instead of hanging on to the elders. So he wilted, pale, under a stone of vivacious brothers and sisters." AWD (Berg) 13 May 1923.

and a strongly argumentative disposition he looked, as might have been expected, to the law for a profession, but it was not to be a lasting vocation.

Virginia found him by turns a depressing or an exasperating companion. He could be maddeningly lethargic, lamentably silent, unable to find interest in anything except the constant rehearsal of old family reminiscences which were, indeed, always his favourite topic. And yet there was another side to his character and he could, on occasion, be gay, enterprising and high-spirited; but such occasions were few and, with his sister, his intelligence and his humour were diverted into a habit of mocking surveillance and quiet irony, a devastating appreciation of other people's faults, and, above all, a merciless vein of pleasantry. Her flightiness brought out his sardonic Stephen matter-of-factness, her enthusiasm his scepticism, her arguments his ridicule. He was a tease and found in Virginia an eminently teasable subject. They were in fact, both of them, highly gifted in the arts of reproach and carried their sallies to great lengths. At Fitzroy Square Sophy used to prepare the butter in little round pats, spheres which Adrian and Virginia used as missiles when other arguments failed, so that the walls were starred with flattened projectiles; there is at least one witness who has seen an argument end in an exchange of butter.

They were genuinely fond of each other—indeed in all that family fraternal sentiments were profound, more profound perhaps than any other, and after Thoby's death brother and sisters were in a new way united. Certain reserves were broken down; they began to talk more freely, above all about the dead, who had hitherto been taboo—so much so that, for years after Stella's death, her name had not been mentioned, but I doubt whether Virginia and Adrian ever hinted at their love for each other. That deep feeling remained unexpressed, in public at all events; it was the arguments in the drawing-room and the butter on the walls that the visitor noticed.

It was all very well for Virginia to go off and live in a perhaps rather disreputable neighbourhood with her younger brother but, said her old friends, that younger brother was by no means so youthful that he could not very well look after himself, and the person who manifestly needed looking after was Virginia. Vanessa's spell of duty was over; Adrian, that irresponsible luggage-loser, was not the man for the job; what Virginia clearly and emphatically needed was a husband. "Virginia," they declared, "must marry."

She was irritated by the suggestion and wrote to Violet, "I wish everyone didn't tell me to marry. Is it crude human nature breaking out? I call it disgusting." Nevertheless she was not so utterly opposed to the very notion as she seems hitherto to have been. Whether it was the spectacle of her sister's felicity, or a new sense of her own loneliness or the disappearance of him who had been, after all, the man she loved best, one cannot tell, but certainly the year 1907 marks a distinct change in her emotional disposition.

Hitherto men, as lovers, seem to have played no role at all in her imagination. There is nothing in her letters or diaries to suggest that any man had inspired her with the slightest erotic excitement. All her passions, her jealousies and tenderness are kept for her own sex and above all for Violet; but now, although very far from falling in love with any man, she was at least ready to flirt.

It is not altogether surprising that the first man with whom she flirted was almost old enough to be her father. Walter Headlam was an old family friend. Born in 1866, he had been one of the younger men whom Julia brought to Talland House. He was now a Fellow of King's, a man with a great reputation amongst Hellenists, a translator who had shown a fastidious delight in the use of English and could, in his own right, be considered a poet. These were qualities to give him an immediate claim upon Virginia's attention: she had a kind of reverence for Greek Scholars, felt them to be rulers over a territory into which she had attempted to journey and, equally, she could not fail to be interested in one who, like herself, was devoted to the art of letters. Moreover his character was in some respects engaging; he had a certain eccentric absurdity which was endearing because it resulted from a complete absorption in his work. The confusion, the learned turmoil of a life spent largely in a single-minded hunt for truth, the occasional reckless sallies into practical affairs, of which he had but the vaguest understanding, the ingenuousness with which he wandered into the most ludicrous misadventures from which he emerged baffled, perplexed but always convinced that the most important thing in his life was, after all, properly to achieve the restoration of Herodas—all this was not unsympathetic.*

Virginia respected and liked him and according to Vanessa he had a great belief in her genius—and this was a lovable trait. But both Vanessa and Violet considered the friendship with some misgivings. Walter Headlam was, in their opinion, a shocking flirt and his real passion in life, so it was said, was for little girls.†

* Headlam may have served as a model for Mr Bankes in *To the Lighthouse*. See George Duckworth to VW, 28 May 1927.

† Violet Dickinson's attitude towards Mr Headlam may have been coloured by Stella Duckworth—who had been her particular friend. In September 1893 he

Not long after Thoby's death–in fact while she was still keeping up the fiction of his survival–Virginia wrote excitedly to tell Violet that she was to send all her "unpublished works" to Walter Headlam "for sober criticism"; further, that he wished to dedicate his translation of the *Agamemnon* to her, instead of to Swinburne, "in gratitude for 3 papers of the finest criticism known to him which I wrote and despatched 4 years ago!" Thereafter they corresponded (he wrote to her "as to a sister") and met frequently; he would come to tea–once with Lytton Strachey, when Virginia complained that she hated "pouring out tea & talking like a lady"; at another time they had "a serious interview"; he declared himself miserable because Virginia didn't marry but sat moping alone, thinking she must be "a d——d failure." They discussed the matter for two hours, greatly to the advantage of their feelings no doubt. She saw him at Cambridge when she went, as she periodically did, to visit her aunt; he took her to the Opera at Covent Garden.

Presently he accused her of being fickle; he was pathetic, dignified, injured and then, so it would seem, the affair petered out with no great harm done to anyone. When he died very suddenly and unexpectedly in June 1908, Virginia's grief was not immoderate.*

---

stayed with the Stephens at St Ives; Stella wrote in her diary (21 September): "Mother & Mr Headlam came home late for dinner, looking tired & unhappy. *Drat* Mr Headlam. What *has* happened?" and (22 September): "Mr Headlam went at 10.30. I cannot think of him without a shudder & yet he is much to be pitied–it is awful."

* Virginia preserved one of Headlam's letters. Erudite and flirtatious, it may serve, probably, as an example of his manner to her.

King's College,
Cambridge.
Saturday.

Dear Virginia

I had thought of writing to say please don't write to thank me for the book, which you had already said thank you for – you talk of me as always giving things away, but this is the only thing I can remember ever asking you to take from me – and now before the letter comes I find this book from you. I thought at first it must be something I had left behind me, though what I knew I had left behind me was not this. I was going in any case to take the Life abroad with me and your MSS. It must seem strange that I have never read them yet, but I want to enjoy them in the holidays.

You musn't say Christian to me: that must be left for me to say to you; it's what you have been in coming to that dismallest of chambers every week and never failing, and it's well there has been Christianity, or I should never be able to say bless you.

$X\alpha\hat{\iota}\rho\epsilon\ \phi\acute{\iota}\lambda\eta$ [Hail Mistress]
Walter Headlam

Virginia had believed, or had affected to believe, that when once Vanessa was married she would be entirely changed and that she and her sister would never meet again on the old footing. Clive would destroy their intimacy. When she returned from her honeymoon Vanessa set herself to reassure Virginia on this point: Virginia must spend a great deal of her time at Gordon Square and she, Vanessa, insisted on coming frequently to see Virginia. They all went off to Paris together, and talked of finding a country house to share for the summer; there were far too many servants at No 46 and if two thirds of them were dismissed it would be easy to finance such a scheme. Discussions such as these, the patent fact that Vanessa was not essentially changed, that they met almost every day, and that they continued to have long tête-à-têtes together–all this had its effect in relieving Virginia from the too gloomy fancies in which she had indulged at the time of Vanessa's marriage.

When they were apart the sisters corresponded daily; together, they discussed Virginia's suitors, Vanessa always fancying that every man whom Virginia met would at once propose to her. Meanwhile, at Fitzroy Square, Virginia was forced to stand on her own feet in her own drawing-room and to talk a little. In the autumn she and Adrian began shyly to entertain and to revive Thoby's Thursday Evenings.

From the first Virginia's ideas of acceptable company were very different from those of Vanessa. She invited Bloomsbury–the word can now be used with a little more confidence–and also other young men who had been at Cambridge and at 46 Gordon Square in Thoby's time–Charles Tennyson, Hilton Young, Theodore Llewelyn Davies–and one rather older Cambridge figure. A scholar, a linguist, a critic, a lawyer, Charlie Sanger was also, according to his friends, a saint; he had been elected to the 'Apostles' at the same time as Bertrand Russell and did, I fancy, exert a considerable influence over his younger friends, with whom he was on terms of perfectly easy familiarity. These, the intellectuals, might find themselves at Fitzroy Square in the company of 'Ozzie' Dickinson (Violet's brother), Lady Beatrice Thynne, Lady Gwendolen Godolphin Osborne, Margaret Vaughan, Janet Case,* Miss Sheep-

Thus by an allusion to the pious inscriptions of the Catacombs, where φίλη has a chaste meaning, Headlam is able boldly to address her as "mistress." (I am much indebted to my colleague Dr Shiel for pointing out to me the extent of Headlam's ambiguous dexterity.)

* "I remember having tea with you one day after the Greek lesson time was over and done with, and V. established in the new odd Bloomsbury life and I didnt

shanks, or any of the Hyde-Park-Gaters—though the latter were more likely I think to be invited to dine than to drop in after dinner on Thursdays.

Virginia was always curious about people and we find her adventuring into decent society there to listen to the current talk of the Establishment: "Country going to the dogs . . . we have no fleet . . . the Germans menace us from without, the Trades' Unions from within . . ." For the Duckworths still represented authority and there were occasions when she felt like a child in their presence, a child who might be scolded because George was 'hurt.' He never saw his family now, he complained; really Clive and Vanessa had treated him very ill; they were drifting apart. And this was true, for things were very different at Gordon Square. Clive was much more easily bored and much more selective in his invitations, while Vanessa enthusiastically slammed the door against old friends and relations. It was almost certainly Vanessa—although the story is told of both sisters—who tried to hide from Mrs Humphry Ward by standing behind a lamp post in the Piazza della Signoria, and it was certainly Vanessa who pushed her neglect so far that Richmond Ritchie—Aunt Anny's husband—cut her dead at the Opera. The Bells really did attempt to be exclusive and it was with a touch of malice that Virginia observed in November 1907 that

> Nessa & Clive live, as I think, much like great ladies in a French salon; they have all the wits & the poets; & Nessa sits among them like a Goddess.

They regarded their drawing-room as a work of art and did not welcome intruders.

Virginia's drawing-room was not a work of art; for one thing it was inhabited by the dog Hans, which delighted in extinguishing visitors' matches with its paw, which interrupted several parties by being sick, and on one occasion, when Virginia was giving Lady Strachey tea, eased itself upon the hearthrug—a performance which both guest and hostess thought it best to disregard.

Despite her training at Hyde Park Gate Virginia was not, I think, in any sense a leader of the society within which she moved. She was often silent, respectfully—or sometimes abstractedly—silent; she affected to feel, and really did feel, awe in the presence of Saxon or of Lytton; even the admirable but unattractive Miss Sheepshanks could

---

think she'd have any further use for me, and felt shy of going [presumably to Fitzroy Square] and *you* told me to stick to her. She'd like it—so thank you for that." Janet Case to Violet Dickinson, 19 April 1937.

put her down with the devastating enquiry: "Miss Stephen, do you *ever* think?" Nevertheless, with her own social life to conduct, Virginia was probably happier than she had expected to be, and, for comfort, she could still turn to her sister.

It was agreed that the two households should spend the summer holidays of 1907 within reach of one another. Virginia and Adrian rented a cottage at Playden, a little to the north of Rye; the Bells, who came a little later after visiting the Bell family residence in Wiltshire, stayed in Rye itself. Guests were to some extent shared and, of course, there were constant meetings. While she was there, in addition to some journalism, Virginia started to write an account of her father and mother, of life in the nursery, of Stella and Jack and her half-brothers; it was in the form of a Life of Vanessa written for her children (Vanessa was by now pregnant). She was also writing descriptions of light and mist, night scenes and rural life, and now also she was attempting, with a novelist's intention, to look at states of mind; she tried to enter the mind of a Sussex farm labourer, she considered the pathetic fallacy in novels, the habit of reading the novelist's sentiments into those of very different kinds of people–or for that matter of animals. Also she was reading Henry James, but without great enthusiasm.*

Amongst the monuments of Rye was the Master himself and a visit was called for. Vanessa had written to Virginia from Wiltshire, hoping that "old Henry James won't be too monumental and difficult." He was monumental enough, as may be seen from the following letter to Violet Dickinson.

. . . we went and had tea with Henry James to-day, and Mr and Mrs Prothero at the golf club and Henry James fixed me with his staring blank eye, it is like a child's marble, and said "My dear Virginia they tell me, they tell me, they tell me, that you–as indeed being your father's daughter, nay your grandfather's grandchild, the descendant I may say of a century, of a century, of quill pen and ink, ink, inkpots, yes, yes, yes, they tell me, a h m m m, that you, that you, that you *write* in short." This went on in the public street, while we all waited, as farmers wait for the hen to lay an egg,–do they? nervous, polite, and now on this foot, now on that. I felt like a condemned person, who sees the knife drop and stick and drop again. Never did any woman hate 'writing' as much as I do. But when I am old and famous I shall dis-

* " I am reading Henry James on America; & feel myself as one embalmed in a block of smooth amber; it is not unpleasant, very tranquil, as a twilight stroll– but such is not the stuff of Genius: no, it should be a swift stream." VW to Clive Bell, [18 August 1907].

course like Henry James. We had to stop periodically to let him shake himself free of the thing; he made phrases over the bread and butter, "rude and rapid" it was, and told us all the scandal of Rye. "Mr Jones has eloped I regret to say to Tasmania leaving twelve little Jones's and a possible thirteenth to Mrs Jones, most regrettable, most unfortunate, and yet not wholly an action to which one has no private key of one's own so to speak." Well, this ceases to interest you . . .

The Bells arrived, also Saxon and Lytton. As we have seen, Henry James did not care for Clive; Saxon he seems to have liked even less. Neither the Bells nor the Stephens returned to Rye, nor did Virginia see very much of Henry James in later years. One may suppose that he was attracted to her on principle–she was Leslie Stephen's daughter–but she hardly conformed then, and was to conform less and less, to his notions of delicacy, decorum and reverence. He could not possibly approve of her scrubby, gritty friends. Virginia, for her part, regarded him with a kind of amused awe, respected his work but respected it with reservations and, as we may perceive from the letter that I have quoted, enjoyed his company only in retrospect.*

On 27 December 1907 there was a meeting at Gordon Square at which Saxon, Vanessa, Clive, Adrian, Lytton and Virginia read Vanbrugh's *The Relapse*. Lytton excelled as Lord Foppington, Virginia was both Berinthia and Miss Hoyden. This was the first of many such meetings. They took place on Friday evenings during the year 1908, usually at Gordon Square, always with the same readers, who may be regarded as the core of Bloomsbury at this period. Walter Lamb, a friend of Clive's, who had been at Trinity and of whom we shall hear more, once took part. He was then a schoolmaster at Clifton and could never have been a regular participant. Saxon kept the minutes for a time, giving the cast and a comment on each reading; Clive, who became Secretary in April 1908, did likewise; the minute book is interesting in that it provides a notion of the taste of the group. It was catholic: the Restoration and the Elizabethans, Milton, Shakespeare, Swinburne, Ibsen. Virginia failed, according to the Secretary, to convey the feeling of concentrated nervous force required in the part of Rebecca West in *Rosmersholm* but she excelled as Althaea in *Atalanta in Calydon*.

* "[Henry James] asked much after Virginia and Vanessa. Can't cultivate Gordon Square because of the unpleasant presence of 'that little image' Clive. 'Tell Virginia–tell her–how sorry I am that the inevitabilities of life should have made it possible even for a moment that I would allow any child of her father's to swim out of my ken.'" Sydney Waterlow, *Diary* (Berg), 10 March 1912.

The Relapse was hardly the kind of play that Sir Leslie would have cared to have heard his daughters reading aloud in the company of young men. Nor, while he was alive, would Virginia, who in her letters ventured no stronger expression than 'd—n,' have imagined herself capable of such an audacity. In the four years that had elapsed since her father's death, there had been a change in the moral climate.

Virginia, after her first relief at finding that the young men from Cambridge did not pursue her, began to find their lack of interest dull; her flirtation with Walter Headlam had inclined her to take a more adventurous attitude. And then Lytton, whose heart had been opened by their common grief and who was now so close a friend, found it intolerable that the pruderies and reserves of the past should be allowed to continue.

It was a spring evening. Vanessa and I were sitting in the drawing room. The drawing room had greatly changed its character since 1904. The Sargent-Furse age was over. The age of Augustus John was dawning. His Pyramus filled one entire wall. The Watts portrait of my father and my mother were hung downstairs if they were hung at all. Clive had hidden all the match boxes because their blue and yellow swore with the prevailing colour scheme. At any moment Clive might come in and he and I should begin to argue–amicably, impersonally at first; soon we should be hurling abuse at each other and pacing up and down the room. Vanessa sat silent and did something mysterious with her needle or her scissors. I talked egotistically, excitedly, about my own affairs no doubt. Suddenly the door opened and the long and sinister figure of Mr Lytton Strachey stood on the threshold. He pointed his finger at a stain on Vanessa's white dress.

"Semen?" he said.

Can one really say it? I thought & we burst out laughing. With that one word all barriers of reticence and reserve went down. A flood of the sacred fluid seemed to overwhelm us. Sex permeated our conversation. The word bugger was never far from our lips. We discussed copulation with the same excitement and openness that we had discussed the nature of good. It is strange to think how reticent, how reserved we had been and for how long.*

---

* MH/A 16. Virginia gives the impression that this occurred in about 1909, but a letter from Vanessa to Virginia which can confidently be dated 11 August 1908 makes it clear that by then Lytton's private life was well known to both sisters, while a letter from Maynard Keynes to Duncan Grant, dated 2 August 1908, contains the following passage:

"Lytton seems to carry on a good deal with his females. He has let Vanessa see his most indecent poems–she is filled with delight, has them by heart, and has made many typewritten copies for Virginia and others."

We may therefore place this *éclaircissement* not later than the summer of 1908;

This was an important moment in the history of the *mores* of Bloomsbury and perhaps in that of the British middle classes; but although Virginia's entire social climate was altered from now on – and this had all sorts of consequences – the libertine speech of herself and of her friends had no radical effect upon her conduct or, I think, upon her imagination. She remained in a profound way virginal and for her the great event of the years 1907–1908 was, not the beginning of Bloomsbury bawdy talk, but the birth of *Melymbrosia*.

Melymbrosia may, indeed, have had its beginnings in Virginia's imagination at some earlier date; perhaps even at Manorbier in 1904. But it is now that we hear it mentioned by name in her letters, now that she asks for advice and gives some indication of her struggle in writing it.

Melymbrosia was to occupy her for the next five years and to become, eventually, *The Voyage Out*. We do not know much about her earlier attempts at what she called "a work of the imagination." She had conceived a play, to be written oddly enough in collaboration with Jack Hills:

> I'm going to have a man and a woman – show them growing up – never meeting – not knowing each other – but all the time you'll feel them come nearer and nearer. This will be the real exciting part (as you see) – but when they almost meet – only a door between – you see how they just miss – and go off at a tangent, and never come anywhere near again. There'll be oceans of talk and emotions without end.

This interesting but remarkably intractable scenario was devised about 1903; so far as I know it never materialised.

A few fragments remain: the beginning of a novel and a short story, to which reference has already been made. There were also, it seems, some works of an unusual kind. We only know of these because Virginia and Madge Vaughan sent each other manuscripts and criticisms. It is clear that Virginia's early attempts at fiction (if that is what they were) disconcerted Madge a good deal and Virginia found it necessary to explain something of her purpose by way of justification.

> My only defence is that I write of things as I see them; & I am quite conscious all the time that it is a very narrow, & rather bloodless point

unless Virginia invented it. That it was not wholly imaginary is made probable by the fact that it was read to the Memoir Club (in about 1922). That audience would not have been troubled by inaccuracies but it would not have accepted a complete invention.

of view. I think–if I were Mr Gosse writing to Mrs Green!–I could explain a little why this is so from external reasons; such as education, way of life &c. And so perhaps I may get something better as I grow older. George Eliot was near 40 I think, when she wrote her first novel–the Scenes [*of Clerical Life*].

But my present feeling is that this vague & dream like world, without love, or heart, or passion, or sex, is the world I really care about, & find interesting. For, though they are dreams to you, & I cant express them at all adequately, these things are perfectly real to me.

But please dont think for a moment that I am satisfied, or think that my view takes in any whole. Only it seems to me better to write of the things I do feel, than to dabble in things I frankly dont understand in the least. That is the kind of blunder–in literature–which seems to me ghastly & unpardonable: people, I mean, who wallow in emotions without understanding them. But, of course, any great writer treats them so that they are beautiful, & turns statues into men & women. I wonder if you understand my priggish & immature mind at all? The things I sent you were mere experiments; & I shall never try to put them forward as my finished work. They shall sit in a desk till they are burnt!

No doubt they were burnt; so, it would appear, were seven different versions of *The Voyage Out*.

She continued to do a good deal of reviewing. A series of *Cornhill* articles published during 1908 gave her the chance to be a little more ambitious than she had been in her contributions to *The Guardian*, *The Times* and other journals, for here she had more room for manœuvre; but she published no fiction until she was thirty-three.

Her literary taciturnity was partly the result of shyness; she was still terrified of the world, terrified of exposing herself. But with this was united another and nobler emotion–a high regard for the seriousness of her profession. To produce something that would meet her own criteria it was necessary to read voraciously, to write and rewrite continually and no doubt, when she was not actually writing, to revolve the ideas that she was expressing in her mind.

Having discovered, more or less, the direction in which she wanted to proceed, she would have lived very close to her work. No one who has any experience of creating a work of art will need to be told how completely such a process, when once started, dominates the mind. It becomes the stuff of one's waking life, more real than anything else, a delight and a torment. Thus, in considering the events of this period in her life, a period in which Virginia embarked with some recklessness and, it must be said, with very little scruple, upon emotional adventures of a sufficiently desperate kind, it is to be remembered that, for the greater part of the time, she lived in a world of her own making and, as will be seen, some of her least creditable actions were related to the necessities of that world.

Chapter Seven

1908-1909

As we have seen, Virginia was always being told that she should marry; but, when one considers the men who formed her immediate circle in the year 1908 it must be allowed that her chances of doing so were not encouraging. The field of search had been narrowed, or at least the pitch had been queered, by her discovery that most of the young men who most interested her were buggers.*

Saxon she would hardly have thought of as a husband; although he did not inspire love in her, she perhaps did in him. In a letter to Lytton, Leonard Woolf speculated on the possibility that she might end by marrying Saxon; but his qualifications as a lover were questionable. He had his peculiarities in love, as in so much else, and it was, perhaps, in order to make his position clear that he discussed them with Virginia.†

On paper, so to speak, Duncan Grant was also a possible husband. Virginia had met him when she was with the Bells in Paris in 1907; he was then an art student in that city. He had liked the Bells and thought that Virginia was extremely witty and "amazingly beautiful." Clive and Vanessa had found him charming and hoped to see a great deal of him when he returned to London.

They did; Duncan Grant was to become a familiar figure in Gordon Square and an even more familiar figure in Fitzroy Square, where he had a studio. He would wander into No 29 at any hour, hitching up his trousers, which always seem to have been in a precarious condition and which, at that time, were frequently borrowed from someone less slim than he; then he would borrow twopence for a tram fare and presently wander out again. He was never unwelcome, although Maud, the housemaid, was slightly scandalized by his informality: "that Mr Grant," she complained,

* Buggers, a coarse and perhaps an inaccurate word. Nevertheless I use it, for Virginia and her friends used it (*q.v.s.* p. 124) and would have thought most of the alternatives over-refined and—in that they do not remind us of persecuted heresy—impoverished.

† "What a very odd talk you seem to have had with Saxon. I cant believe that that mild little man is really a Sadist or whatever its called." VB/VW, [16 March 1909].

"gets in everywhere." I doubt whether Maud remained insensible to his charm; certainly Virginia did not; she would have been pleased to know that Duncan praised her beauty and that he once told his cousin, Lytton Strachey, that he might like to be married to her.★ She would not, however, have taken this remark very seriously; she was well aware that if, at this time, his affections were given— or lent—to any member of the family they were for Adrian.

Probably the person whom Virginia's Bloomsbury friends most frequently thought of her marrying was Lytton Strachey. And yet, considered as a husband, Lytton would appear to have been a non-starter and this for two reasons: he was an impossible character and he was the arch-bugger of Bloomsbury. Nevertheless, Virginia certainly considered the idea of marrying him and he half wanted to marry her. Where both the principals are inclined to make a match it is clear that the spectator cannot dismiss the thing out of hand and it is worth enquiring into the disabilities which, at first sight, made the marriage so unlikely and seeing whether, as stated here, they are not somewhat exaggerated.

That Lytton was a pretty thorough-going homosexual cannot be denied. Once, in considering Virginia's suitors, her sister remarked:

I should like Lytton as a brother in law better than anyone I know but the only way I can perceive of bringing that to pass would be if he were to fall in love with Adrian— & even then Adrian would probably reject him.

Nevertheless, in matters of sex we are few of us entirely consistent; indeed Clive at one moment suggested that Lytton had become a womaniser. Lytton's attentions to Virginia were of a kind to suggest that such a transformation might occur and his later history shows that he could, to some extent, respond to a woman's affection. Conceivably Virginia might have saved him for her sex; but it was not only his sexual inclinations that needed saving.

The picture that we have of him at this period when he was thought of as a possible husband for Virginia is a dark one. I think that it is fair to say that it is the picture of a creature torturing and self-tortured, slipping from one agony to another, a wretched,

★ The remark should be read in its context:
"I think I could almost marry Vanessa, and I could altogether? Clive." Lytton Strachey to Duncan Grant, 6 November 1907.
"I think I might manage to like being married to Virginia—but not to Clive. I suppose you think this odd?" Duncan Grant to Lytton Strachey, [8 November 1907].

sighing, hand-wringing misfit, a quite impossible person. And yet a great many people found him not only possible, but easy and, when he was naughty, as he certainly very often was, they forgave him. Why? The reason is not altogether flattering to Lytton; he was forgiven because neither his sorrows nor his crimes were taken very seriously. Despite his real and sincere emotion at the time of Thoby's death, Virginia felt misgivings about Lytton, not because he was lachrymose but rather because he had so few tears to shed. Socially this made him much easier than the weepy monster of popular imagination. In fact, socially he was easy enough. He might be cruel or spiteful but this ill-humour was as superficial, as histrionic, as his affected groans and his mock lamentations. Virginia thought that he lacked what she called magnanimity, and by this I think that she meant the kind of greatness of feeling which enables one to disregard criticism, the quality, perhaps, that makes a true poet. When Clive sent her some of Lytton's verses to read, she wrote:

> Yes, they are exquisite, & a little anthology I have here of minor Victorian verse shows none better. But (you will expect that but, & relish it,) there is something of ingenuity that prevents me from approving as warmly as I should; do you know what I mean when I talk of his verbal felicities, which somehow evade, when a true poet, I think, would have committed himself? "Enormous month", "unimaginable repose", "mysterious ease", "incomparably dim"; when I come upon these, I hesitate; I roll them upon my tongue; I do not feel that I am breasting fresh streams. But then I am a contemporary, a jealous contemporary, & I see perhaps the marks of the tool where Julian [i.e. the next generation] will see the entire shape. I sometimes think that Lytton's mind is too pliant & supple ever to make anything lasting; his resources are infinite. Jealousy–no doubt!

And no doubt she was jealous; certainly she was critical and her criticism shows some acumen, a just appraisal of Lytton's limitations, if not of his virtues. It was at once the advantage and the difficulty of their relationship that both still had their way to make in the republic of letters and that each divined that the other could become a formidable rival. Virginia must have felt that their union would have been one of competitive powers. But for this very reason it could appear an attractive proposition. As a fellow writer Lytton was a rival but he was also congenial and, from a literary point of view if from no other, he was respectable, more respectable than her other friends; for Saxon, she must by now have suspected, would produce very little, and both she and Lytton were inclined to dismiss Clive as a man of letters. But, for all her strictures, she and her friends had a firm belief in Lytton's potential. She liked him very much; in a way she feared him and perhaps she might–in a way–come to love him.

But, judged by the common standards of marriage, the only one of Virginia's friends who could be regarded as a desirable *parti* was Edward Hilton Young. He was born in 1879, the same year as Vanessa; his father, Sir George Young, had been a friend of Sir Leslie, and Hilton and his brothers had bowled their hoops in Kensington Gardens with the little Stephens. Sir George climbed mountains, sat on Royal Commissions, wrote a study of Homer and the Greek accents and was, in fact, another of those solid Victorian characters who seem to have been so abundant in the older generation.

Hilton seemed to be cast from the same smooth and well-proportioned mould as his father–even, like him, becoming President of the Union at Cambridge; nobody was surprised when in later life he made a name for himself in war and in politics, ending with a peerage, a string of decorations and some estimable volumes of prose and verse. On coming down from the University he read for the Bar and later on, when the Stephen family had moved to Bloomsbury and began to entertain on Thursday evenings, he renewed his acquaintance with them, and became a fairly regular visitor at both Gordon and Fitzroy Squares. He found himself at first rather intimidated by the company with its intellectual brilliance and uncompromising scrutiny of accepted opinions and conventions. He certainly *was* conventional by their standards; but they were tolerant as well as charming and accomplished; he was genial and well-endowed; he grew to value their opinions and they learnt to value him.

He was attracted to Virginia but never–I should suppose–was deeply in love with her; she accepted his attentions with pleasure and yet, when it came to the point, thought him a little unsubtle. As Vanessa characteristically put it, he was "like an elephant in a china shop."* Somehow his perfections bored Virginia; he had all the good qualities and yet failed to be more than interesting. But he *was* interesting and for some years she saw a good deal of him and felt that it might be nice to be married to him or at all events to be proposed to by him. We shall meet him again later but first we must

---

* VB to VW [11 August 1908]. Vanessa's use and misuse of proverbs was an unfailing source of delight to Virginia. "It's an ill worm that has no turning," "to take the bull by the udders," "a stitch in nine saves time" etc. It is uncertain which were invented by Virginia herself.

discuss an admirer of a different kind, a much more agitating and distressing lover than Hilton, Saxon or even Lytton.

In February 1908 Vanessa bore a son, Julian. In April, after the very long convalescence then thought necessary, Clive, Vanessa, and Adrian joined Virginia, who was at St Ives for Easter. With them of course went the baby and his nurse. Virginia had no experience of very young children. The little creature screamed, as it seemed to her, like an ill-omened cat; it seemed a completely inhuman thing, something alien and appalling which created endless bother.

Vanessa felt all that a young mother might be expected to feel; but her maternal sentiments were very highly developed, so much so that they bred a kind of obtuseness, for to her it seemed that the baby was as important, as interesting, as conversable as any adult; all its activities, even its screams, were of delightful interest and she found it almost impossibly hard to believe that there were those who could not share her feelings and would not admit that, the baby being the centre of life, other topics could, for a distraction so entirely charming, be postponed. To Virginia this was incomprehensible; all the comforts of sisterly intercourse were destroyed. She turned to Clive and found that his sentiments were nearly the same as hers. They were both, in a way, jealous of the child.

Clive was in many ways an excellent father, kindly, generous, and if occasionally exasperated beyond endurance by his children, never resentful. But before he could set himself to charm and amuse the young he had to have some common ground on which to meet them. In the case of a small baby he was at a loss. He hated mess— the pissing, puking and slobbering of little children distressed him very much; so did their noise. Naturally anxious and easily alarmed for everyone's health, he was disturbed by the fragility of babies. If a baby howled he would certainly conclude that it was desperately ill and if it continued to howl he would himself be made ill by its noise. So now, at St Ives, tortured alike by compassion and exasperation, he fled the house, taking refuge in long walks through the countryside. With a sense of desertion and of treachery, but to some extent consoled by a sense of her own uselessness, Virginia accompanied him.

Out of earshot of that dreadful caterwauling they could be comfortable again; they could talk about books and friends and they did so with a sense of comradeship, of confederacy, against the fearful tyrannies of family life. In such converse it was easier for Virginia to discover her brother-in-law's good qualities: the real good humour which lay beneath his urbanity, the tenderness for other people's feelings which could make him appear fussy, his almost invariable good temper, his quick sense of the absurd, his charm. He, for his part, had never doubted that she was a remarkable, an exhilarating, an enchanting companion; but perhaps it was now that he noticed, in certain lights and in certain phases of animation, that she was even more beautiful than Vanessa. Clive could never carry on more than five minutes' conversation with a personable woman and refrain from some slight display of gallantry; now perhaps he was a little warmer than mere homage required and–this was the crucial thing–she, who would ordinarily have repulsed all advances with the utmost severity, was now not entirely unkind. An ardent and sanguine temperament such as his was excited by resistance and fortified by the least hint of success. In a word, Clive, after fourteen months of marriage, entered into a violent and prolonged flirtation with his sister-in-law.*

I use the word flirtation, for if I called this attachment an 'affair' it would suggest that Clive succeeded in his object, which was indeed no less, and I think not much more, than a delightful little infidelity ending up in bed. Many years later Virginia accused him of being a cuckoo that lays its eggs in other birds' nests. "My dear Virginia," was his cheerful reply, "you never would let me lay an egg in your nest." In fact I doubt whether the business would have lasted for so long or, for a time, have become so important to them both, if Virginia had given him what he wanted. But this she never did and, in a very crude sense, her conduct may be described as virtuous.

What then did she want? She was not in the least in love with Clive. In so far as she was in love with anyone she was in love with Vanessa. She wrote and received letters daily when they were separated and her letters are much like love letters. If nothing came for her from Vanessa she at once imagined that her sister was ill or dead, or at least in the midst of some fearful calamity. She longed for the comfort of Vanessa's presence. But it was because she loved Vanessa so much that she had to injure her, to enter and in entering to break that charmed circle within which Vanessa and Clive were so happy and by which she was so cruelly excluded, and to have Vanessa for herself again by detaching the husband who, after all, was not worthy of her.

In October 1907 Virginia had written of the Bells "it will be some

* Guesswork: the flirtation may have started earlier; but the date that I suggest is probable.

time before I can separate him from her." This was a lapsus–her ostensible meaning was: "before I can distinguish him from her"—but the slip may have betrayed a velleity of which Virginia herself was unaware at this time. The manifest success of the marriage would have reinforced such feelings. She perceived the happiness of her sister's life as one standing on a cold pavement looks enviously through a window at pleasant firelit intimacies. Her own life with Adrian was a cheerless substitute, nor could she have imagined Lytton, Saxon, or even Hilton Young, making with her the same cheerful domestic blaze that she envied at 46 Gordon Square. Fate had thrust before her a quite exceptionally fair example of normal connubial sensuality; and it left her feeling lonely and frightened by her own loneliness. It was now within her power to make an end of that particular torment and she did not know how to resist the temptation of doing so.

What she must soon have realised, or rather, what she must have known perfectly well from the beginning, was that Vanessa was deeply in love with her husband and that an attempt of this nature, whatever its cause, could not but arouse the deepest resentment in her whom she wished above all things to attach.

Vanessa's situation, as Virginia must have understood, was in the highest degree painful and called for a remarkable exercise in prudence and in fortitude. An outright quarrel with high words and accusations never took place; it is probable that both sisters shrank from the notion of 'a scene.' In letters to Clive and to Virginia, Vanessa takes things lightly, easily, with a show of humour; inwardly she was both hurt and angry; she could, she said, have forgiven Virginia if Virginia had felt any passion, had been genuinely or indeed at all in love with Clive. But this clearly she was not; her conduct was therefore inspired by nothing save a delight in mischief. It made Clive irritable; it made her–Vanessa–very unhappy. What satisfaction did Virginia herself gain from it? None, it may be thought, save that which comes to him who teases an aching tooth with his tongue.*

And yet there was a sense in which Clive's attachment was of real service to Virginia. She was not, I think, of that unamiable temperament which loves to arouse male lust only in order to disappoint it. Her conduct in other affairs of the heart, and indeed all that we know of her temperament, points in a different direction–she was in fact

---

* "My affair with Clive and Nessa . . . For some reason that turned more of a knife in me than anything else has ever done." VW to Gwen Raverat, 22 March 1925.

very shy of arousing any sexual feeling in anyone. But she did enjoy being admired–admired for her looks, her brains, her personality– and being flattered by a man who well understood the art of making himself agreeable to women. It was something quite new in her life, something that she had certainly not had from Madge or Violet, or indeed from Walter Headlam. Clive had the special charm of normality. This meant, not only that he valued Virginia for her sex (whereas Lytton valued her despite her sex), but that he did not belong to that little *cénacle* of Apostolic buggers from which Virginia was necessarily excluded and which she regarded with apprehension, irritation and distaste. I suspect that he succeeded, far more than Walter Headlam, in making her aware of her own normal proclivities, in making her feel the need, which she had not hitherto felt, for a man.

To this was added something of greater moment: Clive believed, as Madge and Violet believed, in Virginia's genius (it was the word that they used), but unlike Madge or Violet, Clive was able to offer acceptable criticism. In this respect he was indeed much more serviceable than Lytton. Lytton was admirable for a discussion of literature in general, but not when it came to the writings of Virginia Stephen. Then he was too serious a rival. With him she was per- petually on her guard, for him she adopted her best literary behaviour, with the result that the letters she sent him were about the dullest and most pretentious that she ever wrote. Clive, though a valuable critic, was more sympathetic and less formidable; with him she could let herself go and he was, therefore, able to offer some useful advice and to make a real contribution to the writing of *Melym- brosia*. (See Appendix D.)

Returning to London from St Ives Virginia forgot her copy of John Delane's *Life* which she was reviewing at some length for *The Cornhill*. She had wanted to read it on the train, but remembered when it was almost too late that she had left it in her lodging house. Clive ran back for it and, rushing after the moving train, tried to thrust it through the window of her compartment, slipped, fell, and hurt himself. The incident furnished a pretext for epistolary gallan- tries: he would not write, he declared, "about the honourable wounds gained in your service. . . ." Half mockingly she com- miserates: "You brought a tear to my eye & a blush to my cheek, by speaking of bandaged hands & crippled knees." "Do you remember," he writes, "our talk about intimacy and the really exciting moments in life? Did we ever achieve the heights?" And "On the top of Rosewall, I wished for nothing in the world but to

kiss you?" "Why?," she responds, "do you torment me with half
uttered and ambiguous sentences?" ". . . though we did not kiss—
(I was willing, & offered once . . .)—I think we 'achieved the
heights' as you put it."

Meanwhile, Vanessa was writing to Virginia:

> I wonder what *you* have said about us—"Of course Nessa was quite
> taken up with the baby. Yes, I'm afraid she's losing all her individuality &
> becoming the usual domestic mother & Clive—of course I like him very
> much but his mind is of a peculiarly prosaic & literal type—And they're
> always making moral judgements about me. However they seem per-
> fectly happy & I expect its a good thing I didnt stay longer. I was
> evidently beginning to bore them." Now Billy*—on your honour
> havent you uttered one of these sentiments?

Presently the Bells followed Virginia back to London and no
doubt the flirtation continued with manœuvres and counter-
manœuvres on both sides; but it is only when the players were
separated that we can get any notion of the state of play.

The 'game' such as it was (for all the participants were losers)
was complicated by irritations and social distresses. There were
moments when general conversation, particularly his style of robust
male conversation, failed to reach Virginia at all and Clive would
find her disconcertingly inattentive; there were times when she
would allow Miss Sheepshanks to spoil a tête-à-tête. Then there was
Lytton; as the summer progressed his interest in Virginia did likewise—or so it appeared. And then, to aggravate Clive's jealous
exasperations, there was Hilton Young. He was certainly regarded
as a serious admirer, and Virginia herself believed that he would
propose to her that summer. When he did not, she was distinctly
disappointed, having hoped at least to have an offer of marriage to
her credit.

For the first part of the summer holidays Virginia was on her own;
Adrian had gone with Saxon to Bayreuth, the Bells as usual were
at Cleeve House. To be within reach of them yet independent, she
settled on Wells, where she went with two dogs on the first of
August, determined to work at her novel. She had finished—or at
least she had written—a hundred pages; Helen Ambrose was coming
to life, so was Rachel Vinrace; but at this moment she was called
Cynthia. At Wells, Virginia decided that this would not do.†

---

* i.e. Billy Goat. Virginia, in writing to Vanessa, contracts this to a 'B.'

† *The Voyage Out* was the only one of Virginia's novels in which she worked
more or less in public, asking for advice, showing portions of her manuscript to

She wrote asking Vanessa to find her another name. Vanessa was willing enough to act as god-mother; she suggested Penelope, Perdita, Chloe, Euphrosyne. "Couldn't you," she added recklessly, "call her Apricot?" Clive, for his part, thought Belinda very suitable. Belinda was too dainty, answered Virginia; besides, the girl's father was a sea captain who would give his child a foreign name–Cintra, perhaps, or Andalusia. "Or Barcelona," exclaimed Clive, rather nettled by the rejection of Belinda, "though Polly or Catherine would be adequate to my taste." Virginia then observed, rather inconsistently, that the changing of names was the most trivial of occupations.

At first it seemed that Mrs Wall's lodging house in Vicar's Close, a place where the fat slumbers of the church seemed gently audible, would provide the tranquillity that Virginia needed; but then she was disturbed by Mrs Wall's attempts to provide her with company in the form of a timid theological student, so she moved to a verger's house in Cathedral Green, abandoned her study of Mrs Wall, for whom she had by now constructed an entire life, and studied the children in the street below. But it was difficult to write in a room without a table or a desk and with Prince Albert staring down at her between his whiskers, and so she removed to Manorbier. Its poor rough austerity compared favourably with Wells and it seems to have been a better place for writing. On 30 August she confided to Violet Dickinson that she had begun to believe that she would "write rather well one of these days," and to Clive:

> I think a great deal of my future, & settle what books I am to write– how I shall re-form the novel & capture multitudes of things at present fugitive, enclose the whole, & shape infinite strange shapes . . . but tomorrow, I know, I shall be sitting down to the inanimate old phrases.

There is a letter to Emma Vaughan written during this stay at Manorbier, a kind of crazy joke of a letter which suggests a sudden lapse into something very near to insanity. But in other respects, and judging by all her other letters of this period, she seems to have been in good health.

Clive and Vanessa had done their duty by Clive's parents by staying with them first in Wiltshire and then in Scotland. In September they were free to take a real holiday. Virginia went

---

others and discussing her progress with her friends. In the later stages of writing the book she was, I think, less communicative. No one was allowed to see anything of her later novels until they were finished.

with them to Milan, Pavia, Siena, Perugia and Assisi. She kept a notebook in which, as usual, she describes the landscape. She also considers with some interest the ceremonies of the Church which, in Siena, seemed very different from those which she had observed in Wells. She describes the characters in hotels: the greedy old spinster who has become a permanent wanderer from *table d'hôte* to *table d'hôte* in foreign lands (Virginia began to make up stories about her and her education in the 'sixties and her family in England), and the thin clean lady with two simple friendly daughters quietly looking for husbands.

Of pictures and architecture she does not usually say much; but she was struck by the frescoes in the Collegio del Cambio in Perugia, and was moved to make certain rapid and disjointed notes which, however, are not uninteresting.

I look at a fresco by Perugino. I conceive that he saw things grouped, contained in certain and invariable forms; expressed in faces, actions—[? which] did not exist; all beauty was contained in the momentary appearance of human beings. He saw it sealed as it were; all its worth in it; not a hint of fear or future. His fresco seems to me infinitely silent; as though beauty had swum up to the top and stayed there, above everything else, speech, paths leading on, relation of brain to brain, don't exist.

Each part has a dependence upon the others; they compose one idea in his mind. That idea has nothing to do with anything that can be put into words. A group stands without relation to the figure of God. They have come together then because their lines and colours are related, and express some view of beauty in his brain.

As for writing—I want to express beauty too—but beauty (symmetry?) of life and the world, in action. Conflict?—is that it? If there is action in painting it is only to exhibit lines; but with the end of beauty in view. Isn't there a different kind of beauty? No conflict.

I attain a different kind of beauty, achieve a symmetry by means of infinite discords, showing all the traces of the mind's passage through the world; achieve in the end, some kind of whole made of shivering fragments; to me this seems the natural process; the flight of the mind. Do they really reach the same thing?

There was equal interest, if less speculation, to be derived from the little collection of India paper novels that she brought with her. She read *Two on a Tower* by Thomas Hardy and considered him too clumsy a writer to be accounted a classic, but there was a kind of bleak force about him, a sort of "rude honesty" which was very much to her taste. She also read *Harry Richmond*. Meredith was, I think, an early enthusiasm; but now "Meredith fails to satisfy me"; she finds in his conceit, his verbal brilliance, the shadow but not the likeness of something magnificent, a world of his own, but a world of flats and flies. Such then were Virginia's intellectual diversions that September.

How her emotional diversions progressed it is harder to say. There was some kind of violent quarrel in Perugia; she and Clive walked through the narrow and precipitous streets of that city screaming at each other, and again in Siena.* But, on the whole, things seem to have gone very well. Clive wrote to Saxon: "Vanessa and Virginia are both well & incredibly charming," to which Saxon replied in characteristic manner: "Does it savour of paradox if I say that I can quite well believe that Vanessa and Virginia are incredibly charming?"

Virginia at the end of the holiday told Violet that Clive was "an admirable man"; from which we may deduce that matters went smoothly enough.

This autumn and indeed during all these years Virginia was busy, not only with her novel and a good deal of journalism, but with her education. Although Janet Case had ceased to be her teacher she remained a friend and Virginia may have profited by her advice. At all events she continued to read the Greek and Roman authors.† In August, when she was at Manorbier, she had attacked that work which her Cambridge friends regarded practically as the gospel of their time: G. E. Moore's *Principia Ethica*. She read it with some difficulty and great admiration. It is a little suprising that she should for so long have postponed what was, one imagines, almost compulsory reading in Bloomsbury (not that Vanessa or Duncan Grant ever attempted it) and I fancy that it was Clive, who rather liked to use Moore in his arguments, who persuaded her to read it.

Clive at this time was her authority, and guided her reading in modern French literature. Also, and this was much more important, he became her literary confidant. Letters have been preserved which show that in 1908 and 1909 he was offering and she was accepting very long and detailed criticisms of the early drafts of *The Voyage Out*. There was a good deal that he did not like, passages which seemed to him crude, immature or derivative. But on the whole he was very enthusiastic; he considered that her words had a force

---

* On a picture postcard showing a view of the Viale della Fortezza in Siena, posted 17 June 1935, to Clive, Virginia wrote: "It was on the spot now marked by a cross that Clive Bell quarrelled with his sister in law in Sept. 1908. I dropped memory's tear there under the orange blossom. V.W."

† In 1907 Virginia was reading Juvenal, in 1908 the *Odyssey* and Plato; in 1909 the *Ion*, the *Ajax* and *The Frogs*; she made a fairly extensive commentary on these works in a notebook. MH/A 21.

"that one expects only in the best poetry" and came "as near the truth underlying them as it is possible for words to come." It is clear that she was fortified by his praise and very glad to have some assurance that her writing was not "all vapour"; also she was able to accept and, it would appear, to use, some of his strictures.*

These exchanges formed the most cheerful and the most constructive part of what was, in other ways, an increasingly unhappy entanglement.

* See Appendix D.

Chapter Eight

1909

ON 17 February 1909 Lytton came to 29 Fitzroy Square, proposed to Virginia and was accepted.

In the very act of proposing, Lytton realised that the idea, an idea which he had been meditating for some time and saw as a solution to the problems of his very complicated private life, was in fact no solution at all. He discovered that he was alarmed by her sex and by her virginity; he was terrified by the notion that she might kiss him. He perceived that his imagined "paradise of married peace" was an impossibility; it would not do at all. He was horrified by the situation in which he had placed himself, all the more so because he believed that she loved him.

She perceived something of this, and with sympathetic tact helped him to escape. After a second meeting, at which he finally declared that he could not marry her, while she assured him that she did not love him, they contrived a gentle disengagement.

For Lytton this was probably the end of the affair; he must have become fully aware of the nature of his feelings and it is hard to suppose that he could again have contemplated such a marriage.

But for Virginia it was different. Although she must have realised that the chances were remote, she still considered the possibility of marrying him. She had told Lytton that she was not in love with him. Nor was she, I think. She might accept his personality but not, when it came to the push, his person. She had always been, as she was later to admit, a sexual coward and her only experience of male carnality had been terrifying and disgusting. But she did want to be married; she was twenty-seven years old, tired of spinsterhood, very tired of living with Adrian and very fond of Lytton. She needed a husband whose mind she could respect; she valued intellectual eminence above everything and in this respect no rival had yet appeared. Lytton's homosexuality might even have been a source of reassurance; as a husband he would not be sexually exigent and a union with him, almost fraternal in character, might perhaps grow by degrees into something real, solid, and deeply affectionate.

But if she continued, as I think she did and as Vanessa certainly did, to hope for such a marriage, her expectations must indeed have been faint when once Lytton's offer had been withdrawn. It was, certainly, a deeply disappointing and saddening experience.*

Lytton retired to Brighton to soothe his agitated nerves; Virginia continued to lead a very busy but, I should guess, a very unhappy life. It was at this time that a stranger, watching her at the Queen's Hall and noticing how lonely and how melancholy she looked, sent her anonymously a ticket for Galsworthy's *Strife* which was then playing at the Haymarket, sat next to her, spoke to her and later wrote asking for her friendship. This she felt that she could not give; but she preserved his letter.

During these early months of 1909 Virginia had embarked upon another and perhaps even more dangerous adventure. Some-one among her friends invented a letter-writing game in which the players—Virginia, Lytton, Walter Lamb, Clive, Vanessa, Saxon and probably Adrian, each took the part of an imaginary character and was provided with a false name—the idea was to produce a novel in letters.† But although the names were imaginary it soon became clear that the characters and the events that they described in their letters were not; it was in fact a kind of epistolary *bal masqué* in which the disguises served only to embolden the partici-pants. From behind his mask Clive felt able to renew his gallantries with unusual openness and ardour; Lytton discusses them frankly with Virginia and adverts to the pain that Vanessa must feel. Virginia replies with agonised evasions; Vanessa chides her for her deplorable weakness with regard to Hilton Young. It is not astonish-ing that the game ended about the time of Lytton's proposal. "Life," wrote Virginia, "is certainly very exciting. . . . Oh how I wish I could write a novel!"

The Bells suggested that she should go with them to Florence for a month towards the end of April. She had planned to take

---

* At the very moment when Virginia seemed in danger of drawing the wrong card the right one emerged momentarily from beneath the pack. Lytton, in a letter to Ceylon, suggested that it was really Leonard Woolf who should marry her. He replied: "Do you think Virginia would have me? Wire to me if she ac-cepts. I'll take the next boat home." [1 February 1909.]

† Virginia was Elinor Hadyng, Clive and Vanessa were James and Clarissa Philips, Lytton was Vane Hatherley, Walter Lamb was Humphry Maitland, Saxon, Mr Ilchester. (Lady Ottoline Morrell, referred to as Caroline Lady Eastnor, Philip Morrell as Sir Julius, and Hilton Young apparently as Roger, were not, I think, participants in the game.) See *Virginia Woolf and Lytton Strachey, Letters*, 1956, p. 28.

ship with Adrian to St Malo, landing "as the first cock rises to crow on Easter Day." But on 7 April Aunt Caroline Emelia, who had been ill for some time, finally died. Between writing an obituary* for *The Guardian* and attending the cremation she sent a postcard to Vanessa saying that she would after all come with them. Clive was of course delighted and wrote ecstatically; she replied with a very flirtatious letter.

But Florence was unsatisfactory. She did not like "that unnatural Florentine Society," in which she met the formidable Mrs Ross, who patronised her—she did not enjoy being patronised—and Mrs Meynell the poetess, lean and bony "like a transfixed hare"—not an encouraging specimen of the literary lady. Virginia was happier scrutinising the less distinguished members of the English colony and, in particular, one Mrs Campbell, an elderly body who had turned the *Life of Father Damien* into verse. It was one of those odd things that stuck in Virginia's mind and found their way into her novels.†

Her diary also contains some preliminary notes for a life of Clive. It looks as though she intended to produce a perceptive and not unsympathetic portrait of a sensitive, honest, kindly man, a little too carefully polished and a little too conscious of his own social gifts. He was, we may surmise, very much on her mind at the time. Their relationship was an unhappy one; how could it be otherwise? Clive's attentions might be a welcome solace after Lytton's evasions; but she, in her own way, was as evasive as Lytton. She would neither take Clive nor leave him; he continued to be exasperated, delighted, thwarted and enraged by her coquetry. She lived, he declared, by the head and not by the heart, and when they were not flirting they were quarrelling. To her it seemed that he took his revenge for her coldness in a way that hurt her abominably, that is to say by the simple expedient of making love to his wife. The slightest, the most natural demonstration of affection—an endearment, a kiss—could make her feel unloved, unwanted, and excluded. "I was," she wrote later, "unhappy that summer and bitter in all my judgments." Probably she was enervated and chafed by the excitements and disappointments of the previous months. No doubt she was quarrelsome, there were scenes; she was, as Vanessa put it, "tiresome" in the Bargello, and after a fortnight she decided that she must cut short the holiday and go home.

* This obituary was published in *The Guardian* on 21 April 1909.
† See *The Voyage Out*, chapter xi, p. 165 and *Jacob's Room*, chapter xxi, p. 263.

Vanessa and Clive urged her to stay: there were strikes in France; she had little French and less Italian; she was miserably bad at catching trains. But she was resolute and she left them.

It was rather melancholy [wrote Vanessa to Margery Snowden] to see her start off on that long journey alone leaving us together here! Of course I am sometimes impressed by the pathos of her position & I have been so more here than usual. I think she would like very much to marry & certainly she would like much better to marry Lytton than anyone else. It is difficult living with Adrian who does not appreciate her & to live with him till the end of their days is a melancholy prospect. I hope some new person may appear in the course of the next year or two for I have come to think that in spite of all drawbacks she had better marry. Still I dont know what she would do with children!

The expedition had been a failure; she returned to England and failure of another kind. In May she visited Cambridge and it was here, in a punt on the Cam, that Hilton Young proposed. There was much to recommend him, she had not discouraged him, his person and his character were admirable; moreover he might have seemed to provide a solution to all her difficulties, for by now her hopes of marrying Lytton must indeed have been faint, while her philandering with Clive had brought more pain than pleasure. But when it came to the point, she knew she did not love him and that she could not marry him. It was perhaps as a kind of excuse that she told him she could marry no one but Lytton.

It was at about this time that her social life received an important addition.

"We have just got to know a wonderful Lady Ottoline Morrell, who has the head of a Medusa; but she is very simple & innocent in spite of it, & worships the arts."

I think that Virginia was right in describing her as innocent and that she was indeed extremely simple and not very clever. But it is hard to believe. Her appearance made one think that she was vicious, devious and complicated to a degree. For she was as decorative and as outlandish as an Austrian baroque church and from the remarkable edifice that she inhabited there issued a voice that had something of the cooing of a dove, something of the roaring of a lion; it seemed to be rolled out upon her improbable Hapsburg chin; and withal she had a certain grace, a certain majesty of address which was at once intimidating and seductive. She arrived at one of Virginia's Thursday Evenings with Dorelia and Augustus John, figures as beautiful and almost as improbable as she (together they must have made a rare spectacle, for Ottoline could by herself draw a sizeable crowd in the street); Philip Morrell, Ottoline's husband, came with them.

Presently Ottoline wrote to ask Virginia for the names and addresses of all her "wonderful friends"; they were all to come and see her at home in Bedford Square. "Then," wrote Virginia—and the word "then" means in the course of the next two or three years—

> we were all swept into that extraordinary whirlpool where such odd sticks and straws were brought momentarily together. There was Augustus John very sinister [?] in a black stock and a velvet coat; Winston Churchill very rubicund all gold lace and medals on his way to Buckingham Palace; Raymond Asquith crackling with epigrams; Francis Dodd* telling me most graphically how he and Aunt Susie had killed bugs: she held the lamp; he a basin of paraffin; bugs crossed the ceiling in an incessant stream. There was Lord Henry Bentinck at one end of the sofa & perhaps Nina Lamb at the other. There was Philip [Morrell] fresh from the House of Commons humming and hawing on the hearth rug. There was Gilbert Cannan who was said to be in love with Ottoline. There was Bertie Russell, whom she was said to be in love with. Above all there was Ottoline herself.

Who, we may add, for the spirit of rumour was reckless in Bedford Square, was said to be in love with Virginia. I don't think that anyone ever suggested that Virginia returned her love; but in sober truth she liked Ottoline, found her comic, fascinating, improbable, like Royalty or the Church, a portent rather than a woman, a character from the fiction of another age; but also quite simply likeable. Certainly she contributed something new to the life of Bloomsbury—a mundane glamour and a very strong heterosexual element which Virginia welcomed. She brought petticoats, frivolity and champagne to the buns, the buggery and the high thinking of Fitzroy Square.

From 6 June to 16 July Adrian kept a diary in which he describes one of his and Virginia's Thursday Evenings and the description seems worth quoting because it gives a notion of what a Bloomsbury party was like at this time, and illustrates Adrian's view of Virginia.

---

* Francis Dodd (1874–1949; R.A. 1935). At his request, Virginia gave him several sittings for her portrait between October 1907 and July 1908. He etched four plates of her from drawings, one of which is in the National Portrait Gallery, London, and another in the collection of Mr Benjamin Sonnenberg, New York. 'Aunt Susie' was Miss Isabel Dacre (1844–1933), a member of the Manchester Academy of Fine Arts, and a close associate of Dodd's.

Thursday July 1st.

On my way home I went to Gordon Square where I found the Goat and walked home with her. We dined alone together and after dinner waited a long time before anybody appeared. Saxon as usual came in first but was quickly followed by Norton and he by James and Lytton Strachey. We were very silent at first, Virginia and Lytton and I doing all the talking, Saxon being in his usual state of torpor and Norton and James occasionally exchanging a whisper. Later on Vanessa and Clive came in bringing with them Duncan Grant. After this the conversation became more lively. Vanessa sat with Lytton on the sofa and from half heard snatches I gathered they were talking about his and James's obscene loves. Whatever it was they were discussing they were brought to an abrupt stop by a sudden silence, this pleased them very much, especially Vanessa, and I kindly added to their joy by asking why they stopped. Soon afterwards Henry Lamb came in having returned from doing some portraits at Oxford. The conversation kept up a good flow, though it was not very interesting, until about half past eleven Miss Cole arrived.

She went and sat in the long wicker chair with Virginia and Clive on the floor beside her. Virginia began in her usual tone of frank admiration to compliment her on her appearance. "Of course, you Miss Cole are always dressed so exquisitely. You look so original, so like a sea shell. There is something so refined about you coming in among our muddy boots and pipe smoke, dressed in your exquisite creations." Clive chimed in with more heavy compliments and then began asking her why she disliked him so much, saying how any other young lady would have been much pleased with all the nice things he had been saying but that she treated him so sharply. At this Virginia interrupted with "I think Miss Cole has a very strong character" and so on and and so on. Altogether Miss Cole was as unhappy and uncomfortable as she could be; it was impossible not to help laughing at the extravagance of Virginia and Clive and all conversation was stopped by their noisy choruses, so the poor woman was the centre of all our gaze, and did not know what to do with herself. At last, a merciful diversion was made and Virginia took my seat and I hers and with, I may say, some skill I managed to keep Clive under control.

James and Lytton Strachey left and we played an absurd game which Vanessa and Clive had learnt at the Freshfields. The principle of the game was as follows: that person won who in half a minute could say the most words beginning with any given letter. Clive held the watch and gave us each a turn. Norton being given G. started off with Jerusalem and Jesus, which I am afraid must have added another pain to poor Miss Cole's already lengthy list. We all had our turns, Vanessa trying to sail as near to the wind as she could, she is always trying to bring out some bawdy remark and is as pleased when she has done it as a spoilt child. Miss Cole went at one and Duncan Grant at about the same time, when a great discussion was started, I know not by whom, about vice. Very soon Virginia with exquisite art made herself the centre of the argument making the vaguest statements with the intensest feeling and ready to snap up anybody who laughed. Her method is ingenious and at first is rather disconcerting for when someone has carefully examined her argument and certainly refuted it she at once agrees with him enthusiastically saying that he has put her point exactly.

The argument such as it was degenerated into mere phrase making and so regarded was quite amusing; this gave way in its turn to the game of bantering Saxon. He was chaffed and laughed at for all his little peculiarities and all the time he kept his silence, only giving an occasional smile. He could not be provoked into saying anything even by Virginia's most daring sallies which never fail of their guffaw when Clive is present. At last everybody went except Saxon. Saxon went on to discuss different ways to Germany having obtained further information from Cooks. Virginia and I were however so sleepy that we managed by sheer indifference to oust him. We got to bed as the dawn was coming up about 5.

Poor Miss Cole was unlucky. It was never easy to know what to do with the image of oneself that Virginia could fabricate and then gaily, publicly, even generously (for she loved her inventions too well not to believe in them) toss back at one's shuffling feet. But it must have been harder still when Clive, whose gallantries were not always well judged, joined forces with her and boisterously amplified the most extravagant of her compliments. The cruelty which sometimes accompanied Virginia's conversational extravagances lay, not in their animus–indeed I do not think that she was (usually) malicious–but rather in their sincerity. The image that she created was fanciful, but the victim–the slender basis upon which she built–could have dismissed such fancies easily enough had they not been advanced with such overwhelming force; and that force arose, not from a desire to misrepresent, but from conviction. Miss Cole may or may not have looked like a sea shell: there was no doubt some elegance about her nacreous enough to stir Virginia's imagination (it was easily stirred), but almost at once Virginia would have come to believe in the reality of the glittering edifice that she had so easily raised. In truth it was she who was being absurd and, in later years at all events, it was she and not her victim who was laughed at when she allowed her fancy to take liberties with people.

Another less guilty anecdote belongs to this period and may be recorded because it shows, in a rather pure form, how Virginia's mythogenic capacity could create distress and confusion.

It was in Cornwall; Virginia, Vanessa and Clive and, I think,

Adrian were having lunch in a lodging house. The maid—a dimmish, timid, mousy maid—came to clear away the remains of mutton and two vegetables.

"What's the pudding?" asked Virginia.

"Mount St Michael's Pudding, Miss."

Virginia's imagination took fire; she saw how it would be and seeing could not but describe her vision. Her exact words are lost; but there was something about a soaring convexity of chocolate surmounted by a castle of dazzling sugar, battlemented, crenellated, machicolated, crowned with banners of crystallized angelica and at its feet a turbulent ocean of lucent jelly, flecked with creamy foam and graced by heaven knows what sweetmeats fashioned to resemble vessels, mermaids, dolphins, nereids. . . . For Virginia's relations the chief interest in listening to this inventory lay in the face of the serving girl, who stood amazed by Virginia's eloquence and appalled by the knowledge that she would, in a few minutes, produce a steamed pudding, not unlike a sand castle in shape and texture, parsimoniously adorned with a dab of strawberry jam.

This was one of the difficulties of living with Virginia; her imagination was furnished with an accelerator and no brakes; it flew rapidly ahead, parting company with reality, and, when reality happened to be a human being, the result could be appalling for the person who found himself expected to live up to the character that Virginia had invented. But even when reality happened to be an umbrella it could cause havoc.

Later in the summer of 1909, when she was at Bayreuth, she went out shopping with Adrian and bought a penholder. This was always an affair of the utmost difficulty, for the actual manual exercise of writing delighted her. She loved the feel of a good stiff nib cutting letters over the paper, and was miserable with inferior implements; from the age of fifteen certainly, probably from an even earlier age, she was continually trying new pens and penholders and was of course madly difficult to please. Thus from Adrian's point of view the expedition started badly. It was made worse by a visit to a bookshop where Virginia created havoc in her search for a Tauchnitz edition of *The Autocrat of the Breakfast Table* which she was reviewing and should have brought from England. Here at least she knew what she wanted. Unfortunately the shop had not got it and had to send to Leipzig for a copy. More unfortunate still, she found it in her bag when she got home. With feminine insouciance she proposed that Adrian should accompany her on a second visit to the shop to countermand the order. Adrian refused; he couldn't face the people again. This however was after the purchase of the parasol, which was an even longer and even more harrowing business. She said that she needed a white parasol and every white parasol in the shop was brought out; but they were not what she had imagined; a white parasol, she explained, was no good without a green lining. There were none of this kind, so then she asked for a coffee-coloured one and eventually bought the cheapest brown holland thing in the shop.

All through her life Virginia was a vague, undecided and exasperating shopper; she must have reduced many poor shop assistants to the verge of blasphemy or of tears, and not only they but her companions suffered intensely when she found herself brought to a standstill by the difference between that which she had imagined and that which in fact was offered for sale.

This digression has taken me to Bayreuth and I must explain why Virginia was there in the month of August 1909. In later years it was the last place in which one would have expected to find her. She was not, in any strict sense, musical. She played no instrument; I do not think that she could follow a score with any deep comprehension. Music, it is true, delighted her; she enjoyed the family pianola (when Adrian did not play it for too long), as she was later to enjoy the gramophone; it formed a background to her musings, a theme for her pen; during the period at which Adrian kept a diary she was frequently at concerts and very frequently at the opera,* which she enjoyed as a spectacle and a social event. But her taste for opera was, as Adrian's had been, probably stimulated by Saxon; certainly he must have been responsible for the marked homage which she now paid to Wagner, for Saxon was, and always remained, a fervent Wagnerian, sitting through cycle after cycle of *The Ring*, relishing every bar of *Tristan* and of *Parsifal* (already, in 1910, he was able to celebrate his 300th operatic performance), and I think it must have been his strong, silent pressure that made Virginia who, even then, would have preferred to listen to Mozart, travel to the shrine of Wagnerism, encountering Germans who seemed to her distressingly ugly, old family friends from England whom she would rather not have met, lodgings and meals that aroused no enthusiasm.

* Adrian records that she went, in a space of six weeks, twice to *Don Giovanni* and twice to *Louise*, to the first performance of *The Wreckers*, to *Aida*, *Madame Butterfly*, *Faust*, and *Orpheus and Eurydice*; she went to several concerts and heard works by Cimarosa and Delius (*The Mass of Life*), to two plays, and also went with the Morrells to see the Russian dancers at the Coliseum.

They remained a fortnight in Bayreuth. Each morning Adrian and Saxon went for a walk while Virginia wrote at a shaky desk made by balancing her box on a commode. They met at lunch, and in the afternoon went to the opera.

We must be a curious sight [wrote Adrian to Vanessa] as we leave the Opera House between the acts; there is the Goat carrying a parasol, a large leathern bag, a packet of cigarettes, a box of chocolates, and the libretto of the opera, in one hand and at the same time vainly striving to hold up a long white cloak & skirt which insist upon trailing in the dust however high she pulls them; then there is Saxon humming to himself with an impassioned voice and gesticulating so wildly that one thinks that every bone in his body must be out of joint; then I come holding my head very high & pretending that nothing particular is happening & at the same time trying to lead the others away from the main body of the crowd.

(". . . There is a great crowd & we get stared at, not for our beauty," wrote Virginia. Remembering Adrian's odd gaunt figure, his awkward manner and the fact that, even without holding his head up high, he would have towered above any crowd, one may wonder whether he did not appear the strangest of the three.)

It is of no use trying to relieve the Goat of any of her burdens because as soon as one makes the attempt half of them are scattered upon the ground. Eventually I conduct them into a large deserted field where Virginia & I sit down and Saxon also when his rheumatics permit of it; here Saxon always becomes doubly mortish* and sour & Virginia begins to expand into the most extravagant images. At last I am driven into contradicting her flatly & she snaps back at me & then we all subside and eat our chocolate in silence & comparative peace.

Nevertheless Virginia and Adrian, driven by Saxon's lethargy to fraternise, were on unusually good terms with each other (although Adrian doubted whether this desirable state of affairs could last if Virginia insisted on doing any more shopping). Virginia also wrote, almost daily, to her sister describing their surroundings, their activities, and their fellow creatures:

The grossness of the [Germans] is astonishing–but they seem very clean & kind. They suit Saxon very well. He thinks them so sensible.

Saxon indeed came under her constant scrutiny:

Saxon is dormant all day long, & rather peevish if you interrupt him. He hops along, before or behind, swinging his ugly stick, & humming,

---

* Mortish, a word invented by Adrian to describe Saxon's deadlier moods.

like a stridulous grasshopper. He reminds me a little of father. He clenches his fists, & scowls in the same way; & stops at once if you look at him. Adrian & I wink at each other, & get caught sometimes. About 11 o'clock at night, when we begin to yawn, he brightens up, & comes out with some very acute & rather acid question. We argued till 1.30 this morning. It was about something Adrian had said two or possibly three Thursdays ago, which Saxon had not understood. He hoards things, like a dormouse. His mind is marvellously accurate; but I am rather surprised by his intellect. . . . We are rather austere, like monks and nuns, speak little, & —— oh I long for you!

And a week later:

Saxon is . . . almost sprightly. His conversation is still odd. "What did you mean, Virginia, when you said, about three years ago, that your view of life was that of a Henry James novel, & mine of a George Meredith?" I had to invent a meaning, & he actually told me that he thought me a very clever young woman–which is the highest praise I have ever had from him.

Saxon himself makes his own characteristic contribution:

. . . it begins to dawn upon me that I have written still another letter merely about letter writing . . . since no doubt Adrian has sent one of his amusing and faithful sketches of actual occurrences, and Virginia several of her brilliant and imaginative pictures of things as they ought to be, there is no need for me to go outside this humble tack and enter into individious and disastrous competition.

Altogether it was Saxon's holiday; in a sense it was his apogee as far as Virginia was concerned. Never again would he persuade her into going to Bayreuth and he, who had been the cleverest of all Thoby's friends, who for six or seven years had exerted a considerable influence and had been regarded by Virginia almost with awe, was already something of a joke and a tedious joke at that. She liked him, and she always continued to like him; but it was becoming more and more apparent that he would never do anything but solve conundrums and cultivate a number of quiet enthusiasms. It was easy to believe that he was a genius; but it was easier still to believe that his genius would never result in anything positive. As he grew older he seemed increasingly to cultivate the art of escape. He might be compared to the cuttlefish which slips silently away beneath a cloud of obfusc sepia, but he might also be likened to the porcupine which not only conceals itself but can wound the too curious investigator. He was not only a solver but

a setter of puzzles; he loved ingenuity and took a natural pride in
his own dexterity; his elliptical utterances, his allusions, his acrostic
letters were proofs of his own erudition but they also humbled and
bewildered the recipient, and this too he enjoyed. He liked to play
games with his friends–games so subtle that they hardly realised
that any sport was afoot. Quietly he laughed at them, but there
was, I fancy, a joke within a joke; at bottom he laughed at a sad
little pleasantry of his own which he made at his own expense
and which had as its theme his own appalling life.

At the beginning of September, after spending a further ten
days with her two companions at Dresden, Virginia returned to
Fitzroy Square. The Bells were still dutifully staying in Wiltshire
with Clive's parents. Virginia met them at Salisbury after arrangements which almost suggest the clandestine contrivances of lovers.
Then she rented a small cottage at Studland and experienced on a
minute scale, and I suppose for the first time, the pleasures and
labours of housework, cooking her own breakfast, taking in the
morning milk and so on. She hired what she called "a bi-sexual"
bathing dress and "swam far out, until the sea gulls played over my
head, mistaking me for a drifting sea anemone." Soon she was
joined by the Bells, who moved into a boarding house nearby and
she was able to enjoy, not only their company, but that of her
nephew Julian who, at the age of eighteen months, was beginning
to manifest charms of a kind that she could appreciate.

The Bells brought other company. Vanessa invited Lytton; but
he was undergoing a cure in a Swedish sanatorium. Walter Lamb
was asked in place of him. A contemporary of Clive's at Trinity,
he was a close friend but perhaps not quite as intimate as he would
have liked to have been. He was an occasional visitor at Gordon
Square on his journeys between Clifton College, where he taught
the classics, and Cambridge or his family home in Manchester.
Earlier in the year, the Bells being away, he was so to speak boarded
out at Fitzroy Square and reported: "I was most agreeably entertained. I had my first good talk with Virginia. The result is . . . that
I agree with everything that you say about her mind: . . . I must
make a further confession of your accuracy; for I was surprised
to find how friendly she made herself appear." Thereafter he made
and sent her a translation of Euripides. Clive commended him,
Adrian cultivated him, it seemed possible that Virginia might
grow fond of him.

But Walter Lamb was not a substitute for Lytton, to whom
Virginia wrote on 6 October:

Now we are back again, living on culture chiefly . . . and the memory-alas it fades!-of conversations with Walter Lamb. I wish (as usual) that earth would open her womb and let some new creature out.

She was, as always, working on her novel; but also throughout 1908 and 1909 she was busy with journalism, busier than she usually was-or than she was to be again for several years; *The Times Literary Supplement* had become her chief employer, although she now wrote some longer reviews for *The Cornhill*. It was for Reginald Smith, the editor of that journal, that she devised what was, for her at all events, an entirely new kind of article. She called it *Memoirs of a Novelist* and it is, ostensibly, a review of Miss Linsett's *Life* of Miss Willatt:

> a book which one may still buy with luck in the Charing Cross Road . . . The volumes had got themselves wedged between Sturm "On the Beauties of Nature" and the "Veterinary Surgeons Manual" on the outside shelf, where the gas cracks and the dust grimes them, and people may read so long as the boy lets them.

Miss Linsett, it becomes clear, is the typical Victorian hagiographer and Virginia has some fun describing her manner of writing a biography. But it is Miss Willatt, a novelist and an almost equally obscure figure, who really interests the reviewer: hers is one of those lives of the obscure which always fascinated Virginia; she regards Miss Willatt with affection, with amusement and with compassion. Marriage was denied to Miss Willatt; she turned to philanthropy, decided that she had no vocation and thereafter devoted her energies to the writing of fiction. It was highly romantic fiction.

> [She] thought it indecent to describe what she had seen, so that instead of a portrait of her brothers (and one had led a very queer life) or a memory of her father (for which we should have been grateful) she invented Arabian lovers and set them on the banks of the Orinoco.

At which point one becomes pretty sure that Miss Willatt is herself an invention and so is Miss Linsett.* *Memoirs of a Novelist* is in fact an attempt to publish fiction under the cloak of criticism, or rather, to combine both genres and, as such, it is interesting and could have been momentous in the history of Virginia's development as a writer. It shows, I think, that the long process of writing and rewriting *The Voyage Out* had in some measure tried her patience, or at all events that she was eager to spread her wings

* I have searched in vain for Miss Linsett and Miss Willatt in the catalogues of the British Museum Library and in that of the Library of Congress.

and publish a work of the imagination; moreover, this was not to stand alone but to be the first of a series.

She showed her manuscript to Clive; he thought it clever, but he clearly had some reservations; later he explained that they were not important and accused himself of being clumsy–his critical stance was affected by the fact that he believed that she had cooled in her feelings towards him and he was anxious to make amends. In November he wrote from Cambridge to say that her series was "expected to be the chef d'oeuvre of the century." Such flattery would have been pleasant enough if it had not been followed, almost at once, by a letter from Reginald Smith who wrote: "My feeling is that you have impaled not a butterfly, but a bumble-bee, upon a pin. It is cleverness itself, but . . ." In short, he rejects it, courteously, regretfully, but most decidedly. The fact that this was a new departure and that her friends had been led to hope so much from it must have added to the bitterness of the occasion. She never published or, I think, tried to publish in *The Cornhill* again.

But the year 1909, which had brought many vexations and disappointments, closed with a new anxiety; for now it appeared that Bloomsbury itself was to be extinguished. Clive and Vanessa, very much pre-occupied by the visual arts and increasingly aware that great things were happening on the other side of the Channel, had begun to feel that they were too far from the capital of the arts, They were both very francophile, they both enjoyed the amenities and liberties of life in France and they decided that they would be happier if they lived in Paris. It would mean leaving their friends behind, but they hoped that Virginia, and perhaps Lytton, might join them. Virginia cannot have welcomed the idea; she did not wish to be separated from Clive and still less from Vanessa; but she was never at home outside her own country, she was not particularly interested in contemporary painting and, when she mentioned the scheme to Lytton, he thought it catastrophic. But if Clive and Vanessa went, then, she declared, she would go too. Vanessa forecast that, when it came to the point, Virginia would stay in England; the move was not to be made for a year or so and by then she would probably have married Lytton–or at least be engaged to him. And yet she hesitated; it was indeed a painful question to decide.

On the last day of the year Vanessa was able to report that Adrian had decided to give up the law and go on the stage, while Virginia had definitely come round to the idea of Paris.

On the morning of Christmas Eve, walking alone in Regent's Park, Virginia suddenly decided to go to Cornwall. According to her, the idea struck her at half past twelve: the train left at one o'clock. Sophy nearly had hysterics, Maud packed her amethyst necklace and left out her handkerchiefs, but she caught her train. Lelant was beautiful, the weather was soft as Spring, and she tramped the countryside, staggered up Tren Crom, and enjoyed her Christmas without festivities. For conversation there was the maid and the Ferryman, for intellectual exercise Dr Meryon's accounts of Lady Hester Stanhope. The fantastic story of that arch-eccentric delighted her, and it was with her in mind that she wrote to Clive:

> Suppose I stayed here, & thought myself an early virgin, & danced on May nights, in the British Camp!—a scandalous aunt for Julian, & yet rather pleasant, when he was older, . . . & wished for eccentric relations. Cant you imagine how airily he would produce her, on Thursday nights "I have an Aunt who copulates in a tree, & thinks herself with child by a grasshopper—Charming isn't it?—She dresses in green, & my mother sends her nuts from the Stores."

The Bells did not leave Bloomsbury, and Adrian never became an actor. Nevertheless he was to give one notable and highly successful impersonation.

Virginia at 29 Fitzroy Square, 1910
By Duncan Grant

Chapter Nine

1910 – June 1912

ON the morning of 10 February 1910, Virginia, with five companions, drove to Paddington Station and took a train to Weymouth. She wore a turban, a fine gold chain hanging to her waist and an embroidered caftan. Her face was black. She sported a very handsome moustache and beard. Of the other members of the party three—Duncan Grant, Anthony Buxton and Guy Ridley–were disguised in much the same way. Adrian was there, wearing a beard and an ill-fitting bowler hat so that he looked, as he himself put it "like a seedy commercial traveller," while the sixth member (and leader) of the party, Horace Cole, was convincingly attired as an official of the Foreign Office.

The object of their excursion was to hoodwink the British Navy, to penetrate its security and to enjoy a conducted tour of the flagship of the Home Fleet, the most formidable, the most modern and the most secret man o' war then afloat, H.M.S. *Dreadnought*.

Virginia came into this impudent and sketchily prepared hoax almost by accident. It had been conceived by Adrian and by Horace Cole. Cole was in fact the person most responsible. He was a rich and in many ways a preposterous young man, the author of many practical jokes, who had become a friend of Adrian's while at Cambridge. The most spectacular of his pranks had been a ceremonious visit to Cambridge by the Sultan of Zanzibar, or rather, by his uncle, who was impersonated by Cole, together with three members of his suite (of whom Adrian was one) and an interpreter. They were formally received at the Guildhall by the Mayor, patronised a Charity Bazaar, were shown the principal Colleges, and seen off at the Railway Station. Cole informed the *Daily Mail*, which published the story; the Mayor was cross about it and asked the Vice-Chancellor to have the culprits sent down. But there were no serious consequences.

The 'Dreadnought Hoax'–to give it the name by which it became famous–was, essentially, to be a repetition of the Zanzibar escapade. Mr Tudor Castle, a friend of Adrian's, was to send a telegram purporting to come from the Foreign Office to the

Commander-in-Chief Home Fleet announcing the impending arrival of the Emperor of Abyssinia. The Emperor would be impersonated by Anthony Buxton and would be escorted by Cole as a Foreign Office official. Adrian was to interpret and there would be a suite of noble retainers. It was here that they encountered their first difficulty. The Abyssinian Court began to melt away until it was reduced to Guy Ridley and Duncan Grant; this seemed altogether insufficient to support the dignity of the Lion of Judah. One more at least was needed. Adrian asked Virginia; she was delighted to take part; she had two days' notice.

Vanessa was dismayed at the whole idea. To her it seemed that the joke would certainly fail, and Virginia should have nothing to do with it. Cole himself already had the deepest misgivings and so, perhaps, had the missing courtiers. Adrian was the only one who seemed happy, confident and quite determined to proceed.

They set off, relying on the Fleet to accept and not to question a telegram *en clair* from the Foreign Office. No one had the vaguest idea of what an Abyssinian, let alone an Abyssinian Emperor, looked like. They depended upon a few words of what may have been Swahili, Mr Clarkson's grease-paint, and a pretty unconvincing wardrobe, intended perhaps for a performance of *Il Seraglio*, to defeat the vigilance of the Navy. And, just to stack the odds impossibly high against them, they had chosen to visit a battleship on which Adrian would almost inevitably encounter his cousin William Fisher, who was flag commander. This indeed, to Adrian's sanguine temper, was an inducement; to tease the Navy would be fun, to do so at the expense of the Fisher family was an irresistible temptation. But if they were detected, what then? They might very well be thrown overboard–not an agreeable experience in the month of February and one for which Virginia was equipped neither in mind nor body.

When the train arrived at Weymouth, a flag lieutenant advanced to their carriage door and saluted the Emperor with becoming gravity. Cole made the proper introductions. There was a barrier to restrain the crowd and the Imperial party proceeded with dignity to where a little steam launch lay in readiness to carry it out to the fleet anchored in the Bay. On H.M.S. *Dreadnought* Virginia found herself shaking her cousin's hand; it was hard not to burst out laughing.

They inspected the Guard of Honour. The Admiral turned to Adrian and asked him to explain the significance of certain uniforms to the Emperor.

"*Entaqui, mahai, kustufani*" said Adrian, and then discovered that his stock of Swahili, if it was Swahili, was exhausted. He sought inspiration. It came, and he continued:

"*Tahli bussor ahbat tahl œsque miss. Erraema, fleet use.* . . ."[*]

The dismembered limbs of a poet would serve the needs of the interpreter, and the Emperor, quickly rising to the emergency, responded with tags from Virgil; Duncan and Virginia may perhaps have spoken a rather different dialect. It is unlikely that Virginia used the opportunity to air her Greek; in fact she spoke very little, and then as gruffly as she could; it was difficult, she said later, to disguise her speaking voice. "A rum lingo they speak," muttered one of the junior officers, but another struck chill into their hearts by announcing that there was a seaman who could talk to the visitors in their own language. Unluckily–most unluckily–he was away on leave.

And so they went round the ship, the captain explaining guns, turrets, range finders, the sick bay and the wireless room to Adrian, and Adrian repeating the explanation in terms of Virgil or sometimes of Homer to the royal party, until there was nothing left to see. Refusing a salute of twenty-one guns and refreshments which might have dislodged the noble Ethiopians' false whiskers, Adrian indicated that the State Visit was over, and the Imperial party was escorted back to Weymouth. Going home, Cole, who had spent the greater part of the visit in the *Dreadnought*'s wardroom, insisted that the waiters attending them in their compartment should wear white gloves.

"Oh Miss Genia, Miss Genia!" exclaimed Sophy as her employer, exhausted, dishevelled, blackened and bewiskered, let herself into No 29 Fitzroy Square late that evening.

The press should be told nothing. This at all events was the view of the majority. They had been charmingly entertained, treated in fact with such kindness that they felt rather guilty, and, at any rate, the joke had gone far enough.

But not for Cole; he had always wanted fame, and here was his chance of it. Without telling his confederates, he went to the newspapers.

The newspapers, and more particularly the *Express* and the *Mirror*, gave the story headlines and full-page photographs. Reporters appeared at 29 Fitzroy Square; they had been particularly interested when they learnt that one of the Abyssinians (according to some accounts it was the appropriately named Ras Mendax) was

[*] "*Talibus orabat talisque miserrima fletus.*" Æneid iv, 437.

a young lady, "very good looking, with classical features"; they wanted her story and they got it. They also wanted her photograph in evening dress, but this, so far as I can discover, they did not get. Leader writers hesitated between indignation and amusement; distressed patriots wrote letters to editors; and at last, when the press grew tired of the matter, the House of Commons took it up.*

The nine days' wonder was over and the public almost forgot about it. But private repercussions continued. Most of Virginia's friends took it as an excellent joke. Vanessa was relieved, although she feared that it would mean they would see even more of Horace Cole, whom she found bumptious and boring. But the Stephen family was outraged. Adrian received a stately rebuke from his cousin Harry, the Indian Judge, who had been much amused by the Zanzibar exploit but felt that, although it was funny to hoodwink a municipal dignitary (the Mayor of Cambridge was a shop-keeper), a naval man-'a man of honour'-must not be made to look ridiculous. Virginia received a letter from Dorothea Stephen in which she declared that it was a silly and vulgar performance; she would not scold, she would merely point out that, clearly, Virginia's life was entirely unsatisfactory and that she stood in need of religion.

Willy Fisher and his brother officers reacted in an appropriately aggressive manner. The honour of the Navy had to be saved, and it could be saved only by the corporal punishment of the hoaxers. After a series of disappointments and of rather absurd arguments on matters of punctilio and propriety, the naval party did succeed in abducting Duncan Grant and taking him to Hampstead Heath, where they were again more than half defeated by the gentle perplexity and mild courage of a pacifist in carpet slippers.

Apart from an account of the business which Virginia wrote in 1940, nearly all of which is lost, Virginia used the 'Dreadnought Hoax' only once in her writings. In a short story entitled *A Society*† she describes how a young woman called Rose "had dressed herself as an Ethiopian Prince and gone aboard one of His Majesty's ships." Discovering the hoax the captain visited her, disguised as a private gentleman, and demanded that honour should be satisfied. The wholly ludicrous manner in which first the Navy and then Rose receive their respective satisfactions occupies no more than five hundred words; but the theme, the theme of masculine honour, of masculine violence and stupidity, of gold-laced masculine

* See Appendix E.
† Published in *Monday or Tuesday*, 1921.

pomposity, remained with her for the rest of her life. She had entered the Abyssinian adventure for the fun of the thing; but she came out of it with a new sense of the brutality and silliness of men. And this perception came, in its turn, to reinforce political sentiments which had for some time been taking shape in her mind.

1910 was a year of crisis in the affairs of the nation. In January the struggle between the House of Lords and the elected majority had entered its final phase with a general election. Ever since January 1906, when Vanessa, Virginia, George and Gerald had gone to Trafalgar Square, the girls to applaud, the gentlemen to deplore, a great Liberal victory, Virginia had, in an imprecise way, known where she stood; but now there was a complicating factor. Virginia desired the defeat of the Conservatives; certainly she was not sorry to see Clive taking an active part in politics on the radical side; but *his* battle was not entirely hers, for while he had two votes she had none. It is not surprising that in the spring of 1910 we find her addressing envelopes, almost always the fate of the youthful volunteer in political causes, on behalf of the Adult Suffrage movement. She had, for a long time, been in sympathy with the feminist cause, but it was not until 1 January 1910, Janet Case having put the arguments for political action with unanswerable force, that Virginia wrote to her saying that she could neither do sums, nor argue, nor speak, but would like in some humbler way to be helpful. Janet Case applied to Margaret Llewelyn Davies, and she in turn spoke to Miss Rosalind Nash, who made some very sensible sounding suggestions. Virginia might like to get up the history of the franchise movement in New Zealand or might make a collection of extracts on representation. Or there were things that might usefully be said in magazine articles. Virginia, it appears, preferred to address envelopes.

Not that she liked the work–she spent "hours writing names like Cowgill on envelopes." Moreover politics, like philanthropy, seemed to her to attract a bloodless, inhuman kind of person. She found work in an office filled with ardent, educated young women and brotherly clerks too much like living in a novel by H. G. Wells. Nevertheless she did do a good deal of work; she even sat on the platform at public meetings and, despite an interval caused by illness, returned to this work at the end of the year.

Whether she addressed too many envelopes, or whether the other effects of the 'Dreadnought Hoax' were to blame, or–and this is more likely–whether she had entered into one of those states of acute nervous tension which usually afflicted her when she was coming to the end of a novel (she was now, she thought, nearing the end of *Melymbrosia*) I do not know. But certainly she fell ill in March and was again on the verge of madness.

Dr Savage was consulted; he, as usual, prescribed a quiet life, early and regular hours, plenty of rest. She went off with the Bells to Studland and tried to obey his orders. At the end of three weeks Clive reported to Saxon that she was cured.

But the cure was not radical. The distractions of London undid all the good that Studland had done; soon she was again suffering from headaches – what she called numbness in the head – insomnia, nervous irritation and a strong impulse to reject food, all the old symptoms in their most severe form. Again Savage was applied to and again he ordered her to leave London and to rest.

Clive and Vanessa rented a house – the Moat House – at Blean, near Canterbury, and here they established themselves with Virginia. They invited Saxon; he could not join them but perhaps he was consoled by the letters which Virginia sent him from the Moat House, for she wrote:

. . . more to mitigate my own lot than to please you. The rain falls, & the birds never give over singing, & hot sulphur fumes rise from the valleys, & the red cow in the field roars for her calf. In these circumstances you would address yourself to Chaucer, & master his habits before tea. I have tried, but cant persist – I pick chocolates out of a box, & worry my sister. Shortly before the rain began, three days ago, we had our windows prized open by a Smith. The decay of centuries had sealed them. No human force can now shut them. Thus we sit exposed to wind & wet by day; & by night, we are invaded by flocks of white moths. They frizzle in the candles, & crawl up my skirt to die, in the hollow of my knee. There is something unspeakably repugnant in the feel of creatures who have lost their legs. However, Nessa has done her best for us. She has invented an old woman who comes before anyone asks her, to stop the chimbleys smoking, & finds eggs, by looking for them, on the common. Then Nessa said at breakfast, "What a very large family Mr LeFevre must have!" & pointed to a photograph of gospel preachers since the time of Wiclif. The poor old man who owns this house, Mr LeFevre, called here the other day; & said that his happiest hours had been spent here, but times were changed. He alluded to the death of his prolific wife, which happened in sad circumstances which I will explain one day. At this, Nessa & Clive suddenly lost their tempers & showed their intolerant brutality in such a way that the old man was led out by his daughter (herself much moved) in tears.

If you should write to me, in one of the living languages [Saxon had a disconcerting habit of writing in Latin], preferably Romance, I should have one happy breakfast. . . .

Saxon took, or affected to take, Virginia's account of the Bells' brutality to Mr LeFevre with so much gravity, seriously considering that Clive and Vanessa were indeed uncommonly hard on any kind of sentimental effusion, that Vanessa felt obliged to protest.

> Virginia since early youth has made it her business to create a character for me according to her own wishes & has now so succeeded in imposing it upon the world that these preposterous stories are supposed to be certainly true because so characteristic.

True or not (and usually there was a scintilla although not much more than a scintilla of truth in Virginia's inventions) she was on good terms with the Bells and particularly with her intolerant and brutal brother-in-law. He indeed had been touched by her unhappiness and her pain and was now particularly considerate and attentive, writing her charming and affectionate letters when he was away, flattering and flirting with her when they were together. His real concern for her health and the absence of any rival who could excite his jealousy made them more happily intimate than they had been for a long time.

Clive was no doubt a stimulating companion, but perhaps it was a sedative that she needed; after a fortnight it was clear that she was getting no better. Vanessa went back to London and told Savage that Virginia was not recovering; worse still, she had to point out that she herself would be unable to look after Virginia much longer, for in July she was expecting another baby. With great misgivings she wrote both to Clive and to Virginia on 23 June to tell them that Savage insisted upon a period of complete rest in a nursing home at Twickenham.

Virginia accepted the decision with dismay, but with resignation; she only wished that Savage had insisted on this in the first place. She wanted to start the cure as soon as possible, to get it over and to get well again. George Duckworth sent her a kindly but fatuous letter; he deplored her ill-health–no doubt she had been smoking too many cigarettes in order to repel the mosquitoes from the moat, and invited her to his country house. She meditated a reply:

> I shall say that I expect to be confined next month & let him muddle it out for himself. He will suspect Saxon, & take immediate steps to have him promoted. He will also run down to Brighton, & negotiate a settlement with Saxon père. How tactful he would be . . . bringing down a basket of plovers eggs, I expect.

But such pleasantries could hardly alleviate the desolating prospect of a month's incarceration at 'Burley,' Cambridge Park, Twickenham, a kind of polite madhouse for female lunatics. Here her letters, her reading, her visitors would all be severely rationed, she would be kept in bed in a darkened room, wholesome foods would be pressed upon her and she would be excluded from all the social enjoyments of London. Faced by the possibility of madness she accepted her fate; but she accepted it in a sullen and rebellious spirit.

Virginia was an exceedingly difficult patient. Vanessa, immobilised by the child which was expected before the end of July but did not appear until the 19th of August, had to wage a continuous war through the post. She had to scold, to exhort, to plead, in order that her sister might behave at all prudently. Sometimes bored to extinction and near to complete despair, sometimes recklessly euphoric about her health, Virginia was always adroit enough to use her charm upon her medical advisers so that she might win them over and make them her allies in whatever plot against routine and good sense she might devise. Savage could be manipulated, so too Miss Thomas, the proprietor of 'Burley,' and also Miss Bradbury, whom Vanessa supposed to be one of the lunatics but was in fact a trained nurse. Virginia declared that they were charming and good women but spoiled by religion: "They reverence my gifts, although God has left me in the dark. They are always wondering what God is up to. The religious mind is quite amazing." But they too were amazed and Miss Thomas in particular was captivated, as Clive, who was allowed to pay visits from time to time during that miserable July and August, observed. She "was transformed . . . suddenly life, which she had found drab and dreary, had become thrilling and precious . . . everything seemed exciting or amusing . . . her own life, coloured by the presence and idle talk of her patient, [had] grown poetical . . . for the first time in her life she felt of consequence to herself; she was aware of her own existence . . . and all the trivial things that made up that existence had significance too. The magician had cast her spell."

All this was in its way pleasing, and Miss Thomas was to repay Virginia with much practical devotion. But it also made it easier for her patient to take unheard-of liberties, to wander in the garden clad only in a blanket, to break rules about rest and food, to plan, if not to effect, a sudden return to London. When attempts were made to keep her in order she wrote accusing Vanessa of plotting against her with Miss Thomas: she was "a dark devil," they were all in a conspiracy behind her back; it was "damned dull being here all alone" and she could not stand much more of it. She would throw herself from a window.

Vanessa answered as one who has reached the end of her forbearance. She quite saw the horrors of Virginia's position; but did she or did she not want to be an invalid (she avoids the frightening word 'mad') for the rest of her life? Presumably she did and she would have her own way; she could get round Savage, who could not bid her do anything that she did not want to do; but if she insisted on coming back to London she would undoubtedly fall ill again. However, she must decide for herself, even though, as Miss Thomas said: "one cannot help having her welfare very near at heart."

In the end Virginia was dissuaded from committing the wilder imprudences. Vanessa, still waiting at Gordon Square for her confinement, wrote every day preaching patience, assuring her that London was hopelessly dull, and grieving over her own shortcomings. "Oh dear," she writes, "how nice it would be if you were quite well again . . . I don't make undue fuss about you . . . really I feel that I have made only too little fuss during the last 3 years."

Virginia remained at Twickenham until the middle of August and then, having had a pretty thorough rest, she tried the effect of healthy exercise. She went to Cornwall; she can hardly have been in a state to go by herself but the devoted Miss Thomas accompanied her, and here they escaped boredom by vigorous walking. Soon Virginia began to complain that she was leading a completely animal existence with no intellectual excitement whatsoever. But Cornwall was her favourite country and it did her good; she began to feel better than she had for a long time, although she still had bad nights and occasional headaches. When early in September she returned to London to see the new baby, Vanessa thought her very much improved. But her state of mind was a little puzzling. She seemed very self-confident, she was elated and excited about the future, looked forward to fame and marriage; at the same time she was irritated by trifles, exaggerated their importance and was unable to shake off her excessive concern with them.

Her cure was to be completed at Studland with the Bells, and in a sense it was; even so, although they should have known better, Clive and Virginia provoked each other to fury (the blame was his rather than hers on this occasion). The trouble was caused, as it often was, by Lytton. Clive thought that Lytton had become insufferably supercilious; he was intimate with and confided in Virginia and Vanessa while taking not the slightest notice of Clive himself. It was not to be borne and Clive announced that in future Lytton would not be welcome at Gordon Square. This squabble agitated Virginia excessively, and they both of them found it hard to avoid the subject.

Vanessa, however, was able to make and keep the peace while they were at the seaside. Here they were distracted by babies and by numerous visitors, including Saxon, Marjorie (the youngest of the Strachey girls), and Sydney Waterlow, another Cambridge intellectual and friend of Clive's, whom Virginia found amiable but not exciting. Presently Clive went to Paris and the two sisters were able to relax and settle down to a long discussion of their favourite topic, which was, of course, Virginia herself. She talked a great deal of Lytton; they would be meeting again in the autumn but now their relationship was to be regarded as entirely platonic. Her obscure and inconclusive connection with Hilton Young still exercised her mind; but her relations with Clive himself were now, she declared, in a satisfactory state. Their former condition was, I should guess, left undiscussed.

Virginia finally came back to Fitzroy Square in the middle of October to take up her London life where she had left it seven months before. She might consider herself cured; but Dr Savage and Miss Thomas, though encouraged and relieved by her good progress, were still fearful of the effect upon their patient of London, late hours, too much company and too much excitement. They uttered appropriate warnings and Miss Thomas drew up a set of rules for Virginia to observe. Vanessa also knew, even if Virginia did not, that her health was still precarious. The question naturally arose—or so I imagine—whether it would not be a good plan if Virginia were to find some quiet and accessible place near London to which she could, when necessary, escape.

Accordingly, at Christmas time, 1910, Virginia began looking for a house in the country.

She found what she wanted in the village of Firle, near Lewes; she could hardly have hit upon a quieter place. But it must be allowed that the house which she actually chose to live in did not contribute to the repose of the village street; it was a raw, red, newly-built, gabled villa. She named it Little Talland House, for even here she could not forget the superior charms of St Ives.

Nevertheless the beauties of Sussex clearly impressed her and the lease of Little Talland began a connection with the neighbourhood which was to last for the rest of her life.

She moved into this country villa early in 1911. Vanessa helped her to make it comfortable and she was frequently there, often with friends to stay, during the Spring and Summer of that year. It would seem that the place had a therapeutic effect; she enjoyed living there, she enjoyed walking on the Downs, she was well enough to go on with her novel and to work for the Adult Suffrage movement. She was staying at Little Talland, very contentedly, in April of the year 1911 when fate suddenly carried her to the shores of the Propontis.

To understand the reason for this unpremeditated excursion we must return to 1910. Early in that year Clive and Vanessa, returning to London after a visit to Cambridge, had travelled up with Roger Fry. Clive and he had not known each other before; now they discovered common interests and common enthusiasms. Clive was excited and impressed; he thought Roger Fry the most remarkable person he had met since he left Cambridge; as a natural consequence his new friend became an intimate and indeed an element in Bloomsbury.

Roger Fry was forty-four, and at an emotional and intellectual turning-point in his life. His wife was going mad, and by the end of the year was incurably insane and in an asylum. Educated as a scientist at Cambridge, he had turned to the arts and become a rather conservative painter and member of the New English Art Club as well as a considerable scholar and connoisseur, qualities he exercised in his capacity as buyer for the Metropolitan Museum in New York, a position from which he had recently resigned. He was in fact a highly respectable and well-established figure until the autumn of 1910 when, as it seemed to many of his old friends and admirers, he had taken leave of his senses and, to his enemies, that he had wilfully and wickedly entered into a conspiracy with hoaxers, crooks and criminals of the Parisian underworld. In short, he had asked the British public to look at and to admire the works of Cézanne.

During the fierce controversy which followed the opening in November 1910 of what is now called 'The First Post-Impressionist Exhibition,' an exhibition for which Roger Fry took the responsibility and the blame, Clive and Vanessa were his fervent supporters. Virginia was not deeply interested in the Post-Impressionists; but with Roger a constant visitor in Gordon Square she could not ignore the commotion that they caused. The atmosphere engendered by him and by the exhibition made her circle a little more centripetal, a little more conscious of being revolutionary and notorious. Bloomsbury had become an object of public disapproval, a centre of disaffection, of Abyssinian Emperors and of incomprehensible aesthetics. Also, the intellectual character of Bloomsbury itself began to change. The doctrines of G. E. Moore no longer seemed quite so important when Cézanne was the chief topic of conversation, and Lytton Strachey might seem less pre-eminent when compared with Roger Fry.

It was, I have very little doubt, under Roger's influence that a party was formed to visit the home of Byzantine art. Early in April 1911 Clive and Vanessa joined H. T. J. Norton (a Cambridge mathematician) and Roger himself in Brussels, from whence they set off together by train for Constantinople. Clive embarked on this expedition with some misgivings. Vanessa had been unwell and this worried him; but his feeling of possessive jealousy for Virginia gave rise to a more intense irritation of the spirit; he had "an irrational foreboding" that something might happen to her while he was away; she might fall in love or someone would fall in love with her. He begged her to assure him that his "own little niche" in her feelings was secure.

A good deal did happen while Clive was away; but not to Virginia. At Broussa Vanessa had fainting fits; she collapsed. The place was at that time remote – a day's journey from Constantinople – the inn was archaic and there was no medical man except a chemist. Virginia, reading between the lines of Clive's letters – letters which Clive tried to make as reassuring as possible – imagined a dreadful repetition of the nightmare of 1906 and, abandoning all other plans, set off across Europe in order to be with her sister.

At Broussa she found Norton in despair, Clive in a state of solicitous and ineffectual agitation, Vanessa convalescent and Roger in command. He was in his element, organising cooks and dragomen, arguing his way with a bottle of medicine in one hand and a Turkish conversation book in the other, cajoling English tourists, constructing a litter, always finding just time enough for another rapid sketch and, as Virginia believed, saving Vanessa's life by his energy, sympathy and practical good sense.

It was now that Virginia got to know Roger really well. During the few days during which all four of them were to remain in Broussa waiting until Vanessa was considered fit to travel, Virginia was able to appreciate the extraordinary richness of his nature.

His conversation, his activity, his delighted interest in ideas, and indeed in everything that he saw or heard, astonished and impressed her. Roger was a tower of strength. He was more, he was a perpetual fount of enjoyment.

Even though he himself was suffering agonies from sciatica Roger was able to take command of his invalid and of her companions and to bring them, together with a considerable collection of paintings, pottery and textiles, successfully to England. But Vanessa's recovery was slow. Her disease was complicated by nervous symptoms and it was many months before she was perfectly well again. For Virginia this was, naturally, a source of unhappiness, all the more so because she depended very much on her sister and needed her support. But Vanessa's fortunes affected Virginia in another way; by the time of their return to England, Roger and Vanessa knew that they were in love. Vanessa did not confide in Virginia; she thought her much too indiscreet for that; but Virginia was pretty well aware of how matters stood and must soon have been conscious that Vanessa's tolerant attitude towards Clive's flirtations was no longer determined by policy but rather by sentiment. Hitherto Clive's passion for Virginia had been a source of severe, though concealed, pain. Now it became a matter of indifference. Now indeed Vanessa would have been only too glad to see Clive more completely obsessed by his sister-in-law, instead of which, such is the perversity of things, that affair seemed to be cooling off. In fact there was a moment—or so I suspect—when Vanessa feared that her much loved but agonisingly exasperating sister might set herself to charm Roger. There was no serious cause for alarm. Virginia was fascinated by Roger and he, undoubtedly, thought from the first that she was a genius; but his passions were pre-engaged and, most unhappily for him, were not to alter for many years. Virginia, for her part, had other things to occupy her mind and heart.

On the whole the break-up of the Bell marriage, that is to say its transformation into a union of friendship, which was slowly accomplished during the years 1911–1914, made for a relaxation of tension between the sisters and a slow dissolution (never quite complete) of Virginia's long troubled relationship with Clive. Perhaps also it created a situation in which she, being no longer preoccupied by her sister's marriage, could begin more easily to contemplate a marriage of her own. For Virginia, who had envied the domesticity of the Bells, need envy it no longer; it was ceasing to exist, things were changing.

In 1908 Bloomsbury had become licentious in its speech, by 1910 it was becoming licentious in its conduct, or rather, licence was no longer the privilege of its homosexual component. Virginia once said that human nature changed in or about December 1910. She is seldom accurate in her use of dates but it is true that the world (or at least her bit of it) was at this time transformed; things were happening which would very much have astonished the maidenly Miss Stephen of 1907. As usual it was Vanessa who gave the lead; she proposed, I do not know how seriously, the creation of a libertarian society with sexual freedom for all. The world at large would not have been surprised to hear it; Vanessa and Virginia had gone to the Post-Impressionist Ball as bare-shouldered bare-legged Gauguin girls, almost—as it seemed to the indignant ladies who swept out in protest—almost naked. And it was whispered that, at Gordon Square, Vanessa and Mr Maynard Keynes copulated *coram publico* in the middle of a crowded drawing-room. The story is improbable, if only because at that time Mr Keynes was pursuing other interests. In fact I believe that there was a certain element of bravado in Vanessa's high-spirited manifestations of sexual anarchy.

The painter Henri Doucet, who was present at one of Bloomsbury's wilder parties, when Vanessa danced with such enthusiasm that she shook off most of her clothes and whirled bare to the waist, remarked—perhaps a little wistfully—"*en France ça aurait fini dans les embrassades*"; for apparently it did not; the game of promiscuity remained only a game. Sex, it was agreed, need no longer be sanctioned by marriage, but it must still be sanctioned by passion. This, for Virginia, was the escape clause. In fact, what Virginia really wanted was someone for whom she could feel passion. Instead, in the month of July, she received another offer of marriage—of a kind.

Walter Lamb, who it will be remembered was one of the party at Studland in 1909 and was a persistent visitor in Bloomsbury, continued to seek Virginia's society. In July he asked her to join him in an excursion to Richmond Park. As she is our only witness we may as well quote the account of it she gave in a letter to Vanessa which can be dated 21 July 1911.

29 Fitzroy Square, W.
Friday.

Beloved,
    It is great devotion to write, as the heat is something awful.
    We had our great expedition yesterday. It was all very odd. First of

all it was rather strained; we lay under the trees & discussed the Bedford Sq. plan.* Then we walked, & he began lamenting the lack of noble souls. We discussed love & women in the abstract. At last he sat down & said "Will you tell me if you've ever been in love?" I asked him whether he knew about the Lytton affair. He said "Clive told me a good deal" which made me angry, but cant be helped. Then I said I would tell him about it if he really wanted to know, & not out of curiosity. He said he wanted to find out what I felt, & would be glad to hear anything. I gave him an abstract. Then he said, "Do you want to have children & love in the normal way?" I said "Yes". He said "I do care for you very much", I said "But you're quite happy?" He said, "There are such dreadful complications." I said, "What". He said, "You live in a hornets nest. Beside[s] marriage is so difficult– Will you let me wait? Dont hurry me." I said "There is no reason why we shouldn't be friends–or why we should change things & get agitated." He said "Of course its wonderful as it is."

Then we went rambling on: & I gathered that he felt he could not let himself fall in love because he doubted what I felt; & he also was puzzled by parts of my character. He said I made things into webs, & might turn fiercely upon him for his faults. I owned to great egoism & absorption & vanity & all my vices. He said Clive had told him dreadful stories to illustrate my faults. (for God's sake, dont repeat this) I said that I liked him, & thought we could be friends. I tried to make this clear. Then he talked a great deal about you–how noble & divine you were–how you frightened him–how he wished to talk to you, how he had an aesthetic love for you &c &c. We talked of general things after that–his gout a good deal–& then had tea & went home, & went to the Opera. There was an enormous crowd of cultivated ones–Sangers, Forster, Rupert, Ka, James, Woolf† &c. Walter walked home, & came in & drank here, as Adrian was out. He began again about our relationship, & said he would like to live near me, in the autumn, but didn't add much. It is uneasy, because he is always trying to find out what I feel, & I can only talk about the beauty of friendship. Of course I liked him much better than I have ever done, as he was quite direct & really felt a good deal (unless I'm too vain to judge). But the thing is left in an uncomfortable state. He wants to come to Firle in September. I do like him, but the prospect of many very long talks, rather appals me. There is something pathetic in him. He's so desperately afraid of making a fool of himself, & yet conscious that his caution is a little absurd. I think I've told all I can remember– at least the gist of it. No doubt some further compliments to you will be washed up. Oh how I'm damned by Roger! Refinement! &

* A plan to make a communal house in Bedford Square which was later realised at Brunswick Square. *q.v.i.*

† i.e. Charles and Dora Sanger, E. M. Forster, Rupert Brooke, Katherine Cox, James Strachey and Leonard Woolf, who had returned from Ceylon in June.

we in a Post Impressionist age. You dont deserve any compliments for sending me that one. By the way, the last thing W. said before we were interrupted was that he could not see that I had a single fault. "Not even as a wife?" I said "No: not even as a wife." In my opinion he is in love with me; but that you must hush up.

I'm in great difficulties with my engagements. Eily wont answer; & I think she must have written to Firle. If she puts me off, I might come down next Thursday or Friday for the night [to Guildford, where Vanessa was convalescing] (if you'll have me). Case comes on Monday, & wont say for how long. Then Savage asks me for Thursday, & I accepted for Wednesday. Jean [Thomas] is in a fury–flings the tele-phone from her ear–because she thinks I'm trying to avoid dining with her–Saxon has become very pathetic about Bayreuth. Altogether, its a hornets nest, as W. said. He meant that we lived in the centre of in-trigues, which distressed him, & he asked about Harry & Roger & Desmond. He asked whether I should flirt if I married. I said "not if I were in love with my husband." But that was bold.

Are you better. Does this heat hurt you ! At lunch I compared you with a South American forest, with panthers sleeping beneath the trees. I also gave a passionate vision of our love–yours for me, I mean.

yrs B.

Virginia was right in supposing that he loved her. He expressed his passion in long and slightly absurd letters, but his cause was hopeless. He was amiable but unimpressive and the only passion that he aroused in her was one of indignation against Clive. She burst out in a furious letter to Vanessa who, as usual, had to try and keep the peace. Then Clive, Walter Lamb and Sydney Water-low became involved in a three-cornered wrangle about who said what to whom about Virginia (she certainly did live in a hornets' nest), and in the end Walter Lamb, having failed to secure a wife, for he must soon have realised that he was getting nowhere with Virginia, discovered also that he had lost a friend, for Clive never spoke to him again.

Vanessa had invited Virginia to stay with her in a cottage she had rented at Millmead, conveniently close to Roger's home at Durbins, near Guildford. She felt some anxiety lest the *sequelae* of Walter's proposals should result in storms between Clive and her sister. But the weather remained fine both literally and metaphoric-ally. Week after week of sunshine made it a time for bathing and landscape painting, for picnics and Neo-Pagans.*

* The term Neo-Pagans was, it would appear, invented in Bloomsbury, perhaps by Vanessa. The first use of it that I have found is in a letter from her to Roger Fry of August 1911.

Of these, some must have been known to Virginia long before 1911, for they were a Cambridge group connected in many ways with Lytton and Maynard Keynes and their friends. But it was now that she began to know a few of them better. One in particular was to be of great practical importance in Virginia's life. She met Katherine Cox – Ka Cox, as she was usually called–for the first time in January 1911 in "the heart of young womanhood"–that is to say in the company of Marjorie Strachey and her Newnham friends, Ray and Karin Costelloe. "Miss Cox is one of the younger Newnhamites," Virginia wrote to Clive, "& it is said that she will marry either a Keynes, or a Brook. She has a superficial resemblance to a far younger and prettier Sheepshanks. She is a bright, intelligent, nice creature; who has, she says, very few emotions. . . ." Virginia used to call her "Bruin" and it is thus that I imagine her–not in the fiercer or gruffer aspects of bearishness–but comfortably furry, slow-moving, warm-hugging, honey-loving, a little clumsy, a little insensitive, but not so insensitive as to be unhurtable–rather, a shade imperceptive, but, unless touched by passion, helpful and dependable. She was a confidant, almost a sister, to many of the Neo-Pagans and in particular to Gwen Darwin and Jacques Raverat (who were married in 1911), to Frances Cornford and, above all, to Rupert Brooke, the luminary of that society, who set its tone rather as Lytton had that of his generation. But the tone was rather different.*

Their background was not unlike that of Bloomsbury; they were, for the most part, the children of eminent Victorian intellectuals; but there was a heartier element, a Bedalian, Rugbeian element; many of the women had received the advantage, which Virginia so much envied, of a university education; they were not so ladylike, more practical, more commonsensical than their seniors. Both the men and the women had reacted sharply and robustly against the decadents and the aesthetes; they felt, far less than Lytton's generation, the influence of G. E. Moore and although they were concerned with and practised the arts, they were also active socialists.

There was a sort of innocent athletic camaraderie about them;

---

* The Neo-Pagans resemble Bloomsbury in that they were intimately connected with Cambridge and were in no sense organised. It is not very easy to say who was and who was not a Neo-Pagan. To the names already mentioned we may add those of Justin Brooke, Dudley Ward, Gerald Shove, Geoffrey Keynes, David Garnett and the four daughters of Sir Sydney Olivier, the Fabian Socialist. Amongst them also were some–as for instance James Strachey and Francis Birrell–to whom the generalisations attempted in the next paragraph hardly apply.

they met, not only in drawing-rooms, but in tents, they navigated canoes, they dressed in jerseys and bandannas, they walked vigorously, they were gay and serious and, in their loves, they looked in general to the opposite sex, with marriage as their ideal.*

Thus, when Virginia went to stay with Rupert Brooke at Grantchester, where she supplied a word for one of his poems and bathed naked with him by moonlight in the Granta, he, one may surmise, considered both these acts as being in the nature of sympathetic gestures; it was decent of her to help him to a simile and decent too not to be prudish about stripping in mixed company; it was treating him like a friend. But for her, I think, this shameless bathing was altogether more eventful; it was an act worthy of Vanessa, a gesture of emancipation. If Adrian is to be trusted, she was a little vexed that it did not create more of a sensation amongst her friends. Whether Adrian was justified in calling their friendship the 'Rupert Romance' is very doubtful. I do not think that there was a serious attachment on either side, although they got on well enough for Rupert to be able to persuade Virginia to join him and some friends in a camp at Clifford Bridge on the banks of the Teign. This visit began badly and uncomfortably. The other campers had made an excursion to Crediton leaving nothing for Ka Cox and Virginia to eat on their arrival save a rotting blackberry pudding–such are the inconveniences of the simple life. There were, however, compensations; the fine weather still held and by the camp fire at night there was music, good conversation and that peculiar serenity which attends a life passed in boundless fresh air and sunlight.

Maynard Keynes was another of the campers at Clifford Bridge that September; he was intimate with, although he certainly could not be said to 'belong' to, the Neo-Pagans; in fact he must have known all Virginia's Cambridge friends and, from 1907, had been a visitor to 29 Fitzroy Square. Although his subsequent election to a Fellowship at King's caused him to live much at Cambridge, in 1909 he took rooms with Duncan Grant at 21 Fitzroy Square and thereafter got to know Virginia very well indeed. Incredibly clever, he had a sensual, affectionate, volatile and optimistic nature which could be very attractive. He was, from the point of view of practical politics, the greatest man Virginia was ever to know

---

* "The group of people we're part of . . . don't copulate without marriage, but we *do* meet in cafés, talk on buses, go unchaperoned walks, stay with each other, give each other books, without marriage." Rupert Brooke to Katherine Cox [? May 1911], *The Letters of Rupert Brooke*, 1968, p. 304.

intimately and in 1911 he might already be considered the most brilliant and the most obviously destined for a great career.

The lease of 29 Fitzroy Square was coming to an end; Virginia and Adrian, tired perhaps of their long and quarrelsome tête-à-tête, proposed a domestic revolution: they would share their home–it would have to be a large home–with other friends; for this purpose they considered a house in Bedford Square, but it was at 38 Brunswick Square that in October they found what they wanted. Here Virginia was to live in rooms of her own on the second floor; Adrian was to have the first, and Maynard Keynes a *pied-à-terre* on the ground floor which Duncan Grant could also use as a studio. The vacant top floor was offered to Leonard Woolf. The expenses of running the house were to be shared, but otherwise the 'inmates' were to be as independent as possible. Service and individual meals were to be supplied by Sophy and the housemaid Maud.★

To modern eyes the arrangement looks unexceptionable, but in 1911 it seemed odd. George protested that Virginia simply could not go off to live by herself with three young men. "Oh, its quite alright, George," Vanessa explained, "you see it's so near the Foundling Hospital." This would do for George: but it was not so easy to find an answer to Violet Dickinson; for Violet, broadminded though she was, thought that her friend was going too far. "Julia would not have liked it." Such an objection, coming from such a quarter, must have brought Virginia, momentarily at all events, to a halt. She liked and respected Violet, she valued Violet's good opinion, Violet was her best friend. Or rather–as we may see in the gradual but decisive diminution of their correspondence– Violet *had* been her best friend. Virginia would always like, trust, and admire her, always be grateful to her; but somehow the vital spirit in their friendship had evaporated and now, when it was put to the test, Virginia found that she could break away and live as she chose, despite Violet's evident disapproval. There was a coolness but no quarrel; their friendship was of too long standing for that; moreover Virginia's conduct, though unconventional, was not immoral. Still Violet had been the most important person in her

★ "Meals are:/Breakfast 9 A.M./Lunch 1./Tea 4.30 P.M./Dinner 8 P.M. Trays will be placed in the hall punctually at these hours. Inmates are requested to carry up their own trays; & to put the dirty plates on them & carry them down again *as soon as the meal is finished.*

"Inmates are requested to put their initials upon the Kitchen Instruction Tablet hung in the hall against all meals required that day before *9.30* A.M."

Extract from the 'Scheme of the house' prepared by VW for Leonard Woolf in December 1911.

life and the incident marks the final extinction of a great passion.

It was indeed a season of terminations and new beginnings; Virginia was leaving, not only Fitzroy Square, but Little Talland. She had found Asham,* a strange and beautiful house in a lonely and romantic situation a few miles to the west of Firle, and planned to rent it from the New Year. Vanessa was enthusiastic and agreed to share the lease. The one thing that seemed endless was her novel. In April 1911 when she was revising it for perhaps the sixth time, she had written to Clive:

> Yesterday I finished the 8th Chapter of Mel[ymbrosia]; which brings them within sight of the South American shore. This is a third of the book done, I think. From sheer cowardice, I didn't bring the other chapters here [to Little Talland]. If I thought "There! thats solid & done with" I'm sure I should have the palsy. Some of it, I'm certain, will have the pallor of headache upon it.

Although the breakdowns of 1910 were not repeated in 1911 there were no doubt plenty of headaches. In June 1911 she wrote to Vanessa describing a moment of depression, when:

> I could not write, & all the devils came out–hairy black ones. To be 29 & unmarried–to be a failure–Childless–insane too, no writer.

How frequent and how important such moods may have been it is hard to say; but if the summer was at times melancholy there is some reason to think that the autumn was happier.

In November Sydney Waterlow†–who had joined them at Studland in 1910–made a declaration of love. She seems to have had no hesitation in rejecting him, kindly though decisively, and his passion soon evaporated. One may presume that the tribute was not unwelcome even though, by then, she was preoccupied by a new and much more important relationship.

When Leonard Woolf returned on leave from Ceylon in June 1911 he naturally sought out those Cambridge friends whom he had left behind him in 1904: Lytton, Saxon, Desmond MacCarthy,

---

* or Asheham.

† Sydney Waterlow was a frequent visitor in Bloomsbury and, as the following Diary entry makes clear, on fairly intimate terms with the Bells:
"Dined with the Clive Bells; what a relief and change [from electioneering]. No one else but Virginia S. We had talk that begins to be really intimate. Vanessa very amusing on pederasty among their circle. I realised for the first time the difference between her and Virginia. Vanessa icy, cynical, artistic, Virginia much more emotional, and interested in life rather than beauty. A glorious evening." Sydney Waterlow, *Diary* (Berg), 8 December 1910.

Clive, Maynard Keynes and Morgan Forster. In so doing he was bound to meet others whom he knew much less well: Roger Fry, Duncan Grant, Vanessa, Adrian and Virginia. He had left Cambridge and had returned to Bloomsbury. Bloomsbury welcomed him easily. "Woolf came to tea," wrote Vanessa, "and we had an argument as to whether colour exists." From which it might appear that things had not changed so very much since he had left Trinity. But of course things *had* changed, and so had he. There was now a difference between him and the rest, to quote again from Vanessa:

> He is of course very clever & from living in the wilds seems to me to have got a more interesting point of view than most of the "set" who seldom produce anything very new or original.

At Cambridge Leonard had been particularly close to Lytton; he was one of the few men whom Lytton liked and trusted but did not love or see as a rival in love. They were both tremendously earnest as Apostles. It was, for them, a kind of religion. Leonard has written of their private Henry-Jamesian language and, when he read *The Golden Bowl* in Ceylon, he was surprised to find how Jamesian they in fact were.* He and Lytton were, with Saxon, notable figures in the G. E. Moore *cénacle*, they were united in their devotion to the great man and, despite their genuine passion for intellectual honesty and their remarkable personal qualities, these young men left Cambridge with a terribly precious esoteric air. They had received the Gospel of *Principia Ethica* and regarded themselves as the elect.

When, therefore, Leonard set sail for Ceylon, Lytton was bereaved and he himself was isolated. Letters from Lytton were his only link with the old world, the "real" part of it. Saxon wrote sometimes, it is true, but usually only to say at considerable length that he had nothing to say, or sometimes–and here he would furnish examples–that he had nothing worth saying. There was always an idea–it was a thing to be talked of rather than actually done, that Lytton would come out to Ceylon some day. Perhaps he ought to have done so. Lytton never got that slight baptism of fire–if we may call it fire–which fate provided for Gibbon. Gibbon knew how practical men managed and mismanaged matters, because he had practical experience of war, or at least of an army. Would

---

* "I have just finished *The Golden Bowl* & am astounded. Did he invent us or we him? He uses *all* our words in their most technical sense & we cant have got them all from him." Leonard Woolf to Lytton Strachey, 23 July 1905.

Lytton have given a sharper edge–a slightly deeper note of com-prehension–to Gordon and to Florence Nightingale if he had sat amidst the flies and dirt of Jaffna and Hambantota? It is hard to say, and hard to imagine Lytton visiting, let alone ruling, a province.

But if Leonard had never left Cambridge and London to fly the Union Jack amongst a wilderness of monkeys it might be hard to imagine *him* as an administrator. As it was he had that experience, the experience of being a sahib amongst natives, utterly removed from all those friends with whom one could be entirely open, the jokes, the high seriousness, the intellectual communion of Cam-bridge. He learnt to travel and to live alone, to undertake the duties of a policeman and to exert the authority of a magistrate, to send men to their deaths and to watch them hang, to perform the endless and endlessly boring tasks of empire. Hardest of all, he had to deal with and to come to terms with compatriots who, in a moment of impatient despair, he described as a "stupid de-graded circle of degenerates and imbeciles." These people, in whose hands lay the administration and the exploitation of the island, the half-educated sahibs and their terrible memsahibs, pointed the difference between Ceylon and Cambridge with dreadful clarity. But to make a success of his job, and he was clearly determined from the outset to do that, it was necessary not merely to live on terms of intimacy, of cordiality even, with people whom as an undergraduate he would easily have avoided, but to cultivate them, to study them, to please them. This he did, and in so doing he became more tolerant, recognised that they were not, after all, homogeneous, that there were many from whom he could learn and some whom he could sincerely like. The arrogance of the young intellectual was tempered, his sympathies were broadened. He found that he could get on with, be tolerated and valued by, people who had no understanding of "good states of mind," and this without ever essentially sacrificing that first fine perception that Cambridge had given him.

It was on this point that Lytton had some misgivings. Leonard, he feared, might become "interested in his work" and in that interest others would be quenched. They almost were.

Even in his early cries of despair Leonard was, consciously or not, adapting his tone of voice to his interlocutor. As time went on and he rose in the Service he found the administrative game fascinating. He purged and reformed offices, he imposed order upon chaos, he made inefficient machinery work smoothly. His superiors soon understood that they had a very useful man in their service. They gave him a kingdom, the Hambantota District of the Southern Province, and for two and a half years he devoted himself to the task of making it peaceful and prosperous. By 1911 he had become an extremely successful colonial servant, and Lytton's fears might have seemed to be justified.

Bloomsbury broke the spell. Leonard returned to find the seeds which he and Lytton had cultivated under Cambridge glass growing tall and no doubt in some ways strange in their flowering. But it was still recognisably the same plant. The old values were still honoured although applied to a greater world than that of Cambridge; despite one melancholy loss, old friends remained, their lives enriched and complicated by new ones and, above all, by the feminine element, that is to say by Vanessa and Virginia.

In this new, but not unfamiliar society, Leonard could discard the reserves and reservations of the intellectual turned Colonial Administrator; he felt at home once more (much more so, I fancy, than at his mother's house in Putney); he was amongst people who respected the same fundamental values, people in whom he could discover congenial characters and qualities. After a seven years' term the holiday was exhilarating; released from the burden of solitude and from the grim pleasures of efficiency he embarked upon an excursive and erratic pursuit of social enjoyments and new experiences (he even took up painting for a time), and then his interests began again to become concentrated; he rediscovered a purpose and it became all-important. Six months after his arrival in England he proposed to Virginia.

On 3 July Leonard had dined in Gordon Square with Clive and Vanessa; after dinner Virginia, Walter Lamb and Duncan Grant came in. A few days later Virginia wrote to "Dear Mr Wolf" and invited him for a week-end at her "cottage in the South Downs." As he was already committed to a series of visits he could not accept and so, while Virginia undertook her 'great expedition' with Walter Lamb and her minor excursion with Rupert Brooke and the Neo-Pagans, Leonard went, firstly to a Somerset rectory, then to a meeting with Lytton and G. E. Moore in Devonshire and finally to Scandinavia. But when he returned he ventured to remind Miss Stephen of her invitation; she repeated it and suggested that it would be nice to use Christian names; she added that "it was not a cottage but a hideous suburban villa." Leonard went there for the week-end of 16 September, together with Marjorie Strachey and Desmond MacCarthy. It was then that Leonard discovered how pleasant it was to walk over the Downs with Virginia; it was in his company that she discovered Asham.

This week-end visit was decisive; from now on Leonard was increasingly at Fitzroy Square and Gordon Square; he continually sought Virginia's company. In November she began living at 38 Brunswick Square and Leonard was by this time so much a part of Bloomsbury that it seemed natural to ask him to join this establishment. On 4 December he moved into two rooms on the top floor at a rent of 35 shillings a week. The rooms had been painted and Virginia assured him that there would be a bookcase.

Thus, for the last three months of 1911 Leonard and Virginia saw a great deal of each other and Leonard found himself falling very deeply in love. She obviously liked him but what her liking amounted to was clear neither to herself nor to him, and his doubts as to the strength and nature of her feelings prevented him from expressing his own.

Early in the New Year Leonard again went to stay with his old friend the Vicar of Frome in Somerset; here, in the quiet of a country parsonage, he saw that he must at once ask Virginia to marry him. On 10 January he sent a reply-paid telegram to Brunswick Square: "I must see you for an hour tomorrow Thursday I shall arrive town 12.50 and leave again 5 if I can come to Brunswick Square 1.15 can I see you then Leonard."

He saw her and asked her to marry him. She cannot have been greatly astonished; but she had prepared no decisive answer; she wanted time in which to get to know him better. Their conversation was interrupted by the arrival of Walter Lamb and Leonard had to go back to Frome. When he arrived he wrote:

Great Elm Rectory
Frome
11 Jan 1912   Somerset

My dear Virginia, I must write to you before I go to bed & can, I think, probably think more calmly.

I have not got any very clear recollection of what I really said to you this afternoon but I am sure you know why I came—I dont mean merely that I was in love but that that together with uncertainty drives one to do these things. Perhaps I was wrong, for before this week I always intended not to tell you unless I felt sure that you were in love & would marry me. I thought then that you liked me but that was all. I never realised how much I loved you until we talked about my going back to Ceylon. After that I could think about nothing else but you. I got into a state of hopeless uncertainty, whether you loved me or could ever love me or even like me. God, I hope I shall never spend such a time again as I spent here until I telegraphed. I wrote to you once saying I would speak to you next Monday but then I felt I should be mad if I waited until then to see you. So I wired. I knew you would tell me exactly what you felt. You were exactly what I knew you are & if I hadnt been in love before I would now. It isnt, really it isnt, merely because you are so beautiful–though of course that is a large reason & so it should be–that I love you: it is your mind & your character–I have never known anyone like you in that–wont you believe that?

And now I will do absolutely whatever you want. I dont think you want me to go away, but if you did, I would at once. If not, I dont see why we cannot go on the same as before–I think I can–and then if you do find that you could love me you would tell me.

I hardly know whether I am saying what I mean or feel: I am extraordinarily tired. A dense mist covered the whole of Somerset & the train was late & I had to crawl my way from the station for 3 miles to the house.

Dont you think that the entrance of Walter almost proves the existence of a deity?

Yr L.

He wrote again the next day:

. . . I can try & write about what, with you sitting there, it was so difficult to discuss calmly & dispassionately. I dont think I'm selfish enough not to be able to see it from your side as well. From mine, I'm sure now that apart from being in love . . . it would be worth the risk of everything to marry you. That of course–from your side–was the question you were continually putting yesterday & which probably you ought to. Being outside the ring of fire, you should be able to decide it far better than I inside it. God, I see the risk in marrying anyone & certainly me. I am selfish, jealous, cruel, lustful, a liar & probably worse still. I had said over & over again to myself that I would never marry anyone because of this, mostly because, I think, I felt I could never control these things with a woman who was inferior & would gradually enfuriate me by her inferiority & submission . . . It is because you aren't that that the risk is so infinitely less. You may be vain an egoist untruthful as you say, but they are nothing compared to your other qualities magnificence intelligence wit beauty directness. After all too we like one another, we like the same kinds of things & people, we are both intelligent & above all it is realities which we understand & which are important to us. . . .

Virginia, rushing to catch a train for what must have been her last visit to Little Talland House, replied:

There isn't anything really for me to say, except that I should like to go on as before; & that you should leave me free; & that I should be honest. As to faults, I expect mine are just as bad–less noble perhaps. But of course they are not really the question. I have decided to keep this completely secret, except for Vanessa; & I have made her promise not to tell Clive. I told Adrian that you had come up about a job which was promised you.

Vanessa had liked Leonard from the first and believed that he had the qualities that could make her sister happy. She wrote at once to say:

. . . how glad I shall be if you can have what you want. You're the only person I know whom I can imagine as her husband.

Also Vanessa hoped that Leonard was coming to her housewarming party at Asham. This he did–in fact he came to two housewarmings there; the first was, according to Virginia, on the

coldest day for 40 years; all the pipes were frozen; the birds were starving against the window panes; some had got in, & sat by the fire; the bottom fell out of the grates; suddenly Marjorie [Strachey], who was reciting Racine, stopped dead & said "I have got chicken pox."

The second and larger party took place a week later, with the Bells, Roger and Duncan, Adrian and Virginia, and again Leonard was there. But despite these gaieties Virginia was in distress. Leonard was anxious not to worry her, she should be free to go on as before; but, inevitably, he imposed a greater strain than had her previous suitors; never before had marriage presented itself as so real, so fair and yet so alarming a possibility. Her nerves gave way; at the end of January she had been in bed for a week–"a touch of my usual disease, in the head you know," and then, after the house-warmings, the symptoms became even more severe and she was obliged to go back to the hateful but convenient shelter of Twicken-ham and Miss Thomas. Vanessa wrote sadly to Leonard to tell him that he must not see or write to Virginia for the time being. She hoped that all would be well in the end. It was not until the end of February that Leonard was allowed to send Virginia a studiously boring letter and when at length she was released, Vanessa dis-missed him with gentle but firm benevolence to Somerset; here he received a letter from Virginia in which she declared:

I shall tell you wonderful stories of the lunatics. By the bye, they've elected me King. There can be no doubt about it. I summoned a con-clave, & made a proclamation about Christianity. I had other adventures, & some disasters, the fruit of a too passionate & enquiring disposition.

I avoided both love & hatred. I now feel very clear, calm, and move slowly, like one of the great big animals at the zoo. Knitting is the saving of life; Adrian has taken to it too. The wondrous thing is that it transmutes Stephenese into Saxonese, so much that the poor old creature thinks himself echoed, & suspects malice.

Today Lytton came to tea, & was very charming & amenable to all the strictures I made upon Cambridge life & the . . . ums.* He practically agreed with me that the Hearthrug was rotten, & the whales a-stink. I said you did too, & he groaned at the spread of light.

. . . I must go out & post this. I have got 5/- which I am going to spend on chocolates & a sleeping draught, if the shops are open, & I escape molestation. I shant want the sleeping draught–in any case.

Leonard cannot have found this letter reassuring; it has a crazy ring although some of its eccentricities probably result from private jokes rather than from a disturbed mind. A tepid lover might have wondered what kind of wife he was wooing and might well have withdrawn from the undertaking; but there was nothing in the least tepid in Leonard's love.

Virginia spent much of her time at Asham living very quietly and working at her novel. It was at this time that Ka Cox, herself in the throes of an agitating and unhappy love affair,† began to devote herself to Virginia and to show her gift for being comfortably useful.

Meanwhile Leonard's situation was becoming very difficult indeed. His feelings for Virginia were complicated by his feelings for Ceylon. His interest in the island and its people was already finding expression in a novel–*The Village in the Jungle*–which he began during the autumn of 1911; at the same time he had begun to wonder whether he ought to return as an agent of the Imperial Government and in fact he had growing doubts about the Empire itself. If Virginia would accept him, this problem would be solved automatically, for it would certainly be impossible to return to Ceylon *with* her; but how, if he lost her, could he go back *without* her? At the same time Colonial Administration had become his profession; he knew that he was good at it and he dreamed sometimes of devoting himself for the rest of his life to some remote Cingalese community; but he had other dreams which made the idea of such a lonely return to a distant station five thousand miles from Bloomsbury and Virginia melancholy indeed. The prospect

* A reference to the 'Apostles.'

† With Rupert Brooke, who had himself been having a nervous breakdown and wrote to Virginia begging her not to follow his example.

however had to be faced and, if Virginia could not love him, might have to be accepted. Virginia herself remained undecided and he was determined not to try to hurry her into a decision; he was therefore obliged to gamble on his fate, for his leave expired on 20 May and before then he had to decide what he should do.

On 14 February, realising that Virginia might need a long time in which to make up her mind, he wrote to the Secretary of State for the Colonies and asked for four months' extension of his leave in order to settle his private affairs. The Under-Secretary answered him and asked politely what these affairs might be. Leonard replied that he could not discuss them. In March the matter was referred to the Governor of Ceylon, who decided that unless Leonard could be more explicit the extension could not be granted. On 25 April Leonard sent in his resignation.

Such a renunciation could hardly be accomplished without some natural regrets. Whatever misgivings he may have felt cannot but have been increased by a week-end at Asham when, clearly, Leonard realised that things were going very wrong between him and Virginia. On 29 April, four days after he had despatched his final letter to the Under-Secretary, Leonard wrote in a rather different manner (for under the influence of passion his style became most uncharacteristically diffuse and unpunctuated) to Virginia:

. . . I want to see you to talk with you & now though I suppose I shouldn't I'm going to write utterly miserable what I should want to say to you & probably couldn't.

Since yesterday something seemed to rise up in you against me. It may be imagination on my part: if it is, you must forgive me: I dont think even you realise what it would mean to me. God, the happiness I've had by being with you & talking with you as I've sometimes felt it mind to mind together & soul to soul. I know clearly enough what I feel for you. It is not only physical love though it is that of course & I count it the least part of it, it isn't only that I'm only happy with you, . . . : It's that that I want your love too. It's true that I'm cold & reserved to other people; I dont feel affection even easily: but apart from love I'm fond of you as I've never been of anyone or thing in the world. We often laugh about your lovableness but you dont know how lovable you are. Its what really keeps me awake far more than any desire. It's what worries me now, tears me two ways sometimes—for I wouldn't have you marry me, much as I love you, if I thought it would bring you any unhappiness. Really this is true though it hurt me more than the worst physical pain your mere word, that you told Vanessa that probably you would never marry anyone.

There was much more. It was a long repetitive letter in which he seemed almost to be talking to himself, wandering from hope to despair and back again; but always beset by the fear that there was some dreadful psychological barrier which he could not surmount.

And while he was writing in this vein to Virginia a Semi-Official letter was being written to him on behalf of the Secretary of State offering him the means whereby the extension of leave might yet be granted. On receipt of this he wrote at once to Asham to ask Virginia if he might speak to her before sending a reply.

... what a career you're ruining! [she answered and then]:

It seems to me that I am giving you a great deal of pain–some in the most casual way– & therefore I ought to be as plain with you as I can, because half the time I suspect, you're in a fog which I dont see at all. Of course I *cant* explain what I feel–These are some of the things that strike me. The obvious advantages of marriage stand in my way. I say to myself, Anyhow, you'll be quite happy with him; & he will give you companionship; children, & a busy life. Then I say By God, I will not look upon marriage as a profession. The only people who know of it, all think it suitable; & that makes me scrutinise my own motives all the more. Then, of course, I feel angry sometimes at the strength of your desire. Possibly, your being a Jew comes in also at this point. You seem so foreign. And then I am fearfully unstable. I pass from hot to cold in an instant, without any reason; except that I believe sheer physical effort & exhaustion influence me.

All I can say is that in spite of these feelings, which go chasing each other all day long when I am with you, there is some feeling which is permanent, & growing. You want to know of course whether it will ever make me marry you. How can I say? I think it will, because there seems no reason why it shouldn't–But I dont know what the future will bring. I'm half afraid of myself. I sometimes feel that no one ever has or ever can share–something–Its the thing that makes you call me like a hill, or a rock. Again, I want everything–love, children, adventure, intimacy, work. (Can you make any sense out of this ramble? I am putting down one thing after another.) So I go from being half in love with you, & wanting you to be with me always, & know everything about me, to the extreme of wildness & aloofness. I sometimes think that if I married you, I could have everything– & then–is it the sexual side of it that comes between us? As I told you brutally the other day, I feel no physical attraction in you. There are moments–when you kissed me the other day was one–when I feel no more than a rock. And yet your caring for me as you do almost overwhelms me. It is so real, & so strange. Why should you? What am I really except a pleasant attractive creature? But its just because you care so much that I feel I've got to care before I marry you. I feel I must give you everything; & that if I cant, well, marriage would only be second-best for you as well as for me. If you can still go on, as before, letting me find my own way, that is what would please me best; & then we must both take the risks. But you have made me very happy too. We both of us want a marriage that is a tremendous living thing, always alive, always hot, not dead & easy in parts as most marriages are. We ask a great deal of life, dont we? Perhaps we shall get it; then how splendid! One doesn't get much said in a letter, does one?

But she had said enough; for all his doubts–and they must have been considerable–Leonard was now fixed in his determination not to return to Ceylon. His resignation was finally accepted on 7 May.

Now indeed his boats were really burnt and in fact she had not given him very much reason to hope. The best that she could say was that she was half in love with him, wanted to love him and to marry him if only she could. This, to be sure, was something quite different from her previous flirtations.

"No, I shan't float into a bloodless alliance with Lytton–though he is in some ways perfect as a friend, only he's a female friend." This she wrote in March 1912, and in the same letter:

I began life with a tremendous, absurd, ideal of marriage; then my bird's eye view of many marriages disgusted me, and I thought I must be asking what was not to be had. But that has passed too. Now I only ask for someone to make me vehement, and then I'll marry them!

But could Leonard make her "vehement"? Clearly she had the gravest doubts about it. It was something gained, however, that she was by this time anxious to give him every chance of doing so. When she returned again to Brunswick Square he was her neighbour. She began to know him thoroughly and could now understand how admirably his character suited hers. He had the intellectual eminence that she had found hitherto only in Lytton, and with it a reliable strength that Lytton did not possess. Leonard too was a writer, a novelist, and he had told her, after reading one of her manuscripts that one day she "might write something astonishingly good"; every morning at Brunswick Square each sat down to write 500 words–it was an agreed programme. And when their writing was done they were free; they might lunch together or wander out into the Square to sit quietly beneath the shade of the trees and find new pleasure in each other's company. The more she saw of him the better she liked him and the amenity of their intercourse may well have been increased by the fact that Vanessa, Clive and Roger were in Italy. It was an advantage to be out of sight of those quizzical spectators. From Italy Vanessa wrote: "I hope you aren't getting too much worried by the Leonard question. I should let it slide on & see what happens. Its sure to be all right in the end."

And it was all right. As their intimacy progressed Virginia's fears melted away, her confidence grew, her feeling for Leonard became more definite and at length, on 29 May, she was able to tell him that she loved him and would marry him. It was the wisest decision of her life.

APPENDIX A
Chronology

1878
26 March

Marriage of Leslie Stephen and Julia Prinsep Duckworth (*née* Jackson). They settle at 22 Hyde Park Gate, Kensington, where their four children are born

1879
30 May

Birth of Vanessa Stephen

1880
8 September

Birth of Julian Thoby Stephen

1881
September

Leslie Stephen buys the lease of Talland House, St Ives, where his family spend each summer from 1882 to 1894

1882
25 January

Birth of Adeline Virginia Stephen

November

Leslie Stephen begins work as the Editor of the *Dictionary of National Biography*

1883
27 October

Birth of Adrian Leslie Stephen

1888
April

The Stephen children all have whooping cough; in May they convalesce in Bath with their grandmother Mrs Jackson

1889/90
Winter

Margaret (Madge) Symonds, aged 20, stays at 22 Hyde Park Gate for some months

1891
January

Thoby goes to Evelyn's Preparatory School, Hillingdon

February

The *Hyde Park Gate News* begins publication

April

Leslie Stephen gives up the editorship of the *D.N.B.*

1892
January

Adrian goes to Evelyn's School

3 February

Death of J. K. Stephen

2 April

Death of Mrs Jackson at 22 Hyde Park Gate

1894

February	Vanessa and Virginia go to stay with Mr and Mrs G. F. Watts at Limner's Lease, Guildford
11 March	Death of Sir James Fitzjames Stephen
September	Thoby goes to Clifton College, Bristol

1895

Mid-February	Mrs Leslie Stephen ill with influenza
11 April	George, Stella and Gerald Duckworth go abroad
5 May	Death of Mrs Leslie Stephen
Summer	Stephen family at Freshwater, Isle of Wight
	Virginia's first breakdown
November	Caroline Emelia Stephen settles in Cambridge; Vanessa and Virginia stay with her there fairly often, particularly after Thoby goes up to Cambridge in 1899
	The lease of Talland House, St Ives, is sold

1896

	Vanessa begins to go to Drawing Classes
Summer	Stephen family at Hindhead House, Haslemere (let by Mrs John Tyndall)
22 August	Stella Duckworth accepts J. W. Hills, after two refusals
24 September	Adrian enters Westminster School
November	Virginia and Vanessa travel for a week in Northern France with George and Miss Duckworth (Aunt Minna)

1897

3 January	Virginia begins to keep a regular diary
8–13 February	Virginia goes to Bognor with Vanessa, Stella and Jack Hills
15 February	Virginia allowed to start lessons again
10 April	Marriage of Stella Duckworth to John Waller Hills at St Mary Abbots Church, Kensington
14–28 April	Stephen family at 9 St Aubyns, Hove; daily communication with the Fisher family
28 April	Return to 22 Hyde Park Gate to find Stella ill with peritonitis at her new home, 24 Hyde Park Gate
2 May	Stella pronounced "out of danger"
9 May	Virginia examined by Dr Seton; her lessons are stopped and she is prescribed milk and medicine
5 June	Stella again ill
22 June	Queen Victoria's Diamond Jubilee; Vanessa, Virginia and Thoby watch the procession from St Thomas's Hospital

APPENDIX A

1897

11 July	Virginia feverish and ill
19 July	Death of Stella
28 July–	Stephen family at Painswick Vicarage, Gloucestershire
23 September	
25 September–	Vanessa and Virginia go with Jack Hills to visit his
2 October	parents at Corby Castle, Carlisle
November	Virginia attends Greek and History classes at King's College, London

1898

1 January	Virginia concludes her diary
	Greek classes with Dr Warre at King's College
April	Stephen family spend Easter holidays at 9 St Aubyns, Hove
21/22 May	Vanessa and Virginia visit their aunts at Cambridge and Godmanchester
25 June	Vanessa and Virginia go to Clifton to see Thoby
9 July	Vanessa, Virginia and others go for the day to the Fens to hunt for moths
28 July	Marriage of William Wyamar Vaughan, Virginia's cousin, to Madge Symonds at All Saints, Ennismore Gardens; Vanessa a bridesmaid
August and September	Stephen family at the Manor House, Ringwood. Guests include Rezia, Guido and Nerino Rasponi, Charles and Cordelia Fisher, Susan Lushington, and Dermod O'Brien
21 September	Return to 22 Hyde Park Gate
17 October	Term begins at King's College; Virginia takes Latin with Miss Pater and Greek with Dr Warre

1899

12–28 April	Stephen family at 9 St Aubyns, Hove. Thoby has pneumonia
August and September	Stephen family at the Rectory, Warboys, Huntingdonshire. Guests include Emma and Margaret Vaughan, and Susan Lushington
21 September	Return to 22 Hyde Park Gate
3 October	Thoby enters Trinity College, Cambridge, together with Lytton Strachey, Saxon Sydney-Turner, Leonard Woolf and Clive Bell

1900

March	Virginia has measles
April	Easter(?) at 9 St Aubyns, Hove. Vanessa goes to Paris for a week on 18 April

1900

12(?) June	Virginia goes to the Trinity May Ball with Thoby and Vanessa, the Maitlands, and Cordelia Fisher
	Dictionary of National Biography completed in 63 volumes
6 July	Vanessa and Virginia go to Henley with Jack Hills
7 July	Vanessa and Virginia go with George Duckworth to Crabbet for the sale of Blunt's horses
August and September	Stephen family at Fritham House, Lyndhurst, Hampshire. Guests include Margaret Booth and Austen Chamberlain. Leslie Stephen in poor health
17 September	Return to 22 Hyde Park Gate
October	Virginia attends classes at King's College

1901

4 April	Stephen family spend a fortnight at Little Park, Lyme Regis; Madge and Will Vaughan near, staying with her mother, Mrs. A. J. A. Symonds
8–9 June	Vanessa and Virginia at Cambridge
1 August– mid-September	Stephen family go to Fritham House, Lyndhurst. Guests include Miss Pater, Filippo and Rezia Corsini (on their honeymoon), and Margery Snowden
September	Vanessa enters the Royal Academy Schools
October	Virginia takes up bookbinding
25–26 November	Vanessa and Virginia accompany Leslie Stephen to Oxford, where he receives an Hon. D.Litt.

1902

(?)January	Virginia starts private lessons in Greek with Miss Janet Case
1 April	Leslie, Thoby, Virginia and Adrian Stephen go to Hindhead Copse, Haslemere (Sir Frederick Pollock's house); Vanessa and George Duckworth go to Rome and Florence for three weeks; visit cut short by Leslie Stephen's illness
26 June	Leslie Stephen created K.C.B. in the Coronation Honours
31 July	Stephen family to Fritham House, Lyndhurst. Guests include Theodore Llewelyn Davies, Emma Vaughan, Margery Snowden, Clive Bell, and Violet Dickinson, who now becomes, and for many years remains, Virginia's most intimate friend
19 September	Return to 22 Hyde Park Gate. The Stephen family acquires a pianola
October	Adrian enters Trinity College, Cambridge; Thoby returns there for a further year

APPENDIX A

1902

12 December   Leslie Stephen operated by Sir Frederick Treves in a nursing home in Duchess Street, W.1

1903

6 January   Leslie Stephen returns to 22 Hyde Park Gate

February   Owing to his ill health, Leslie Stephen receives his insignia at home

16–30 April   Stephen family at Blatchfield, Chilworth, Surrey

31 July   Stephen family go to Netherhampton House, Salisbury. Guests include Susan Lushington, Violet Dickinson, Ronald Norman, J. W. Hills. The Fisher family stay in The Close, Salisbury. Visits to Wilton, Stonehenge, Romsey Abbey &c

18 September   Return to 22 Hyde Park Gate. Sir Leslie slowly dying

October   Virginia resumes Greek lessons with Miss Case; Vanessa at the Royal Academy Schools; Thoby reading for the Bar

14 November   Sir Leslie dictates the last entry in the 'Mausoleum Book' to Virginia

1904

22 February   Death of Sir Leslie Stephen

27 February– c. 25 March   Vanessa, Thoby, Adrian and Virginia with George Duckworth at Manorbier, Pembrokeshire

1 April   Vanessa, Thoby, Virginia and Adrian go to Venice with Gerald Duckworth

13 April   Stephens to Florence, where they are joined by Violet Dickinson. Adrian returns to Cambridge on 20 April; Thoby departs on a walking tour. Vanessa, Virginia and Violet Dickinson visit Prato, Siena, Genoa

1 May   Vanessa and Virginia with Violet Dickinson rejoin Thoby in Paris, where they are entertained by Clive Bell and Gerald Kelly, and meet Lady Beatrice Thynne. Visits to Rodin's and Kelly's studios

9 May   Vanessa and Virginia, escorted by George Duckworth, return to 22 Hyde Park Gate

10 May   Beginning of Virginia's second serious breakdown; at first she is under the care of Dr Savage and three nurses; later with Nurse Traill she spends almost three months at Violet Dickinson's house, Burnham Wood, Welwyn; here she also has scarlet fever

2nd half of August   Stephens at The Manor House, Teversal, Nottinghamshire, for the summer holiday; Virginia with Nurse Traill rejoins her family there; she is convalescent and able to study a little and go for walks

1904

September	Violet Dickinson stays at Teversal
10 September	Marriage of George Duckworth to Lady Margaret Herbert at Dulverton, Somerset. Vanessa, Thoby and Adrian attend
Late September	Margery Snowden and Clive Bell stay at Teversal
c. 8 October	Stephens return to London. Virginia and Vanessa stay with the Booths during the move from 22 Hyde Park Gate to 46 Gordon Square, Bloomsbury
c. 18 October	Virginia goes to Cambridge to stay with her aunt Caroline Emelia Stephen at The Porch; she is helping F. W. Maitland with his *Life* of her father
8–18 November	Virginia at 46 Gordon Square; begins to send articles to Mrs Lyttelton, editor of the Women's Supplement of *The Guardian*. Leonard Woolf dines with the Stephens on 17th before sailing for Ceylon
18–29 November	Virginia stays with Madge and Will Vaughan at Giggleswick; returns to 46 Gordon Square
3–10 December	Virginia at The Porch, Cambridge; returns to Gordon Square
14 December	Virginia's first publication, an unsigned review, printed in *The Guardian*
21 December	The Stephens go to Lane End, Bank, near Lyndhurst (lent by Miss Minna Duckworth), for a Christmas holiday

1905

4 January	Return to Gordon Square
14 January	Virginia 'discharged cured' by Dr Savage; she undertakes to give a weekly class at Morley College
16 February	Thoby Stephen starts 'Thursday Evenings' at 46 Gordon Square
1 March	Formal housewarming party at 46 Gordon Square
5 March	The 'Sultan of Zanzibar' hoax by Adrian, Horace Cole and others, at Cambridge
29 March	Virginia and Adrian sail from Liverpool to Oporto by Booth Line, landing 5 April; they visit Lisbon, Seville and Granada; on 20th, they embark at Lisbon on the SS *Madeirensa* and reach Liverpool on Easter Sunday, 23 April
24 April	Return to 46 Gordon Square
June and July	Virginia pays brief visits to Herbert and Lettice Fisher at Oxford; to Cambridge (Trinity College Ball); to the Freshfields at Forest Row Sussex; and to Sir George Young's family at Formosa Place, Cookham
	Clive Bell proposes to Vanessa and is refused

APPENDIX A

1905

10 August Stephens go to Trevose View, Carbis Bay (near St Ives) for the summer holidays; they are visited there by Kitty and Leo Maxse, Gerald Duckworth, Imogen Booth, Sylvia Milman, Jack Hills and Saxon Sydney-Turner

5 October Return to 46 Gordon Square

1905/6

Autumn and Winter All four Stephens in residence at Gordon Square: Virginia writing, reviewing and teaching at Morley College, Thoby and Adrian studying Law. Vanessa organises the Friday Club. 'Thursday Evenings' continue

1906

12–25 April Virginia at Giggleswick, Yorkshire, lodging with Mrs Turner, near Madge and Will Vaughan; Vanessa joins her on 21st after painting Lord Robert Cecil's portrait at Chelwood Gate

June and July Virginia pays brief visits to her aunt at Cambridge; to Lady Robert Cecil at Chelwood Gate; to Violet Dickinson at Welwyn; and to Eton for the wedding of Desmond MacCarthy and Mary Warre Cornish on 10 July

3–31 August Vanessa and Virginia at Blo' Norton Hall, East Harling, Norfolk; Thoby and Adrian stay two days, then return to London and leave for Trieste on 10 August. Guests include George Duckworth, Hester Ritchie and Emma Vaughan

8 September Virginia, Vanessa and Violet Dickinson leave London for Greece; they meet Thoby and Adrian at Olympia on 13th. They all go *via* Corinth to Athens, thence to Nauplia by boat for Epidaurus, Tiryns and Mycenae; Vanessa ill at Corinth on return journey

1–5 October Virginia and her brothers visit the Noels at Achmetaga, Euboea; Vanessa goes with Violet Dickinson to Athens, where she is ill for two weeks

21 October Thoby returns to England; the others go to Constantinople, where Vanessa is again ill

29 October Vanessa, Virginia, Adrian, and Violet Dickinson return to England by Orient Express, reaching London on 1 November

November Thoby and Vanessa both ill in bed at 46 Gordon Square

20 November Thoby Stephen dies of typhoid fever

22 November Vanessa agrees to marry Clive Bell

1906

December | Walter Headlam offers to criticise Virginia's writings, and asks to dedicate his translation of the *Agamemnon* to her

21 December | Virginia and Adrian go to Lane End, Bank, for Christmas. Vanessa is at Cleeve House, Seend, Wiltshire, with Clive Bell's family

31 December | Virginia and Adrian go to Cleeve House

1907

3 January | Virginia and Adrian return to 46 Gordon Square for a night, and then make a brief visit to the Booths at Gracedieu Manor, Leicestershire

7 February | Marriage of Vanessa Stephen to Clive Bell at St Pancras Registry Office

February | Virginia house-hunting. 16–18th she visits Caroline Emelia Stephen at Cambridge; she also stays with Violet Dickinson at Welwyn. Meetings and correspondence with Walter Headlam

23–25 March | Virginia and Adrian sleep at Violet Dickinson's house in Manchester Square while their move to 29 Fitzroy Square takes place

28 March | Virginia and Adrian go to Paris with Clive and Vanessa Bell; meetings with Duncan Grant

10 April | Virginia and Adrian return to London and take up residence in their new home, 29 Fitzroy Square, W.1

May–July | Virginia pays brief visits to Cambridge and to Cleeve House, Seend

8 August | Virginia and Adrian go to The Steps, Playden, Rye, for the summer holidays; Beatrice Thynne, Pernel Strachey and Katherine Stephen each stay a few days

26 August | Bells to Curfew Cottage, Rye; Margery Snowden, Walter Lamb, Lytton Strachey and Saxon Sydney-Turner stay at Playden or Rye

26 September | Virginia returns to 29 Fitzroy Square. She resumes teaching at Morley College; and agrees to sit to Francis Dodd for a portrait

October–December | Virginia works on her novel (*Melymbrosia*); she and Adrian begin 'Thursday Evenings' at Fitzroy Square; she stays with H. A. L. and Lettice Fisher at Oxford; and decides to give up teaching

21 December | Inception of the Play Reading Society at 46 Gordon Square: Vanessa and Clive Bell, Virginia and Adrian Stephen, Lytton Strachey and Saxon Sydney-Turner; nine subsequent meetings till 24 May 1908

APPENDIX A

1908

4 February	Birth of Julian Heward Bell at 46 Gordon Square
17 April	Virginia goes to Trevose House, St Ives; joined there by Adrian on 23rd and Bells on 24th
2 May	Virginia returns to 29 Fitzroy Square
Summer	Virginia and Adrian have German lessons with Miss Daniel
20 June	Death of Walter Headlam
July	Day visits by Virginia to her aunt Lady Stephen at Godmanchester, and to Violet Dickinson at Welwyn. Sits to Francis Dodd
1–17 August	Virginia (with two dogs) in lodgings in Wells; expeditions to Glastonbury and Cheddar; and twice to meet Clive and Vanessa Bell in Bath
18–31 August	Virginia lodges at Manorbier, Pembrokeshire; expedition to Tenby. 100 pages of *Melymbrosia* completed
3 September	Virginia goes with the Bells to Italy; they stay in Siena and Perugia; and visit Pavia and Assisi. On the 24th they return to Paris for a week
1 October	Return to London. 'Thursday Evenings' at Fitzroy Square begin again
27 October	Play Reading Society resumes its meetings after five months' break; five meetings during the winter
12(?)–17 November	Virginia and Adrian at The Lizard with Lytton Strachey
November	Virginia pays a brief visit to Lady Stephen at Godmanchester
Christmas	Virginia and Adrian at 29 Fitzroy Square

1909

15 January	Last meeting of the Play Reading Society until its revival on 29 October 1914
Late January– mid-March	Letter-writing game with Virginia, Vanessa and Clive Bell, Lytton Strachey, Walter Lamb, Saxon Sydney-Turner and Adrian Stephen
Early February	Seven chapters of *Melymbrosia* read and criticised by Clive Bell
13–15 February	Virginia stays with the H. A. L. Fishers at Oxford
17 February	Lytton Strachey proposes marriage to Virginia
End of February	Virginia's last visit to her aunt Caroline Emelia Stephen at Cambridge
2(?) March	Virginia goes with the Bells to The Lizard; she returns to Fitzroy Square on the 9th; the Bells remain until the 19th

1909

30 March	Virginia dines for the first time with Lady Ottoline Morrell
7 April	Death of Caroline Emelia Stephen; Virginia attends her cremation at Golders Green on 14th; is left a legacy of £2500
23 April	Virginia goes with Clive and Vanessa Bell to Florence
9 May	Virginia returns alone to 29 Fitzroy Square
15–17 May	Virginia goes to Cambridge to stay with the Verralls; Hilton Young's proposal(?)
22–24 May	Virginia and Adrian stay with the Freshfields at Forest Row
6 June–16 July	Adrian keeps a diary
Summer	Lady Ottoline Morrell comes to 'Thursday Evenings' at 29 Fitzroy Square
5 August	Virginia goes to Bayreuth with Adrian and Saxon Sydney-Turner for the Wagner Festival
22 August	They go on to Dresden
3(?) September	Virginia and Adrian return to 29 Fitzroy Square
10–13 September	Virginia meets the Bells in Salisbury; she returns to London, the Bells to Cleeve House
c. 16 September– 2 October	Virginia at Studland, where she rents a cottage near the Bells' lodgings; Adrian comes; and Walter Lamb stays with the Bells from 23rd September
10 November	*The Cornhill* rejects *Memoirs of a Novelist*
27–29 November	Virginia stays with the George Darwins at Cambridge; she attends a performance of *The Wasps*; lunches and spends the afternoon with Lytton Strachey before returning to London
24–28 December	Virginia alone at Lelant, Cornwall

1910

January	Virginia volunteers to work for Women's Suffrage
10 February	'The Dreadnought Hoax'
25 February	Roger Fry talks to The Friday Club
c. 5–10 March	Virginia with Clive and Vanessa Bell makes an unpremeditated excursion to Lelant, Cornwall; Virginia ill in bed after her return
26 March	Virginia goes with the Bells to lodgings at Harbour View, Studland, for three weeks' rest
16 April	Virginia returns to 29 Fitzroy Square; her health remains uncertain throughout the summer
Early June	Virginia with Adrian visits George and Margaret Duckworth for the day at Chalfont St Giles; also goes with Clive Bell for a day with the Youngs at Formosa Place, Cookham

APPENDIX A

1910

7 June — Virginia goes with the Bells, their child and domestic staff to The Moat House, Blean, near Canterbury

21 June — Vanessa returns to London and consults Dr Savage about Virginia's health

30 June–
c. 10 August — Virginia undergoes a rest cure at Miss Thomas's private Nursing Home, Burley Park, Twickenham

c. 16 August1
6 September — Virginia goes on a walking tour in Cornwall with Miss Jean Thomas

19 August — Birth of Claudian [Quentin] Bell at 46 Gordon Square

6 September — Virginia returns to London

10 September — Virginia goes to Studland with Saxon Sydney-Turner to join Clive and Julian Bell; Vanessa and baby arrive on 13th. Visitors include Desmond and Mary (Molly) MacCarthy, Sydney and Alice Waterlow, Marjorie Strachey, and H. T. J. Norton

10 October — Virginia returns to 29 Fitzroy Square

15–18 October — Virginia stays at Court Place, Iffley, Oxford, with Pearsall Smiths and Costelloes

8 November–
15 January — The first Post-Impressionist exhibition (*Manet and the Post-Impressionists*), organised by Roger Fry, shown at the Grafton Galleries, London

November–
December — Virginia resumes her activity on behalf of Women's Suffrage; she visits Miss Thomas at Twickenham; she spends a week-end with the Cornishes at Eton; and one with Violet Dickinson at Welwyn

24 December — Virginia and Adrian stay at The Pelham Arms, Lewes, for a week; she visits Saxon Sydney-Turner and his parents at Brighton; Miss Thomas joins her for a day; she finds a house to rent in Firle

1911

1 January — Virginia and Adrian return to 29 Fitzroy Square. During January she takes possession of, and starts to furnish, Little Talland House, Firle

19–23 January — Virginia stays at Court Place, Iffley, and Bagley Wood, near Oxford, with Ray and Karin Costelloe and Marjorie Strachey; she meets Katherine (Ka) Cox

4–6 February — Virginia and Vanessa at Firle completing the furnishing of Little Talland House

April — Virginia at Firle with two servants; her guests include Ray Costelloe, Ka Cox. Elinor Darwin. Eight chapters of *Melymbrosia* completed

c. 22 April — Virginia sets out for Broussa, Turkey, where Vanessa, travelling with Clive Bell, Roger Fry and H. T. J. Norton, has fallen ill

1911

29 April	Virginia with Bells and Roger Fry return by Orient Express to London
May-June	Virginia mostly at 29 Fitzroy Square, with visits to Firle, where Ka Cox stays with her; to Cambridge for the wedding of Jacques Raverat and Gwen Darwin on 27 May; and to Durbins, Guildford (Roger Fry's house)
3 July	Leonard Woolf, on leave from Ceylon, dines with the Bells at 46 Gordon Square; Virginia, Duncan Grant and Walter Lamb come in after dinner
July	Virginia and Adrian plan to give up 29 Fitzroy Square in favour of a new system of living; they consider sharing a house in Bedford Square with friends
20 July	Virginia and Walter Lamb make an excursion to Richmond Park; his 'declaration'
22–25 July	Virginia at Firle; Janet Case to stay for two days
27 July and 9 August	Virginia visits Vanessa at Millmead Cottage, Guildford, where she is convalescing
12–14 August	Virginia stays with Philip and Lady Ottoline Morrell at Peppard Common
14–19 August	Virginia stays at The Old Vicarage, Grantchester, with Rupert Brooke
19–26 August	Virginia at Firle with her servants, Sophia and Maud
c. 27–30 August	Virginia and Ka Cox go to camp near Clifford Bridge, Drewsteignton, Devon, with Rupert Brooke, Maynard Keynes and others
31 August	Virginia back at Firle
16–19 September	Leonard Woolf and Marjorie Strachey to stay with Virginia at Firle
19–27 September	Virginia in lodgings at 2 Harmony Cottages, Studland, near the Bells; Lytton Strachey and Roger Fry with his family also at Studland
October	Virginia engages in negotiations over Asham House, Beddingham, and 38 Brunswick Square, Bloomsbury. She goes to the *Ring* cycle at Covent Garden; and sees Leonard Woolf frequently
4–6 November	Virginia goes to Cambridge to stay with Francis and Frances Cornford
11–14 November	Virginia with Vanessa and Adrian (and Duncan Grant?) go to Firle; they go to see and measure Asham House
14–19 November	Virginia sleeps at 46 Gordon Square during the establishment of her new home
20 November	Virginia starts living at 38 Brunswick Square, W.C.1, a house shared with Adrian, Maynard Keynes, Duncan Grant and, after 4 December, Leonard Woolf

APPENDIX A

1911

9 December	Virginia writes to Sydney Waterlow to say that she cannot love him. To Firle for the week-end with Vanessa
Christmas Day	Luncheon party at 46 Gordon Square: the Bells, Virginia, Leonard Woolf, Maynard Keynes and Duncan Grant. Adrian is in a Nursing Home

1912

11 January	Leonard Woolf comes up from Somerset and proposes to Virginia at 38 Brunswick Square
13–15 January	Virginia at Firle
16–19 January	Virginia goes to Niton, Isle of Wight, to stay with Vanessa; on her return to London she falls ill
3–5 February	Virginia's housewarming party at Asham, with Adrian, Marjorie Strachey and Leonard Woolf
9–12 February	The Bells' housewarming party at Asham, with Virginia, Adrian, Duncan Grant, Roger Fry and Leonard Woolf
16 February	Virginia enters Miss Thomas's Nursing Home at Twickenham for a rest cure
28 February	Virginia goes to Asham for further rest and quiet
March	Virginia spends three week-ends at Asham: one with Vanessa, one with Ka Cox, and on the 16th with Vanessa, Adrian, Leonard Woolf, Roger Fry and Marjorie Strachey
9 March	Virginia sees a psychologist, Dr Wright
April	Virginia mostly at Asham; her guests there include Leonard Woolf and Ka Cox
2 May	Virginia returns to 38 Brunswick Square
7 May	Leonard Woolf's resignation accepted by the Colonial Office
29 May	Virginia Stephen agrees to marry Leonard Woolf

Report on Teaching at Morley College

This report, a heavily corrected draft in Virginia's handwriting, is headed:

July 1905

This is the season for another report upon that class of working women whom I have already mentioned.

It was to be a class of history this time; in spite of the fact that those in authority looked rather coldly on it; history they told me, was the least popular subject in the College; at the same time they could not confute me when I asserted that it was also one of the most important. My class it is true dropped instantly to half its previous size; I had four instead of a possible eight; but then those four were regular attendants, & they came with one serious desire in common. The change then, was to my liking.

I have already described those four working women; so that my remarks this time are merely a development of that tentative sketch. Only in one instance did I find that I must reconsider my judgment. That Miss Williams whom I described as the 'least interesting of my class' 'rather handsome & well dressed–with wits sharpened in the streets, inattentive & critical' came to the first history class, & to my surprise hardly missed a Wednesday throughout the term. One night, too, I so far cornered her as to make her reveal herself; she then told me that she was a reporter on the staff of a Religious paper–reported sermons in shorthand–did typewriting, & also wrote reviews of books; the germ of a literary lady in short! & a curious one. Here was literature stripped of the least glamour of art: words were handled by this woman as that other one manipulated the bottles of a patent mouth wash. She was a writing machine to be set in motion by the editor. For some reason, unconnected with the author, the notice was to be favourable or unfavourable; but to record this notice it was not necessary by any means to read the book; that indeed would be impossible, considering the number of reviews to be turned out; but with a little practise it was easy to get sufficient material to support your statements by a rapid turning of the pages with a keen eye; quotations picked up at random need only be linked together by a connecting word, & the column was filled out of someone else's pocket. But at the same time, as she made no pretence that her work was of any higher nature than this so there seemed to be no reason to condemn it; indeed she was certainly of a higher level of intelligence than the other women.

The three other girls have been described already: the two friends, &

one of the two sisters, who came last term. This sister, Burke was her name, had been as I found, writing that account of her own life which I had suggested before. It did not take up many pages, & only described certain memories of childhood; it was a curious little production, floundering among long words, & involved periods, with sudden ponderous moral sentiments thrown into the midst. But she could write grammatical sentences, which followed each other logically enough; & she had evidently some facility of expression; in other circumstances I suppose, she would have been a writer!

The faithful pair of friends sat receptive & open mouthed as usual. Meanwhile, I had to administer each week some semblance of English history. Each week I read through a reign or two in Freeman or Green; noting as I went. Each time I tried to include one good 'scene' upon which I hoped to concentrate their interest. I talked from notes, with as little actual reading as possible. I found it not difficult to skim along fluently–though superficially; & I tried to make the real interest of history–as it appears to me–visible to them. Then they were provided with a sheet of hard dates to take home with them; so that they might have something solid to cling to in the vagueness of my speech. So we made our way through Early British, & Romans, & Angles Saxons & Danes, & Normans, till we were on the more substantial ground of the Plantagenet Kings. I do not know how many of the phantoms that passed through that dreary school room left any image of themselves upon the women; I used to ask myself how is it *possible* to make them feel the flesh & blood in these shadows? So thin is the present to them; must not the past remain a spectre always? Of course it was not possible in the way I took to make them know anything accurately; my task, as I conceived it, was rather to prepare the soil for future sowers. Pictures I showed them, & I lent them books; sometimes they seemed to gape not in mere impotent wonder, but to be trying to piece together what they heard; to seek reasons; to connect ideas. On the whole they were possessed of more intelligence than I expected; though that intelligence was almost wholly uncultivated. But of this I am convinced; what it would not be hard to educate them sufficiently to give them a new interest in life; They have tentacles languidly stretching forth from their minds, feeling vaguely for substance, & easily applied by a guiding hand to something that [they] could really grasp.

But like all other educational establishments, Morley College has to effect compromises & to prefer the safeness of mediocrity to the possible dangers of a high ideal. That is one way of saying that they would rather that a great number should learn a less valuable subject, like English Composition, than that a few should be encouraged to the study of English History. Accordingly I am to stop at King John: & turn my mind next term to essay writing & the expression of ideas. Meanwhile, my four women can hear eight lectures on the French Revolution if they wish to continue their historical learning. And what,

I ask, will be the use of that? Eight lectures dropped into their minds, like meteors from another sphere impinging on this planet, & dissolving in dust again. Such disconnected fragments will these eight lectures be: to people who have absolutely no power of receiving them as part of a whole, & applying them to their proper ends.

(MH/A 22)

Virginia Woolf and the Authors of *Euphrosyne*

Euphrosyne was published in the summer of 1905. Virginia wrote the following commentary on its authors and dated it 21st May 1906. The manuscript contains a great many deletions and corrections (which I have not attempted to reproduce); it appears to be unfinished.

Among all the advantages of that sex which is soon, we read, to have no [dis]advantages,* there is much to be said surely for that respectable custom which allows the daughter to educate herself at home, while the son is educated by others abroad.

At least I am fain to think that system beneficial which preserves her from the omniscience, the early satiety, the melancholy self satis-faction which a training at either of our great universities produces in her brothers. You see a pink cheeked boy whose only talk is of cricket, & whose most ardent admiration is kept for some champion of the ball or bat, enter upon his first term at Oxbridge, & you predict in your mild maidenly way, all kinds of manly triumphs for him there, & assure him that this will be the happiest time in his life, that is the phrase which parents use, & Aunts, & elderly bachelors; & from this un-animous Chorus one would think that life was a very poor business save for those three or four years at College & that if he failed to enjoy those, you had not much to promise him in this world or the next—unless indeed there is some kind of university in the fields of Paradise.

But it must be either that this is one of those parental fictions, like the existence of the Good Santa Claus, with which it is thought fit to veil the dreary truth from the eyes of the young, or, times have changed very much since our parents & uncles & elderly bachelor friends were happy at Oxbridge.

For when those three years of happiness are over, the result is one that suggests that the word has taken on a new, & peculiar meaning. They come from their University, pale, preoccupied & silent; as though in their three years absence, some awful communication had been made them, & they went burdened with a secret too dreadful to impart. Such a one is S.T., & G.L.S. & C.B. & W.L.;† others I might name if I chose to continue the dismal catalogue. But they entered the College, young & ardent & conceited; pleased with themselves, but so well pleased with the world that their vanity might be forgiven them. They return not less impressed with their own abilities indeed, but that

---

* The text reads: ~~There is certainly one advantage in~~ Among all the ~~dis~~ advantages of that sex which is soon, we read, to have no advantages.

† i.e. Saxon Sydney-Turner, Lytton Strachey, Clive Bell and Walter Lamb.

is the last illusion that is left to them. The things they once found pleasing, please them no longer; they neither play nor work. They fail to pass their Examinations, because they say, that success is failure & they despise success.

It is perhaps because they fear to fall a victim to its snares that they are generally silent, & express for the most part a serene & universal ignorance; which does not disqualify them however to pronounce the opinions of others absurd.

They admire, however, the works of minor French poets, & crown certain English authors with the epithets "supreme" & "astounding"; but if the public show signs of appreciating the same things [they dexterously transfer their praise to some more obscure head].*

But their most permanent & unqualified admiration is reserved for the works which, unprinted as yet, "unprintable" they proudly give you to understand, repose in the desks of their immediate friends. For it is characteristic of them, that they live closely in one 'set', & made but few acquaintances outside it. They met on Sundays, when it was pleasant to picture the respectable world on its knees, & read these astoundingly brilliant & immoral productions; or, with the help of a table cloth, acted the clergyman himself, & annihilated the Christian faith in the doctrines that fell from his lips.

Some few songs & sonnets that were embedded in these gigantic works, were graciously issued to the public some little time ago, carelessly, as though the Beast could hardly appreciate such fare, even when simplified & purified to suit his coarse but innocent palate, but ought perhaps to be allowed the chance of tasting it. The poets sang of Love & Death, & Cats, & Duchesses,† as other poets have sung before, & may, unless the race is extinct, sing yet again. [It was melodious/ But such sadness, they said had never been known before; & it was/ the work was/ it marked an era; a decadence that was beyond the decadence of Swinburne himself. its significance was something they only could understand/ so tremendous.‡] But when taxed with their melancholy the poets confessed that such sadness had never been known, & marked the last & lowest tide of decadence.

(MH/A 13b)

* This phrase is partly deleted in the text but seems necessary.

† The allusion is to Lytton Strachey's poem *The Cat*. Love and Death abound in the pages of *Euphrosyne*, and the *Song* by Walter Lamb is addressed to a Duchess.

‡ These phrases are deleted in the original text.

APPENDIX D
Clive Bell and the Writing of
The Voyage Out

Virginia Stephen to Clive Bell

29, Fitzroy Square, W. [n.d.]

My dear Clive,
   Will you think me a great bore if I turn to the dreary subject again,
& ask you whether you have anything to say about that unfortunate
work? I have a feeling at this moment that it is all a mistake, & I believe
you could tell me.
   At any rate I put myself in your hands with great confidence: I dont
really think you will be bored by my demands, & I believe you do
speak the truth.
   At the same time, I groan over my egoism that wont let me or anyone
else think of better things.

yr aff^{nt} AVS

Dont bother to write at length–in fact, dont write if you had rather not.

Clive Bell to Virginia Stephen

Sunday night.   46, Gordon Square,
[? October 1908]   Bloomsbury.

My dear Virginia,
   I find it hard to believe that you really attach importance to my
opinion of your work. But to relieve myself rather than you I send
this note which will be of greater interest when you have recovered
your manuscript.
   To my apprehension, the wonderful thing that I looked for is there
unmistakeably: one can always recognise it when one gets that glimpse
of the thrilling real beneath the dull apparent. Surely there can't be the
least doubt, even in your own mind, about Geranium's (sic) entry with
his wife Lucila (or Helen), page 36, and the description on page seven,
nor yet about the Daloways' first night on board and pages 76 & 77.
So, in spite of the immaturity–crudity even–and some places jagged
like saws, that make my sensitive parts feel very much what the Christian

207

martyrs must have felt, I believe this first novel will become a work that counts. 'Become', I say, because seven chapters never are, or never ought to be, a work of any sort.

Of course there are things such as page, 23, spots in the Sir T.B. conversation, ('Death soft and dark as velvet'), page 33, and other simillar or smaller excrescences, which fill me with horror and some fear; and I don't know how far they can be mended.

To give a sense of matter need one make so much use of words like 'solid' and 'block'–they become irritating: imaginations too, must they glimmer & shimmer always or be quite so often 'shadowy'.

But the style, the general form, (in its extreme oddity the lucidity of which however I believe I can appreciate & which will, I fancy develope & unroll itself quite harmoniously) the presentation of your ideas, seem to me an immense improvement on all your other descriptive writing. The first 3 pages are so beautiful as almost to reconcile me with your most feverish prose.

There are a hundred things that I long to talk or ask about, but I have time for this only; your power (to which I think I have always done justice) of lifting the veil & showing inanimate things in the mystery & beauty of their reality appears once or twice to equal–to excel rather–well never mind–; it is all very exciting and delightful, but in a day or two I hope to feel more securely critical.

Yrs ever
CB.

Clive Bell to Virginia Stephen

Friday   46, Gordon Square,
[? 5 February 1909]   Bloomsbury.

My dear Virginia,

if you really expected me to be disappointed with Melymbrosia, it must have been, I suppose, that you thought I might be disappointed with the last volume, that I should feel you have compromised with the Conventional & fallen away from the high–transcendent almost,– task, that you set yourself at the beginning. I do not feel that, and presently I will tell you why. My quarrels are all, or nearly all, with Vol. 1. and that is still so far from being finished that one hesitates to criticise it. But I do think it will be a difficult matter to make it supple, and I don't know that I like the new draft as well as the old. We have often talked about the atmosphere that you want to give; that atmosphere can only be insinuated, it cannot be set down in so many words. In the old form it was insinuated throughout, in the new it is more definite, more obvious, &, to use a horrid expression–'less felt'–by the reader I mean.

To give an example; Rachel's day-dreams flood one's mind with an exquisitely delicate sense of Rachel on a ship, alone; the sea-gulls conjure up nothing but rather commonplace visions of sea-voyages for health & pleasure. The conversations, stiff though they were, created wonderful pictures of the speakers' surroundings; the conversations have for the most part gone, and that first difficult forenoon has gained in consequence; but the two letters from Helen, most interesting in themselves, are as stiff and unreal as the old conversations, and coming on the mind in the state which you have been able to produce, by what has gone before, they seem inappropriate. For the first volume, I suggest, less definition, and a reversion to the original plan of giving an atmosphere, which atmosphere you must remember has got to serve through chapters of incident & criticism which are coming later. In this part of your book I shouldn't bother much about the characters of your people; I think they tell their own story beautifully along with the ship, and the less one knows about their antecedents the better, perhaps. Then, I must tell you again that I think the first part too didactic, not to say priggish. Our views about men & women are doubtless quite different, and the difference does'nt matter much; but to draw such sharp & marked contrasts between the subtle, sensitive, tactful, gracious, delicately perceptive, & perspicacious women, & the obtuse, vulgar, blind, florid, rude, tactless, emphatic, indelicate, vain, tyrannical, stupid men, is not only rather absurd, but rather bad art, I think.

To sum up my animadversions, then;–I feel, in the first part, that to give more 'humanity' to your work, you have sacrificed the 'inhuman',–the super-natural–the magic which I thought as beautiful as anything that had been written these hundred years; in so far as the book is purely Virginia, Virginia's view of the world is perfectly artistic, but is'nt there some danger that she may forget that an artist, like God, should create without coming to conclusions; lastly, I think you should be careful not to wonder how some other novelist would have written your book,–as if he could have written it! If you can manage to extract all the meaning from this short paragraph (about 6 pages full) you will know all I have to say against Melymbrosia.

I can now say, with a clear conscience, what I really think about your novel–that it is wonderful. As I read it I was perhaps most struck by what I took for the improvement in its prose. It seemed to me that you gave your words a force that one expects to find only in the best poetry; they came as near the truth underlying them as it is possible for words to come I should think. This refers, of course, to particular passages; in some places the style was quite bald, but these I took to be mere notes; I don't think I need retract a word of my praise from any at all finished passage. Though Helen is by far the best character, the Dalloways enjoy the advantage of being more like the people whom the world knows. They are very amusing, and more than life-like; them you have stripped quite naked at all events, I am stunned & amazed by your insight, though you know I have always believed in it. Of Helen I cannot trust myself to speak, but I suppose you will make Vanessa believe in herself. Rachel is, of course, mysterious & remote, some strange, wild, creature who has come to give up half her secret; but she is quite convincing as one reads, and in no true sense of the word unreal. I am not so sure about Valentine & Vinrace, though they are both good characters & interesting. Now about the last part, it is of course, at first sight, less startling – more customary. But the whole situation is seen in such a new, such a curiously personal way, by Rachel, that I think it is really the best part of the book. I cannot tell you how interested I am in all the new old figures – the inmates of the hotel – seen so differently by Rachel, as entities, and as combinations. At first I thought it a mistake to put Rachel outside the hotel, later I saw the genius of it. And then the pic-nic; that is why I say the novel has lost none of its early promise. Honestly, I think it challenges comparison with Box Hill & holds its own, & something more. Nothing could be more alive, or more subtle. Nothing is said to show that it was just half a failure, but everybody feels it, except Rachel who is thinking about better things. How on earth, by telling us what it was like at noon, do you show us what it was like at five, at sunset, and at night? Believe me the pic-nic is your master-piece, it surpasses anything in the first volume. Now, how are you going to finish it? Surely the Dalloways must appear again, & the Mary Jane? Unless, indeed, you have invented some new, undream't of form? Well, I shall see some day.

If parts of your novel are notes, what is to be said about this letter? You must consider it the merest jotting down of stray ideas. It is sure to be full of stupidities, and almost unintelligible I'm afraid in parts. I have had no time to give it a semblance of form or even to find the right word, I hope you will be able to make something of it, but besides being rather unintelligible it is probably also illegible.

Yours affectionately

CB

Virginia Stephen to Clive Bell

29 Fitzroy
Sunday [? 7 February 1909]

My dear Clive,

You are really angelic to take so much pains to give reasons & advice. They seem to me excellent; for you have laid your finger on spots already suspected by me. I will only offer some explanation of the wretched first volume. Those bare passages of biography were not meant to remain in the text: they are notes, to solidify my own conception of the peoples characters. I thought it a good plan to write them down; but having served their purpose, they shall go. Helens letter also was an experiment. When I read the thing over (one very grey evening) I thought it so flat & monotonous that I did not even feel 'the atmosphere': certainly there was no character in it. Next morning I proceeded to slash & rewrite, in the hope of animating it; & (as I suspect, for I have not re-read it) destroyed the one virtue it had–a kind of continuity: for I wrote it originally in a dream like state, which was at any rate, unbroken. My intention now is to write straight on, & finish the book; & then, if that day ever comes, to catch if possible the first imagination & go over the beginning again with broad touches, keeping much of the original draft, & trying to deepen the atmosphere–Giving the feel of running water, & not much else. I have kept all the pages I cut out; so the thing can be re-constructed precisely as it was. Your objection, that my prejudice against men makes me didactic 'not to say priggish', has not quite the same force with me; I don't remember what I said that suggests the remark; I daresay it came out, without my knowledge: but I will bear it in mind. I never meant to preach, & agree that like God, one should'nt. Possibly, for psychological reasons which seem to me very interesting, a man, in the present state of the world, is not a very good judge of his sex; and a 'creation' may seem to him 'didactic'. I admit the justice of your hint that sometimes I have had an inkling of the way the book might be written by other people. It is very difficult to fight against it; as difficult as to ignore the opinion of one's probable readers–I think I gather courage as I go on. The only possible reason for writing down all this, is that it represents roughly a view of one's own. My boldness terrifies me. I feel I have so few of the gifts that make novels amusing.

I expect your praise is immensely exaggerated: you (I guess) have so much more of the dramatic instinct than I have that you see it into my scenes. But I take praise very gratefully; long for some assurance that all my words are'nt vapour. They accumulate behind me in such masses– dreadful, if they are nothing but muddy water. I think myself that the last part is really the best; at least I have written it with far greater relish, & with the sense of having the thing before me. What vanity these sheets will seem, one of these days, when Melymbrosia is a dirty book on your shelves, which Julian tries to read, but can't! However, there are numbers of things that I should be interested to say about the book; & we need not always be thinking of posterity. I too write in haste, just before dressing to go out; I will only add that I have blind faith in my power of making sentences presentable, so that I leave bald patches gaily, to furbish up next winter.

I was a little afraid that you would accuse me of compromise; but I was also quite sure that, made as I am, that sequel was the only one possible. I want to bring out a stir of live men & women, against a background. I think I am quite right to attempt it, but it is immensely difficult to do. Ah, how you encourage me! It makes all the difference. Are you really interested? I suppose so, since you say it; but you have no notion how pale & transparent it reads to me sometimes—though I write with heat enough. That will do, for one evening! . . .

On 19 July 1917 Clive Bell wrote a very enthusiastic letter to Virginia praising 'The Mark on the Wall'; he concluded by saying: "Shall I post this letter now and risk having said something terribly ridiculous, or shall I wait for the sober morning mood?"

Virginia Woolf to Clive Bell

Hogarth House, Paradise Road, Richmond, Surrey.
Tuesday [24 July 1917]

My dear Clive,

I've always thought it very fine – the way you run risks, though I don't see that there's much risk in sending such a letter to such a woman. You know you always told me I was notorious for vanity, & its still a fine plant, though growing old.

But please dont put it all down to vanity. I do like you to praise me, not only because of your gift for knowing whats what, but for what you would call sentimental reasons too—as for instance that you were the first person who ever thought I'd write well. We talked so much about writing too. . . .

Clive Bell to Leonard Woolf

Charleston, Firle, Sussex.
24 August 1956.

. . . I have a notion that the earlier and less 'gossipy' letters—the letters in which Virginia talks about her writing and her difficulties as an artist—are the most interesting. I will confess that I very much hope you will print a letter dated "Tuesday, Hogarth House, and beginning "I've always thought it very fine etc". Vanity? Not exactly perhaps. But there is a sentence—"you were the first person who ever thought I'd write well", which seems to me the finest feather I shall ever be able to stick in my cap. . . .

See also Clive Bell on Virginia Woolf in *Old Friends*, 1956, p. 93.

APPENDIX E
The Dreadnought Hoax

Hoax on Naval Authorities.

Colonel LOCKWOOD asked the First Lord of the Admiralty, whether a hoax has been played upon the naval authorities by the pretended visit of some Abyssinian princes; and, if so, whether he will take steps to prevent such conduct in future?

The FIRST LORD of the ADMIRALTY (Mr McKenna): I understand that a number of persons have put themselves to considerable trouble and expense in pretending to be a party of Abyssinians, and in this disguise visited one of His Majesty's ships. The question is being considered whether any breach of the law has been committed which can be brought home to the offenders.

Mr WILLIAM REDMOND: Will the right hon. Gentleman include in his inquiry an inquiry as to whether it is not a fact that these gentlemen conferred the Royal Abyssinian Order on the Admiral, who wrote to the King to know whether he could wear it, and will he wear it?

Mr McKENNA: I shall be relieved from the necessity of inquiring into that matter because I know it not to be true.

Colonel LOCKWOOD: Does the right hon. Gentleman think with me that the joke was a direct insult to His Majesty's flag?

Mr McKENNA: I think I have answered the question on the paper fully. The hon. and gallant Gentleman will not ask me to go further into a matter which is obviously the work of foolish persons.

Hansard, 24 February 1910

H.M.S. "Dreadnought" (Officers' Reception)

Captain FABER asked the First Lord of the Admiralty, if he would state what were the circumstances which led to the giving of an official reception by the commander-in-chief, Vice-Admiral Sir W. May, and the officers of H.M.S. "Dreadnought", to certain reputed Abyssinian princes and their staff; whether these reputed Abyssinians were received by the admiral and the officers of the ship with full naval honours; whether by the admiral's orders they were furnished with a special train on the return journey to London; and whether an inquiry had yet been held?

The FIRST LORD of the ADMIRALTY (Mr McKenna): With regard to the first part of the question, I would refer the hon. and gallant Gentleman to the reply given to the right hon. and gallant Gentleman the Member for Epping last Thursday. No flags were hoisted or salutes fired, and no special train was ordered by the Admiral.

Captain FABER: Is it not a fact that certain pairs of white kid gloves were actually purchased for the occasion, and can the right hon. Gentleman say who will pay the expense?

Mr McKENNA: I am afraid that the hon. and gallant Gentleman is better informed than I am, but if he will kindly give me notice of his question I will inquire into the matter.

Hansard, 2 March 1910

Virginia wrote an account of her part in this hoax in the form of a paper which she read to the Women's Institute in Rodmell during the summer of 1940. The Memoir Club heard it soon afterwards; E. M. Forster mentions it: 'an unpublished paper which she herself once wrote for a Women's Institute, leaving it helpless with laughter', in his Rede Lecture, *Virginia Woolf* (Cambridge, 1942, p. 7). Only three pages of erratic typescript have been found. These I give.

friends we were told that the best thing we could do was to go to Mr McKenna who was then First Lord of the Admiralty and make a clean breast of it. We were told by a friend of Mr McKenna's that if we took all the blame on ourselves they would not take any steps against the admiral or the other officers. The House of Commons would be told that we had apologised and there would be an end of it. So my brother A. & D. go to McKenna. and Duncan Grant went to the Admiralty and were shown in to Mr McKenna. And there they had a very queer interview. They tried to explain that they didn't want to get the admiral into trouble; and Mr McKenna dismissed the idea that such foolish people could get so great a man into a scrape, and pointed out that one of them had committed a forgery and was liable to go to gaol. So they argued at loggerheads. The truth was I think that Mr McKenna was secretly a good deal amused, and liked the hoax, but didn't want it repeated. At any rate he treated them as if they were school boys, and told them not to do it again. But we heard afterwards that

Rules made. one result of our visit had been that the regulations were tightened up; and that rules were made about telegrams that make it almost impossible now to repeat the joke. I am glad to think that I too have been of help to my country. With that interview with

W.W.'s visit on Sunday. the First Lord of the Admiralty we hoped that the affair was over. But no–there was still the navy to reckon with.

I was just getting out of bed one Sunday morning soon afterwards when there was a ring at the bell; and then I heard a man's voice downstairs. I seemed to recognise the voice. It was my cousins. It was Willy Fisher. And though I could [not] hear what he said I could tell that he was saying something very forcible. At last the voices ceased and my brother appeared. He was in his dressing gown. He looked very upset.

W.F.'s rage And he told me that Willy Fisher had been in a towering rage; had said he had found out who we were. And he was horrified. Did we realise that all the little boys ran after Admiral May in the street calling out Bunga Bunga? Did we realise that we owed our lives to the British Navy? Did we realise that we were impertinent, idiotic? Did we realise that we ought to be whipped through the streets, did we realise that if we had been discovered we should have been stripped naked and thrown into the sea? And so on and so on. My brother thought he was going to whip a knife out of his sleeve and proceed to blows. But no, Willy Fisher explained that since my brother's mother was his own Aunt, the rules of the Navy forbade any actual physical punishment. Then he asked: 'I know who the others were; and

A. gives addresses. now you've got to tell me their addresses.' This my brother did. The next moment he realised his mistake. But it was too late. And Willy Fisher dashed out of the house brushing aside the hand which my brother–who was after all his first cousin–held out to him. We hadn't long to wait before we

Officers call on D. heard what happened next. Three naval officers were waiting outside in a taxi. They drove off to the address in Hampstead where Duncan Grant lived. Duncan Grant was just sitting down to breakfast with his father and mother. They sent word that a friend was outside and wished to speak to him. Duncan Grant got up and went down into the street. One of the young men tipped him up and flung him head foremost into [the taxi.] Mrs Grant, who was looking out of the window saw her son disappear head foremost and turned back in alarm. "What on earth are we to do" she asked her husband. "Someone's kidnapping Duncan." Major Grant who had been in the army himself merely smiled and said "I expect its his friends from the Dreadnought." Duncan Grant found that he

D.G. alone. was sitting on the floor at the feet of three large men who carried a bundle of canes. Duncan asked where they were taking him?

"You'll see plenty of Dreadnoughts where you're going" said Willy

Fisher. At last they stopped somewhere in a lonely part of Hampstead Heath. They all got out. Duncan Grant stood there like a lamb. It was useless to fight. They were three against one. And this rather upset them. Won't fight. "I can't make this chap out" said one of the officers. He doesnt put up any fight. You can't cane a chap like that". My cousin however ordered them to proceed. He was too high in the service to lend a hand himself. And so, very reluctantly, one of the junior officers took a cane and gave Duncan Grant two ceremonial taps. Then they said the honour of the navy was avenged. There was Duncan Grant standing without a hat in his bedroom slippers. They at once conceived an affection for him and I am not surprised. They were really sorry for him. "You can't go home like that" they said. But Duncan Grant felt that he would much rather go home in the tube in his slippers than be driven back by the officers. And so he shuffled off; and the officers disappeared in their car.

(MH/A 27.)

In 1937, when Admiral Sir William Wordsworth Fisher died, Virginia wrote to Ethel Smyth:

Yes, I'm sorry about William–our last meeting was on the deck of the Dreadnought in 1910, I think; but I wore a beard. And I'm afraid he took it to heart a good deal. . . . (28 June 1937).

VOLUME II

Mrs Woolf

1912-1941

ACKNOWLEDGMENTS

In the first volume of this Biography I expressed my gratitude to those individuals and corporate bodies without whose aid or encouragement it would not have been undertaken at all; and to those others whose help in one way or another advanced its progress. With the completion of this volume my obligations are further extended. I should like to express or repeat my thanks to the following for the help that they have given and the permissions they have granted:

Christabel Lady Aberconway; Lord Annan; Dr Igor Anrep; Mr Mark Arnold-Forster; Mrs Barbara Bagenal; Mrs Mary Bennett; Miss Mary Bennett of the Walker Art Gallery, Liverpool; Professor John W. Bicknell of Drew University; Miss Elizabeth Bowen; Mr Gerald Brenan and Messrs Hamish Hamilton Ltd; the British Broadcasting Corporation; Mr Noel Carrington; Mr John Carter; Lord David Cecil; Mr Angus Davidson; Mrs Pamela Diamand; Mrs Beata Duncan; Mrs David Garnett; Mr Duncan Grant; Professor Leon Edel; Mrs T. S. Eliot; the late E. M. Forster and King's College, Cambridge; Mr Nicholas Furbank; Mr Philip Gaskell, Librarian of Trinity College, Cambridge; Miss Winifred Gill; Dr and Mrs A. D. Harris; Lady Hills; Mr Michael Holroyd; the staff of the India Office Records; Mr Julian Jebb; Lady Roderick Jones; Mr David Jolley; Sir Geoffrey Keynes; Miss Jacqueline Latham; Mr John Lehmann; Mrs Su Hua Ling; Longman Group Ltd for permission to quote from *Ethel Smyth, A Biography* by Christopher St John; Mr Michael MacCarthy; M. Georges Mevil-Blanche; the late Charles Mauron; Mrs Louie Mayer; the late Mrs Robin Mayor; Dr A. N. L. Munby, Librarian of King's College, Cambridge; Mrs Lyn Newman; Mr Benedict Nicolson; Mr Nigel Nicolson; Miss Lucy Norton; Mr Stanley B. Olson; Mrs Ian Parsons; Mrs Ralph Partridge; Mr Kenneth Phelps; Sir Edward Playfair; Mr William Plomer; Mrs Sophie Pryor; Miss Berta Ruck; Mr George Rylands; Miss Daphne Sanger; The Society of Authors as the Literary representative of the Estate of Katherine Mansfield; Mr George A. Spater; Mr Stephen Spender; the late Sebastian Sprott; Mrs James Strachey; Mrs Lola Szladits, Curator of the Berg Collection, New York Public Library; Mr Barry Till of Morley College; Mr Julian Trevelyan; Dame Janet Vaughan; Mrs Julian Vinogradoff; and Mr C. J. White.

Chapter One

1912–1915

Virginia and Leonard are engaged. They appeared this morning to
tell me so and seemed very happy. It happened some days ago but
they kept it secret till we returned.

(Vanessa Bell to Roger Fry, 2 June, 1912)

IT was not a very well-kept secret nor in any way a surprise for
their friends, who had been discussing the possibility of such an
engagement for a long time. Vanessa had undoubtedly been hoping
for it; she saw well enough that Leonard was the only one of
Virginia's suitors whom she could respect both as a man and as an
intelligence. For their friends the marriage had the double advantage
of keeping him in England while giving her a husband whom they
liked. Of these, one, Lytton, received the news in the form of a
postcard bearing the words:

> Ha! Ha!
> Virginia Stephen
> Leonard Woolf

One may suppose that he was both amused and relieved.

Clive was the only person whose feelings were in some measure
to be pitied. His passion for Virginia was much less acute than it
had been two years earlier, and his infidelities had taken a new
direction; but he still felt, and was always to feel, that he had a
special relationship with and a special claim upon her. He wrote to
her to say that he would always cheat himself into believing that
he appreciated and loved her better than did her husband. This, it
would appear, was not unkindly received; but unfortunately Clive's
feelings for Virginia were equally compounded of love and of
exasperation. This, if it was not clear to her already, was certainly
made so when Adrian showed her letters in which Clive, giving
vent to his frustrations, had said some very bitter things indeed.
Virginia and Leonard were incensed and there was the devil to pay
in Brunswick Square and Gordon Square where everyone seemed
to be cross with everyone else. Vanessa had the thankless role of

peacemaker and in the end succeeded in her task; Leonard and Virginia were too happy to remain angry for long and there was a general reconciliation. But, as Vanessa remarked: "an engagement seems an exhausting and bewildering thing even to the bystanders."

The principals certainly found it so. There were a great many people whom Leonard had to meet: George and Gerald Duckworth, Aunt Minna, Aunt Mary, Aunt Anny, Jack Hills, Nelly Cecil. All these belonged to the past and their disapproval might be endured with philosophy. But there were others of greater consequence; above all there was Violet Dickinson. At one time Virginia had felt that Violet's good opinion of her was essential to her happiness; this was no longer the case; but it was still necessary that Violet should be informed and her approbation solicited. Virginia wrote to her, almost in a spirit of bravado:

38 Brunswick Square W.C.
June 4, 1912

My Violet,

I've got a confession to make. I'm going to marry Leonard Woolf. He's a penniless Jew. I'm more happy than anyone ever said was possible—but I *insist* upon your liking him too. May we both come on Tuesday? Would you rather I come alone? He was a great friend of Thoby's, went out to India—came back last summer when I saw him, and he has been living here since the winter. You have always been such a splendid and delightful creature, whom I've loved ever since I was a mere chit, that I couldn't bear it if you disapproved of my husband. We've been talking a great deal about you. I tell him you're 6 ft 8", and that you love me.

My novel's just upon finished. L. thinks my writing the best part of me. We're going to work very hard. Is this too incoherent? The one thing that must be made plain is my intense feeling of affection for you. How I've bothered you—and what a lot you've always given me

your Sp[arroy]

Fortunately Leonard and Violet were ready enough to like each other, although Virginia's marriage could not but increase a separation which was already becoming evident.

The case of Madge Vaughan was different; Leonard could not understand what Virginia had ever found to admire in such over-scented sensibility. But Madge no longer counted for much in Virginia's life and her husband, Will Vaughan, whom Leonard frankly disliked, counted for even less. Then there were the Vaughan sisters, Emma and Marny; the meeting with Emma was no more than a formality; but Marny, working for the Care Committee amongst the poor of Hoxton, became, in her way, influential. Leonard, who had returned to England with a considerable sense of social duty, was sufficiently interested in Marny's efforts to offer to take a part in them. He paid several visits to the East End; what he saw of the horrors of urban poverty and of the futile charities to which poor Marny devoted her life made him a socialist. Another of Virginia's acquaintances whom he now met for the first time was to give a more precise direction to his developing political understanding. This was Margaret Llewelyn Davies, a woman of enormous energy and intelligence which she devoted largely to the organisation of the Women's Co-operative Guild, of which she was Secretary. Virginia had come to know her through Janet Case, her Greek teacher, and these two, Margaret and Janet, not only remained her loyal friends for life but were to prove amongst Leonard's best allies in the calamities of the ensuing years.

Virginia for her part had to meet the Woolf family. It was a daunting experience. Leonard himself was sufficiently Jewish to seem to her disquietingly foreign; but in him the trait was qualified. He had become so very much a citizen of her world that, unless she had married Lytton, she could hardly have remained more completely in Bloomsbury. But Leonard's widowed mother, a matriarchal figure living with her large family in Colinette Road, Putney, seemed very alien to Virginia. No place could have been less like home than her future mother-in-law's house.

And how did the Woolfs regard her? Did they perceive that she thought their furniture hideous? Did she seem to them a haughty goy thinking herself too good for the family of their brilliant son? I am afraid that probably they did.

When in *Night and Day* Ralph Denham brings Katherine Hilbery to visit his family in Highgate, Virginia is surely remembering that first visit to the Woolf family. Whether the situation was saved, as in the novel it was saved, must be doubted. Virginia seems to have disgraced herself.

"A sandwich, Miss Stephen–or may I call you Virginia?"

"What? Ham sandwiches for tea?"

"Not *Ham*: potted meat. We don't eat Ham or bacon or Shellfish in this house."

"Not Shell fish? Why not shell fish?"

"Because it says in the Scriptures that they are unclean creatures & our Mr Josephs at the Synagogue–&–"

It was queer.

3

Virginia was ready to allow that Mrs Woolf had some very good qualities, but her heart must have sunk as she considered what large opportunities she would have for discovering them.

"Work and love and Jews in Putney take it out of me," she wrote, and it was certainly true. She and Leonard undertook many excursions that were purely delightful: walking, riding, listening to the Opera or watching the Russian dancers, but she still had her novel to finish: it was always about to be finished. It is not surprising that she was at times unwell.

The wedding had been planned for 12 August, but it was moved forward to suit the Bells. It therefore took place on Saturday, 10 August, the official business being conducted at St Pancras Registry Office. (It was perhaps for this reason that Mrs Woolf did not attend.) To Virginia it seemed a very good way of getting married, very simple and soon done. Nevertheless the Registrar found it trying, partly because he was, or so it seemed to Virginia, half blind, partly because a violent thunderstorm was raging and partly because, when it came to witnessing the marriage, he got muddled by names which were, to him, unfamiliar: Virginia and, still worse, Vanessa. And then, in her vague but deliberate way, Vanessa interrupted the proceedings. She wanted to change the name of her younger son; how should she set about it?

George and Gerald, in frock coats and everything else that the occasion could demand, attended the wedding breakfast given by the Bells at 46 Gordon Square. They must have been somewhat distressed by the appearance of Duncan Grant which, in intention, was equally ceremonious but somehow failed in its effect, and by a conversation which turned upon the best manner of pawning clothes. Those which Duncan wore could not have been pawned; he could never have redeemed them. They were, only too evidently, borrowed from wearers of very different sizes. The other guests were Roger Fry, Saxon Sydney-Turner, Aunt Mary Fisher (carrying a crutch) and Frederick Etchells, who came bearded, bespectacled and uncouth, to lend a final touch of oddity to the scene.

Although she had been agitated earlier in the morning, Virginia enjoyed both the ceremony and the party. When this was over she and Leonard left for Asham in high spirits. They spent the night there and then went to stay for a few days in the Quantocks before going abroad. They had had the idea of taking their honeymoon in Iceland; but it was too late in the season and they set off from Somerset in a more orthodox direction, to Avignon and Vaucluse and thence to Spain.

In Barcelona the food was bad, in Madrid the heat was over-powering; they went on to Toledo and Saragossa. They were desperately hot and often tired; but the bareness and the beauty of the country amazed them. They rode on mules and took dilatory trains. Virginia read Dostoevsky and Charlotte M. Yonge. Presently they found themselves in Valencia and by now she was reading *Le Rouge et le Noir*. From Valencia a boat took them to Marseilles; they travelled on into northern Italy and Venice, which, after Spain, seemed comfortable but decidedly tame. At last on 3 October* they returned to London. They had, so they declared, talked incessantly and become "chronically nomadic and monogamic."

They were wrong in thinking of themselves as nomads. Never again were they to travel so far or for so long; but certainly they were, in comparison with most of their friends, monogamous. In two months of wandering they had discovered that their personalities were complementary, their sympathies extraordinarily close. Their love and admiration for each other, based as it was upon a real understanding of the good qualities in each, was strong enough to withstand the major and the minor punishments of fortune, the common vexations of matrimony and, presently, the horrors of madness. It is a proof of their deep and unvarying affection that it was not dependent upon the intenser joys of physical love. Even before her marriage, they must have suspected that Virginia would not be physically responsive, but probably they hoped that Leonard, whose passionate nature was never in question, could effect a change. A letter written from Saragossa to Ka Cox shows clearly enough that, if this hope was entertained, it was also disappointed.

> Why do you think people make such a fuss about marriage & copulation? Why do some of our friends change upon losing chastity? Possibly my great age makes it less of a catastrophe; but certainly I find the climax immensely exaggerated. Except for a sustained good humour (Leonard shan't see this) due to the fact that every twinge of anger is at once visited upon my husband, I might still be Miss S.

Thus, with placid conversational ease, Virginia alludes to her frigidity. It was, nevertheless, a cause of worry to both of them, and when they were back in England they sought Vanessa's advice.

---

* "... at the end of November ..."–Leonard Woolf (*Beginning Again*, p. 83). For once he is at fault, perhaps owing to the fact that he kept no diary during the autumn of 1912. See VB/VW, 19 August 1912 and VW/VD, 11 October 1912.

They seemed very happy, but are evidently both a little exercised in their minds on the subject of the Goat's coldness. I think I perhaps annoyed her but may have consoled him by saying that I thought she never had understood or sympathised with sexual passion in men. Apparently she still gets no pleasure at all from the act, which I think is curious. They were very anxious to know when I first had an orgasm. I couldnt remember. Do you? But no doubt I sympathised with such things if I didnt have them from the time I was 2.

Vanessa, Leonard and, I think, Virginia herself were inclined to blame George Duckworth. George certainly had left Virginia with a deep aversion to lust; but perhaps he did no more than inflame a deeper wound and confirm Virginia in her disposition to shrink from the crudities of sex, a disposition which resulted from some profound and perhaps congenital inhibition. I think that the erotic element in her personality was faint and tenuous. Of the two women who knew her best, one, as we have seen, said that she had no understanding of sexual passion in men, the other – Vita Sackville-West – was to note many years later that "She dislikes the possessiveness and love of domination in men. In fact she dislikes the quality of masculinity." I would go further and suggest that she regarded sex, not so much with horror, as with incomprehension; there was, both in her personality and in her art, a disconcertingly aetherial quality and, when the necessities of literature compel her to consider lust, she either turns away or presents us with something as remote from the gropings and grapplings of the bed as is the flame of a candle from its tallow.

But although Virginia was sexually frigid, in other respects she seems to have entertained all the hopes and fears of any normal bride. About a week after her return to London she wrote:

> 38 Brunswick Square, W.C.
> Oct 11 1912

My Violet,

Yesterday, happening to go into one of the bachelor sitting rooms, I discovered a cradle, fit for the illegitimate son of an Empress. When I brought forth my theory, however, they fathered the cradle on me. I blushed, disclaimed any intention, and so on: and blushing leant my elbow on a table. "What a beautiful table this is anyhow!" I exclaimed, thinking to lead the conversation away from my lost virginity and the probable fruits of it. The table was disclaimed too. Bit by bit I pieced together the story–how a great packing case had arrived, how Miss Dickinson etc etc. Nobody but Miss Dickinson could deal with the facts of life so boldly of course. Nobody else ever routed old shops to such effect. My baby shall sleep in the cradle. I'm going to eat my dinner off the table tonight.

At this time, Virginia was still cheerfully expecting to have children. Leonard already had his misgivings but I do not think that Virginia became aware of them until the beginning of 1913. Before that time the Woolfs (to use a term which passed into common use amongst their friends) had moved out of Brunswick Square, their place being taken by Maynard Keynes's brother Geoffrey, and had found rooms in Clifford's Inn, just off Fleet Street. This took them out of Bloomsbury, and had the double advantage that they were more exclusively in each other's company and that they had more time for work.

There was plenty of work to be done. Leonard on his return had accepted a part-time job at the Grafton Galleries until the end of the year; here Roger Fry was showing his Second Post-Impressionist Exhibition. It was Leonard's duty to deal with the indignant art-lovers who exploded with mirth or with rage before the works of Picasso and Matisse. It must have been an exasperating and a depressing job. Virginia was irritated on Leonard's behalf and also because, as sometimes happened, she found herself out of patience with the art of painting. Artists, she declared, "are an abominable race. The furious excitement of these people all the winter over their pieces of canvas coloured green and blue, is odious." I think she resented the fact that Leonard should be engaged in the service of "an inferior art." By this time she must surely have realised that he might excel in a more serious art form: the novel. *The Village in the Jungle* was finished before their marriage. At what point Virginia read it we cannot tell (it was accepted for publication by Edward Arnold in November); when she did see it she admired it very much. In fact they both intended to make their living by writing. They entertained the idea of starting a magazine of their own, but this, like all such notions, required money; they hoped but failed to raise £2000 for it. In addition Leonard had certainly decided that he must be politically active and was, by the beginning of 1913, strenuously undertaking his own political education. At the same time, when the job at the Grafton Galleries came to an end, he began to look for some other equivalent employment.

Virginia's own work continued to present formidable difficulties. Leonard has described her as writing with "a kind of tortured intensity" during the months of January and February, when *The Voyage Out* was almost completed. Already, by the time of their return from the honeymoon, he was worrying about her health. She needed rest and quiet and clearly there was more chance of these in the country. They went to Asham for Christmas and discussed the possibility of living there altogether, of buying horses and a cow, chickens and some pigs. These plans resulted in nothing more than a little strenuous gardening; the Woolfs had, as they were always to have, too many interests drawing them back to London.

In January they were joined at Asham by Vanessa; she also was unwell:

> Virginia has been very nice to me. She saw that I was depressed yesterday & was very good – & cheered me up a great deal. Do you think I sometimes laugh at her too much? I dont think it matters, but really I am sometimes overcome by the finest qualities in her. When she chooses she can give one the most extraordinary sense of bigness of point of view. I think she has in reality amazing courage & sanity about life. I have seen so little of her lately that it has struck me here.

And yet, at the very time when Vanessa was remarking on Virginia's "sanity about life," Leonard was anxiously noting in his diary the variations in her health, and although I think that Vanessa was not altogether wrong in what she said and that there was a kind of sanity about Virginia, it was certainly a quality which could be submerged by other internal forces and these, as the year advanced, grew stronger.

At the end of January Virginia and Vanessa were discussing the question of whether Virginia should have children. Leonard talked to Dr (now Sir George) Savage, and Sir George, in his breezy way, had exclaimed that it would do her a world of good; but Leonard mistrusted Sir George; he consulted other people: Maurice Craig, Vanessa's specialist, T. B. Hyslop, and Jean Thomas, who kept a nursing home and knew Virginia well; their views differed but in the end Leonard decided and persuaded Virginia to agree that, although they both wanted children, it would be too dangerous for her to have them. In this I imagine that Leonard was right. It is hard to imagine Virginia as a mother. But it was to be a permanent source of grief to her and, in later years, she could never think of Vanessa's fruitful state without misery and envy.

Perhaps comparison between Vanessa and herself may occasionally have soured a relationship which, at most other times, was very happy and which could no longer be damaged by Clive. There were some sisterly bickerings in the Spring of 1913. Adrian and Leonard got on badly and Vanessa tended to take Adrian's side. The feelings of jealousy which had hurt Virginia so much when Vanessa married may have sounded a tiny echo when Virginia found a husband.

8

Neither sister could really think that anyone was quite good enough for the other. "I wish Woolf didn't irritate me so," Vanessa once observed, and Leonard might have said the same about her. They were both strong characters; neither was easily convinced that he or she might be mistaken. And if there were a difference of opinion between Vanessa and Leonard, Virginia would side with her husband. Marriage, so Vanessa discovered, had made Virginia part of an alliance. Leonard had his own particular moral and intellectual position and this she accepted. She was perfectly in sympathy with the high seriousness of Cambridge which Leonard, in the arid climate of an eastern exile, had fragrantly preserved but which others, in the softer and more corruptive atmosphere of London–the London of Clive and Lytton, Lady Ottoline and Maynard Keynes– had half lost. The difference between him and them was a slight one. Leonard accepted the irreverent scepticism of his friends but he did not quite accept their frivolity or their worldliness. Having finished *The Village in the Jungle* he set to work upon a novel which he called *The Wise Virgins.** The story is that of a young man (Leonard himself) who oscillates between two young women; they come from very different social backgrounds; one belongs–more or less–to the same milieu as the Woolf family in Putney, the other is more or less Virginia. She is carefully described and there are fairly recognisable portraits of Vanessa and Clive. The hero brings the ideas of Bloomsbury to the young woman in Putney and without being himself really in earnest, gets her with child and is obliged, although it is really Virginia whom he loves, to marry without affection. "The whole moral significance of the book," as Leonard put it to his publisher, was that his hero was "living in a circle of somewhat unnatural cultured persons and like them he indulges in a habit of wild exaggerated talk which he believes that he believes." The effect of such talk is disastrous for all concerned.

The novel obviously does not represent Leonard's considered opinion of people who were, after all, to be his closest friends for

* *The Wise Virgins/A Story of Words, Opinions and a few Emotions*, by L. S. Woolf, Edward Arnold, 1914. According to Leonard it appeared at the very beginning of the war and was one of the first casualties. Vanessa deprecated the resemblance of the characters in this novel to Leonard's friends (VB/LW, 14 January 1914) and Morgan Forster seems to have felt similar misgivings (EMF/LW, 7 November 1914): ". . . it's a remarkable book: very bad in parts; first rate in others. A writer's book, I think, because only a writer perhaps can see why the good parts are so very good and why the very bad parts aren't very bad . . . I like the poetic side of L[eonard] and it gets a little smothered in Blue Books and organisations." *AWD (Berg)*, 31 January 1915.

the greater part of his life; but it does accurately reflect his mood in 1913, his impatience with a certain amount of brittle talk in Gordon Square and, above all, his attitude towards Clive.

Leonard was of course perfectly aware of Virginia's long flirtation with Clive and although, in later years, he would not defend her part in it, at that time, ardent, impatient and in love, he might have found it hard to blame her and easy to find fault with his brother-in-law. When he went to Ceylon he had left Clive in a peripheral situation on the fringes of intellectual Cambridge; he returned to find him a central figure in Bloomsbury and, as such, a rather unwelcome newcomer. He thought that Clive was not disinterested, that he was altogether too preoccupied by the social decorations of life, by little questions of vanity and decorum; and like Virginia he felt that Clive was not really good enough for Vanessa. Probably he was aware that Clive, on his side, felt that Leonard was not nearly good enough for Virginia. Leonard was, in Clive's opinion, provincial and puritanical, an enemy to all that was charming and amusing in life. Moreover, his effect on Virginia was disastrous. She was, he declared, losing her looks, drifting away from her old friends and being led into the dreary routines of politics. He didn't object to her being a Socialist–at that time he was not far from being a Socialist himself; but he didn't like a beautiful woman to be anything but charming. He was vexed to see her carried into Committee rooms and Co-operative halls, wearing 'sensible' clothes and stout boots. And of course he might object, with a fair show of reason, that she had neither the abilities nor the stamina for such work.

Virginia did indeed go with Leonard on the first of his political tours of investigation, although she confessed that economic problems were beyond her, and for ten days in March 1913 they travelled through the industrial north, visiting Liverpool, Manchester, Leeds, York, Carlisle and Leicester. So far as I know, this strenuous journey did her no harm. Later in the year a further political excursion was accompanied by a sudden deterioration in her health, but for this there may well have been another cause.

In March *The Voyage Out* was at last finished. Leonard read it through and on 9 March, before setting out on their Northern tour, he took the manuscript to Gerald Duckworth, Virginia's half-brother, who had his own publishing house. "I expect to have it rejected," wrote Virginia to Violet Dickinson, adding that this might "not be in all ways a bad thing." However, Gerald's reader, Edward Garnett, gave an extremely favourable report upon it, and on the morning of 12 April Virginia went herself to Henrietta Street to hear from Gerald how pleased he would be to publish her novel.

It is fair to suppose that she immediately had misgivings. Almost anyone who has attempted to create a work of art will have an inkling of what she then felt. A book is so much a part of oneself that in delivering it to the public one feels as if one were pushing one's own child out into the traffic. If it be killed or hurt the injury is done to oneself, and if it be one's first-born, the product of seven years' gestation, if it be awkward and vulnerable and needing all the tenderness and all the understanding that no critic will ever give, anxiety for its fate becomes acute.

Virginia already knew whither such anxieties might lead her. She knew that she had to be sensible and to exert self-control if the horrors of 1895 and 1904 and 1910 were not to be repeated. But how does one learn to be sensible? How, when one longs for sleep, does one command the brain to lie still and lose consciousness? Most people have experienced this inhibition. Quite a little thing – a social blunder, the prospect of an unpleasant interview – can keep one awake at night. The topic that one orders oneself to forget returns again and again into the mind which, at one level, desires only to dismiss the unwelcome trifle, but at another insists on bringing it back again and again so that, for a time, the spirit is at war with itself and, while the unhappy body begs for oblivion, insists that there shall be no respite until at last exhaustion brings a truce or the clock turns the mind to the business of the day. But Virginia was not tormented with a trifle; her sleepless nights were spent in wondering whether her art, the whole meaning and purpose of her life, was fatuous, whether it might not be torn to shreds by a discharge of cruel laughter.

After such nights the days brought headaches, drilling the occiput as though it were a rotten tooth; and then came worse nights, nights made terrible by the increasing weight of anxiety and depression, "those interminable nights which do not end at twelve, but go on into the double figures – thirteen, fourteen, and so on until they reach the twenties, and then the thirties, and then the forties . . . there is nothing to prevent nights from doing this if they choose."*

---

* *The Voyage Out*, p. 403. Here, and in subsequent passages, I have attempted to describe Virginia's madness from her point of view; such an attempt seems necessary if one is to write her biography but, obviously, it must be very largely a matter of conjecture. I have used *The Voyage Out*, *Mrs Dalloway* and also Leonard Woolf's description of her symptoms in *Beginning Again*.

Something of this sort is, I suppose, concealed beneath the laconic daily record of Virginia's condition in Leonard's diary for 1913: V.f.w., V.sl.h., g.n., f.g.n., b.n. and so on: Virginia fairly well, Virginia slight headache, good night, fairly good night, bad night. Clearly he was increasingly worried. They remained prudently at Asham for the greater part of April and May, but went back to London to attend the *Ring* at Covent Garden, which Virginia then vowed she would never do again: "My eyes are bruised, my ears dulled, my brain a mere pudding of pulp—O the noise, the heat, & the bawling sentimentality, which used once to carry me away, & now leaves me sitting perfectly still." But once in London, the social pressures were irresistible: their friends called, they dined out, went to concerts, ballets, theatres. Again they retreated to Asham and again were seduced by London. During the summer days of late June and early July their friends joined them in Sussex and shared their country pleasures: riding, walking, talking and gardening. Oliver and Ray Strachey, Lytton and Norton, Morgan Forster and Molly MacCarthy—all these came to stay at Asham. Each day Leonard noted down his wife's state: fairly well, fair night, good night, fairly good night. On 1 July she was thrown from her horse which bolted and was brought back in the evening. On 7 July they were again in London, going to Ottoline's after dinner, to Gordon Square, to the Russian Ballet, to *Don Giovanni*. They returned to Asham, and by now Leonard was very seriously alarmed: Virginia's headaches, her sleeplessness, her depression and sense of guilt, her aversion to food, had all increased to a frightening degree, and he began to realise that the danger of suicide was now very real.

Leonard, who by this time had been enlisted by Sidney and Beatrice Webb, was committed to speaking at a Fabian Society conference at Keswick on 22 July. Virginia insisted that there was nothing the matter with her and that she should go with him; but when they reached the Lodore Hotel she was barely able to leave her bed. Leonard took her back to London on the 24th and, convinced that she was on the brink of disaster, sought the advice of the specialist who knew her entire history, Sir George Savage.

. . . he seems to have thought Virginia rather bad [wrote Vanessa to Roger Fry.] . . . He said it was just the same thing as usual & she would get all right but must have the rest. So she was going off to Jean [Thomas] at Twickenham yesterday afternoon. Its too wretched I'm afraid. . . . Please be *very* careful not to say a word to *anyone* about her worrying over what people will think of her novel, which seems really to be the entire cause of her breakdown. I told Duncan simply that she had been worried about her proofs, which seems the easiest thing to say & that Asheham hadn't been very successful. I suppose she must be in a state where anything which made her think about herself in this way would get on her nerves. Oh God, I cant help being rather worried lest I ought to have done more, but after all one cant do much with married people.

Savage could see, as Leonard saw, that Virginia was very ill indeed, but I doubt whether he had more understanding of the causes or cure of her illness than Leonard. For him it was the same thing as usual, and the same remedy was prescribed. A few weeks in bed in Jean Thomas's Twickenham nursing home appeared to have cured her in 1910; it therefore seemed best, in spite of her own remonstrances, to repeat this treatment. And since on that previous occasion the rest cure had been fortified by a holiday in Cornwall, Savage promised, if she now would do as he ordered, she might afterwards go with Leonard to Somerset on the holiday they had already planned.

In retrospect both these recommendations seem disastrous. The rest cure proved worse than useless; it separated Virginia from the one person who could now help her; the holiday in Somerset made it more difficult to restrain the suicidal impulse fostered by her seclusion in Twickenham.

And yet at this distance one cannot but wonder whether there *was* a better remedy–then at all events. The doctors with their prescriptions of rest and food, "Robin's Hypophosphate," and mulled wine at night, could at least relieve the symptoms of Virginia's disorder. It was something of which they understood almost as little as did their great-grandfathers. The disease was in control: it struck when its hour had come.

Virginia went to Twickenham on 25 July and remained there until 11 August. A few miserable shaky pencil-written notes to Leonard survive from that time. They make one think of a child sent away by its parents to some cruel school. Everything, she complained, seemed so cold, so unreal. Childlike, she burst out against the husband who had put her away in this awful place. But then, seeing his worn and distressed face, she was overcome with guilt and misery. Again and again they expressed to each other the hope that somehow the cure would work, that somehow they would yet be able to make a happy life together.

But this time, although she tried to think otherwise, it did not work. She left Twickenham shaky, desperate, and so intolerably driven that the temptation to end it all by suicide became acute.

They returned to Asham, and during the ten days they were there Leonard introduced two new terms into his abbreviated records of Virginia's daily health: *worry*-"Virginia good deal worried," "less worry,"-and *cheerful*, which word indeed occurs but rarely among the worries and the good and bad nights-nights when he had to give her veronal for her sleeplessness. From 20 August he kept his diary in cypher; he had invented a code composed of a mixture of Sinhalese and Tamil characters which he had employed on occasions before his marriage when he wished to be discreet (not that it concealed anything very scandalous); now however he used it regularly to note Virginia's state.

On the morning of 22 August the Woolfs returned to London, where they were to spend the night with Vanessa at Gordon Square. Leonard was by this time thoroughly frightened by the prospect of taking Virginia alone to Somerset and, when he saw Savage, he expressed his fears. Sir George pooh-poohed them, and insisted that, since this holiday had been promised as a reward, the promise must be kept; to break it would be psychologically disastrous. Meanwhile Virginia had been at 46 Gordon Square with Vanessa. "Virginia," she reported to Clive, "seems to me pretty bad. She worries constantly and one gets rid of one worry only to find that another crops up in a few minutes. Then she definitely has illusions about people." After his interview with Savage, Leonard was able to talk things over with Vanessa, and also with Roger Fry, who being himself a man of science and the husband of a mad wife, was able at least to suggest an alternative to Savage, in whom Leonard had now lost all faith. Henry Head, a very distinguished scientist and a man of culture (he had translated Heine), seemed altogether a more suitable consultant. Leonard arranged to see him at once. But there was little that Head could do at this juncture. He had to agree with Savage that the promised holiday must be undertaken; it might possibly work a cure. If it did not, and Virginia's condition deteriorated, Leonard should summon help and, if it got worse still, they must return to London.

This in fact was the sequence of events. On 23 August Leonard and Virginia took the train to Bridgewater and motored out to the Plough Inn at Holford in the Quantock Hills, where they had stayed just after their wedding. It was a lovely and peaceful place, and the people who kept the Inn showed the utmost consideration to their uneasy guests; but Virginia was by now oblivious to such attentions. The entries in Leonard's diary suggest an alternation of moods; bad mornings and good evenings, delusions by day and peaceful nights, bad nights and cheerful days; but the worries, the delusions, the arguments about food, the necessity for sleeping-draughts, increased, and on 1 September Leonard telegraphed for Ka Cox. That warm, sensible and kindly woman arrived at Holford on 2 September and could at least relieve the strain on him.

But the pressures on Virginia did not relax: she thought people were laughing at her; she was the cause of everyone's troubles; she felt overwhelmed with a sense of guilt for which she should be punished. She became convinced that her body was in some way monstrous, the sordid mouth and sordid belly demanding food–repulsive matter which must then be excreted in a disgusting fashion; the only course was to refuse to eat. Material things assumed sinister and unpredictable aspects, beastly and terrifying or–sometimes–of fearful beauty.

And yet, dimly, like things seen through a dirty window pane, ordinary life was going on. It was one of the horrors of Virginia's madness that she was sane enough to recognise her own insanity, just as one knows that one is dreaming when one begins to wake. But she could not wake.

At length Leonard determined that they really must go back and see a doctor. At first Virginia demurred, too afraid to go; but then, to his astonishment, suggested that they might see Dr Head, which was what he had secretly wanted. She had not been a party to the discussion concerning Head at Gordon Square, but no doubt she had been affected, as most people were affected, by the conversation of Roger Fry. So, on the afternoon of 8 September they travelled back with Ka to London; by now his wife's condition was such that Leonard expected her at any moment to try to throw herself from the train. They arrived however at Brunswick Square, where they spent the night in Adrian's rooms. The next morning they went to see Dr Maurice Wright, whom Leonard had more than once consulted on his own account and in whom he had considerable faith. Dr Wright told Virginia that she must accept the fact that she really was ill; and in the afternoon Dr Head repeated this opinion, saying that she would get perfectly well again if she followed advice and re-entered a nursing home.

Virginia, believing that there was nothing wrong with her, that her anxieties and insomnia were due simply to her own faults, faults which she ought to overcome without medical assistance, was silent. They returned to Brunswick Square; Vanessa came and had tea with them; Virginia seemed more cheerful, and presently lay down to rest. Then Leonard, who had committed the indiscretion of consulting Dr Head without the prior agreement of Sir George Savage, went off with Vanessa to make his excuses. He was with Savage when at 6.30 Ka telephoned to tell him that she had found Virginia unconscious on her bed.

He ran for a taxi and, arriving at Brunswick Square, realised what had happened. Virginia had found the case in which he kept drugs. It was unlocked. She had taken 100 grains of veronal–a mortal dose.

Dr Head, nurses, Vanessa, were sent for; Ka stood by. Lodging on the top floor was Maynard Keynes's younger brother Geoffrey, a house surgeon at St Bartholomew's. He drove Leonard at high speed through the London traffic shouting: "Urgent! Doctor!" got a stomach-pump from his hospital and raced back. The doctors and nurses pumped the veronal out of Virginia and then watched through the night. At 12.30 Leonard went exhausted to bed and slept. At 1.30 Virginia nearly died; at six in the morning Vanessa woke Leonard to tell him that she was better; at nine Dr Head returned and was able to say that she was practically out of danger. She remained unconscious all that day.*

But the nightmare did not end with her return to consciousness. "She is" wrote Ka Cox to Janet Case, "a little quieter and eating more, but the symptoms continue very bad." As her strength returned so did her manias, and Leonard had now to face the question whether she should be certified and put into an asylum. He looked at some "homes" only to dismiss the idea. The doctors agreed that if she could be cared for by Leonard and trained nurses she need not be certified. But for this their rooms at Clifford's Inn were out of the question. Here George Duckworth intervened, and with great kindness offered them Dalingridge Place, his large and well-appointed house near East Grinstead in Sussex, where there

---

* "It is the novel which has broken her up. She finished it and got the proof back for correction . . . couldnt sleep & thought everyone would jeer at her. Then they did the wrong thing & teased her about it and she got desperate–and came here a wreck. It was all heart rending. . . . They will blame Sir George [Savage] probably, but they have never really done what he advised, except get married. And the marriage brought more good than anything else till the collapse came from the book–and as the doctors say, it might have come to such a delicate brilliant brain after such an effort *however* much care and wisdom had been shown." Jean Thomas to Violet Dickinson, 14 September 1913 (*Berg*).

According to Leonard, one of the difficulties of the situation was that Jean Thomas felt an unconscious but violent homosexual passion for Virginia and was also devoted to Sir George Savage; this made her awkward and quarrelsome. (p.i. LW)

Virginia Stephen, 1903

Mrs Leslie Stephen
with Virginia, 1884

Sir Leslie Stephen, K.C.B., 1902

Virginia and Vanessa,
St Ives, 1894

Vanessa, Stella,
and Virginia, c. 1896

Vanessa Stephen

Thoby Stephen

George Duckworth

Stella Duckworth

Adrian and Virginia, 1900

Violet Dickinson
and Virginia, 1902

Clive Bell, c. 1906

The Emperor of Abyssinia and his suite.
Seated: Virginia Stephen, Anthony Buxton. Standing: Guy Ridley,
Horace de Vere Cole, Adrian Stephen, Duncan Grant

Virginia with Clive and Julian Bell, Blean, 1910

Virginia Woolf by Stephen Tomlin,
lead, 1931
The National Portrait Gallery, London

Adrian Stephen,
at Fitzroy Square

Virginia by Vanessa
By permission of Alex Reid & Lefevre Ltd., London

Virginia and
Leonard Woolf, 1914

Vanessa, 1914

Virginia walking in
Cornwall, 1916

Duncan Grant,
Maynard Keynes,
and Clive Bell,
Charleston, 1919

Virginia, c. 1925

V. Sackville-West
By courtesy of Nigel Nicolson

Katherine Mansfield, 1920
By courtesy of Miss I. C. Baker

Lady Ottoline Morrell
by Simon Bussy

Lytton Strachey and Virginia

Julian Bell, 1932

Leonard and Virginia, Cassis, 1928

Roger Fry, Desmond MacCarthy, and Clive Bell, Charleston, 1933

Carrington, Ralph Partridge, and Lytton Strachey, Ham Spring, 1930

Virginia with John Lehmann, c. 1931

Virginia with
Ethel Smyth,
Monk's House, 1932

Virginia with
Angelica Bell, 1934
By Lettice Ramsey

Virginia Woolf

was plenty of room, a staff of servants, and every material comfort.

On 20 September Ka and a nurse went ahead to Dalingridge, followed by Leonard and Virginia and a second nurse in a motor-car. Virginia was worse than ever; she could not sleep, she would not eat, she was by turns deeply depressed and violently excited.* The faithful Ka remained for a week, and while she was there, Leonard took a day off and went over to Asham, where he found Clive and Vanessa. Clive wrote to Molly MacCarthy:

> Woolfe bicycled over to lunch yesterday, looking ill and very much tired, I thought, and in very low spirits. Virginia seems to have been even worse since the veronal affair and is intractable about food – the key to the situation so they say. The nurses they took with them seem to be powerless to persuade her to do anything; they are seeking others; meanwhile the bulk of the really hard work falls on Woolfe. One begins to wonder whether she will ever get really sound again.

Very slowly Virginia began to improve. The days of "excitement" became rather less numerous, she was gradually persuaded to eat a little. There were more quiet days and more good nights until at last, after two months, her doctors agreed that she might be moved, still with two attendant nurses, to Asham. Here the Woolfs settled, giving up their rooms at Clifford's Inn, here they remained almost continuously from 18 November 1913 until August 1914; and here, despite numerous setbacks, Virginia seemed to recover.

In his autobiography Leonard describes Virginia's state of mind;

---

* The entries concerning Virginia in Leonard's diary at this time suggest but do not describe the day-to-day strain under which he was living:

Sept 10: V. unconscious all day. *Sept 11*: Saw V. morn. Spoke to me. Saw V. even. more consc. *Sept 12*: V fully conscious. V. fairly happy even. *Sept 13*: V. fairly cheerful. V. very cheerful even. *Sept 14*: V. fairly calm & cheerful. Sat w V. 6–7.30. Very worried at first. *Sept 15*: W. V. morn. Talked V. aftn. Sat w V. aft dinner cheerful. *Sept 16*: W V. even. rather cheerful Not good night. *Sept 17*: W V. aft tea much worry. V. had bad night. *Sept 18*: Tea w V. walked w her in sq. V. depressed & much worry V. slept v badly. *Sept 19*: W V. morn. V. much worry bad night. *Sept 20*: Motor w nurse & V. to Dalingridge. V. v bad night. *Sept 21*: V. very excited & worried. Gr trouble w food bad night. *Sept 22*: V. v depressed, continual trouble w food v. bad night. *Sept 23*: V. v depressed great trouble w all meals 5 hrs sl. paraldahide. *Sept 24*: V. fair day. diff. lunch, great diff. dinner. 5 hours sl. w sl. dr. paral. *Sept 25*: V. excited all day 2 hrs over each meal. Did not sleep at all. *Sept 26*: Some diff w br. None w 11.30 milk. Ka left 11.47 trn. V. v queer on walk, cd hardly walk for a moment, & then jumpy. Lay down. Nurse got her eat 1½ courses lunch, I did rest without diff. Walk w me aftn. much calmer. Ate good tea. Nurse got her eat dinner 2½ hours sleep Adalin. *Sept 27*: Some diff w br. None w 11.30 milk. Marg [Llewelyn] D[avies]. arrived lunch. V. v excited. Nurse succeeded w ½ lunch I w rest Ditto dinner. V. violent w nurses at times 5½ hrs nat sl. asperine. [And so on.]

he does not describe his own. He does not pause in order to indulge in self-pity nor—and this would have been much more in character—does he pause to shake an angry fist at Jehovah, just in case Jehovah should be there to take notice. All complainings and whinings were omitted from his book as they were from his life. And yet he might well have complained of those who, unlike Jehovah, could be called to account.

Leonard had undertaken the care of a woman who had twice been mad and had once attempted suicide without—as far as I can discover—any serious and wholly unequivocal warning of what he was letting himself in for. Neither Vanessa nor Adrian gave him a detailed and explicit account of Virginia's illnesses or told him how deadly serious they might be, until this greatest and worst crisis occurred. Her insanity was clothed, like some other painful things in that family, in a jest.

"Oh you know very well the Goat's mad." That was easily said and easily disregarded. Virginia herself, then and later on, would cheerfully allude to the times when she was "off her head." Thus, in effect if not in intention, Leonard was allowed to think of Virginia's illnesses as something not desperately serious, and he was allowed to marry her without knowing how fearful a care such a union might be. In fairness to all parties it must be said that, even if Virginia's brother and sister had been as explicit and circumstantial as they ought to have been, Leonard certainly would not have been deflected from his purpose of marrying Virginia; but his subsequent treatment of one who was, in fact, already dangerously ill might well have been different. As it was, he learnt the hard way and one can only wonder, seeing how hard it was, and that he had for so long to endure the constant threat of her suicide, to exert continual vigilance, to exercise endless persuasive tact at mealtimes and to suffer the perpetual alternations of hope and disappointment, that he too did not go mad.

In fact he nearly did, although he does not mention it. The strain upon him was intense and continuous. Now and then he had been able to escape for a day or a night to London, to see his friends or his family, to visit a theatre or to attend a meeting. But after almost six months of unremitting vigilance the burden became too great. During the early part of 1914 he was troubled by bad headaches; they became so violent and disabling that, early in March, it was arranged that Ka Cox and Janet Case should come by turns to Asham to be with Virginia so that Leonard might have ten days' holiday. He went to Wiltshire to stay in an uncomfortable cottage with Lytton, who read him his *Cardinal Manning* and argued about Ulster – a strange cure, but it seems to have worked.*

By April 1914 the Woolfs felt well enough to venture upon a change of scene, and Maurice Craig, whom they now consulted and whose opinions and advice Leonard respected (Savage was by now only referred to as a matter of courtesy), agreed that Virginia was sufficiently improved to justify the undoubted risk of removing her from her familiar surroundings. They went for three weeks to Cornwall – to Lelant, St Ives and Carbis Bay. Leonard found the excursion a pretty nerve-wracking affair; Virginia was very fearful of strangers, still difficult over food, and liable to bursts of excitement or bouts of despair. But on the whole the holiday did her good; her nostalgic delight in the scenes of her childhood soothed her overwrought nerves, and her progress towards recovery, though erratic, was maintained during the summer months at Asham.

In mid-June Leonard, who had to some extent been able to continue his political studies and interests, went to Birmingham to attend a Women's Co-operative Guild meeting. Before going, he drew up a kind of treaty, comic in form but serious in intention, the articles of which bound Virginia to rest on her back with her head on the cushions for a full half-hour after luncheon, to eat exactly as much as if he were there, to be in bed by 10.25 each night and settle off to sleep at once, to have her breakfast in bed, to drink a whole glass of milk during the morning, in certain contingencies to rest on the sofa and not walk about the house or garden, to be wise and to be happy. These injunctions were to be observed on the 16th, 17th and 18th of June 1914. Virginia signed with a flourish. And in fact, though she was still liable to bad days or bad nights, the empirical method, which consisted of rest, food, calm, and the avoidance of intellectual excitement, was yielding good results.†

* "Leonard *is* better . . . I think if only I can behave now, he will soon be quite right. . . . By occupying myself with typewriting & Co-operative manuals, I keep cheerful, which I see does more to inspirit L. than anything else." VW/Janet Case, March 1914.

Leonard and Virginia's friends did what they could to help them; Lytton Strachey showed his sympathy and concern by offering hospitality and conversation to Leonard, and the menial tasks of her own profession to Virginia. She was typing his short story, *Ermyntrude and Esmeralda*. We do not know *how* she occupied herself with the Co-operative manuals.

† In May 1914, Leonard was reading Freud's *Interpretation of Dreams* as a preliminary to reviewing his *Psychopathology of Everyday Life* for *The New Weekly*. He was a good deal impressed and it is possible that, if he had read Freud two years earlier, Virginia's medical history might have been different. It is however doubtful whether she could have been analysed or whether analysis would have

She was able to read and to write short letters, to sew, to some extent to manage her household of cook and housemaid (the nurses were gone), and to go for long walks with her two dogs Shot and Mike. Vanessa reported from Asham at the end of July that Virginia was certainly very much better and was indeed bent upon returning to London. This idea filled Leonard with despair. London would certainly be bad for her and would lead, inevitably, to another breakdown.

Shortly after the declaration of war he did take Virginia to London, but only for a night on their way to Northumberland. They stayed at Wooler in the Cheviots. From thence Virginia wrote to Ka Cox:

It is thought that you are probably doing service somewhere, either as a nurse, or part of the military. I never felt anything like the general insecurity. We left Asheham a week ago, & it was practically under martial law. There were soldiers marching up and down the line, & men digging trenches, & it was said that Asheham barn was to be used as a hospital. All the people expected an invasion–Then we went through London–& oh Lord! what a lot of talk there was! Roger, of course, had private information from the Admiralty, & had been seeing the German Ambassadress, & Clive was having tea with Ottoline, & they talked & talked, & said it was the end of civilisation, & the rest of our lives was worthless. I do wish you would write & tell me what you hear–They say there must be a great battle, & here, where we are 15 miles from the North Sea, they expect to be in the midst of it, but then so they did at Seaford.

Your future is practically blasted, because you will be on 20 different committees. The very earnest & competent are already coming to town, with their practical habits–but I never could see the use of committees.

We have struck about the most beautiful country I've ever seen here.

---

been an appropriate treatment. Analysts are usually reluctant to treat patients who have actually been mad and Virginia's first breakdown could hardly have been treated even by Freud himself: it was contemporaneous with his *Studien über Hysterie* (1895). The Freudian techniques of analysis would barely have been heard of in this country at the time of her second breakdown (1904), and even in 1913 cannot have been at all well known. (Ernest Jones began to practice in London in 1913.) The Japanese psychiatrist Mme Miyeko Kamiya is, I believe, preparing a pathography of Virginia Woolf and this may enable us to know whether psychiatry could have helped her. To a lay observer it would appear, as to Leonard himself it appeared, that her symptoms were of a manic-depressive character, which would not have responded to analysis. In her later years she showed little interest in and less enthusiasm for the discoveries of Freud and could not have been persuaded to consult a psychiatrist.

Except that it has no sea, I think that it is better than Cornwall – great moors & flat meadows with very quick rivers. We are in an Inn full of north country people, who are very grim to look at, but so up to date that one blushes with shame. They discuss Thomson's poetry, & post impressionism, & have read everything, & at the same time control all the trade in Hides, & can sing comic songs & do music hall turns – in fact the Bloomsbury group was stunted in the chrysalis compared with them. But why did you never prepare me for the Scotch dialect, & the melodious voice which makes me laugh whenever I hear it?

This northern holiday was undoubtedly a success. Leonard's diary records their expeditions and an almost unbroken series of good nights. They returned to London on 15 September and Virginia remained in excellent health, so much so that, in the month of October, his daily record ceases.

This marked improvement in her condition made it easier for Virginia to insist that they should live in London. She and Leonard spent much of that autumn looking for a house. They tried Hampstead and Highgate, Westminster, Holborn, Chelsea and Twickenham; finally they decided that Richmond would suit them best of all. Richmond was near enough to London for Leonard's political work and far enough out to prevent the social distractions of town from becoming too much of a threat to Virginia's health. They took lodgings there in October with a Belgian lady, Mrs le Grys, at 17 The Green, and sent for their own furniture and books which had been in storage since Clifford's Inn was given up. While househunting in Richmond they came across a beautiful eighteenth-century mansion, Suffield House, which had been divided into two, one half keeping the original name, the other now called Hogarth House. This they liked very much; they tried to get a lease of it; but there were difficulties and delays, so that they alternated between hope and resignation, and continued their search elsewhere.

Virginia could again be active and she felt, as the wife of a poor man, that she ought to have some domestic skills; she began to attend a school of cookery in Victoria Street:

> At one end of the room are sailors & then there are a few greyheaded ladies of great culture & refinement, dabbling in the insides of chickens, & some very smart, come to improve their knowledge of dinner-party soup. I distinguished myself by cooking my wedding ring into a suet pudding!

She found it all great fun, but it is doubtful whether she put her training to much practical use at that time, since their meals were provided by their landlady.

She began again to enjoy a little social life, having friends to tea or dinner, and sometimes going up to London to see people, to get books from a library, or to hear a concert or a play. Bloomsbury had been scattered by the onset of the war, though its remnants were being gathered up and reinforced by Lady Ottoline Morrell; her brilliant and hectic parties in Bedford Square were exactly the kind of social event which Leonard was anxious that Virginia should avoid. The Woolfs did not look for excitement; their visitors came singly or perhaps in pairs–Janet Case, Margaret Llewelyn Davies, Saxon or Ka, Leonard's family, Sydney Waterlow and Walter Lamb; he was now Secretary to the Royal Academy, lived near them at Kew and was regarded as a figure of fun.

By the end of the year Virginia was writing again–a novel or a story which has been lost; she also began to keep a diary. It is the record of a perfectly sane woman leading a quiet but normal life:

Saturday, January 2nd [1915]
This is the kind of day which, if it were possible to choose an altogether average sample of our life, I should select. We breakfast: I interview Mrs Le Grys. She complains of the huge Belgian appetites and their preference for food fried in butter. "They never *give* one anything" she remarked. The Count, taking Xmas dinner with them, insisted, after pork and turkey, that he wanted a third meat. Therefore Mrs Le G. hopes that the war will soon be over. If they eat thus in their exile, how must they eat at home, she wonders? After this, L. and I both settle down to our scribbling. He finishes his Folk Story review and I do about four pages of poor Effie's story; we lunch and read the papers; agree that there is no news. I read Guy Mannering upstairs for 20 minutes and then we take Max for a walk. Halfway up to the Bridge, we found ourselves cut off by the river, which rose visibly, with a little ebb and flow, like the pulse of a heart. Indeed, the road we had come along was crossed, after five minutes, by a stream several inches deep. One of the queer things about the suburbs is that the vilest little red villas are always let and that not one of them has an open window or an uncurtained window. I expect that people take a pride in their curtains and there is great rivalry among neighbours. One house had curtains of yellow silk, striped with lace insertion. The rooms inside must be in semi-darkness and I suppose dank with the smell of meat and human beings. I believe that being curtained is a mark of respectability. Sophie used to insist upon it. And then I did my marketing. Saturday night is the great buying night and some counters are besieged by three rows of women. I always choose the empty shops, where I suppose one pays

¼d a lb. more. And then we had tea and honey and cream; and now L. is typewriting his article; and we shall read all the evening and go to bed.

Mrs le Grys complained a good deal of her refugee lodgers. The Count spat in his bath (a fact which was to be remembered in *The Years*). Her servants were also a source of interest, distress and amusement to Virginia. Lizzy, the house-maid, nearly set the house on fire and on another occasion made the boiler, which had no water in it, red hot; also she broke the crockery. Maud, her successor, claimed that she was a Colonel's daughter; she attempted genteel talk when she brought in the coals. Visitors are recorded: Sydney Waterlow came and talked about philosophy; Walter Lamb came and talked about royalty; Marjorie Strachey came and talked about herself. Molly MacCarthy brought gossip from Bloomsbury, described Clive's latest love affair, Desmond's resolve to live in the country and, at last, to write his novel.

Leonard was now able to devote considerably more time to his own writing and other activities; he was increasingly in demand on committees and as a speaker on Co-operative and International subjects. "The Sidney Webbs ask us to dinner about once a week, & Leonard has got to go tomorrow, though it sounds too dismal. They've clawed him for a huge job* . . ." wrote Virginia in December. She went with him to political meetings and much admired his speeches, his clarity, and the complete lack of condescension with which he addressed himself to working men and women. She herself now became a member of the Fabian Society. Interest in the progress of the war is barely manifested in her diary, though she noted the sinkings of the *Formidable* and of the *Blücher*.

On 25 January, her 33rd birthday, Leonard gave her a green purse and a square brown parcel containing a first edition of *The Abbot*. In the afternoon they went for a treat to a Picture Palace, and to tea at Buszards; and that evening they decided that if they possibly could they would live at Hogarth House; they would buy a printing press; and a bulldog. Virginia was delighted by her birthday and greatly excited by the idea of having their own press.

Two days later Virginia noted in her diary that she and Janet Case had discussed the novel "which everyone, so I predict, will assure me is the most brilliant thing they've ever read: and privately condemn, as indeed it deserves to be condemned." It is her only reference to *The Voyage Out* and if, as I suspect, the diary

* Leonard was asked by the Fabian Society to prepare a report on International Relations, which was the germ of the League of Nations.

was at this time intended partly as a sedative, a way of proving to herself how normal she now was, then this reticence, so unlike the anxious speculations of later years, is not astonishing. The novel was to appear at the end of March; in the middle of February Leonard took Virginia to the dentist, and afterwards to look at printing presses in Farringdon Street; the following day he came home to find her with a bad headache. He began the usual treatment; rest, seclusion, veronal at night; and, as before, recorded her progress in his diary.

But one morning, while she was breakfasting in bed, Virginia began to talk to her mother; she became very distressed and more and more excited and incoherent. A day or two later she seemed–to herself at any rate–to have stepped back from the abyss and, re-membering the nightmare of the previous year, tried to express something of what she felt she owed to Margaret Llewelyn Davies:

> 17, The Green, Richmond.
> Thursday [25 February 1915]
>
> My dear Margaret
> Thank you so much for troubling about the Morris. [She had asked if Margaret could lend her *The Pilgrims of Hope*.] I shd. very much like to see it.
> I want just to tell you how wonderfully things have changed in the last few days. I am now all right though rather tired. It is so wonderful that I can hardly believe it. And I wanted to say that all through that terrible time I thought of you, & wanted to look at a picture of you, but was afraid to ask! You saved Leonard I think, for which I shall always bless you, by giving him things to do. It seems odd, for I know you so little, but I felt you had a grasp on me, & I could not utterly sink. I write this because I do not want to say it, & yet I think you will like to know it. Our happiness now is something I cannot even think about.
> Please come. We have given up the Shaws, & Saturday afternoon about 4 would suit me. I can't do much but lie still, but I should like immensely to see you & gossip about Madame Tournier and other friends.
> Dear Margaret, I so often think of you, & thank you for what you have done for us both, & one cd do nothing to show what it meant.
> Yrs V.W.
> I wanted to tell Janet [Case] what I have told you but Leonard thought better not. Her goodness was so great

This letter, rather hurriedly, rather wildly but quite firmly written in pencil, may possibly express a sentiment of rational guilt and remorse resulting from agonies of irrational fury, and the reasons why Margaret Llewelyn Davies should inspire such feelings need to be explored. She had indeed saved Leonard and, during the past two years had become, after Virginia, the most important woman in his life. She was, as Leonard has said, a born leader, energetic, enthusiastic, likeable and handsome; she brought Leonard into the work of her own particular organisation-the Women's Co-operative Guild; Virginia came too and was indeed very much impressed. Nevertheless it must have been clear from the outset that Leonard would move further and faster on this excursion than Virginia. With Margaret as his guide, Leonard had soon adventured deep into politics and, as Virginia realised, this was what he needed at a time when her illness would otherwise have driven him to despair.

But the influence of this wholly benevolent, altogether virtuous, 50-year-old Egeria cannot have been altogether welcome. Virginia was never drawn to female politicians and Margaret, with all her fine qualities, was something of a bore.* That Leonard should be so dependent upon her-and Virginia too, for Margaret's kindness was such during Virginia's illness that Leonard found his gratitude too deep to express-was not altogether a recommendation.

Virginia believed that she had recovered when she wrote to Margaret on 25 February, but it was no more than a respite. Two letters which followed, both oddly frivolous, were dictated to Leonard, who added postscripts saying that he thought her a little better; but in fact she grew rapidly worse. It was quite unlike the first phase of her madness when she was depressed, languid and, though sometimes violent, more often quietly suicidal. Now she entered into a state of garrulous mania, speaking ever more wildly, incoherently and incessantly, until she lapsed into gibberish and sank into a coma. Doctors and nurses were sent for. It was clear that the Woolfs couldn't remain indefinitely in their lodgings. Mrs le Grys was a nice woman but she could hardly be expected to cater for a raving lunatic and her attendants. The negotiations for the lease of Hogarth House were completed, and on 25 March, the day before the publication of *The Voyage Out*, Virginia was taken to a nursing home; she remained there for a week while Leonard made the move to their new home, and was then installed under the

---

* Leonard compares Margaret Llewelyn Davies with Robert Owen, the founder of the Co-operative Movement (*Beginning Again*, pp. 104/5) and in so doing quotes Leslie Stephen's description of that great man: "one of those intolerable bores who are the salt of the earth"—but Leonard omits the word "intolerable."

care of four mental nurses. Life at Hogarth House began with the dreary and all too familiar alternation of good days and bad days, exasperating mealtimes and sleepless nights, but with even more harrowing symptoms, for now Virginia was violent and screaming, and her madness culminated in virulent animosity towards Leonard himself. On 20 May Leonard's diary reads: "Exc. & irritable all day but not as bad as yest Marg. came tea. Nurse Missenden came. Did not see V." For almost two months he scarcely saw her. Vanessa reported to Roger Fry:

> I saw Woolf yesterday. He too was very dismal. Virginia seems to go up & down, at times being pretty reasonable & at others very violent & difficult. The only thing to do is to hang on as long as possible he thinks in the hope that she may get well enough to be able to go to some nursing home & not have to go to an asylum which he thinks might have a disastrous effect on her. The question is whether the nurses will stand it. Woolf himself seemed to have reached a state when he didnt much care what happened which was rather dreadful; & one couldn't say anything much.

Very, very slowly Virginia began to improve. That is to say there were fewer moments of violence and excitement. She became more lucid and more rational. But it seemed that there would be no real recovery from this second bout of the disease; it had inflicted a wound which appeared to be incurable. In April, Jean Thomas told Violet Dickinson that Virginia's mind seemed "played out" and that it was not only her mind but her entire personality which had deteriorated. At the end of June Vanessa wrote:

> Ka had been to see Virginia & thinks she's really getting better slowly, but it sounds most depressing as she seems to have changed into a most unpleasant character. She won't see Leonard at all & has taken against all men. She says the most malicious & cutting things she can think of to everyone & they are so clever that they always hurt. But what was almost the worst thing to me was a small book of new poems by Frances Cornford which has just come out which Virginia has annotated with what are meant to be stinging sarcasms & illustrations. They are simply like rather nasty schoolboy wit, not even amusing. I had just been reading a lot of her old letters & it is really terrible. The early ones are so brilliant, better than her novel–perhaps I told you about them before–& the later ones during the last year or two are so dull by comparison–it looks as if she had simply worn out her brains.

Thus by the summer of 1915 it was clear that Virginia, however completely she might seem to recover from her insanity, could easily relapse into madness, and each attack seemed worse than its predecessor. After two years of intermittent lunacy it appeared that her mind and her character were permanently affected.

Chapter Two

1915–1918

WHEN *The Voyage Out* appeared in March 1915 it was greeted cordially by Virginia's friends and, on the whole, by the Press. E. M. Forster (and there was no one whose opinion mattered more to her) published his criticism in the *Daily News*.

"Here at last is a book which attains unity as surely as *Wuthering Heights*, though by a different path."

Other reviewers were equally enthusiastic. Several used the word "genius."

That is not a word [wrote the critic of the *Observer*] to use inadvisedly, but there is something greater than talent that colours the cleverness of this book. Its perpetual effort to say the real thing and not the expected thing, its humour and its sense of irony, the occasional poignancy of its emotions, its profound originality–well, one does not wish to lose the critical faculty over any book, and its hold may be a personal and subjective matter, but among ordinary novels it is a wild swan among good grey geese to one reviewer, to whom its author's name is entirely new and unknown.

At what point in the summer of 1915 Virginia was able to read these words I do not know; but when she did read them they must have given her lively pleasure and, what was more important, reassurance.

In December 1914, she had told Molly MacCarthy that she was relieved to find that one sentence "more or less followed another"; that her book "though long and dull" was not, as she sometimes feared, pure gibberish. I do not think that this was simply false modesty. Her novels were very close to her own private imaginings; she was always conscious that, to the outside world, they might simply appear to be mad, or, worse still, that they really were mad. Her dread of the ruthless mockery of the world contained within it the deeper fear that her art, and therefore her self, was a kind of sham, an idiot's dream of no value to anyone.* For her, therefore, a

---

* "Suppose one woke and found oneself a fraud? It was part of my madness that horror." *AWD* (Berg), 16 May 1927.

favourable notice was more valuable than mere praise; it was a kind of certificate of sanity. The point is one that should be borne in mind when we consider her extreme sensitivity to criticism, a sensitivity which may be considered morbid and which indeed in a sense *was* morbid, in that it arose from a diseased condition. The critical thrusts and buffets which could easily have been resisted by a more robust organism might, in her case, reopen wounds that had never quite healed and had never ceased to be acutely tender.

I believe then that Virginia's gradual return to health in 1915 was helped by the favourable notices given to her first novel. But it was a very slow and unsteady recovery; in whatever other ways it may have been assisted it would not have been possible without a long regime of tedious inertia on her part and Leonard's infinite patience. His success was such that in August he no longer felt it necessary to keep a daily record of her health. In that month he began to take her for drives or wheel her out in a Bath chair; she was seeing one or two friends, and beginning to be allowed to read more and write a little; a postcard to Margaret Llewelyn Davies postmarked 31 August is much in her old style:

> Your letter still delights me. I take it up at intervals to get into closer touch with Madame T. [presumably Margaret had passed on a compliment about *The Voyage Out*]. But my dear Margaret, what's the use of *my* writing novels? You've got the whole thing at your fingers ends–& it will be envy not boredom that alienates my affections. I saw Forster, who is timid as a mouse, but when he creeps out of his hole very charming. He spends his time in rowing old ladies upon the river, & is not able to get on with his novel. Also I saw Ray Strachey, but, alas, she makes me feel like a faint autumnal mist, she's so effective & thinks me such a goose.

In September she was well enough to be moved, still with an attendant nurse, to Asham, where she lived very quietly. They had few visitors–Vanessa, the Waterlows, her cousin Fredegond with her husband Gerald Shove*–and this regime was so beneficial that by the middle of October she was writing to Lytton: "I think it is about time we took up our correspondence again. . . . I am really all right again, and weigh 12 stone!–three more than I've ever had, and the consequence is I can hardly toil uphill."

On 4 November the Woolfs returned to Hogarth House, and a

---

* Gerald Shove, a Cambridge economist and pacifist, married Fredegond Maitland in 1915; she was a daughter of Florence, *née* Fisher, Virginia's first cousin, and F. W. Maitland, the Cambridge historian and biographer of Leslie Stephen.

few days later the last nurse left. Now, very cautiously, they began once more to lead a normal life. This they spent mainly at Richmond, but they kept Asham and went there usually for Christmas and Easter, with perhaps a week or so in May and, always, a prolonged summer holiday, lasting sometimes from late July until October. I am speaking here of the war years and a time when publishing had not put a limit to their holidays.

At Hogarth House, during the years 1915 and 1916, Virginia was very much isolated from London – one cannot say from Bloomsbury for Bloomsbury hardly existed. "It has vanished like the morning mist," wrote Virginia to Ka Cox. In so far as it revived at all its reassembly was due to the development of the war. The year 1915 had been inconclusive and bloody (Rupert Brooke died in that year) and so, in order to continue the *jeu de massacre* fresh soldiers had to be found. In January 1916 a Conscription Bill was introduced. Nearly all Virginia's friends were in one way or another affected by it; most of them were conscientious objectors, all of them reacted against the chauvinism and the hysteria of the home front and many of them faced the alternatives of fighting for a cause in which they did not believe or of facing a Tribunal which, having passed judgement on their sincerity, might send them to do war work, or to prison, or into the armed services where there was always the possibility that they might be court-martialled and shot. In the face of this common peril Bloomsbury was reunited.

Leonard had decided that he was not a conscientious objector; he was therefore in immediate danger of being called to the colours. This would undoubtedly have meant the end of all hopes of permanent recovery for Virginia. He suffered from a trembling of the hands which prevented him from filling tea cups with any ease or, on occasions, from signing his own name. Dr Maurice Wright,* whom Leonard had consulted about this ailment and on Virginia's behalf, must have known very well that the health of both his patients depended upon Leonard's ability to stay at home. He provided Leonard with a certificate which secured exemption by the medical board.

Lytton's obvious debility made it impossible that he could be

* Although Leonard says (*Beginning Again*, p. 178) that it was Dr Maurice Wright who gave him the certificate, Virginia wrote on 14 May 1916 to Vanessa: "Leonard went to Craig who said that he would give him a certificate of unfitness on his own account, as well as mine. He has written a very strong letter, saying that L. is highly nervous, suffers from permanent tremor, & would probably break down if in the army. Also that I am still in a very shaky state, & would very likely have a bad mental breakdown if they took him."

effectively pursued by the military and he used the Tribunal as a platform on which to tease the tribunes. Clive, whose opinions had hardened more rapidly than those of his friends,* slipped through the official net without too much difficulty; he agreed to do agricultural work and found employment on Philip Morrell's farm at Garsington. Philip Morrell, one of the few Members of Parliament to be openly opposed to the war, employed a number of pacifists as farm workers on his estate without, one imagines, much profit to his land.

Adrian, who early in the war had married Karin Costelloe (Virginia and Vanessa thought her not nearly good enough for their brother), was the most convinced and the most active of the Bloomsbury pacifists and defended conscientious objectors before the Tribunals. Maynard Keynes's position was the most equivocal; he held a position of major responsibility in the Treasury and was out of reach of the Tribunals; his sympathies were given to the pacifists, his efforts to the war.

Virginia's chief concern was, of course, for Leonard. But she had other cares. During her madness there had been a change in the affairs of the Bells. Clive lived his own life at 46 Gordon Square and at Garsington; Vanessa lived with Duncan Grant, and when the local Tribunal refused him exemption, she turned to Virginia for assistance. In her efforts to get the verdict set aside Vanessa did not hesitate to ask her sister to use improper influence. She hoped that Virginia might be able to persuade Lady Robert Cecil to speak on Duncan's behalf to Lord Salisbury, who in his turn could sway the judgement of the Tribunals. Nor might Virginia – who could not be insensible to anything that touched Vanessa so deeply – refuse to act in the matter. Representations *were* made to Lady Robert and Lady Robert *did* write to her brother-in-law; but he could not intervene and the matter went no further.

It was soon after the failure of this intrigue, in July 1916, that Leonard and Virginia went to stay with Duncan, David Garnett and Vanessa, who were then attempting to manage a farm at Wissett in Suffolk. For Virginia the visit was important, for it had an effect upon her next novel.

She was again able to write but it would appear that her writing was very strictly rationed. After her visit to Wissett she told Lytton:

---

* *Peace at Once*, a pamphlet in which Clive urged the necessity of a negotiated settlement, was published during the spring of 1915 by the National Labour Press. In the summer of 1915 it was destroyed by order of the Lord Mayor of London (see Clive Bell, *Warmongers*, published by the Peace Pledge Union [1938], p. 1).

My industry has the most minute results, and I begin to despair of finishing a book on this method–I write one sentence–the clock strikes –Leonard appears with a glass of milk. However, I daresay it don't much matter. Wissett seems to lull asleep all ambition–Don't you think they have discovered the secret of life? I thought it wonderfully harmonious.

This may probably be translated into the statement that she was allotted one, or perhaps two, hours for work every morning. At all events her mind was certainly active and on returning home from Wissett she wrote to Vanessa:

I am very much interested in your life, which I think of writing another novel about. Its fatal staying with you–you start so many new ideas.

And in fact the new ideas which Vanessa started were to develop into *Night and Day*.

Despite the failure of Virginia's *démarche* with the Cecil family, Duncan Grant and David Garnett, who was in a similar predicament, were granted exemption from military service on condition that they undertook full-time agricultural work. For a variety of reasons it seemed best to leave Suffolk and they thought, naturally enough, of Sussex. Already in May Virginia had written to Vanessa:

I wish you'd leave Wissett and take Charleston. Leonard . . . says it is a most delightful house & strongly advises you to take it. . . . It is about a mile from Firle . . . under the Downs. It has a charming garden, with a pond, & fruit trees, & vegetables, all now rather wild, but you could make it lovely. The house is very nice with large rooms . . . There is a w.c. & a bathroom, but the bath only has cold water . . . It sounds a most attractive place–& 4 miles from us, so you wouldn't be badgered by us.

This was premature. But in July when the question of the future of Vanessa's household again arose in more urgent form, Virginia was active in making enquiries on her behalf. In September Vanessa herself came to Sussex and settled the matter, rented Charleston, found work on a neighbouring farm for Duncan and David Garnett, and in October moved in. It seemed an eminently convenient disposition and it meant that the sisters would be able to see much more of each other. If this was desirable then the propriety of the arrangement was obvious. But was it desirable? Vanessa obviously thought that it was or she would hardly have applied to Virginia in the first place; Virginia, in letter after letter, had urged Vanessa to leave Suffolk and come to Sussex. Nevertheless a doubt persists.

I think the Woolves have a morbid terror of us all [wrote Vanessa to Lytton]—I can't think why. They seem to think we should contaminate the atmosphere & bring wicked gaieties into Virginia's life. If they could only see the quiet lives we lead! Surely the downs are wide enough for us all & they needn't fear a constant flow in & out of Asheham as long as Woolf is in it–of course it might provide useful spare rooms when they were away.

To Lytton, Leonard explained that his objection to Vanessa's presence in the neighbourhood was that Virginia was sure to insist on walking over to see Vanessa every Sunday, four miles there and four miles back, which would be bad for her health. But although that was what Leonard said, there was, in Lytton's view, "some pollution theory in the background."

Lytton may have been making mischief; but he may also have been right–up to a point. Virginia and Leonard would hardly have objected to having Duncan and Vanessa as neighbours had they been the only neighbours; but they were not coming by themselves. They were bringing children and they were bringing David Garnett.

David Garnett's first visit to Asham had been, to put it mildly, unfortunate. When he came to Sussex to interview the farmer who was to employ him and Duncan he brought with him two young women art students, Barbara Hiles and Dora Carrington. The party was overtaken by nightfall somewhere near Asham and, the Woolfs being away, they broke into the house and slept the night there. They were observed leaving in the early morning and this burglarious exploit was reported before David Garnett's explanation, or rather the explanation which he asked Vanessa to concoct for him, could be received.

There are people who don't mind having their houses broken into by friends or even by intruders such as these, who were hardly more than acquaintances; but the Woolfs did not like it. Virginia was upset. The case was made worse by Garnett's explanation, which was, as Vanessa herself said, disingenuous, and by the fact that he had taken the Oxford book of poetry which Virginia kept by her bedside.*

* "Carrington has been asked to dine with Virginia who wants to hear all about Asheham! I expect she'll worm every detail out of her so Bunny's letter will be exposed. I don't believe Carrington will be a match for Mrs Woolf as one knows her powers if she wants to find out something. However I told Carrington she must stick to Bunny's account, which may be true in the letter but hardly in the spirit." VB/DG, [?17 October 1916]. ". . . I went yesterday evening to

Were these then the kind of neighbours whom Vanessa intended to bring with her? The "Cropheads," the "Bloomsbury Bunnies," the semi-intellectual underworld? "We are not at all anxious," said Virginia, "to have neighbours (unless you)." Was Charleston to become another Garsington filled with casual, carefree Slade students, amoral, anti-social and noisy?

Vanessa would probably have allowed that, under the circumstances, Leonard and Virginia had a case. Virginia was in no condition to be bothered by such people and Leonard would not in any case much want to see them. In fact the menace was imaginary; David Garnett was too discreet to offend in future and it was, in the event, the Woolfs themselves who were to encourage Barbara Hiles as a visitor. But there was another objection that Vanessa could not see and which was real enough; it was impossible for Virginia to resist or for Leonard not to resent the visits of Vanessa's children and their nurse and these, for some years, were to be a real menace to the peace of Asham.

Leonard was cast in the ungrateful role of family dragon. He had to make sure that Virginia did not have too many visitors, to keep her from exhausting excursions, to see to it if she were away from home that she should leave early, or if she received a guest that the guest should not stay too long. In 1916, with Virginia still slowly recovering, he could take no chances and neglect no precautions. This made him seem fussy, and indeed curmudgeonly. Usually it was hard to believe–hard for the visitor and hard for Virginia herself–that there was anything wrong with her. But a few days in company, a party or two or an excursion to London, might bring back headaches and sleepless nights which could be cured only by long periods of rest and seclusion.

But there was more to it than this; even if Virginia had been in good health, Leonard would still have been more domestic and more serious-minded than the younger members of Ottoline's circle. His temper was more severe, his habits more sober than theirs and, in that the inhabitants of Charleston were more tolerant of the kind of frivolity that verges on silliness, there was also a difference between

Virginia. What an examination!!! But I was rigid and denied everything. Even to Bunny taking a book which of course was true. But she asked me if Bunny did take a book, which I denied. So you *must* say you borrowed it the weekend before, & give it to her back. She asked if we spent the night at Firle. So I supported Bunny's story and said yes. I thought her indeed charming and also the grissily wolf." Carrington to VB, n.d. [? October 1916]; see also VW/VB, [24 October 1916]. See also Carrington, *Letters*, p. 45.

him and them. He would hardly have condemned his sister-in-law's 'way of life,' but he might have considered it a trifle ramshackle, a little desperate. His attitude, I surmise, was marked by an almost imperceptible shade of disapproval and in a way this sentiment was shared by Virginia–but not entirely.

Virginia believed that she was quite capable of bicycling over to Charleston and back; she was pretty sure that a visit to Vanessa could do nothing but good, and she may even have accepted her nephews at their mother's valuation–for an afternoon at all events; if she curtailed her visits and put off the children it was (in writing to Vanessa at all events) out of deference to a husband who got into unreasonable 'states' when she lived a reasonably social life. In fact she was not quite consistent in these matters; she liked to be (from Leonard's point of view) naughty, and yet she respected his views. In all serious matters they were united, and even in small things she would usually allow, on reflection, that he was in the right.

These considerations have taken me somewhat beyond the year 1916, for in fact Vanessa did not settle at Charleston until October of that year (after David Garnett's blunderings at Asham), while the subsequent social transactions belong rather to the years 1917 and 1918. In fact the autumn and winter months of 1916 were quiet and uneventful, and Leonard and Virginia evolved a pattern of life at Hogarth House to which they adhered more or less all their lives. They wrote in the morning, they walked in the afternoon, they read in the evening; once or twice a week political or publishing business would take Leonard up to London; once or twice a week Virginia would accompany him and visit libraries, shops, concerts or friends. They would meet again at tea time and dine out or go home together. Their friends came out to Richmond to tea or to dine and often to spend the night. On Sundays their afternoon walk would very likely turn into a rather more ambitious expedition and they would take a bus or train and go further afield–it might well end in a visit to Leonard's family.

In the autumn Virginia became an active member of the Richmond Branch of the Women's Co-operative Guild, and presided once a month at a meeting held in her own house, at which she was responsible for providing the speaker.

This function she continued to fulfil for the next four years, after which she rather thankfully resigned. In that time she prevailed upon Leonard and upon many of her friends ("we have had nothing but brilliancy and charm the last 3 months–Morgan Forster on India, Bob Trevelyan on China, Mary Sheepshanks on Peru") to speak. The Guild members liked a change of subject, but at times the subject was too much for them. On 23 January 1917, they were addressed by Mrs Bessie Ward from the Council of Civil Liberties. She spoke on the subject of Conscription and, in particular, of the possible conscription of women. Noting the presence in the audience of two quite young girls she said that she was going to touch on "moral" questions and asked whether she should continue. No one objected, so she proceeded to describe, in some detail, the dangers of venereal disease, the risks to young soldiers of infection and so on. There was a queer silence when the talk ended and Virginia had thanked Mrs Ward. Two ladies left immediately, one very fat woman sat and wept; the company dispersed except for a Mrs Langston, an active and valuable member, who expressed her sense of outrage. Only a childless woman, she said, could have made such a speech, "for we mothers try to forget what our sons have to go through." She then burst into tears.

Virginia was quite unrepentant. Writing an account of the whole affair to Margaret Llewelyn Davies, she said she had never heard such nonsense; poor Mrs Ward on the other hand was well used to it–she had gone up and down the country provoking tears and indignation wherever she went. Margaret seems to have replied that the women's anxiety for their sons was quite natural and with this, in a second letter, Virginia agreed, although she still found it surprising that working women should choose to remain ignorant of a matter which might well concern them closely. Her cook, Nelly Boxall, who admitted that she had been shocked, acknowledged that it was right that women should know about such things. And indeed, in time, the other members did too, and told her so; they even asked for a lecture on Sex Education–all of which Virginia thought did them great credit.*

It cannot have been very long before Mrs Ward's lecture that Virginia made a new and important friend. It was Lytton who had suggested that she might like to meet Katherine Mansfield–

* "... I went to the Guild, which pleased me by its good sense, and the evidence that it does somehow stand for something real to these women. In spite of their solemn passivity they have a deeply hidden and inarticulate desire for something beyond the daily life. I believe they relish all the pomp of officers and elections because in some way it symbolises this other thing. They recanted their abuse of the woman on syphilis, which I think to their credit. Since then they have learnt, they said, that she only spoke the truth. They wish me to get them a speaker on Sex Education, Mrs Hiscoke telling us that she had had to get a friend to explain the period to her own daughter, and she still feels shy if the daughter is in the room when sexual subjects are discussed. She's 23 years old." *AWD* (*Berg*), 18 April 1918.

" . . . decidedly an interesting creature, I thought – very amusing and sufficiently mysterious. She spoke with great enthusiasm about *The Voyage Out*, and said she wanted to make your acquaintance more than anyone else's. So I said I thought it might be managed. Was I rash?" The lady was said to be in Cornwall. "If," said Virginia, who was to spend a fortnight near St Ives at the end of September, "I see anyone answering to your account on a rock or in the sea I shall accost her." She did not, and presumably their meeting took place in London later in the year.* By this time Katherine Mansfield and John Middleton Murry were living, with Carrington and Dorothy Brett, at 3 Gower Street, a house rented from Maynard Keynes, who himself had taken over the Bells' house at 46 Gordon Square. By February 1917 they were on such terms that Virginia could write to Vanessa: "I have had a slight rapprochement with Katherine Mansfield; who seems to me an unpleasant but forcible & utterly unscrupulous character."

They were always to disagree and never to disagree finally. United by their devotion to literature and divided by their rivalry as writers, they found each other immensely attractive and yet profoundly irritating. Or at least these were certainly Virginia's sentiments. She admired Katherine; she was also fascinated by that side of Katherine's life which was beyond her own emotional capacity. Katherine had knocked about the world and had been hurt by it; she had given rein to all the female instincts, slept with all kinds of men; she was an object of admiration – and of pity. She was interesting, vulnerable, gifted and charming. But also she dressed like a tart and behaved like a bitch. Or so it sometimes seemed to Virginia and in rather the same way she admired her stories, so sharply observed, so perceptive, at times so tragic and yet, at others, so cheap and so obvious. Katherine Mansfield, I think, returned Virginia's admiration and also her animosity. Probably she was rather frightened and at the same time half amused by her, and not displeased to discover that she could give Virginia not only pleasure but pain. Their doubts and reservations about each other were considerable; but in each other's company they were at ease and felt themselves to be fellow-workers.

Virginia certainly thought well enough of Katherine's talents to

* Leonard Woolf (*Beginning Again*, p. 203) says that it was at Garsington that they first came across Katherine Mansfield and Middleton Murry; but the Woolfs' first visit to Garsington was in November 1917. They are first mentioned in Leonard's *Diary* on 12 January 1917: "Katherine Mansfield, Murry & S. Waterlow to dinner."

want to print one of her stories. It will be remembered that, in
1915, before Virginia's collapse, the Woolfs were thinking of buying
a printing press. Now that she was better the idea was revived.
Leonard's purpose in this was to some extent therapeutic: it would
be good for Virginia to have some manual occupation; but of course
they were both of them writers, and the idea of printing and publishing their own works, even on the small scale dictated by a hand press,
was very seductive. In October 1916 Virginia was again talking of
getting a press, and she and Leonard began to consider whether
they ought not to take lessons in printing. It was not easy, for Schools
of Printing would not take middle-aged amateurs, and in the end
they had to learn from a book. Then another difficulty arose;
they had not enough money to buy a press.

It has been said, and the story has been repeated more than once,
that the Hogarth Press was founded upon Leonard's winnings in the
Calcutta Sweepstake. It sounds a pleasantly substantial foundation
on which to build a business; but those winnings had been gained
long before Leonard married Virginia and in fact the Press started
on a capital outlay of £41. 15s. 3d—and this was not easily raised.

When, in 1912, Virginia told Violet Dickinson that she was
marrying a penniless Jew she was not, if we understand the word
penniless as Violet's friends would have understood it, overstating
the case. For they would have considered an income of less than
£600 a year as something like penury and Leonard, who had been
earning £260 a year from the Colonial Office, was, as a result of
his resignation, reduced to something very much less. His mother,
at the time of her husband's death, had been left with just enough
money to keep herself and her nine children and to give the sons
a good education. Once educated they had to fend for themselves.
With his salary, and no doubt his sweepstake winnings, Leonard
was able to save some money and this he increased by speculation.
According to his diary his investments on 1 January 1912 amounted
to £517. 15s. 2d, which would yield—but here I have no exact
figures—something like £30 a year—not affluence, even by the
standards of 1912. He and Virginia had hoped to make money by
writing, but their novels in 1916 were bringing in less than £25 a
year, and although Leonard was earning something by journalism,
Virginia since 1913 had been unable to earn anything at all, while
her illnesses were extremely expensive.

Fortunately Virginia had money of her own. It is not easy to
know how much. When Sir Leslie Stephen died in 1904 and his
children set up house together at 46 Gordon Square Vanessa, who

looked after the money, was asked by an old family friend what their income amounted to.

> When I said I thought about £300 a year each she said all was well– £200 would have been too little but with £1,200 between us we need not worry. Nor did we–but in fact our income was largely imaginary, depending on the successful letting of the Hyde Park Gate house, which remained obstinately empty for years owing to Duckworth mismanagement: not only that but Adrian was still at Cambridge, Thoby reading for the Bar, neither Virginia nor I earning anything. Then there were our old family servants who took it for granted all should go on as before, as did we ourselves. Sometimes I had a vague suspicion we were heading for bankruptcy, but all my life I had heard my father say gloomily that we should soon be in the workhouse & I had got used to not taking it seriously.

Virginia, who had inherited some money from Thoby and some from her aunt Caroline Emelia Stephen, had–"theoretically," as Leonard puts it–an invested capital of some £9,000; and this yielded less than £400 a year.*

In 1914 the Woolfs were living just within their income; doctors' bills were no doubt high in that year and, when they took a holiday in Northumberland, Virginia had to ask Vanessa for an advance of £15 on her share of the rent of Asham. In 1915 Leonard cast the following account of his and Virginia's expenses:

	£
Rooms	130
Food	156
Pocket Money	52
Doctors (this includes patent foods and medicaments for Virginia)	25
Dress	50
Miscellaneous	30
TOTAL	443

The payments to doctors, which seem comparatively reasonable, were probably largely postponed until 1916. By this time the Woolfs were established with their own servants at Asham and

---

* After their half-sister Stella's death in 1897 her husband Jack Hills made over the income on her marriage settlement to Vanessa and Virginia, and continued this until his second marriage (in 1931). Virginia inherited one-third of Thoby's estate (valued at £6,681) in 1906, and £2,500 from Caroline Emelia in 1909. She tried to persuade Adrian to take a half of this legacy, but I think without success.

Hogarth House, and the pattern of spending had changed; at the same time Virginia was beginning to earn money once more while Leonard's takings decreased a little.

	Estimate £	Expenditure £		
Houses	140	129.	5.	8.
Misc. House. (including fuel, furniture, etc.)	50	69.	0.	8.
Food	220	220.	5.	2.
Servants	60	67.	2.	2.
Doctors	25	81.	3.	3.
Dress (Virginia)	36	30.	8.	7.
Dress (Leonard)	14	14.	1.	5.
Miscellaneous	50	66.	17.	9.
TOTAL	595	678.	4.	8.

Leonard's estimate was made at the beginning of the year 1916, and as will be seen was exceeded by £83. 4s. 8d, largely owing to the unexpectedly heavy bills from the doctors. For the rest the Woolfs seem to have practised economies with some care; that Leonard exceeded his estimate of £14 for dress by 1s. 5d shows, I think, that it was exiguous. The servants were a new item; it will be noted that their joint wages came to less than the doctors' fees or the rent of the two houses, but of course, the increased expenditure on food must have been largely on their account. In that year, realising that the Woolfs were in difficulties, Violet Dickinson tried, but failed, to lend them money. The highly detailed accounts that Leonard kept (Virginia attempted to keep them but soon gave up) show that he counted every penny. Expenditure on newspapers and cigarettes was carefully entered and continued to be noted long after there was any need for such strict accounting; undoubtedly Leonard took pleasure in such exactitude and it became an end in itself; but in the early years of their married life such care was necessary. It is not easy to find items that can be classed as luxuries; in fact I think that there must have been some separate fund for the rare visits to music halls and cinemas, indulgences which they did occasionally allow themselves but which I cannot find mentioned. The nearest to luxuries that I can discover in the year 1916 are a total of 5s. 1d on cigarettes, 1s. 7d on flowers, £2. 5s. 6d on tips and presents, 3s. 4d on coloured papers (for which Virginia had a passion) and 1s. 9d on a dog collar. They spent £5. 3s. 5d on books and library subscriptions, but these can hardly be classed as luxuries. There is no mention of wines and spirits, gramophone records, cigars, taxis or concerts–all things that they were to enjoy in later years.

Keeping two houses and two servants the Woolfs cannot be described as poor; but neither, by the standards of their class, were they prosperous. In 1914, 1915 and 1916 they were what their friends would have called very hard up. The printing press could no doubt have been purchased by selling securities,* but clearly they were reluctant to do this. Their intention was to use an income tax rebate of £35 which they expected in December 1916. But the rebate amounted to only £15. More money had to be found and they thought that it could be raised by selling some inherited Thackeray manuscripts to the Pierpont Morgan Library. Adrian was to manage this business but before the sale was completed they found the capital elsewhere. On 23 March Leonard and Virginia went to the Farringdon Road and ordered a press.

It arrived a month later. They unpacked it with enormous excitement and carried it up to the drawing-room, only to discover that an essential part was broken. Leonard sent for a replacement. With all the excitement of children on Christmas morning, they began to divide the blocks of type into separate letters. Some got lost in the drawing-room carpet and Virginia managed, almost at once, to get the lower case h's mixed with the n's.

"I see that real printing will devour one's entire life. I am going to see Katherine Mansfield, to get a story from her, perhaps," wrote Virginia to Vanessa, and after a week Leonard was telling Margaret Llewelyn Davies that he wished he had never bought the cursed thing for now he would do nothing else but print. They decided that their first publication should be a joint effort and by 7 May they were able to post off to likely subscribers the hand-printed announcement: "It is proposed to issue shortly a pamphlet containing two short stories by Leonard Woolf and Virginia Woolf (price, including postage 1s. 2d)."

Virginia was by this time working hard for *The Times Literary Supplement*;† at the same time the idea which she had conceived at Wissett in July 1916 was sprouting into a novel which increasingly

* The Woolfs may have sold securities in order to pay the doctors. There is no evidence of this and it appears that they had other resources: ". . . it meant selling my few earrings and necklaces." VW/ES, 1 May 1931.

† Kirkpatrick (*A Bibliography of Virginia Woolf*, 1967) lists 12 contributions in 1916, 32 in 1917.

occupied her mind. On Easter Day 1917 Duncan and Vanessa came over from Charleston to tea at Asham, and Virginia was able to have a comfortable, intimate talk with her sister and tell her "all about her new novel."

> I am the principal character in it & I expect I'm a very priggish & severe young woman but perhaps you'll see what I was like at 18–I think the most interesting character is evidently my mother who is made exactly like Lady Ritchie down to every detail apparently. Everyone will know who it is of course.

Night and Day was, and was intended to be, a fairly pedestrian affair. Virginia wanted to see if she could achieve a perfectly orthodox and conventional novel. Also she wanted to do something which would not bring her too close to the abyss from which she had so recently emerged. In the final chapters of *The Voyage Out* she had been playing with fire. She had succeeded in bringing some of the devils who dwelt within her mind hugely and gruesomely from the depths, and she had gone too far for comfort. That novel and the final effort of giving it to the world had taken her over the edge of sanity and she could not yet risk a repetition of that appalling operation. Deliberately therefore she embarked upon something sane, quiet and undisturbing. She was to use this expedient again and to follow a particularly exacting novel with something lighter and easier; thus *Orlando* follows *To the Lighthouse*, *Flush* follows *The Waves* and *Three Guineas* follows *The Years*; the heavyweight novel is succeeded by a lightweight book–what she called "a joke." *Night and Day* was more than a joke, but despite its ambitious proportions it was a recuperative work. She did not altogether enjoy working on it. She compared it, writing to Ethel Smyth many years later, to drawing from the cast–an academic exercise. She began to promise herself a holiday–a kind of trip into those perilous areas that were forbidden.

> ... they were the treats I allowed myself when I had done my exercise in the conventional style. I shall never forget the day I wrote the *Mark on the Wall*–all in a flash, as if flying, after being kept stone-breaking for months. The *Unwritten Novel* was the great discovery however. That– again in one second–showed me how I could embody all my deposit of experience in a shape that fitted it ... *Jacob's Room* ... *Mrs Dalloway* &c. How I trembled with excitement–& then Leonard came in & I drank my milk, concealed my excitement, & wrote I suppose another page of that interminable *Night & Day*.

In the summer of 1917 *Night and Day* was not nearly finished and, even if it had been, it would have been far too large an undertaking for the Woolfs' little hand press. It was *The Mark on the Wall* which, together with Leonard's *Three Jews*, appeared in July from the Hogarth Press under the title *Publication No. 1. Two Stories.*

This publication and its favourable reception* (by a very small public, for only 150 copies were printed) were both the result of and a contribution to Virginia's steady return to health. By this time she was leading almost as normal a life as she was ever to do, seeing a good many people in London and Richmond and, in August and September, at Asham. Henceforward it became a habit of many of their friends to spend a few days with the Woolfs at Asham and then proceed to Charleston to stay with Vanessa—or *vice versa*, and there was a continual to-ing and fro-ing between the households. This summer Virginia's guests at Asham were Roger Fry, Lytton Strachey and Desmond MacCarthy, who came from, or went on to Charleston, as well as Katherine Mansfield, Sidney Waterlow, G. Lowes Dickinson, Pernel Strachey and Philip Morrell, whom Leonard had insisted upon inviting on the grounds that he was never asked away on his own account without Lady Ottoline. "And then," as Virginia wrote to Margaret Llewelyn Davies,

> we've seen a lot of the younger generation, who seem to me the essence of good sense, honesty, sobriety & kindliness . . . [they] walk across the downs in brown corduroy trousers, blue shirts, grey socks, & no hats on their heads, which are cropped, so that as I sit on the terrace, I really don't know Barbara Hiles from Nick Bagenal, who is in the Irish Guards.

Leonard's invitation to Philip Morrell may be considered a sort of reply to one of Virginia's more reckless social adventures. This summer, for the first time since her marriage, she met Ottoline again—a reunion which seems to have been highly gratifying to both ladies. Virginia wrote to Vanessa:

> I was so much overcome by her beauty that I really felt as if I'd suddenly got into the sea, & heard the mermaids fluting on their rocks. How it was done I can't think; but she had red-gold hair in masses, cheeks as soft as cushions with a lovely deep crimson on the crest of them, & a body really shaped more after my notion of a mermaid's than I've ever

---

* "The *Two Stories* was a most cheering production. I could never have believed it possible. My only criticism is that there doesn't seem to be quite enough ink. Virginia's is, I consider, a work of genius. The liquidity of the style fills me with envy: really some of the sentences!—How on earth does she make the English language float and float? And then the wonderful way in which the modern point of view is suggested. *Tiens!*" Lytton Strachey to Leonard Woolf, 17 July 1917.

seen; not a wrinkle or blemish, swelling, but smooth.

Our conversation was rather on those lines, so I'm not surprised that I made a good impression. She didn't seem so much of a fool as I'd been led to think; she was quite shrewd, though vapid in the intervals. I begged her to revive Bedford Sqre. & the salon, which she said she would, if anyone missed her. Then came protestations, invitations – in fact I don't see how we can get out of going there, though Leonard says he wont, & I know it will be a disillusionment. However, my tack is to tell her she is nothing but an illusion, which is true & then perhaps she'll live up to it. She was full of your praises . . .

She & Virginia [wrote Roger Fry] have fallen into each others arms and each flatters t'other to the top of their bents. What a lot of temporary mischief it'll brew, that liaison – I s'pose it'll cut me off Virginia, & Ott. will get in some fine whacks at you too. But it won't last long.

Roger was perhaps writing to please Vanessa, who was not sorry to hear him speak ill of Ottoline and, at an earlier period, seems to have caused a breach between them. He took Virginia's infatuation a little too seriously; she never fell into Ottoline's arms so violently as to lose her balance. Certainly she was delighted to renew the acquaintance and certainly she was inclined to disregard the protests of Leonard and the aspersions of Vanessa, Clive and Roger. But this didn't prevent her from making fun of Ottoline and perhaps something that was not quite fun. Ottoline appealed to the snob in her; she had the grand manner and she was also one of the grand entertainments. Virginia liked to think that anything so improbable existed.

Their meeting in May did result in an invitation to Garsington. The visit had to be postponed because Ottoline caught the measles and, for one reason or another – perhaps Leonard managed to defer the evil day – it did not take place until November.

Meanwhile there had been a change, if not exactly in Virginia's life, at least in the manner in which that life was henceforth to be recorded. Returning from Asham on 5 October she discovered the diary she had written during her interval of sanity in 1915; it made her laugh and she was pleased enough by what she read to begin again. The record which she now kept was often to be neglected for days, for weeks, or indeed for months; but she never abandoned it altogether. She found in it an outlet for her immediate feelings, a source which she hoped, one day, when she had grown old, might enable her to write an autobiography. She fell into the habit of opening her book after tea and writing perfectly freely: she believed that this practice of spontaneous composition helped to give her more pondered works greater force and directness. This spontaneity makes her diary biographically interesting; it also makes it hard to publish. She wrote with the passion of the moment in her heart and at times she relieved her feelings with bitter ferocity. But despite their uncalculating sincerity I do not believe that these volumes give an entirely true picture of their author. There were times when she wrote in her diary because she could not read, and when she could not read it was usually because she was nervous, cross, or in some way disturbed and wanted, as she put it, "to write out the pain." Thus she often shows herself in a rather sad light, catching anxious and fearful moods rather than the gaiety and fantasy (which was equally a part of her character) which becomes more evident in her letters. Nevertheless, with the aid of these volumes it should be possible to give an accurate idea of her life.

Here are three entries from October 1917:

Wednesday, October 10th

No air raid; no further disturbance by our country's needs [Leonard had again been summoned for a medical inspection]; in fact L. made out in his bath that he deserved some good fortune, and opening his letters found a cheque for £12 from a Swedish paper which never was born and yet pays its debts. And I had 4/- for myself. Late last night, I was told to have my Henry James [review for *The Times Literary Supplement*] done if possible on Friday, so that I had to make way with it this morning and as I rather grudge time spent on articles, and yet can't help spending it if I have it, I am rather glad that this is now out of my power. And another article upon the country in Hardy and E. Brontë is suggested. We walked down the river, through the park and back to an early tea. At this moment L. is bringing the [19]17 Club into existence. I am sitting over the fire, and we have the prospect of K. Mansfield to dinner, when many delicate things fall to be discussed. We notice how backward the leaves are in falling and yellowing here as compared with Asheham. It might still be August, save for the acorns scattered on the path–suggesting to us the mysterious dispensation which causes them to perish, or we should be a forest of oaks.

Thursday, October 11th

The dinner last night went off: the delicate things were discussed. We could both wish that our first impression of K. M. was not that she stinks like a–well, civet cat that had taken to street walking. In truth, I'm a little shocked by her commonness at first sight; lines so hard and cheap. However, when this diminishes, she is so intelligent and inscrutable that she repays friendship. ... We discussed Henry James, and K. M. was illuminating, I thought. A munition worker called Leslie Moor came to fetch her–another of these females on the border land of propriety and naturally inhabiting the underworld–rather vivacious, sallow skinned, without any attachment to one place rather than another. Today poor L. had to go the round of Drs. and committees, with a visit to Squire thrown in. His certificates are repeated. He weighs only 9 [stone].6 [lbs]. I bought my winter store of gloves, got a reference in the London Library, and met L. at Spikings for tea. Heaven blessed us by sending a quick train and we came home very glad to be home, over our fire, though we had to light it and cook up our dinner, owing to the servants' off day.

Sunday, October 14th
That is an awful confession, and seems to show the signs of death already spreading in this book. I have excuses though. We were rung up and asked to dine with the Bells in Soho, and this, I regret to say, led to much argument; we put off going to Kingston [i.e. to see Leonard's mother]; the night was wet, and L. didn't want–old arguments in short were brought out, with an edge to them. So we went dolefully enough, found the place, behind the palace, dined with Roger, Nina Hamnett, Saxon, Barbara [Hiles] and a party such as might figure in a Wells novel: I enjoyed it though, and L. was a model of self control. . . . Saturday was entirely given over to the military. We are safe again and, so they say, for ever. Our appearance smoothed every obstacle; and by walking across Kingston we got to the doctor about 12, and all was over by half past. I waited in a great square, surrounded by barrack buildings and was reminded of a Cambridge College–soldiers crossing, coming out of staircases and going into others; but gravel and no grass. A disagreeable impression of control and senseless determination; a great boarhound, emblem of military dignity, I suppose, strolled across by himself. L. was a good deal insulted: the doctors referred to him as the "chap with the senile tremor", through a curtain. Mercifully the impression slowly vanished as we went about Richmond. Herbert [Woolf, Leonard's brother] came to tea, bringing the dog, Tinker, a stout, active, bold brute, brown and white with large humourous eyes, reminding me a little of Dominic Spring-Rice. We have taken him for a walk, but directly he is loosed he leaps walls, dashes into open doors and behaves like a spirit in quest of something not to be found. We doubt rather if we can cope with him. Have I put down our Manx cat, also presented to us, one day this week?

These three entries may serve to announce those themes which in 1917 and 1918 recur most frequently in her diary: the air raids, Katherine Mansfield, the "Underworld" and the 1917 Club. The fact that she frequently adverts to them does not mean that they were, for her, of supreme importance. Virginia's mind was so constituted that it is very hard to know what would have been supremely important to her and, although it may sound ludicrous, her acquisition, at a rather later date, of a green glass jar from a chemist-one of those great flagons that glow or used to glow in pharmacy windows-was for her, it having been coveted perhaps since childhood, an event possibly as important as Katherine Mansfield's friendship or the German air raids. The point is not one that can be decided or, in any exhaustive way, discussed, but it should be borne in mind. More obviously important than either Katherine Mansfield or the chemist's jar was the continual progress of *Night and Day*. But during the autumn of 1917 she says nothing about it.

On the other hand she says a good deal about her journalism; at this time her book reviews were appearing in *The Times Literary Supplement* almost every week. This journalism was a source of mixed pleasure and vexation. If the Editor stopped sending her books she complained that she had been dismissed; if on the other hand he gave her a great deal of work then of course it took time from her novel. Virginia's ephemeral writing, if one may use such a word of contributions to *The Times Literary Supplement*, was never easily accomplished; she made several drafts, sometimes a great many drafts, before she was satisfied with a review.

. . . this sort of writing is always done against time; however much time I may have. For example here I have spent the week (but I was interrupted 2 days, & one cut short by a lunch with Roger) over Hakluyt: who turns out on mature inspection to justify over & over again my youthful discrimination. I write & write; I am rung up & told to stop writing: review must be had on Friday; I typewrite till the messenger from the Times appears; I correct the pages in my bedroom with him sitting over the fire here.

"A Christmas number not at all to Mr Richmond's taste, he said. Very unlike the Supplement style."

"Gift books, I suppose?" I suggested.

"O no, Mrs Woolf, its done for the advertisers."

But to retrace. On Thursday I lunched with Roger in order to hear the following story.

Mrs MacColl to Mr Cox of the London Library:

"Have you *The Voyage Out* by Virginia Woolf?"

"Virginia Woolf? Let me see; she was a Miss Stephen, daughter of Sir Leslie-her sister is Mrs Clive Bell I think. Ah, strange to see what's become of those two girls. Brought up in such a nice home too. But then, they were never *baptised*."

If she were to write reviews it was of course necessary to use the London Library, a good hour's journey from Hogarth House, and having gone so far she might go further and buy herself a pen or a pair of gloves or stockings, or take tea with Vanessa (if she happened to be in London), and thus an entire afternoon would be expended. Afternoons at home were now almost entirely devoted to printing. The Woolfs had started work on Katherine Mansfield's *Prelude*, Virginia setting up type–it came to 68 pages–Leonard doing the heavier work of machining. Printing was a constant source of delight and of misery; the actual processes and operations frequently perplexed them. Leonard consulted a local jobbing printer, who convinced him that he needed a larger press; they also began to look for an assistant. They thought that one of those sensible and well-disposed young women whom Virginia had noticed might help them.

On 10 October Virginia had written in her diary: "At this moment L. is bringing the 17 Club into existence." This club* had a local habitation in Gerrard Street, Soho. Leonard and other socialist intellectuals thought that it might provide a congenial meeting place. It very soon became a centre, not only for the politically-minded, but for a kind of second-generation Bloomsbury. The old pre-war Bloomsbury was already beginning to acquire a sort of mythical existence, to be admired and imitated or denigrated by younger people who were, for the most part, non-conformists in a nation at war. Many in fact were not seriously interested in politics, but they were all deeply and decidedly hostile to the faith and morals of those Victorians and Edwardians who, they thought, had led their generation to catastrophe. When *Eminent Victorians* appeared in June 1918 it found in them a ready and responsive audience. There was in fact what Leonard was to call an "element of unadulterated culture" amongst the members of the 1917 Club. In the visual arts they were naturally on the side of the *avant-garde*; but painting had had its great explosive flowering in 1910. It was the writers who seemed to be just within sight of new possibilities. Ezra Pound, James Joyce, T. S. Eliot and Katherine Mansfield were beginning to be read and discussed; and Roger Fry came back from France with news of an undoubted literary genius; admittedly he was rather apt to return from France with news of this kind, but on this occasion the genius was Marcel Proust.

The writer of *The Voyage Out* also had her place among the nascent stars–stars, it must be borne in mind, visible only to a very few. She was half pleased, half irritated by the attention shown her in the 1917 Club. She found it a convenient place at which to meet Leonard. After delivering her article to *The Times* she would collect books from Mudie's, or Day's or the London Library,

* The club took its name from the Russian Revolution, presumably the February Revolution.

drink tea in Gerrard Street and find company to engage her interest. Many of the people whom Virginia met at the club were already known or half known to her; there were some whom she referred to as: "Cropheads" or "Bloomsbury Bunnies;" others she referred to as "the Underworld." * It was among the former that she sought a helper in the quite considerable task of printing and binding *Prelude*. Their first assistant, a tall and grave young woman called Alix Sargant-Florence, came to start work on 16 October 1917. After showing her what to do, Leonard and Virginia left her on her high stool and took their dog for a walk. When they returned Alix said that she found the work totally without interest and saw no point in continuing. Their next apprentice was much less critical and considerably more persevering. Barbara Hiles had been one of the thoughtless trio who had broken into Asham and spent the night there. She came, trotting like a little pony, into the lives of the Bells and the Woolfs (sometimes, it must be said, on the wrong side of the road), pretty, practical and sensible, eager to be of service to everyone; she was ready and willing to be helpful in the Hogarth Press and turned up on a bicycle, bright as a button, on 21 November.

She set to work with more enthusiasm than competence, so that often enough Leonard had to take down and re-set the formes after she had gone home. She chattered, she was lively and decorative and never grumbled–as well she might have, for her wages amounted only to a meat meal on the days when she worked, an assurance of shelter in case of air raids and a proportion of the profits, which proportion she received after two months' work, when Leonard pressed half a crown into her hand. The real wages, one imagines, were Virginia's company and the opportunity of talking about her rather agitated life to a sympathetic listener.

Virginia had plenty of opportunity for getting to know Barbara fairly well during the next weeks. She and her friend Carrington –both ex-Slade students, with their bobbed hair and thick fringes, their free and independent ways, their healthy high spirits and bright sensible clothes, their passion for culture–represented Virginia's archetypal Cropheads. "The Bloomsbury hypnotism," she wrote to Vanessa, "is rank, & threatens the sanity of all the poor Bunnies, who are perpetually feeling their hind legs to see if they haven't turned into hares." Carrington fell in love with

* These terms were of course extremely imprecise. "Bloomsbury Bunnies" was invented by Mrs Desmond MacCarthy, "Cropheads" was Virginia's own word.

Lytton Strachey and devoted her life to serving him. Barbara's artless charms touched some chord in Saxon's heart and disturbed his deeply entrenched celibacy; his devotion–which was to be lifelong –promised access to the imagined Empyrean of Bloomsbury, though when it came to marriage she settled for a younger and more human admirer, Nicholas Bagenal. The movements of this *pas de trois*, as described by Barbara herself and by her friends, were for Virginia a source of endless fascination and speculation. Nick Bagenal's sister Faith, the austere and melancholy Alix (desperately, but in the end successfully, engaged in the pursuit of James Strachey), and her own cousin Fredegond, a very intense and poetic young woman, helped also to provide the company and the youthful indiscretions which enlivened Virginia's visits to the 1917 club. There too she was able to observe many examples of what she called "the Underworld." She used this term with malicious intent and certainly with a kind of snobbery, sometimes with a purely social meaning, but also to classify those who were not so much creative artists as critics and commentators–people who could write a clever essay or a smart review; people who were more interested in reputations than in talents. For them the important thing was success; they would know who was on the way up or the way down; they could measure one author against another in terms of copies sold and retail the latest scandal in the world of journalism or of publishing. Their ambition was to be on the winning side. Thus, to anticipate a little, when Conrad published *Victory* Virginia found it hailed by the Underworld as a masterpiece: Conrad was very much 'the thing.' But when she expressed her doubts, finding the book below his best level, there was a kind of uneasy shift of opinion–perhaps Conrad was going out, perhaps the moment had come to disparage him. One must tack, shift, reinsure, turn and come again.

Grub Street, I suppose, has always been like this, and the Squires and Lynds, Sullivans or Swinnertons of Virginia's Underworld were no worse and probably better than most. But for her the perpetual president and oracle of the Underworld was John Middleton Murry, for he added another ingredient–a high moral tone, a pretentious philosophy borrowed in part from his friend D. H. Lawrence– which allowed the game to be played under the cover of deep, manly, visceral feelings and virtuous protestations. I think that most of Virginia's generalisations about the Underworld are really based upon Murry; he was so very much 'the coming man.' She and Lytton agreed that he would probably end as Professor of English Literature at Oxford or Cambridge.

The Cropheads and the Underworld met and to some extent fused at the 1917 Club; some of them were also to be found at Garsington Manor near Oxford, where Philip and Ottoline Morrell kept open house and whither, it may be remembered, the Woolfs were invited during the summer of 1917.

Long before she finally persuaded Leonard to accompany her there, Virginia had gained a pretty accurate notion of what Garsington was like. Here, since the introduction of conscription, Philip Morrell had offered easy employment on his farm to pacifists and conscientious objectors, and here there was in consequence a resident population which included at different times Clive Bell, Gerald and Fredegond Shove, Middleton Murry's younger brother, and the painter Mark Gertler; this was reinforced by the visits for longer or shorter periods of Middleton Murry and Katherine Mansfield, Carrington and her friend Brett,* Lytton Strachey and relays of young men who came out from the University to extend their education. The atmosphere was not a happy one and may be illustrated by one story which was told by Clive Bell and in the truth of which he firmly believed.

On one occasion he had had to go unexpectedly to London on a Sunday leaving on the hall table several letters to be posted on Monday morning. Gertler and Carrington thought that it would entertain a dull Sunday evening if they were to steam these letters open and read the contents aloud. Ottoline protested too little or not at all, which was unwise of her, for the company was entertained by an account, no doubt in Clive's best Walpolian manner, of all that was mean, base or ridiculous in her Ladyship. There was, in particular, the story of a peacock which, having died of old age complicated by various disgusting maladies, reappeared pompously accoutred on the dining-room table. There was, not unnaturally, an awkward coolness when Clive returned from London, all the more awkward in that its cause could not be avowed.

True or false, the story is significant in that it gives a notion of the moral atmosphere of Garsington at that time.

When, on 19 November 1917, Virginia returned from her first visit there she wrote:

> We came back from that adventure two hours ago. It's difficult to give the whole impression, save that it wasn't much unlike my imagination. People strewn about in a sealingwax coloured room. Aldous Huxley

---

* The painter Mark Gertler, unhappily in love with Carrington, watched with bitter jealousy her infatuation for Lytton; Brett (the Hon. Dorothy Brett) had been at the Slade with Carrington and Gertler.

toying with great round disks of ivory and green marble–the draughts of Garsington: Brett in trousers: Philip tremendously encased in the best leather: Ottoline, as usual, velvet and pearls: two pug dogs: Lytton semi-recumbent in a vast chair. Too many nicknacks for real beauty, too many scents and silks and a warm air which was a little heavy. Droves of people moved about from room to room–from drawing room to dining room, from dining room to Ottoline's room– all Sunday. At moments the sense of it seemed to flag; and the day certainly lasted very long by these means. Fredegond was admitted in the morning; and then after tea I had perhaps an hour over a log fire with Ottoline. . . . On the whole I liked Ottoline better than her friends have prepared me for liking her. Her vitality seemed to me a credit to her and in private talk her vapours give way to some quite clear bursts of shrewdness. The horror of the Garsington situation is great of course, but to the outsider the obvious view is that O. and P. and Garsington house provide a good deal, which isn't accepted very graciously. How- ever to deal blame rightly in such a situation is beyond the wit of a human being: they've brought themselves to such a pass of intrigue and general intricacy of relationship that they're hardly sane about each other. In such conditions I think Ott. deserves some credit for keeping her ship in full sail, as she certainly does. We were made immensely comfortable, a good deal of food; the talk had frequent bare patches, but then the particular carpet had been used fairly often. By talking severely to Philip, L. made him come up to Parliament today. He is a weak amiable long-suffering man who seems generally to be making the best of things, and seeing the best of people whom by nature he dislikes.

The "horror" of Garsington lay in the fact that it was a refuge. The angular and difficult characters whom Ottoline entertained were bound–or should have been bound–to their hostess by a sentiment of gratitude. But the consciousness of an obligation does not engender affection. The refugees quarrelled with her and with each other; having done so, they could not go away but had to stay and live with the objects of their discontent. They could not leave Garsington precisely because it offered a refuge from the war, and for the same reason they could not be happy while they remained there. Visitors, like Virginia, could enjoy the pleasures of what one may almost call "neutral territory," and like it the better by reason of the fact that they returned to the abominable moral atmosphere, the increasing hardships, and the dangers of a capital at war.

Air raids came–or were expected–each month with the full moon, and when they did, they drove the inhabitants of Hogarth House into the basement. On these occasions bedding and blankets were brought down and disposed in passages and pantries; Leonard would lie like a funerary image upon the kitchen table, Virginia lay beneath it. The servants had regular bunks, preferring to sleep below ground every night; they chattered and giggled at Virginia's jokes until Leonard called for silence. Then they all slept as best they might while Zeppelins or aeroplanes cruised overhead dropping bombs on what they no doubt supposed to be Slough or Staines, and the anti-aircraft guns added to the general noise and discomfort of the night. On one occasion however, when their dinner party had to adjourn to the cellar, their friend R. C. Trevelyan continued his discourse in so loud a voice that friend and foe were alike inaudible.*

The Woolfs went to Asham for Christmas and on their return to town at the New Year found that a great many people were talking about the possibility of peace. "This talk . . .," Virginia noted, "comes to the surface with a kind of tremor of hope once in three months: then subsides: then swells again." It was a regularly renewed disappointment and this time Virginia found no great consolation in the knowledge that she had been given a vote. Despite her efforts on behalf of Women's Suffrage in the years before the war the triumph, now that it had come, did not appear very considerable. It was altogether a rather gloomy time. She was, however, working fast and had written over 100,000 words of *Night and Day* by March 1918; but she felt depressed, and in February she fell ill with influenza. When she was well enough Leonard took her to Asham for ten days to recuperate, and they seriously discussed the possibility of remaining there until the war was over. They returned to Hogarth House but were back again at Asham three weeks later for an Easter holiday. The late March days were blazing hot, and the sound of artillery fire in Flanders was clearly audible upon the hill as the Germans pushed the Allies back towards Amiens. One of Leonard's brothers had been killed over there before Christmas, and now Barbara's new husband was in the fighting;† Virginia felt uneasy and unhappy and it seemed to her there was an odd and unhealthy pallor in those days of spring sunshine.

---

* "We had a raid last night – Bob was dining with us & talked so loud that we couldn't hear the guns; but Saxon says it was rather bad in London. We ate most of our dinner in the coal cellar." VW/VB, 19 December 1917 (Berg).

When I first read this it seemed typical of Virginia's exaggerated style; but compare it with Leonard's diary entry for 18 December 1917: "Aft. tea Bob Trevelyan came to spend night. At 6.45 air raid began but Bob's raucous voice never stopped & drowned the sound of guns. Dined between dining room & cellar. But it went on so long that we got tired & settled upstairs. Played & won a game of chess. Raid over at 10."

† He was in fact seriously wounded on Easter Saturday, 30 March 1918.

Lytton came to Asham and perhaps did something to relieve her melancholy, but Lytton presented problems. *Eminent Victorians*, much of which had been read to her (to her shame she fell asleep during the reading of one chapter), was now in the press. It would soon appear, and Lytton tactfully but repeatedly suggested that she should review it for *The Times Literary Supplement*, until at length, much against her better judgement, she consented and wrote to Bruce Richmond. He replied that she could review the book if she could keep her authorship secret; but this she felt that she could not do and the book fell into other hands.

A rather different literary transaction began on 14 April, by which time the Woolfs had returned to Richmond. Miss Harriet Weaver, owner and editor of the *Egoist Press*, came bearing the manuscript of *Ulysses*; she hoped that the Hogarth Press might publish it.* It was a work which Virginia could neither dismiss nor accept. Its power and subtlety were sufficiently evident to arouse her admiration and, no doubt, her envy. It seemed to her to have a kind of beauty but also a kind of cheap, smart, smoking-room coarseness. Joyce made use of instruments not dissimilar to her own and this was painful, for it was as though the pen, her very own pen, had been seized from her hands so that someone might scrawl the word fuck on the seat of a privy. Also she felt that Joyce wrote for a clique; and when she refers to him she writes of "these people," classing him perhaps with Ezra Pound and I know not what other figures of the "Underworld." Her reaction is perhaps significant; the gratuitous and impudent coarseness of Joyce made her feel suddenly desperately lady-like. Nevertheless she was quite perceptive enough to see that this was clearly something well worth publishing; equally clearly it was wholly beyond the technical capacity of the Hogarth Press. Professional printers would have to be employed; and it was the impossibility of finding one to undertake such a task–for those whom Leonard consulted insisted that they would court certain prosecution–which obliged the Woolfs to give up the attempt.

Eminent Victorians appeared in June. Lytton's friends were in

* According to Leonard Woolf Miss Harriet Weaver came to Hogarth House on the recommendation of T. S. Eliot (*Beginning Again*, pp. 245 /6). This is no doubt the case; but when he says: "He told us at the end of 1917 or the beginning of 1918 that Miss Harriet Weaver . . . was much concerned about a MS by James Joyce . . ." he suggests a degree of intimacy between Virginia and T. S. Eliot which did not then exist. A diary entry in November 1918 makes it hard to believe that she had ever met Mr Eliot before the 15th of that month.

some ways disappointed. It was, of course, brilliant–it had always been taken for granted that Lytton would achieve brilliance. But was it quite worthy of him? Vanessa and Virginia thought not. Clive was more enthusiastic; he also declared that Virginia was jealous–absurdly and disgracefully jealous–of Lytton's success. If she was, she didn't tell her diary, but probably she did feel a pang. Inevitably when a friend, one's obvious rival in the literary game, with whom one has, so to speak, run neck and neck for years, all at once draws ahead–even though it only be in public estimation, so that people say "Do you really know Lytton Strachey?" rather than "Are you *the* Virginia Woolf?" – a superhuman degree of detachment and a quite exceptional degree of moral superiority –qualities no-one could possibly claim for Virginia–are required if the distanced runner is to remain entirely calm. And Clive, it must be said, would not have hesitated to rub salt into the wound. He still enjoyed teasing Virginia and relations between them were strained that autumn, so much so that there was, as we shall see, a rather violent break. For a time, too, relations with Vanessa were little better; but in order to explain their embroilment it is necessary to enter a rather long digression, for it arose from what Vanessa called "the servant problem."

It was a practical problem, a moral problem, a personal problem, and it was of agonising importance to Vanessa, Virginia and, I suppose, to a great mass of people like them. In order to understand it I must remind the reader of some very obvious facts which we tend to forget. If you can afford to buy this book it is probable that when you take it home with you in the evening you can make a light with which to read it by pressing a switch. The room is warmed by central heating, you turn a tap and hot water pours into your bath or into your sink, you pull a plug and cold water gushes into your lavatory. You may do your own cooking and your own housework, but you are probably assisted by dozens of mechanical devices, tins and tin-openers, frozen foods, refrigerators and plastic containers. Heaven knows how many thousand horses give their power every day at the touch of your fingers. No very serious effort is demanded of you when ovens have to be heated, foods ground and mixed, floors swept, rooms lighted and fires made.

Now, when Virginia Woolf went to Asham she found none of these commodities. To get there at all she had to walk or to bicycle for several miles or to go to the expense of a taxi or a fly. To make a light she had candles which dropped grease on the carpet, or lamps which smoked and had to be refilled with oil and trimmed every morning; heat was supplied by wood or coal–and coal was in short supply from 1916 to 1919; the coal had to be carried about in scuttles, grates had to be cleaned, fires laid, and if they were not competently managed they would fill the room with smoke or die miserably. In the country you got hot water by boiling it over a stove. Cold water had to be pumped up into a tank every day and Asham was furnished only with an earth closet. There were no refrigerators or frozen foods, a tin-opener was a kind of heavy dagger with which you attacked the tin hoping to win a jagged victory. All the processes of cooking and cleaning were incredibly laborious, messy and slow. There are still plenty of people who live in conditions of this kind or worse–far worse–but obviously in these circumstances someone must be perpetually at work if any kind of comfort or cleanliness is to be maintained.

Before 1914 a surprisingly large number of people could employ, at all events, one indoor servant. Labour was plentiful and girls would accept places for their keep and a pittance. The rich, who might afford a ratio of say six servants to one master, probably found them more efficient than we our mechanical appliances.

The Woolfs before the war kept two servants, the Bells four– the minimum for a household in which the wife had a full-time occupation and, as in the case of the Bells, two children. During the war the condition of the market changed radically. There were good wages to be earned in factories and female labour became scarce. Younger women were unwilling to go into service; the isolation of domestic work in the country was very discouraging.

At the same time there was a moral problem. In Hyde Park Gate, with its army of servants, the situation had been frankly patriarchal. Leslie Stephen was the head of the house. Minny, Julia, Stella or Vanessa were his deputies and the servants were immediately responsible to them. Everyone knew their respective place. The system had the faults and the virtues of benevolent despotism. During the years between 1904 and 1914 that system began to break down; the Stephen sisters lacked the social assurance of their parents; they disliked the servant/mistress relationship, but they did not know how to avoid it. Paternalism only works when both sides accept it as proper and natural. When it breaks down, injustices may be removed, but the moral situation becomes extremely uncomfortable. Mrs Bell and Mrs Woolf looked for, felt for, some other and more equal form of contract between employer and employed. With Sophia Farrell–a family treasure if ever there was one–they were particularly uneasy. It was hard either to take her or to leave her. They could neither live up to her standards nor play the matriarchal part which she expected of them. On the other hand, if she needed employment, clearly the family had to provide it. She went from one household to another, ending at last with the George Duckworths who still played the game in the old way.

Her successors did not have the same traditional background and in that sense were easier, but the personal relationship was if anything more difficult than before. In Bloomsbury the domestic servants were not offered the servile status of the Victorian age, but neither had they the businesslike employer/employee relationship which can be established today between the "daily" woman who "helps" and the woman who is "helped." They were part of the household, in a sense a part of the family, but they were also independent human beings, equals with feelings to be respected. Ideally, hopefully, they were friends. But how many of one's friends are there whom one can see daily, who are dependent on one for a livelihood, who hold one's comforts in their hands, and with whom one is never bored or cross? And how hard to base a friendship on a written character, an interview, and no similarity of upbringing, of interests, of education or of class. Class is today almost a dirty word, and one hopes represents less than it did fifty years ago in English society, but to imagine that anybody at that time was not class-conscious would be crazy.

Class divisions produce incomprehension on both sides. In Bloomsbury the servants had to deal with neurotic and unusual people who wore the wrong clothes, hung the wrong pictures, held the wrong views and had the most peculiar friends. (Thus in 1917 Vanessa's cook found herself having to discuss with her mistress the relationship between one of the guests in the house and a particularly seductive stable-boy on the adjacent farm. The guest, of course, was Lytton Strachey.)

Virginia's household did not present quite the problems that Vanessa's did, but undoubtedly she puzzled and at times infuriated her servants.

Early in 1916, when Virginia was recovering, Leonard had engaged Nelly Boxall and her lifelong friend Lottie Hope as cook and housemaid. They had previously been in the service of Roger Fry at Guildford. The two girls were very devoted to one another. Lottie, a foundling, was a simple character, generous, impulsive, untruthful and passionate. She passed easily from high spirits to rage. Nelly was quieter, gentler and, at bottom, even more passionate than her friend.

Nelly was to recall her first interview in 1916, when she came into the drawing-room at Hogarth House and found Virginia lying on the sofa in an old dressing-gown and thought her "so sweet" and knew that she would like working for her. What she didn't know, poor Nelly, was that she would be so enchanted by Virginia and so aggravated by her that, for the next eighteen years, she could neither live with her nor live without her, nor that Virginia was to be so exasperated and at the same time so touched by *her* changing moods that she could neither endure her nor dismiss her. Nelly and Lottie quarrelled and were reconciled, sulked and were mollified, complained and gave notice, over and over again. They were torn between an extreme terror of air raids in town and despair at the tedium of living in the country. They provided a constant source of drama. Virginia was fascinated but infuriated by them; they brought out the best and the worst in her.

In April 1918, Vanessa found that she was pregnant. There were then living at Charleston Vanessa, Duncan, David Garnett, a governess and her lover, four children, including the governess's daughter and nephew, a cook and a kitchen-maid. Clearly the burden of work in this household was heavy. Then the cook gave notice. It seemed almost impossible to get another. In this crisis, Virginia, not for the first time, made herself useful by visiting domestic agencies, while Vanessa made enquiries in her immediate district, all to no avail. Then Virginia had the idea that Nelly and Lottie should go to her sister, at all events for two weeks. Privately she thought that they might remain there, for the Woolfs were getting so short of money that it seemed impossible to go on keeping servants; there was, however, the chance that Leonard might be offered an editorship, in which case, of course, they would want to have Nelly and Lottie back. At all events the possibility that they might not return was concealed from them. The negotiations between Vanessa and Virginia and between Virginia and her servants and between the servants and Vanessa, in which figured the suspicions of Nelly and Lottie that they might be leaving for good, Vanessa's hesitations about coming to an agreement which might not be permanent, with the added complication of a Miss Ford, a local girl who would obviously not be as good as Nelly and Lottie, but was momentarily available, fill page after page of the almost daily correspondence between the sisters in May and June 1918. In the end Vanessa, being unwell, had to send Trissie, the cook who was leaving her, to Richmond to conclude negotiations, and she managed matters so ill that Nelly and Lottie declared that nothing would induce them to leave the Woolfs or go to Charleston at all. This *dénouement* came just too late for Vanessa to secure Miss Ford; she was snatched up by somebody else. In her anxious and exasperated state Vanessa asked whether it was not Leonard who all along had been opposed to her having Nelly and Lottie? This brought a rather stiff rejoinder from Leonard, followed by explanatory peace-making letters from both sides.

Virginia could always make her peace with Vanessa easily enough. But not with Clive; and during the autumn of 1918 she was again at odds with him.

Clive always accused Virginia of being a mischief-maker and he believed, perhaps rightly, that the unkind remarks which he and Desmond MacCarthy had made about Katherine Mansfield at Hogarth House were repeated to Katherine by his hostess. This of course led to some trouble; but there was worse to come.

At this time the most important person in Clive's life was neither Virginia nor Vanessa, but Mrs St John Hutchinson, and this of course meant that she became, if not a "member," at least a very frequent visitor in Bloomsbury. Both Vanessa and Virginia admired her; but Clive demanded more of his friends than that they should like Mary. In his enthusiasm he insisted that they should recognise in her the most infinitely subtle and civilised being in their society—a du Deffand with the charms of a Pompadour. She herself had no such pretensions and probably realised that, in making these claims, Clive injured rather than advanced her cause and succeeded only in spoiling what would otherwise have been a sufficiently warm welcome. In fact Virginia's feelings about Clive's friend varied a great deal. There was no-one whose stock did not rise and fall in the uncertain market of her regard; but if this issue sometimes crashed to fearful depths it was because Clive had drawn up a wholly misleading prospectus.

It is within this context that we should consider Virginia's mischief-making (if it was she who made it) in the autumn of 1918.

It was at this time that Mrs Hutchinson was told—by whom it is not clear—that Clive's friends, and Vanessa in particular, thought her a great bore and only tolerated her for his sake. Naturally this ill-natured report distressed her very much. Clive and Vanessa jumped to the conclusion that this story must have come from Virginia and have been repeated by Mark Gertler, who had been at Asham in September. "Whatever you may have said to Gertler was at once repeated by him . . ." wrote Vanessa, adding: "Do be careful what you say . . . & please dont let him or in fact anyone think that I don't like Mary for as you know I do."

Virginia replied with some heat: yes, Mary had once been the subject of conversation between her and Gertler at Asham–Leonard was there, and could testify that all she had said was that she scarcely knew Mary, who always seemed very silent in her company, and that yes, she supposed she was equally silent with Vanessa. As for Gertler, he had been neither inquisitive nor malicious, being ("as usual") entirely absorbed in himself and in his own affairs.* Some of Mary's friends might have a motive for making mischief; she certainly had none. She objected very strongly to "being made the victim of this infernal spy system" and resolved in future to steer clear of Clive and his new set.

A letter from Clive to Vanessa suggests that Virginia's indignation was justified:

> I just want to put you right on one point. It was not I who said that Virginia had been telling Gertler tales. I merely said that tales had been told and it was someone else–you I rather think–who suggested Virginia as the *fons et origo*. We all agreed that this was probable and I think so still, but I'm quite sure I didn't say the tales came from Virginia because to this day I don't know how they reached Mary. I will find out. It isnt that I in the least mind being embroiled with Virginia. I am well used to it and rather like it, but let it be on a real issue.

She had been accused on suspicion, and not on evidence, and the evidence, as far as it goes, tends to exonerate her. It may however be argued that Vanessa (if it was Vanessa) would not have suspected her if she had not already earned a bad reputation. Certainly she was indiscreet. She herself recalls an occasion on which she told secrets, not realising they would be blurted out in company, so that, as she puts it, she found herself in "hot water." On another occasion Vanessa thought it necessary to warn her when she was going to see Lady Strachey, "Do, for God's sake, be careful about what you say. . . . Remember, she's *not* up to date in morals–has never heard of buggery–at any rate not in her own family. You have the wildest ideas about such things." Indeed she had an alarming

---

* In her diary Virginia records that she was at Charleston on 17 September when Clive and Mrs Hutchinson arrived by car. "She was," she wrote on the 23rd, "as usual, mute as a trout–I say trout because of her spotted dress–also because, though silent, she has the swift composure of a fish." And on the same day she writes: "We have been talking about Gertler to Gertler for some 30 hours; it is like putting a microscope to your eye. One molehill is wonderfully clear; the surrounding world ceases to exist." *AWD (Berg)*.

tendency to say whatever came into her head. But this is not the same thing as the kind of deliberate, pointlessly cruel mischief-making of which she was here accused.

These private dramas must be imagined against a background of large public events, events towards which Virginia's attention was increasingly directed. For the Gertler-Mary Hutchinson row took place in mid-October 1918 and by then it had become clear that the war really was at last coming to an end. Leonard was much occupied by the political struggles that resulted from the search for an international peace-keeping organisation to be established after the war, and something of these efforts is recorded in Virginia's diary. When Beatrice and Sydney Webb had come to stay at Asham in September, a visit which for Virginia involved a considerable social effort, their incessant talk was largely concerned with re-construction and the new social order that would be established.

"The work of government," declared Sidney Webb, "will be enormously increased in the future."

"Shall I have a finger in the pie?" asked Virginia.

"Oh yes, you will have some small office no doubt. My wife and I always say that a railway guard is the most enviable of men. He has authority and is responsible to a government. That should be the state of each one of us."

As the weeks passed these fair visions of the future became brighter.

"Whatever we have done this week," wrote Virginia on 12 October, "has had this extraordinary background of hope; a tremendously enlarged version of the feeling I can remember as a child as Christmas approached." The following Sunday her cousin, H. A. L. Fisher, then a Cabinet Minister, appeared unheralded at Hogarth House at tea-time and announced: "We've won the war today."

In fact there was still a month to wait, and Virginia noted, not without anger, Lord Northcliffe's anxiety to prolong the slaughter. She wrote in her diary:

Wednesday, October 30
Just in from a walk in the Park on this incredibly lovely autumn day. Various houses have orange berries growing upon them; the beech trees are so bright that everything looks pale after you have looked at them. (How I dislike writing directly after reading Mrs. H. Ward!– she is as great a menace to health of mind as influenza to the body). We talked of peace: how the sausage balloons will be hauled down and gold coins dribble in; and how people will soon forget all about the

war and the fruits of our victory will grow as dusty as ornaments under glass cases in lodging house drawing rooms. How often will the good people of Richmond rejoice to think that liberty has been won for the good people of Potsdam? I can believe though that we shall be more arrogant about our own virtues. The Times still talks of the possibility of another season, in order to carry the war into Germany and there imprint a respect for liberty in the German peasants. I think the distance of the average person from feelings of this sort is the only safeguard and assurance that we shall settle down again neither better nor worse.

And later:

Monday, November 11th.
Twentyfive minutes ago the guns went off, announcing peace. A siren hooted on the river. They are hooting still. A few people ran to look out of windows. The rooks wheeled round and wore for a moment the symbolic look of creatures performing some ceremony, partly of thanksgiving, partly of valediction over the grave. A very cloudy still day, the smoke toppling over heavily towards the east; and that too wearing for a moment a look of something floating, waving, drooping. We looked out of the window; saw the housepainter give one look at the sky and go on with his job; the old man toddling along the street carrying a bag out of which a large loaf protruded, closely followed by his mongrel dog. So far neither bells nor flags, but the wailing of sirens and intermittent guns.

Chapter Three

November 1918 – December 1922

NOVEMBER 1918, which brought the armistice, brought also the end of *Night and Day*–the last words were written on 21 November; it also brought Virginia a new friend, T. S. Eliot. He came to Hogarth House on 15 November bringing with him three or four poems. Mr Eliot himself appeared to Virginia a polished, cultivated, elaborate young American, and almost too decorous; but very intelligent and very much a poet. He was very firm in his opinions, which were not Virginia's, for he thought Ezra Pound and Wyndham Lewis great men, and admired James Joyce immensely. Leonard and Virginia agreed that the Hogarth Press should publish his latest poems and she began to set them up towards the end of January 1919.

But most of January Virginia spent in bed. She had a tooth extracted and then a headache; her nephews, whom she had undertaken to house during Vanessa's *accouchement*, had to be sent off to their father at Gordon Square. The armistice did not end but seemed rather to have intensified shortages of every sort. Life was made more difficult by a wave of industrial unrest. In a letter to Ka Cox, who had now become Mrs Arnold-Forster and had settled in Cornwall, she describes the inconveniences of that time:

... to be ill at the Lizard seems to me better than to be well here. You can't conceive what existence is like without trains or tubes, a heavy snow falling, no coal in the cellar, a leak in the roof which has already filled every possible receptacle, & probably no electric light tomorrow. We in Richmond can still get to Waterloo; but Hampstead is entirely cut off. Leonard's staff of course live upon the northern heights, & hardly get to the office at all, so the poor man has to go up himself, & here I sit waiting, & God knows, what with the snow & the fog, when he'll be back. Then the experts say that the working classes have behaved with such incredible stupidity that the Government will beat them; & this strike is only the beginning of others far worse to follow. They say we are in for such a year as has never been known. Sensible people like you go & live in Cornwall. I wish you'd go to Gurnards Head & see if there's a cottage there to let, as I've been told. We are faced with the appalling prospect of having to give up Asheham. It's wanted for the farm probably; there's still a ray of hope but I'm afraid not much. . . .

I'm quite well again, though slightly restricted in my jaunts to London, so I haven't a great deal of gossip . . . Have you heard of the catastrophes at Charleston? I cant go into them in any detail, since they would fill volumes. But imagine a country doctor ordering some medicine for the baby [Vanessa's daughter Angelica, born on Christmas Day, 1918] which made it ill by day and by night–Nessa commands him to stop–he refuses–he wont say what it is–the gamp has to obey him–child loses more & more pounds–Duncan goes over to Brighton & interviews Saxon's father about the quality of Nessa's milk–without result–Noel [Olivier] telegraphed for–lady doctor arrives secretly –finds the doctor is ordering some form of poison–Mrs. Brereton [the governess] thinks it her duty to inform the Dr. of his rival's presence– scenes, explosions, dismissal–triumph of Nessa & the lady doctor & partial recovery of the Baby. Just as this was over, the servants took to drink or worse, & had to be got rid of; frantic efforts of course to get others; none to be had; telegrams sent, interviews arranged, cook discovered, fails at the last moment–whole thing begins over again; more cooks discovered; just about to start when their father falls dead in the street, upon which both Nessa & I rush about in a fury, with the result that we each engage cooks without telling the other, and one has to be dismissed at enormous expense & terrific cost of energy. You can't think what a lot of time this has all taken up, or how sick I am of beginning my letters, "Jane Beale, I am writing for my sister–" For one thing I detest that style of sentence, & then the bold abrupt handwriting is what I can't compass.

The catastrophes at Charleston had in fact involved Virginia in a great deal of fatiguing exertion at a time when she was not at all well. She could not resist, but could not but be exasperated by the demands which her sister made (demands which were all the more eloquent for being unspoken). When things got too bad, Nelly was sent to Charleston to save the situation but, as usual, Leonard had to intervene in order to protect Virginia from the effects of her own generosity.

It was not until early March that Virginia was able to go to Sussex to inspect her new niece and see for herself how Vanessa was managing. Living, she noted, was rather bare at Charleston –"nothing but wind and rain and no coal in the cellar." All the same there was something attractive and soothing about that bleak interior. It was disorderly and might fairly be called disreputable; but the atmosphere was congenial and in some moods, comparing

it with her own relatively well-regulated and completely irreproachable domesticity, Virginia could find it enviably romantic.

On the first of June Virginia again spent a night at Charleston.
This visit was important, for reasons which must be explained
by returning to the events of the spring.

It will be remembered that, in her letter to Ka, Virginia was
deploring the probable loss of Asham, though there was then still
a ray of hope. This hope was extinguished on 1 March when Mr
Gunn the farmer gave them six months' notice. Leonard and
Virginia at once began house-hunting–an occupation which she
confessed was always a source of great pleasure to her–hoping to
find something in the same district. From Katherine Mansfield
however she heard of three adjacent cottages near Zennor to let
at £5 a year each. D. H. Lawrence had lived in them, and this
was the only occasion that the two novelists entered into any kind
of correspondence. Virginia could not resist the temptation of
Cornwall, and took them, but must soon have recognised that
Higher Tregerthen was too far from London to be a practical
proposition. I do not think the Woolfs ever went there, and no
more was heard of this plan.

Meanwhile they had printed three small books: T. S. Eliot's
Poems, Middleton Murry's *The Critic in Judgment*, and Virginia's *Kew
Gardens*–and these were all published on 12 May. By 31 May only
49 copies of *Kew Gardens* had been sold, while business in Eliot and
Murry was fairly brisk. Virginia blamed Leonard a little for having
persuaded her that *Kew Gardens* was worth publishing.

Thus it was in a rather discontented frame of mind, her book
unwanted, her house problem unsolved, that she returned to
Charleston. The domestic situation there had by this time more
or less resolved itself, but another sisterly dispute arose. This time
it was aesthetic and concerned the production of *Kew Gardens*.
Vanessa, who had made the woodcuts for this book, did not at
all like the way in which they had been printed. According to
Virginia, who was rather inclined to exaggerate the gravity of
Vanessa's strictures, she went so far as to question the use of having
a Press that could print so badly, and to say that for her part, if that
was the best they could do, she would never work for it again.
The effect of this conversation, to judge again by Virginia's account
of the matter,★ was strange. She went to Lewes, found a house
for sale, and bought it outright.

★ "Did you realise that it was your severity that plunged me into the recklessness of buying a house that day? Something I must do to redress the balance, to

65

It was an odd thing to do and an odd house to buy. It had once been a windmill and stood high upon Lewes Hill near the Castle Wall. Being in the middle of the town it was not really what they wanted at all. She returned to London in a rather defiant mood; she was always upset by a quarrel with Vanessa and by this time it is likely that the purchase, for £300, of a small cylindrical edifice in the middle of Lewes had begun to appear a less crushing reply to her sister's criticisms of the printing techniques of the Hogarth Press than she had first supposed; nevertheless it was a course of action which had to be defended.

That evening, when the Woolfs opened the front door of Hogarth House, they found a snowdrift of mail. It consisted of orders for *Kew Gardens*: orders from distributors, from shops and from private people. Suddenly everybody wanted it; there had been a very favourable review in *The Times Literary Supplement*.

It should have been a wholly joyful occasion; but the repercussions of the Charleston visit made a cantankerous evening; and then, what was Leonard going to say about the house?

He was in fact magnanimous, but they both realised that it was a mistake when Leonard was able to look at it a few weeks later. What they really wanted was a house in the country. On their way through Lewes to inspect the Round House they had noticed a poster which announced the forthcoming sale of a property at Rodmell, a village lying about three miles south of Lewes. "That would have suited us exactly," said Leonard, ruefully.

Monk's House lay at the bottom of the village street that winds down from the high road between Lewes and Newhaven and on which nearly all of Rodmell has been built. It was a modest brick and flint dwelling, weather-boarded on the street side, two stories high with a high-pitched slate roof; inside, many low small rooms opened one from another; the ground floors were paved with brick, the stairs were narrow with worn treads; there was of course neither bath nor hot water nor W.C. Rising behind the house was a profuse and untidy garden, with flint walls and many out-houses, and beyond the garden was an orchard and beyond the

---

give myself value in my eyes, I said: & so I bought a house; the blood will there-fore be upon your head. Did anyone ever suffer as I did? You might have seen my soul shrivelling like a —— I cannot remember the image exactly, but its something one does by rubbing a piece of sealing wax & then everything curls up–as if in agony. Not that there was any imagery about it in my case. But the immanent greatness of my soul formed, as it were, a cream upon the surface. I survived."
VW/VB, [18 June 1919], Berg.

orchard the walled churchyard. The more Leonard and Virginia looked at the place, the more they liked it. They tried their best to find faults, but only succeeded in liking it better. They decided they must try to buy it and sell the Round House. The sale by auction of Monk's House took place in Lewes on 1 July. They gave their agent, Mr Wycherley, a limit of £800, which he thought should give them a good chance of success.

> I don't suppose many spaces of five minutes in the course of my life have been so close packed with sensation. Was I somehow waiting to hear the result, while I watched the process, of an operation? The room at the White Hart was crowded. I looked at every face and in particular at every coat and skirt, for signs of opulence, and was cheered to discover none. But then, I thought, getting L. into line, does *he* look as if he had £800 in his pocket? Some of the substantial farmers might well have their rolls of notes stuffed inside their stockings. Bidding began. Someone offered £300 . . . Six hundred was reached too quick for me.

After this figure, there were only two competitors; they were allowed to bid in twenties; then in tens; then in fives; at £700 there was a pause; an appeal from the auctioneer. The hammer fell. The Woolfs had bought Monk's House.

Of the two remaining months before they need make the move to Rodmell, they managed to spend the whole of August at Asham. It was a mournful interval, particularly for Virginia. Asham, so beautiful, so melancholy and so haunted, had a quality which suited her exactly. She had celebrated its gentle ghosts in words which, for one who has lived there, are almost painfully evocative. It was no doubt exciting to move into a new home, but really, compared to Asham, Monk's House was only a pleasant cottage with some nice views and a pretty garden.

She wrote her last letter from Asham on 29 August 1919 to Vanessa:

Asheham,
Friday.

Dearest,

Many thanks for the cheque. Leonard quite agrees with you that I shall be merely in the way during the move. I, on the other hand, think myself indispensable. I don't see how they could manage without me. But I am very grateful for the offer. Perhaps I might come over one day later in my shay, if you have any horse accommodation at Charleston.

The move begins on Monday; we are already strewn with old boxes full of the most interesting letters—yours & Madge's & Walter Lamb's, and I see a very tart one from Maynard about my arrangements at Brunswick Square. We shall be in by Wednesday; but I'm afraid I shant be able to ask Lytton to stay, as the servants will be distracted, and I suppose, giving notice. Tell him I'm much disappointed.

When will you come over & see Monks? If you took train to Lewes my shay would meet you & bring you out; & then take you back. I shall be doing a good deal of brush work on the house, but without any false shame.

Every one felt that Mrs. Dolphin [i.e. Vanessa] was the soul of the party the other night. Morgan said he was going to tell you that he thought you beautiful & charming, but he might be too shy. What struck me most was the farewell—every one feeling a little sentimental about Asheham—old mother Bell hurrying about the Terrace looking for her Badmington set. "It's no good being sentimental on these occasions. Now Leonard, wasn't there a bit of old carpet —?" Immortal woman!

Yr.
B.

Monk's House was only two or three miles from Asham. On 1 September the two waggons on which the Woolfs' possessions were loaded might easily cross the river Ouse and discharge all their business within the space of a morning; and that night Leonard and Virginia were able to sleep in their own home.

Being thus translated Virginia did her best to dwell upon the advantages of her new situation. In addition to the superiority of the garden, the views were more extensive and offered greater variety; but she was obliged to admit to herself that she was depressed. Whether this melancholy arose from the comparative imperfections of her new house or from the fact that Duckworth was about to publish *Night and Day* is not easily determined.

As always, she found publication an agitating business, and, as usual, tried to be philosophic about it. When on 20 October she received her own six copies, she at once sent five of them off—to Vanessa, Clive, Lytton, Morgan Forster and Violet Dickinson. She waited anxiously for their comments. Clive immediately declared it a work of the highest genius, Violet and Vanessa were eulogistic, Lytton enthusiastic. She accepted their praise with great pleasure if a little dubiously. But Morgan wrote to say that he preferred *The Voyage Out*; he couldn't really sympathise with her characters; *Night and Day* seemed to him (as it seems to most subsequent critics) less successful than its predecessor. But his verdict was delivered with such discernment and so much kindness that she was only momentarily cast down.

Katherine Mansfield hated *Night and Day*. Her private opinion was that it was "a lie in the soul." "The war never has been: that is what its message is. . . . I feel in the *profoundest* sense that nothing can ever be the same–that, as artists, we are traitors if we feel otherwise: we have to take it into account and find new expressions, new moulds for our new thoughts and feelings." Thus Katherine to Middleton Murry; and, three days later: "Talk about intellectual snobbery–her book *reeks* of it. (But I can't say so). You would dislike it. You'd never read it. It's so long and so tahsome." Writing in the *Athenaeum* Katherine Mansfield was discreet; but she said enough to inflict pain. Virginia thought it a spiteful review; so did Leonard. "He could see her looking about for a loophole of escape. 'I'm not going to call this a success–or if I must, I'll call it the wrong kind of success.'"

And yet this review was in many ways perceptive. In that *Night and Day* was a deliberate evocation of the past it might seem unreasonable to complain that it lacked actuality; but it belonged to the past in another way: it was a very orthodox performance and Katherine Mansfield does no more than anticipate the bewilderment of many later critics at finding in it none of the audacity of *The Voyage Out* or of *Kew Gardens*. "We had thought that this world was vanished for ever, that it was impossible to find on the great ocean of literature a ship that was unaware of what has been happening; yet there is *Night and Day*, new, exquisite–a novel in the tradition of the English novel. In the midst of our admiration it makes us feel old and chill. We had not thought to look upon its like again."

Virginia's feelings about Katherine Mansfield were as always mixed, and the question of their relationship continued to interest her very much:

> . . . I should need to write a long description of her before I arrived at my queer balance of interest, amusement and annoyance. The truth is, I suppose, that one of the conditions, unexpressed but understood, of our friendship has been precisely that it was almost entirely founded on quicksands. It has been marked by curious slides and arrests; for months I've heard nothing of her; then we have met again upon what has the appearance of solid ground. We have been intimate, intense perhaps rather than open; but to me at any rate our intercourse has been always interesting and mingled with quite enough of the agreeable personal element to make one fond–if that is the word–as well as curious.

This Virginia had written in her diary in February 1919 in a rather chagrined mood, because Katherine, whom she had visited almost weekly in Hampstead before Christmas, had since fallen totally silent. She was in fact ill, and when they did again meet Virginia noted:

> The inscrutable woman remains inscrutable–I'm glad to say; no apologies or sense of apologies due. At once she flung down her pen and plunged, as if we'd been parted for 10 minutes, into the question of Dorothy Richardson; . . . as usual, I find with Katherine what I don't find with the other clever women–a sense of ease and interest, which is, I suppose, due to her caring so genuinely if so differently from the way I care, about our precious art.

Through the summer of 1919 they had continued to meet, though often enough Murry was there too; his presence inhibited them both. But Murry was then editing the *Athenaeum;* Virginia was pleased to be asked for contributions; she wrote some seventeen articles for it in the next two years. Katherine was in France when her review of *Night and Day* appeared; returning to England in the summer of 1920 she made no attempt to see Virginia and it was Virginia who made the first move. When at last they did meet there was

> a steady discomposing formality and coldness at first. Enquiries about house and so on. No pleasure or excitement at seeing me. It struck me that she is of the cat kind; alien, composed, always solitary–observant. And then we talked about solitude and I found her expressing my feelings as I never hear them expressed. Whereupon we fell into step, and as usual talked as easily as though 8 months were minutes–till Murry came in. . . . A queer effect she produces of someone apart, entirely self-centred; altogether concentrated upon her 'art': almost fierce to me about it.

Virginia was unable to refrain from mentioning *Night and Day*. "An amazing achievement," declared Katherine, with pardonable disingenuity. "Why, we've not had such a thing since I don't know when——"
"But I thought you didn't like it?"

> Then she said she could pass an examination in it. Would I come and talk about it–lunch–so I'm going to lunch; but what does her reviewing mean then? Or is she emotional with me? Anyhow, once more as keenly as ever I feel a common understanding between us–a queer sense

of being 'like', not only about literature and I think its independent of gratified vanity. I can talk straight out to her.

For the rest of Katherine's life, and indeed for long after her death, Virginia was to regard her with feelings nicely compounded of sympathy and jealousy. Their last meeting was in August 1920. Virginia went from Rodmell to London in order to say goodbye, for Katherine was going abroad again. Virginia wondered how much she really minded losing her; and came to the conclusion that she did mind a good deal.

The year 1919 ended in vexation. Nelly and Lottie gave notice, as they so often did, only to withdraw it; Leonard returned from a meeting of the Oxford University Socialist Society with a fever, and this, which proved to be malarial, made him unwell for about three weeks. Before he had recovered Virginia went down with influenza. She was still in bed on Christmas Day, when Adrian and Karin (not the guests whom Leonard would have most wished to see) came to tea and dinner at Hogarth House. When, at the end of December, the Woolfs were able to get to Rodmell the weather was atrocious and Leonard, who went out to prune the fruit trees, very nearly pruned off a finger.

"We think we now deserve some good luck," wrote Virginia at the end of her diary for 1919. "Yet I daresay we are the happiest couple in England."

1920, which was to be a momentous year, began with no grand stroke of good luck, but it began well. The Woolfs stayed on at Monk's House for some days and on 7 January Virginia wrote:

This is our last evening. We sit over the fire, waiting for the post–the cream of the day, I think. Yet every part of the day has its merits–even the breakfast without toast. That, however it begins, ends with Pippins; most mornings the sun comes in; we finish in good temper; and I go off to the romantic chamber [one of the garden buildings which she used as a work-room] over grass rough with frost and ground hard as brick. Then Mrs. Dedman comes to receive orders–to give them, really, for she has planned our meals to suit her day's cooking before she comes. We share her oven. The result is always savoury–stews and mashes and deep many coloured dishes swimming in gravy thick with carrots and onions. Elsie aged 18 can be spoken to as though she had a head on her shoulders. The house is empty by half past eleven, empty now at five o'clock. We tend our fire, cook coffee, read, I find, luxuriously, peacefully, at length.

This is but a little part of an entry that is almost entirely devoted to the pleasures of country life: Leonard's activities in the garden and her own walks–Monk's House offered a greater variety of walks than Asham–through landscapes of astonishing beauty. Here, and in succeeding passages, she sounds a rare note of contented serenity.

She has very little, in these early days of 1920, to say about her writing. After finishing *Night and Day* she must have been mainly occupied by those short stories which were to be published for the first time in *Monday or Tuesday* and by *An Unwritten Novel* which appeared in *The London Mercury* in July. Also she was extremely active as a journalist★; but she seems to have had no full-scale work in mind, or at least in her conscious mind.

In November 1919 she had written:

> It is true that I have never been so neglectful of this work of mine [her Diary]. I think I can foresee in my reluctance to trace a sentence, not merely a lack of time and a mind tired by writing, but also one of those slight distastes which betoken a change of style. So an animal must feel at the approach of spring when his coat changes.

By the end of January the spring to which Virginia refers began to approach. By that time the Woolfs were back in Richmond and Virginia celebrated her birthday by listening to Mozart and Beethoven, and on the following day, Monday, 26 January, she wrote:

> The day after my birthday; in fact, I'm 38. Well, I've no doubt I'm a great deal happier than I was at 28; and happier today than I was yesterday, having this afternoon arrived at some idea of a new form for a new novel. Suppose one thing should open out of another–as in An Unwritten novel–only not for 10 pages but 200 or so–doesn't that give the looseness and lightness I want; doesn't that get closer and yet keep form and speed, and enclose everything, everything? My doubt is how far it will enclose the human heart–Am I sufficiently mistress of my dialogue to net it there? For I figure that the approach will be entirely different this time: no scaffolding; scarcely a brick to be seen; all crepuscular, but the heart, the passion, humour, everything as bright as fire in the mist. Then I'll find room for so much–a gaiety–an inconsequence–a light spirited stepping at my sweet will. Whether I'm sufficiently mistress of things–that's the doubt; but conceive *Mark on the Wall*, *K. G.* and *Unwritten Novel* taking hands and dancing in unity. What the unity shall be I have yet to discover; the theme is a

---

★ Not since 1905 or 1906 had her book reviews appeared so frequently as in the years 1918 to 1920. In 1920 she had articles in *The Times Literary Supplement*, the *Athenaeum* or the *New Statesman* every month except September.

blank to me; but I see immense possibilities in the form I hit upon more or less by chance two weeks ago. I suppose the danger is the damned egotistical self; which ruins Joyce and Richardson to my mind: is one pliant and rich enough to provide a wall for the book from oneself without its becoming, as in Joyce and Richardson, narrowing and restricting? My hope is that I've learnt my business sufficiently now to provide all sorts of entertainments. Anyhow, I must still grope and experiment but this afternoon I had a gleam of light. Indeed, I think from the ease with which I'm developing the unwritten novel there must be a path for me there.

It is rare to find an author who sees so clearly and suddenly, not the plot, or indeed the method, of a particular novel, but the whole programme for a decade.

During the spring of 1920 *Jacob's Room* began to take shape, and although in May, after the initial rush had spent its force, the novel proceeded more steadily, still she was enjoying it, feeling her renewed strength and noting that it was the most amusing novel-writing that she had ever done.

June brought one of those psychologically charged sequences of events which for her were of capital importance, not so much by reason of their intrinsic character as because she received their impression with a heightened power of perception.

She had what she called one of her "field days": took an afternoon train into town from Richmond, went to the National Gallery and there met Clive, who, as his habit was, took her to eat ices at Gunter's, where she observed her fellow patrons with fascinated interest. Then she dined with Vanessa at Gordon Square and heard the whole story of Mary. Mary was one of the servants, a girl of some beauty and very great charm. Misfortunes had fallen upon her with dreadful suddenness; first her father, then her brother, then her fiancé, were killed in accidents. Her grief was frightening in its intensity and naturally with each blow it increased. The tale of her misfortunes became more and more appalling and more and more highly complicated until at length, after some quite startling peripeteia, it was discovered that she had invented her own calamities, and that the relatives and friends who left messages of bad news for her at Gordon Square or who wrote to advise or to admonish her, were herself, using a disguised hand or voice. After a dramatic flight, she was brought back raving and then removed to St Pancras Infirmary. The sight of her being taken away, watched from every window by all the other servants in the Square, made a most sinister impression upon Virginia.

This made my drive to Waterloo on top of a bus very vivid. A bright night, with a fresh breeze. An old beggarwoman, blind, sat against a stone wall in Kingsway holding a brown mongrel in her arms and sang aloud. There was a recklessness about her; much in the spirit of London. Defiant–almost gay, clasping her dog as if for warmth. How many Junes has she sat there, in the heart of London? How she came to be there, what scenes she can go through, I can't imagine. O damn it all, I say, why can't I know all that too? Perhaps it was the song at night that seemed strange; she was singing shrilly, but for her own amusement, not begging. Then the fire engines came by–shrill too; with their helmets pale yellow in the moonlight. Sometimes everything gets into the same mood; how to define this one I don't know. It was gay and yet terrible and fearfully vivid. Nowadays I'm often overcome by London; even think of the dead who have walked in the city. Perhaps one might visit the churches. The view of the grey white spires from Hungerford Bridge brings it to me; and yet I can't say what 'it' is.

That old blind woman appears in *Jacob's Room*; and perhaps it is she who sings "Lay by my side a bunch of purple heather" in *Mrs Dalloway*.

On that memorable evening in 1919 when the Woolfs found the front hall at Hogarth House littered with demands for *Kew Gardens*, the Hogarth Press began to change from a hobby into a business. In some ways they found its rapid growth alarming and they wondered whether they should allow it to expand. But at the same time it offered large opportunities and substantial advantages which they could not easily disregard. Virginia, who hated submitting her novels to Gerald Duckworth–he had what she called "a clubman's view of literature"–began to think what a comfort it would be to publish her own books. Friends who had been amused and sceptical at the time of their first amateurish efforts made suggestions or sent them manuscripts. They attracted some remarkable authors. Katherine Mansfield, T. S. Eliot, Middleton Murry, E. M. Forster, Logan Pearsall Smith, and Maxim Gorki had all appeared, or were soon to appear, beneath their imprint. The possibilities were interesting, and the Press continued to grow. They began to farm out some of the setting and printing, although they continued to do a great deal themselves at Hogarth House.

But the Press made work, and as the volume of work increased the time available for it diminished. Virginia, as we have seen, was occupied not only by her novel but by a great deal of journalism. Leonard, who in 1919 had finished his book *Empire and Commerce in Africa*–a book which Virginia greatly admired–was now busy with another (*Socialism and Co-operation*); he was also editing a monthly paper, *The International Review*, and in May 1920 was adopted as a parliamentary candidate for one of the two Combined University seats. It was clear that they needed an assistant who could undertake more responsibility and do more business than had been required of Barbara Hiles. They needed an intelligent young man, and there were surely a number of intelligent young men to whom an apprenticeship leading perhaps to an eventual partnership in the Hogarth Press would seem a most attractive proposition–an ideal arrangement for all parties.

It was, in fact, a trap into which all parties fell headlong. For the aspiring young men, publishing was above all a matter of discrimination, of choosing the right authors and presenting them beautifully to the world. For Leonard–and Leonard was necessarily the effective power in the management of the Press–it was a matter of setting and distributing type, of printing page after page after page, of cleaning up the machinery, of binding and pasting, of doing up and addressing parcels and delivering messages and writing letters; and although this was no doubt explained to the applicants when they came to the Hogarth Press, somehow they continued to hope that all this menial business was but a purgatory leading to the heaven of aesthetic direction. Presently, however, they would discover that such hopes were vain. Leonard had his own idea about the literary policy of the Press and if he was in any doubt he would turn to Virginia. Leonard was an excellent man of business and drove a hard bargain–a cruelly hard bargain it seemed to some–and of course there was plenty of work for the assistant to do. Leonard and even more Virginia regarded publishing as a part-time business, but for the assistant it was to be very much more than that. He was, in fact, expected to do everything except the few things that he wanted to do. Thus the situation was, in its nature, difficult. It was made worse by the fact that, as Leonard himself says, he was a perfectionist, and still young enough to be hot-tempered. The Press was his child and as time went on he was not perfectly rational about it. Perhaps it might be more true to say that it was his mistress. He could at a pinch share it with a woman but not with a man. Leonard and the succession of young men who came to work at the Hogarth Press did not usually get on well together, while the women assistants were, I think, much more easily and happily accommodated.

The first of the young men whose difficult passage through the Press Virginia was to observe with sympathy, amusement, and some irritation was Lytton's friend Ralph Partridge. It was arranged that he was to work at Hogarth House three days a week. Ralph Partridge was an engaging and vigorous person, handsome, intelligent, with considerable drive and a marked talent for business.

In October 1920 Virginia noted that he was "putting his ox's shoulder to the wheel, and intends to do 'hurricane' business." Clearly great things were hoped of him. By the end of the year Virginia's enthusiasm had waned a little; he was indomitable, but he was also rather domineering and increasingly there was friction with Leonard. It was only at moments of crisis, or in matters that concerned the fate of her own books, that Virginia made an effort fully to understand the disputes between Leonard and his collaborators in the Press; there was much that she did not notice or did not bother to examine; but whatever the dispute and whatever the degree of attention that she brought to it, she never had any doubt that Leonard was in the right.

Friday, February 18th [1921]

I have been long meaning to write a historical disquisition on the return of peace; for old Virginia will be ashamed to think what a chatterbox she was, always talking about people, never about politics. Moreover, she will say, the times you lived through were so extraordinary. They must have appeared so, even to quiet women living in the suburbs. But indeed nothing happens at one moment rather than another. The history books will make it much more definite than it is. The most significant sign of peace this year is the sales; just over. The shops have been flooded with cheap clothes. A coat and skirt that cost £14 in November went for 7 perhaps 5. People had ceased to buy and the shops had to dispose of things somehow. Margery Strachey who has been teaching at Debenhams foretells bankruptcy for most of the shopkeepers this very month. Still they go on selling cheaply. Pre-war prices, so they say. And I have found a street market in Soho where I buy stockings at 1/- a pair, silk ones (flawed slightly) at 1/10. A hundred yards down the road they ask 5/6 to 10/6 for the same things, or so they seem. Food has fallen a penny here, a penny there, but our books scarcely show a change. Milk is high–11d a quart. Butter fallen to 3/- but this is Danish butter. Eggs–I don't know what eggs are. Servant girls aged 20 get £45 wages. And the Times pays me 3 guineas instead of 2 guineas for a column. But I think you'll find all this written more accurately in other books, my dear Virginia; for instance in Mrs. Gosse's diary and Mrs. Webb's. I think it is true to say that during the past two months we have perceptibly moved towards cheapness–*just* perceptibly. It is just perceptible too that there are very few wounded soldiers abroad in blue, though stiff legs, single legs, sticks shod with rubber, and empty sleeves are common enough. Also at Waterloo I sometimes see dreadful looking spiders propelling themselves along the platform–men all body–legs trimmed off close to the body. There are few soldiers about.

It is true that in her diary she was "always talking about people, never about politics," or at least when she does talk about politics –as for instance when she mentions the great railway strike of 1919 and her active support of the strikers–it was an exceptional effort. In the same way it was an interruption of her life, a life which in the spring of 1921 was mainly devoted to *Jacob's Room*, *Monday or Tuesday* and an abortive effort to learn Russian, when she went electioneering with Leonard in March of that year. They went together to Manchester and Virginia, as usual, admired Leonard's masterly way of dealing with public meetings. But the socialist academics of Manchester filled her with despair. She saw, clearly enough, that they were good, brave and earnest people, fighting against fearful odds, against strong, blind and wicked forces. But they were dreadfully dull; she despised them and was ashamed of her own snobbery in doing so, and she was depressed by Manchester itself. She did not accompany Leonard on his other electoral excursions.

Monday or Tuesday★ appeared at the beginning of April, but owing, as Virginia believed, to a blunder by Ralph, who made a mistake about the date of publication, the book was inadequately reviewed by *The Times*, Doran (the American publisher of *The Voyage Out*) refused it, and altogether it seemed to have fallen very flat. Meanwhile Lytton's *Queen Victoria* was received everywhere with deafening applause. Ralph Partridge gave a celebration dinner party for him and the Woolfs in Gordon Square at which Lytton never so much as mentioned *Monday or Tuesday*, so that from Virginia's point of view the evening would have been a total failure had they not gone on to the Old Bedford Music Hall and seen Marie Lloyd:–"a mass of corruption–long front teeth–a crapulous way of saying 'desire', and yet a born artist."

Virginia's depression, though severe, was not of long duration for soon praise started to arrive. She began again at once to feel "important"–"and its that that one wants"–and by the middle of April she was able to consider Lytton's continued success–he was

★ *Monday or Tuesday* was a book of Virginia's stories which included *An Unwritten Novel*, *Kew Gardens*, and *The Mark on the Wall*, and five new pieces, as well as four woodcuts by Vanessa.

said to have sold 5,000 copies in a week while she had sold 300 in all–with decent philosophy. Moreover Lytton might be forgiven for a great deal; Ralph had repeated to her what he had said about *The String Quartet* (one of the stories in *Monday or Tuesday*)–he thought it marvellous. This did for a moment flood her every nerve with pleasure.*

With Ralph Partridge at the Hogarth Press, Virginia became involved in the affairs of the ménage at The Mill House, the country home which had been established for Lytton at Tidmarsh in Berkshire. Since her role in one of the dramas which distracted that household has been rather harshly described, it requires particular attention.

Life at Tidmarsh was, as Lytton told Virginia, "very complex"; it was conducted by a nearly incomprehensible trinity consisting of Ralph Partridge, Dora Carrington and Lytton himself, three persons who were all more or less in love with each other but each in a rather different way. Carrington was deeply and devotedly in love with Lytton and, at this period, sufficiently fond of Ralph Partridge to sleep with him and be, at all events, unwilling to lose him. But when he pursued her she fled from him, sometimes into the arms of other gentlemen. When he retired, she advanced. Partridge, although he could see her faults well enough, was obsessed by her and wished, passionately, to marry her; he was also very attached to Lytton, and Lytton, who in his turn was in love with Ralph, felt a tender, almost paternal, regard for Carrington–upon whom, moreover, he entirely depended for the domestic comforts of his life at Tidmarsh.

I do not think that Virginia knew, or perhaps she did not want to know, how important Carrington really was to Lytton. Carrington had good qualities–a kind of debauched innocence which was at once entertaining and touching–and in fact Virginia liked her; but at the same time she was very ignorant and rather silly; her charm was the charm of youth. "Carrington grows older," Virginia noted in her diary, "and her doings are of the sort that age." She felt, I suspect, that Lytton deserved and needed the companionship of a more informed and a more powerful intellect than you would find in a Crophead. Carrington, it appeared, was not altogether good

---

* "And Eliot astounded me by praising *Monday or Tuesday*! This really delighted me. He picked out the String Quartet, especially the end of it. 'Very good' he said, and meant it, I think. The Unwritten Novel he thought not successful; Haunted House 'extremely interesting.'" *AWD (Berg)*, 7 June 1921.

for Lytton.* Lytton himself, perhaps in deference to the ghost of an old attachment, perhaps half agreeing with Virginia's views, encouraged her to under-estimate the strength of his affections.† In December 1920, meeting by chance in Gordon Square, they spoke of the possibility of a marriage between Ralph and Carrington.

"Well," Virginia observed, "I wouldn't marry Ralph. A despot."

"True. But what's to happen to C[arrington]? She can't live indefinitely with me–perhaps with him?"

And again, when Lytton dedicated *Queen Victoria* to Virginia, a compliment which delighted her, she objected nevertheless that it should have been dedicated to Carrington.

"Oh dear no," he replied, "we're not on those terms at all."

In May 1921 Ralph Partridge, now desperate and made positively ill by Carrington's evasions and equivocations, laid all his troubles and perplexities before Leonard and Virginia.

He was very shrewd and bitter about C[arrington]. "She thinks herself one of the little friends of all the world" he said. Then he said she was selfish, untruthful, and quite indifferent to his suffering. So people in love always turn and rend the loved, with considerable insight too. He was speaking the truth largely. But I expect he was biassed; and also I expect–and indeed told him–that he is a bit of an ogre and tyrant. He wants more control than I should care to give–control I mean of the body and mind and time and thoughts of his loved. There's his danger and her risk; so I don't much envy her making up her mind this wet Whit Sunday.

This in fact was what Carrington had now to do, for Ralph's state of mind was such that Leonard and Virginia told him that he must, as Leonard said: "put a pistol to Carrington's head"–that is to say, tell her that if she would not marry him he would break with her altogether and go abroad.

Faced by the alternatives of marrying Ralph or, as she felt, of

* In 1928, commenting upon *Elizabeth and Essex*, Virginia remarks: "So feeble, so shallow; and yet Lytton himself is neither. So one next accuses the public; and then the Carringtons and the young men?" *AWD (Berg)*, 28 November 1928. Vanessa, in the same year, wrote: "Carrington has a funereal effect on Lytton who loses all interest in her presence." VB/CB, 23 May 1928.

† "He [Lytton] spoke of her [Carrington] . . . with a candour not flattering, though not at all malicious. 'That woman will dog me,' he remarked. 'She won't let me write I daresay,' 'Ottoline was saying you would end by marrying her.' 'God! The mere notion is enough. One thing I know–I'll never marry anyone.' 'But if she's in love with you?' 'Well, then she must take her chance.'" *AWD (Berg)*, 12 December 1917.

being parted from Lytton altogether–for she knew that her life with Lytton was inextricably bound up with his affection for Ralph, Carrington capitulated. They were in fact married ten days later. In a moment of unreserve Ralph revealed to her that his resolve had been strengthened by the Woolfs' advice. Virginia had told him that Lytton was afraid that Carrington might feel she had some claim on him; everyone was surprised that he could have stood her for so long, for obviously she had nothing in common with him, either intellectually or physically. Carrington, in a very moving and unhappy letter to Lytton, described the feelings and motives that had led her to marry; she also gave Ralph's version of what the Woolfs had told him. In a postscript she added: "You musn't think I was hurt by hearing what you said to Virginia and Leonard and *that* made me cry. For I'd faced that long ago with Alix in the first years of my love for you." Lytton answered:

> You must not believe, too readily, repeated conversations. I think that possibly some bitterness of disappointment makes you tend to exaggerate the black side of what you are told. . . . Certainly, I thought that it was generally agreed that one didn't believe quite everything that came through Virginia!

Virginia's part in this affair has been misunderstood and misrepresented. She has been credited with the most odious motives and to Lytton has been ascribed a denunciation of her conduct which is almost pure invention. When Ralph told the Woolfs of his feelings for Carrington, Virginia, it is said, "with her love of stirring up trouble, and knowing only too well that everything she said would be repeated, interposed a few poisonous comments of her own." Lytton's gentle and perhaps slightly guilty disclaimer (for, after all, it was he who had given Virginia the impression that Carrington might bore him) has been altered out of all recognition: "He told her that Virginia, with characteristic neurotic malevolence, had lied about his feelings and intentions."

Virginia *did* have some qualms of conscience; but they were not related to any remarks of hers that Ralph might have repeated. What disturbed her was the thought that she could have helped to promote an imprudent marriage.

> So Carrington did make up her mind to become Partridge–no, that is precisely what she is determined not to do; and signs herself aggressively Carrington for ever. If people ever took advice I should feel a little responsible for making up Ralph's mind. I mean I am not sure that this marriage is not more risky than most.

Her doubts were well-founded; within a year there were violent rows and recriminations, and Virginia then found herself very much on Carrington's side.

Although at first, no doubt, she had been a little piqued and puzzled by Lytton's attachment, Virginia was fond of Carrington for her own sake. And when it became clear how important that attachment was to Lytton, she loved Carrington for his sake too. In all these transactions – in which she was certainly unwise to become involved – Virginia's and Leonard's concern was with Lytton; he was, after all, one of their oldest and dearest friends, and it was his happiness that was their chief object.

Three days before Ralph Partridge married Dora Carrington at St Pancras Registry Office, Virginia and Leonard conducted an experiment, the subject of which was Desmond MacCarthy. In 1919 Virginia had written of him:

I'm not sure he hasn't the nicest nature of any of us – the nature one would soonest have chosen for one's own. I don't think that he possesses any faults as a friend, save that his friendship is so often sunk under a cloud of vagueness; a sort of drifting vapour composed of times and seasons separates us and effectively prevents us from meeting. Perhaps such indolence implies a slackness of fibre in his affections too – but I scarcely feel that. It arises from the consciousness which I find imaginative and attractive that things don't altogether *matter*. Somehow he is fundamentally sceptical. Yet which of us, after all, takes more trouble to do the sort of kindnesses that come his way? Who is more tolerant, more appreciative, more understanding of human nature? It goes without saying that he is not an heroic character. He finds pleasure too pleasant, cushions too soft, dallying too seductive and then, as I sometimes feel now, he has ceased to be ambitious. His "great Work" (it may be philosophy or biography now, and is certainly to be begun, after a series of long walks, this very spring) only takes shape, I believe, in that hour between tea and dinner, when so many things appear not merely possible but achieved. Comes the daylight, and Desmond is contented to begin his article; and plies his pen with a half humorous half melancholy recognition that such is his appointed life. Yet it is true, and no one can deny it, that he has the floating elements of something brilliant, beautiful – some book of stories, reflections, studies, scattered about in him, for they show themselves indisputably in his talk. I'm told he wants power; that these fragments never combine into an argument; that the disconnection of talk is kind to them; but in a book they would drift hopelessly apart. Consciousness of this, no doubt, led him in his one finished book to drudge and sweat until his fragments were clamped together in an indissoluble stodge. I can see myself, however, going through his desk one of these days, shaking out unfinished pages from between sheets of blotting paper, and deposits of old bills, and making up a small book of table talk, which shall appear as a proof to the younger generation that Desmond was the most gifted of us all. But why did he never do anything? they will ask.

Those who knew him may still ask themselves that question. Desmond, in the imagination of his friends, was going to be the successor of Henry James. Hearing him talk you could believe that. Even when he had sunk beneath repeated failures to float magazines, to produce copy on time, to meet the demands of bailiffs, to cope with life at all, still he had only to speak in order to command, not so much attention, as affection, to fill one with delight, and, when he was in the vein, to convince one that he was the master of some prodigious treasury. He had only to put his hand into his pocket and draw out whatever you might wish–subtlety, brilliance or deep imaginative richness. It was "ask and have," for he was the most carelessly generous, the most intellectually spendthrift of men. How few plays have ever enchanted one half so much as Desmond's small talk.

Conversation was his art, and for him the tragedy was that he should have chosen so ephemeral a medium. For Virginia there was an inconvenience of another kind; he would turn up at Richmond for dinner, uninvited very probably, and probably committed to a dinner elsewhere, charm his way out of his social crimes on the telephone, talk enchantingly until the small hours, insist that he be called early so that he might attend to urgent business on the morrow, wake up a trifle late, dawdle somewhat over breakfast, find a passage in *The Times* to excite his ridicule, enter into a lively discussion of Ibsen, declare he must be off, pick up a book which reminded him of something which, in short, would keep him talking until about 12.45, when he would have to ring up and charm the person who had been waiting in an office for him since 10, and at the same time deal with the complications arising from the fact that he had engaged himself to two different hostesses for lunch, and that it was now 1 o'clock and it would take forty minutes to get from Richmond to the West End. In all this Desmond had been practising his art– the art of conversation. Unfortunately, in order to do so he had to prevent Virginia from practising hers, and there would be occasions when she looked back on a wasted morning with some bitterness of spirit.

And yet, it was impossible to think of Desmond without affection or without a lively regret that his words could not be given a permanent form. A great many efforts had been made to persuade him to achieve something more serious than journalism. It is said that he was once locked into a room in an attempt to make him at least start his novel. More subtly, his wife invented the Novel Club, which was to lure him into literature, and in 1920 the Memoir Club* was devised with a similar purpose. This club lasted for many years without ever extracting from Desmond that masterpiece which it was still hoped that he might produce.

The Woolfs' experiment was different in its means but similar in its general purpose. The aim was, quite simply, to record Desmond's conversation. Desmond was invited to dine at Hogarth House. Roger Fry was asked too. Miss Green, Leonard's secretary at *The International Review*, whom Virginia unkindly, but accurately, likened to a chest of drawers, was posted in a convenient place with paper and pencils, and Desmond, ignorant of the plot and fortified with two bottles of Chablis, was encouraged to talk. He talked magnificently and Miss Green set down every word. There was only one flaw in the scheme: the record of Desmond's conversation was completely uninteresting.

On 10 June Virginia went to a concert and that night she could not sleep. On the next day she kept to her bed and it soon became depressingly clear that she was in for one of her bouts of illness. The next two months she spent more or less in bed. Leonard took her to Monk's House for a time, but she did not improve, and it was not until 8 August, again at Rodmell, that she was well enough to write in her diary.

> These, this morning, the first words I have written–to call writing–for 60 days; and those days spent in wearisome headache, jumping pulse, aching back, frets, fidgets, lying awake, sleeping draughts, sedatives, digitalis, going for a little walk, and plunging back into bed again–all

* The Memoir Club met for the first time on 4 March 1920. The members were: Desmond and Molly MacCarthy, Leonard and Virginia Woolf, Saxon Sydney-Turner, Maynard Keynes, Lytton Strachey, Duncan Grant, Clive and Vanessa Bell, Morgan Forster, Sydney Waterlow and Roger Fry. David Garnett became a member fairly soon afterwards. The club had no rules, save that there was an understanding that members were free to say anything they pleased, nor did it keep any records. Leonard Woolf suggests (*Downhill . . .*, p. 114) that the membership was identical with the original thirteen members of Bloomsbury. But it is arguable that if the club had been started in 1912 it would have included Adrian Stephen, and I am not sure that Sydney Waterlow can really be considered a member of Bloomsbury. The Novel Club, so far as I can find out, existed only briefly in 1913.

the horrors of the dark cupboard of illness once more displayed for my diversion. Let me make a vow that this shall never, never, happen again; and *then* confess that there are some compensations. To be tired and authorised to lie in bed is pleasant; . . . I feel that I can take stock of things in a leisurely way. Then the dark underworld has its fascinations as well as its terrors.

She recovered slowly, but she was irritable. Rodmell, she declared, was becoming a colony for Georgian poets, and the village children made a hideous noise playing in the meadow beyond their orchard. She began to think that they had better look for a new house. For the first time she thought of making a will.

Finding that she could write again her morale improved and she returned to Richmond with her equanimity restored; Ralph and the new printing machine were working well, Nelly and Lottie were at peace and even a visit by her cousin Dorothea Stephen, stamping and trumpeting across the carpet of Hogarth House like some obscene relic of the Ice Age, did not disturb her too much. Moreover Dorothea intended to spend the next five years improving the moral sense of the Indians. On Friday, 4 November Virginia wrote the last words of *Jacob's Room*, noting that she had begun it on 16 April of the previous year.

At the beginning of the new year she decided that she would do no more reviewing; it consumed altogether too much time and energy, Bruce Richmond tampered with her copy, and she felt that she was now able to make as much money by other forms of writing. Also, as Leonard must have observed, she was by no means really recovered.

Putting the revision of *Jacob* aside she began a new work which she had for some time been meditating and which she called *Reading*. She began it with the greatest enjoyment but almost at once she was struck down with influenza and was back in bed for a fortnight. Dr Fergusson forbade her to work for another two or three weeks. Dr Fergusson was their General Practitioner at Richmond and clearly a man of sense. He needed to be, for now Virginia's erratic pulse "had passed the limits of reason and was in fact insane." Her temperature too behaved very abnormally. She was sent to two specialists, one of whom pronounced that her heart was affected and that she had not long to live; the other said it was her lungs. Dr Fergusson decided to disregard them and Leonard did likewise. But the first three months of 1922 were spent as an invalid. She had her bed moved into the drawing-room beside the fire, and there wrote a little and read a great deal, received her visitors, and observed the worsening relationship between Leonard and Ralph over the Hogarth Press.

Virginia, however, was not such an invalid that she could not again undertake a mild flirtation with Clive.

> . . . I am seeing Clive rather frequently. He comes on Wednesdays; jolly, and rosy, and squab; a man of the world; and enough of my old friend, and enough of my old lover, to make the afternoons hum. Once a week is probably enough. His letters suggest doubts. But, oh dear me, after 9 weeks of claustration, I want to vault the wall and pick a few flowers.

> . . . We talked from 4.30 to 10.15 the other day. It is clear that I am to rub up his wits; and in return I get my manners polished. I hear of supper parties; elicit facts about drink and talk and goings on. . . . He enjoys *everything*-even the old hag in the doorway. There is no truth about life, he says, except what we feel. It is good if you enjoy it; and so forth. Obviously we reach no heights of reason. Nor do we become completely intimate. A little colour is added to taste. We have our embrace; our frill of sentiment,-impossible, as Nessa says, to talk without it. But I perceive . . . that once a fortnight is the pitch of our relationship.

Clive for his part had written to Vanessa to say that "as usual" he had fallen slightly in love with Virginia and, ten days later: "I hope I shan't fall more deeply in love. However its a great compliment for a woman of forty don't you think?"

Neither of them was in much danger. Clive's affections were at this time engaged elsewhere; as for Virginia, her feelings for him fluctuated, but the pendulum of her heart never swung anywhere near to passion. Dining with him and Vanessa, she reflected that they had all become happier, more tolerant, more secure, since those days when meals *à trois* at Gordon Square had been a habit and Clive had been the most important man in her life. Now she could enjoy his company and his gallantries, which stemmed from a natural kindness and a genuine desire to please; even his absurdities, which only the year before she had severely condemned, she now could laugh at. At that time his mundane life, his dinings-out and little luncheon parties, his duchesses and his fine French phrases, his name-dropping, his fancy waistcoats, his bawling voice and his balding head, had exasperated and slightly shocked her. Now she still disapproved of him, but liked him better.

The variations in Virginia's comments upon Clive are in themselves an indication that her strictures should not be taken too seriously. But it was true that, since the war, Clive had become more worldly, and at the same time she herself had become both more interested in and more critical of worldliness. Being herself a snob she was able to understand the subtle corruption of values which she discerned in Clive and which she herself was to describe with some particularity in *Mrs Dalloway*.

In June 1922 T. S. Eliot came to Hogarth House and read a new work.

> He sang it and chanted it and rhythmed it. It has great beauty and force of phrase; symmetry; and tensity. What connects it together, I'm not so sure. But he read till he had to rush—letters to write about the London Magazine—and discussion thus was curtailed. One was left, however, with some strong emotion. The Waste Land, it is called; and Mary Hutch[inson], who has heard it more quietly, interprets it to be Tom's autobiography—a melancholy one.

To Virginia, as to many others, it seemed wrong that so serious and original a poet should have to spend his days working for his livelihood in a bank, and she became involved in one of the periodic attempts that were made to release Eliot from this necessity. An Eliot Fellowship Fund was set up, the intention being to raise £300 a year for him for five years. An account was opened in the names of E. G. Aldington, Lady Ottoline Morrell and Mrs Virginia Woolf at Lloyds Bank and Ottoline, who was a prime mover in the matter, prepared a circular inviting regular contributions from likely supporters. It fell to Virginia to discuss the matter with Mr Eliot; he was invited to Monk's House, together with E. M. Forster, for the week-end of 23 September 1922. Their talk was largely about *Ulysses*; and Virginia was both impressed and illuminated by Eliot's analytical defence of the book, which she summarised in her diary.

> After Joyce, however, we came to ticklish matters—the Eliot Fund; the upshot of it was (and we were elliptical, tactful, nervous) that Tom won't leave the Bank under £500 and must have securities, not pledges. So next morning, when Ott.'s letter & circular arrived, aiming at £300, on a 5 year basis of pledges, I had to wire her to stop and then to draft a long letter giving my reasons; and another to Tom, asking him to confirm my information. I shall be scalded in two separate baths of hot water no doubt.

Subscriptions did come in; but the poet's reticence, his reservations and embarrassment, made benefaction an uphill task. As a gesture the Fund sent him £50 for Christmas, but even that Virginia expected him to refuse.*

* After some five years the subscribers were re-imbursed; Eliot had by then liberated himself from the Bank by other means.

T. S. Eliot and his finances have taken me too far into the year 1922. The pleasures and embarrassments of knowing Mr Eliot were but a minor incident in the events of that year. It began badly with the coldest spring on record and Virginia's health was not good; she had trouble with her teeth–three were extracted–she had trouble also with her heart and her persistent high temperature. But she managed to work hard and by June she was making a fair copy of *Jacob's Room* for Miss Green to type out: Harcourt, Brace, who had published *Monday or Tuesday* in America, asked to read it, and the copy was promised for July. On the 23rd of that month Leonard read it, and declared it to be her best work–"amazingly well written" and unlike any other novel. Virginia was excited and grew increasingly anxious as the prospect of publication approached. She speculated as to other people's reactions and began the usual soliloquy in her diary. The book would fail, it would be abused by the critics, and she told herself that she would not mind, or would not mind very much.

She devised a plan to guard herself against the expected wounds of criticism: she would go on with *Reading* and write a story or two for magazines; if people disliked her fiction, they could read her criticism; if they thought *Jacob* merely a clever experiment she would produce *Mrs Dalloway in Bond Street*.

Mrs Dalloway had made a brief appearance on board the *Euphrosyne* in *The Voyage Out*; now she re-emerged from the shadows of Virginia's imagination. She was connected with several short stories which Virginia invented at Rodmell that summer. To some extent she may be identified with Kitty Maxse, and Kitty's sudden death in October 1922–she fell from the top of a flight of stairs and Virginia believed that she had committed suicide–almost certainly helped to transform the stories into a book and to give that book its final character.

By the time the Woolfs came back to Richmond early in October the future of the Hogarth Press had become a matter of critical concern. It had become obvious that Leonard and Ralph could not work together–but Ralph would not leave. The whole question was complicated by Lytton's interest in Ralph and Ralph's career. At one time he had thought of purchasing, with Maynard Keynes, the *English Review*, largely so that Ralph might manage it. Lytton let it be known that if Ralph were able to stay on at the Hogarth Press they might publish his, Lytton's, books. This bait, which could not be ignored, created a certain awkwardness in the continual discussions which took place; and so too did Lytton's next idea of establishing a rival Tidmarsh Press for Ralph. Roger produced a rich and cultured young man who would put money into, and make money for, the Press; Logan Pearsall Smith tried to negotiate an arrangement between the Woolfs and Constable; Heinemann made a most tempting takeover offer. The uncertainty was said by Lytton to be trying to Ralph's nerves and yet, Virginia burst out, "this nervous man makes no attempt to do the most ordinary things for us. L. has to tie parcels every morning. Ralph catches no earlier or later trains. Monday morning he spent at the tailor's."

After endless and wearing discussions they opted for freedom—freedom from commercial publishers, freedom from Ralph, and freedom from the perpetual strain of hurting Lytton's feelings. By pure chance they came upon a young woman who longed to become a printer and would work full time for a salary; she came in January, and, in March 1923, Ralph Partridge left.

Jacob's Room was the first full-length book to be published by the Hogarth Press (it was printed by R. & R. Clark of Edinburgh). It was published on 27 October 1922. To Virginia it seemed at first that the press reviews were against her and the private people enthusiastic. Of these, one, T. S. Eliot, shall be quoted:

> You have freed yourself from any compromise between the traditional novel and your original gift. It seems to me that you have bridged a certain gap which existed between your other novels and the experimental prose of *Monday or Tuesday* and that you have made a remarkable success.

And this, it seemed presently, was the opinion both of the reviewers and of the public. Virginia was satisfied; *Jacob's Room* marks the beginning of her maturity and her fame.

Chapter Four

1923–1925

VIRGINIA began the new year in a mood of depression and of introspection. She imagined herself, rather in the style of Mr Ramsay,

> . . . forging ahead, alone, through the night . . . suffering inwardly, stoically; . . . blazing my way through to the end–and so forth. The truth is that the sails flap about me for a day or two on coming back; and not being at full stretch I ponder and loiter. And it is all temporary; yet let me be quite clear about that. Let me have one confessional where I need not boast. Years and years ago, after the Lytton affair, I said to myself, walking up the hill at Bayreuth, never pretend that the things you haven't got are not worth having; good advice, I think. At least it often comes back to me. Never pretend that children, for instance, can be replaced by other things. And then I went on . . . to say to myself that one must (how am I to convey it?) like things for themselves; or rather, rid them of their bearing upon one's personal life. One must throw that aside; and venture on to the things that exist independently of oneself. Now this is very hard for young women to do. Yet I got satisfaction from it. And now, married to L., I never *have* to make the effort. I do it, if I enjoy doing it. Perhaps I have been too happy for my soul's good? Perhaps I have become cowardly and self-indulgent? And does some of my discontent come from feeling that? I could not stay at 46 [Gordon Square] last night, because L. on the telephone expressed displeasure. Late again. Very foolish. Your heart bad, and so my self reliance being sapped, I had no courage to venture against his will. Then I react. Of course it's a difficult question. For undoubtedly I get headaches or the jump in my heart; and then this spoils his pleasure and if one lives with a person, has one the right–So it goes on.

It is possible to disengage a number of connected elements from Virginia's melancholy reflections: a perennial and incurable regret that she had no children; a natural jealousy of Vanessa in this respect and–a further source of envy–Vanessa's ability, despite her parental commitments, to lead a freer, a more adventurous life than Virginia. This again was related to her feeling, as she approached her forty-first birthday, that life was slipping away and that it could in some manner be arrested, or more effectively detained in its flight, by one who lived in town than by an inhabitant of the suburbs. She wanted to return to London.

Her longing for social adventures was in part assuaged, but also in part exacerbated, by the acquisition of new friends. In December 1922 she had met Vita and Harold Nicolson at Clive's dinner table, a meeting which shall be discussed in a later chapter; at this time too she began to see a number of young and brilliant people: George Rylands and Angus Davidson (both of whom she was to know well), F. L. Lucas and Frank Ramsay from Cambridge, Raymond Mortimer and Lord David Cecil from Oxford. Most of them might be met at 46 Gordon Square, which, in 1916, had been taken over by Maynard Keynes. Maynard was a genial and energetic host, and he made Gordon Square the centre of an enlarged and altogether more amorphous "Bloomsbury" (the term is very loosely used). Here too one might be certain to find Lydia Lopokova.

Lydia had come to London as a principal dancer in Diaghilev's company in 1918, 1919 and 1921, and had danced very beautifully in *Boutique Fantasque*, *Les Sylphides* and *The Sleeping Beauty*. Maynard, like most of his friends, was a passionate devotee of the ballet; he became an equally passionate devotee of Lopokova. His devotion was very understandable. But supposing he were to marry her? Lydia as a friend, Lydia as a visiting bird hopping gaily from twig to twig was, Virginia thought, very delightful. She was pretty, high-spirited, a comic, a charmer and extremely well-disposed.* In that gay, peripatetic capacity she was altogether irreproachable. But how, without two solid ideas to rub together, could she fail to destroy the intellectual comforts of Maynard Keynes's friends, and indeed of Maynard himself?

> I can foresee only too well [wrote Virginia to Vanessa], Lydia stout, charming, exacting; Maynard in the Cabinet; 46 [Gordon Square] the resort of dukes and prime ministers. Maynard, being a simple man, not analytic as we are, would sink beyond recall long before he realised his state. Then he would awake, to find 3 children, & his life entirely and for ever controlled.

The nature of Bloomsbury was such that the fine web of intimate friendships upon which it depended for its existence could be snapped by any intruder. Thus Adrian had married himself away from his sisters and his friends, and thus Clive's mistresses formed a constantly

---

* On 11 September 1923 Virginia noted, after staying with Maynard Keynes and Lydia Lopokova at Studland: "I wanted to observe Lydia as a type for Rezia; and did observe one or two facts." *AWD (Berg)*.

disturbing element. Eventually, however, Maynard decided, and decided wisely, that his happiness could best be secured by marrying Lydia. Friends must take the two of them together–and in fact they did.

But in January 1923 Lydia was still, so to speak, one of the decorations of Bloomsbury. Her dancing was one of the delights of Maynard's Twelfth Night party at Gordon Square; Marjorie Strachey gave her own obscenely comic renderings of nursery rhymes, Sickert acted Hamlet; Virginia found herself among all her friends and her spirits rose wonderfully. The evening was immensely enjoyable.

But it was no more than an interlude. She returned to her work, her cares, her depression and her suburb.

"Mrs. Murry's dead! It says so in the paper." Nelly made the announcement dramatically at breakfast on 12 January. Virginia's feelings were mixed and, on the whole, painful. It was a rival struck down; she could not repel that thought or refrain from recording it. But Katherine and Katherine's injunction "do not quite forget me" were remembered, and her loss–a loss genuinely felt despite all the vicissitudes and jealousies of their relationship–was one more unhappiness in an unhappy season.

Berta Ruck was also dead. She had been killed in *Jacob's Room*.

Yet even in this light the legends on the tombstones could be read, brief voices saying: 'I am Bertha Ruck, I am Tom Gage'. And they say which day of the year they died, and the New Testament says something for them, very proud, very emphatic or consoling.

Somewhere Virginia must have seen that odd name and unconsciously distorted it a little, adding an *h*, an addition which did not save her from a lawyer's letter pointing out that the real Berta Ruck was very much alive and inclined to be litigious on the subject of her literary extinction. She was, it appeared, in the same line of business as Virginia, the authoress of *The Lad with Wings*, *Sir or Madam* and *The Dancing Star*; but whereas Virginia might be content to sell a few hundred copies of *her* works, Miss Ruck, who very skilfully combined the qualities of the *feuilleton* writer with those of an authority on social behaviour, sold by the thousand and tens of thousands. Like Virginia, she was married to a literary man, Oliver Onions, and it was he, indignant on his wife's behalf, who refused to believe Virginia's disarming reply to their solicitors' letter: how could Mrs Woolf never have heard of Berta Ruck, whose name and fame were emblazoned even on the tops of London omnibuses? Fortunately his rage evaporated, and peace was made. The two authoresses exchanged letters, were reconciled, and later found that they had a common friend in Lydia. Virginia and Berta Ruck both found Mlle Lopokova amusing and, at times, disconcerting;* she formed a tenuous link between them. When a year or so later at a Bloomsbury party, Berta Ruck gave a most spirited rendering of "Never allow a Sailor an inch above your knee"–a performance which filled Virginia with amazement and delight–all differences over tombstones had long been forgotten.

There was a further annoyance in the early weeks of 1923. *The Nation* was changing hands. H. W. Massingham, the editor, had employed Leonard as a salaried contributor; but now Maynard Keynes had emerged as a major shareholder and Chairman of the new Board of Directors. He wanted to change the style and policy of the paper. The result might be injurious, in a financial sense, to the Woolfs, but it was not so much this as the feeling of uncertainty, and perhaps even more, the feeling of subordination which demoralised not only Virginia, but Leonard.

> Leonard thinks himself a failure. And what use is there in denying a depression which is irrational? Can't I always think myself one too? It is inevitable. But there was Maynard arrived and trim, yet our junior. The absurd unreality of this as a standard strikes me, but it is not easy to make these truths effective. It is unpleasant waiting in a dependent kind of way to know what Massingham will do.

The weather was wet and wan. The Hogarth Press was in a most

* Miss Ruck recalls a performance of *The Frogs* to which she and Virginia were taken by Lydia Lopokova. They sat in the front row of the stalls and the two novelists were greatly enjoying themselves.

"Lydia, however (invariably one to speak her mind in her enchantingly original English) said, 'This is so doll.'

'Lydia! It's *not* dull! It's very very *funny*.'

'It is doll. We will go out.'

'We can't' said your Aunt [Virginia] in a whisper, 'At least wait until the Interval.'

'We will go out *now*. It is too doll to bear. Now. Come.'

'We can't, possibly ——'

'No one will see.'

'Lydia, *everybody* will see us! We are all much too noticeable ——'

We were, you know. Your famous Aunt wore a very large black sombrero hat, I was as tall as she, and had fat black plaits done over my ears, Lydia between us was small, but always outstandingly striking in movement and manner, you might not see what she wore, but she drew every eye.

Fortunately she allowed herself to be persuaded to sit down and see it out before the audience joined in!"

Miss Berta Ruck to the author, 11 September 1971

uncomfortable condition; Ralph, who was not to leave until Easter, was defiant and argumentative; the drawling voice of the new aspirant, Marjorie Joad, grated on Virginia's ears. But they had to work together, they had to be given lunch and tea, and the need to maintain some kind of conversation between them all imposed a heavy burden upon her. Her melancholy mood was intensified by a fever and a violent cold and, to add to her anxieties, there seemed, in the remodelling of *The Nation*, to be a chance of solving Mr Eliot's financial problems by making him Literary Editor.

Virginia pulled strings, rang people up, exhorted and advised; but she found herself wishing that "poor dear Tom had more spunk in him, less need to let drop by drop of his agonised perplexities fall ever so finely through pure cambric." Finally *The Nation's* demand for a quick decision, and the fact that it could not guarantee more than six months' employment settled the matter. Eliot found that he could not take the risk of accepting. The job was offered to Leonard and he took it.

Virginia was a good deal taken aback by this surprising turn of events. She could see the disadvantages of such an employment, but at the same time it offered security and she was immensely relieved.

It was on Friday, 23 March that Maynard offered the post of Literary Editor of *The Nation* to Leonard; on 1 April the Woolfs were in Madrid. It was many years since they had crossed the Channel; the experience was exhilarating and therapeutic and I think that something of Virginia's delight in that holiday is preserved in a contribution (it is not easy to know whether one should describe it as a story or an article) to the refurbished *Nation* entitled *To Spain*. Their journey took them–partly on muleback–to Yegen in the mountains south of Granada, where they were entertained by Ralph Partridge's friend Gerald Brenan, at that time a rather earnest young man who was devoting himself very seriously to the art of writing. The Woolfs stayed with him for a fortnight and, according to Virginia, they discussed literature twelve hours a day. She called him a mad Englishman and liked him very much. Forty years later he remembered not only the beauty and distinction of her appearance and her voice, not only the brilliance, gaiety and irony of her conversation, but her real friendliness and her insatiable curiosity.

Perhaps because Virginia lacked the novelist's sense for the dramatic properties of character and was more interested in the texture of people's minds, she was much given to drawing them out and documenting herself upon them. She asked me a great many questions–why I had come to live here, what I felt about this and that, and what my ideas were about writing. I was conscious that I was being studied and even quizzed a little, and also that she and Leonard were trying to decide whether I showed any signs of having literary talent. If so, I must publish with them. Yet it must not for a moment be thought that she was patronizing. On the contrary her deference to the views of the callow and rather arrogant youth with whom she was staying was quite surprising. She argued with me about literature, defended Scott, Thackeray, and Conrad against my attacks, disagreed with my high opinion of *Ulysses* on the grounds that great works of art ought not to be so boring, and listened humbly to my criticisms of her own novels. That was the great thing about 'Bloomsbury'—they refused to stand on the pedestal of their own age and superiority. And her visit was followed by a succession of highly characteristic letters in which she continued the theme of our discussions.

The Woolfs returned by way of Paris, where Virginia hoped to meet Vanessa. She stayed for a few days, while Leonard went on alone to Richmond and *The Nation*.

Whenever they were apart, which was seldom enough, Leonard and Virginia wrote to each other every day. Her letters usually give a faithful account of her activities; they did so on this occasion. Vanessa did not come. Virginia saw Paris as a tourist might see it; she was lonely, and without her husband everything seemed pointless and second-rate; his absence was acutely felt. The tenderness of her feelings was well expressed in an earlier letter:

> I lie & think of my precious beast, who does make me more happy every day & instant of my life than I thought it possible to be. There's no doubt I'm terribly in love with you. I keep thinking what you're doing, & I have to stop—it makes me want to kiss you so.

Virginia's friends would hardly have been surprised by such an avowal. Seeing the Woolfs together the observer certainly received a very strong impression of happiness and unity in their marriage. Their affection, despite much teasing and some tiffs, was manifest; so too was Virginia's dependence upon Leonard in practical matters and all judgements requiring calculation and solid good sense. What was less generally apparent was *his* need of her, particularly in moments of disappointment and pain. Certainly in the early part of that year he had needed her sympathy and she his; they were united in their discouragement. But by May 1923, and in the following year, the solidarity that is born of misfortune was unnecessary.

Returning to England with the prospect of being a Literary Editor, of undergoing all the fatigues and exasperations incidental to an employment in which, as in a treadmill, the last step of the old week is but the first step of the new, Leonard required no sympathy; he was never in the least dismayed by the prospect of hard work. His discontents at this time, and they were not very serious, did not arise from calamities but from success.

Jacob's Room had been well received; Virginia felt a certain buoyancy in her situation; she was, as she herself put it, being "pushed up"; she had become, almost, a celebrity.

The growth of her reputation showed itself in social terms. Lady Colefax (a sensitive barometer of fame) began to issue invitations. At first Virginia refused them. She was still socially timid, she still felt that it took a good deal of courage to go into strange rooms "properly dressed"; she was still visited by horrid doubts as to whether she *was* properly dressed and, when she had mastered her fears well enough to enable her to go into Lady Colefax's dining-room, she might well find herself placed next to Sir Arthur, who always seemed to imagine that his neighbour took a passionate interest in the fate of the Dye-stuffs Bill. Nevertheless, Lady Colefax was persistent and Lady Colefax was persuasive, and of course Virginia half wanted to be persuaded. Moreover, although she thought that Lady Colefax was rather like a glossy artificial cherry stuck on a hat, she had her perceptions, she had her character. When she came to tea and left her umbrella, Virginia referred to it as "glowing and gleaming among my old gamps." She was taken up sharply. "Mrs. Woolf, I know what you think of my umbrella—a cheap, stubby, vulgar umbrella, you think my umbrella: and you think I have a bag like it—a cheap flashy bag covered with bad embroidery." Since this was precisely what Virginia did think, she considered Lady Colefax with a new respect.

Virginia's social adventures became part of a game which she used to play with Clive: the game of "boasts". Two postcards give a notion of what Virginia's boasting was like. One: "My boast: 2 invitations: one to stay with Cecils & meet Lady Gwendolen; the other to spend 5 days at Easter playing Badmington & discussing fiction with H. G. Wells. Yes—this sort of thing *does* give me pleasure." Or, again to Clive: "Lady Londonderry gave a party and did ask me—at which my heart leapt up, as you can imagine, until I discovered that it was to meet 500 Colonial dentists and to hear Mr. Noyes read his own poetry aloud. Not a distinguished gathering." Virginia had certainly not outgrown her snobberies and, unlike her husband, succumbed easily to the blandishments of hostesses. She was welcomed by the world of fashion, and she enjoyed it. "Leonard," she wrote in her diary, "Leonard thinks less well of me for powdering my nose and spending money on dress. Never mind, I adore Leonard."

Writing to her old art student friend, Margery Snowden, in April 1923, Vanessa said that Virginia was now more like what she used to be, and in saying this I think that she meant that her sister was completely cured. She had regained her serenity, her moral and intellectual balance. Physically she showed signs of the ordeal of the past ten years. She had grown more angular, more bony, more austere; she had lost whatever prettiness she may have possessed; but certainly she continued to be very beautiful. In her dress, there was only a passing and reluctant acceptance of the demands of fashion, and not the least coquetry; those frivolities which, as she believed, were condemned by Leonard were certainly on a very minute scale.* Her powder was minimal, her dress allowance stringent. Looking for some analogy to the style of her appearance I come nearest to finding it in the art of the Sienese masters of the fourteenth century: in everything she was linear, elegant, dignified, graceful, with very little high renaissance bulk about her, no Raphaelesque sweetness or softness, no Correggioscity. In her attitudes there was the oddest mixture of grandeur and clumsiness. Imagine a Simone Martini dismissing the annunciate angel to roll a cigarette or take a hearty four-mile walk over the hills, and you may perceive something of the fine incongruity that I am trying to suggest. The pictures and photographs of this period are unreliable; a ciné-camera could in ten seconds have caught the essential quality that is lacking in the still image; for it was in movement that she was most truly herself. Then she reminded one of some fantastic bird, abruptly throwing up her head and crowing with delighted amusement at some idea, some word, some paradox, that took her fancy. Her conversation was full of surprises, of unpredictable questions, of fantasy and of laughter – the happy laughter of a child who finds the world more strange, more absurd and more beautiful than any-

* "Her hair was allowed to drift about in all directions, she never wore any make-up–she seemed quite devoid of personal vanity, and yet she never appeared anything but beautiful. Sometimes in the summer when I was working in the printing room she'd wander in and set up type or distribute it with her quick, sensitive fingers, looking like a dishevelled angel–her bare feet shuffling about in bedroom slippers, in a nightdress with a great tear down the side, and a dressing-gown vaguely thrown over it, but her mind far, far away from her mechanical task. . . ." Ralph Partridge, *Portrait of Virginia Woolf*, BBC Home Service, 29 August 1956.

one could have imagined possible; laughter seemed in those years to be her natural element.

For children she was a treat. The announcement: "Virginia is coming to tea" was like a warm capricious breeze blowing in from the south-west and bringing with it a kind of amazed joy. Of the miseries of her life, they were allowed to know nothing, nor did it seem, in their company, that she could be unhappy.

She could, though, inspire terror. Not that she ever set herself to terrify children; but I can remember listening to a conversation between her and Vanessa when Virginia described two old ladies—I don't know who—living quietly in one of those London streets which are closed at one end to traffic by means of solid iron posts. A house further up the street was burgled. The thieves were surprised; they slipped out of the front door, leapt into a fast car and crashed against the barrier. The old ladies heard this and heard the men shrieking in mortal pain until the ambulance arrived. The story was told simply but with such incredible power that my blood ran cold—it still does a little when I recall it and the way Virginia told it. But, of course, a child wants to be frightened. One would have liked to have heard more. I can't remember that I did. Usually it was all jokes and fun.

She seems to have had a natural sympathy with the young, accepting their fantasies, joining in their games without effort and without condescension, exercising a purely benevolent power of enchantment. But in speaking here of "the young" I refer to the inhabitants of the nursery rather than to those of the campus. If you were old enough to regard her as a celebrity (a role in which the nursery did not see her) her incantations might be of a different kind. She could charm and she could terrify; but her magic was not purely benevolent. It is said that she could behave with some ferocity, that she had claws and could bite, that several young men and women had been mauled.

> ... her social approach to young people was thoroughly intimidating. She was particularly hard on innocent young women with any intellectual pretensions; she would question them in a relentlessly encouraging way, get them to air all their high-minded views and then expose their utter ignorance and ineptitude to the assembled company in her low, mocking voice, without ever losing the benign expression on her face. Yet the relish with which she punctured their poor aspirations to partake in intelligent conversation was only too evident. Pretty girls, who only wanted to attract the men present physically, were spared these snubs—the silly nincompoops could flirt as much as they

liked with impunity. But it was *lèse-majesté* for a girl to think herself clever enough to talk to Virginia as an equal. Aspiring young men weren't so obviously maltreated. They too were encouraged by her to speak what was in their callow, shallow minds, but they were not publicly humiliated; they were just left to go home with the uncomfortable sensation that in some inscrutable way they'd made utter fools of themselves.

Certainly there is an element of truth in this, although I think that, in a matter of this kind, Ralph Partridge cannot be considered a reliable witness. He was very much inclined to make large generalisations upon rather slender material and I strongly suspect that he was doing so in this instance. Nor do I think that his analysis of Virginia's motives is a correct one; indeed the evidence on which it is based is highly questionable, for of those who charged Virginia with cruelty to the young, there was one–Clive–who always took the view that it was young *men* who suffered at her hands and that she was indulgent, almost too indulgent, to the claims of young women. But having made these reservations the charge itself must be accepted. Like many people who have been socially terrified, Virginia could be and probably rather enjoyed being socially terrifying; as her reputation grew, as the success of *Jacob's Room* was followed by the acclaim of *Mrs Dalloway*, her ability and her opportunities for social misbehaviour of this kind increased.

As we have seen, in 1922 Virginia hit upon the plan of writing two books simultaneously: her novel and a work of criticism which she had at first called *Reading* and now *The Common Reader*. The one, she calculated, would provide relief from the other. *The Common Reader* was based, largely, upon articles which she had already published, but to this she added some new material and, notably, the long essay entitled *On Not Knowing Greek*. It was with this theme in mind that she planned, in October 1922, to read Sophocles, Euripides and the first five books of the *Odyssey*. (Her usual practice was to read the original Greek text, consulting a crib when she had to.) She was also intending to read the lives of Bentley and of Jebb, and a little later she decided that she must also read Zimmern and Aeschylus.*

* Sir Alfred Eckhard Zimmern, 1879–1957. Virginia probably read *The Greek Commonwealth – Politics and Economics in 5th Century Athens*, Oxford, 1911. *The Life and Letters of Sir R. C. Jebb*, by Caroline Jebb, Cambridge, 1907, contains an essay by A. W. Verrall which might have been useful; in other respects the book seems barely relevant to Virginia's topic and she may have had in mind Jebb's edition of the *Trachiniae* (1892) which belonged to Leonard (see Holleyman & Treacher Ltd., *Catalogue of important and association books from the Library of the late Leonard and*

That autumn of 1922 both books seem to have hung fire. In late October and in November Virginia was rethinking *Mrs Dalloway*. On 7 November she planned to tackle her Greek chapter before the end of the month, although she felt that she had not done half enough reading and had still to tackle Aeschylus, Bentley and the *Odyssey*. On 23 January she notes that she wants to get *Mrs Dalloway* into full talk. By the month of May the Greeks were still unwritten. Early in June she spent a week-end at Garsington and this visit, showing her, as it must have done, a striking though singular vision of the British social apparatus, directed her mind to the main theme of her novel (which she now called *The Hours*).

"I am a great deal interested suddenly in my book," she wrote on 4 June. "I want to bring in the despicableness of people like Ott. I want to give the slipperiness of the soul. I have been too tolerant . . ." The reflection may have been unkind and unjust, but it was not unproductive. A fortnight later she examined herself and her novel with some care.

I took up this book with a kind of idea that I might say something about my writing – which was prompted by glancing at what K. M. said about her writing in *The Dove's Nest*. But I only glanced. She said a good deal about feeling things deeply: also about being pure, which I won't criticise, though of course I very well could. But now what do I feel about *my* writing? – this book, that is, *The Hours*, if that's its name? One must write from deep feeling, said Dostoievsky. And do I? Or do I fabricate with words, loving them as I do? No, I think not. In this book I have almost too many ideas. I want to give life and death, sanity and insanity; I want to criticise the social system, and to show it at work, at its most intense. But here I may be posing. . . . Am I writing *The Hours* from deep emotion? Of course the mad part tries me so much, makes my mind squirt so badly that I can hardly face spending the next weeks at it. It's a question though of these characters. People, like Arnold Bennett, say I can't create, or didn't in *Jacob's Room*, characters that survive. My answer is – but I leave that to the *Nation*: it's only the old argument that character is dissipated into shreds now; the old post-Dostoievsky argument. I daresay it's true, however, that I haven't that "reality" gift. I insubstantise, wilfully to some extent, distrusting reality – its cheapness. But to get further. Have I the power of conveying the true reality? Or do I write essays about myself? Answer

Virginia Woolf, May 1970, III, 12). The Woolfs also owned a copy of Monk's *Life of Bentley* (1883) (*ibid.* VII, 4) and this served not only Virginia's purposes in her essay *On Not Knowing Greek* but was used too in the writing of *Dr Bentley* (also in *The Common Reader*). It was lent to Lytton Strachey and was his main, perhaps his only, source, in *The Sad Story of Dr Colbatch*. (*Portraits in Miniature*, 1931; p. i.)

these questions as I may, in the uncomplimentary sense, and still there remains this excitement. To get to the bones, now I'm writing fiction again I feel my force glow straight from me at its fullest. After a dose of criticism I feel that I'm writing sideways, using only an angle of my mind. This is justification; for free use of the faculties means happiness. I'm better company, more of a human being. Nevertheless, I think it most important in this book to go for the central things. Even though they don't submit, as they should, however, to beautification in language. No, I don't nail my crest to the Murrys, who work in my flesh after the manner of the jigger insect. It's annoying, indeed degrading, to have these bitternesses. Still, think of the 18th Century. But then they were overt, not covert, as now.

I foresee, to return to *The Hours*, that this is going to be the devil of a struggle. The design is so queer and so masterful. I'm always having to wrench my substance to fit it. The design is certainly original and interests me hugely. I should like to write away and away at it, very quick and fierce. Needless to say, I can't. In three weeks from today, I shall be dried up.

In July she was still confronted by the unwritten Greek chapter of *The Common Reader*; but *Mrs Dalloway* was going well. At Monk's House she found herself in good health and able to work. But on 6 August she re-read what she had written. It seemed to her "sheer weak dribble." Middleton Murry had said that with *Jacob's Room* she had reached a dead end and could go no further. Was he perhaps right? His criticism had worried her a good deal and she adverts to it frequently in her diary. But the check was overcome; she had confidence enough to go on and began to discover new ways of doing so. At the end of August she drew up a systematic scheme for *The Common Reader*.

Then, on 18 September, she suffered a short but violent mental tremor.

And I meant to record for psychological purposes that strange night when I went to meet Leonard and did not meet him. What an intensity of feeling was pressed into those hours! It was a wet windy night; and as I walked back across the field I said Now I am meeting it; now the old devil has once more got his spine through the waves. (But I cannot re-capture really). And such was the strength of my feeling that I became physically rigid. Reality, so I thought, was unveiled. And there was something noble in feeling like this; tragic, not at all petty. Then cold white lights went over the fields; and went out; and I stood under the great trees at Iford waiting for the lights of the bus. And that went by; and I felt lonelier. There was a man with a barrow walking into Lewes, who looked at me. But I could toy with, at least control, all this until suddenly, after the last likely train had come in, I felt it was intolerable to sit about, and must do the final thing, which was to go to London. Off I rode, without much time, against such a wind; and again I had a satisfaction in being matched with powerful things, like wind and dark. I battled, had to walk; got on; drove ahead; dropped the torch; picked it up; and so on again without any lights. Saw men and women walking together; thought you're safe and happy; I'm an outcast; took my ticket; had three minutes to spare, and then, turning the corner of the station stairs, saw Leonard, coming along, bending rather, like a person walking very quick, in his mackintosh. He was rather cold and angry (as perhaps was natural). And then, not to show my feelings, I went outside and did something to my bicycle. Also, I went back to the ticket office and said to the humane man there "It's all right. My husband caught the last train. Give me back my fare" which he did. And I got the money more to set myself right with Leonard than because I wanted it. All the way back we talked about a row (about reviewers) at the office; and all the time I was feeling My God, that's over. I'm out of that. It's over. Really, it was a physical feeling of lightness and relief and safety, and yet there was too something terrible behind it – the fact of this pain, I suppose; which continued for several days, and I think I should feel it again if I went over that road at night; and it became connected with the deaths of the miners and with Aubrey Herbert's death next day.* But I have not got it all in, by any means.

There were no ill effects – indeed no effects at all, unless it be that this odd experience had something to do with the work on which she was engaged during the weeks that followed it, for at that time she was describing the madness of Septimus Warren-Smith.

Thereafter there is no record of *Mrs Dalloway*'s progress for some months, but *The Common Reader* was not neglected and in November the necessities of the Greek chapter required that she should read Sophocles; the amount of reading and writing that went into the production of that essay, an essay of about 7,000 words, was remarkable.

On 23 January 1924 she wrote:

back again tomorrow to *The Hours*, which I was looking at disconsolately – oh the cold raw edges of one's relinquished pages – when the House business started this morning. But now I am going to write till we move – 6 weeks straight ahead. I think it's the design that's good this time – God knows.

* "the deaths of the miners." On 25 September 1923 the No. 23 Redding Pit near Falkirk was flooded and 41 men lost their lives. Lt.-Col. Aubrey Herbert, M.P. (b. 1880), died on 26 September 1923; he was a half-brother of Lady Margaret Duckworth.

The "move" to which Virginia refers was a move from Richmond to London, for, in the autumn of 1923, Virginia won her long struggle with Leonard. It had begun in the summer when she suggested that really the time had come to leave Hogarth House. She was, surely, well again. She found the incessant journeying to and from Richmond tiresome, time-consuming and exhausting. Leonard, however, was worried and made the old objections; London life was too rackety for her. He thought a move unwise—or at least, premature.

For a time Virginia was in despair. How could she argue against a husband to whom she owed so much, who had proved so wise in the past, who had devoted himself so greatly? I don't know, but she did—and she won her argument. In October she began house-hunting and eventually, on 7 January 1924, found what she wanted in No. 52 Tavistock Square, Bloomsbury. The Woolfs moved there on 13 March.

No. 52 was part of an early nineteenth-century block forming the southern side of Tavistock Square, a characteristic specimen of its district and period; its plain façade was of darkened brick rising four storeys above a railed area which illuminated the basement. When the Woolfs bought the ten-year lease from the Bedford Estate, they took on the sitting tenants on the ground and first floors; their relations with this firm of solicitors, Messrs Dollman and Pritchard, were so harmonious that when eventually they had to leave Tavistock Square on the expiry of their (extended) lease, old Mr Pritchard and his staff moved with them. The two floors above these offices became the Woolfs' London home for the next fifteen years. Their rooms were light and spacious and well-proportioned, and Virginia commissioned decorations by Vanessa and Duncan. The basement, originally the domestic offices—kitchen, scullery, pantries and so forth—housed the Hogarth Press. A long passage led to the back of the house where, in place of the garden, was a huge room with a skylight which had been a billiard room. This Virginia used as her workroom, and referred to as the Studio. It had also to serve as a storeroom and repository for Hogarth Press publications, and here, among the heaped-up parcels of books and piles of paper, in conditions of dirt and disorder, surrounded by what the Stracheys called "filth packets"—accumulations of old pen nibs, paper-clips, buttons and fluff, empty ink bottles and un-emptied ashtrays, used envelopes and galley proofs—Virginia could be found in the morning, seated beside the gas fire in an old arm-chair, the stuffing of which emerged in disembowelled confusion upon the floor, a board of three-ply on her lap, writing and re-writing her books.

Every now and again someone would creep in apologetically and remove what was needed from the store of books; but Virginia, sensitive though she normally was to noise of any kind, took no notice.

But she took a great interest in the Press and in the afternoons she would go and work there. She had become an able compositor and she enjoyed exercising her skill in the company of her fellow-workers. When they first came to Tavistock Square, only Marjorie Joad was working with them, but Leonard had already broken it to her that there was to be a new regime in the Hogarth Press. George Rylands was soon to leave Cambridge; he wanted to learn about printing and publishing from the Woolfs while working upon his Fellowship dissertation. The idea was that he might gradually relieve Leonard of the burden of management. (It was not the last time that they were to entertain this completely unrealistic idea.)

Rylands came to the Hogarth Press at the beginning of July 1924; his connection with the firm was comparatively short (he was awarded his Fellowship at the turn of the year). He and Virginia got on like a house on fire; she teased and questioned him, they chattered together about words and parties and people; when she was working there, the basement office was full of gaiety and laughter. There were times, however, when the new recruit found his duties less congenial; he had to tie up parcels, calculate discounts for waiting customers, oil, ink, operate and clean the machinery of the press itself. But the worst of his trials came when he had to go out and face booksellers and try to sell them modern poetry or the *Collected Works* of Freud, both of which were likely to be contemptuously dismissed, the former as nonsense, the latter as pornography. And Leonard seemed to take his efforts so much for granted; there seemed to be no praise for the struggling novice. Leonard who, with Virginia, was quite happy to take a holiday selling his publications to country bookshops, probably did not realise what agonies might be involved in such negotiations.

George Rylands returned to Cambridge and to a very distinguished academic career, and the Woolfs found another very charming young man, Angus Davidson, to take his place. The retiring assistant wrote with great tact and modesty: "Thank God, Angus is at once a soothing and a responsible person whose tranquil labours will do far more than my moments of frantic toil alternating with lackadaisical interims. I am terrified lest I shall not see a great deal of you and Leonard now I am out of the Press: I must. I depend upon you. A thousand thanks for the last six months." But in fact Angus was to have a much stormier passage.

In May 1924 Virginia went to Cambridge to speak on "Character in Modern Fiction" to a society called the Heretics. The result was *Mr Bennett and Mrs Brown*. It was as near as she came to an aesthetic manifesto. She speaks to the young and for the future–"we are trembling on the verge of one of the great ages of English literature." "We" means the *avant garde*. As always happens in manifestos of this kind, it appears that the only way in which we can enter that great age is by pushing aside a certain number of human obstructions which clutter the road: the writers of "those sleek, smooth novels, those portentous and ridiculous biographies, that milk and watery criticism, those poems melodiously celebrating the innocence of roses and sheep which pass so plausibly for literature at the present time," as well as Bennett, Galsworthy and Wells. These indeed were the real enemies, for they obscured the true end of writing, which is the discovery of reality personified by the intriguing but obfusc person of Mrs Brown, the unknown lady in the railway carriage. Mr Bennett does no more than tell us about her rent; Mr Wells tells us rather what her rent ought to be; Mr Galsworthy, that she cannot possibly pay it. None of them captures the real Mrs Brown because none of them is interested in the real character of human beings–in the essential Mrs Brown, which is . . . At this point I hesitate, but so, I think, did Virginia, for she perceived that Mrs Brown was a chameleon, a creature which changes its colour according to its situations and the angle from which you look at it, so that in the end the best one can say is that Mrs Brown is a human being–an object largely composed I believe of water with certain added salts and so on–but also, and for Virginia, eminently a collection of memories, some ever present, others mysteriously varied, others capriciously available. The waking Mrs Brown knows very well she is Mrs Brown and can probably remember her age, certainly cannot remember her first meal, yet does recall the appearance of a teddy bear and more precisely the particular black buttons which served for its eyes when she smells a certain kind of furniture polish–this, I think, is the kind of Mrs Brown with whom Mr Bennett never comes to grips–a kind of awareness, sometimes luminous, sometimes intelligible, sometimes wholly awake, sometimes completely asleep. One day when the collection of water and salts is dissolved perhaps, who knows, this cloud, those memories, loosely tied by a wisp of semi-consciousness, may be the only Mrs Brown.

This, then, is the business of what Virginia calls the "Georgian novelists," to look past the circumstantial evidence of Bennett, the preaching and moralising of Wells and Galsworthy, and approach that central mystery, Mrs Brown herself. But having declared that this is the true battle, this the victory that has to be won, Virginia looks at the troops on her own side and, like Wellington, declares: "I don't know whether they will frighten the enemy but by God they frighten me." E. M. Forster and D. H. Lawrence were both of them brave and brilliant, but both spent much of their time marching in the wrong direction. Eliot and Joyce did not fall into that fault, but the former was guilty of indiscipline and the latter of atrocities. Strachey's heart was not really in the fight. Victory would be won and triumph was assured, but who would gain it? She never gives the answer but it is obvious, and indeed a manifesto, unless it be written at a time when there is a real coherent and unanimous doctrine amongst artists, is bound to be a personal confession and likely to be little else. *Mr Bennett and Mrs Brown* is, in fact, Virginia's own private manifesto. She outlines her programme for the next decade. To some extent she outlines her own life work.

In May 1924 she resolved to finish *Mrs Dalloway* in four months; then it would be done, or sufficiently done, to be put away for the next three months, which would be devoted to *The Common Reader*. The essays would be published in April 1925, the novel a month later. This she accomplished. That summer she worked swiftly and well; by 2 August she had reached the death of Septimus Warren Smith. It is true that, on the following day, she was contemplating what she supposed must be the eightieth systematic beginning of *The Common Reader* and was modestly proposing to read *Clarissa* as well as *The Pilgrim's Progress*, the *Medea* and Plato; but she returned to the novel and by September saw the end in sight. On 9 October just after her return to London, *Mrs Dalloway* was finished, and she congratulated herself on the speed with which it had been done. Already she could see the "Old Man"—and by this she almost certainly meant *To the Lighthouse*. But the last months of 1924 were spent in preparing *Mrs Dalloway* for the press (Leonard saw the typescript in January 1925) and in finishing *The Common Reader*. She does not seem to have done more than think about her next novel until the summer of 1925.

Virginia did not often discuss her own writing in letters; but she came near to doing so in a letter which she wrote to the French painter Jacques Raverat. He had asked her what she was writing. She, refusing to be drawn, replied:

> I don't think I shall tell you, because, as you know perfectly well, you don't care a straw.... I'm terrifically egotistic about my writing, think practically of nothing else, and so, partly from conceit, partly shyness, sensitiveness, what you choose, never mention it, unless someone draws it out with red hot pincers ... (however, I've almost finished 2 books).

His reply, received at Rodmell while she was deeply absorbed in the writing of *Mrs Dalloway*, was of a kind to interest her greatly, for his ideas were to some extent congruous with those which she had tried to formulate in *Mr Bennett and Mrs Brown*. The difficulty about writing was that it has to be–as he put it–"essentially linear"–one can only write (or read) one thing at a time. Writing a word–the word "Neo-Pagan" for instance, which Virginia had thrown at him–was like casting a pebble into a pond: "There are splashes in the outer air in every direction, and under the surface waves that follow one another into dark and forgotten corners...." But this phenomenon was one which could only be represented by some graphic expedient such as placing the word in the middle of a page and surrounding it radially with associated ideas. Thus, in a fashion, a writer might achieve that simultaneity which the painter enjoys by reason of the nature of his art. Moreover, the mind cannot carry all the complexities of a literary design because such a design is, of necessity, sequential. "Surely, when you are writing you are not clearly conscious on Page 259 of what there was on Page 31? But perhaps that's only because I'm not a writer, & in fact do not naturally think in words."

"Certainly," Virginia replied, "the painters have a great gift of expression. A highly intelligent account you seem to me to give of the processes of your own mind when I throw Neo-Paganism in." But she would not allow that the circumstances of their art gave them a power of vision denied to an author; on the contrary: "I rather think you've broached some of the problems of the writers too, who are trying to catch and consolidate and consummate (whatever the word is for making literature) those splashes of yours." Indeed it was precisely the task of the writer–that is to say her task– to go beyond the "formal railway line of sentence" and to disregard the "falsity of the past (by which I mean Bennett, Galsworthy and so on)." The literary artist has to realise that "people don't and never did feel or think or dream for a second in that way; but all over the place, in your way." In other words she is claiming for herself the ability, or at least the intention, to see events out of time, to apprehend processes of thought and feeling as though they were pictorial shapes.

It is possible in *Mrs Dalloway* to find an attempt of this nature, a desire to make literature "radial" rather than "linear," to describe at once the "splashes in the outer air" and the "waves that follow one another into dark and forgotten corners." It may be that she acknowledges the extreme difficulty of such an undertaking when, in her next novel, she places a painter and a painting so near to the heart of her literary design and ends it with: "a line there, in the centre."

But most of Virginia's letters to Jacques Raverat are frivolous and uninhibited gossip. He–a Frenchman educated in England–had been one of the Neo-Pagans and had married another–Gwen Darwin–in 1911. A letter from Jacques to Virginia praising *Monday or Tuesday* began a correspondence which lasted until his death in March 1925. He was now unable to walk or to write (his letters were dictated to his wife); in fact he was slowly and painfully dying. Virginia's instinctive response to suffering was always to write; and her way of showing practical sympathy in illness or distress was to write letters. She wrote long and fairly frequent letters to Jacques, and he wrote some extremely good letters in reply. "I like to please Jacques," she confided to her diary, and clearly Jacques was pleased. "Your letters," he wrote in December 1924, "particularly the last 3 or 4, have given me something, which very few people have been able to give me in these last years." They planned to meet again, but they never did; perhaps Virginia did not really want it. The pleasure of their friendship lay in its epistolatory character. In February 1925, a month before he died, Virginia did something that, so far as I know, she never did for anyone else. She sent him proofs of her unpublished novel. Gwen read *Mrs Dalloway* to him on his death-bed, omitting, for she found them too unbearably poignant, the passages describing the suicide of Septimus Warren-Smith.

On 8 April Virginia wrote in her diary:

> Since I wrote, which is these last months, Jacques Raverat has died; after longing to die; and he sent me a letter about *Mrs Dalloway* which gave me one of the happiest days of my life.

With Jacques' death, nothing seemed to remain of the Neo-Pagans. As Gwen wrote, it was "all over long ago." It died in 1914, though it was sick before. Rupert Brooke was gone; Frances Cornford had found another faith. The Olivier girls were married or had drifted away into very different worlds. Ka Cox too was married, to Will Arnold-Forster; "I feel you'll probably not like Will," she had written to Virginia; and she was right.

The Common Reader appeared on 23 April, *Mrs Dalloway* on 14 May. Virginia suffered the usual vicissitudes of feeling, winced at bad notices and rejoiced at good ones. By the end of May the worst was over: Morgan Forster liked *Mrs Dalloway*; Thomas Hardy had read *The Common Reader* with great pleasure. "Never," she was able to write in her diary, "have I felt so much admired."

Chapter Five

June 1925–December 1928

BETWEEN June 1925 and December 1928 Virginia wrote *To the Lighthouse* and conceived *The Waves*, the books which, in the opinion of many critics, are her greatest achievements. This may therefore be a suitable point at which to attempt an examination of her mind at work, even though, in such a scrutiny, we must abandon all pretence at chronological method and must adventure into an area which, manifestly, is not easily negotiated.

She herself has pointed out the dangers of such an undertaking.

Many scenes have come and gone unwritten, since it is today the 4th September. A cold grey blowy day, made memorable by the sight of a kingfisher and by my sense, waking early, of being again visited by 'the spirit of delight'. "Rarely, rarely, comest thou, spirit of delight." That was I singing this time last year; and sang so poignantly that I have never forgotten it, or my vision of a fin rising on a wide blank sea. No biographer could possibly guess this important fact about my life in the late summer of 1926: yet biographers pretend they know people.

They don't, or at least they ought not to. All that they can claim is that they know a little more than does the public at large and that, by catching at a few indications given here and there in recollections or writings, they can correct some misconceptions and trace, if they are very skilful or very lucky, an outline that is consistent and convincing, but which, like all outlines, is but tenuously connected with the actual form of the sitter in all lights, poses, moods and disguises.

To know the psyche of Virginia Woolf, and this is what she is in effect asking of a biographer, one would have to be either God or Virginia, preferably God. Looking from outside, one can go no further than what I have called the outline and for the rest one may guess, one may even build upon one's divinations, but never for a moment allowing oneself to forget that this is guesswork and guesswork of a most hazardous kind.

When, in September 1927, Virginia recalled Shelley's lines, we may fairly deduce that she was looking back at a period of unhappiness. The "fin rising on a wide blank sea"–one of her recurrent images–was a signal of disaster and she had seen it on that night in September 1923 when Leonard was so late coming home. Possibly these recollections are associated with another diary entry headed "A State of Mind" which she made on 15 September 1926:

> Woke up perhaps at 3. Oh it's beginning, it's coming–the horror–physically like a painful wave swelling about the heart–tossing me up. I'm unhappy, unhappy! Down–God, I wish I were dead. Pause. But why am I feeling this? Let me watch the wave rise. I watch. Vanessa. Children. Failure. Yes; I detect that. Failure, failure. (The wave rises).

This may be interpreted as: "Vanessa has three children; I have none."

Oh they laughed at my taste in green paint!

So, we may be fairly sure, did she; this being–in broad daylight–some tease at Charleston, laughingly uttered, laughingly rebutted, and barely felt at the time. But now, in the small hours:

> Wave crashes. I wish I were dead! I've only a few years to live, I hope. I can't face this horror any more. (This is the wave spreading out over me.) This goes on; several times, with varieties of horror. Then, at the crisis, instead of the pain remaining intense, it becomes rather vague. I doze. I wake with a start. The wave again! The irrational pain; the sense of failure; generally some specific incident, as for example my taste in green paint, or buying a new dress . . . tacked on.

She was still desperately shy in dress shops, and although at about this time she congratulated herself on having at last learnt to face a shop assistant with nonchalant authority, it was but a temporary victory; she still hated buying clothes, particularly underclothes, and, when her purchases were criticised, she was mortified.

> At last I say, watching as dispassionately as I can, Now take a pull of yourself. No more of this. I reason. I take a census of happy people and unhappy. I brace myself to shove, to throw, to batter down. I begin to march blindly forward. I feel obstacles go down. I say it doesn't matter. Nothing matters. I become rigid and straight and sleep again and half wake and feel the wave beginning and watch the light whitening and wonder how, this time, breakfast and daylight will overcome it; and then hear L. in the passage and simulate, for myself as well as for him, great cheerfulness; and generally am cheerful by the time breakfast is over. Does everyone go through this state? Why have I so little control? It is not creditable, nor lovable. It is the cause of much waste and pain in my life.

During the 1920s Virginia's friends often remarked upon her exuberant high spirits.* She was a great social success but, reading her diary, one would hardly suspect that this was the case. In 1926 Roger Fry records a dinner at the Commercio Restaurant when "Virginia was in her grandest vein"; Virginia herself noted, on the previous day, "I tremble and shiver all over at the appalling magnitude of the task I have undertaken – to go to a dressmaker recommended by Todd [Miss Todd was then editor of *Vogue*], even, she suggested, but here my blood ran cold, with Todd." Or again, in 1928 Clive wrote: "The Woolves are in great glory" (19 February) and "Virginia is still on the crest of the wave" (2 March). She herself writes, on 18 March: "Since February I have been a little clouded with headache."

I suppose that most people, if their morale could be measured throughout the day, would show a fluctuation of psychic temperature which would astonish their friends. In Virginia's case the curves of the graph were, one suspects, unusually abrupt and the impression unusually deep and lasting, so that the despair of 1926 was vividly recalled in 1927.

But was it simply despair? The fin that rises above the water may indeed belong to an evil monster armed with razor teeth, but the monster is unseen, it lies in the depths, its character is uncertain.

Here, plunging recklessly, let us suppose that the wave, the fin, the creature from the abyss, was a signal that something was again quickening within her. To return to the autumn of 1926:

. . . it is not oneself but something in the universe that one's left with. It is this that is frightening and exciting in the midst of my profound gloom, depression, boredom, whatever it is. One sees a fin passing far out. . . . All I mean to make is a note of a curious state of mind. I hazard the guess that it may be the impulse behind another book. At present my mind is totally blank and virgin of books.

And a month later:

Monday, Ozzie Dickinson; Wednesday, Lady Colefax; Thursday, Morgan to meet Abel Chevalley, dine Wells to meet Arnold Bennett; Friday to Monday, Long Barn. So the week slips or sticks through my pages; rage, misery, joy, dulness, elation mix. I am the usual battlefield of emotions; alternately think of buying chairs and clothes; plod with some method revising To the Lighthouse; quarrel with Nelly (who was

* This was particularly true when she was with her immediate circle of friends; but she did not depend upon their presence. Professor William Empson recalls that "the only time I had the luck to meet her, which was when I was an undergraduate, I was quite ill with laughing at her jokes." BBC, 24 November 1953.

to catch the afternoon train today because I told a lie about a telephone) and so we go on. Maurice Baring and the Sitwells send me their books; Leonard forges ahead, now doing what he calls "correspondence"; the Press creaks a little at its hinges; Mrs. C[artwright]. has absconded with my spectacles; I find buggers bores, like the normal male; and should now be developing my book for the Press. All these things shoulder each other out across the screen of my brain. At intervals I begin to think (I note this, as I am going to watch for the advent of a book) of a solitary woman shaping a book of ideas about life. This has intruded only once or twice, and very vaguely; it is a dramatisation o my mood at Rodmell. It is to be an endeavour at something mystic, spiritual; the thing that exists when we aren't there.

The Waves, if it was *The Waves,* which Virginia had now begun vaguely to envisage, had not yet assumed a form sufficiently precise for her purpose and five years were to elapse before she could make her notions into a novel. When, in September 1927, she found herself echoing Shelley's despair the sequel, if one may call it a sequel, was to be something different. A month later a whole galaxy of ideas suddenly took shape in the most light-hearted and easily written of her novels.

The evidence suggests (it does no more) that moments of depression were followed by moments of creativity. Virginia, as will be seen in a later chapter, could profit by her illnesses. She needed to "float with the sticks on the stream; helter-skelter with the dead leaves on the lawn, irresponsible and disinterested and able, perhaps for the first time for years, to look around, to look up-to look, for example, at the sky." But she also needed, if she were to cope with the exacting task of describing that which she had seen in the heavens, to be well. In 1913 she had not been strong enough to cope with her vision, but in the years between 1925 and 1932 she was just healthy enough to cope with her own maladies. Nevertheless the effort was considerable and the balance between her illnesses and her constitution was a fine one, as she was to discover in the summer of 1925.

Although she was eager to begin work upon her novel, Virginia decided to postpone writing it until the beginning of August when she would be at Monk's House. The reception of *Mrs Dalloway* and *The Common Reader* had been of a kind to make society and the flatteries of society agreeable. She resolved to give her working time to journalism.*

* She had an additional motive: "I'm out to make £300 this summer by writing and build a bath and hot water range at Rodmell." *AWD*, p. 74, 19 April 1925.

... my mornings have all been spent writing–Swift or letters. So a
whole tribe of people and parties has gone down the sink to oblivion –

Thus she wrote in her diary in July 1925. With the aid of Leonard's
pocket book it is possible however to restore a fairly detailed
calendar of these forgotten engagements. The record for the month
of July will suffice.

On 1 July the Woolfs had Philip and Irene Noel-Baker to tea and
dined out. On the 2nd Lytton's sister Dorothy Bussy came to tea;
that evening was George Rylands' party, the party at which Berta
Ruck performed. On 3 July Raymond Mortimer and Hope Mirrlees
dined at Tavistock Square, Leo Myers and Daphne Sanger came in
afterwards. On 5 July (Sunday) they went to a performance of *The
Rehearsal*; on 6 July Virginia dined with Clive; on the 9th Lady
Colefax and George Rylands came to tea, T. S. Eliot after dinner;
on the following day, Friday 10th, they went to Rodmell, returning
on Sunday to see Lytton's play, *The Son of Heaven*, at the Scala
Theatre; on the 14th Julian Morrell, Ottoline's daughter, and
Edward Sackville-West came to dinner, and the Thomas Marshalls
(she had been Marjorie Joad when she worked in the Hogarth
Press), John Hayward and Philip Morrell came after. On 15
July Virginia dined with the Morrells; on 16 July Angus came
upstairs to tea; on the 17th Virginia, accompanied by Edward
Sackville-West, joined a river party and dined at Formosa Place,
Cookham, their host being George Young, the brother of Hilton
Young; on the following day she saw Gwen Raverat and on the day
after that, the 19th, she and Leonard lunched out with Morgan
Forster and had Clive to dinner; after dinner Adrian came in to see
them and he was followed by Ottoline, Julian and Philip Morrell.
On the 21st Jack St John Hutchinson and Frances Marshall came to
dinner; Francis Birrell and C. H. B. Kitchin, the novelist, joined
them afterwards. On the 22nd Ann Watkins from New York came
on business; Edith Sitwell also came; on the 23rd Stella Benson and
Angus Davidson came to tea; on the 24th the Harcourts–I do not
know which Harcourts–came to tea and the Woolfs and Harold
Nicolson dined with Raymond Mortimer. During the last week in
July Leonard was suffering from sciatica and this put an end to their
social engagements. Nevertheless this did not save them from some
uninvited visitors, viz.: Roger Fry, Mary Hutchinson, Gwen
Raverat, Geoffrey Keynes, Julian and Quentin Bell.

The work of the Press continued. Business, Virginia noted, had
been brisk. She still worked as a compositor and a packer, and for

her Maynard Keynes's pamphlet *The Economic Consequences of Mr Churchill** meant long hours in the basement with Leonard and the other workers in the Press,† answering the telephone, doing up parcels and attempting to meet the demand for the 10,000 copies printed. (Maynard Keynes, it may be noted, was married at St Pancras Registry Office on the 4th July that summer.) It is hardly surprising that, as she later observed, she was "riding on a flat tyre."

There was bound to be a reckoning. It came at Charleston on 19 August, when in those years there was always a birthday party. This anniversary fell so fortunately – all the family being there, the grouse being just high enough for eating, the weather usually propitious – that it was for some years celebrated with considerable brio. Brio, or at least noise – noise induced by good food and drink, by Clive's social volubility, by Virginia's sallies – describes the tone of the evening, until the clamour in that hot candle-lit room was suddenly stilled by Virginia, who rose, staggered, turned exactly the colour of a duck's egg and tried blindly and inefficiently to make her way out of the room. At that juncture, when most of the company sat in stupid amazement, two persons acted promptly: Leonard and Vanessa moved swiftly and decisively, with the efficiency of long training, to do what was necessary – to take Virginia away from the room to fresh air, to a bed, and to administer whatever medicines experience had shown to be useful.

This sudden collapse marked the beginning of a long bout of ill-health, with headaches and exhaustion, partial recoveries and new relapses, which lasted on and off through the rest of the year and was not finally overcome until the spring of 1926. Virginia realised that she had been overdoing it, that her life in London brought with it dangers which she could ignore only at her peril, and she resolved that she would in future see rather less of society and, when she did see it, take less trouble over it. This resolve was not altogether kept, but neither was it altogether broken. In subsequent years she was rather more careful about her social commitments.

The process of recovery was enlivened, but no doubt in some ways made more difficult, by the realisation that she had no lack of material for *To the Lighthouse*. The idea of it had come suddenly two

---

* *The Economic Consequences of Mr Churchill*, a pamphlet dealing with the return by Britain to the Gold Standard and its probable consequences.

† These were: Angus Davidson, who came to the Press in December 1924 and stayed until the end of 1927; Bernadette Murphy, who arrived about the same time as Angus and was replaced the following July by Mrs Cartwright, who was to remain until 1930.

years earlier at Tavistock Square and it was now in a manner of speaking only waiting to be written. All that she needed was to be well enough to commit it to paper.

But that autumn, despite a promising start, she could do very little work; she remained idle and frustrated, first at Monk's House and then at Tavistock Square, leading what she called an "amphibious" life, half in, half out of bed; and when she could write something it was an essay *On Being Ill*. In addition she suffered from various vexations; one of these was connected with T. S. Eliot, another with Mrs Harold Nicolson.

In the autumn of 1925 T. S. Eliot, as Virginia put it, deserted the Hogarth Press. It was a rather unfair description of his conduct. What Eliot had done was to accept an editorship from the publisher who was reviving *The Criterion*. This gave him the financial security which Virginia had always wished him to have (and indeed the disposition of the Eliot Fellowship Fund became a matter of some difficulty), but, as a natural consequence, he was published by his new employer; and as a further consequence, he competed with *The Nation* for contributors. This, to Virginia, seemed conduct becoming only to the Underworld and it was some months before he was completely forgiven.

Mrs Harold Nicolson, who wrote under and indeed preferred to use the name of V. Sackville-West, was, in Virginia's words, "doomed to go to Persia." This, in more prosaic terms, meant that she was going, for a time, to join her husband in Teheran where he was Counsellor at the British Embassy. Of her, who must for convenience' sake be referred to as Vita, something has to be said, for at this time and for some years to come she was the most important person – apart from Leonard and Vanessa – in Virginia's life.

Vita would seem to have been invented for Virginia's pleasure. In her Virginia found a person of high lineage, but also one in whom there was something better – or at least more romantic than the blood of plain territorial magnates – a certain literary heritage; the child of an historic house, but also a house where the art of letters had been worthily cultivated – a Kentish *Academe* – and to crown it all, an exotic strain, the blood of disreputable Spanish gypsies, showing itself in the finest dark eyes imaginable, or perhaps in a certain grace of bearing, which might be called aristocratic but might equally well come from the streets of some Andalusian town.

Vita was certainly a very beautiful woman, in a lazy, majestic, rather melancholy way, charming with a charm which was largely unconscious–and the more lovable for that, intelligent and yet at the same time in an odd way stupid, blundering through life rather, with excellent intentions but without the acuteness, the humour, the malice, of Virginia. Add to these qualities the fact that she had a great admiration for the novels of Virginia Woolf and that she was herself a writer and she appears irresistible.

And yet for a time Virginia did resist her. Their first encounter, as we have seen, was at Clive's table, for Clive, despite the fact that she had no eyes for him, could not but admire Vita's rank, her beauty and her amiability of temper. He was quick to see her merits and to report to Virginia that Mrs Nicolson admired her, despite which, when she met "the lovely gifted aristocratic Sackville-West" she found her "Not much to my severer taste–florid, moustached, parakeet coloured, with all the supple ease of the aristocracy, but not the wit of the artist. She writes 15 pages a day–has finished another book–publishes with Heinemann's–knows everyone. But could I ever know her?"

I fancy that Virginia was a little frightened. No doubt she knew that Vita was a frank and unequivocal Sapphist. She probably became aware of Vita's feelings and perhaps acquired an inkling of her own at that first encounter; she felt shy, almost virginal, in Vita's company, and she was, I suspect, roused to a sense of danger. Since her marriage, no-one save Katherine Mansfield had touched her heart at all, and Katherine but slightly. She was still in love with Leonard. But suppose now, in middle age, someone else were to claim a place in her affections, might it not lead to something terrifying, something disastrous? Under the circumstances it was necessary that she should be indifferent, cold, hostile even, to Vita's charms.

Nevertheless, she was ready to see her again and although the friendship did not develop very fast, the Woolfs met the Nicolsons (mark those plurals) four times in the early months of 1923 and more frequently during 1924. In September 1925 Virginia writes to Vanessa of "our (Clive and my) Vita." By this time the friendship was well-established and Virginia, turning back to her diary entry for 15 December 1922, would, I think, have been slightly shocked and very much astonished.

The word 'friendship' has a coy look on this page and I would use the word 'affair' if I were perfectly certain of not being misunderstood. But, in fact, I myself know too little. What should or does one imply if one quite baldly says: "Virginia Woolf and Vita Sackville-West had a love affair between, shall we say, 1925 and

1929"? Vita was very much in love with Virginia* and being, I suspect, of an ardent temperament, loved her much as a man might have loved her, with a masculine impatience for some kind of physical satisfaction–even though Virginia was now in her forties and, although extremely beautiful, without the charm of her youth, and even though Vita herself was a little in awe of her. But the little evidence that we have suggests that Vita found Virginia unkind. Speaking of the seals of the General Post Office, Vita remarked in a letter to Virginia that they "are inviolable (like Virginia)." Again she accused her–this was in 1924, early in their relationship–of regarding their affections as literary material. "Look on it, if you like, as copy–as I believe you do on everything, human relationships included. Oh yes, you like people better through the brain than through the heart." The accusation was indignantly rejected but was not I think without truth. But not the whole truth–things are never so simple. Virginia felt as a lover feels–she desponded when she fancied herself neglected, despaired when Vita was away, waited anxiously for letters, needed Vita's company and lived in that strange mixture of elation and despair which lovers–and one would have supposed only lovers–can experience. All this she had done and felt for Katherine, but she never refers to Katherine, never writes of her as she does of Vita.

> Vita for three days at Long Barn, from which L. and I returned yester-day. These Sapphists *love* women; friendship is never untinged with amorosity. In short, my fears and refrainings, my 'impertinence', my usual self-consciousness in intercourse with people who mayn't want me and so on–were all, as L. said, sheer fudge; and partly thanks to him (he made me write) I wound up this wounded and stricken year in great style. I like her and being with her and the splendour–she shines in the grocer's shop in Sevenoaks with a candle lit radiance, stalking on legs like beech trees, pink glowing, grape clustered, pearl

* Two undated letters from V. Sackville-West to Clive Bell give a notion of her sentiments:

"Virginia is just gone. She came back here with me–more entrancing than ever. Isn't it odd, dear Clive, how often our tastes (yours & mine) seem to coincide? But that is because we both have very good taste, or so I like to think."

And again:

"I saw Virginia today; incredibly lovely and fragile on two chairs under a gold cloak; with a weak voice and tapering hands; saying that she "felt stupid" and then giving vent to earthquaking remarks; but recovering, I think,–only *such* a liar about her own health that one doesn't know what to believe; but Leonard (a saner & more truthful barometer) seemed optimistic. My devotion increased; Virginia brilliant, one is inured to; but Virginia defeated is newly & surprisingly endearing. Dear Clive, I would go to the ends of the earth for your sister-in-law."

hung. That is the secret of the glamour, I suppose. Anyhow she found me incredibly dowdy. No woman cared less for personal appearance. No one put on things in the way I did. Yet so beautiful, etc. What is the effect of all this on me? Very mixed. There is her maturity and full breastedness; her being so much in full sail on the high tides, where I am coasting down backwaters; her capacity I mean to take the floor in any company, to represent her country, to visit Chatsworth, to control silver, servants, chow dogs; her motherhood (but she is a little cold and off-hand with her boys) her being in short (what I have never been) a real woman. Then there is some voluptuousness about her; the grapes are ripe; and not reflective. No. In brain and insight she is not as highly organised as I am. But then she is aware of this and so lavishes on me the maternal protection which, for some reason, is what I have always most wished from everyone. What L. gives me, and Nessa gives me and Vita, in her more clumsy external way, tries to give me. For of course, mingled with all this glamour, grape clusters and pearl necklaces, there is something loose fitting. How much, for example, shall I really miss her when she is motoring across the desert? I will make a note on that next year. Anyhow, I am very glad that she is coming to tea today and I shall ask her whether she minds my dressing so badly? I think she does. I read her poem; which is more compact, better seen and felt than anything yet of hers.

And to Vanessa, who wouldn't see Vita's perfections, she wrote:

Vita is now arriving to spend 2 nights alone with me & L. is going back. I say no more; as you are bored by Vita, bored by love, bored by me, & everything to do with me, except Quentin and Angelica; but such has long been my fate, & it is better to meet it open-eyed. Still, the June nights are long and warm; the roses flowering; and the garden full of lust and bees, mingling on the asparagus beds.

All of which might be a form of bravado and sisterly one-upmanship. Finally, considering the case for – what is it, the prosecution? – take the evidence of Vita's monument, *Orlando*, of all Virginia's novels the one that comes nearest to sexual, or rather to homosexual, feeling; for, while the hero/heroine undergoes a bodily transformation, being at first a splendid youth and then a beautiful lady, the psychological metamorphosis is far less complete. From the first the youth is a little uncertain of his sex; when he puts on petticoats he becomes, not simply a woman, but a man who enjoys being a woman. Orlando is also Virginia's most idealised creation; he/she is modelled near to the heart's desire (and not only to the heart) – near, in fact, to the glamorous creations of the novelette. Compare Virginia's treatment of him/her to the cool ironies of *Mrs Dalloway* or to the floral metamorphosis of Jinny in *The Waves*—a bouquet on a gilded chair—or the discreet glimpses of Jacob's loves.

There may have been—on balance I think that there probably was —some caressing, some bedding together. But whatever may have occurred between them of this nature, I doubt very much whether it was of a kind to excite Virginia or to satisfy Vita. As far as Virginia's life is concerned the point is of no great importance; what was, to her, important was the extent to which she was emotionally involved, the degree to which she was in love. One cannot give a straight answer to such questions but, if the test of passion be blindness, then her affections were not very deeply engaged.

Virginia certainly had her illusions about Vita; she could credit her with an almost impossible degree of charm and distinction, she could believe in her as a Kentish nymph, a blue-blooded dryad, an aristocratic goddess—but not as an author. She writes, says Virginia, "with complete competency, and a pen of brass." Usually Virginia was not unkind about Vita's writing, she found what she could to admire in the novels and the poetry, but she never extends her indulgence to the limits of what her conscience would allow, as she was always ready to do for Leonard. The reason, I think, is clear. She admired Leonard in a way that she could never admire Vita; she was not insensible to physical perfections and moral qualities but she could not really love without feeling that she was in the presence of a superior intellect.

And Vita comes to lunch tomorrow, which will be a great amusement and pleasure. I am amused at my relations with her: left so ardent in January—and now what? Also I like her presence and her beauty. Am I in love with her? But what is love? Her being 'in love' (it must be comma'd thus) with me, excites and flatters and interests. What is this 'love'? Oh and then she gratifies my eternal curiosity; who's she seen, what's she done—for I have no enormous opinion of her poetry.

It was, she felt, all rather a bore for Leonard—but not enough to worry him. Harold wrote to her to say how glad he was that Vita should have such a friend. The husbands took it all with admirable calm. It is perhaps significant that whereas neither Vanessa nor any other of Virginia's friends, except Clive, was really devoted to Vita, the closest, the nearest to devotion, was in fact Leonard.

How then, when all is said and done, shall we describe their relationship? I think we may call it an affair of the heart, but so far as Virginia was concerned that was where it began and that was where it ended. Nevertheless, when she returned from Sussex to London in the autumn of 1925, cured as she imagined but at once to be sent to bed by her doctor and not allowed to make her first sortie (to the Ballet) until 27 November, and learned that her friend was "doomed to go to Persia," she concluded that she was genuinely fond of Vita and minded her going very much indeed.

The Woolfs spent Christmas that year with the Bells at Charleston. Vita drove over from Long Barn to lunch on Boxing Day. "How beautiful she is," said Clive to Virginia after the guest had gone. "An aristocrat of ancient race," said Virginia to Clive. Leonard turned to Julian, then a freshman at King's. "What snobs they are," he said.

This remark unleashed, as it was intended to unleash, furious expostulations and an argument which lasted the rest of the evening.

The early months of 1926 brought an improvement in Virginia's health. "Never," she reports, "never have I written so easily, imagined so profusely." *To the Lighthouse* seemed to be composed without effort; by 16 March she had written 40,000 words.

She was able to become more sociable and even to explore new territory, for, despite her excursions into Mayfair, Virginia believed that she was too much in Bloomsbury and that it would be good for her to measure herself against the standards of another milieu. These, in the Spring of 1926, were provided by Miss Rose Macaulay, a novelist and a person sufficiently close to and yet sufficiently distant from Virginia to be at once a welcome—in some lights a superior—friend and an effective assessor. It was therefore in a spirit, as one may suppose, not only of friendship but of enquiry that Virginia accepted an invitation to dine with Rose Macaulay at a restaurant on the evening of Wednesday 24 March.

It was a disastrous evening.

The Woolfs were very late. They had been machining and they hurried from Tavistock Square without changing the clothes or removing all the printer's ink that they had on. Virginia had assumed that they would dine at what she called a "pothouse"; but this was no Bloomsbury dinner. Miss Macaulay received her guests in a very superior establishment. There were a dozen guests, all ladies and gentlemen of letters, all in pearls and white waistcoats; there was a platoon of waiters to serve them.

Leonard and Virginia were utterly unprepared for such a party; it was not the kind of party that they themselves would ever have given; they were conscious of being late, of having kept everyone waiting, of making a very bad impression. When Leonard was unnerved, the habitual trembling of his hands became wild and ungovernable. He now made conversation impossible by beating violently upon his soup plate, his spoon behaving as though it were a drum stick. It was not until he had drunk, or to speak more accurately, had distributed his soup (for but little can have reached his mouth) that the talk became audible. In Virginia's opinion it was none the better for that; it was what she called the "pitterpatter" of "baldnecked chickens." Who was to get what literary prize? Was Gerhardi as good as Tchekhov? Might *Shining Domes* by Mildred Peake be voted the best novel of 1926? To her it all seemed a whirl of meaningless jargon; presently her neighbour, Mr O'Riordan, made a remark about the Holy Ghost.

"Where is the Holy Ghost?" asked Virginia with sudden interest. The table fell silent.

"Wherever the sea is," replied Mr O'Riordan.

Am I mad? she wondered, or is this wit? and could only repeat: "The Holy Ghost?"

"The whole coast!!" shouted Mr O'Riordan.

It was all very awkward and everyone felt that Virginia had disgraced herself. But Leonard was to have his turn too. Observing his neighbour's napkin upon the floor, he bent gallantly and picked it up only to discover that he was lifting her petticoat. The gesture, it seems, was misunderstood and the Woolfs crept home as soon as they decently could.

Virginia had said after a previous meeting with Rose Macaulay that it showed her own position "a good deal lowered and diminished," and this, she continued "is a part of the value of seeing new people." On this occasion she certainly got full measure; but I do not think that she was anxious to repeat the experience.

That same day had brought a more comfortable event and one more likely to have lasting consequences. For some time Virginia and her friends had felt that Leonard was wasting his talents as Literary Editor of *The Nation*. He ought, they felt, to be writing his own books instead of being tied down to this game of pursuing or putting off contributors—a dreary life with few rewards and few holidays. Then, on the morning of the Rose Macaulay party, Leonard, to whom Virginia had as yet said nothing, remarked as he made the coffee for breakfast: "I am going to hand in my resignation this morning."

"To what?"

"*The Nation*."

So that was that.

In April, Virginia finished the first part of *To the Lighthouse* and attacked Part II (Time Passes); she found it difficult but she was in good spirits and progressed. Nelly had given notice for, shall we say, the fiftieth time. This time it was to be final: it was no good going on, the work was too much for her, too many people came to the house. Virginia was desolate, but she was firm; she accepted it, and began seriously looking for someone else. Then on 27 April Nelly stopped her on the landing with a request: "Please, Ma'am, may I apologise. I am too fond of you ever to be happy with anyone else," which Virginia thought the greatest compliment she could receive. But, of course, it meant a return to the old emotional switchback, with this difference, that she would not, she swore, ever believe poor Nelly again when she threatened to leave. Nelly for her part had also probably come to the conclusion that she would never believe Virginia again when she threatened dismissal.

> I saw this morning 5 or 6 armoured cars slowly going along Oxford Street; on each two soldiers sat in tin helmets, and one stood with his hand at the gun which was pointed straight ahead ready to fire. But I also noticed on one a policeman smoking a cigarette. Such sights I daresay I shall never see again; and don't in the least wish to.

But I think that, in a way, she was glad to have seen them. It was curious, strange, and perhaps historic, perhaps it was the beginning of the British Revolution; in fact it was the end of the General Strike. But in the anxious weeks that preceded the strike there were some of her friends who thought there would be civil war. 52 Tavistock Square became a centre of unusual activity, petitions were drawn up and cyclostyled, people came and went on bicycles carrying messages; Mr Pritchard, their tenant, genially declared that he was being trained to shoot Leonard. Friends came to listen to the Woolfs' wireless set, the only source of news apart from rumours.

Virginia discovered that she differed from Leonard; she thought him a tub thumper, he thought her an irrational christian; she wanted peace, he wanted victory. She was glad when the strike collapsed but saddened by the fate of the miners who were left to struggle alone, and by what she considered the vindictive spirit of the employers.

Time Passes, the second part of *To the Lighthouse,* was finished on 25 May. She hoped to have the whole book done by the end of July. But once again she over-estimated her strength. Vita returned from Persia as the strike ended and with her, other social claims. There was a week-end at Garsington, when Virginia met Robert Bridges, and a meeting with H. G. Wells. She must have met him before this – Leonard knew him well – but this was a prolonged and clearly an interesting encounter. They did not like each other's books and Virginia had made her views clear in public, but they got on well enough. She thought him an odd mixture of bubble and solidity. He gossiped about Hardy and Henry James and outlined his plans for a ten-day week, unaware perhaps that Max Beerbohm had already put this notion into his mouth. From these encounters Virginia went to one which meant much more to her, with Thomas Hardy. I think she respected Hardy more than she respected any other living writer, and clearly she was delighted when she heard that he approved of *The Common Reader*. The meeting was a success, although, as so often happens when one meets the great, she was unable to frame the kind of question or elicit the kind of reply that she would have liked.

London in the summer of 1926 offered its usual attractions but Virginia, remembering her experience of the previous year, did manage to exercise some self-restraint, and was at all events less exhausted by this summer than she had been by its predecessor. Even so she had "a whole nervous breakdown in miniature" at Monk's House at the end of July. The delights of the summer (it was a beautiful August), and even of new possessions, were in some degree spoilt by nervous irritability. It was, to be sure, very pleasing that *Mrs Dalloway* and *The Common Reader* had earned them lavatories and running hot water;* hitherto they had had an earth-closet and when Leonard and Virginia bathed they did so in a tin hip-bath on the kitchen floor. But Leonard planned to spend a part of their new wealth on his own kingdom, the garden, while Virginia wanted it to be devoted to more domestic comforts; and there was friction. Altogether it was a rather anxious and difficult time. She was trying to finish *To the Lighthouse*, and the end of a novel always gave her great trouble. In September she had moments of deep depression in which she described herself in her diary as an "elderly dowdy fussy ugly incompetent woman; vain, chattering and futile" and then she had her vision of a fin rising on a wide blank sea, and she woke in the early mornings with feelings of complete and utter despair.

Despite these vexations, *To the Lighthouse* made good progress. She wrote with heat and ease every morning. She did her two pages,

---

* "We are having two water closets made, one paid for by Mrs. Dalloway the other by the Common Reader: both dedicated to you." VW/VSW, 17 February 1926.

It has frequently been said that the MSS of Virginia's novels were put to a base use in the lavatories of Monk's House. My own recollection is that galley proofs were provided and these would, for a variety of reasons, have been more suitable.

and although her hope of finishing by the end of September was over-sanguine, she had reached the stage of rewriting in November and was planning another critical work on literature–a successor to *The Common Reader*. Finally, early in 1927, *To the Lighthouse* was ready for Leonard's approval and the proofs were read by March of that year.

1927 saw an evolution in the lives of people who were close to Virginia, which should be mentioned. Early in the year Duncan had gone to Cassis, where his mother and his aunt were staying, and there had fallen ill. His temperature soared alarmingly; Vanessa was told that he almost certainly had typhoid. It seemed a repetition of old horrors. She turned naturally to Virginia and Leonard; with their assistance she packed, settled outstanding affairs in London and transported Angelica, her servant and herself to Cassis within forty-eight hours of receiving the news. She arrived to find that Duncan had made a substantial recovery; it was not typhoid, but he was very weak. Vanessa established herself at Cassis, discovering what madness it was to remain in England during the winter months and how admirable a place Cassis was for a painter. Presently Clive announced his intention of joining them. On 28 January 1927 he had written to Vanessa to say that he was at last going to write that book about civilisation which had for so long been planned as a part of his magnum opus *The New Renaissance* and, furthermore, that he was very unhappy. He felt that he could not be comfortable unless he joined Vanessa and Duncan at Cassis. The reason for his unhappiness was that his long affair with Mary Hutchinson was coming to an end. The circumstances of that schism do not concern us apart from the fact that the break was not easily made (it caused great unhappiness to both parties), and that in the month of February there were still doubts and reservations on both sides.

Clive had always maintained that there was no-one more untrustworthy than Virginia and no more perfect model of indiscretion. It is therefore interesting that at this juncture, in many ways the most serious crisis of his life, he turned to Virginia for sympathy and advice. Almost at the same time Mary Hutchinson, divining perhaps that this would be the case and knowing that, in a way, Virginia was still one of the most important persons in Clive's life, telephoned her to ask her to soothe Clive–who was by now in a great state, talking wildly at parties and saying that he was miserable. Thus Virginia became, in some sort, the confidante of both.

"You'll get into trouble with the principals, one always does," wrote Vanessa. She was perfectly right. Virginia was already in trouble. What happened is not perfectly clear. It seems that she had a long interview with Clive. He came to tea; he described the situation and he asked her for her advice. Should he leave Mary and leave London, should he go to Cassis and write his book? Virginia thought he should. She did not like what she supposed to be Mary's influence upon Clive; she did not think the social whirl, the smart suppers and smart week-ends which she imagined to be Mary's natural milieu, were at all good for him.

Virginia I think had invented a character for Mary Hutchinson–a worldly glittering character which was far removed from the truth. As Mary herself put it, Virginia saw her as "a mere popinjay of fashion," a judgement which she found heart-breaking in its injustice. From her diaries and her letters it is clear that, at times, Virginia saw that this was unjust and was struck by the high moral qualities and serious character of Clive's friend; but the imaginary picture that she had drawn was equally real to her and it was on this that she relied at the present juncture. To Mary it must have appeared that, having applied to Virginia for help, she now found her maliciously and consciously plotting against her. There were some acrimonious exchanges culminating in an interview. The full dramatic impact of this encounter was muffled by the unexpected arrival of Vita's cousin Edward Sackville-West, a new friend of Virginia's, and so, while the two ladies glared at each other, for they were both angry, there was tea and a polite conversation about books until at length Mr Sackville-West departed. The discussion which then ensued began on a high note; but it ended in a renewal of friendship and confidences. Mary Hutchinson rebutted the charge that it was her mundanity which had lead Clive astray; Virginia was touched and convinced by her evident sincerity and they parted friends.

The rest of the affair does not concern us save that Clive, after a period of indecision, did go to Cassis, where Virginia was to meet him later in the year. In February the Woolfs had considered going to America to lecture and gave it up when they found that their expenses, which would not be covered, would leave practically nothing out of the lecture fees. They then thought of Greece and finally compromised on Sicily, stopping at Cassis on the way. The details of the tour may be omitted. We should however notice that the sea passage from Naples to Palermo was made memorable by the company, in Virginia's cabin, of a Swedish lady who complained that there was no lock to the door. "Madam," observed Virginia, "we have neither of us any cause for fear," which, happily, she took in good part. It was on this holiday that Virginia began to smoke cheroots. Rumour says that she smoked a pipe. I have found no evidence of this.

"I don't think I've ever enjoyed one month so much," she told her diary, and she said as much to Vanessa in a series of enthusiastic letters describing her travels. Vanessa read the letters aloud, which indeed she usually did with Virginia's letters, and Clive, then staying at Cassis and not making much headway with *Civilisation*, carried certain details with him back to Paris where, so Virginia believed, her enthusiasm was made fun of. She was cross enough to say that she would write no more letters to her sister. Luckily she did not persist in this resolve, and presently there was an epistolary exchange which was to be of some importance.

On 3 May Vanessa wrote from Cassis:

It is a work of absolute heroism to write to you. All my writing paper has been taken by Angelica to write a poem beginning The Robin hops on the window sill. Then having rescued one sheet I sit with moths flying madly in circles round me & the lamp. You cannot imagine what its like. One night some creature tapped so loudly on the pane that Duncan said "Who is that?" "Only a bat" said Roger "or a bird", but it wasn't man or bird, but a huge moth–half a foot, literally, across. We had a terrible time with it. My maternal instinct which you deplore so much, wouldn't let me leave it. [Vanessa's children were as enthusiastic in collecting butterflies and moths as their parents and relations had been before them.] We let it in, kept it, gave it a whole bottle of ether bought from the chemist, all in vain, took it to the chemist who dosed it with chloroform for a day–also in vain. Finally it did die rather the worse for wear, & I set it, & now, here is another! a better specimen. But though incredibly beautiful I suspect they're common–perhaps Emperor moths. Still I know how one would have blamed one's elders for not capturing such things at all costs so I suppose I must go through it all again. Then I remembered–didn't Fabre try experiments with this same creature & attract all the males in the neighbourhood by shutting up one female in a room?–just what we have now done. So probably soon the house will be full of them.

However, you'll only tell me its what comes of allowing instinct to play a part in personal relationships. What a lot I could say about the maternal instinct, but then also what a lot about Michael Angelo & Raphael. I wish you would write a book about the maternal instinct.

Virginia's reply ended thus:

By the way, your story of the Moth so fascinates me that I am going to write a story about it. I could think of nothing else but you & the moths for hours after reading your letter. Isn't it odd?–perhaps you stimulate the literary sense in me as you say I do your painting sense. God! how you'll laugh at the painting bits in the Lighthouse!

To the Lighthouse had, in fact, been published on 5 May. Vita, returning from Persia, found a copy awaiting her. Virginia had promised she would have a new book ready for her. It was inscribed: *Vita from Virginia (In my opinion the best novel I have ever written).* Vita was a little surprised at such shameless immodesty, but that night when she opened the book to read it in bed, she found that the inscribed copy was a dummy. Two copies had gone to Cassis–one for Vanessa and one for Duncan. And now, so far from wishing to break off the correspondence with her sister, Virginia became more and more anxious for a letter. By 15 May, unable to bear the suspense any longer, she wrote:

Dearest, no letter from you–But I see how it is–scene: after dinner: Nessa sewing: Duncan doing absolutely nothing.

Nessa (throwing down her work) Christ! There's the Lighthouse! I've only got to page 26 & I see there are 320. Now I cant write to Virginia because she'll expect me to tell her what I think of it.

Duncan Well, I should just tell her that you think it a masterpiece.

Nessa But she's sure to find out. They always do. She'll want to know why I think its a masterpiece.

Duncan Well Nessa, I'm afraid I cant help you, because I've only read 5 pages so far, & really I dont see much prospect of doing much reading this month, or next month, or indeed before Christmas.

Nessa Oh its all very well for you. But I shall have to say something: And I dont know who in the name of Jupiter all these people are (turns over some pages desperately). I think I shall make a timetable: its the only way: ten pages a day for 20 days is . . .

Duncan But you'll never be able to keep up ten pages a day.

Nessa (rather dashed) No. I suppose I shant. Well then, we may as well be hung for a sheep as for a goat–though whats the sense of saying that I never could see: a sheep is almost identical with a goat in some countries; except that one can milk a goat of course. Lord! I shall never forget Violet Dickinson at Athens & the Goat's milk But what was I saying when you interrupted me? Oh yes: I shall take the bull by the horns. I shall write to Virginia & say "I think its a masterpiece–"(she takes the inkpot & prepares to write, but finds it full of dead & dying insects). Oh Duncan, what have you done with the inkpot? Used it to catch flies in? But thats a beetle! Yes it is. Beetles have 12 legs: flies only 8. D'you mean to say you didnt know that? Well, I suppose you're one of those people who think a spider's an insect: Now if you'd been brought up in Cornwall you'd know that a spider's not an insect; its–No I dont think its a reptile: its something queer I know. Anyhow, I cant write to Virginia, because the ink is nothing but a mass of beetle or spider legs–I really dont know what they are: but one man's meat is another man's poison; & if you will use the inkpot to catch flies in, then I dont see how even Virginia herself could possibly expect, or even wish me to write to her–(they settle down again to discuss spiders etc.) etc. etc. etc.

Vanessa had in fact already written:

I think I am more incapable than anyone else in the world of making an aesthetic judgement on it–only I know that I have somewhere a feeling about it as a work of art which will perhaps gradually take shape & which must be enormously strong to make any impression on me at all beside the other feelings which you roused in me–I suppose I'm the only person in the world who can have those feelings, at any rate to such an extent–So though probably they don't matter to you at all you may be interested to know how much you did make me feel. Besides I daresay they do show something about aesthetic merits in your curious art of writing. Anyhow it seemed to me in the first part of the book you have given a portrait of mother which is more like her to me than anything I could ever have conceived of as possible. It is almost painful to have her so raised from the dead. You have made one feel the extraordinary beauty of her character, which must be the most difficult thing in the world to do. It was like meeting her again with oneself grown up & on equal terms & it seems to me the most astonishing feat of creation to have been able to see her in such a way–You have given father too I think as clearly, but perhaps, I may be wrong, that isnt quite so difficult. There is more to catch hold of. Still it seems to me to be the only thing about him which ever gave a true idea. So you see as far as portrait painting goes you seem to me to be a supreme artist & it is so shattering to find oneself face to face with those two again that I can hardly consider anything else. In fact for the last two days I have hardly been able to attend to daily life. Duncan & I have talked about them, as each had a copy, whenever we could get alone together, Roger too furious at being out of it for us to be able to do so when he was there.

Roger, however, was able to write six days later:

You won't want or expect criticisms from me–I'm not du métier. How little, I realized when I tried to imagine how I should describe the problems of a writer à la Lily Briscoe (in which by the by Vanessa and I both think you come through unscathed and triumphant though a little breathless and anxious perhaps). I know I should make a great mess of that.

So you won't get a criticism–only you can't help my thinking it the best thing you've done, actually better than Mrs. Dalloway. You're no longer bothered by the simultaneity of things and go backwards and forwards in time with an extraordinary enrichment of each moment of consciousness.

I'm sure that there's lots I haven't understood and that when I talk it over with Morgan he'll have discovered a lot of hidden meanings. I suspect for instance that arriving at the Lighthouse has a symbolic meaning which escapes me. But I wonder if it matters.

And to this Virginia replied regretting that she had not dedicated *To the Lighthouse* to Roger and acknowledging a debt of gratitude for his aesthetic guidance; he had kept her, she felt, on the right path. She continues:

I meant *nothing* by *The Lighthouse*. One has to have a central line down the middle of the book to hold the design together. I saw that all sorts of feelings would accrue to this, but I refused to think them out, & trusted that people would make it the deposit for their own emotions— which they have done, one thinking it means one thing another another. I can't manage Symbolism except in this vague, generalised way. Whether its right or wrong I don't know; but directly I'm told what a thing means, it becomes hateful to me.

Clive, back in London, wrote to Vanessa in May that the town seemed particularly dull and sad. "Only Virginia is sublimely happy, as well she may be–her book is a masterpiece." The view was pretty generally held by the critics, and a great many people wrote enthusiastically, although one complained that her descriptions of the fauna and flora of the Hebrides were totally inaccurate. The book sold better than its predecessors–3,873 copies (two of which were purchased by the Seafarers' Educational Society) in the first year.

That summer Virginia acquired a motor-car and a lover. The motor-car was an important addition to her life. The lover was Philip Morrell. Amiable and amorous, still handsome and with an honourable career behind him, he was nevertheless somehow ridiculous (or at least Virginia found him so). He pursued her briefly and cumbrously with unexpected visits and tentative love-letters; she eluded him without much difficulty. Neither Vita nor Leonard can have felt a moment's uneasiness on account of Philip.

The motor-car was considered a great luxury. Leonard at once became a skilful and knowledgeable driver; Virginia also took driving lessons and, as she considered, made good progress. But after taking their Singer through a hedge she decided (although no substantial damage was done) to let herself be driven. This indeed she found most enjoyable. The whole Sussex countryside, with its castles, seashores and great houses, suddenly became accessible; so too of course was Charleston and the Keynes's new home at Tilton. The social possibilities of the automobile were such that Vanessa, much to Virginia's amusement, placed a large notice on the gate leading to Charleston drive, bearing the word OUT.

Another important addition to Virginia's life was the gramophone. I do not think that the Woolfs had one until Leonard, who reviewed records for *The Nation*, purchased an expensive model. Virginia, who had a fairly catholic taste, developed a particular interest in Beethoven's late quartets, and they assisted those meditations which resulted finally in *The Waves*.

The pleasures of driving were country pleasures, the gramophone belonged also to the town and must have formed an ingredient of what was on the whole to be one of Virginia's happiest autumns. Not that, when the Woolfs returned to Tavistock Square at the end of September, they were particularly happy. They were troubled by that perennial problem, the young man in the Hogarth Press. Since the end of 1924 the young man had been Angus Davidson. He was one of the most amiable characters whom you could hope to meet. Unfortunately it was not amiability that Leonard was looking for. Already in 1926 Virginia was writing to Vanessa to say that the Press was going to make a loss that year and could not she, Vanessa, talk to Angus: he really ought to be more energetic. Vanessa did no doubt carry Virginia's message to Angus, who was taking his holiday with her and Duncan in Venice. But no amount of talking was going to remedy a situation in which Leonard and Angus continually got on each other's nerves.

One morning early in October 1927, Virginia left her studio at the back of No. 52 Tavistock Square, walked through into the offices of the Press, found Leonard and Angus together there and asked them the time.

She saw at once that she had made an unfortunate, or perhaps too apposite, a remark. Mrs Cartwright, the secretary, lowered her head over her typing and laughed. Virginia realised that she had come at the tail end of some terrific quarrel. She had in fact interrupted an argument which Leonard had begun by telling Angus that he was late for work. Angus denied the charge. Leonard persisted and produced his watch. Angus replied that his own watch was the better time-keeper. Leonard denied this; Angus refused to be outfaced. Leonard was sure of his facts; Angus doubted them. And so, the thing going on in this fashion – ding-dong, hammer and tongs, no one able to prove his point and time passing all the while unnoticed – they had got to the point at which there was nothing for it but to sally out and consult I know not what public monument—Euston Station, it may be—when Virginia, as though cued by a comic dramatist, put her head through the door and asked the time of day. They were both too vexed for laughter but it ended the dispute.

A few months later Angus and Leonard agreed, very wisely, that it would be best to part and, in November, the Woolfs wondered whether it might not be best to make an end of the Hogarth Press itself.

It was also at the beginning of October that Virginia's mind, which had for some time been simmering, suddenly boiled over. She had been contemplating two books: on the one hand that work of literary criticism which was to make a second volume to *The Common Reader*, which she had thought she would begin at Monk's House in August and with luck have finished by January, and on the other hand an imaginative work—the book she had vaguely seen dealing with a solitary woman shaping a book of ideas about life, or a semi-mystical, very profound life of a woman—a kind of play, it might be, she thought in February 1927. Then in May Vanessa had given this conception a slightly more definite form when she wrote about the moths. Connected with this was an idea for "Lives of the Obscure," or possibly of her friends—it was a favourite theme. This in turn had hardened into something much more definite in March—*The Jessamy Brides*—a comic version of the serious novel which still lay inchoate at the back of her mind. There were to be two poor solitary women at the top of a house with a view of Constantinople. The idea was still secondary—a pastime—when suddenly it presented itself in its final form. She wrote to Vita:

> Yesterday morning I was in despair. You know that bloody book which Dadie [Rylands] and Leonard extort, drop by drop, from my breast? Fiction, or some title to that effect. I couldn't screw a word from me; and at last dropped my head in my hands; dipped my pen in the ink, and wrote these words, as if automatically on a clean sheet: Orlando: A Biography. No sooner had I done this than my body was flooded with rapture and my brain with ideas. I wrote rapidly till 12. But listen; suppose Orlando turns out to be Vita. . . .

It was Vita—as she knew very well, for she had already told her diary that it was to be

> a biography beginning in the year 1500 and continuing to the present day called *Orlando*: Vita; only with a change about from one sex to another. I think, for a treat, I shall let myself dash this in for a week. . . .

The treat became an orgy. The work on fiction was abandoned

and in a state of high exhilaration she rushed into the writing of *Orlando*.

The book is interesting biographically, partly because it commemorates Virginia's love for Vita, and partly because we can trace so many of its elements to the incidents of Virginia's daily life in those years; for whereas *To the Lighthouse* was made from the passions and tragedies of her youth, *Orlando* was composed of materials which she noted hurriedly in her diary: Vita at Knole, showing her over the building–4 acres of it–stalking through it in a Turkish dress surrounded by dogs and children; a cart bringing in wood as carts had done for centuries to feed the great fires of the house; Vita hunting through her writing desk to find a letter from Dryden; Vita sailing through the Mediterranean in January 1926, with gold-laced captains off Trieste; Vita standing gorgeous in emeralds; a description of Vita and Violet Trefusis meeting for the first time upon the ice; Vita dressing her son as a Russian boy and his objection –"Don't," he said, "it makes me look like a girl"; Vita courted and caressed by the literary world; the homage of Sir Edmund Gosse, and indeed of Virginia herself.*

Then, early in September, Maynard and Lydia Keynes gave a party at Tilton. Jack (later Sir John) Sheppard enacted the part of an Italian *prima donna*, words and music being supplied by a gramophone. Someone had brought a newspaper cutting with them; it reproduced the photograph of a pretty young woman who had become a man, and this for the rest of the evening became Virginia's main topic of conversation.

Never had she worked so fast. She threw in everything that so beautifully, as it seemed so inevitably, lay to hand. In that autumn, "that singularly happy autumn," *Orlando* shoved everything aside.

Nevertheless she did have time to write an article for the *Atlantic Monthly* on E. M. Forster. Forster was the English contemporary for

---

* Sir Nicholas Greene is certainly a Gosse-like figure. Virginia had noticed how, at a gathering in Cambridge, Vita was "fawned upon by the little dapper grocer Gosse, who kept spinning round on his heel to address her compliments and to scarify Bolshevists; in an ironical voice which seems to ward off what might be said of him; and to be drawing round the lot of them thicker and thicker the red plush curtains of respectability." (*AWD* (*Berg*), 30 October 1926). Obviously Nick Greene in his earlier avatar is less closely drawn from life and, if I am right in supposing that Virginia made use of a mirror in drawing him, it was for his pose rather than for his features, and the pose might have been provided by another model. Nevertheless something of Virginia's attitude in Vita's company is recorded in *Orlando*. She did then show a slight tendency to talk about the de l'Etang family. Vita, on the other hand, was rather inclined to dwell upon the humble origins of her Spanish forbears. (Cf. *Orlando*, p. 80.)

whom she had most respect. His view of the world was not unlike hers. They loved and detested many of the same things. And yet there was between them a considerable barrier. Morgan was established as a novelist before she had published anything, but his career in fiction had ended, though she did not realise this, just when she was really beginning to find her voice. In a sense he belonged to an older generation. He was not deeply interested in–could not entirely sympathise with–her experiments in the handling of time, her probings into the mind. *Kew Gardens* and *The Mark on the Wall* had seemed to him "lovely little things," he had seen that *Night and Day* was a blind alley, but he was astonished to find the method used in these exquisite trifles also used, and, as it seemed to him, successfully used, in *Jacob's Room*, *Mrs Dalloway* and, his favourite to date, *To the Lighthouse*. And yet she had sacrificed a great deal–she had gone away from narrative, away from life.

They were a little afraid of each other. Morgan Forster was, I think, happier with his own sex. He found Virginia's feminism disturbing and felt that there was something a little too sharp, a little too critical, about her. "I don't think," he said, "that she cared for most people. She was always very sweet to me, but I don't think she was particularly fond of me, if that is the word." He was more at ease with Leonard; it was Leonard who urged him on when he despaired of finishing *A Passage to India* and believed it to be a failure. In a way I think that Forster was almost jealous of Leonard's affection for Virginia. He felt that Leonard was under-valued by Virginia's friends and resented, as Leonard did not, her growing eminence, the growing tendency to think of him as "her husband." And yet there was affection between them. Virginia was grateful for his praise, was touched when he informed her, before anyone else, that he had at last finished *A Passage to India*, and had, when all was said and done, a great admiration for his writings.

Still, a good deal had to be said and done. In *Mr Bennett and Mrs Brown* she had hailed Forster as one of the younger Georgians who were in revolt against Wells, Galsworthy and Bennett, but felt that somehow he had compromised. He had contrived to combine his own direct sense of the oddity and significance of character with Galsworthy's knowledge of the Factory Acts and Mr Bennett's knowledge of the Five Towns.

In 1927 Virginia wrote two rather severe articles about E. M. Forster. He saw one of them–at least–before publication and raised objections which led Virginia to feel, or at least to express, astonishment that this aloof, self-possessed man could be as sensitive, more sensitive indeed than she who had such a reputation for being thin-skinned.

In the first of her articles* she discussed E. M. Forster's critical work *Aspects of the Novel*. He seemed to her to be too ready to dismiss the claims of art as opposed to those of what he called "life"; it was an attitude which permitted him to do less than justice to Henry James.

But at this point the pertinacious pupil may demand: What is this "Life" that keeps on cropping up so mysteriously and so complacently in books about fiction? Why is it absent in a pattern and present in a tea party? Why is the pleasure that we get from the pattern in *The Golden Bowl* less valuable than the emotion which Trollope gives us when he describes a lady drinking tea in a parsonage? Surely the definition of life is too arbitrary, and requires to be expanded.'

To this E. M. Forster replied in a letter:

Your article inspires me to the happiest repartee. This vague truth about life. Exactly. But what of the talk about art? Each section leads to an exquisitely fashioned casket of which the key has unfortunately been mislaid and until you can find your bunch I shall cease to hunt very anxiously for my own.

I find the Continentals greater than the English not because Flaubert got hung up but because Tolstoy etc. could vitalise guillotines etc. as well as tea tables, could command certain moods or deeds which our domesticity leads us to shun as false. And why do you complain that no critic in England will judge a novel as a work of art? Percy Lubbock does nothing else. Yet he does not altogether satisfy you. Why?

Virginia replied:

Dear Morgan, I'm not particularly inspired to repartee by your letter. But I reply:—You say "Each sentence leads to a . . . casket of which the key has unfortunately been mislaid, and until you can find your bunch I shall cease to hunt very anxiously for my own."

Very well—but then I'm not writing a book about fiction. If I were, I think I *should* hunt a little. As a reviewer, which is all I am, it seems to me within my province to point out that both bunches are lost.

I agree that Tolstoi "vitalises the guillotine" &c. But by means of art I think; admitting that I can't define the word.

No; Percy Lubbock doesn't "altogether satisfy" me. But then I don't agree with you that he's a critic of genius. An able and painstaking pedant I should call him; who doesn't know what art is; so,

* *Is Fiction an Art?* first published in the *New York Herald Tribune*, 16 October 1927. Reprinted (revised) as *The Art of Fiction* in *Nation* and *Athenaeum*, 12 November 1927; VW, *Collected Essays*, II, p. 51. *The Novels of E. M. Forster*, published in *Atlantic Monthly*, Boston, November 1927; VW, *Collected Essays*, I, p. 342.

though his method of judging novels as works of art interests me, his judgments don't. V.

The above is official & impersonal. Unofficially & personally I'm afraid I've hurt or annoyed you (perhaps I imagine it). I didn't mean to. The article was cut down to fit the Nation, and the weight all fell in the same place. But I'm awfully sorry if I was annoying.

Forster, it seems, was able to reassure her: she was not annoying, merely wrong. Right or wrong, her next article, *The Novels of E. M. Forster*, must surely have been annoying, for, while finding much to admire in his work she also finds much to blame and indeed finds fault with his entire method.

After Virginia's death, in his Rede Lecture, Morgan Forster returns to his side of the argument. She has all the aesthete's characteristics, selects and manipulates her impressions and is not a great creator of character, enforces pattern on her books, has no great cause at heart. She stands, therefore, at the very entrance of that bottomless cavern of dullness, the Palace of Art. She keeps out, says Forster, but I would surmise that he thought her too close for comfort–for his comfort anyhow. In much the same way she, I think, took the view that although Morgan comes very close to the pulpit, where he would be a bore, and terribly close to the Groves of Eleusis, where he would have been an embarrassment, he is saved from both these fates by a hair's breadth. In other words, each admired and each found a good deal to deplore in the work of the other.

About this time Virginia found herself engaged in a controversy – but it was a controversy of a very different kind–with T. S. Eliot. In February 1928 we find that she has been talking to him for two hours about God. Unfortunately the details of this conversation are not recorded. By all rights this should have been a far more momentous discussion than that slight difference concerning the character of the novel which preceded it. For Eliot had become an Anglo-Catholic, for him the whole universe was changed–his life was but an instant's preparation for eternity, he was (potentially at all events) saved for Heaven–while Virginia and Leonard were quite certainly damned. But in fact it seemed to her that his religious views need not be treated very seriously. She used to tease him about his beliefs and, with some ribaldry, beg him to explain them; but from such assaults he would retire, smiling, unruffled but unwilling to engage. Her own views never changed; after a momentary conversion in childhood she lost all faith in revealed religion and, while never committing herself to any positive declaration, she maintained an attitude sometimes of mild, sometimes of aggressive agnosticism. Using the word in a very wide sense we may find a "religious" element in her novels; she tended to be, as she herself put it, "mystical"; but she entertained no comfortable beliefs. That the Universe is a very mysterious place she would certainly have allowed, but not that this mysteriousness allows us to suppose the existence of a moral deity or of a future life.

Orlando went through the usual vicissitudes of her novels, but within a shorter space of time than most. Virginia began with an impetuous rush. Then there had been a loss of momentum. By December she had come to the conclusion that *Orlando* was bad. It would not be out, if it came out at all, until the autumn. In February she believed that she was finishing it and she had in fact finished writing it by 18 March 1928. Then the Woolfs set out again for Cassis by motor, reaching the Mediterranean on 2 April. It was on the whole a delightful holiday, although the return journey across the *Massif Central* was almost too adventurous. "Often," she declared, "we were suspended on a precipice with the crows ogling us. Often only a hairsbreadth was between the left side wheel & a drop of some 80,000 feet." In fact it was a pretty agitating and tiresome journey, with many punctures, but at Cassis there had been agitations of a kind to worry her more. There was "Clive (who smacked me in public – curse him for an uneasy little upstart)."* This incident, the exact character of which is dubious, for it would have been unlike Clive to have resorted to actual physical demonstrations in public, and no-one seems to remember it, brought a contrite letter of apology in which he pointed out that he was very unhappy; to which Virginia replied that she for her part had been not only unhappy but insane. After all these years Virginia could still be driven to desperation by Clive. Twenty-four hours could be ruined – were ruined – and made utterly miserable simply because Clive made fun of her hat. It seems astonishing that he should have teased her so, or that she should so deeply have resented being teased by him. But on his part there was a kind of irritability and jealousy – a sense that she had no right not to be elegant, a sense that she was (as indeed she was) highly critical of him, so that in this way he could take his revenge; but also a more disinterested feeling that it was a part of everyone's duty to look as beautiful – and by beautiful he meant attractive, *soigné*, desirable – as possible. He resented and

---

* Cf. *Orlando*, p. 194. "Mr Pope left her with a bow. Orlando, to cool her cheeks, for really she felt as if the little man had struck her, strolled in the nut grove at the bottom of the garden."

always had resented the Stephen sisters' proud indifference to ornament–rather a kind of indifference which was in part modesty and
in part sartorial incompetence–so that although they were sometimes
beautifully dressed they were never well dressed. George, I suppose,
had felt something the same about his half-sisters.

Virginia for her part really more than half wanted to be invisible.
The whole business of clothes was a nightmare to her; and she was
happiest when she could forget that anyone looked at her. It was
when she was more or less in this happy condition that Clive could
tumble her back into a state of self-conscious insecurity in what
seemed to her an utterly merciless fashion, but to him was no more
than a passing pleasantry.

This particular quarrel was in a way a continuation of the tensions
which began in January of the previous year, when Clive, it may be
remembered, had sought refuge from the miseries of love by applying himself to the composition of his book on civilisation. He had
sent the first part of his manuscript to Virginia in November 1927,
and she had called the opening chapters "brilliant, witty and
suggestive." During the first months of 1928 they had seen a good
deal of each other. But then at some point–perhaps when they were
both at Cassis in April–Virginia had seen the rest of *Civilisation* and
came to the conclusion, which she voiced privately after its publication, "that he has great fun in the opening chapters but in the end
it turns out that Civilisation is a lunch party at no. 50 Gordon
Square"–a just criticism, but one which, if given to the author in
that form–and it was given in some form–must have been exceedingly mortifying. The quarrel was ended, or at least mended, when
Clive wrote, and Virginia accepted, an elegant dedicatory chapter
which prefaced the book when it appeared at the end of May.

In that month of May Virginia, rather shamefacedly, received the
Femina Vie Heureuse prize (£40). Interest in her work was growing
and has always persisted amongst the French. The ceremony itself
was portentously dull; there was an eulogy by Hugh Walpole,
which he himself described as "a rotten speech." To her it seemed
that he was explaining at some length just why he disliked her novels
so much. Nevertheless, she wrote a fulsome letter of thanks and
invited him to dinner. Such formal insincerities are pardonable. But
there was about her whole relationship with Walpole a certain lack
of candour; that is to say, she praised his novels to his face rather
more than she would have praised them to anyone else, and she made
fun of him behind his back, though not unkindly. She was wrong in
thinking that he did not like her work. He had in fact enormous

admiration for her writing–for everything that she had written so far–and dreamed wistfully of producing novels which, like hers, would appeal to the intellectuals of Bloomsbury, to the happy few, instead of to the enormously lucrative public which he managed somehow always to capture. He admired her, was genuinely fond of her, any meeting with her was a delight–a special treat–for him. But also she terrified him. She for her part found him, as did everyone, a simple, lovable, faintly absurd and very teasable character. For all his terrors he found her approachable, he confided in her, described his life, his character, and the most intimate details of his sexual history, so that when she died he was almost relieved that certain of his secrets could now never be divulged.

In May 1928 Leonard saw the final version of *Orlando*; he liked it and Virginia was surprised to find that he took it more seriously than she expected; she of course found plenty of fault with it and, reading Proust, everything else appeared insipid and worthless. I think that she saw well enough that *Orlando* was not "important" among her works, but also she was content, feeling that, of its kind, it was good. That summer and autumn were not unhappy. With *Orlando* out of the way she began to prepare some lectures on Women and Fiction, to be delivered at Cambridge in October.

Morgan was here for the weekend; timid, touchy, infinitely charming. One night we got drunk and talked of sodomy and sapphism, with emotion–so much so that next day he said he had been drunk. This was started by Radclyffe Hall and her meritorious dull book. They wrote articles for Hubert [Henderson, editor of *The Nation*] all day and got up petitions; and then Morgan saw her and she screamed like a herring gull, mad with egotism and vanity. Unless they say her book is good, she won't let them complain of the laws. Morgan said that Dr Head can convert the sodomites. "Would you like to be converted?" Leonard asked. "No" said Morgan, quite definitely. He said he thought Sapphism disgusting: partly from convention, partly because he disliked that women should be independent of men.

Radclyffe Hall's "meritorious dull book" was called *The Well of Loneliness*, and it created a good deal of excitement when it first appeared. It was a story of Sapphist love which today would hardly cause a moment's surprise; but in 1928 it was seized by the police. Those were the days when the Home Secretary, Joynson Hicks, was trying to cudgel the British public into purity and the question arose whether evidence of the book's literary merits was admissible. Hugh Walpole, Desmond MacCarthy and Virginia were all ready to go into the witness-box and testify in its favour. The difficulty, as will be seen, was that Miss Hall wanted her witnesses to declare that *The Well of Loneliness* was not only a serious, but a great work of art. This seemed too large a sacrifice in the cause of liberty.

However, the matter was compromised. Virginia went to testify at Bow Street but the magistrate, Sir Chartres Biron, ruled literary evidence out of court and the novel, a sincere though feeble effort, was condemned as though it had been any other piece of cheap pornography.

The case came on six days before the publication of *Orlando* and five days after Virginia had, in another manner, identified herself with the cause of homosexuality by spending a week in France alone with Vita. They set out from Monk's House on 24 September and the complexity of Virginia's affections is well illustrated by the fact that when the tour, which was to take them to Saulieu for a week, was imminent, she wrote to Vita, "I am melancholy, and excited in turn. You see, I would not have married Leonard had I not preferred living with him to saying goodbye to him." And yet on the morning of their departure the journey caused a small and sudden row between husband and wife. And yet again, when after three days' absence Virginia had no news from Leonard, she sent a telegram to make sure that all was well with him. And to Harold Nicolson she wrote:

> . . . I was going to thank you for having married Vita; & so producing this charming & indeed inimitable mixture. . . . Anyhow we had a perfect week, & I never laughed so much in my life, or talked so much. It went like a flash–Vita was an angel to me–looked out trains, paid tips, spoke perfect French, indulged me in every humour, was perpetually sweet tempered, endlessly entertaining, looked lovely; showed at every turn the most generous & magnanimous nature, even when there was only an old jug in the W.C. & she had lost her keys–in short it was the greatest fun.

It was a pleasant, and it may have been a perfectly innocent, excursion. Virginia returned refreshed, able to face the magistrate and, what was even more alarming, the critics.

"The great excitement," wrote Vanessa from London, "is Virginia's new book," and London was indeed well prepared, for the success of *To the Lighthouse* was recent in the public mind. *The Well of Loneliness* had given the sexual theme of the book topicality. The book itself was, from a publisher's point of view, perfect. By this time a great many people had discovered that Virginia Woolf was a novelist who must be tackled if one were to lay any claims to intellectual alertness. On the other hand, her manner of writing was still unfamiliar. For these *Orlando* came like an answer to prayer. Here was a work by a highbrow—a 'difficult' novelist—which nevertheless was easy, amusing, and straightforward in its narrative.

Vanessa had her doubts, so had Morgan; but the volume of praise, the enthusiastic letters, were impressive; so were the sales. It was, as Leonard said, the turning point in Virginia's career as a successful novelist. *To the Lighthouse* had sold 3,873 copies in the first year. *Orlando* sold 8,104 copies in the first six months. Financial anxieties were at an end. When in late October Virginia went to Cambridge and gave her lectures at Newnham and Girton there was, as Vanessa remembered, an atmosphere of triumph—a kind of ovation; Maynard Keynes came up with what seemed to her unnecessary *empressement*, saying, "Well there can be no doubt who is the famous sister now." Virginia's sales were still lower than those of Lytton, who published his *Elizabeth and Essex* in November of that year, but to her friends it was now clear that her genius burnt brighter. That autumn she was tempted by the idea of repeating her performance, of writing another *Orlando*. People felt that it was spontaneous and natural and this was a quality which she wanted to cultivate, but in fact she was waiting for something else. She was still haunted by the moths.

Chapter Six

1929–1931

IN January 1929 Leonard and Virginia travelled to Berlin. Harold Nicolson was now *en poste* there and Vita was with him; this, no doubt, supplied the chief motive for their journey. Vanessa and Duncan, who wanted to see the Berlin picture galleries, decided that they would go too.

> The Woolves [Vanessa observed] are enjoying themselves very much– Leonard is I think far more at home here than in Provence & Virginia finds all change fascinating. They don't of course quite know what to do. They walk miles rather than take a cab & go to the hotel restaurant where one pays about 10 marks for lunch rather than to some far better place where one could feed for a third as much. But it doesn't matter. I think Leonard has already got involved with socialists & Virginia with Vita who has a car & will whisk her about.

Vanessa disliked Germany, and Berlin did nothing to make her change her opinion; she found the Berliners kind but utterly unattractive (a view with which Virginia concurred) and was in a state of profound irritability most of the time. Something of her irritation finds its way into the letters which she addressed to Roger Fry. What she says in those letters of the disasters of the Berlin holiday is true enough, but her reflections on people are unusually severe and cannot be considered objective.

> The human situation here keeps us amused at odd moments. Virginia is of course a good deal involved with the Nicholsons [sic]. Vita is miserable here it seems. She hates Berlin & the Germans & I suspect will soon have to face a terrific crisis with Harold. He seems to me to be cut out for the diplomatic world to which he belongs. He reminds me of all the old official world I used to hate so & is really much like them, only perhaps he is nicer & I suppose must have more wits somewhere. Vita hardly ever comes to Berlin & when she does objects to the social duties, so that I suspect in the end he will have to give it up & then he'll be done for–Meanwhile the situation seems to be extremely edgy & is not improved by the Woolves' behaviour. Leonard swore he would go to no parties here & told Virginia to make this clear. She *says* she did so, but as soon as they arrived Harold announced that he had arranged two lunch parties for them, one to

meet a politician who specially wished to see Leonard. They shuffled and agreed to go to one & left the other vague till last night, when Leonard announced at supper after a concert (we were all there) that he did not mean to go. Harold was very cross–it was all most painful–& the Ws put it all on to our wishing to go to Potsdam that day. I think it was so transparent that we didn't get much blame, but it was very uncomfortable. However the Nicholsons seem to me such an unnecessary importation into our society that I can only leave Virginia to deal with them. We spent one of the most edgy & badly arranged evenings I can remember with them. We were to meet for dinner, all of us, & their two boys, so that we were 9. They hadn't ordered a table & of course none was to be had. It was horrid thawing weather, the streets covered with thick slush, & we hurried about from one restaurant to another trying to find room. At last we found it and had dinner. Then we went to see a Russian film called Storm over Asia. As we went in the younger boy was stopped by the man at the door who said he was too young to be allowed in–he's 11 or 12. Vita was furious & only made matters worse & enraged Leonard by pretending the people at the box office had told her it would be all right. We were all held up on the stairs & finally the wretched child had to be taken home by Vita. The film seemed to me extraordinary–there were the most lovely pictures of odd Chinese types, very well done. I enjoyed it immensely & was under the impression that everyone else did too until we got out into the street when it appeared that feeling was running very high on the question whether it was anti-British propaganda! No doubt it was–at least the feeblest part of it consisted of the flight of soldiers in British uniforms flying from Asiatics. Vita again enraged Leonard by asking him 6 times whether he thought they were meant for Englishmen – she and Harold both thought they weren't but managed to quarrel with each other all the same.* This discussion went on & on, all standing in the melting snow, & the general rage & uneasiness was increased by Eddy [Sackville-West] who was also of the party, who got into one of his regular old maidish pets, unwilling to stay or go home, flitting about from group to group like a mosquito. He always irritates the Nicholsons which I quite understand, but at the same time he's so far more intelligent than they are that I can't help sympathising with him. He had offered to take Duncan to see a little of Berlin night life & his one object was to avoid having to take Harold with them. But when at last the cold became too intense & Leonard and I between us managed to get a move on Eddy found

---

* I think that Vanessa was mistaken on this point; I do not think that Harold Nicolson doubted that the film was an attack upon British Imperialism in Asia. Vita may have had her doubts. Harold's position was made painful by the fact that he was his country's representative and that at the end of the film there was a small demonstration in the audience which could have been considered anti-British.

himself landed with Harold as well! Never have I spent such a thundery evening. As I was quite uninvolved however I got a good deal of amusement out of it. . . .

Virginia also was rather amused by the recollection of that disastrous but interesting entertainment, but, as Vanessa remarked, "Virginia lives in a world of her own."

As things turned out, Leonard's fears that the Berlin excursion might be too much for Virginia were fully justified. On 24 January they recrossed the North Sea. For the purpose of the voyage Vanessa gave Virginia a drug called *Somnifène* which she, Vanessa, had found an excellent preventive for seasickness. It was a fairly strong sedative and Vanessa warned Virginia on no account to exceed the stated dose. Virginia, according to her own account, took less than Vanessa had prescribed. Unfortunately the medicine clearly affected her with peculiar force. At Harwich she could hardly be roused. Leonard had to haul her like a sack into the train. There she relapsed at once into an unconscious condition, and upon reaching London was put to bed.

As in 1925, we find that what for someone else might have been a temporary set-back was for her the beginning of a long bout of ill-health. She was in bed for three weeks; she had one of her "first rate headaches," with all the usual symptoms—"pain, and heart jumps and my back aches, and so on." For six weeks she couldn't work. Vita wrote anxious half-apologetic letters, Virginia replied reassuringly; Vanessa felt some guilt about the *Somnifène*, and Leonard had to set her mind at rest. Altogether the *post mortem* on the Berlin visit was a good deal longer than the visit itself.

But this illness was another of those long fallow periods—fallow in the true sense—a period when her mind was ploughed and harrowed and made ready for its next sowing and harvesting. In January she was already beginning to compose *The Moths* in her head, and later she wrote to the author: "I am writing an entirely new kind of book. But it will never be so good as it is now in my mind—unwritten."

Perhaps I ought not to go on repeating what I have always said about the spring. One ought perhaps to be forever finding new things to say, since life draws on. One ought to invent a fine narrative style. Certainly there are many new ideas always forming in my head. For one, that I am going to enter a nunnery these next months; and let myself down into my mind; Bloomsbury being done with. I am going to face certain things. It is going to be a time of adventure and attack, rather lonely and painful I think. But solitude will be good for a new book.

Of course, I shall make friends. I shall be external outwardly. I shall buy some good clothes and go out into new houses. All the time I shall attack this angular shape in my mind. I think *The Moths* (if that is what I shall call it) will be very sharply cornered. I am not satisfied though with the frame. There is this sudden fertility which may be mere fluency. In old days books were so many sentences absolutely struck with an axe out of crystal: and now my mind is so impatient, so quick, in some ways so desperate.

There were other unwritten books to which she had committed herself, and of these the one that interested her most was the one concerned with women and fiction; it was based upon the two lectures which she had given in Cambridge in October 1928. She addressed herself to the task of turning them into a book with some enthusiasm. It was finished by the middle of May and in October the book was published under the title *A Room of One's Own*. It is, I think, the easiest of Virginia's books, by which I mean that it puts no great burden on the sensibilities. The whole work is held together, not as in her other works by a thread of feeling, but by a thread of argument–a simple well-stated argument: the disabilities of women are social and economic; the woman writer can only survive despite great difficulties, and despite the prejudice and the economic selfishness of men; and the key to emancipation is to be found in the door of a room which a woman may call her own and which she can inhabit with the same freedom and independence as her brothers. The lack of this economic freedom breeds resentment, the noisy assertive resentment of the male, who insists on claiming his superiority, and the shrill nagging resentment of the female who clamours for her rights. Both produce bad literature, for literature–fiction, that is–demands a comprehensive sympathy which transcends and comprehends the feelings of both sexes. The great artist is Androgynous.

This argument is developed easily and conversationally, striking home in some memorable passages but always lightly and amusingly expressed. It is that rare thing–a lively but good-tempered polemic, and a book which, like *Orlando*, is of particular interest to the student of her life. For in *A Room of One's Own* one hears Virginia speaking. In her novels she is thinking. In her critical works one can sometimes hear her voice, but it is always a little formal, a little editorial. In *A Room of One's Own* she gets very close to her conversational style.

If truth is not to be found on the shelves of the British Museum, where, I asked myself, picking up a notebook and a pencil, is truth?

Thus provided, thus confident and enquiring, I set out in pursuit of truth. The day, though not actually wet, was dismal, and the streets in the neighbourhood of the Museum were full of open coal-holes, down which sacks were showering; four-wheeled cabs were drawing up and depositing on the pavement corded boxes containing, presumably, the entire wardrobe of some Swiss or Italian family seeking fortune or refuge or some other desirable commodity which is to be found in the boarding-houses of Bloomsbury in the winter. The usual hoarse-voiced men paraded the streets with plants on barrows. Some shouted; others sang. London was like a workshop. London was like a machine. We were all being shot backwards and forwards on this plain founda-tion to make some pattern. The British Museum was another depart-ment of the factory. The swing-doors swung open; and there one stood under the vast dome, as if one were a thought in the huge bald forehead which is so splendidly encircled by a band of famous names. One went to the counter; one took a slip of paper; one opened a volume of the catalogue, and . . . . .

It is tempting to continue, and indeed those who wish to know what kind of a person Virginia Woolf was in the autumn of 1928 should do so. But because it is, after all, a book, because she is leading us through London and into that perplexing labyrinth, the Reading Room of the British Museum, in order to say some very trenchant things about the relationship of men to women, she must make an argument, and resist the temptation of following her fancies. Swiss families entering Bloomsbury boarding-houses, men with plants on barrows, were to her infinitely seductive; she could fill them with romance. The Italians might be refugees flying from Fascism or perhaps from the Austrians (she was sometimes a little uncertain about dates). The men with barrows might collect lizards or play the harp. She is too good an advocate to wreck her arguments by pushing such enquiries further, as she might have done when talking. They are only tentatively suggested, but the conversational tone of voice is there. It is a serene voice, the voice of a happy woman who loves life, loves even the rattle of coal down the pavement coal-hole, and loves, how much more, that "subtle and subterranean glow which is the rich yellow flame of rational intercourse. No need to hurry, no need to sparkle," when you can light a cigar, blow that dense satisfying cloud of vapour into the air and talk nonsense about the underlying music of conversation, the absurdities of dogs, the peculiarities of Manx cats. . . .

A mongoose had just run into the bathroom at Monk's House– Nelly is terrified. Or, driving from Lewes to Sevenoaks: "We met an elephant on the road here only the other day–I fancy they are common in this part of Kent. Why, there is another. Well, perhaps it is only an old sow. But you wouldn't usually find a sow that looked so much like an elephant in any other part of England."

"She lives," said Clive, "half in a world of solid reality, half in a Victorian novel" (and she could make others do likewise); but she did so adventuring gaily, noting advancing age without too much distress, conscious always of the flight of time, "reckoning how many more times I shall see Nessa," but with great good humour, with always the comforting reflection–important, I think, for Leslie Stephen's daughter–that she was richer than she had ever been before. Now she could go into a shop and buy a pocket-knife if she wanted one without thinking about the cost. It might not be the noblest of pleasures, but to those who have had to stint and save and calculate it may be one of the most solid. "I like printing in my basement best, almost," she wrote about this time; "no, I like drinking champagne and getting wildly excited. I like driving off to Rodmell on a hot Friday evening and having cold ham, and sitting on my terrace and smoking a cigar with an owl or two." And yet she could also write: "What a born melancholic I am"; and in a sense this also was true.

She had worries. She made the most of them. She invented others. There was Vita. Vita remained admirable and charming; it was a pleasure to see her and it was a pleasure too when that summer Harold finally decided to quit the diplomatic service. He had written to Leonard and Virginia to ask if they would think it disgraceful if he were to accept a post on Beaverbrook's *Evening Standard*. Presumably they did not. Indeed they congratulated him warmly when on 15 September they heard of his decision to leave the Service for good. But Vita had friends–a Sapphist circle–which Virginia found decidedly unsympathetic. Perhaps Vita found in them a relief from the too-chaste, the too-platonic atmosphere of 52 Tavistock Square and Monk's House, and perhaps Virginia was jealous. At all events Virginia found them second-rate; they engendered a school-girl atmosphere, and although she was conscious of being unkind to Vita she was unable to resist the temptation of telling her what she thought. Poor Vita discovered a certain acidity in her friend's com-munications–"adders' tails or viper's gall," as Virginia put it (with considerable zoological inexactitude). And so their friendship was for a time agitated.

It was perhaps also a vexation that the Hogarth Press now made its one bad blunder, rejecting *Brothers and Sisters* by Ivy Compton-Burnett, which Leonard, it is said, did not like. It is uncertain whether

Virginia ever saw the manuscript but she admitted later that they had made a mistake.

Then there was Vanessa. Between her and Virginia there was a kind of tacit competition; the one was brilliantly articulate and a successful artist, the other was silent, and as a painter somewhat overshadowed by Duncan Grant's growing fame. But she had three children; she had that ruthless artistic egotism which could say: "I need sunlight and peace at Cassis even more than I need my sister's company" (not that she probably said it out loud); she had, in a word, things that Virginia did not have and she led a life, even though it was devoted to what Virginia called "a low art," which seemed enviably enjoyable and romantic. When, early in June 1929, the Woolfs went to Cassis for a week and tasted the delights of intense heat, cheap wine and cigars and that peculiar languid serenity which is induced by the ease and abundance of Mediterranean life as the visitor knows it, Virginia entered into negotiations for a house, "La Boudarde," a few hundred yards from "La Bergère" where Vanessa lived. She wanted it, I think, in order to be even with her sister and at the same time to experience something which Vanessa had and which she, Virginia, had not. It was another example, too, of the way in which they were drawn together as though by some capillary attraction. Thus Vanessa had followed Virginia to Sussex, thus Virginia had made her way back from Richmond to Bloomsbury. But "La Boudarde" was not a realistic proposition, as Leonard, I imagine, saw from the beginning. Virginia could live in two establishments but not in three. Nor, without impossibly exhausting journeys, could she live so far from London and the Press. Leonard was not really as fond of Cassis as were the Bells, and neither, Virginia discovered later on, was she. The attempts to furnish the Cassis house became more and more half-hearted and in 1930 the enterprise was quietly dropped.

> Of course there are the Woolves too, whom I have seen twice since you were here, and in my opinion Virginia is in a bad way and ought to stay in the country. She will not of course; and so I daresay will go into a madhouse instead. And then what will all the ladies say? (*Clive Bell to Frances Marshall*, Charleston, 11th September 1929).

Clive was unduly pessimistic (if he really meant what he said), but it was true that Virginia's health had not been good. The return from Cassis had been followed by what she described as a "helter skelter random rackety summer," and at Monk's House there had been some unusually unpleasant scenes with Nelly. Also the page proofs of *A Room of One's Own* demanded particular attention. But, when these and other matters had been disposed of:

> . . . I must think of that book again and go down step by step into the well. These are the great events and revolutions in one's life–and then people talk of war and politics. I shall grind very hard; all my brakes will be stiff; my springs rusty. But I have now earned the right to some months of fiction and my melancholy is brushed away, so soon as I can get my mind forging ahead, not circling round.

And three days later:

> And so I might fill up the half hour before dinner writing. I thought on my walk that I would begin at the beginning: I get up at half past eight and walk across the garden. Today it was misty and I had been dreaming of Edith Sitwell. I wash and go into breakfast which is laid on the check tablecloth. With luck I may have an interesting letter; today there was none. And then bath and dress; and come out here and write or correct for three hours, broken at 11 by Leonard with milk and perhaps newspapers. At one, luncheon–rissoles today and chocolate custard. A brief reading and smoking after lunch; and at about two I change into thick shoes, take Pinker's lead and go out–up to Asheham hill this afternoon, where I sat a minute or two, and then home again along the river. Tea at four, about; and then I come out here and write several letters, interrupted by the post, with another invitation to lecture; and then I read one book of the Prelude. And soon the bell will ring and we shall dine and then we shall have some music and I shall smoke a cigar; and then we shall read–La Fontaine I think tonight and the papers–and so to bed. . . . Now my little tugging and distressing book and articles are off my mind my brain seems to fill and expand and grow physically light and peaceful. I begin to feel it filling quietly after all the wringing and squeezing it has had since we came here. And so the unconscious part now expands; and walking I notice the red corn and the blue of the plain and an infinite number of things without naming them; because I am not thinking of any special thing. Now and again I feel my mind take shape, like a cloud with the sun on it, as some idea, plan or image wells up, but they travel on, over the horizon, like clouds and I wait peacefully for another to form, or nothing–it matters not which.

These words, surely, were written in an interval of fruitful tranquillity. But even her illnesses could yield spiritual dividends. On 10 September she wrote: "Six weeks in bed now would make a masterpiece of *Moths*"; it was a thought to which she was to return some months later when the *Moths* had been rechristened *The Waves* and she was again ill.

If I could stay in bed another fortnight (but there is no chance of that) I believe I should see the whole of *The Waves*. . . . I believe these illnesses are in my case–how shall I express it?–partly mystical. Something happens in my mind. It refuses to go on registering impressions. It shuts itself up. It becomes chrysalis. I lie quite torpid, often with acute physical pain–as last year; only discomfort this. Then suddenly something springs.

But the process of gestation was slow and there was very little progress that autumn either at Rodmell or in London. The Woolfs had decided to see as few people as possible in Sussex, and in fact they did see rather less of their old friends that summer; but some younger ones were invited: Janet Vaughan, Madge's daughter, then beginning her career as a scientist; Lyn Irvine, a young Cambridge graduate who, with considerable competence and enterprise, was trying to make a living by her pen; and William Plomer. In 1925 Plomer had sent a manuscript from Zululand to the Hogarth Press which both Leonard and Virginia had thought extraordinarily good, and which they published. In 1929 he reached England and they met and liked him; they asked him to Rodmell for a week-end in August and Virginia persuaded him to talk about himself. She was much interested by what he had to say and considered him a more solid and a more serious character than most of the young men of her acquaintance. Nevertheless, when she brought him over to Charleston her behaviour was abominable. "Mr. Plomer," she began, "has been telling me all about himself. He is descended from Shakespeare and also from William Blake." Needless to say he had said nothing of the kind and, indeed, he shyly attempted to explain what he *had* said, but it was no good. Virginia had imagined so fascinating and so astonishing a conversation that she could not keep it to herself. The result, of course, was to make it appear that he, who was the quietest and most modest of men, had been outrageously self-important and vainglorious.

"I am afraid," he said to her next day, "that I was very inadequate last night." Virginia apologised for the Bell family party. He replied that it had been delightful. I hope he was not too insincere. Certainly the family party attacked Virginia very severely when they next met, but she seemed perfectly unconscious of any cruelty to the guest whom she had brought, and to whom, judging from her diary entries, she certainly wished no ill.

The Woolfs returned to London on 3 October. Here they seemed to have lived pretty quietly, with few social engagements and no great excitement other than the publication of *A Room of One's*

Own on the 24th, which brought the usual crop of appreciative letters. Clive was one of the few who didn't like it; he thought that Virginia should stick to works of the imagination. It sold extremely well.

That autumn, which was devoted to *The Waves*, was distracted by Nelly; she again gave notice and did so as Virginia was attempting to dismiss her (which was provoking). She was to leave on 12 December; on 2 December she asked to be allowed to stay and a compromise was reached: they would try one more month. And then there was an excavator's pumping machine which made a spasmodic and exasperating noise; and to the thumping of the pump was added the far worse noise of dance music from the hotel which had arisen behind them in Woburn Place; every night No. 52 Tavistock Square shook with the din and this of course drove Virginia frantic. In the end they had to go to law to get it silenced.

More agreeable, but hardly less destructive of the peace that she needed for the composition of *The Waves*, were her social duties. As an aunt, as a sister, she felt obliged to go to a New Year party in Vanessa's studio at No. 8 Fitzroy Street; it was for her niece Angelica, who was twelve years old – a fancy-dress affair, everyone being disguised as a character from *Alice in Wonderland*. Roger had most appropriately dressed himself up as the White Knight. He was wearing white Jaeger pants, chain armour, cricket pads, his whiskers were green, he had fastened to his person an infinity of objects – candles, mousetraps, tweezers, frying-pans, scales jingling from a brass chain. The children crowded round him; he was the *pièce de résistance* of a highly successful evening. Returning from the party by way of Francis Street, the Woolfs witnessed a social injustice of the kind that made Leonard's blood boil. Two men passing on the other side of the road jeered at a rather tipsy middle-aged tart. She retorted fiercely, shrieking out something about bollocks, bulls and buggers. "Whore," they roared back, and then, perceiving a policeman, bolted. A bottle of beer crashed behind them on the pavement. The woman was not so agile and the policeman began to bully and goad her into saying something for which she might be arrested. Leonard found this intolerable. Flinging himself between the policeman and the woman he said, "Why don't you go for the men who began it? My name's Woolf and I can take my oath that the woman is not to blame." A small crowd accumulated, as such crowds do; moved by Leonard's eloquence it took the woman's side. Immediately she lost her head and nearly spoilt her case by abusing the policeman. The ex-District Officer of Hambantota Province told someone to take her away. The policeman was cowed. "We parted almost amicably," said Leonard in his account of the affair, "and as the crowd broke up I saw Lydia standing on the outskirts under a gas-lamp gazing with amazement at me and the policeman."

Mrs Keynes had good reason to be amazed, for not only was the scene unusual, but it was made more so by the fact that Leonard was still in his party dress. He was Lewis Carroll's Carpenter, complete with paper hat, green baize apron and chisels, while Virginia wore the paws and ears of the March Hare. It was typical of Leonard that this aspect of the matter never occurred to him. What the effect of so strange an apparition may have been on the policeman one cannot tell.

It is a wonder, when one considers the number of interruptions, pleasant and unpleasant, that Virginia made any progress at all with *The Waves*. Nevertheless, in January 1930, she found herself rather more fluent than she had been throughout the autumn. When, in February, she was again ill, her imagination was busy with the Hampton Court scene. But in February she encountered the most disastrous interruption of all – Ethel Smyth.

"An old woman of seventy-one has fallen in love with me," wrote Virginia. "It is at once hideous and horrid and melancholy-sad. It is like being caught by a giant crab."

And yet it was not all hideous and horrid and melancholy-sad. Ethel was, as Virginia said more than once, a game old cock. Her vitality was so terrific. She fumbled and blustered and bawled her way through life, without vacillations or hesitations or doubts of her own tremendous genius as a musician. Virginia admired the headlong impetuosity of her conversation and of her writing, her startling freedom of expression. She was absurd – grotesque even, brave as befitted a General's daughter, one who would ride straight to a bullfinch, tumble, remount, ride on regardless of either pain or ridicule – a gallant figure whom it was impossible not to admire, perhaps to love. And then, how could Virginia resist so much admiration? "I don't think," Ethel wrote, "I have ever cared for anyone more profoundly . . .", "for eighteen months I really thought of little else." Ethel admired Virginia for her beauty – "for her most wonderful speaking voice and the distinction and the fascination no words can describe" – and yet from a very early date she could see another side to Virginia.

I think she has very grave faults. Absolutely self-absorbed and (no wonder), jealous of literary excellence; (couldn't see the point of D. H.

Lawrence until he was dead). Ungenerous, indeed incapable of knowing what generosity means, I had almost said, but she recognizes it in others. In Vita, for instance, who I think is the only person except Vanessa Bell . . . and Leonard, . . . whom she really loves. . . . She is arrogant, intellectually, beyond words yet absolutely humble about her own great gift. Her integrity fascinates me. To save your life, or her own, she could not doctor what she thinks to be the truth. Of religion she has no conception. Her views, and the views of all that Bloomsbury group, about it are quite childish. Also their political views. They think all aristocrats are limited and stupid, and swallow all the humbugging shibboleths of the Labour Party. . . .

This entry in Ethel's diary–written about 1933–is in many ways interesting. It shows some of the misunderstandings and some of the perceptions that made the relationship between the two women difficult. The references to Virginia's socialism were written, I fancy, with Leonard in mind. I doubt whether Ethel herself was deeply religious or very deeply political, but she saw in the tenets of what she was pleased to call Bloomsbury an affront to her own notions of good form, and this difference, social rather than ideological, was one of the things that separated her from Virginia. Virginia did not refrain from mocking at and abusing Ethel's beliefs.

Virginia's arrogance, the kind of arrogance that made her contemptuously dismiss the novels of Maurice Baring which Ethel considered masterpieces of the highest order, or, worse still, some of Ethel's friends, was real enough. For rather the same reason she could appear ungenerous, although to me the charge seems the most unjust that Ethel makes. Nor were Virginia's affections so limited as her friend supposed, although here again we may see a personal application: undoubtedly Virginia never loved Ethel half so much as Ethel herself wished to be loved. And of course she *was* self-absorbed. But in this accusation there is something more than a little comic, for here indeed it was a case of Greek meeting Greek. Ethel was a fascinating person but also incredibly demanding. Vita Sackville-West tells us:

how angry she could get when her friends didn't answer her letters in detail. Poor Virginia Woolf, endlessly patient under this loving persecution, had to endure long questionnaires: "You haven't answered my questions one, two, three, four–right up to twenty. Please reply by return of post." Ethel seemed to command endless time, and to expect her friends to command equal leisure. Blinkered egoism could scarcely have driven at greater gallop along so determined a road. But although often a nuisance, Ethel was never a bore.

Ethel and Virginia appear to have met on 20 February 1930, and thereafter, as was usual in any matter which concerned Ethel, things went on at a thundering pace. She burst into the room at four in the afternoon, in a three-cornered hat and a tailor-made suit, and found Virginia resting on a sofa. "Let me look at you . . . I have brought a book and a pencil. I want to ask . . . First I want to make out the genealogy of your mother's family. Old Pattle–have you a picture? No, well now–the names of his daughters." Fifteen minutes later they were on Christian name terms. She had thought of nothing for ten days but of seeing Virginia; she was in rhapsodies about *A Room of One's Own*, and didn't much care for Vita's friends. She said writing music was like writing novels, that orchestration was colouring. She lived in the country because of her passion for games, for golf. She had been thrown off her horse two years ago while hunting. She rode a bicycle. She was very strong. And so it went on until half-past seven, when she had to leave for Woking.

Virginia was impressed. There was something fine and tried and experienced about Ethel besides the rant and the riot and the egoism; and perhaps after all she was not such an egotist as people made out. As for Ethel, she, I think, was in love with Virginia before she even met her.

The honeymoon period was short. Virginia could not keep up with Ethel's demands or conform to the reckless pace of her friendship. Towards the end of April Ethel declared that she was disillusioned. Virginia replied that she was glad of it; she hated illusions.

With this exchange the friendship might have come to an end, but there was a reconciliation on the 1st of May. Ethel came to tea, she met Vanessa, who became her confidante–she wrote innumerable letters to both sisters, often twice a day to Virginia–and later that month, after Leonard and Virginia had returned from a business holiday, travelling their books in Devon and Cornwall, there were more meetings, and so it continued throughout the summer. When in August the Woolfs were at Monk's House, Ethel wrote to Virginia and told her that in getting to know her, she had felt an emotion comparable only to that which she had experienced when first she heard the music of Brahms.

Then she came to spend a night at Rodmell and Virginia meditated on "this curious unnatural friendship. I say unnatural because she is so old, and everything is incongruous." There had been, as Virginia said, some interesting moments.

"D'you know, Virginia, I don't like other women being fond of you."

"Then you must be in love with me Ethel."

"I have never loved anyone so much. . . . Ever since I saw you I have thought of nothing else. . . . I had not meant to tell you. But I want affection. You may take advantage of this."

And some affection Virginia was ready to give her. She was such a splendid old thing—"an indomitable old crag"—so assured, sometimes so quick, so practical, and she had a certain smile, very wide and benignant.

Ethel, Vita, Vanessa and Duncan, and writing *The Waves* were what she called the "elements" of that summer of 1930, and it was surely Ethel who made her describe it as "a very violent summer." Being violent it was, of necessity, exhausting and one afternoon in late August when Maynard and Lydia Keynes had come to Monk's House, Virginia, having placed a sprig of white heather in a vase (it had been sent by an admirer), walked down the path with Lydia:

> If this don't stop, I said, referring to the bitter taste in my mouth and the pressure like a wire cage round over my head, then I am ill: yes, very likely I am destroyed, diseased, dead. Damn it! Here I fell down—saying "How strange—flowers". In scraps I felt and knew myself carried into the sitting room by Maynard. Saw L. look very frightened; said I will go upstairs; the drumming of my heart, the pain, the effort got violent at the doorstep; overcame me; like gas; I was unconscious; then the wall and the picture returned to my eyes; I saw life again. Strange, I said, and so lay, gradually recovering, till 11, when I crept up to bed. Today, Tuesday, I am in the lodge and Ethel comes—valiant old woman! But this brush with death was instructive and odd. Had I woken in the divine presence it would have been with fists clenched and fury on my lips. "I don't want to come here at all!" so I should have exclaimed. I wonder if this is the general state of people who die violently. If so, figure the condition of Heaven after a battle.

It is possible that this "brush with death" gave Virginia an idea of how she would finish *The Waves*. She continues:

> I will use these last pages to sum up our circumstances. A map of the world.
>
> Leaving out the subject of Nelly, which bores me*, we are now much

* It may bore the reader too; but it seems only proper to note that Nelly had an operation in May 1930 and was convalescent throughout the summer. In her absence Virginia employed daily servants and was so well pleased by the arrangement that, while continuing to pay her wages, she refused on grounds of her health to let Nelly return to work. In November 1930 Virginia wrote dismissing her finally; but Nelly's dismay and her arguments, supported as they were by Leonard, overcame Virginia's resolution, and she returned for a further trial period from 1 January 1931. Nelly's fellow-servant, Lottie, had left the Woolfs and taken service with the Stephens in 1924.

freer and richer than we have ever been. For years I never had a pound extra; a comfortable bed, or a chair that did not want stuffing. This morning Hammond delivered 4 perfectly comfortable armchairs–and we think very little of it.

I seldom see Lytton; that is true. The reason is that we don't fit in, I imagine, to his parties, nor he to ours; but that if we can meet in solitude all goes as usual. Yet what do one's friends mean to one, if one only sees them 8 times a year? Morgan I keep up with in our chronically spasmodic way. We are all very much aware of life and seldom do anything we do not want to. My Bell family relations are young, fertile and intimate. . . . Julian is publishing with Chatto and Windus. As for Nessa and Duncan, I am persuaded that nothing can be now destructive of that easy relationship, because it is based on Bohemianism. My bent that way increases–in spite of the prodigious fame (it has faded out since July 15th; I am going through a phase of obscurity: I am not a writer; I am nothing; but I am quite content) I am more and more attracted by looseness, freedom and eating one's dinner off a table anywhere, having cooked it previously. This rhythm (I say I am writing the Waves to a rhythm, not to a plot) is in harmony with the painters'. Ease and shabbiness and content therefore are all ensured. Adrian I never see. I keep constant with Maynard. I never see Saxon. I am slightly repelled by his lack of generosity; yet would like to write to him. Perhaps I will. George Duckworth, feeling the grave gape, wishes to lunch with Nessa; wishes to feel again the old sentimental emotions. After all, Nessa and I are his only women relations. A queer cawing of homing rooks this is. I daresay the delights of snobbishness somewhat fail in later life–and we have done–"made good", that is his expression.

My map of the world lacks rotundity. There is Vita. Yes. She was here the other day, after her Italian tour with 2 boys; a dusty car, sandshoes and Florentine candlepieces, novels and so on tumbling about on the seats. I use my friends rather as giglamps: There's another field I see–by your light–over there's a hill. I widen my landscape.

George (now Sir George) came to lunch at Charleston, corpulent, complacent and gluttonous. Virginia used to describe his demeanour on that occasion with a kind of amused horror. It was not an enlivening reunion; neither was Mrs Woolf's annual visit to Monk's House which took place at the end of September and consumed a day that might have been given to *The Waves*. It was most unwillingly sacrificed, for she was a vain, querulous, utterly commonplace old person connected to Virginia only by the circumstance of marriage. She had to be fed on sweet cakes and conversational bromides; she demanded sympathy and admiration and, if denied these treats, might dissolve into reproachful tears.

These were only some of the time-consuming interruptions of what Virginia described nevertheless as the happiest, the most satisfactory summer since they came to Monk's House.

The Woolfs returned to London on 4 October and Virginia set to work to finish *The Waves*. On 15 October she records a bad start and felt that she must return to Rodmell, which she did, apparently with good results. "Alas, too numb brained to go on with Bernard's soliloquy this morning"—this she wrote on 8 November, and on 2 December: "No, I cannot write that very difficult passage in the Waves this morning." She took a week off before attempting to tackle the last lap—Bernard's final speech. The Woolfs spent Christmas at Rodmell and the end seemed in sight when Virginia was struck down by influenza; at the very end of the year she was able, cautiously, to resume work. But there were difficulties: the cold at Monk's House was intense and she found that her wits were frozen; all she could do was to write a few staggering sentences. A visit to Charleston brought little comfort. She found it depressing; the painters teased her, so did Clive; the young reminded her of her age—they seemed to sneer, to mock, and certainly they did not help her to write *The Waves*.

Again at Tavistock Square, Bernard's speech continued to present difficulties.

> I could perhaps do B[ernard]'s soliloquy in such a way as to break up, dig deep, make prose move—yes I swear—as prose has never moved before; from the chuckle, the babble to the rhapsody. . . .
> Now this is true: *The Waves* is written at such high pressure that I can't take it up and read it through between tea and dinner; I can only write it for about one hour, from 10 to 11.30. And the typing is almost the hardest part of the work.

Still *The Waves* had to be written. It ground on somehow until 20 January when, lying in her bath, Virginia was struck by an idea. It excited her so much that, for a time, *The Waves* became more impossible than ever. It was to be a sequel to *A Room of One's Own*. It would be called *Professions for Women* perhaps. For a week she could think of nothing else and Bernard remained tongue-tied. The idea was triggered off by a speech that she delivered on 21 January at a meeting organised by Philippa Strachey and the London National Society for Women's Service. Virginia spoke to an audience of two hundred people; Ethel, in a blue kimono and a wig, spoke also. It was on the whole a successful occasion, although Leonard, so it appeared to Virginia, was somewhat exasperated by it all. Possibly he foresaw that she would have a temperature of 99 on the following morning and again be unable to work.

By 26 January she had shaken off the feminist pamphlet and hoped to finish *The Waves* within three weeks. By 2 February she believed she would have finished by the 8th. "Oh Lord the relief when this week is over." It had, she felt, been at least a brave attempt and oh, the delight to be free again. But on that very day she had to go and hear Ethel rehearse *The Prison*. This was a fascinating experience – an audience of fat, elderly, satin-swathed ladies in a vast Adam house in Portland Place and Ethel, shabby, vigorous, impetuously conducting with a pencil, convinced that she was as great as Beethoven. And who knows, reflected Virginia, perhaps she *was* a great composer? And then on the 4th, Leonard's day was ruined by jury service and Virginia's by the fact that her doctor, Ellie Rendel, who was to have come to enquire into her persistent high temperature at 9.30 sharp, thus leaving the morning free for writing, was an hour and a half late. It was a little thing, the reader may think – a morning's work lost – but the frustrations that such a delay can cause, the accumulated exasperation when one is interrupted again and again as one attempts to finish a task, is one of the major miseries of life. It is as though one were crushed beneath a multitude of counterpanes unable to breathe until at length they are cast off and with each attempt to throw them away something happens, they fall back again, stifling, oppressive, inevitable.

But now at last the end really was in sight, and indeed she was able to keep exactly to the timetable she had proposed for herself on 2 February. On the morning of the 7th she wrote:

Here in the few minutes that remain, I must record, heaven be praised, the end of *The Waves*. I wrote the words O Death fifteen minutes ago, having reeled across the last ten pages with some moments of such intensity and intoxication that I seemed only to stumble after my own voice, or almost, after some sort of speaker (as when I was mad). I was almost afraid, remembering the voices that used to fly ahead. Anyhow, it is done; and I have been sitting these 15 minutes in a state of glory, and calm, and some tears, thinking of Thoby, and if I could write Julian Thoby Stephen 1881-1906 on the first page. I suppose not. How physical the sense of triumph and relief is! Whether good or bad, it's done; and, as I certainly felt at the end, not merely finished, but rounded off, completed, the thing stated – how hastily, how fragmentarily I know; but I mean that I have netted that fin in the waste of water which appeared to me over the marshes out of my window at Rodmell when I was coming to an end of *To the Lighthouse*.

If, as many critics assert, *The Waves* was Virginia's masterpiece, then that morning of Saturday, 7 February 1931, may be accounted the culminating point in her career as an artist.

This chronicle of Virginia's final efforts to finish her novel has obliged me to pass over an event of some importance in her life.

On 27 October 1930 Leonard and Virginia decided to make an end of the Hogarth Press. They might perhaps continue to publish their own works and those of a few friends, together with those which they actually printed themselves; but the Press would cease to be a large business. The motives which governed this resolution were not new. The Press deprived the Woolfs of liberty and imposed altogether too much labour. If Virginia could have had her way the decision would not have been reversed; she found the work, and particularly her own employment as a reader, onerous and dispiriting. But Leonard could not easily destroy the remarkable edifice which he had built. I have little doubt that it was he who decided to try once more to enlist an intelligent adjutant. The young man whom he found this time was Julian's friend John Lehmann. He had recently left Cambridge; they had just accepted his poems for publication. He was to become manager, to run the press under Leonard's supervision and eventually to become a partner.

Virginia met him early in the New Year: "a tight aquiline boy, pink, with the adorable curls of youth; yes, but persistent, sharp."

The arrangement lasted less than two years, although it was not to be the end of the connection between John Lehmann and the Hogarth Press. It strengthened the first tenuous contacts between the Woolfs and those remarkable young writers of the Left–Stephen Spender, C. Day Lewis, W. H. Auden and Christopher Isherwood–whose work John Lehmann promoted through the Press. And of course it meant that the idea of bringing the whole business to an end was quietly dropped.

Virginia went out and had her hair curled. Vanessa didn't like the effect and Virginia was chagrined. Then she quarrelled with Ethel. They were both in a state to quarrel with anyone. Virginia, depressed and exhausted by so much effort, wrote on 11 April: "I have finished the worst novel in the language," which, of course, was partly fake modesty but also contained, I think, a germ of real despair, the knowledge that she had not after all achieved that perfect work of art which must always remain unachieved. Ethel's work, *The Prison*, after a successful performance in Edinburgh, was not well received in London. She displayed, as it seemed to Virginia, a tawdry, paltry vanity. Moreover, the things that Virginia and Ethel did not like about each other were becoming more and more obvious to each of them. Ethel's overwhelming egotism and incessant raucous demands for attention gave Virginia headaches. She felt she was being attacked, overwhelmed, submerged, and she reacted fiercely in defence of her own personality. Each saw the other as the aggressor, each felt some misgivings about the other's friends. Ethel disapproved of Bloomsbury, what she knew of it – although she did like Duncan and Vanessa and she was amiable with the younger generation, but there was little love lost between her and Leonard and I think that she saw a vague background of frivolous long-haired atheists and socialists who were not impressed by her music, who perhaps made fun of her – that potent hostile unnamed Bloomsbury of the imagination, which has enraged so many unsuccessful artists. Virginia was equally, if not even more, un-appreciative of Ethel's friends and relations. Matters seem to have come to a head in June 1931. Again Virginia was unwell, despite the fact that in May the Woolfs had taken a memorable but wet holi-day carrying them as far as Brantôme and Montaigne's house. Ethel irritated her by saying that there was nothing wrong with her save her liver. No doubt it was kindly meant, and the postcard decorated with a picture of a sick monkey which accompanied it was intended obviously as a joke, but Virginia was in no mood for such joking. With a headache which gnawed like a rat as she retyped *The Waves*, and then the correction of the retyping, no, it didn't seem to her a bit funny. Their relations deteriorated until on 29 June Ethel seems to have burst out in a letter which Virginia called sordid and ridicu-lous. She meditated a scathing reply, or so it seems, and finally con-tented herself with a laconic note. "I suppose from your tone that you don't want to come here on Monday." She didn't. There was an interval of hurt silence. At the end of it Ethel came, in a sense, to apologise – that is to say, to explain, to defend, to extenuate, while her tea grew cold and her parentheses grew endless. When she had gone Virginia wrote to her saying in effect: this must not happen again. Ethel, she explained, demanded too much sympathy. It was a fault into which Sir Leslie had fallen in his dealings with his children. The result would inevitably be estrangement. Virginia had, in fact, discovered that she was the stronger of the two. She could up to a point dictate the terms of their friendship. Ethel could loom and strut and talk her head off, but when Virginia was silent, Ethel was undone; she needed Virginia. Virginia liked, was entertained by and in a way sympathised with her, but she could do perfectly well without her. On these terms the friendship could, and indeed did, continue, but not without altercations.

All this must be imagined against the final miseries of correcting the typescript copy of *The Waves*.

On 17 July she wrote: "Yes, this morning I think I may say I have finished." The novel could be submitted to Leonard. Would he perhaps condemn it, no doubt in some qualified fashion, and find it too difficult, too incoherent? Two days later he came out to her in the garden house at Rodmell and said that the first hundred pages were indeed very difficult, but: "It is a masterpiece, the best of your books." She felt inexpressible relief, and walked off in the rain "as light as a trout." Now she could count her blessings—so hard to count when they really need counting: what with the Press and her work, she had a "hoard"* of £860, and material luxuries: a Heal's bed, a wireless, electric light, a Frigidaire; she could make a dress allowance to her niece Angelica, who would soon be old enough to value such things—and set herself to write something light and easy and untroubling—a biography of Mrs Browning's dog, Flush.

Moreover she had settled not only Ethel's hash but Stephen Tomlin's, for Tomlin, a charmer whose charm totally failed to work upon Virginia, had nevertheless persuaded her to sit to him for a sculptured head. Posterity may be glad that he did so. No-one else had any cause to be glad. For somehow Virginia managed to forget, in agreeing to the proposal, that the sculptor must inevitably wish to look at his sitter and Virginia should have recollected that one of the things she most disliked in life was being peered at. A very few friends had been allowed to make pictures; some were made by stealth. She didn't like being photographed, but if a painter or a photographer is unwelcome, how much more so a modeller? The man with the camera may be offensive but his offence is swiftly committed. The painter is worse in this respect, but he may, like Lily Briscoe, be supposed to regard you as no more than a part of the composition—an interesting but perhaps not an essential accent. But a sculptor has but one object: yourself—you from in front, you from behind, you from every conceivable angle—and his is a staring, measuring, twisting and turning business, an exhaustive and a remorseless enquiry. Virginia couldn't stand it. His face staring

* "At the end of the year I worked out what the actual expenditure had been and also the total actual combined income, and then the excess of income over expenditure was divided equally between us and became a personal 'hoard', as we called it, which we could spend in any way we liked." Leonard Woolf, *Downhill . . .* p. 142.

into hers appeared ugly, obscene and impertinent. It seemed an insult to her personality, pinning her down, wasting her precious time–insufferable.

In vain Vanessa tried to ease matters by coming with her and making a sketch of her own. Ethel came too. Nothing answered. Tomlin was intolerable. He insisted on making plans to suit his own convenience. Then he was not punctual and she, Virginia, had to plod along dusty streets–a proceeding which if the object had been different she would have found delightful–to reach his studio, and in short she was, as Vanessa said, in "a state of rage and despair," so that after four short sittings–how short time seems to those who paint and how long to those who sit–she struck. Two further sessions were by some prodigy of persuasion vouchsafed, and then she would have no more of it. She was free of the affliction. Poor Tomlin was miserable. The work had to be left unfinished without any hope that it would ever be brought to a satisfactory conclusion.

Now the final irony is this: Stephen Tomlin's best claim to immortality rests upon that bust. It is not flattering. It makes Virginia look older and fiercer than she was, but it has a force, a life, a truth, which his other works (those I have seen) do not possess. Virginia gave him no time to spoil his first brilliant conception. Irritated, despondent, reckless, he pushed his clay into position and was forced to give, while there was still time, the essential structure of her face. Her blank eyes stare as though in blind affronted dismay, but it is far more like than any of the photographs.

So far as Virginia herself was concerned, by August 1931 the business was over. And so she could face the proofs of *The Waves*, Mrs Woolf for lunch, Lady Colefax come to cadge an invitation to Monk's House, and Maynard, foretelling doom, destruction, crisis and war so eloquently that she wondered whether she was not fiddling while Rome burned.

On 19 August she writes, "My proofs did go–went yesterday; and I shall not see them again." And so *The Waves* was committed to the public and she took to her bed with a headache and slept and read *Ivanhoe*, with which she found fault. How could her father have taken the archery scene seriously? And all those unreal heroines? And yet she still liked it better than *Judith Paris* by Hugh Walpole.

It is worth looking for a moment at her reactions to this book, for they provide a test of her sincerity. On 1 September 1931 she noted:

. . . it's a London Museum book. Hugh bouncing with spurious enthusiasm–a collection of keepsakes–bright beads–unrelated. Why? No central feeling anywhere–only "I'm so vital–so big–so creative".

True, it's competent enough, spare in the wording–but words without roots. Yes that's it. All a trivial litter of bright objects to be swept up.

A fortnight later, when the first copies of *The Waves* had been sent out, the first reactions came from Hugh, not directly, and probably in a distorted form. They were unfavourable. Virginia's latest novel, he told his friends, was a disappointment–"all about nothing –exquisitely written, of course." The report gave Virginia a day of acute anguish, which was to turn to acute delight when on the following day John Lehmann wrote an enthusiastic letter. It was the first of many and thereafter she was once more floated on a tide of success. On 4 November Hugh wrote and congratulated her on the second edition. Her sales were almost half those of *Judith Paris*.

I was delighted to see that *The Waves* went into a second edition so quickly. Much of it beat me because I couldn't feel it to be real. Very odd this reality–so personal and unreasonable–but some of it is lovely and I feel that I am wrong about my "reality".

To which she replied:

My dear Hugh, And I'd been meaning to write to you, but unlike you, I never, never do what I mean to. How d'you get the time? . . . Well– I'm very much interested about unreality & *The Waves*–We must discuss it (I mean why do you think *The Waves* unreal, & why was that the very word I was using of *Judith Paris*). "These people aren't *real* to me"–though I do think; & you won't believe it, it had all kinds of qualities I admire & envy. But unreality does take the colour out of a book, of course; at the same time, I don't see that it's a final judgment on either of us–You're real to some–I to others. Who's to decide what reality is? Not dear old Harold, anyhow, whom I've not heard [Harold Nicolson had been broadcasting about both *Judith Paris* and *The Waves*], but if as you say, he sweeps us all into separate schools, one hostile to the other, then he's utterly–damnably wrong, & to teach the public that's the way to read us is a crime & a scandal, & accounts for the imbecility which makes all criticism worthless. Lord– how tired I am of being caged with Aldous, Joyce & Lawrence! Can't we exchange cages for a lark? How horrified all the professors would be!

This seems to me a temperate reply–no doubt it would have been less temperate if it had been written at the time when Hugh's reported chatter had cast her into a tumult of anguished feelings. By November she could write with a growing assurance of success. Presently Morgan Forster wrote to say that he felt he had encountered a classic, something which, I surmise, he would hardly have said about *Judith Paris*. Nevertheless, Hugh had given her deep pain and she found in his words a confirmation of the gossip which had reached her. Her retort omits that which would have been needlessly offensive–her sense of Hugh's posturing; it mentions and exaggerates the good qualities which she notes in her diary and it goes to the root of the matter as she saw it–the fundamental unreality of Hugh's imagined world.

"But Oh the happiness of this life." Thus she wrote on 16 November, and although she goes on to note some minor vexations–differences with Vita and with Leonard, whose own book *After the Deluge*, was not quite the success that they had hoped for, still, "my happiness is too substantial to be tarnished." Ethel was, for the time being, on her best behaviour, Vita was really very agreeable. The General Election had, it was true, been disastrous for Labour and the country was in a condition of economic crisis. In Sussex the Labour Party candidate had disgraced himself by building the ugliest imaginable house on the top of Rodmell Hill–a feat which brought from Leonard the memorable statement: "You have done the impossible–you have ruined the view for everyone else without getting a view for yourself" and led Virginia to declare that she would not vote for him. But none of this counted against Morgan's words, against the solid fact that her extraordinary venture into fiction had succeeded. Yes, that autumn she was happy, although exhausted, and there were more things to write. *Flush* was going well. She meditated a book to be called *The Tree*, and the feminist pamphlet and a second *Common Reader*. But her happiness was to be short.

On 6 December she had agreed, no doubt at Leonard's request, to lead an invalid's life until Christmas–no writing, no parties. On 10 December she did, however, amuse herself by writing a letter to Lytton. She had dreamed of him the night before and in her dream they were both young again and in fits of laughter. She had no news, nothing to say except "when you're in London with the tulips & Waley's white flannels, please come and see your old and attached friend Virginia." During the past few years they had met infrequently. She found him charming when they did meet–mellowed, his eyes twinkling behind his spectacles, altogether benign and at peace with her. *Elizabeth and Essex* she had not liked; she found it a disappointing book. Virginia, though she still felt some envy, could all the same regret this and welcome *Portraits in Miniature*, for in these essays she thought that Lytton dealt with congenial material in the form which exactly suited his pen. When she wrote to him in December 1931 he was ill. By the time that her letter reached Ham Spray his illness had become acute. By Christmas Eve all hope seemed gone. Virginia and Leonard sat over the fire at Monk's House and wept unashamedly. They talked about death, the coming of old age, the loss of friends. Then on Christmas Day a telephone message revived their hopes. Lytton was rather better, and this improvement was maintained; the relief was exquisite. And so, agitated but hopeful, Lytton's state seeming to go up and down, they waited for news, and on 14 January drove down to Ham Spray. The Bear at Hungerford was full of melancholy Stracheys reading detective novels or solving crossword puzzles. Pippa sobbed on Virginia's shoulder: "He is so ill, how can he get better?" The house was full of nurses, very efficient, very orderly; the routine of illness had been well established. Carrington moved about scarcely knowing people. They did not see Lytton, but were told he was pleased at their coming.

A fancy dress party in Vanessa's studio had been planned for 21 January. Should it go on? James Strachey telegraphed "Much better again" and the party took place. But already when the guests were arriving, the noise and laughter beginning, Virginia, Duncan and Vanessa were sobbing quietly in a corner, for they knew now that James's telegram had been wrongly transmitted: "much better" should have read "much weaker"—in fact Lytton had died that afternoon.

Chapter Seven

1932–1934

ON 25 January 1932, Virginia was fifty years old, she had written six novels, she was famous, and Lytton was dead. She felt physically and morally exhausted. She was distressed by the loss of an old friend, and Leonard, whose friendship went further back, was perhaps even more saddened. They both felt, I think, that the world had lost an artist who had never quite found himself, never quite justified the hopes of his Cambridge contemporaries, never written that "supreme" book of which they had believed him capable.

The idea of a biography of Lytton was discussed and, some time later, his sisters–some of them–suggested that Virginia might write "something." But to give any notion of what Lytton had really been like, it was, everyone agreed, necessary to deal frankly with his sexual adventures. At that time this seemed completely impossible. It was taken for granted that no true life could be written and Virginia did not want to write anything else.

Meanwhile the *sequelae* of Lytton's death were causing anxiety and sorrow. As we have seen, Carrington had married Ralph Partridge largely because she could in this way continue to be with Lytton; thereafter she had remained his devoted companion. Before his death she had talked of following him; when it was imminent she had tried to kill herself and now there could be no doubt that she would make a second attempt. Oliver Strachey, dining with the Woolfs, took a very commonsensical view of the matter. If she really wanted to kill herself why should anyone try to stop her? She had a right to dispose of her own life. It might be a good plan for her to wait until the shock of the thing had worn off but then . . . Suicide seemed to him a perfectly sensible act. Why could not the other inhabitants of Ham Spray leave her alone?

This is the kind of view that it is more easy to take when one is not actually in touch with the person who contemplates death. Ralph Partridge, at all events, was determined to save his wife if he could; he believed that it was important that she should see people and not mope alone at Ham Spray. He asked the Woolfs to visit her. And so, one fine cold morning in March, they motored out to Wiltshire and came to that pretty house with its long verandah facing the downs. Carrington opened the door in her little jacket and socks; she wore a twisted necklace; her great blue eyes were pale with anguish. She had not expected them to come, there had been a muddle; she had sent a telegram . . . "But I do everything wrong."

They entered. The house was cold, Lytton's room very neat. She had wanted to keep it just as Lytton had left it, but the Stracheys thought this morbid. She contrived a good lunch for them, brightened a little and even managed to find a laugh or two. After lunch Leonard suggested a walk. She took them to "her grove"; the trees there, she said, had a flower that smelled very sweet in summer. Then she left them; she had some letters to write. Leonard went to do something to the car; Virginia wandered for a time in the garden, and then returned to the sitting-room; presently Carrington found her there, and offered tea. Together she and Virginia went upstairs to Lytton's room and there she broke down and wept in Virginia's arms.

> She sobbed and said she had always been a failure. "There is nothing left for me to do. I did everything for Lytton. But I've failed in everything else. People say he was very selfish to me. But he gave me everything. I was devoted to my father. I hated my mother. Lytton was like a father to me. He taught me everything I know. He read poetry and French to me."

Carrington's intention was clear. Virginia's was not. She, who had twice attempted to kill herself, could neither preach nor lie. She would not, she could not, pretend that there was no sense in what Carrington said.

> I said life seemed to me sometimes hopeless, useless, when I woke in the night and thought of Lytton's death. I held her hands. Her wrists seemed very small. She seemed helpless, deserted, like some small animal left. She was very gentle; sometimes laughing; kissing me; saying Lytton had loved his old friends best. She said he had been silly with young men. But that was only on the top. She had been angry that they had not understood how great he was. I said I had always known that. And she said I made too much of his young friends. . . . And this last year Lytton made up his mind to be middle aged. He was a realist. He faced the fact that Roger [Senhouse] could not be his love. And we were going to Malaga and then he was going to write about Shakespeare. And he was going to write his memoirs, which would take him ten years. It was ironical, his dying, wasn't it. He thought he was getting better. He said things like Lear when he was ill. I wanted to take you to see him the day you came, but I was afraid to. James and

Pippa said one must not run any risk and it might have upset him. " No, of course not " I said. " Roger will take the books of course – he will have to." And what else did we say? There was not much time. We had tea and broken biscuits. She stood by the fireplace. Then we said we must go. She was very quiet and showed no desire for us to stay.

As they were going she produced a little French box.

"James says I mustn't give away Lytton's things. But this is alright. I gave it to him."

She seemed frightened of doing wrong, like a child that has been scolded. At the door she kissed Virginia repeatedly.

"Then you will come and see us next week – or not – just as you like?" "Yes, I will come, or not" she said. And kissed me again and said goodbye. Then she went in.

On the following evening Stephen Tomlin came round to break the news. Early that morning Carrington had shot herself. Even in this she had half failed and she died slowly, in great pain. It was impossible for Virginia not to feel in some measure responsible. It would have been wrong to lie to Carrington; but she might have argued more strongly in favour of life. One may doubt whether any arguments could have deflected Carrington from her purpose.

There had to be an inquest; but the Coroner was a sensible man, and he accepted Carrington's story of an accident. Neither Leonard nor Virginia was called as a witness. They went, as they had already planned, on a short excursion by car to East Anglia, spending nights at Cambridge and at Cromer and with Roger Fry near Ipswich. Virginia noted Carrington's married name, Partridge, on tombstones and over grocers' shops. On 15 April they set off with Roger and his sister Margery Fry for Greece.

Yes, but what can I say about the Parthenon – that my own ghost met me, the girl of 23, with all her life to come. . . .

A lot of things had changed, the country seemed more beautiful than before, the inhabitants seemed nicer, the inns cleaner and of course Greek art was quite different with Roger to talk about it, to draw their attention to Byzantine work, to prevent too whole-hearted an acceptance of classical sculpture, to praise the architecture, to see that nothing of importance was passed over.

"It's all likely to end in bugs, quarrels, playing chess, disputing about expeditions & so on," wrote Virginia to Vanessa and in fact, on the face of it, this did seem a danger, all the more so because

Margery was the kind of female philanthropist whom Virginia tended to admire rather than to like. But it was all right; Margery fell in love with Virginia and told her the entire story of her life which, though melancholy in the extreme, was of course fascinating. And the spectacle of the two Frys, who between them seemed to know everything that could be known about the art, architecture, folklore, fauna, flora, geography, geology and history of Greece, was amusing, as also was their energy which, despite Roger's usual ill-health, was prodigious. Roger's audacity in attempting impossible roads and dealing with unruly mules and muleteers, visiting inaccessible monasteries, climbing mountains and playing continual games of chess with Leonard who, to his vexation, continually won them, was diverting yet admirable. There was even, to Virginia's perception, some charm in the discovery that when Roger with one Demotic Grammar and Leonard with another and Virginia herself with tags from the classical tongue attempted to ask the way, they had purchased two black kids and a bowl of sour milk. It was above all Roger's character, "so humane, so sympathetic, so indomitable," that she appreciated and that made the pleasure of the holiday. For the rest, a postcard to Julian Bell may serve to suggest their activities.

> We have seen vultures, buzzard, eagles, bee eaters, blue thrushes, temples, ruins, statues, Athens, Sparta, Corinth—& are just off to a monastery. So goodbye.

The homecoming was not agreeable. In the Hogarth Press the differences between John Lehmann and Leonard were now such that, after an increasingly contentious summer, it seemed best to bring the arrangement to an end. Then there was a hostile review in *Scrutiny* which made Virginia think that, from now on, she would be under attack. But this does not quite account, nor could she herself account, for the fact that by the end of May she felt "nearer to one of those climaxes of despair that I used to have than at any time these ten years." I think that her health had been bad ever since she reached the concluding passages of *The Waves*; the tragedies of the winter must have been psychologically unhealthy and she needed, not a holiday, but a rest.

The trouble was that she hardly knew how to rest, to rest voluntarily, that is; when a "headache" knocked her down and out and it became too painful to do anything but rest, she would lie on a sofa; she could even be persuaded to do so for a little time after the pain itself had ceased to issue commands; but in general she found it exceedingly hard to be doing nothing. There was always a book, usually a good deal of journalism, numerous letters to write, and a diary to keep. In addition to this, she was by nature physically energetic. The picture of continual illnesses, headaches, exasperation and despair is a true one, but it may suggest another picture of languid and lethargic debility; and this would be false. She was still, at this time, working in the Hogarth Press, often enough parcelling up books. And although this exercise was irregular, her walks—seven, eight or more miles every afternoon leaping over ditches, climbing up hills, negotiating barbed-wire or brambles if she were in the country–continued to be an habitual pleasure whenever she had health enough to undertake them.

During these years, however, her walks from Monk's House became less agreeable to her than her long rambles through London. The reason was simple. The country was being spoilt. All along the valley, it seemed, from Lewes to the sea, villas, dog-racing tracks and other ugly incongruities were creeping into the valley; what its ultimate fate might be was made very clear by the creation of Peacehaven. This had once been a very lovely and wild-looking stretch of downland between Rottingdean and Newhaven. Now the whole sea coast had been made into a kind of holiday slum, a hopelessly ugly agglomeration of mean squat bungalows. But, from Virginia's point of view, there was worse to come. Asham, which they might have regained for a thousand pounds soon after their establishment at Monk's House, was now sold to a cement-making Company and so, bang in the middle of their view from the grassy terrace of Monk's House, bang in the middle of the loveliest stretch of the South Downs and that to which Virginia was nostalgically attached, went tractors, lorries, excavators and scaffolding. Asham itself was blotted out of sight by vast corrugated iron sheds, the valley was coated with toxic white dust, the air with nauseating fumes, the grass became foul, trees died and the hill itself was hollowed out as though it had been a diseased tooth.

Virginia, coming across such evidence of 'progress' on her afternoon walks, was in despair. Writing to Ethel Smyth in January 1932 she uses coarser language than is usual in her letters when she describes the capitalists responsible for these works as "damnable buggers." Duncan and Vanessa, with the usual perversity of painters, found a certain beauty in the new buildings at Asham and Virginia tried, pathetically enough, to share their view; "I intend to see them," she said, "as Greek temples." But it was no good. Maynard's confident belief that the Cement Company was utterly unsound and would certainly go smash even before its buildings were complete (it prospers to this day) was much more comforting and, if it had not been for his assured optimism, the Woolfs, who had often talked of leaving Rodmell, might actually have done so.

"I don't like old ladies who guzzle," said Virginia; she referred to Ethel,* who certainly champed and chawed at her food with some ferocity. It is perhaps worth noting that Virginia was always critical of her friends' behaviour at table. Her sensitivity on this point was perhaps connected with her own phobias about eating, phobias which, when she was ill, could make her starve herself and, at ordinary times, made her always very reluctant to take a second helping of anything. George Duckworth, Julian Bell, Kingsley Martin were all, at various times, severely condemned for eating with too little grace and too much enthusiasm. From this we may perhaps conclude that Virginia's condemnation of Ethel was not wholly rational. Certainly, at this time, Ethel had a real grievance against her friend. For Ethel was still in love with Virginia, and so inevitably made scenes, scenes which Virginia found disgusting, repellent and tedious. In self-defence she chased Ethel away and declared that she would have nothing more to do with her. For a time she *did* break off relations altogether.

Ethel, her woes and her demands, form a *leitmotif* of these years, an important and an exasperating part of Virginia's life. There were crises in July 1932 and again in February 1933 and early in 1934, when Ethel celebrated her 75th year and there was a kind of Smyth Festival with special performances of her compositions and a lunch, at which Sir Thomas Beecham made facetious remarks which reduced Virginia to despair. Her *Mass* was performed before Royalty, and the nobility and gentry were subsequently entertained by Ethel at Lyons' Corner House. This brought on another quarrel. In June 1934 Ethel wrote to Vanessa, "I rather think she's through with me"; but she wasn't. In July Ethel discovered that she owed the Inland Revenue £1,600; she was ruined. Virginia's sympathies were aroused. And so it went on.

For a time Ethel seemed to transfer her affections from Virginia to Vanessa. Vanessa was to do the décor for Ethel's ballet *Fête Galante*.

★ " The reason why Ethel Smyth is so repulsive, tell Nessa, is her table manners. She oozes; she chortles; and she half blew her rather red nose in her table napkin. Then she poured the cream – oh the blackberries were divine – into her beer; and I had rather dine with a dog. But you can tell people they are murderers; you cannot tell them that they eat like hogs. . . . She was however full – after dinner – of vigorous charm; she walked four miles; she sang Brahms; the sheep looked up and were not fed. And we packed her off before midnight." VW/QB, 19 September 1933.

The vicissitudes of that project, detailed in endlessly loquacious letters, were something appalling. And here too Ethel began to feel a sentimental attachment and to resent the fact that her passion was not returned. "You are a little like your sainted sister in some respects," wrote Ethel tartly. This was true; they both liked Ethel in small doses and neither wanted to swallow her whole; but Vanessa could manage her better and was more ready, if necessary, calmly and finally to shut the door in Ethel's face.

To return to 1932: at the beginning of the year Virginia had written her *Letter to a Young Poet*, which arose out of discussions with John Lehmann, and which was published as No. 8 in a series of shilling booklets, *The Hogarth Letters*, in July 1932. The second *Common Reader* made its appearance in October and was reprinted in November. The preparation, revision and correction of this "bunch of articles" was virtually the only writing, save for a little journalism and one or two experimental stories, that she undertook during the first nine months of 1932. She completed it with "no sense of glory; only of drudgery done." *Flush*, which she had started in August 1931, before *The Waves* was published, was taken up again after she had finished work on the *Common Reader*; on 16 September she was at work on the penultimate chapter.

In November 1931 she had written to George Rylands, thanking him for his kind remarks about *The Waves*.

> . . . I'm full of ideas for further books, but they all develop from *The Waves*. Now if *The Waves* had seemed to you a barren and frigid experiment—merely Virginia hanging to a trapeze by her toenails—then I should have felt, Why go on? and as I can't go back, even so far as *Mrs. Dalloway* and *The Lighthouse*, I should have come to an awkward pass, and have probably taken a vow of silence for ever. That's why your encouragement is a draught of champagne in the desert and the caravan bells ring and the dogs bark and I mount—or shall in a few months—my next camel. Not that I mean to begin another of these appalling adventures yet awhile.

A year later she had found her theme; but it does not appear to have developed from *The Waves*. Indeed *The Pargiters* was to be completely different from *The Waves*; it was to be what she called a novel of fact, a narrative, and almost as much of a conventional story as *Night and Day*. It was:

> . . . to take in everything, sex, education, life etc.: and come, with the most powerful and agile leaps, like a chamois, across precipices from 1880 to here and now. That's the notion anyhow, and I have been in

such a haze and dream and intoxication, declaiming phrases, seeing scenes, as I walk up Southampton Row that I can hardly say I have been alive at all, since 10th October.

Everything is running of its own accord into the stream, as with *Orlando*. What has happened of course is that after abstaining from the novel of fact all these years–since 1919–and N[ight] & D[ay] is dead–I find myself infinitely delighting in facts for a change, and in possession of quantities beyond counting: though I feel now and then the tug to vision, but resist it. This is the true line, I am sure, after *The Waves*–the Pargiters–this is what leads naturally on to the next stage– the essay novel.

Monday, December 19th

Yes, today I have written myself to the verge of total extinction. Praised be I can stop and wallow in coolness and downs and let the wheels of my mind–how I beg them to do this–cool and slow and stop altogether. I shall take up *Flush* again, to cool myself. By Heaven, I have written 60,320 words since October 11th. I think this must be far the quickest going of any of my books. . . .

It is impossible to read these words without pain and pity; it is as though one saw Virginia run gaily and swiftly out upon a quick-sand. For, whatever we may think of the final result (*The Pargiters* became *The Years*), it was for her a pitfall, very nearly a death trap. She entered with delight into most of her novels, but never with such lighthearted confidence as now; and never was she to be so thwarted, baffled, anxious and miserable in her writing.

In January 1933 she had to deal with *Flush*. She prided herself on the care that she took in making this trifle fit for the Press, but she was anxious to be rid of it–she wanted to get back to *The Pargiters*. When she did so the book ran without a check until April.

In March 1933 Virginia was offered an Honorary Degree by the University of Manchester; she refused it as she had previously refused to give the Clark lectures at Cambridge.*

The Clark lectures had tempted her considerably and she half

---

* "It is an utterly corrupt society I have just remarked, speaking in the person of Elvira Pargiter, and I will take nothing that it can give me etc. etc.: Now, as Virginia Woolf, I have to write–oh dear me what a bore–to the Vice-Chancellor of Manchester University and say that I refuse to be made a Doctor of Letters. And to Lady Simon, who has been urgent in the matter and asks us to stay. Lord knows how I'm to put Elvira's language into polite journalese. What an odd coincidence!" *AWD*, p. 195, 25 March 1933.

The Clark lectures were offered and refused in February 1932. In March 1939 Virginia refused a Doctorate from the University of Liverpool. *AWD* (*Berg*), 3 March 1939.

regretted it when she had posted her letter to the Master of Trinity; how pleased, she reflected, her father would have been if he could have known that his daughter was to be asked to succeed him. Her friends also felt that she was rather absurd to refuse the Doctorate, but in both cases she felt that one of the dangers of becoming an established writer was that one would come to terms with the academic machine; and she had it in mind to attack that machine in her next book. She was a little caustic about Roger when he became Slade Professor at Cambridge.

Perhaps she still felt something of the old jealousy which had consumed her when she saw her brothers going to Cambridge and herself left behind. Young women were admitted to the campus but they were still unfairly treated and the Universities remained to a large extent a preserve of the other sex. But also she distrusted academic criticism altogether.* During the summer of 1933 she was able to discuss the point with T. S. Eliot. Eliot was at this time painfully disengaging himself from his first marriage and Virginia was the sympathetic auditor (perhaps not always sympathetic for there were moments when she thought that Vivien was being badly treated) of his domestic troubles. By September 1933, however, these were in a fair way to solution and the two authors were able to discuss other questions. Eliot interested her by saying that he was now no longer so sure that there was a science of criticism; the critics had exaggerated the intellectuality and the erudition of his poetry, he found that they got things very wrong. They agreed—or perhaps it might be more true to say that Virginia persuaded him to agree—that the teaching of English in Universities was idiotic. I believe also that she felt, in the case of certain teachers of English, that they showed in their writings so little understanding of the language that they could hardly discuss their betters, the genuine masters of English, without being guilty of arrogance.

If this was the case she was not wholly consistent, for, during that autumn of 1933, she attempted to criticise an art in which she herself had no skill. Sickert was having an exhibition in London and she went to it with Vanessa. She was delighted by what she saw. She had always liked his work—it seemed to her all that painting ought

* To her nephew Julian, when he took a chair of English at Wuhan University, she wrote: "But why teach English? . . . all one can do is to herd books into groups, and then these submissive young, who are far too frightened and callow to have a bone in their backs, swallow it down; and tie it up; and thus we get English Literature into A B C; one, two, three; and lose all sense of what its about." VW to Julian Bell, 1 December 1935.

to be. Vanessa, who was very fond of Sickert, said that Virginia ought to write to the artist and tell him what she thought. In his reply Sickert said: "I have always been a literary painter, thank goodness, like all the decent painters. Do be the first to say so."* Clive gave a dinner-party for them to meet again–a highly successful evening. Fortified by wine and turkey, cigars and brandy, Sickert kissed the ladies' hands, sang a French song, told the story of his life, made jokes about Roger, repeated that he was a literary painter–a romantic–and assured Virginia that she was the only person who understood him.

The result was *Walter Sickert: a Conversation*, a small pamphlet and no doubt a minor work, but interesting in that it shows Virginia adventuring into an unfamiliar field. She was very conscious of her own temerity, was careful to explain her own limitations, but determined nevertheless to advance her own view of painting. What she admired in Sickert was his "literature"–"Not in our time will anyone write a life as Sickert paints it," and she compares him as an artist with Dickens, Balzac, Gissing and the earlier Arnold Bennett. It would have been difficult to choose an approach to the art of painting more completely opposed to that of her sister, and I fancy that she was rather frightened of what Vanessa would say. From Sickert himself she had nothing to fear. When in the following year the pamphlet was published, he turned up at tea-time wearing a green peaked cap, sang a few bawdy songs over his cake, smoked a cigar and exclaimed against the criticism of Clive and Roger. They didn't know a picture from a triangle whereas she, Virginia (kissing her hand), was an angel: her criticism had been the only criticism that had ever been worth having in all his life.

Flush appeared in October 1933. It was, as she had foreseen, a success; but on this occasion she feared success almost as much as she usually feared blame. The critics would like it for reasons which did her no credit; she would be admired as an elegant lady prattler. Judging from the reviews she was not far wrong. Her problem now, she felt, would be how to cope with the kind of popularity that lady prattlers achieve. In spite of which, such is human perversity, I do not believe that she would have welcomed the comments of Ethel Smyth, who wrote to Vanessa saying that it was the kind of book that gave her "the kick screams." One may be fairly sure that this criticism never reached Virginia's ears.

---

* "I would suggest that you *saute pardessus* all paint-box technical twaddle about art which has bored and will always bore everybody stiff." Walter Sickert to VW, n.d.

Biographically *Flush* is interesting, for in a way it is a work of self-revelation. As it is, I imagine, one of the least read of her novels, it may be useful to tell the reader that Flush was Elizabeth Barrett Browning's spaniel, given her by Miss Mitford; he was stolen and Miss Barrett had to retrieve him from a thieves' den in the East End of London; she took Flush with her when she eloped with Browning, and he ended his days in Florence. The narrator is Virginia herself but an attempt is made to describe Wimpole Street, Whitechapel and Italy from a dog's point of view, to create a world of canine smells, fidelities and lusts.

Ottoline, writing to congratulate Virginia, said: "Don't you sometimes *hug* your dog–I did my darling Socrates–hugged him & hugged him–and kissed him a thousand times on his soft cheeks." "No," would have been Virginia's truthful reply to this question. She was brought up with dogs in the home, she had always kept dogs and liked them; but she was not, in the fullest sense of the word, a dog lover.

The original of Flush was a golden cocker spaniel called Pinka which had been given to Virginia by Vita. It became, essentially, Leonard's dog. Neither Leonard nor Virginia ever "hugged it and hugged it." Leonard had a feeling for animals which was, on the surface at all events, extremely unsentimental. He was gruff, abrupt, a systematic disciplinarian, extremely good at seeing that his dogs were obedient, healthy, and happy. Whenever one met Leonard there would be a brief shouting match between him and whatever dog or dogs happened to be there, at the end of which the animals would subside into whining passivity and Leonard would be transformed from a brutal Sergeant-Major into the most civilised of human beings.

But Virginia's attitude was much less understandable. She nearly always had a dog, she took a dog with her when she went for a walk and did, up to a point, control the creature. Sometimes, when talking, she would slowly caress Pinka's nose, thoughtfully stroking it in the wrong direction. She was fascinated by all animals but her affection was odd and remote. She wanted to know what her dog was feeling–but then she wanted to know what everyone was feeling, and perhaps the dogs were no more inscrutable than most humans. *Flush* is not so much a book by a dog lover as a book by someone who would love to be a dog. In all her emotional relationships she pictured herself as an animal; to Vanessa she was a goat or sometimes a monkey, sometimes even a cartload of monkeys–*les singes*; to Violet Dickinson she was half monkey, half bird–Sparroy;

to Leonard she was–surprisingly enough–Mandrill (and he Mongoose); to Vita she was Potto (a cocker spaniel, I think). These animal *personae*, safely removed from human carnality and yet cherished, the recipients indeed of hugs and kisses, were most important to her, but important as the totem figure is to the savage. Her dog was the embodiment of her own spirit, not the pet of an owner. Flush in fact was one of the routes which Virginia used, or at least examined, in order to escape from her own human corporeal existence.

1934 began with the great Ethel festival and a burst of work in which Virginia wrote the air-raid scene in *The Pargiters*. This effort ended with ten days in bed and then, on 15 February, there was a tremendous row with Nelly, who flatly refused to cook dinner so that the Woolfs were driven out raging to a restaurant. Virginia swore that this should be the end. She would dismiss Nelly on 27 March before they went to Rodmell for Easter. Leonard, who was often Nelly's advocate, might protest; but neither should deflect her from her purpose. She had been weak too often; now at last, she told herself, she was absolutely determined. But, as the moment approached, she looked forward to the interview with growing dismay, counting the days before it was due, longing to have it over, unable to concentrate upon her novel. The day came. The interview took place; it was a miserable business but at last it was done and, when they returned to Tavistock Square on 10 April, Nelly was out of the house. Even so she made some efforts to return, until she found another job and the long unhappy association was over at last.

Despite some real affection and sympathy on both sides and despite some acts of true generosity, it had been an uneasy and an agitating relationship. Nelly could bring out the worst in Virginia and when, in her diary, she writes of Nelly in anger Virginia is at her least sympathetic. The relationship, as she knew, was a mischievous one and at times they both made the worst of it.

Henceforth, in London Nelly was replaced by a daily–steady, silent, unselfish Mabel–and in the country by another, and it says something for the personal relationship that they there established, and which lasted for the rest of Virginia's life, that Louie Everest, who came and 'did' for them at Rodmell, was able to risk a fairly exasperating joke on her employer and to be, and know that she would be, forgiven.* Here however tempers were not tried by the

---

* "... another year, I thought well you've had me two or three times, I'm going to have Mrs. Woolf April Fool. Whether she will like me after or not I don't know. But we had a certain lady lived in the village who ran the Women's

difficulty of having a resident. It was this I think that made it so hard to deal with Nelly; she was so much a part of the family. Life without indoor servants, which they had seen as the possible result of their poverty in 1918, was now a sign of their increasing wealth. They were beginning to be able to afford the kind of appliances which made indoor servants unnecessary.

At the end of April they took a fortnight's holiday in Ireland; it was pleasant, though wet and on the whole uneventful. But at Waterville Leonard opened *The Times* and saw George Duckworth's obituary. It was years since Virginia had escaped from George and so she could indulge in some slightly sentimental reminiscences; he had after all been extremely kind to them when they were little. The period of revolt, that time when he stood for the kind of life which they felt must either crush them or be thrown aside, was long past.

To the younger generation, the generation of Virginia's nephews and nieces, George was no more than a name and the 'Georgian' view of life no more a menace than the megatherium. But were they perhaps lacking in something that had been granted to their elders? Were they altogether fortunate in not having had to struggle against Victorian morality? Maynard Keynes said that they lacked a religion. It was, he continued, addressing a dinner party in Clive's flat at 50 Gordon Square, it was a fine thing to fight against, but a still finer thing to be brought up in the Christian tradition. They, the young, would never get so much out of life as their elders. They were trivial and, in their lusts, like dogs. T. S. Eliot agreed from the other side of the table, whereupon Virginia asked him to define his belief in God; as usual he evaded her. And then, as dinner came to an end, Julian came blundering in, and Maynard, reminded of his theme, remarked that the young had no religion save Communism and this was worse than nothing. Moreover, it was founded upon nothing better than a misunderstanding of Ricardo. Given time he would deal thoroughly with the Marxists, and indeed all the other economists, and then there would be no more economic stress.

Institute. Who had a very loud domineering voice. Which frightened the life out of Mrs. Woolf, she couldn't bear the voice of this lady. So I went up to her study and said, this lady was here and could she speak to her about the Women's Institute. So she rushed out of her room, down into her bedroom, combed her hair, made herself look tidy and come and sat in the dining room, and then discovered there was no lady in the dining room. So I was able to get on back at her; she really laughed and laughed about it; but I didn't think she really would." Mrs Louie Mayer, BBC/TV, *Omnibus*, 18 January 1970.

"And then," asked Maynard, "how will you live, Julian, you who have no moral strictness?"

"We miss your morality," Julian admitted. "But I prefer *my* life in many ways."

"The young are too anxious to publish, you publish too soon."

"That's to make our names and make money; we want to chip in before the talk has changed."

"It's because you have no sense of tradition, of continuity. It was different in my day," said Maynard. "I could take 15 years over a book. I wanted to take longer and longer. You write and publish at 18."

Eliot agreed, and so, I imagine, did Virginia. Then the talk wandered to the morals and beliefs of the Jews, to Montagu Norman, Major Douglas and Social Credit. It was all very much Maynard's monologue that evening; he ended by describing the manner in which new Fellows were made at King's. He was, at this time, very much in love with tradition, with the idea of moral stability, with a conservatism which some of his younger friends found increasingly distasteful. For them tradition, conservatism, the respectability of ancient ceremonies, was at best an irrelevance, at worst the cloak for something much more sinister.

In January 1933 Hitler had become ruler of Germany and in April of that year Virginia met Bruno Walter, the conductor. "Our Germany," he exclaimed, "our Germany, which I loved, with our tradition, our culture. We are now a disgrace." But it was not until after the events of 30 June 1934 that Virginia became imaginatively aware of what was happening in Germany. It was then, when General von Schleicher, his wife and others, were dragged out of their beds and slaughtered without the pretence of a trial, without a thought of mercy, that Virginia, like a great many people in this country, felt that Germany was in the hands of thugs, of people without scruples, decency or pity, and she was horrified, all the more so when she read articles in the British press in which the Führer was extolled as a truly great man, a real leader.

For Virginia's juniors, those who were politically conscious, the massacres of 30 June were something completely different. To them it was a matter of hope, almost of rejoicing, that the Nazis should be at each other's throats. When these rogues started to kill each other it seemed as though, for the first time in their lives, they were usefully employed. For us the shock had come earlier, in the first weeks of Hitler's tyranny, or even before that, when the political murders of 1932 showed us, not only what stuff the Nazis were made of, but how the German people, by supporting the murderers, had abandoned the cause of human decency.

But as yet Virginia was not really worried about politics. In 1934 she was much more worried about her novel, which in January had been renamed *Here and Now*. The honeymoon period was coming to an end; there were still moments when, as she put it, she was in "full flood," but such moments were becoming more and more infrequent.

At Rodmell on 27 August she wrote: "I am trying to start the nameless book again; and of course find it grinding, to try to get back into those stiff boots"; on the 30th: "After three days' grind, getting back, I am I think floated again"; on 2 September:

I don't think I have ever been more excited over a book. . . . I wrote like a–forget the word–yesterday; my cheeks burn; my hands tremble. I am doing the scene where Peggy listens to their talking and bursts out. It was this outburst that excited me so. Too much perhaps. I can't make the transition to Elvira's speech easily this morning.

And then came a piece of news that swept everything aside.

Roger died on Sunday. I was walking with Clive on the terrace when Nessa came out. We sat on the seat there for a time. On Monday we went up with Nessa. Ha [Margery Fry] came. Nessa saw Helen [Anrep].* Tomorrow we go up, following some instinct, to the funeral. I feel dazed; very wooden. Women cry, L. says: but I don't know why I cry,–mostly with Nessa. And I'm too stupid to write anything. My head all stiff. I think the poverty of life now is what comes to me; and this blackish veil over everything. Hot weather; a wind blowing. The substance gone out of everything.

* Since 1926 Helen Anrep had been living with Roger Fry as his wife. As Roger put it: "il n'y a que la formule qui manque." See VW, *Roger Fry*, p. 255.

Chapter Eight

1934–1936

They played Bach. Then the coffin moved slowly through the doors. They shut. They played again—Anon, I think; old music. Yes, I liked the wordlessness; Helen [Anrep] looking very young and blue eyed and quiet and happy. That is much to remember her for. I kissed her on the lips in the courtyard. Then Desmond came up: said "Wouldn't it be nice to walk in the garden? Oh we stand on a little island" he said. "But it has been very lovely" I said. For the first time I laid my hand on his shoulder and said "Don't die yet." "Nor you either" he said. "We have had wonderful friends" he said.

ROGER'S death was a more intimate and a more desolating event than the death of Lytton. Lytton was her past, Roger her present. It was, as she said, "a horrid time," and the worst of it was that she had to suffer, not only from her own sense of loss, but from Vanessa's grief.

It was more than twenty years now since the affair with Roger had come to an end; but Vanessa could make a friend of her lover and so, despite some very painful transitional periods, Roger had, bit by bit, come back into the family circle on a new, happier and less romantic footing. He brought his own contribution to the symposium of Bloomsbury, a vintage old and dry, but generous and heart-warming. In his presence people became at once more lively and more serious, livelier because there was something naturally cheerful and ebullient in his nature, more serious because, behind the gaiety, certain things were taken so very much for granted—the need for intellectual honesty, for aesthetic probity, a respect for certain values: tolerance, charity, good humour. Roger had always believed in them, as his friend Lowes Dickinson believed in them, but in a more robust way, and without that kind of weak and whimsical hopelessness which made Lowes Dickinson at once so charming and so exasperating. Roger was altogether more earthy, more sensual, more resilient, and yet, in his way, just as unworldly, just as "pure."

To these qualities of humour and integrity he joined, and it was this that made him so important to Virginia and to Bloomsbury, a gift for friendship. This was surprising in him, for certainly he was not tractable; he could, and did, impose his will upon others; he was capable of spending six hours on end in a picture gallery and of making his friends do likewise, and at the same time he was, in a way, a figure of fun. He was laughed at by his friends for his scientific open-mindedness which verged upon sheer credulity, for his panaceas, for his prophecies of cosmic doom, for his White-Knightly inventions. But neither his tyrannies nor his absurdities put any real strain upon his friends or his friendships. He knew well enough that he was mocked at; he could laugh at his own gullibility—though usually *after* he had been disillusioned—and he could smilingly allow that he might be a dictator, although it made him no less dictatorial. But Roger's genius for friendship could stand a much more severe strain than this. All his life he had wanted to be a painter. The critic, the art historian, the lecturer, were roles forced upon him, disguises which he cast away as soon as he could get back to his easel. He wanted to paint great pictures and—love apart—I should say that the happiest moments of his life were spent in front of a canvas while the unhappiest were those when the picture hung unsold, damned with the faint praise of the critics and the unspoken condemnation of his friends. Virginia, however, dealt neither in unspoken condemnation nor in faint praise; seizing a trowel (an instrument which she would not have employed in literary criticism) she laid on her praise in thick creamy slabs.

So my dear Roger, don't go palming yourself off on me as a broken down failure, because such shifts are utterly unworthy; & I now can't, for very shame, tell you how much I liked—but I know I liked all the wrong things, the colour, the charm, the sentiment, the literary power —your little landscape at Heals.

Or again:

I could trace so many adventures & discoveries in your pictures, apart from their beauty as pictures—& some seemed to me surprising in their beauty—but then as you know I'm a partial & imperfect judge of that. What intrigued me & moved me to deep admiration was the perpetual adventure of your mind from one end of the room to the other. How you have managed to carry on this warfare, always striding ahead, never giving up or lying down & becoming inert & torpid & commonplace like other people, I can't imagine.

Roger was grateful and perhaps it was her praise which led him, half seriously, to express the hope that she might one day be his biographer.

When on 18 November Margery Fry came to tea to discuss the matter with Virginia, this suggestion had already been canvassed, but they were both half inclined to think that a collection of essays written by different hands might be better. Margery should describe his youth, Nathaniel Wedd should write about Roger at Cambridge, Clive and Sickert should describe his later life in London, Desmond, and Virginia herself, his place in Bloomsbury and Julian, Anthony Blunt and Gerald Heard might write about his later years.

This scheme never came to anything, but the idea of a 'Life' persisted. In July 1935 there was a Memorial Exhibition of Roger's paintings at Bristol. Virginia was asked to speak at the opening; she found it a heavy and an unrewarding task, for the Fry family—Roger's daughter and five sisters—did not seem to like what she said. She realised also that, if there were to be a 'Life,' the relations would want to manage everything. And then she asked herself, "Have I the indomitable courage" to start another book? For by now *The Years* had become a nightmare.

The manner in which Virginia finally got committed to this task is not perfectly clear. Helen Anrep was strongly in favour of her writing Roger's biography and took credit for the result. Margery Fry, who was literary executor, seems to have been undecided. Vanessa I think favoured the idea; Ottoline on the other hand was against it and so was Julian Bell. What Leonard advised, or whether at this stage he offered any advice, I do not know. At a later date he expressed the view that Virginia had undertaken a task for which she was not well equipped. ". . . she could deal with facts and arguments on the scale of a full-length book only by writing against the grain, by continually repressing something which was natural and necessary to her peculiar genius." I imagine that most critics would agree. But in addition to the difficulties inherent in the form that she had chosen, Virginia had to tackle problems which were peculiar to this particular subject.

There was a side of Roger's life which needed to be described by an artist or by an art historian and this was a task which might be, perhaps will be, accomplished by some author who can stand away from the passions, prejudices and fashions of our time. This was a study for which Virginia had not, and did not pretend to have, the equipment. The other story that might have been told was the tragic—but at times comic—story of Roger's love affairs. A great part of this story was well known to Virginia. But this she could not make public. "How," she wrote to Vanessa, "how to deal with love so that we're not all blushing?" "I hope you won't mind making us all blush, it won't do any harm," Vanessa bravely replied. But Virginia was born in 1882 and I do not think that she, or anyone else that I can think of born before 1900, could in cold print have set down the tale of a sister's adulterous passion.* But even if she could have brought herself to be perfectly unreserved, the Fry sisters would have been deeply distressed. It was only when Helen Anrep insisted that the truth about her should be told that Virginia was able to deal frankly if briefly with Roger's last love affair.

The effect of these inhibitions was bad for the book. A crucial period of Roger's life was made tremendous by Cézanne and by Vanessa. I doubt whether Virginia could have given the whole of Roger's feelings and of his adversaries' feelings about Cézanne. Vanessa she did understand, and she might have described her love affair with Roger beautifully; but she was prevented from doing so. Thus in the end she was thwarted both by what she knew and by what she did not know; and the life of Roger, which should have been a rest after *The Years*, became a further torment. This, however, is an anticipation.

The last months of 1934 and the beginning of 1935 were made unhappy and constituted a period of what Virginia called "human emptiness," not only because Roger was dead, but also for another reason. On 10 March the Woolfs drove in a snowstorm from Rodmell to Sissinghurst to see Vita. As they took their leave Virginia realised that their passionate friendship was over. There had been no quarrel, no outward sign of coldness, no bitterness, but the love affair – or whatever we are to call it – had for some time been quietly evaporating, and that particular excitement had gone out of her life, leaving a blankness, a dullness.

At about this time Virginia began, as she had anticipated, to suffer from a good deal of hostile criticism. Prince Mirsky and Frank Swinnerton attacked her, the one as a peddler of capitalist narcotics, the other as a clever intellectual snob. They caused pain; but a deeper and a more lasting wound was inflicted by Wyndham Lewis.

Men Without Art was advertised on 11 October 1934 in *The Times Literary Supplement*. Virginia knew at once that she would be attacked, nor was she mistaken. A chapter was devoted to her and she was dismissed as a nonentity – she is "extremely insignificant . . .," she is "taken seriously by no-one any longer today." These criti-

* "If I could have shirked all the relations, I might have said more – but as it is, No, I don't think one can so disregard human feelings: – a reason not to write biographies, – yet if one waits the impression fades." VW to Shena Simon (Lady Simon of Wythenshaw), 25 January 1941.

cisms concern us only in so far as they were a psychological event in her life. She read the chapter on 14 October and for the next two days was completely miserable. She certainly took Wyndham Lewis very seriously; she acknowledged that he made "tremendous and delightful fun" of *Mr Bennett and Mrs Brown*, she considered whether she ought not to attend to and to act upon his strictures; then, having faced her critic, she assured herself that the pain was over. But it was not and, on the next day, 15 October, she opened her heart to Leonard, walking with him in Kensington Gardens, and then again to Ethel Smyth. They were both, in their different ways, kind and comforting and she was grateful to them. On the 16th she again told herself that she was cured. On 2 November a letter by Wyndham Lewis to *The Spectator*, where he had been accused of malice by Stephen Spender, brought all the pain back again.

The disquieting thing about Wyndham Lewis's criticism was not simply that it was clever, ably written and severe, but that it was in a quite special way belligerent. This belligerence showed itself–paradoxically–in passages which can only be described as apprehensive. Lewis was a man with a grievance, he believed that he had been driven to lead "the life of the outlaw." Virginia, so far as I can discover, never referred to him in print; but she might easily be regarded as a representative of that ill-defined and largely imaginary body which, so Lewis imagined, had as its chief object the destruction of Wyndham Lewis. Of this sinister gang he was, it would seem, terrified. Therefore, although willing enough to wound, he was half afraid to strike and, when he did strike, he tried to shirk the responsibility for his words–"I don't say it–others do."

This timorous quality in the criticism of Wyndham Lewis should not have disturbed Virginia but I suspect that, in her more anxious moments, it did. Criticism by stealth is more contemptible, but it is not for that reason less injurious than outright, straightforward condemnation. The idea that she had an enemy who was waiting for his opportunity, a critic who wanted to hurt rather than to argue, to impugn rather than to judge, was I believe a contributory factor in Virginia's almost hysterical attitude to criticism, or, more exactly, to the potentialities of criticism, during the next three years.

Hostile criticism was now to become more and more frequent. She tried to be indifferent to it, she tried to profit by it, and sometimes she tried to answer it with her pen. She failed in all three endeavours. She could never really be indifferent either to praise or to blame (and this I suspect is true of nearly all artists, although it was particularly true in her case); the critics had not very much to offer her that she would or could use, and she was not a good controversialist. Leonard had often to persuade her not to rush impetuously into the correspondence columns of the papers. Criticism was a thing that had to be endured, like headaches and insomnia.

She had a sense at this time that her reputation must decline, nor was it an unreasonable supposition, apart from the fact that she felt deeply apprehensive about the reception of *The Years*. There was the equally important fact that she had reached a position the eminence of which made her an obvious target for those critics who like to take a shy at the Establishment. In writing *Mr Bennett and Mrs Brown* Virginia had seen as her natural antagonists Wells, Bennett and Galsworthy, while her natural allies were (not without some reservations) E. M. Forster, D. H. Lawrence, T. S. Eliot, James Joyce and Lytton Strachey. It was possible, in 1924, to see the party warfare of literature in those terms. Ten years later it was no longer possible. Wells was now the only survivor of the old guard and, of what had been the younger generation, Lawrence was dead, Lytton was dead, E. M. Forster had ceased to write novels and there had been no major work from Joyce since 1922. The English novelists of roughly her own generation were Compton Mackenzie, Aldous Huxley, J. B. Priestley, Hugh Walpole, David Garnett and Rose Macaulay; they none of them seemed to be carrying forward the revolution which, in 1924, she had believed to be imminent. Having lost both her adversaries and her collaborators she stood very much alone. I don't think that this, in itself, worried her. But, as the survivor of a movement that had spent its impetus, she might fairly be regarded as being, in her turn, a reactionary and the natural adversary of the young. To me the wonderful thing is not that she was the object of criticism, but that those criticisms were for the most part so mild and so limited. For her manner of writing was not one to arouse the enthusiasm of young people in the 'thirties. To many she must have appeared as an angular, remote, odd, perhaps rather intimidating figure, a fragile middle-aged poetess, a sexless Sappho and, as the crisis of the decade drew to its terrible conclusion, oddly irrelevant—a distressed gentlewoman caught in a tempest and making little effort either to fight against it or to sail before it. She made far less of an attempt than did Forster to contribute something to the debates of the time, or rather, when she did, it was so idiosyncratic a contribution that it could serve no useful purpose.

This is a picture which requires some qualification, as the following pages will show. But it is true that during these years the temper of literature was changing, or at all events that a large and important contingent of young poets and novelists was calling for a literature that would lead to effective political action.

Here it is perhaps necessary to remind the reader that in 1933 – the year of the publication of *Flush* – Hitler came to power and the Japanese were overrunning Manchuria; in the following year there was what looked like the first stage of a Fascist revolution in France; in 1935 the Italians invaded Abyssinia, in 1936 the Spanish Civil War began, in 1937 the Japanese took Shanghai and Pekin and in 1938 the Nazis annexed first Austria and then the Sudetenland. As the reactionaries went from strength to strength those who opposed them had to consider whether force should be countered by force. Virginia hated violence – she associated it with masculine assertiveness. But were we then to scuttle like frightened spinsters before the Fascist thugs? She belonged, inescapably, to the Victorian world of Empire, Class and Privilege. Her gift was for the pursuit of shadows, for the ghostly whispers of the mind and for Pythian incomprehensibility, when what was needed was the swift and lucid phrase that could reach the ears of unemployed working men or Trades Union officials.

And yet her critics were on the Right rather than on the Left. There were many of the younger writers who knew her personally; through Julian and through John Lehmann she knew Isherwood, Stephen Spender and Day Lewis and her relationship with the anti-Fascist poets was, on the whole, easy, friendly and cordially appreciative. They, knowing her, must also have known that although her prose could never be an effective vehicle for conveying political ideas, her attitude to politics was of a kind that they found sympathetic.

Of course, in a sense, she had been in Left-Wing politics for much longer than they had. But then her attempts to deal with political reality were bewildering, and at times exasperating, both to her and to those who had to collaborate with her. I recall her during these years at the meetings of the Rodmell Labour Party, a small group of which she was, for a time, the Secretary, and I remember my despair, when I was trying to get the party to pass resolutions urging the formation of a United Front – or something equally urgent, vital and important – and Virginia managed to turn the debate in such a way that it developed into an exchange of Rodmell gossip. In this of course she was much nearer to the feelings of the masses, if one may thus describe the six or seven members of the Rodmell Labour Party, than I was. I wanted to talk politics, the masses wanted to talk about the vicar's wife.

After one such meeting Virginia did ask me why, in my opinion, things had gone so very wrong with the world during the past few years. I replied with what I suppose was the stock answer of any young socialist: the world economic crisis, of which the American stock-market crash was the grand symptom, was the prime cause; it had bred unemployment, revolution, counter-revolution, economic and political nationalism, hence Communism, Fascism and war . . . all these things were but the effects of an economic cause. She was frankly amazed, neither agreed nor disagreed, but thought it a very strange explanation. To her, I think, it appeared that the horrible side of the universe, the forces of madness, which were never far from her consciousness, had got the upper hand again. This to her was something largely independent of the political mechanics of the world. The true answer to all this horror and violence lay in an improvement of one's own moral state; somehow one had to banish anger and the unreason that is bred of anger. Thus she tended, unlike Leonard, to be an out-and-out pacifist; she never made this clear in terms of policy, but it was her instinctive reaction, the feminine as opposed to the masculine—"the beastly masculine"—reaction.

When in October 1935 she and Leonard went to the annual Conference of the Labour Party in Brighton, they witnessed the celebrated debate between Ernest Bevin, representing Collective Security, and George Lansbury, the Pacifist leader. Bevin demolished Lansbury. They were both horrified by his methods—"like an enormous frog crushing a smaller frog," said Virginia; but whereas Leonard distinguished carefully between Bevin and his policy (of which on the whole he approved), Virginia thought only of the drama and horror of the occasion.*

In December of that year she attended a gathering of anti-Fascist intellectuals. Such gatherings provided one of the many disheartening political spectacles of the time—the supposed demonstration of unity and solidarity invariably ending in a vicious dispute between Communists and Pacifists. Virginia felt amazed admiration at the competence and loquacity of the politicians, but her chief reaction was dismay that Leonard would have to serve on yet another committee. She had already got into trouble with her more conservative friends by lending her name to a Communist-inspired anti-Fascist exhibition, and with the Left by her unwilling-

---

* She also noted Leonard's political shrewdness. When the meeting rose to its feet and sang "For he's a jolly good fellow" (referring to George Lansbury), Leonard turned to Virginia and said, "Now they can get rid of him." (p. i., QB)

ness to advocate the use of violence. She was persuaded by the charming secretary of the Artists' International Association in 1936 to write an article for the *Daily Worker*, and was then attacked by the Editor of that paper for her lack of Marxism. She could not quite keep out of politics–how could she when she detested Fascism and Fascism was becoming every day more menacing?

But the machinery of politics exasperated and bewildered her. As a celebrity and one whose sympathies were with the Left she was continually approached by politicians who wanted to use her name. She might be, and indeed was, expected to give an immediate reply to a journalist who rang up to know what she thought of the Supreme Court's verdict in the Scottsboro Case;* she was asked, very frequently, to lend her name to organisations which might or might not be controlled by the Communist Party. In such cases she could usually turn to Leonard for advice. But sometimes she herself was persuaded to serve on committees or to be present at conferences. In 1935 we find E. M. Forster trying to induce both her and Leonard to attend a meeting of anti-Fascist intellectuals in Paris.

Oh my dear Virginia, fancy if you and Leonard came after all! What a delight, and what a fortification against communists who will probably try to do the silly! Yes, I am going, so is Aldous, we are trying to persuade Gerald Heard, and there is even a hope of Desmond. Charles Mauron will be there. I do beg you both to come, if only for a day or two. I don't suppose the conference is of any use–things have gone too far. But I have no doubt as to the importance of people like ourselves *inside* the conference. We do represent the last utterances of the civilised.

On this occasion Forster failed. But she could not always resist his appeals, witness a letter to Ethel Smyth written in August 1936.

I was pressed by E. M. Forster to be on a committee–they bothered me to take part–endless correspondence: I refused to budge, finally resigned. But it was harrowing. A woman called Ellis Williams ran amok. Gide and other famous French abused me.

She had to have a problem presented in personal terms before it could capture her imagination. When a fainting girl came down the area steps of 52 Tavistock Square and begged for a glass of water– she had not eaten all day and had been tramping from place to place looking for work–the horrors of unemployment became real to

* I.e.: the finding of the Supreme Court in 1935, when the verdict of an all-white Alabama jury upon two Negroes accused of rape was reversed.

her. Dynastic dramas were of course immediately acceptable; she enjoyed the Abdication crisis of 1936 immensely.

Critics and politicians played a growing part in Virginia's existence; they were both unwelcome interruptions in a life which was principally devoted to the increasingly miserable business of trying to write *The Years*. But there were, of course, other interruptions, pleasant and unpleasant, which should be noted.

In January 1935 *Freshwater*,* a play which she had begun twelve years before and had then entirely rewritten, was acted in Vanessa's studio. The performance was somewhat marred by Clive and his brother Cory, spectators who laughed so loud and so long that the dialogue was practically inaudible.

In the spring of 1935 the Woolfs, taking what had become their annual excursion abroad, decided to drive to Rome, there to meet Vanessa and some of her family. I was astonished then (I am astonished still) that Leonard chose to travel by way of Germany.

It is true that the Woolfs had the privileges of foreigners and that they were armed with a letter from Prince Bismarck at the German Embassy in London; it is also true that, in the event, Mitz, Leonard's marmoset (which bore a striking likeness to the late Dr Goebbels), created so strong and so favourable an impression that the Woolfs never had to use their letter of recommendation. Nevertheless, only a slight misfortune was needed in order to create a frighteningly unpleasant incident. In fact they came very near to such a misfortune when they blundered into a Nazi demonstration near Bonn. Not, I think, that they had to fear arrest or physical brutality; but for Virginia a mere show of hostility, of truculence, or of Aryan arrogance, would have been sufficiently shattering. It was the only time, so far as I know, when Leonard took an unjustifiable risk with Virginia's nerves.

Leaving Germany they drove through the Alps to Verona, and thence by way of Bologna, Florence, Perugia and Spoleto to Rome, where Vanessa awaited them. From Rome they made excursions to

* *Freshwater, a Comedy in Three Acts*, deals with the home life of Virginia's great-aunt Mrs Cameron (the photographer) and her friends on the Isle of Wight. There are two versions: the first was written about 1923 (MH/A 25a); the second (MH/A 25b) is the one performed in 1935. A copy in Vanessa Bell's hand (MH/A 25c) has, in addition, a list of props and the cast which acted at the first and only performance at No. 8 Fitzroy Street. Vanessa Bell took the part of Mrs Cameron, Mr Cameron was played by Leonard Woolf, Lord Tennyson by Julian Bell, Ellen Terry by Angelica Bell, G. F. Watts by Duncan Grant, John Craig by Ann Stephen and Eve Younger doubled the parts of Mary (the maid) and Queen Victoria.

the Villa d'Este and to Monte Cassino and in Rome itself there was not only the Vatican and the Borghese but the rag market to be visited; here Vanessa was in her element, purchasing cheap crockery with splendid avidity and reminding Virginia of other journeys in the days when they were young.

At the *Poste Restante* there was a letter from No. 10 Downing Street; the Prime Minister would be glad to recommend to His Majesty . . . In fact it was the offer of a C.H.* Virginia's comment in her diary was a simple No.

Soon after their return to Tavistock Square Julian Bell arrived in a state of high excitement; he had been offered and had accepted a Chair of English at the University of Wuhan. He would be in China for three years. Virginia regretted his going, yet approved of it; he had been too long in Cambridge and London, now he would grow up and it would be good for him. Her nephews, unlike her nieces, were a cause of exasperation, and exasperation brought a sense of guilt. She never failed to be irritated by Vanessa's silliness, as she thought it, on the subject of her children. Even at a dinner which she and Leonard had purposely arranged to cheer Vanessa up at a time when she was very much saddened by the loss of Roger, the unlucky subject of Julian's poems could produce a wrangle in which the sisters hurt each other when each only wanted to be comforting and comfortable. In the same way, when I had an exhibition of pictures, Virginia was grieved by her inability to find anything to say to Vanessa in praise of them. It was a constant cause of sadness, this friction between the childless and the maternal sister.

On 5 November 1935 Virginia again recorded what she called "a specimen day."† By this she meant not a normal day but rather, I think, a specimen of the distractions, worries, absurdities, that make up one's life. In other passages she complains that she has had no time in which to write her diary because there had been too many "specimen days."

A specimen day, yesterday: a specimen of the year 1935, when we are on the eve of the Duke of Gloucester's wedding: of a general election: of the Fascist revolution in France; and in the thick of the Abyssinian War: it being mild warm November weather: at 2.30 we went to the B.B.C. and listened to some incomparable twaddle soliloquy which the B.B.C. requests me to imitate (a good idea, all the same, if one were free), with all the resources of the B.B.C. behind one: real railway

* Companion of Honour. This order consists of the Sovereign and not more than 65 members.
† Possibly a reference to Walt Whitman.

trains; real orchestras; noises; waves, lions and tigers etc. At 3. we reach Dorland Hall*; a loudspeaker proclaiming the virtues of literature, the Princess Louise having just declared the show open and said that books are our best friends. There we meet old stringy Rose Macaulay, beating about like a cat a-hawking odds and ends; Gerald Duckworth, covered with small prickly red squares, as if he had fallen on his face in a bramble bush; Unwin; and so out: home: at 5.15, telephone: the Baroness Nostitz has arrived early: will we see her now: up she comes; a monolithic broad faced Hindenburg, bulky; can't get in and out of my chair; says Germany is the better for Hitler–so they say: but of course I'm not a politician: I want to get some young man to lecture on English poetry: has a rather hard, dominating impassive eye: slow; stately; must have been a beauty; statuesque; aristocratic; then a card: in comes the Indian: stays till 7.30; was turned out of a carriage in Bengal. "That's an Indian!" the lady cried. "If you don't go, I shall kick you". He jumped out, happily into bushes, as the train was going 15 miles an hour. Liberty, justice. A girl who shot at the Governor. Hatred of the British rule: still, it's better than the Italian. Mussolini is paying their fare and hotel bills in order to get them to side with him. "You are our allies. The British will be turned out." And now Morgan rings up–what about Jules Romains? Will you meet him? [This was politics.] May 1 lunch to discuss the French question. And so we go on. Another specimen day.

But the "specimen day" began at 2.30; by that time the real day, the working day, was done. Usually it was devoted to *The Years*; but there were distractions. In 1935 Virginia was reading and making some preliminary notes for the Roger Fry biography, also she was anxious to write *Three Guineas*–at times very anxious. In April 1935 she had met E. M. Forster on the steps of the London Library, the Committee of which had, he told her, been discussing whether to admit ladies as Committee members. Virginia supposed that she was about to be invited to serve; but she was not. Having raised her expectations Forster proceeded to disappoint them. Ladies were troublesome, ladies were impossible, the Committee wouldn't hear of it. Virginia was furious and her projected book, which at this point was called *On Being Despised*, received a new impetus.

Nevertheless, although she could be distracted, she could not for long be diverted from the task of finishing her novel.

The history of the writing of *The Years* was something like this: it began very joyously in the autumn of 1932 and proceeded without a check until June of the following year (1933). Then Virginia's efforts became more spasmodic. She was "in flood" in June, and

* I.e. the Sunday Times Book Exhibition.

again in July; there were difficulties in August and a rearrangement
of all the first part. "I have stopped inventing the Pargiters," she
writes on 20 August; then she began to rewrite but there was not a
word done in October, and on 29 October she declares, "No, my
head is too tired." But Part 4 was finished in December and 1934
began with another burst of creative energy; she was at work on the
air-raid scene in February, in March she was checked again: Nelly's
dismissal hung over her and there were decorators in the house; and
then in May, despite influenza on her return from Ireland, she
started Part 7 and things went fairly well; in June she lost momentum
and regained it; in July "that particular vein" was worked out, and
she rested, priming herself for a further effort, getting "a little fresh
water" in her well. By August she believed that she could at last see
the end of it and, at the time of Roger's death, she was working on
the last chapter with some excitement and enthusiasm; the last
words of the first draft were written on 30 September 1934.

This was the end of the beginning; so far the progress of *The Years*
had been not unlike that of her other novels, apart from the fact that
the draft was so very long. Too long, she felt, and decided that
drastic cuts must be made. In October, as we have seen, she was
very much unnerved by Wyndham Lewis's criticisms; they reinforced doubts that she already felt about the "nameless book"; for
a moment she thought of recasting it in the light of the criticisms
that had been made of her other work. She rejected the notion, but
still felt thrown out of gear so that she could not work again until
November, when she started the rewriting. By 2 December she was
so far recovered as to think it rather good. But 1935 brought a set-
back. "I am taking a fortnight off fiction. My mind became
knotted" (23 January). "Sara is the real difficulty" (20 February),
and then, a week later, "writing and writing and rewriting the
scene by the Round Pond. . . . It won't be done before August." It
was all revision and like many authors she found this the hardest and
the saddest part of writing. "Since October 16 I have not written
one new sentence but only copied and typed" (6 March). And then
later in that month came more hostile criticism and she makes a
rather grim observation: "The only thing worth doing in this book
is to stick it out." Accordingly she rewrote the entire chapter, and
not without some satisfaction. "I think I have actually done the
Raid this morning" (28 March).

The difficulty of the work was bad for her nerves and her temper.
What Leonard suffered from Ethel Smyth she began to suffer from
Kingsley Martin, who was perpetually telephoning or calling to lay

his problems before Leonard. He, like Ethel, was a gross feeder, he shovelled the grub into his mouth; he was a bore, a time-waster, and how Leonard could endure so much of his company she could not conceive. In April, when he appeared at Monk's House, his visit was followed by a violent headache and *The Years* had to be given up until after their tour of Holland, Germany and Italy. But that excursion did not cure her. On their return they found their dog Pinka had just died; this depressed Leonard. Virginia complained of "the fidgets"—her name, since childhood, for bouts of intense nervous irritability; she found it very hard to get back into the mood for working at her novel: "I wish for death," she exclaims on 5 June. Mrs Woolf had to be entertained, and then Leonard, as though his family were not affliction enough, complained of Mabel's cooking and her carelessness (she had broken the gramophone) and found Mabel herself a poor substitute for Nelly. There was a domestic explosion and Virginia, with the insouciance of a well-blackened kettle, accused Leonard of not knowing how to deal with servants. The dispute did not last long—their disputes never did—but it produced headaches, despite which she finished what she called a "wild retyping" on 15 July, and in August at Rodmell was making a further typed version at the rate of 100 pages a week and clearly felt a resurgence of energy. Eleanor's day was concluded "with the usual pangs and ecstasies" on the 29th. But this effort had to be paid for: on 5 September she had to stop work; "I can't pump up a word"; on the 6th she declares that she will wrap her brain in green dock leaves, just as she had wrapped her legs in them as a child when they were stung by nettles. She had never had such a "hot balloon" in her head as rewriting *The Years*: it was so long, and the pressure so terrific. Towards the end of September she was dealing with Sally and Maggie in the bedroom; it was, she thought, the most difficult writing she had ever undertaken; but still she hoped to finish by Christmas.

Almost every day of their two months at Monk's House had brought some distraction or interruption in terms of visitors or excursions. On 30 September Virginia went with Leonard to the first day of the Labour Party Conference at Brighton and as a result of this she was so preoccupied with ideas for the book which was finally to emerge as *Three Guineas* that she could hardly think of her novel. But in London again she settled down to regular work on it and set herself a target; she would deliver the completed manuscript by February. It had been decided that *The Years* should be put into galley before Leonard was asked to read it. This was something new and the reasons for it are not clear; perhaps she was afraid of what he might say and wanted to defer the evil moment for as long as possible. Certainly she was terribly anxious about the book and it was making her unwell. On 18 December she writes: "I've had a bad morning at *The Years*," and ten days later: ". . . almost extinct, like a charwoman's duster; that is my brain; what with the last revision of the last pages of *The Years*." Two days later: ". . . it's no go. I can't write a word: too much headache" (30 December). For three days she lay still and tried to vegetate. "My head," she observed on 4 January "is still all nerves; and one false move means racing despair."

The *Life* of Roger Fry was now beginning to become a counter-attraction; she longed to be at it and to abandon this wearing and wearying work of fiction. Already she had read a great many of Roger's letters. In December she had tackled his aesthetic theories. She determined that she would make herself work at *The Years* until midday each day and then relax with the biography. One morning she caught herself cheating: she had contrived to read 11 as 12 on her watch and had stolen an hour from the novel. A few days later she re-read what she had written and was appalled: "Seldom have I been more completely miserable," she wrote; it was feeble twaddle. But there seemed nothing for it: she went on working and she went on getting headaches and on 10 March, 132 pages went to the printer.

Then, for a few days, things seemed to go rather better. But March was a bad month. Hitler was on the Rhine and, suddenly, Virginia recognised that the nightmare of war had returned. The growing international crisis aggravated her own private worries and they were now acute. Her diary records violent alternations of feeling concerning the value of her novel. On 18 March she believed that *The Years* might be very good, on the 19th it seemed hopelessly bad, on the 20th she regained courage, on the 21st she lost it, and so on. Never had she worked so hard at a book and never, since the days when she was finishing *The Voyage Out* and slipping fast towards madness, had she experienced such acute despair on re-reading what she had written. On 24 March she realised, as she was walking in the Strand, that she had begun to talk to herself aloud. She became increasingly alarmed by her own state but managed never-theless to totter on; she rewrote the passage dealing with Eleanor in Oxford Street for the twentieth time on 29 March and on 8 April posted the last batch of typescript to the printer from Rodmell.

Now will come the season of depression, after congestion, suffocation. . . . The horror is that tomorrow, after this one windy day of respite—

oh the cold north wind that has blown ravaging daily since we came, but I've had no ears, eyes, or nose: only making my quick transits from house to room, often in despair–after this one day's respite, I say, I must begin at the beginning and go through 600 pages of cold proof. Why, oh why? Never again, never again . . .

Although Leonard was not to read the novel in manuscript, he read some of the galley proofs as they came from the printer, and, without at all committing himself, he gave Virginia the impression that he was disappointed. Nor was this an entirely false impression: Leonard read enough to have his doubts; he was seriously alarmed by Virginia's condition. "It's terrible about Virginia," wrote Duncan to Vanessa. "It's much better to put the book away. But I wonder why Leonard thinks it may not be so good." Virginia's own doubts and the doubts that she divined in Leonard were enough to bring her to the verge of collapse. All her novels were a cause of anxiety and depression, but this one was by its very nature particularly shattering to her nerves. She had been content, and the critics had been content, with *Jacob's Room*; *Mrs Dalloway* had been the logical outcome of that achievement and, having written *Mrs Dalloway*, she could adventure in the same direction: *To the Lighthouse* and *The Waves* followed naturally, each novel consolidating the ground for its successor. She had known where she was going and she became increasingly certain, as did her public, that she had taken the right path.

But *The Years* was something different, a step back, or at least a step in another direction. It could easily be a wrong direction–a *cul-de-sac*–and if it were, then her friends would be saddened and her enemies–she had recently become well aware that she had enemies–would rejoice. The old nightmare that had visited her when she finished *The Voyage Out*, the nightmare of the jeering crowd, returned. And so, faced by six hundred pages of cold proof, fearful of Leonard's judgement, tortured by repeated and incapacitating headaches, she felt madness coming upon her.

Leonard took her to Cornwall, and as usual Cornwall did her some good. But when she returned to London she was ordered by her doctor to rest at Monk's House. For two months her diary was left untouched. She lost half a stone in weight. A letter to Ethel Smyth written at the end of this time gives a notion of what she was suffering:

. . . never trust a letter of mine not to exaggerate that's written after a night lying awake looking at a bottle of chloral & saying No, no no, you shall not take it. It's odd how sleeplessness, even of a modified kind, has the power to frighten me. It's connected I think with those awful times when I couldn't control myself.

This was written on 4 June 1936; a week later she wrote in her diary:

> . . . at last after two months dismal and worse, almost catastrophic illness–never been so near the precipice to my own feeling since 1913–I'm again on top.

But it was scarcely true. Very slowly, very painfully, she set about the task of correcting her proofs. She had to take a great deal of rest, and was continually obliged to stop–the pain in her head, her feelings of complete despair and failure–were too intense. Writing again to Ethel she said: "I have to consider the appalling nuisance that I am to Leonard–angel that he is." Leonard's angelic qualities were soon to be tested. For at length, on the 2nd of November, after pains and difficulties which it would be otiose to record, the proofs were all corrected and handed to him for inspection. Virginia herself had made up her mind, or at least she thought she had. She had re-read *The Years* and concluded that it was impossibly bad. The proofs would have to be destroyed; it was throwing away two or three hundred pounds, and four years of her life had been wasted. But it was better, in a way it was a relief, to face the situation frankly. All this she said to Leonard, who answered that she might perhaps be wrong; he would read it and tell her what he thought.

Leonard was not able to start his reading until late in the day. After a round of weary trivialities and excursions they came home in the evening and Leonard began to read. He read in silence. Leonard's silences could be pretty frightening and certainly Virginia was frightened; as he read on she fell into a kind of feverish doze, a sort of miserable half-sleep. Meanwhile Leonard was feeling both disappointed and relieved. The book was a failure–but it was not so disastrous a failure as Virginia supposed. It would therefore be possible to tell a lie; if he told her the truth he had very little doubt that she would kill herself.

Suddenly he put down the proof and said, "I think it's extraordinarily good."

Chapter Nine

November 1936–September 1939

ON 24 November 1936 Virginia noted in her diary:

> . . . I've been on the whole vigorous and cheerful since the wonderful revelation of L[eonard]'s that night. Now I woke from death–or non being–to life! What an incredible night–what a weight rolled off!

But although Leonard's duplicity had succeeded in its main purpose, Virginia needed more reassurance than he could give; she had been severely shaken; nor were her ills to be ascribed simply to her novel and the state of mind that her novel engendered. She suffered from swollen veins, a sense of falling, a feeling that the blood was not reaching her head, and a tendency, when she was alone, to fall into a sort of trance or coma, symptoms which she attributed, no doubt correctly, to the change of life.

She welcomed distractions now; was glad that she had Lord Robert Cecil to tea, glad to be lunching with Mme de Polignac and Nadia Boulanger, glad of the company of Ethel Smyth, of Dorothy Wellesley and of older friends, glad of the Abdication crisis with all its picture-book absurdities, glad in fact of anything which could make her forget that she had, with her own hands, lit a fuse which would burn steadily for the next few months and explode a charge beneath her feet when *The Years* was thrown upon the world. Under the circumstances, work and society might both be used as opiates, and so she saw a great many people and returned to *Three Guineas*. Whatever else may be said for or against that work it was certainly therapeutic; she had always to be writing something; but *this* writing induced none of those aesthetic miseries which always accompanied her novels. It enabled her to let off steam, to hit back at what seemed to her the tyrannous hypocrisy of men.

The New Year opened with misfortunes. Stephen Tomlin died early in January, and two weeks later Miss West, one of the employees of the Hogarth Press. Both these deaths left Virginia with a feeling of guilt–she felt now that she had been unreasonable in the matter of Tomlin's sculpture, and recalled his good qualities; she felt also that she should have been more sociable, more accessible, to the workers in the Press. But a far more serious disaster threatened when Leonard was taken ill at the beginning of February 1937. It seemed to be a serious liver complaint, or diabetes, or perhaps prostate–the doctors didn't know what. Leonard himself remained calm, took to his bed, lived upon rice pudding and continued, as always, to work very hard at politics, journalism and the business of the Press. But it was not so easy for Virginia to remain calm; if Leonard were in hospital, or worse, she would be left alone to face the crisis which now lay hardly more than a month ahead. So that when, on 12 February, they drove off together to Rodmell with a complete medical pardon, it was with a sense of relief, of sheer overflowing joy, such as she does not often record during these years. And three days later she noticed with complacency that 38 pages of *Three Guineas* were now written.

Saturday, February 20th
I turn my eyes away from the Press as I go upstairs, because there are all the review copies of *The Years* packed and packing. They go out next week: this is my last week-end of comparative peace. What do I anticipate with such clammy coldness? I think chiefly that my friends won't mention it; will turn the conversation rather awkwardly. I think I anticipate considerable lukewarmness among the friendly re-viewers–respectful tepidity; and a whoop of Red Indian delight from the Grigs who will joyfully and loudly announce that this is the long-drawn twaddle of a prim prudish bourgeois mind, and say that now no one can take Mrs. W. seriously again. But violence I shan't so much mind. What I think I shall mind most is the awkwardness when I go, say to Tilton or Charleston, and they don't know what to say. And since we shan't get away till June I must expect a very full exposure to this damp firework atmosphere. They will say it's a tired book; a last effort. . . . Well, now that I've written that down I feel that even so I can exist in that shadow. That is if I keep hard at work. . . .

Monday, March 1st
I wish I could write out my sensations at this moment. They are so peculiar and so unpleasant. Partly T[ime]. of L[ife]. I wonder? A physical feeling as if I were drumming slightly in the veins: very cold: impotent: and terrified. As if I were exposed on a high ledge in full light. Very lonely. L. out to lunch. Nessa has Quentin, don't want me. Very useless. No atmosphere round me. No words. Very apprehensive. As if something cold and horrible–a roar of laughter at my expense were about to happen. And I am powerless to ward it off; I have no protection. And this anxiety and nothingness surround me with a vacuum. It affects the thighs chiefly. And I want to burst into tears,

but have nothing to cry for. Then a great restlessness seizes me. I think I could walk it off–walk and walk till I am asleep. But I begin to dislike that sudden drugged sleep. And I cannot unfurl my mind and apply it calmly and unconsciously to a book. And my own little scraps look dried up and derelict. And I know that I must go on doing this dance on hot bricks till I die. This is a little superficial I admit. For I can burrow under and look at myself displayed in this ridiculous way and feel complete submarine calm: a kind of calm moreover which is strong enough to lift the entire load: I can get that at moments; but the exposed moments are terrifying. I looked at my eyes in the glass once and saw them positively terrified. It's the 15th March approaching I suppose–the dazzle of that head lamp on my poor little rabbit's body which keeps it dazed in the middle of the road. (I like that phrase. That gives me confidence.)

Tuesday, March 2nd
I'm going to be beaten, I'm going to be laughed at, I'm going to be held up to scorn and ridicule–I found myself saying those words just now. Yet I've been absorbed all the morning in the autobiography part of *Three Guineas*. And the absorption is genuine: and my great defence against the cold madness that overcame me last night. Why did it suddenly point itself like a rain cloud and discharge all its cold water? Because I was switched off doing Pictures in the morning: and then at the play★, I suddenly thought the Book Society has not even recommended *The Years*. That's true; but the B.S. is not an infallible guide. Anyhow these days of waiting must be a dull cold torture. I shall be happy enough this time next month I've no doubt. Meanwhile, suffer me now and again to write out my horror, this sudden cold madness, here. It is partly T. of L. I think still. And it won't be anything like so bad in action as in prospect. The worst will be that the book will be treated with tepid politeness, as an effusive diluted tired book. All my other books have stirred up strife; this one will sink slowly and heavily. But when that's said, need I fear more? I may get praise from some people. Indeed I think there must be some 'seriousness' in it. And I can feel a little proud that I have faced the music; that we have sold 5,000 before publication: that we shall get some money; that I'm doing my share, and not merely subsiding into terrified silence. Also my own psychology interests me. I intend to keep full notes of my ups and downs for my private information. And thus objectified, the pain and shame become at once much less. And I have proved to my own conviction that I can write with fury, with rapture, with absorption still.

On the morning of Friday, 12 March, Leonard brought *The Times Literary Supplement* to Virginia as she lay in bed. It carried a

★ *Le Misanthrope.*

favourable review; and so, later in the day, did *Time and Tide*; on Sunday the *Observer* added two columns of praise; it became obvious that *The Years* was a success, so far as the newspapers were concerned at all events. Virginia's old friends were less enthusiastic; Maynard, so far as I know, was the only one of them to give his unqualified approval. But Virginia's fears had been so intense, the public acclaim was so great, the triumph of the book, in terms of copies sold, was so emphatic that she could feel little save relief. There were some unfavourable notices to be sure; but they were nothing to what she had expected.

The success of *The Years* became news to such an extent that the *New York Times* sent a journalist to get personal details; he rang up and was told that he could look at the outside of 52 Tavistock Square if he chose. But he was not to be denied. He appeared at Monk's House in a Daimler and Virginia found that he had walked into her sitting-room and was coolly taking notes. She fled unobserved, and presently Leonard managed to get rid of him. Virginia was incensed by such behaviour, as I suppose anyone might be. But her reaction was odd. She burst into an almost hysterical outburst of half-rhymed prose, rather like a parody of Joyce.*

The Woolfs had arranged to take a holiday early in May; but before leaving for France Virginia had the satisfaction of accomplishing two pieces of business. On 29 April she broadcast. It was not her only broadcast but it is of interest as it was the only one to be recorded; and it seems worth noting, for the benefit of posterity, that this record is a very poor one. Her voice is deprived of depth and resonance; it seems altogether too fast and too flat; it is barely recognisable. Her speaking voice was in fact beautiful–though not so beautiful as Vanessa's–and it is sad that it should not have been immortalised in a more satisfactory manner.

On the day of her broadcast, while Leonard was checking the stock in Virginia's studio, the Woolfs once again discussed the question of the Hogarth Press and resolved that they must either give it up altogether or radically change its organisation. It was by no means the first time that they had decided this; but now, they were in earnest. The little hobby, involving a hand press and a few pounds of type, had become a considerable business. But for Virginia it was inconvenient and worse than inconvenient. It kept her in London when she should have been in the country; it obliged her to read manuscripts when she should have been writing them. It was a worry, a distraction, it had been a source of endless disputes

* See Appendix B.

between Leonard and the young men whom he had brought in as apprentice managers, and, because it was emotionally important to him, it was a source of agitation to her.

In October 1937 a solution presented itself:

> . . . suddenly L. developed the idea of making the young Brainies take the Press as a co-operative company (John [Lehmann]: Isherwood: Auden: Stephen [Spender]). All are bubbling with discontent and ideas. All want a focus: a manager: a mouthpiece: a common voice. Would like L[ehmann] to manage it. Couldn't we sell and creep out?

Only John Lehmann was sufficiently interested in the possibilities of the Hogarth Press to consider buying them out altogether. But by this time it was so large a concern that he could afford only fifty per cent of the business. He bought out Virginia. It was not a very good arrangement–indeed it had all the disadvantages of the old one, with the added drawback that Leonard and his new partner were bound by a commercial marriage from which neither could easily escape. "There were," writes John Lehmann, "checks and clashes . . . though Virginia's presence helped to cool our fevers and bring us back to the understanding that really underlay our differences." But in April 1937 these plans and these mistakes were still in the future, and Virginia could take her holiday with the comforting assurance that the burden of the Press was to be lifted off her back and that *The Years* had, after all, not been a total disaster.

On the other hand there were still abundant causes for unhappiness. Janet Case was ill; she had taught Virginia Greek and was one of the few people who had known her intimately during the opening years of the century; she had remained a steadfast friend. Now it was clear that she was dying. "No one," wrote Virginia to Margaret Llewelyn Davies, "not Leonard even, knows how much I have to thank Janet for." And now Virginia sent her letters, visited her, and at last, when she died in June 1937, wrote her obituary for *The Times*. When the Woolfs were in France in May, news came that Maynard Keynes was desperately ill, and they drove through the Dordogne expecting, in every newspaper, to read that he was dead. He recovered, thanks largely to Lydia's care, but there was another calamity in preparation, one which was, in a way, more dreadful.

Julian Bell had written from China late in 1936 to say that he was coming home in the Spring. His main object was to take an active part in politics, and soon it appeared that he intended to go to Spain to fight for the Republic. Virginia, as soon as she became aware of this, wrote begging him to remain where he was; but in vain.

From this time Vanessa's happiness was at an end. The spectacle of her dumb despair added to the horror of those weeks in the Spring of 1937 when Virginia was preparing herself as best she might for the publication of *The Years*. She certainly felt some anger against her nephew; she felt that he must know what torture he was inflicting, and it was very hard for her to sympathise with the emotions of a young man who felt that he could not leave other people to do his fighting for him; still less could she sympathise with the excited interest of one who saw in warfare itself an art form to be enjoyed for its own sake. To her, therefore, Julian's attitude seemed quite incomprehensible.

Things were made worse by the fact that Julian allowed himself to be deflected a little from his purpose. His first idea, that he would leave the boat at Marseilles and go straight to Spain, was abandoned. He returned to England in March and other political occupations, suggested by Leonard, were proposed as substitutes and not altogether rejected. Nevertheless, when he came home, it was at once clear to Virginia that something had happened to him. He had grown up. There was a new authority, a new tension in his manner. Presently he declared that he must go to Spain, if not as a soldier, then as an ambulance driver. For Vanessa it was as though a small window of hope were shuttered and bolted; she continued, in a sense, to enjoy Julian's company–now he was her dearest child– though with an intolerably aching heart. Virginia saw and understood everything and could do nothing about it; like Vanessa, she was convinced that if he did go to Spain he would not return.

They were right: he left for Spain on 7 June; he was killed on 18 July. The matter concerns us only in as much as it concerned Virginia. She was appalled by her own loss; but it was Vanessa's affliction that hurt her most. Virginia, being in London, was of necessity a witness of her sister's first shocking paroxysms of grief. Thereafter she was a daily visitor at Vanessa's bedside, giving what consolation she could, trying with every device of her imagination to make Vanessa's existence bearable.

Discussing Julian's action with Leonard's friend W. A. Robson, Virginia could allow that "there is a kind of grandeur . . . which somehow now & then consoles one. Only to see what she has to suffer makes one doubt if anything in the world is worth it." The spectacle of this daily renewed torture was something that might shake the reason and the nerves of anyone, especially of Virginia. But like Thoby's death thirty years earlier it was a challenge to which she rose. She was hardly aware of how well she did and it was a surprise to her when she discovered–at a later date–that while Vanessa lay in bed in what she herself called "an unreal state," it seemed to her that Virginia's voice was the only thing that kept life from coming to an end.

Throughout August and September Vanessa was an invalid. Only very slowly was she able to return to something like normal life and to paint a little. "I shall be cheerful, but I shall never be happy again," she told Virginia. The Woolfs drove her down to Charleston late in July and themselves moved to Monk's House so that Virginia might see her daily: "the only point in the day," as Vanessa said, "that one could want to come." Thus Virginia continued to be the witness of a misery that she could not cure. She had to prevent herself from thinking about it too much. Any day when she could not get to Charleston she wrote, and Vanessa, receiving these notes, would sometimes remark with a wintry little smile, "Another love letter from Virginia," and went on to say sadly that she found it difficult to respond to Virginia's affection: "When she is demonstrative I always shrink away." Not that Virginia's affection was unimportant–far from it. Virginia had helped her more than she could say; but she was unable to express her gratitude to Virginia herself. She had to write to Vita who, as Vanessa knew, would see that her message reached its destination.

Seven months later Vanessa did manage to be rather more explicit: Virginia, remembering that Julian's birthday fell on 4 February, wrote a line of affection. Vanessa replied: "I couldn't get on at all if it weren't for you," and went on to regret that she was such an emotional wet blanket.

Virginia, at the time of Julian's death, had been getting on very well with *Three Guineas*; now for some weeks she found this work impossible and instead wrote an account of her nephew and of their last meetings.* Later on, when she returned to her book during the autumn, she found that it became in a large measure a kind of argument with Julian, or rather with what she supposed to be Julian's point of view.

That autumn *The Years*, having sold very well in England, became a best-seller in the United States and for the first time she found herself really wealthy. As she observed, in October, "We have the materials for happiness, but no happiness." She had but two consolations: the continued easy progress of *Three Guineas*, and Leonard. In October she felt a sudden impulse to take a holiday in Paris. She looked up trains, she asked Vanessa about hotels. Then Leonard

* See Appendix C.

said that he didn't want to go and she discovered, to her enormous satisfaction, that if he didn't come with her it wasn't worth going. It was like falling in love again and the pleasure was exquisite. But even the joy which derived from a solid and happy marriage had its Janus head. Early in 1938 Leonard had a return of the malady which had so alarmed Virginia a year before. The scare on this occasion was greater than before, and lasted longer, although it brought the same happy conclusion. Virginia was impatient with the doctors, and Helen Anrep, who was seeing a good deal of her (for now the *Life* of Roger was beginning in earnest), was touched by this concern and by her evident pride in doing things for Leonard.

This evil brought another in its train. Vanessa, who had been genuinely and unaffectedly distressed when Leonard seemed dangerously ill, grew bored and impatient with the description of his symptoms when once he was out of danger; nor, I think, did she altogether conceal her impatience. She was in fact profoundly irritated by Leonard at this time and throughout 1938, for in the preparation of a memorial volume* devoted to Julian she was continually encountering Leonard's not unreasonable caution concerning the work that he was to publish, and his dislike of what he rather impatiently called "Vanessa's necrophily." In fact her anxiety that Julian's genius should be recognised, and the Woolfs' scepticism concerning that genius, was even more likely to breed quarrels after his death than they had been during his lifetime. To make matters more difficult, the inevitable administrative disputes with John Lehmann over the Press were now beginning. Some of these disputes were concerned with the memorial volume and Vanessa tended to take John's side.

Three Guineas was published in June 1938. It is the product of a very odd mind and, I think, of a very odd state of mind.† It was intended as a continuation of *A Room of One's Own*, but it was written in a far less persuasive, a far less playful mood. It was a protest against oppression, a genuine protest denouncing real evils and, to the converted, Virginia did not preach in vain. A great many women wrote to express their enthusiastic approval; but her close

---

* *Julian Bell. Essays, Poems and Letters.* Edited by Quentin Bell, with contributions by J. M. Keynes, David Garnett, Charles Mauron, C. Day Lewis and E. M. Forster. The Hogarth Press, 1938.

† ". . . the book which was like a spine to me all last summer; upheld me in the horror of last August: and whirled me like a top miles upon miles over the downs. How can it all have petered out into diluted drivel? But it remains, morally, a spine: the thing I wished to say, though futile." *AWD (Berg)*, 12 March 1938.

friends were silent, or if not silent, critical. Vita did not like it, and Maynard Keynes was both angry and contemptuous; it was, he declared, a silly argument and not very well written. What really seemed wrong with the book–and I am speaking here of my own reactions at the time–was the attempt to involve a discussion of women's rights with the far more agonising and immediate question of what we were to do in order to meet the ever-growing menace of Fascism and war. The connection between the two questions seemed tenuous and the positive suggestions wholly inadequate.

The book was pretty severely attacked; but on the whole Virginia does not seem to have minded very much. There was, however, one critic of whom she was obliged to take notice, for she was a woman and a very eloquent woman. Her name was Agnes Smith and she lived near Huddersfield. At the time of the publication of *Three Guineas* she was unemployed. In a long, fluent and forceful letter she objected that Virginia had said nothing about working women. Of what use was it to suggest that women should refuse to manufacture arms when they were only too glad to have the opportunity to manufacture anything? She herself was living on a dole of 15s. a week, and she described how when her nephew, a small child, cried for an extra piece of cake, and got it, it had meant that she herself had nothing more to eat for the rest of the day. From Agnes Smith's next letter it is clear Virginia replied that *Three Guineas* had been explicitly addressed to women in a more fortunate social position; but the tone of that letter must also have encouraged her correspondent to write again and, although I think that they never met, they continued to write to each other, at intervals, until the end of Virginia's life.

But the true criticism of *Three Guineas* came from events; for the events of 1938 did not turn upon the Rights of Women but upon the Rights of Nations. In March, when Hitler invaded Austria, Virginia had written in her diary: "When the tiger . . . has digested his dinner he will pounce again." It was indeed becoming difficult to think of anything save the growing menace of war. *Roger Fry* was not a very potent diversion.

In April, however, she was struck by the idea of a book about England and English literature to be called, perhaps, *Poyntzet Hall*. In June, after the publication of *Three Guineas*, the Woolfs took a holiday in Scotland. Virginia wrote to Vanessa:

> Well, here we are in Skye, & it feels like the South Seas–completely remote, surrounded by sea, people speaking Gaelic, no railways, no London papers, hardly any inhabitants. Believe it or not, it is (in its

way, as people say) so far as I can judge on a level with Italy, Greece or Provence. No one in Fitzroy Street will believe this; & descriptions are your abhorrence–further the room is pullulating & popping with Edinburgh tourists, one of whom owns spaniels, like Sally [her dog], but "all mine are gun trained, the only thing they won't carry being hares"–so I can't run on, did you wish it. Only–well, in Duncan's highlands, the colours in a perfectly still deep blue lake of green & purple trees reflected in the middle of the water which was enclosed with green reeds & yellow flags, & the whole sky & a purple hill–well, enough. One should be a painter. As a writer, I feel the beauty, which is almost entirely colour, very subtle, very changeable, running over my pen, as if you poured a large jug of champagne over a hairpin. I must here tender my congratulations to Duncan upon being a Grant. We've driven round the island today, seen Dungevan [sic], encountered the children of the 27th Chieftain, nice red headed brats: the Castle door being open I walked in; they very politely told me the Castle was shut to visitors, but I could see the gardens. Here I found a gamekeepers larder with the tails of two wild cats. Eagles are said to abound & often carry off sheep: sheep & Skye Terriers are the only industries; the old women live in round huts exactly the shape of skye terriers; & you can count all the natives on 20 feet: but they are very rapacious in the towns, & its no use trying to buy anything, as the price, even of Sally's meat, is at least 6 times higher than in our honest land. All the same, the Scotch are great charmers, & sing through their noses like musical tea kettles. The only local gossip I've collected for you is about your Mr Hambro's wife–the one who was drowned in Loch Ness. We met a charming Irish couple in an Inn, who were in touch, through friends, with the Monster. They had seen him. He is like several broken telegraph posts & swims at immense speed. He has no head. He is constantly seen. Well, after Mrs Hambro was drowned, the Insurance Company sent divers after her, as she was wearing 30,000 pounds of pearls on her head. They dived & came to the mouth of a vast cavern, from which hot water poured; & the current was so strong, & the horror they felt so great, they refused to go further, being convinced the Monster lived there, in a hollow under the hill. In short, Mrs Hambro was swallowed. No drowned body is ever recovered & now the natives refuse to boat or to bathe. That is all the local gossip. And I will NOT describe the colour.

They returned at the beginning of July to find that *Three Guineas* was selling very well, to the "fearful niggling drudgery" of the biography, and to a different kind of monster.

They were at Rodmell in September when war began to seem inevitable. Kingsley Martin, who, so it appeared to Virginia, sought Leonard in every crisis, much as a timid bothering child might come running to its Nanny, telephoned on the 26th in a state of panic and implored Leonard to return to London. The Woolfs drove up together. It was raining; men were digging trenches. Kingsley was melodramatic and tedious; it never became clear why he wanted Leonard; the telephone rang continually.

Virginia escaped to the London Library to look up *The Times* of 1910 on the first Post-Impressionist exhibition. There, in the basement, an old man came gently dusting.

"They're telling us to try on our masks, Madam."

"Have you got yours?"

"No, not yet."

"And shall we have war?"

"I fear so, but I still hope not. I live out at Putney. Oh they've laid in sandbags; the books will be moved; but if a bomb strikes the house . . . May I dust under your chair?"

She went to the National Gallery; someone was lecturing to quite a large audience on Watteau. Then she returned to Tavistock Square; plans had to be made to evacuate the Press. They drove back through torrential rain to Monk's House. It seemed curiously sane and beautiful after London. At 10.30 that night the local Air Raid Warden brought their gas masks.

On 28 September they expected a declaration of war; instead they heard that Mr Chamberlain was on his way to Munich; the 'Settlement' was made on the following day. "We have peace without honour for six months," said Leonard, and the postman expressed the same opinion at much greater length on the doorstep. Virginia felt that it was probably true; still, the sense of reprieve was tremendous and she could work again.

But the work on which she was engaged could not please her. The discipline of facts, facts pure and simple, without a novelist's licence or the opportunity for polemics, bored her. *Pointz Hall* was now her relaxation; it was beginning to become *Between the Acts* and it could on occasion give her a day's pleasure. But *Roger Fry* had somehow to be written. Difficulties accumulated; there was the unspoken censorship of the Fry sisters, that of her own feelings, and there was Helen Anrep. She was sorry for Helen Anrep; she liked her (most of the time), but Helen could be trying. Encouraged by Vanessa, she had persuaded Virginia to become one of the guarantors of a new School of Drawing and Painting (which later became known as "The Euston Road School"). This didn't worry Virginia—she was rich now—neither should it have worried her that she lent Helen £150; but it did.

The lamentable story of that loan, which amused Vanessa a good deal, began in October 1938 when Helen Anrep dined with the Woolfs at Tavistock Square. After dinner, she and Virginia discussed the progress of Roger's biography; they talked about his ruthlessness—yes, he was ruthless, although his motives were pure and good; they discussed the breach between Roger and Sir William Rothenstein (whom Virginia was later to interview and to find very agreeable). Then, most unluckily, the talk turned to the subject of *Three Guineas*. Helen Anrep, who prided herself on speaking her mind and was always ready, with a kind of mock imperiousness, to tax her friends with their faults, told Virginia what she thought of her book. Helen's overbearing way amused some people; it annoyed others. Virginia was one of the others. With apparent humility she told Helen that probably she was right; she, Virginia, was not gifted for any writing save fiction or criticism; ought she not then to abandon the *Life* of Roger? Helen, I surmise, was appalled by this application of her criticisms; but worse was to come. Virginia now became solicitous about Helen's financial situation. It appeared that she could not meet her commitments. Virginia offered to pay off her overdraft. Helen, after some hesitation, accepted.

Virginia had attempted to redress the balance of her ruffled feelings by a large gesture; she regretted it almost at once, particularly when she discovered that the overdraft was not, as she had supposed, a matter of some fifty pounds but one hundred and fifty. All the old Stephen money terrors awoke within her; she was shooting Niagara; she had been reckless; she would be ruined. It gave her sleepless nights and, even though she must have known that her alarms were absurd and that the sales of *The Years* made such generosities perfectly safe, she could not be easy in her financial conscience until she had rewritten and sold an old story, *Lappin and Lapinova*, to America.

Meanwhile Helen herself was far from easy. Somehow, she felt, she must repay Virginia. In 1939 she was trying to economise for this purpose. In the Spring of 1940 she wrote to Vanessa, "if only I could ever get enough money ahead to pay Virginia even a small instalment I should breathe more happily"; and at length, in February 1941, she managed to save £25 and sent it to Virginia. To crown the sad absurdity of the transaction it appears that Helen's insolvency, like Virginia's terrors, was purely imaginary. The muddle of her accounts was so great that she had imagined a deficit which never existed.

"We have reached a time of life," said Duncan, "when we must expect our friends to die." In the year 1938 it must have seemed to

Virginia that this was indeed the case. Ottoline died in April, Ka Cox in May. The death of Ka affected her chiefly because she felt it so little; for many years now they had met to remember rather than to renew their friendship. The loss of Ottoline was much more felt. Virginia wrote an obituary of her for *The Times*. The world seemed greatly impoverished by the disappearance of that fantastic being; there had been something grand about her and, in later years, something rather touching and loveable.

At the end of the year Jack Hills died – but he indeed was "a figure from the past"; and in June 1939 Mark Gertler committed suicide. Public events were not of a kind to dissipate the general gloom. Franco was in Barcelona in January 1939; he was in Madrid (and Hitler in Prague) by March. Julian's life seemed, more than ever, to have been thrown away. "Maynard, even Maynard," wrote Virginia, "can't find much that's hopeful now." England was full of refugees. Freud was in Hampstead and the Woolfs went to see him. He gave Virginia a narcissus and talked, as everyone then talked, about Hitler. It would take a generation, he said, to work out the poison. And what were they, the English, going to do? He struck Virginia as an alert, "screwed up shrunk very old man," an "old fire now flickering" and, as they all knew, near to extinction.

And all the time she was working on Roger; she brought what she called the "first sketch" to an end on 11 March 1939, and hoped to have it all finished by July; but it was not. On 12 July, "For the first time for weeks, after being so damnably down in the mouth . . . I've worked with some pleasure at R[oger]." In that month there was yet another death, that of old Mrs Woolf, Leonard's mother. It did not touch Virginia deeply, and yet she was saddened. The poor old creature had been very silly and very boring, she had wasted a lot of Virginia's time and yet, in a way, Virginia was fascinated by her and deeply sorry for her, for she was a lonely self-pitying person who tried to keep up a fiction of intense family affection to which Leonard, despite a strong sense of filial duty, could not respond. With Virginia, she played an odd, unreal game, in which each tried to act out the not very suitable part allotted to them by fate.

But there was still plenty of fun. That is a fact which must be stated but which it is difficult to convey. Virginia's diaries, it is true, become increasingly despondent; private miseries and public events struck with overwhelming force, but still, she was not overwhelmed. Neither Vanessa nor Virginia ever courted sorrow, or wallowed in grief as their father had done when *he* was bereaved.

It was their instinct to remain as cheerful as they could, and the new friends whom Virginia made in the 'thirties–as for instance Elizabeth Bowen, Shena Simon, Stephen Spender–did not carry away with them the impression of an old and gloomy authoress, frustrated in her work, bereaved and menaced. At Monk's House and at 52 Tavistock Square the prevailing sound was still one of laughter; it might take some courage to go on laughing at that time, but an appearance–and indeed a reality–of gaiety was maintained.*

In June 1939 the Woolfs took a holiday in Brittany. Virginia had always wanted to visit Les Rochers and pay her respects to a great predecessor.† They returned to face the business of moving house. No. 52 Tavistock Square was to be pulled down and the area redeveloped. Together with their friendly tenants the solicitors Messrs Dolman and Pritchard, they looked for and found a suitable house in Mecklenburgh Square. They left their old home on 25 July. At the same time various new additions to Monk's House were completed. The Bells simultaneously were making further additions to Charleston. There was a general atmosphere of retreat and fortification in the country, of making all secure and shipshape before the coming of the storm.

Virginia spent much time walking about the City of London; it was almost as though she were saying goodbye to it. There was not much time in which to do so, for in August "last year's mad voice" was heard again; and this time a defiant answer had become inevitable.

* Virginia wrote one of the gayest and one of the most hilarious of her letters to Vanessa at the height of the Munich crisis. Unfortunately it is not a letter which can, at present, be published.

† *Madame de Sévigné*, which was published, together with other essays, in *The Death of the Moth* (1942), was almost certainly written at this period.

Chapter Ten

1939–1941

ON the morning of 3 September 1939, Virginia and Leonard sat arguing in their new sitting-room at the top of Monk's House while they waited for Mr Chamberlain to speak to the nation. Virginia said it was 'they' who made wars; 'we' as usual remained outside and had no voice in our fate. And supposing the Allies were to win–then what?

"Better to win the war than to lose it," replied Leonard. This in fact had become the only choice. Virginia more than half agreed and yet, to face those harsh alternatives was difficult for her–difficult also for the nation at large, and for nine months we most of us refused to do so.

At Monk's House the first effect of the war was to produce a kind of peace. Yards of blackout material were bought and made into curtains (Virginia's blackout was not very efficient and she was in trouble with the police at least once). Pregnant mothers, hurriedly evacuated from the capital, were decanted from buses and presently drifted disconsolately back to London; the first sirens sounded the first false alarm. Virginia and Leonard returned to their usual tasks and diversions; throughout that wonderfully fine autumn they played bowls up and down their undulating green. But Virginia was under no illusions, or at least she had fewer illusions than most of us. The war, it seemed to her, was beginning in cold blood, the killing machine was starting silently, but it was not the less deadly for that. It was working very efficiently in Poland and, when the Poles had been conquered, "we shall be attended to." And, while the newspapers indulged in the kind of jolly hubristic patriotism which Virginia particularly disliked, Kingsley Martin brought dark rumours of chaos, inefficiency and despair.

The biography still had to be finished; that ungrateful task plagued her all through the autumn and winter, and from time to time she took refuge in *Pointz Hall*, which she had been writing intermittently all through 1939. She also began to write her memoirs, which, unfortunately, are incomplete.

When war broke out she decided to return to journalism and to write for *The New Statesman*. She did this partly because she took it for granted that she and Leonard would be impoverished by the war, partly for reasons which are not easy to understand. Journalism represented, in some way, a kind of patriotic gesture, or at least a way of meeting the emergency, though in what way the war effort, or indeed her private income, would benefit by the fact that she now gave time to articles on Sir Walter Scott or Horace Walpole, it would be hard to say. I think also that she simply felt that she wanted to be doing something different. Everyone else, it seemed, had found or was looking for a new employment; so would she. T. S. Eliot wrote to say that he half expected to meet her in Russell Square directing the traffic and wearing an Air Raid Warden's tin hat.

In that 'phoney' period of the war there were no air raids, but raids were expected and when, in October, the Woolfs drove to London and were confronted by large posters at Wimbledon declaring "THE WAR BEGINS. HITLER SAYS: NOW IT'S ON," Virginia remarked to Leonard that it seemed foolish to have chosen that particular day for their visit. They appeared to be driving into a trap and she was frightened; but not for very long; later she felt that there was sufficient community of sentiment in the capital to allow her to merge her private emotions with those of others. London seemed sober and businesslike. At night it was dark and so unsocial that she wondered whether she might not be seeing the end of urban life and the beginning of a time when badgers and foxes, owls and nightingales would populate the darkened city. But by day there were more familiar manifestations. Mrs Sidney Webb–"like the veins of a leaf when the pulp has been eaten away"–presiding over lunch in a spacious Victorian room with sideboards and maids; the ordered conversation: ten minutes for Virginia and ten for Leonard; sharp remarks about Wells and Shaw. Mrs Webb said she was thankful for her Victorian training in morality; "I said we were moral in fighting that morality. Now there's a morality to make again." The old Fabian marched on and Virginia, as usual, found her uncommonly depressing and was glad to leave her.

She tried to bring some order into their new home in Mecklenburgh Square, which was still in a state of confusion and most uncomfortable. The kitchen seemed too small, everywhere else too large, the stairs were bad, there were no carpets. The staff of the Press were uneasy, Sally the spaniel was unwell. Virginia felt useless, fretful and *désœuvrée*. After a week of London they returned to the peace of Monk's House.

In the ensuing months–until their house became uninhabitable in

September 1940-Leonard and Virginia would drive up to London every other week and spend a few days there.

Nevertheless it was many years since Virginia had spent so much of her winter in the country-not in fact since 1913. It was an experience which interested, depressed and exalted her. In a way it was the fulfilment of a dream, the dream of escaping from London, of getting away from Colefax and her like and from the Press, of having abundant leisure in which to read and to write and very little company save their own. Better still, she need no longer feel, as she usually did in the country, that she was "out of things." "Things" seemed to have vanished, or at all events to have left town. Moreover at this time Virginia seems to have wanted, or half wanted, to be "out of things." She had, she decided, come to a stage in her career in which fame would leave her. She would become "an outsider"–it might be just as well. Living in the country she might claim to be living the part. However, living alone in the country, particularly if you have a book on your hands that won't come right and won't get finished, can be boring. Monk's House at that time was a decidedly cold house and the winter of 1939/40 was quite dramatically cold.* Snow made roads impassable, the brooks froze solid, and there was ice even on the tidal Ouse. Then there was a sudden thaw, followed by an even more sudden frost, so that all the country seemed glazed with diamond-clear ice which at sunset and sunrise gave it a prismatic splendour of unbelievable beauty.

After Christmas there was one last Bloomsbury celebration, Angelica's twenty-first birthday party which, since wartime shortages had not yet made themselves felt, could be celebrated with some *éclat*. Lydia danced for the last time and Duncan danced with her, Marjorie Strachey sang *The Lost Chord*, a young German refugee gave a parody of the Führer, and Virginia obliged with *The Last Rose of Summer*, of which she knew, or invented, a great many verses. Everyone was gay, everyone knew that there would be no more such gaieties.

---

* The cold at Monk's House was so intense that Morgan Forster, vainly seeking to warm himself by the "Cosy Stove" in his bedroom, burnt his trousers. At Charleston he was warmer; but here the house caught fire. He celebrated these events on the back of a National Gallery Concert programme:

> "*To a cosy stove, installed in a hospitable homestead*
>
> "O hearth benign! O decent glow!
> My trousers, blackened down below,
> Accuse not thee, but praise the zest
> Which burns the host before the guest."

"Oh, it's a queer sense of suspense, being led up to the spring of 1940." Virginia wrote this in her diary on 8 February; she felt that we were all being led to an altar, a sacrificial altar garlanded with blossoms of flame. Towards the end of February she had influenza and for a long time was unable to shake it off; nevertheless Leonard clearly thought her well enough–morally and mentally–to endure a very severe criticism of *Roger Fry*. It was, he said, merely analysis, not history; she had chosen the wrong method, seen it from a dull angle made even more dull by so many dead quotations. No doubt he added that, like everything of hers, it had things in it which could only have been hers, and very good they were; but this, characteristically, she does not record. It was a painful conversation; she felt as though she were being pecked with a very strong, hard beak. Although Leonard had not been enthusiastic about *Three Guineas*, this was the first time that he had given her an entirely adverse criticism. He was rational, impressive, definite and emphatic; and he convinced her that she had failed–almost. She was not certain however that his motives were quite pure; unconsciously he might be moved by a lack of sympathy for Roger, a lack of interest in his personality. She had sent her manuscript, or parts of it, to two other judges, Margery Fry and Vanessa. She would await their verdict.

"It's *him* . . . unbounded admiration," wrote Margery, with more enthusiasm than grammar. And Vanessa wrote:

> Since Julian died I haven't been able to think of Roger. Now you have given him back to me–Although I cannot help crying I can't thank you enough.

These judgements prevailed. Vanessa's commendation was, in its way, sufficient. To bring back Roger to those who knew him was a great part of Virginia's intention. Whether Leonard's verdict may not have been nearer to that of those who did not know Roger is another matter. Virginia was certainly made happy again by these assurances. She could go ahead with the dreary task of correcting proofs without too much despair, and on 13 May they were posted back to the printer.

On 10 May the Germans had invaded Belgium and Holland, on the 14th the Dutch army surrendered, on the 28th the Belgians followed suit and on 14 June, Paris fell.

Virginia, as we have seen, had not been living in a fool's paradise; she had suspected that things would go badly and she saw in these events, I think, no more than the continuance and intensification of a nightmare that had been going on for five or six years. She was still instinctively opposed to the idea of armed resistance; she was not uncritical when Leonard announced his intention of joining the Local Defence Volunteers. That he should wear an arm-band, a bandolier or a uniform seemed ridiculous. But her qualms about fighting the enemy did not make the enemy himself appear any less terrifying. It was disturbing to find that the bestial stupidity of the Fascist, his belief in the most puerile nonsense, was allied to immense military science and valour. Our own leaders seemed elderly, dull-witted and timorous. Nor could she take comfort from the oratory of our leaders, or from the new sense of desperation and resolution in the British people. Old Ethel Smyth stoutly declaring "of course we shall fight *and* win," two days after the fall of Paris, could excite her admiration, but she brought no comfort and no conviction. Neither did Winston Churchill, and still less the newspaper myths of laughing heroic tommies, the cheery brittle optimism of the BBC and of the politicians. There might be something in it not wholly false; but it was tainted with falsehood and there was an uglier side to our conduct in the national emergency. Refugees, as she knew from personal experience, were being incarcerated for no fault save their nationality, and a soldier came limping home from Dunkirk to Rodmell with stories of panic, demoralisation, looting, and utter military incompetence.

As the battle approached, and it became more and more likely that we should be defeated, Virginia's existence seemed to become unreal or at least incongruous; the activities and sentiments of her daily life were completely at variance with the appalling struggle on which her fate depended. Thus, when she sent off the proofs of the *Life* of Roger, she could speak of "peace and content" well knowing how grotesquely such a statement must read on the third day of the Battle of France; "So my little moment of peace comes in a yawning hollow." A week later, when the drama in the Low Countries was reaching its climax, Desmond MacCarthy and G. E. Moore came to stay at Monk's House–Desmond battered and dishevelled, but charming and talkative as ever; Moore, at sixty-five a shade less impressive than he had seemed in the days when Virginia Stephen had listened to him in mute reverence at the Sangers, but still noble in his disinterestedness. Desmond read him *The Hound of the Basker-villes* in the garden before lunch and in the afternoon they all went over to Charleston. There they discussed Moore's famous taci-turnity: he was accused of silencing a generation. "I didn't want to be silent," he replied. "I couldn't think of anything to say." And at any rate he had never silenced Desmond, who presumably started talking to the cat and the towel-horse in his nursery. And over the hills came the reverberation of the cannon-fire.

Still more unreal was the Woolfs' jaunt to Penshurst with Vita. They visited the house, with its banqueting hall, its disappointing furniture, its memories of Elizabeth and Essex, the shell of Lady Pembroke's lute and Sidney's shaving glass, its tidy lawns, goldfish ponds and the old lord, garrulous, excruciatingly bored by his life, living for his game of cards in Tonbridge. On that day Paris fell.

July brought the publication of *Roger Fry* and something of the usual anxieties which Virginia always felt on such occasions. With it also came the fear of invasion. For Virginia and Leonard this meant something worse, in a way, than the universal annihilation which awaits us today if our rulers decide to destroy us. Leonard, in the last of his autobiographical volumes, gives an account of what the Fascist menace must have meant for him. I quote it, because it supplies the image that stared Leonard and Virginia in the face in July 1940.

> Jews were hunted down, beaten up, and humiliated everywhere publicly in the streets of towns. I saw a photograph of a Jew being dragged by storm troopers out of a shop in one of the main streets in Berlin; the fly-buttons of the man's trousers had been torn open to show that he was circumcised and therefore a Jew. On the man's face was the horrible look of blank suffering and despair which from the beginning of human history men have seen under the crown of thorns on the faces of their persecuted and humiliated victims. In this photograph what was even more horrible was the look on the faces of respectable men and women, standing on the pavement, laughing at the victim.

This then was the quality of the enemy who now had victory almost within his grasp and who, having achieved it, would be released from all restraints. Even if one were optimistic enough to believe that there might be a grain of pity or magnanimity in the heart of such an enemy, it was quite certain that there would be none for a Jewish socialist and his wife; for them the gas chamber would be an unlooked-for mercy. Leonard and Virginia had the advantage, if it was an advantage, of knowing enough about their adversary to be free from illusions. On 13 May, when the battle was at its height, they had discussed the question of suicide. They decided to poison themselves with the fumes of their car and Leonard kept enough petrol for this purpose in his garage; later they managed to get sufficient morphia from Adrian for a lethal dose. Throughout May and June Virginia refers frequently to the question of how and when they should make an end of themselves. Believing the war to be lost, she hardly doubts the necessity will arise, and looking into the future she sees nothing: "I can't conceive," she wrote, "that there will be a 27th June 1941."

And so, for three months, she lived on the brink of a precipice, always tensed to throw herself over. But towards the end of this period, fate provided a sort of cure, or so it seems, in the form of actual rather than imagined dangers. Throughout August and September she witnessed those odd scraps of air fighting which were all that people on the ground were usually able to perceive of the Battle of Britain. These contests in the sky were, as often as not, incomprehensible to the onlooker. Tiny sharp accents of light wheeled and vanished high in the air and then a great plume of smoke, with perhaps, an elegant botanical parachute above it, signified that someone, English or German, one could not tell which, had been shot down. But at times the events were more understandable and more dramatic; one might see a low-flying plane with enemy markings, hear the pop-pop-pop of cannon-fire, the disconcerting noise of bullets ripping the air, the whistle and crash of bombs.

They came very close. We lay down under the tree. The sound was like someone sawing in the air just above us. We lay flat on our faces, hands behind head. Don't close your teeth, said L. They seemed to be sawing at something stationary. Bombs shook the windows of my lodge. Will it drop I asked? If so, we shall be broken together. I thought, I think, of nothingness–flatness, my mood being flat. Some fear I suppose. Should we take Mabel to garage. Too risky to cross the garden L. said. Then another came from Newhaven. Hum and saw and buzz all round us. A horse neighed in the marsh. Very sultry. Is it thunder? I said. No, guns, said L., from Ringmer, from Charleston way. Then slowly the sound lessened. Mabel in kitchen said the windows shook. Air raid still on: distant planes . . . The all clear 5 to 7. 144 down last night.

Shattering, nerve-racking though such experiences must have been, unfit though Virginia was to be at the periphery, let alone the centre of a battle, I think that the effect may have been therapeutic. From the time when she came literally under fire, the talk of suicide ceased.

I remember her at this time reading aloud to the Memoir Club the account which she had written for the Rodmell Women's Institute of the Dreadnought Hoax; there was much laughter and applause, she seemed cheerful and certainly not at all suicidal. No doubt it was different when she rang up Sissinghurst and heard Vita's voice with the bombs falling all around her and did not know, when she rang off, whether she would ever hear Vita again.

The war moved inland; Rodmell was by no means out of danger but London was now the chief target. Both Virginia and Vanessa suffered material damage in the bombardment. And now the old competition between them was, in the strangest way, renewed. When Mecklenburgh Square was blasted Virginia was in despair for two reasons: it was exasperating to have moved into what was now an uninhabitable house while still paying rent for No. 52 Tavistock Square which remained untouched; it was also annoying when Vanessa's studio (and Duncan's next door) was entirely destroyed so that her own broken windows and fallen ceilings seemed but a paltry disaster. She was positively relieved when No. 52 Tavistock Square shared the fate of No. 8 Fitzroy Street and she felt, as Vanessa did when her studio went up in flames, an odd, unaccountable sense of exhilaration. But when they went to London to see what could be done about the damage and to arrange for the removal of the Hogarth Press, she experienced different emotions: amazement at the stouthearted stoicism of old Mr Pritchard and his sister, and, to quote a letter to Ethel Smyth:

> . . . what touched and indeed raked what I call my heart in London was the grimy old women at the lodging house at the back, all dirty after the raid, & preparing to sit out another . . . And then the passion of my life, that is the city of London – to see London all blasted, that too raked my heart.*

On top of all this came a private trouble, perfectly silly and petty and unnecessary, but worth mentioning if only to show how Virginia was torn between the cosmic disasters of war and the little ennuies of private life. There was a furnished cottage to let at Rodmell. Helen Anrep wanted to be near her friends and Vanessa told her about it. In a telephone conversation between Vanessa and Virginia, Virginia understood that Helen was coming to live in Rodmell permanently. For a moment the dangers of invasion were forgotten, or rather the threat of invasion now came from the Anrep family, a prospect equally grim. There was a sisterly quarrel as heated as any for years. It was soon over; Helen only intended a short stay anyway; but while the altercation lasted it was violent and painful.

In May 1940, speaking to the Workers' Educational Association

---

* "When the Germans bombed London, she [Virginia] calculated the serious damage in terms of decreased book-sales." (Michael Holroyd, *Lytton Strachey*, Vol. I, p. 404.) I have found no record of these singular calculations.

in Brighton, Virginia gave expression to her irritation with some of the poetry of the Left Wing intellectuals. Her lecture was published later under the title of *The Leaning Tower*. *The Leaning Tower* got her into a great deal of trouble with Left Wing writers, and this is natural enough, for she was rude, and for all I know mistaken, about their poetry. But it is in many ways a thoughtful essay, the final statement of a socially conscious writer, and it expresses much that is true. Virginia saw how intimately the history of English literature is conditioned by the English class structure, and how even the Left Wing movement of the 'thirties derived its nature from an essentially bourgeois society. She believed that the young socialist writers of her time did not, despite their ideological stance, transcend the boundaries of class and were indeed condemned to a certain obliquity of vision by reason of their class origins, and always would be so condemned unless they could create a classless society.

Where Virginia differed from most of the younger socialists was in her frank and unequivocal acceptance of the importance of the class structure in literature. Where others attempted to cross the barriers of class, or even to deny their existence, she frankly recognised them and, in so doing, recognised that she herself was in an isolated position within a divided society. As she makes clear in *The Leaning Tower*, she did not consider that this was a desirable state of affairs; but neither did she think that it was a state of affairs which could be altered by pretending that it did not exist. It was here that she parted company, not only with the Left, but with the Right.

The point is well brought out by an earlier essay. In *The Niece of an Earl* she wrote:

> ... our ignorance of the aristocracy is nothing compared with our ignorance of the working classes. At all times the great families of England and France have delighted to have famous men at their tables, and thus the Thackerays and the Disraelis and the Prousts have been familiar enough with the cut and fashion of aristocratic life to write about it with authority. Unfortunately, however, life is so framed that literary success invariably means a rise, never a fall, and seldom, what is far more desirable, a spread in the social scale. The rising novelist is never pestered to come to gin and winkles with the plumber and his wife. His books never bring him into touch with the cat's-meat man, or start a correspondence with the old lady who sells matches and boot-laces by the gate of the British Museum.

As a sympathetic critic puts it:

> The subject of her writing was the little world of people like herself, a small class, a dying class, ... a class with inherited privileges, private

incomes, sheltered lives, protected sensibilities, sensitive tastes. Outside of this class she knows very little.

This, for a novelist, is certainly a limitation, but there is some advantage in being aware of one's own limits.

Commenting on *The Niece of an Earl*, Jacques Emile Blanche wrote:

> . . . je me permets de vous avouer que m'étonne une autre phrase de cet essai où vous exprimez comme une certitude, que les gens de notre classe ne connaissent pas l'ésprit du peuple, "of the old woman who sells matches and bootlaces at the gates of the British Museum." J'ai beaucoup causé avec "the plumber and his wife"—avec toutes sortes d'ouvriers, à la ville et à la campagne—et il est facile de sé mettre a leur niveau; ou mieux; c'était facile. La guerre de classes, qui fait rage ici, sous le souffle de Moscou, transforme les plus gentils en des brutes effrayantes.

This may serve as a classic instance of the writer who believes that he knows the lower classes, knows how he can bring himself "to their level," loves them quite genuinely so long as they play the role that he expects of them but whose affection, when that role changes, turns to hatred.

Virginia's attitude is the exact opposite. She did not demand love from her social inferiors or feel hatred when love was refused. She felt so little love for the proletariat that she wanted to abolish it and in abolishing it to abolish the class society. Her attitude, in that it resulted from a correct assessment of the character of the society in which she lived, enabled her in *The Leaning Tower* to make a very penetrating analysis. At the same time it was politically sterile in that it ignored those social affections on which political action usually depends. This, for those who suffered from the political blunders of her generation, was profoundly irritating. Benedict Nicolson, Vita's son, who was at that time on active service, read her biography of Roger while he was living in conditions of great stress and danger. He wrote to Virginia to express his exasperation. Bloomsbury, it seemed to him, had been living in a fool's paradise, enjoying cultivated pleasures while it neglected the first duty of the intellectual, which is to save the world from its follies. That disagreeable task had been left to him and his generation.

Virginia was clearly both irritated and impressed by his arguments. She wrote her reply with some care and, when it was finished, her letter was quite as fierce as his. In a subsequent exchange they both regained their tempers and the correspondence ended in a spirit of charity, if not of agreement. Apart from its acerbities and

some points which related simply to Roger Fry's achievements as a critic, the argument turned on the social responsibility or irresponsibility of Bloomsbury in the years between the wars. Virginia did not defend Bloomsbury, as she might have done, by questioning the validity of the term in such a connection and pointing out that, if Leonard and Maynard Keynes belonged to Bloomsbury, it would be hard to accuse that body of total indifference to public affairs.*
She rested her case on the view that artists are unable, substantially, to influence society and that this was true even of the greatest writers: Keats, Shelley, Wordsworth or Coleridge. And this was the defence most applicable to her. As we have seen, she had attempted to be politically active; it was the ability, not the inclination, that was lacking. Only in *A Room of One's Own* does she exhibit any great persuasive power and, politically, she was a much less influential writer than Harriet Beecher Stowe.

This exchange took place in August 1940; by that time the Battle of Britain was approaching its climax and Virginia was passing from a mood of apprehension to one of quiet imperturbability.

Her serenity was perhaps a necessary prelude to the storm–by which I mean that the workings of Virginia's mind may have been such that she had to pass from the terror of June 1940 to the final agony of March 1941 by way of an euphoric interval, and that this may have been just as much a part of her mental illness as all the rest. At the same time we may note that the happier phase of that autumn–though not the subsequent relapse–could be directly related to public events. In August and September the threat of invasion continued; but at least it was clear that this island was capable of resistance, the enemy was not going to win command of the air without a tremendous struggle; and presently it began to look as though he were not winning it at all. Invasion was postponed from week to week until, clearly, it would be delayed until the Spring. London might be bombed and blazing but Leonard was not yet compelled to wear a yellow star. And, at the end of the year, a pale star of Victory shone over Africa.

It was satisfactory that Mabel went off to live with her sister. Mabel was the London maid; she had never played as important a role in Virginia's life as had Nelly; she was an easier, more placid, less disastrously interesting character. Nevertheless the Woolfs were

---

* In a draft for her letter of 24 August 1940 she does make this point, and, defending herself, alludes to her own work for Morley College, the Suffrage movement, and the Women's Co-operative Guild. This is omitted in the letter that she sent to Benedict Nicolson.

glad when she left; she was only at Rodmell because it was impossible to ask anyone to stay in London at that time. All the work that the Woolfs needed doing at Monk's House could be done by Louie, who lived in the village and with whom they both got on very well (Louie indeed was to remain with Leonard for the rest of his life). Thus the great servant problem was solved at last.

Bombs went on falling, and on 29 September one fell very close to Monk's House. Virginia swore at Leonard for slamming the window so noisily and then, realising what it was, went out on the lawn to see the raider chased back over Newhaven; but such things no longer worried her. She reflected that she was leading a lazy life. Leonard brought her breakfast in bed, as he had done for so many years, and there she read a book; she took a bath, then she saw Louie and made her household dispositions; then she went out to her lodge in the garden to work at *Pointz Hall*. Never had a novel of hers flowed so rapidly, so effortlessly from her pen; there were no checks, doubts, despairs, struggles or revisions. There was another book. Several drafts for a first chapter remain and two chapters are complete. It was called *Anon*, and was to be a kind of history of literature; it was to be written for Duncan in order to explain to him what English Literature was about. The difficulty was, she said, that she had reached a point at which she had to explain Shakespeare; his genius was universal and her book might therefore be rather long. In the intervals of writing she took pleasure in observing the landscape; she altered the position of her table in order to get a new aspect of the very beautiful flat country that lay between her and Mount Caburn. In November it became more beautiful than ever before; a bomb had burst the river bank and the waters of the Ouse, pouring out over the water-meadows, swept right up to her garden and formed a lovely inland sea visited by multitudes of water fowl. This was a source of great delight. Having surveyed the view and lighted a cigarette – "to tune up" as she put it – she would write until midday. Then came a pause to look at the newspapers, then she typed until one o'clock. Their lunch was frugal, the food shortage was now becoming acute; but with an appetite so sharply set, she ate whatever there was to eat more heartily than ever before; she even confesses at this period to an occasional guzzle, when guzzling was possible. Vita, having a farm, could make handsome presents and in November 1940 was thanked in the following terms:

> I wish I were Queen Victoria. Then I could thank you. From the *depths* of my *Broken* WIDOWED heart. *Never* NEVER NEVER have we had such a *rapturous* ASTOUNDING GLORIOUS – no, I can't get the hang

of the style. All I can say is that when we discovered the butter in the envelope box we had in the household–Louie that is–to look. That's a whole pound of butter I said. Saying which, I broke off a lump & ate it pure. Then in the glory of my heart I gave all our week's ration–which is about the size of my thumb nail–to Louie–earned undying gratitude: then sat down & ate bread and butter. It would have been desecration to add jam. You've forgotten what butter tastes like. So I'll tell you–its something between dew & honey. Lord, Vita!–your broken po, your wool; & then on top your butter!!! Please congratulate the cows from me, & the dairymaid, & I would like to suggest that the calf should be known in future (if its a man) as Leonard if a woman as Virginia.

Think of our lunch tomorrow! Bunny Garnett and Angelica are coming: in the middle of the table I shall put the whole pat. And I shall say: Eat as much as you like. I can't break off this rhapsody, for its a year since I saw a pound, to tell you anything else. I don't think anything else seems important. Its true all our books are coming from the ruined house tomorrow: all battered & mildewed. Its true I've been made Treasurer of the Women's Institute. Also I want to ask you about lantern slides of Persia; & will you come and talk; but this is mere trifling. Bombs fall near me–trifles; a 'plane shot down on the marsh–trifles; floods damned–no, nothing seems to make a wreath on the pedestal fitting your butter.

They've never sent me your book from the Press, damn them.

Here L[eonard] breaks in: If I'm writing to you, will I add his deepest thanks

> for the
>> Butter. V.

After lunch Virginia read the newspapers more seriously, went for a walk and perhaps did a little manual work, gathering and storing apples, or bread-making. Tea followed, and after tea there might be letters to write, followed by some more typing and reading or writing in her diary. Then it was time to cook the dinner and to eat it, to listen to some music on the gramophone, to read, doze, or embroider until it was time for bed.

She compared this life to the scramble, the frustrations, the interviews, telephonings, social engagements and social prevarications of her life in London. Here she was happy, very free, disengaged–"a life that rings from one simple melody to another. Yes: why not enjoy this after all those years of the other?"

Such an existence provided few incidents worthy of record. Their continued residence and the necessities of war brought the Woolfs much more into village life, and on the whole Virginia enjoyed this, although there were some village bores whom she grew to dread.

But in this period of no headaches, no exasperations, and smoothly running work, she seemed almost imperturbable. She enjoyed it when Morgan wrote asking her to join the Committee of the London Library, as she had said that he would one day, and she was able to take a little revenge for herself and her sex by refusing to be "a sop" to public opinion. She enjoyed it when Lady Oxford sent her a statuette of Voltaire and letters of some absurdity written from the Savoy Hotel during the Blitz. In the New Year she enjoyed going to Charleston and to Cambridge and, clearly, she enjoyed a visit from Elizabeth Bowen.

Miss Bowen was at Rodmell on 13 and 14 February 1941 and has recorded her memories of that visit. She describes Virginia kneeling on the floor – they were mending a torn curtain –

> and she sat back on her heels and put her head back in a patch of sun, early spring sun, and laughed in this consuming, choking, delightful, hooting way ... and it has remained with me. So that I get a curious shock when I see people regarding her entirely as a martyred, or a definitely tragic sort of person claimed by the darkness.

When did the laughter end and the darkness begin? It is hard to say. She finished *Between the Acts* on 23 November, and the ending of a novel was always a period of danger for her; but throughout December she seems to have been happy enough. There are passages in her diary for January, February and March which, with hindsight, may be considered ominous. From the middle of January Leonard was very anxious about her; but there is no entry in his diary relating to her health until 18 March, when he writes: "V.n.w." [Virginia not well]. Six days later, on 24 March, she wrote to John Lehmann to say that she did not want *Between the Acts* to be published. By that time it was clear to Leonard that her situation had become critical.

It was a symptom of Virginia's madness that she could not admit that she was mentally ill; to force this knowledge upon her was, in itself, dangerous. But by 26 March Leonard had become convinced that the risk must be taken and that she must be persuaded to see a doctor. For this purpose it was far better that she should see someone whom she knew and liked. As it happened the Woolfs had a friend who was also a physician with a practice in Brighton. Octavia Wilberforce lived with Elizabeth Robins, the actress, who had been a friend of Virginia's mother. Both ladies were clearly fascinated by Virginia. Miss Robins returned to America in 1940, but Octavia, who owned a farm and had seen that Virginia was growing thin and pallid, would send presents of butter and cream to Monk's House. Virginia declared that she would like to write Octavia's portrait and appears to have begun something of the sort, Octavia coming now and then to sit–that is to say, to talk with her.

On March 21 she came to tea and Leonard told her what the situation was.

For the next five days Octavia herself was ill in bed. On the 27th Leonard rang her up. He had persuaded Virginia to see Octavia as a friend and as a doctor. He sounded desperate. Octavia also was desperate. She could only just crawl out of bed, but, heroically, she concealed this fact from Leonard, and it was arranged that he should bring Virginia over to Brighton that afternoon.

The interview was difficult. Virginia at once declared that there was nothing the matter with her. It was quite unnecessary that she should have a consultation; she certainly would not answer any questions.

"All you have to do," said Octavia, "is to reassure Leonard." Then she added that she knew what kind of symptoms Virginia felt, and asked to examine her. In a kind of sleep-walking way Virginia began to undress and then stopped.

"Will you promise, if I do this, not to order me a rest cure?"

"What I promise is that I won't order you to do anything that you won't think it reasonable to do. Is that fair?"

Virginia agreed and the examination continued, but not without many protests. She was like a child being sent up to bed. In the end she did confess some part of her fears, fears that the past would come back, that she would be unable to write again. Octavia replied that the mere fact that she had had this trouble before and that it had been cured should be a reason for confidence. If you have your appendix removed, she said, nothing will remain but the scar; a mental illness can be removed in the same way if you don't inflame the wound by dwelling upon it.

At the end she took Virginia's hand, a cold thin hand she found it, saying: "If you'll collaborate I know I can help you and there's nobody in England I'd like more to help." At this Virginia looked a little happier–"detachedly pleased," as Octavia put it.

Then there was a private consultation between Octavia and Leonard. What were they to do; should Virginia be under the surveillance of a trained nurse? It might easily be a disastrous measure. It seemed, both to Leonard and to Octavia, that the consultation had done some good. The Woolfs went back to Rodmell and Octavia returned to bed. She wrote Virginia a note, as gentle and as reassuring as she could make it, and on the following evening rang up, but by that time it was too late.

On the morning of Friday 28 March, a bright, clear, cold day, Virginia went as usual to her studio room in the garden. There she wrote two letters, one for Leonard, one for Vanessa–the two people she loved best. In both letters she explained that she was hearing voices, believed that she could never recover; she could not go on and spoil Leonard's life for him. Then she went back into the house and wrote again to Leonard:

> Dearest,
> I feel certain I am going mad again. I feel we can't go through another of those terrible times. And I shan't recover this time. I begin to hear voices, and I can't concentrate. So I am doing what seems the best thing to do. You have given me the greatest possible happiness. You have been in every way all that anyone could be. I don't think two people could have been happier till this terrible disease came. I can't fight any longer. I know that I am spoiling your life, that without me you could work. And you will I know. You see I can't even write this properly. I can't read. What I want to say is I owe all the happiness of my life to you. You have been entirely patient with me and incredibly good. I want to say that–everybody knows it. If anybody could have saved me it would have been you. Everything has gone from me but the certainty of your goodness. I can't go on spoiling your life any longer.
> I don't think two people could have been happier than we have been.
>   V.

She put this on the sitting-room mantelpiece and, at about 11.30, slipped out, taking her walking-stick with her and making her way across the water-meadows to the river. Leonard believed that she might already have made one attempt to drown herself; if so she had learnt by her failure and was determined to make sure of it now. Leaving her stick on the bank she forced a large stone into the pocket of her coat. Then she went to her death, "the one experience," as she had said to Vita, "I shall never describe."

APPENDIX A
Chronology

1912

4–6 June
Virginia unwell and in bed; for the rest of June and July she is much occupied, introducing Leonard to her friends and relations, meeting his family, spending week-ends at Asham and one at Walberswick

10 August
Marriage of Virginia Stephen and Leonard Woolf at St Pancras Registry Office. They go to Asham for two days, return to London, and then stay at the Plough Inn, Holford, Somerset

18 August
Leonard and Virginia leave *via* Dieppe for their honeymoon, spent travelling in Provence, Spain and thence by sea to Italy; on 28 September they are in Venice

3 October
The Woolfs return to 38 Brunswick Square. On 8th Leonard starts work as Secretary to the 2nd Post-Impressionist Exhibition at the Grafton Galleries (until 2 January)

Late October
The Woolfs move to rooms at 13 Clifford's Inn; they divide their time between these and Asham

December
Virginia unwell with headaches, Leonard with malaria. They are at Asham for Christmas and again early in the new year

1913

January
Leonard consults medical advisers as to the wisdom of Virginia having a child. She is suffering from headaches and sleeping badly. On 13th he begins to keep a daily record of her state of health

25 January–
1 February
The Woolfs stay at Harbour View, Studland, for Virginia's health, returning to London for two weeks and then spending a long week-end at Asham

22–23 March
The Woolfs stay at Ditchling with the Gills

9 March
The manuscript of *The Voyage Out* is delivered to Gerald Duckworth. Virginia goes to Liverpool, Manchester, Leeds, York, Carlisle and Leicester with Leonard, who is studying the Co-operative movement; they return to London on 19 March, and then go to Asham for Easter with Adrian Stephen and Saxon Sydney-Turner

1–11 April	At Asham with Marjorie Strachey and Sydney-Turner
12 April	*The Voyage Out* accepted for publication by Duckworth
19 April	The Woolfs go to Asham for a fortnight. Back in London, they attend *The Ring* at Covent Garden
16 May–2 June	At Asham; Desmond MacCarthy and Lytton Strachey stay one week-end and Janet Case another
6–8 June	The Woolfs are at Cambridge, staying at Newnham with Virginia's cousin the Principal
9–12 June	The Woolfs go to Newcastle-upon-Tyne to attend Women's Co-operative Congress, returning to London with Margaret Llewelyn Davies. Virginia not well
19 June–7 July	The Woolfs are at Asham. Guests are Oliver and Ray Strachey, H. T. J. Norton, E. M. Forster, Lytton Strachey and Molly MacCarthy
12 July	The Woolfs lunch with Beatrice and Sidney Webb during a week's stay in London
16–21 July	At Asham; Lytton Strachey to stay. Virginia increasingly depressed and unwell
22 July	The Woolfs go to Keswick for Fabian Society Conference; Virginia ill. They return to London on 24th and next day consult Sir George Savage. Virginia enters nursing home at Twickenham
11 August	Virginia leaves nursing home for Asham
22 August	Leonard takes Virginia to London to see Drs Savage and Head; they go next day to the Plough Inn, Holford. Virginia's depression, delusions and resistance to food increase
2 September	Katherine Cox joins the Woolfs at Holford; on 8th they all return to London, to 38 Brunswick Square
9 September	Virginia sees Drs Wright and Head; in the evening she attempts suicide
20 September	Virginia is taken by Leonard to Dalingridge Place, Sussex, where she remains until November under the care of Leonard and nurses
18 November	Virginia is moved with two nurses to Asham; her condition slowly improves
3–5 December	Leonard is in London arranging to vacate Clifford's Inn rooms
1914	
January	Virginia is now able to read and write letters; she undertakes typewriting for Lytton Strachey, whom Leonard visits in Wiltshire
16 February	Virginia's last nurse leaves

APPENDIX A

7–18 March	Ka Cox, Janet Case and Vanessa Bell each come to stay with Virginia at Asham while Leonard is away
6 April	The Woolfs go to London to consult Dr Craig; they stay with Janet Case in Hampstead
8–30 April	In Cornwall–St Ives, Carbis Bay and Godrevy
1 May	Return *via* London to Asham, where they remain all summer save for a visit to London in June (dentist) and Leonard's visits to Birmingham and Keswick for conferences
7 July	Leonard buys Virginia a bicycle
4 August	Declaration of war
6 August	The Woolfs spend a night in London and then go to Northumberland, staying at Wooler and Coldstream until 15 September, when they return to London. House-hunting
30 September	To Asham for a week
9 October	The Woolfs go into lodgings at 65 St Margaret's Road, Twickenham; and on 16th they move to 17 The Green, Richmond
November– December	Virginia is apparently recovered, seeing friends, attending cookery classes. The Woolfs spend a week end at Lytton Strachey's cottage in Wiltshire, and Christmas near him at Marlborough

1915
1 January	Virginia starts to write a diary
25 January	Virginia's 33rd birthday; she and Leonard resolve to buy a printing press and to take Hogarth House, Richmond
18 February	Virginia has headache and sleeps badly; early stage of recurrence of mental breakdown. By 4 March she is excited and violent, and nurses are called in
25 March	Virginia is taken to nursing home, while Leonard undertakes the move to Hogarth House
26 March	Publication of Virginia's first book, *The Voyage Out*
1 April	Virginia is brought to Hogarth House; four nurses in attendance. April and May are the most violent and raving months of her madness
June	Beginning of gradual improvement in Virginia's condition. By August Leonard is able to take her out for drives or in a wheel-chair
11 September– 4 November	The Woolfs live at Asham with one nurse, a cook and a housemaid
4 November	Return to Hogarth House. Virginia is gradually returning to normal life; the nurse leaves 11 November

22–30 December	Christmas at Asham; James Strachey and Noel Olivier are guests

1916

January	Virginia leads a comparatively normal life at Hogarth House
1 February	Nelly Boxall and Lottie Hope come as cook and housemaid. The Woolfs are at Asham for a week-end in February
6–15 April	Virginia has influenza, after which she goes to Asham for three weeks. Lytton Strachey and C. P. Sanger are guests for Easter
5 May	The Woolfs return to Hogarth House
20–22 May	The Woolfs stay with Roger Fry at Durbins near Guildford
30 May	Leonard is examined and rejected by Army Medical Board
17–19 June	The Woolfs spend week-end in Sussex with Mr and Mrs Sidney Webb; George Bernard Shaw is a fellow guest
7 July	The Woolfs go to Asham until mid-September, interrupted by a visit to Vanessa at Wissett in Suffolk (21–24 July) and the succeeding week at Hogarth House
15–19 August	G. E. Moore and Pernel Strachey at Asham. Subsequent guests include Adrian and Karin Stephen, Alix Sargant-Florence, James Strachey, R. C. Trevelyan, the Waterlows and Roger Fry
16 September	The Woolfs return to Richmond and go on 18th to Carbis Bay
2 October	Return to Hogarth House
c. 4 October	David Garnett, Carrington and Barbara Hiles spend a night at Asham (uninvited)
17 October	Virginia lectures to Richmond Branch of Women's Co-operative Guild
20–24 October	The Woolfs are at Asham. Vanessa has recently moved to Charleston, four miles away, but they are unable to meet
21 December	The Woolfs go to Asham; Ka Cox comes for Christmas

1917

2 January	The Woolfs visit Charleston; Virginia stays the night. On 4th they return to Hogarth House. Virginia is again writing for *The Times Literary Supplement*

APPENDIX A

23 March	The Woolfs order a printing press in Farringdon Road
3–17 April	Easter holiday at Asham. C. P. Sanger and Marjorie Strachey to stay
24 April	Printing press delivered to Hogarth House. The Woolfs remain at Richmond until August, with short visits to Asham and to R. C. Trevelyan
July	Publication No. 1 of The Hogarth Press: *The Mark on the Wall* and *Three Jews*
3 August– *5 October*	The Woolfs are at Asham. Virginia enters brief notes in a diary (*Berg*). Guests include G. Lowes Dickinson, Lytton Strachey, Katherine Mansfield, Philip Morrell, Sydney Waterlow, Desmond MacCarthy
8 October	Virginia starts regularly writing a diary (*AWD* (*Berg*)). Emma Vaughan gives her bookbinding equipment to Virginia
10 October	Foundation of the 1917 Club; Leonard on committee
29 October	Virginia goes to Asham with Saxon Sydney-Turner, then on to Charleston, while Leonard goes to Bolton, Manchester and Liverpool
2 November	Return to Hogarth House
17–19 November	The Woolfs first visit to Garsington Manor, home of Philip and Lady Ottoline Morrell; Lytton Strachey and Aldous Huxley are fellow guests
15 November	The Woolfs buy a larger second-hand press; on 21st Barbara Hiles starts work as part-time assistant in the Hogarth Press
19 December	First General Meeting and Dinner of the 1917 Club
20 December	The Woolfs go to Asham for Christmas holiday; visits to Charleston and *vice versa*; Ka Cox to stay
1918	
3 January	Return to Hogarth House. Virginia is setting type, writing for *TLS*, and making frequent visits to London, to libraries, 1917 Club, etc.
8 February	Virginia is in bed for a week with influenza; she goes with Leonard to Asham on 19th, thence to Charleston on 1 March, returning to Hogarth House on 2nd
12 March	Over 100,000 words of *Night and Day* written
21 March–5 April	The Woolfs are at Asham for Easter; Lytton Strachey to stay
14 April	Harriet Weaver comes to tea at Hogarth House with the manuscript of *Ulysses*
May	Publication of Lytton Strachey's *Eminent Victorians*
16–28 May	The Woolfs are at Asham; Roger Fry to stay
15–17 June	The Woolfs stay with the Waterlows at Oare, Wiltshire

10 July	First copies of Katherine Mansfield's *Prelude*, printed at the Hogarth Press, are sent out
20–22 July	The Woolfs stay at Tidmarsh with Lytton Strachey and Carrington
27–29 July	The Woolfs stay at Garsington with the Morrells
31 July	The Woolfs go to Asham for summer. Guests include Adrian and Karin Stephen, Sidney and Beatrice Webb, Mark Gertler
7 October	Return to Hogarth House; on 13th H. A. L. Fisher calls with news of the war ending
11 November	Armistice Day; guns announce peace
15 November	T. S. Eliot comes to Hogarth House; first meeting with Virginia
21 November	Virginia finishes *Night and Day*. Printing *Kew Gardens*; frequent visits to Katherine Mansfield at Hampstead
14–16 December	Virginia stays week-end at Durbins, near Guildford, with Roger Fry
20 December	Virginia goes to Asham; Leonard comes next day
25 December	Birth of Angelica Bell at Charleston; on 28th Julian and Quentin Bell are brought to Asham

1919	
1 January	The Woolfs return to Hogarth House with Julian and Quentin Bell
2 January	Virginia has a tooth extracted and is subsequently in bed for a fortnight; on 9th the Bell children are sent home to Gordon Square
January–March	Domestic crises at Charleston; Virginia sends Nelly to help
26 February	Death of Lady Ritchie (Aunt Anny)
28 February	The Woolfs go to Asham; are given notice to leave the house
4 March	Virginia spends a night at Charleston and returns next day to Hogarth House. Printing T. S. Eliot's *Poems*
1 April	*Night and Day* submitted to Gerald Duckworth
25 April	The Woolfs go to Asham for ten days; house-hunting in district
7 May	Virginia takes three cottages in Cornwall. Duckworth accepts *Night and Day*
12 May	*Kew Gardens* by Virginia, *The Critic in Judgment* by J. M. Murry and *Poems* by T. S. Eliot published by the Hogarth Press
27 May	The Woolfs go to Asham; house-hunting
2 June	Leonard returns to town; Virginia goes to Charleston for the night; next day she buys the Round House in Lewes and returns to Hogarth House

APPENDIX A

21–23 June	Virginia stays at Garsington for the week-end; G. L. Dickinson, Aldous Huxley and Mark Gertler are also there
26 June	The Woolfs go to Lewes to look at the Round House and on to Asham; on 27th and 28th they look at Monk's House
1 July	Auction sale of Monk's House, Rodmell; bought by the Woolfs for £700
19 July	Peace Treaty signed
29 July	The Woolfs go to Asham for the whole of August; guests include Hope Mirrlees and E. M. Forster
1 September	The Woolfs move to Monk's House, Rodmell
6 October	The Woolfs return to Hogarth House
20 October	*Night and Day* is published by Duckworth
8–10 November	The Woolfs stay at Tidmarsh with Lytton Strachey and Carrington; Saxon Sydney-Turner is also there
1–19 December	Leonard ill with malaria
20–27 December	Virginia in bed with influenza
29 December	The Woolfs go to Monk's House

1920	
8 January	Return to Hogarth House
18 January	Virginia goes to Guildford to stay overnight with Roger Fry
7–9 February	The Woolfs go to Aldbourne for week-end with Ka (*nee* Cox) and Will Arnold-Forster
21 February– *1 March*	The Woolfs are at Monk's House
4 March	First meeting of the Memoir Club
25 March–7 April	The Woolfs are at Monk's House for Easter; from 30 April–4 May; and for a week-end at end of May
11 May	Leonard is offered nomination as Labour candidate for the Combined English University Constituency
7 June	Virginia goes to London; has tea with Clive Bell, dinner with Vanessa; story of "Mad Mary" and vivid bus ride to Waterloo
24–28 June	The Woolfs are at Monk's House
22 July	The Woolfs go to Monk's House for two months. On 2 and 23 August Virginia goes to London to see Katherine Mansfield (their last meeting)
28 August	Carrington and Ralph Partridge stay the week-end; the latter is invited to join the Hogarth Press
September	Lytton Strachey stays several days and T. S. Eliot one night at Monk's House. Virginia is writing *Jacob's Room*

1 October	The Woolfs return to Hogarth House. Ralph Partridge starts part-time work in the Press on 6th
22 December	The Woolfs go to Monk's House for Christmas holiday

1921

2 January	Return to Hogarth House, whence they make two excursions: to Woodcote (Philip Woolf) and on to Tidmarsh (Lytton Strachey) on 28–29 January; and to Monk's House on 22–28 February
16–18 March	Virginia accompanies Leonard to an adoption meeting in Manchester
23–31 March	The Woolfs stay at Zennor, near the Arnold-Forsters
April	Publication of Lytton Strachey's *Queen Victoria*
7 or 8 April	Publication of *Monday or Tuesday*
22–25 April	The Woolfs are at Monk's House
18 May	Desmond and Molly MacCarthy and Roger Fry dine at Hogarth House; Desmond's conversation written down
21 May	Marriage of Ralph Partridge and Dora Carrington
June–July	Virginia unwell; no diary entries between 7 June and 8 August. The Woolfs are at Monk's House from 18 June to 1 July; and return there on 28 July
August–September	Virginia is convalescent; she is unable to work or see visitors until mid-September. T. S. Eliot stays 24–25 September
6 October	Return to Hogarth House
4 November	Last words of *Jacob's Room* written
November	Excursions to Monk's House on 5th, and to see Philip Woolf and then Lytton Strachey on 19th
1–3 December	Leonard goes on political business to Manchester and Durham
20 December	The Woolfs go to Monk's House for Christmas holiday

1922

2 January	Return to Hogarth House
January–February	Virginia has influenza on 7 January, a relapse on 22 January and is an invalid throughout February; she is visited frequently by Clive Bell
25 February	Richmond G.P. Dr Fergusson recommends that Virginia see a heart specialist; she has a persistent high temperature throughout March
7–27 April	The Woolfs are at Monk's House
May	Virginia's temperature and heart still causing anxiety. She has three teeth extracted

APPENDIX A

27–29 May	The Woolfs go to Tidmarsh to visit Lytton Strachey, Carrington and Ralph Partridge; E. M. Forster and Gerald Brenan are also there
c. 2–10 June	The Woolfs are at Monk's House, whence they attend the Co-operative Conference at Brighton presided over by Margaret Llewelyn Davies
July	Virginia is finishing *Jacob's Room*; anxiety about her lungs
15–17 July	Virginia stays at Garsington, where she meets Augustine Birrell and J. T. Sheppard
1 August–5 October	The Woolfs are at Monk's House. On 9 August Virginia sees a specialist in London, who finds no tuberculosis, but identifies pneumonia germs in her throat. House guests are Sydney Waterlow, Lytton Strachey, E. M. Forster and T. S. Eliot; question of the Eliot Fellowship Fund is discussed
27 October	*Jacob's Room* is published by the Hogarth Press
4–5 November	The Woolfs stay at Tidmarsh with Lytton Strachey; the future of Ralph Partridge and the Hogarth Press under consideration until the end of the year
17 November	General Election; Leonard fails to win a University seat
14 December	The Woolfs dine with Clive Bell; first meeting with Vita Sackville-West (Mrs Harold Nicolson)
21 December	The Woolfs go to Monk's House for Christmas holiday
1923	
1 January	Return to Hogarth House
9 January	Death of Katherine Mansfield
15 January	Virginia is ill in bed with a temperature; unwell for rest of the month. On 29th Marjorie Joad comes to work full-time at the Hogarth Press; Ralph Partridge leaves in March
3–5 February	The Woolfs go to Cambridge for the week-end; they dine at King's, see *Oedipus Rex*, visit Newnham, and dine with Maynard Keynes
February–March	*The Nation* remodelled; Virginia attempts to get the literary editorship for T. S. Eliot; it is offered to and accepted by Leonard on 23 March
27 March	The Woolfs go to Spain *via* Paris, reaching Granada on 31st. They stay with Gerald Brenan at Yegen from 4–13 April, then travel by stages back to Paris. Leonard returns home on 24th; Virginia follows on 27th April. Leonard starts work on *The Nation*
25–27 May	The Woolfs are at Monk's House

2–3 June	The Woolfs stay at Garsington; Lytton Strachey is also there; "37 people to tea," including Lord David Cecil, E. Sackville-West, L. P. Hartley, Mrs Asquith
Late June	Virginia retires from her task of providing speakers for the Richmond Branch of the Women's Co-operative Guild
1 August–30 September	The Woolfs are at Monk's House; house guests include Francis Birrell and Raymond Mortimer, Mrs Mary Hamilton, E. M. Forster, Lytton Strachey and the Partridges; from 7–10 September they stay at Lulworth with Maynard Keynes; Lydia Lopokova, George Rylands and Raymond Mortimer are also there. Virginia is writing first version of *Freshwater*, and *The Hours* (*Mrs Dalloway*)
October–November	Virginia looks for a London house
December	The Woolfs are at Monk's House from 1–3 December and again from 21st

1924
1 January	Return to Hogarth House
January–March	Virginia finds 52 Tavistock Square, Bloomsbury on 8 January, buys the lease on 9 January, and moves there on 13–15 March
17–28 April	The Woolfs are at Monk's House for Easter
9–10 May	The Woolfs stay at Tidmarsh with Lytton Strachey and the Partridges
17–19 May	The Woolfs stay at Cambridge; they lunch with George Rylands at King's; plan of his joining Hogarth Press considered. Virginia lectures to The Heretics on Modern Fiction (*Mr Bennett and Mrs Brown*)
5–9 June	Whitsun holiday at Monk's House
28–29 June	The Woolfs stay at Garsington; fellow guests include Lord Berners and T. S. Eliot
2 July	George Rylands starts work at the Hogarth Press
4 July	Virginia taken by V. Sackville-West to Knole; she meets Lord Sackville, Lady Dorothy Wellesley and Geoffrey Scott
30 July–2 October	The Woolfs are at Monk's House; Virginia is working on *Mrs Dalloway*. Guests include George Rylands, Norman Leys, V. Sackville-West and Karin and Ann Stephen
8 October	*Mrs Dalloway* finished. The Woolfs visit Lytton Strachey in his new home, Ham Spray House, near Hungerford
30 October	*Mr Bennett and Mrs Brown* is published

APPENDIX A

25 November	George Rylands decides to leave the Hogarth Press at the end of the year; Angus Davidson interviewed to succeed him
24 December	The Woolfs go to Monk's House; Angus Davidson stays for Christmas

1925

3 January	Return to Tavistock Square; the Woolfs remain there until 26 March with one week-end at Monk's House, 6–8 February. Angus Davidson is working in the Hogarth Press
22 January	Virginia is ill and in bed for about two weeks
February	Marjorie Joad leaves the Hogarth Press; Bernadette Murphy comes
6 February	Virginia sends proofs of *Mrs Dalloway* to Jacques Raverat; he dies on 7 March
26 March–7 April	The Woolfs go to Cassis, and stay at Hotel Cendrillon
9–13 April	Easter at Monk's House
23 April	*The Common Reader* is published
2–3 May	The Woolfs stay at Cambridge; they meet John Hayward and Richard Braithwaite and many old friends
14 May	*Mrs Dalloway* published. Virginia thinking of *To the Lighthouse*
May–July	Virginia leads a very social life in London, with two week-ends at Monk's House and one at Thorpe-le-Soken with Adrian and Karin Stephen
July	Bernadette Murphy leaves the Hogarth Press; Mrs Cartwright comes
4 August	Marriage of John Maynard Keynes and Lydia Lopokova
5 August–2 October	The Woolfs are at Monk's House. On 19 August Virginia collapses at Charleston, and is unwell, seeing few visitors, throughout the holiday
October–November	Virginia is unwell and inactive at Tavistock Square
7 November	Death of Madge Vaughan
2 December	Virginia goes to the ballet; her first night out for two months
17–20 December	Virginia stays with V. Sackville-West at Long Barn, near Sevenoaks; Leonard joins them on 19th
22–28 December	The Woolfs stay with the Bells at Charleston (builders at Monk's House); V. Sackville-West to lunch there on 26th

1926

8 January	Virginia starts German measles at Tavistock Square and is unwell for the rest of the month; she begins

237

	again on *To the Lighthouse*. V. Sackville-West goes to Persia
6–8 February	The Woolfs are at Monk's House
16 March	40,000 words of *To the Lighthouse* written
24 March	Leonard gives in his resignation as Literary Editor of *The Nation*. Disastrous "literary" dinner with Rose Macaulay
13–18 April	The Woolfs go to Iwerne Minster; sell travel books in Dorset
29 April	Virginia finishes first part of *To the Lighthouse* and begins Part 2, which she finishes on 25 May
3–12 May	General Strike.
27–30 May	The Woolfs go to Monk's House, to which improvements have been made
11–15 June	Virginia is at Monk's House; Leonard stays two days and V. Sackville-West the next two
26–27 June	The Woolfs stay at Garsington; fellow guests include Aldous Huxley, Siegfried Sassoon, E. Sackville-West. They visit Robert Bridges at Boar's Hill
23 July	The Woolfs go to Dorchester to visit Thomas Hardy
27 July	The Woolfs go to Monk's House; Virginia exhausted and resting. Very few visitors; among them Rose Macaulay, Angus Davidson and Stephen Tomlin. Virginia depressed
14 October	Return to Tavistock Square
23–25 October	The Woolfs stay at Cambridge; they see Edmund Gosse, Pernel Strachey, F. L. Lucas and V. Sackville-West
4 November	The Woolfs dine with H. G. Wells to meet Arnold Bennett; the following day they go to Long Barn to spend the week-end with V. Sackville-West
22–28 December	The Woolfs spend Christmas with the Arnold-Forsters in Cornwall
1927	
January	Virginia finishing *To the Lighthouse*. She and Leonard at Monk's House from 5–9 January; 15th–17th she is at Long Barn and visits Knole; on 29 January V. Sackville-West returns to Persia. The Woolfs consider and reject the idea of going to America
9 February	Virginia has her hair shingled
25–27 February	The Woolfs are at Monk's House
Mid-March	Virginia conceives the idea of *The Jessamy Brides*
30 March–28 April	The Woolfs spend a week with the Bells at Cassis and then travel to Palermo, Syracuse, Naples and Rome, where they stay for a week

30 April	Vanessa writes to Virginia describing the moths at Cassis
5 May	*To the Lighthouse* is published
18–19 May	Virginia visits Oxford with V. Sackville-West and then goes to Monk's House for the week-end
Early June	Virginia is in bed for a week with headache; she goes to Monk's House for a week on 8th; on 16th she sees V. Sackville-West presented with the Hawthornden Prize
28–29 June	The Woolfs with the Nicolsons and others travel to Yorkshire to see the total eclipse of the sun
July	Virginia spends two week-ends with V. Sackville-West at Long Barn. The Woolfs buy a Singer car. Virginia broadcasts
27 July–1 August	Virginia stays with Ethel Sands and Nan Hudson at the Château d'Auppegard, near Dieppe; she meets J. E. Blanche
August–September	The Woolfs are at Monk's House. House guests include V. Sackville-West, Raymond Mortimer, E. M. Forster. Numerous excursions by motor car
5 October	Virginia starts to write *Orlando* "as a joke." The Woolfs return to Tavistock Square on 6th
8 November	Clive Bell sends Virginia first part of *Civilisation*. Correspondence with E. M. Forster about art and life
9 December	Angus Davidson is to leave the Hogarth Press
24 December	The Woolfs go to Charleston for Christmas; and on to Monk's House on 27th
1928	
2 January	Return to Tavistock Square. Virginia is working on *Orlando*. On 14–15 January she stays at Long Barn. Towards the end of the month she is in bed with headache, and again, with influenza, in mid-February
9–12 March	The Woolfs are at Monk's House. *Orlando* is finished on 17 March
26 March	The Woolfs cross to Dieppe and drive to Cassis, arriving on 2 April. They stay at Colonel Teed's house, Fontcreuse, near the Bells and Duncan Grant. They start home on 9 April, reaching London on 16th
April–June	Virginia is awarded the *Femina Vie Heureuse* prize. The Woolfs spend the last week-ends in April, May and June at Monk's House
9–11 June	The Woolfs visit Janet Case at Lyndhurst

24 July	The Woolfs go to Monk's House. V. Sackville-West stays on 29th and 30th; other guests this summer are E. Sackville-West, E. M. Forster, Richard Kennedy and Mrs Woolf. They buy the field adjoining Monk's House
24 September	Virginia and V. Sackville-West travel to Paris, Saulieu, Vézelay and Auxerre, returning to Monk's House on 1 October
2 October	The Woolfs return to Tavistock Square
11 October	*Orlando* is published
20 October	The Woolfs with V. Sackville-West, Vanessa and Angelica Bell, go to Cambridge. In this and the following week Virginia reads to the women's colleges two papers which are revised to become *A Room of One's Own*
9 November	*The Well of Loneliness* case is heard at Bow Street
November– December	Virginia and Vanessa organise a series of parties. On 10 November the Woolfs go to Cambridge to see Lydia Lopokova act; on 24–25 November they are at Rodmell, where they buy a cottage; and again on 15–16 December. Third edition of *Orlando* ordered
27 December	The Woolfs go to Monk's House; Richard Kennedy comes for one night
1929	
3 January	Return to Tavistock Square
16 January	The Woolfs travel to the Prinz Albrecht Hotel in Berlin, where they are joined on the 18th by Vanessa and Quentin Bell and Duncan Grant. Harold Nicolson is *en poste* at the Embassy; Vita and E. Sackville-West are also in Berlin
24–25 January	Return journey *via* Harwich; Virginia suffers from the effects of *Somnifène* and is ill for several weeks; she is further affected by the noise of a pumping machine near Tavistock Square
March	Virginia is writing the final version of *A Room of One's Own* and thinking about *The Moths*
3–7 April	The Woolfs go to Monk's House; and again later in the month, making arrangements to have two new rooms built on
3–6 May	To Monk's House, and again at Whitsun, 17–23 May
30 May	General Election. The Woolfs drive to Rodmell to vote; return next day *via* Long Barn to Tavistock Square
4–14 June	The Woolfs go to Cassis for a week, by train; they

	stay at Fontcreuse. Vanessa Bell and Duncan Grant are there
19–23 June	The Woolfs are at Monk's House. Virginia has a bad throat and headache
July	At Monk's House 5th–8th, 12th–14th and 20th–23rd
27 July–6 October	At Monk's House; guests include Ka Arnold-Forster, William Plomer, Janet Vaughan, Lyn Irvine, F. L. Lucas. Virginia suffers from intermittent headaches and melancholy. Visits to Long Barn to see V. Sackville-West and to Worthing to see Mrs Woolf
September	Harold Nicolson resigns from the Diplomatic Service
30 September	The Woolfs attend the Labour Party Conference in Brighton
24 October	*A Room of One's Own* is published
20 November	Virginia broadcasts. The Woolfs are disturbed by dance music from an hotel in Woburn Place and take legal action
21 December	To Monk's House; Virginia's new bedroom ready. They see the Keyneses and V. Sackville-West

1930

5 January	The Woolfs return to Tavistock Square. On 15th Virginia dines with Henry Harris in Bedford Square to meet the Prime Minister, &c; on 18th to Angelica Bell's party at 8 Fitzroy Street. On 31st the case against the Imperial Hotel Company is decided in the Woolfs' favour
9 February	Death of C. P. Sanger. On returning from two days at Monk's House, Leonard is ill, succeeded by Virginia, who has an intermittent temperature for the rest of the month
February	Plans for a new periodical are discussed between Woolfs, Bells, Roger Fry and Raymond Mortimer (unrealised)
20 February	Virginia's first meeting with Ethel Smyth, who henceforth is a constant visitor
1–8 March	The Woolfs are at Monk's House; and again from 21st–24th. Virginia is writing *The Waves*
31 March	Mrs Cartwright leaves the Hogarth Press
April	The Woolfs are at Monk's House 4th–6th; and again at Easter, 16th–27th
29 May	Virginia finishes first version of *The Waves*
4–11 May	The Woolfs make a tour of Somerset, Devon and Cornwall travelling books, returning through Hampshire to Monk's House. Nelly Boxall is ill all the month and on 29th goes into hospital

5–10 June	The Woolfs are at Monk's House; and again 20th–21st. Virginia is rewriting *The Waves*; and seeing a good deal of V. Sackville-West and Ethel Smyth, both of whom she visits
July	The Woolfs are at Monk's House 4th–6th, 12th–14th and from 29th. They make short visits to Cambridge, to Woking to see Ethel Smyth, and to Long Barn
August–September	At Monk's House. Leonard drives to London about once a week, Virginia sometimes accompanies him. Guests are Ethel Smyth, V. Sackville-West, Alice Ritchie, E. M. Forster. On 29 August Virginia faints in the garden and is ill for ten days. Her new bedroom becomes the sitting-room. On 10 September the Woolfs go to Sissinghurst Castle, V. Sackville-West's new home, for the day
1 October	The Woolfs lunch with the Bells at Charleston to meet George and Margaret Duckworth
4 October–December	Return to Tavistock Square. Four week-ends are spent at Monk's House. Virginia is leading a sociable life in London, dining out with Lady Rhondda, Lady Colefax, etc., as well as seeing old friends and family
23 December	The Woolfs go to Monk's House for Christmas; Virginia is ill in bed from 24th–30th
1931	
7 January	Return to Tavistock Square. Nelly Boxall returns to work as cook-housekeeper
12 January	Virginia meets John Lehmann, the prospective partner in the Hogarth Press; he starts work on 21st
23–25 January	The Woolfs are at Monk's House. Henceforth their general intention is to spend every other week-end (from Friday to Sunday), usually rather longer at Easter, Whitsun and Christmas, and the whole of August and September, at Rodmell
7 February	Virginia records the end of *The Waves*
14–15 February	The Woolfs drive with Vanessa to Cambridge to see Purcell's *Faery Queen*; they see E. M. Forster, George Rylands and others
27 February	Virginia goes to Sissinghurst to stay overnight with V. Sackville-West
28–29 March	The Woolfs drive to Liphook to stay with Sidney and Beatrice Webb

2–9 April	Easter at Monk's House
16–30 April	The Woolfs tour western France by car, from Dieppe to La Rochelle, Brantôme, Poitiers, Le Mans, Dreux, Caudebec and back
3 May	Return to Tavistock Square after Virginia has spent two days at Monk's House
21–28 May	Whitsun holiday at Monk's House after Virginia has spent two days in bed with a headache blamed on Ethel Smyth
July	Virginia sits to Stephen Tomlin for a sculptured head
17–19 July	The Woolfs are at Monk's House. Virginia finishes correcting and retyping *The Waves*, which Leonard reads and declares a masterpiece
25–26 July	The Woolfs stay at Oare with Sydney and Margery Waterlow
30 July	The Woolfs go to Monk's House for the summer. Virginia begins writing *Flush* and corrects proofs of *The Waves*; some days of headache. Visitors include V. Sackville-West, Lady Colefax, Ethel Smyth, John Lehmann, Sir George and Lady Margaret Duckworth, Kingsley Martin and Lyn Irvine
1 October	Return to Tavistock Square. Leonard gives six broadcasts at weekly intervals
8 October	*The Waves* is published
24 November	Virginia has headaches and has to remain inactive for a month
22 December	The Woolfs go to Monk's House for Christmas. Lytton Strachey is dangerously ill
1932	
10 January	Return to Tavistock Square
14 January	The Woolfs drive to Ham Spray to visit Lytton Strachey, who is too ill to see them; lunch with Pippa Strachey
21 January	Death of Lytton Strachey
31 January	Virginia finishes writing *A Letter to a Young Poet*; she works on *The Common Reader: Second Series*
February	Virginia is invited to deliver the Clark Lectures at Cambridge, but declines
10 March	The Woolfs drive to Ham Spray to see Carrington, who the following day kills herself
12–15 March	The Woolfs drive to Cambridge to see *Hamlet* with George Rylands; then to King's Lynn, Cromer, Norwich and to spend a night with Roger Fry near Ipswich

23 March–3 April	Easter at Monk's House; the Woolfs visit V. Sackville-West at Sissinghurst Castle and Ethel Smyth and Maurice Baring at Rottingdean. Cement works being erected at Asham
15 April	The Woolfs, with Roger and Margery Fry, set out for Greece, *via* Paris and Venice, reaching Athens on 20th; they return by Orient Express *via* Belgrade and reach Monk's House on 12 May
15 May	Return to Tavistock Square. Discussions concerning organisation of the Hogarth Press; John Lehmann is to stay as adviser, Miss Scott Johnson as manager, with three clerks
June–July	Virginia leads a very sociable life, going to Monk's House every other week-end
1 July	*A Letter to a Young Poet* is published; on 11th *The Common Reader: Second Series* is finished
26 July	The Woolfs go to Monk's House. Very hot August weather: on 11th Virginia faints from heat and is unwell for some days. Visitors include Stella Benson, Mrs Woolf, Mr and Mrs T. S. Eliot, V. Sackville-West, Ethel Smyth and William Plomer
25–26 August	The Woolfs go to Thorpe-le-Soken to visit Adrian and Karin Stephen, returning to Monk's House *via* Tavistock Square
31 August	John Lehmann leaves the Hogarth Press
October	The Woolfs return to Tavistock Square; on 3–5 October they attend the Labour Party Conference at Leicester
13 October	*The Common Reader: Second Series* is published. Virginia begins "making up" *The Pargiters* (*The Years*)
1 November	Virginia's heart "galloping", which restricts her activity
20 December	The Woolfs go to Monk's House for Christmas; the Keyneses come to lunch and tea on Christmas Day
1933	
2 January	The Woolfs go to London for one night, to Vanessa's party
15 January	Return to Tavistock Square. Virginia is correcting *Flush*
February	Virginia begins twice weekly Italian lessons
March	Virginia is offered, and refuses, an Honorary Doctorate of Manchester University
13–23 April	The Woolfs are at Monk's House for Easter
5–27 May	The Woolfs drive through France and *via* the Grande

	Corniche and Pisa to Siena, returning by Lucca, Lerici, Avignon and Chartres to Monk's House
28 May	Return to Tavistock Square. Virginia is working on *The Years*
1–7 June	Whitsun at Monk's House
June–July	The Woolfs are very active and sociable; there is a revival of intimacy with Lady Ottoline Morrell, whom Virginia encourages in writing her memoirs
27 July	To Monk's House for the summer. Virginia is completely exhausted and in bed early August. Visitors include Elizabeth Read, Ethel Smyth, Kingsley Martin, V. Sackville-West, Leopold Campbell-Douglas, W. A. Robson, T. S. Eliot, E. M. Forster. Virginia begins again on *The Years*
Early September	Virginia is offered the Leslie Stephen lectureship at Cambridge, which she declines
23 September	The Memoir Club meets at Tilton (the Keyneses); E. M. Forster stays with the Woolfs; on 24th there are eleven people for tea at Monk's House
3–4 October	The Labour Party Conference at Hastings; Leonard attends both days, Virginia the first
5 October	*Flush* is published; the Woolfs go to Sissinghurst for the day
7 October	Return to Tavistock Square. Fortnightly visits to Monk's House continue (Friday to Sunday). On 11–12 November the Woolfs go to Ipsden to stay with Rosamond (Lehmann) and Wogan Philipps; on 30 November Virginia goes to Oxford to visit H. A. L. Fisher
15 December	Virginia dines with Clive Bell to meet Walter Sickert
21 December	The Woolfs go to Monk's House for three weeks. The Keyneses and V. Sackville-West and her sons come on Christmas Day
1934	
7 January	The Woolfs go to London for the day, Leonard to the funeral of his sister Clara
14 January–end March	Return to Tavistock Square. Fortnightly visits to Monk's House continue. Virginia is suffering from recurrent headaches. In February she finishes revising *Sickert* and returns to work on her novel. Vanessa is painting her portrait
28 March	Nelly Boxall finally leaves the Woolfs' service. They go to Monk's House for a fortnight over Easter. E. M. Forster comes to stay for the Memoir Club meeting at Tilton on 8 April

22 April	The Woolfs drive to Monk's House and thence, by Salisbury and Fishguard, to Ireland; they visit Elizabeth Bowen at Bowen's Court; at Waterville on 1 May they read of George Duckworth's death; they go to Galway and Dublin and return by Holyhead and Stratford-on-Avon
9 May	Return to Tavistock Square. Virginia has influenza and is in bed for a week, after which they go to Monk's House for Whitsun (17–22 May). She is again ill in London, so they return to Monk's House for another week. They go to *Figaro* at Glyndebourne
11 June	Return to Tavistock Square. Virginia has French lessons with Janie Bussy twice a week; she returns to work on *The Years*
25 July	Leonard acquires a marmoset
26 July	The Woolfs go to Monk's House for the summer; Mabel comes as their new cook, Louie Everest as daily help. Visitors include Enid Bagnold, Saxon Sydney-Turner, William Plomer, Lyn Irvine, Karin, Ann and Judith Stephen, George Rylands
9 September	Death of Roger Fry; the Woolfs go to his funeral at Golders Green on 13 September
30 September	Virginia finishes first draft of *The Years* and is unwell for several days
7 October	Return to Tavistock Square. Virginia is depressed over her novel and Wyndham Lewis's detractions
20–21 October	The Woolfs go to a New Fabian Research Bureau conference at Maidstone. On 25th *Walter Sickert: a Conversation* is published. Virginia meets W. B. Yeats at Lady Ottoline Morrell's house
15 November	Virginia starts rewriting *The Years*
21 December	The Woolfs go to Monk's House for Christmas; very wet
1935	
2 January	Death of Francis Birrell
13 January	The Woolfs return to Tavistock Square
18 January	Virginia's play *Freshwater* performed before friends in Vanessa's studio at 8 Fitzroy Street
February–April	Alternate week-ends at Monk's House. Virginia is revising *The Years* and seeing a great many people
18–24 April	Easter at Rodmell
1 May	The Woolfs set out *via* Harwich for a tour of Europe by car. They spend a week in Holland, three days in Germany and cross the Brenner Pass into Italy

on 13 May; they reach Rome on 16 May and find Vanessa, Angelica and Quentin Bell there; they start home on 24th and drive through France, reaching Monk's House on 31 May

2 June   Return to Tavistock Square until 6th, when they go back to Monk's House for Whitsun. Two visits to Glyndebourne

2 July   Virginia goes to spend a night with the Tweedsmuirs (Susan Buchan) in the Cotswolds

12 July   The Woolfs drive to Bristol, where Virginia opens an exhibition of Roger Fry's paintings; they return by Avebury, Lechlade and Kelmscott

24 July   "Reconciliation dinner" for John Lehmann

25 July   The Woolfs go to Monk's House for the summer. Visitors include Stephen Tennant, Leonard's relations, W. A. Robson, Margery Fry and T. S. Eliot. They make day visits to London, to Worthing, to Sissinghurst, to Dorking (to see Margaret Llewelyn Davies).

29 August   Julian Bell leaves Newhaven for China. Exceptionally stormy weather

September   Virginia decides to call her book The Years; she is rewriting it

30 September–2 October   The Woolfs attend the Labour Party Conference in Brighton; they hear Bevin's attack on Lansbury

5 October   Return to Tavistock Square. Virginia is reading Roger Fry's letters and making notes for a possible biography

14 November   General Election. The Woolfs vote at Rodmell and drive voters to the poll at Patcham

20 December   To Monk's House for Christmas holiday. Very wet

1936

1 January   Virginia is in bed with headache; three bad days

8 January   Return to Tavistock Square. Virginia is revising The Years and reading for Roger Fry

20 January   Death of King George V; accession of Edward VIII

24–26 January   The Woolfs go to Monk's House and on to Canterbury, where Leonard lectures to the Workers' Educational Association

9 February   The Woolfs attend a meeting of Vigilance, an organisation of anti-Fascist intellectuals, at Adrian Stephen's home

February   Virginia is working very hard, is not very well, and limits her social engagements

March   The Woolfs go to see Lydia Lopokova playing in

	Ibsen. There is a general preoccupation with the worsening political situation. Part of *The Years* is sent to the printer, but the greater part is still being revised and retyped
3 April	The Woolfs go to Monk's House for Easter. Virginia sends last batch of manuscript of *The Years* to the printer on 8th, collapses into bed and remains at Rodmell for a month, able to do nothing
3 May	Return to Tavistock Square; Virginia sees Dr Rendel. They then set out by car for a tour of the south-west, to Weymouth, Lyme Regis and to Cornwall, where they stay three nights with the Arnold-Forsters at Zennor; they return *via* Coverack and Shaftesbury to Monk's House and Tavistock Square, which they reach on 22 May
23 May	Virginia begins work again–not more than 45 minutes a day permitted by her doctor
29 May–10 June	The Woolfs return to Monk's House, following the doctor's recommendation
10–25 June	Return to Tavistock Square for a fortnight's trial. Virginia is correcting proofs of *The Years* with great suffering
25–30 June	The Woolfs are at Monk's House. After a further week in London they return there and remain until October. Virginia is very unwell; no entry in her diary from 23 June to 30 October; few visitors–mostly family to play bowls with Leonard
11 October	Return to Tavistock Square. Virginia seems much better; on 19th she goes to stay a night with Ethel Smyth at Woking, and begins to entertain and to go out again
2 November	Virginia is in despair; Leonard reads proofs of *The Years* and reassures her; she finishes work on it on 30 November
November	Roger Fry's friend Charles Mauron is in London and meets the Woolfs. Virginia begins writing *Three Guineas*
December	The Abdication crisis; King Edward abdicates on 10th
17 December	The Woolfs go to Monk's House for Christmas; Christmas lunch with the Keyneses
1937	
1–4 January	Ann and Judith Stephen stay at Monk's House. On 8th the Woolfs have tea with Elizabeth Robins and Octavia Wilberforce in Brighton
9 January	Funeral of Stephen Tomlin

16 January	Return to Tavistock Square. On 21st Miss West, the manager of the Hogarth Press, dies
February	Virginia is working on *Three Guineas*; Leonard is not well and sees specialists; by 22nd he is given a clean bill of health
12–15 March	The Woolfs are at Monk's House. Julian Bell returns from China with the intention of enlisting in the International Brigade in Spain
15 March	Publication of *The Years*
25 March–4 April	The Woolfs are at Monk's House for Easter. On 1 April they drive to Minstead in the New Forest to see Janet Case, who is dying
29 April	Virginia broadcasts
7–25 May	The Woolfs tour south-western France by car, staying some days at Souillac and visiting Les Eyzies, Albi, George Sand's house at Nohant, and Maintenon. Maynard Keynes is seriously ill
29 May–6 June	The Woolfs are at Monk's House
6 June	Farewell dinner for Julian Bell at 50 Gordon Square; he leaves next day to drive an ambulance in Spain
June–July	Virginia is again active and sociable; some week-ends are spent at Monk's House
15 July	Death of Janet Case
20 July	The news is received of Julian Bell's death on 18 July
29 July	The Woolfs drive Vanessa to Charleston, and then go to Monk's House until October. Virginia is a constant support to her sister and family. Dorothy and Janie Bussy, Judith Stephen and T. S. Eliot stay at Monk's House. Day visits to London, to Dorking to see Margaret Llewelyn Davies, and to Sissinghurst. Virginia is working on *Three Guineas*
10 October	Return to Tavistock Square. On 12th Virginia finishes *Three Guineas*
October–December	The Woolfs go once a fortnight to Monk's House; 12–13 November they are at Cambridge, Leonard speaking at the Union. Virginia is unwell at the beginning of December, and anxious about Leonard's health
22–29 December	The Woolfs are at Monk's House for Christmas; Leonard is ill, so returns to London and is examined at the Royal Northern Hospital on 31 December

1938

1–11 January	Leonard stays in bed; specimens found "normal"
14–23 January	To Monk's House for Leonard's convalescence

24 January	Virginia is ill at Tavistock Square with a temperature
1 March	John Lehmann takes over Virginia's share of the Hogarth Press
12 March	Hitler invades Austria
14–24 April	The Woolfs are at Monk's House for Easter. Lady Ottoline Morrell dies on 21 April. Virginia is working at *Roger Fry* and thinking about *Poyntz Hall* (*Between the Acts*)
14–15 May	The Woolfs go to Haslemere to stay with Ray and Oliver Strachey
22 May	Death of Mrs Arnold-Forster (Ka Cox)
1–11 June	The Woolfs are at Monk's House. *Three Guineas* is published on 2 June
16 June–2 July	The Woolfs go by car *via* the Roman Wall to Scotland and the Western Isles
28 July	The Woolfs go to Monk's House for the summer; guests include V. Sackville-West, Lady Colefax, E. M. Forster and Molly MacCarthy (for Memoir Club meeting, 11 September), Noel Olivier Richards and Richard and Ann (Stephen) Llewelyn Davies. Weekly visits to London, and for one night (26–27 September) during the Munich crisis
16 October	Return to Tavistock Square; the Woolfs make fortnightly visits to Monk's House
20 December	To Monk's House for Christmas. Snow. On 24th Jack Hills dies; also Leonard's marmoset, Mitz. To Tilton and Charleston on Christmas Day.
1939	
15 January	Return to Tavistock Square. The Woolfs go twice a month to Rodmell for week-ends
28 January	The Woolfs visit Sigmund Freud at Hampstead
2 March	Virginia speaks at an exhibition of book jackets at the Central School of Arts and Crafts
3 March	Virginia is offered and refuses an Honorary Doctorate of Liverpool University
6–24 April	The Woolfs are at Monk's House for Easter. Virginia is not very well
25 May	At Monk's House for Whitsun
5–20 June	The Woolfs go from Rodmell to France, to make a tour by car in Brittany and Normandy
22 June	Return to Tavistock Square
2 July	Death of Mrs Woolf, Leonard's mother
25 July	The Woolfs go to Monk's House for the summer
17 August	To London to move the Hogarth Press to 37 Mecklenburgh Square, W.C.1; on 24th they move their

	personal possessions there, and return to Rodmell. Crisis atmosphere in London
1 September	Germany invades Poland; on 3rd England declares war
September	Hogarth Press clerks each stay two or three days at Monk's House; other guests are Kingsley Martin, Stephen Spender, John Lehmann and Judith Stephen
13–20 October	The Woolfs stay at Mecklenburgh Square. Henceforward they live at Monk's House, going to London usually once a week, sometimes for the day, sometimes staying a few days
October–December	At Monk's House. Regular meetings of the Rodmell Labour Party are held there. Guests are T. S. Eliot, E. Sackville-West, W. A. Robson, John Lehmann

1940

6 January	Party for Angelica Bell at Charleston; guests include the Woolfs, the Keyneses, Marjorie Strachey and Duncan Grant
12–13 January	E. M. Forster stays at Monk's House
February	6th–7th, John Lehmann to stay; 12th–16th, in London; 17th–19th, Sally Graves (Mrs Chilver) stays at Monk's House; 24th, Virginia is ill with influenza, but on 26th goes to Mecklenburgh Square, where she stays in bed
2 March	Return to Monk's House. The manuscript of *Roger Fry* is sent to Margery Fry and to Vanessa. Virginia is mostly ill and in bed until 21 March. 27th–28th, Margery Fry stays at Monk's House
9 April	German invasion of Norway and Denmark
23–24 April	V. Sackville-West stays at Monk's House
27 April	Virginia lectures to the Workers' Educational Association in Brighton (*The Leaning Tower*)
10 May	Germany invades Holland and Belgium
18–21 May	Desmond MacCarthy and G. E. Moore stay at Monk's House
10 June	Italy enters the war
14 June	The Woolfs visit Penshurst with V. Sackville-West; Paris falls to the Germans
17–20 June	The Woolfs stay at Mecklenburgh Square; Adrian Stephen provides them with a lethal dose of morphia
25–27 June	Elizabeth Bowen stays at Monk's House
15–16 July	St John and Jeremy Hutchinson stay at Monk's House
23 July	Virginia reads her account of the Dreadnought Hoax to the Women's Institute in Rodmell

25 July	Publication of *Roger Fry: A Biography*
August–September	Battle of Britain; daily air raids. John Lehmann, Ann and Judith Stephen, Benedict Nicolson stay at Monk's House. The Memoir Club meets at Charleston on 1 September. Helen Anrep stays in Rodmell
10 September	The Woolfs drive to London; Mecklenburgh Square has been bombed, their house severely damaged, and they cannot reach it
23 September	The Hogarth Press is moved from Mecklenburgh Square to Letchworth, Hertfordshire
18 October	The Woolfs drive to London for the day; see 52 Tavistock Square in ruins
7 November	Virginia refuses E. M. Forster's request to propose her for the Committee of the London Library
4 December	Furniture and books arrive from Mecklenburgh Square for storage at Monk's House and in the village
14 December	The Hogarth Press printing machine is delivered to Monk's House

1941

1 January	Dr Octavia Wilberforce has tea at Monk's House; she now comes fairly often from Brighton, bringing cream, etc.
11–13 February	The Woolfs drive to London and go by train to Cambridge, where they see Pernel Strachey and George Rylands; they also visit the Hogarth Press at Letchworth
13–15 February	Elizabeth Bowen stays at Monk's House
17–18 February	V. Sackville-West stays at Monk's House
26 February	Virginia finishes *Pointz Hall* (*Between the Acts*)
8 March	To Brighton; Leonard lecturing to the Workers' Educational Association, Virginia fighting despondency
18 March	Leonard becomes seriously alarmed by Virginia's deteriorating state
27 March	The Woolfs go to Brighton to consult Dr Wilberforce about Virginia's condition
28 March	Virginia Woolf drowns herself in the River Ouse

APPENDIX B

The Years was published on 15 March 1937; on Easter Sunday, 28 March, Virginia Woolf made the following entry in her diary (AWD (Berg)) at Monk's House, Rodmell

. . . Yesterday a reporter for the New York Times rang up: was told he could look at the outside of 52 [Tavistock Square] if he chose. At 4.30 as I was boiling the kettle a huge black Daimler drew up. Then a dapper little man in a tweed coat appeared in the garden. I reached the sitting room: saw him standing there looking round. L. ignored him. L. in the orchard with Percy. Then I guessed. He had a green notebook and stood looking about jotting things down. I ducked my head–he almost caught me. At last L. turned and fronted him. No, Mrs W. didn't want that kind of publicity. I raged: a bug walking over one's skin–couldn't crush him. The bug taking notes. L. politely led him back to his Daimler and his wife. But they'd had a nice run from London–bugs, to come and steal in and take notes.

The typescript original (MH/A 19) of the following contains a certain number of typing errors which have been corrected in accordance with Virginia's obvious intentions.

FANTASY UPON A GENTLEMAN WHO CONVERTED HIS IMPRESSIONS OF A PRIVATE HOUSE INTO CASH

He wished to see, J.B., the lady of the house, did he?
There he sat, in the morning, the precious morning,
in the spring of the year, on a chair; J.B.
Yes, I see; I see, the unbaked crumpet face;
with a hole for a mouth; and a blob at the lips;
the voluble half closed lips; gooseberry eyes;
his lack of attraction; his self satisfaction;
sitting there, in the chair in the spring of the year;
taking time, air, light, space; stopping the
race of every thought; blocking out with his tweeds
the branches; the pigeons; and half the sky.
Monarch of the drab world; of the shifting shuffling
uneasy, queasy, egotist's journalist's pobbing and
boobling, like a stew a-simmer, asking for sympathy
dousing the clean the clear the bright the sharp in
the stew of his greasy complacency; his self satisfaction
his profound unhappy sense of his lack of attraction;
his desire to be scratched cleansed, rubbed clean of
the moss and the slime; demanding as a right,

other people's time; sitting there on the chair;
blocking out the light with his rubbed grease stained tweeds.
Why did he want to be 'seen'. What corkscrew
urge from the surge of his stew, his gobbets and
gibbets forced him out of the here, to this chair,
to be seen? when the spring was there?
to be seen sitting there, sprawling, self conscious,
conscious only of nothing, blear eyed, blubber
lipped, thick thumbed, squirming, to be seen,
Brown like a bug that slips out on a lodging house
wall; J.B. John Bug; James Bug Bug bug bug, as he
talked he slipped like a bug malodorous glistening
but only semi transparent; as if while he talked he
sipped blood. my blood; anybodies blood to make a
bugs body blue black. There he sat on the chair,
with his hair unbrushed; his mouth dribbling; his eyes
streaming with the steam of some lodging house stew.
A bug; Always on the wall. The bug of the house
that comes. But if you kill bugs they leave marks
on the wall. Just as the bug's body bleeds in pale
ink recording his impressions of a private house
in the newspapers for cash.

APPENDIX C
Virginia Woolf and Julian Bell

Julian Bell was killed in Spain on 18 July 1937. Virginia's memoir of him is dated 30 July 1937. The manuscript (MH/A 8) runs to some 7,000 words, and was made use of by Peter Stansky and William Abrahams in their dual biography of Julian Bell and John Cornford, Journey to the Frontier (1966). It is printed here in the belief that it illuminates Virginia's own character and personality: some less relevant passages have therefore been omitted.

I am going to set down very quickly what I remember about Julian, – partly because I am too dazed to write what I was writing: & then I am so composed that nothing is real unless I write it. And again, I know by this time what an odd effect Time has: it does not destroy people – for instance, I still think perhaps more truly than I did, of Roger, of Thoby: but it brushes away the actual personal presence.

The last time I saw Julian was at Clive's, two days before he went to Spain. It was a Sunday night, the beginning of June – a hot night. He was in his shirtsleeves. Lottie* was out, & we cooked dinner. He had a peculiar

They reminded one of a sharp winged bird – one of the snipe here in the marsh

way of standing: his gestures were, as they say, characteristic. He made sharp quick movements, very sudden, considering how large & big he was, & oddly graceful. I remember his intent expression; seriously looking, I suppose at toast or eggs, through his spectacles. He had a very serious look: indeed he had grown much sterner, since he came back from China. But of the talk I remember very little; except that by degrees it turned to politics. L. & Clive & Julian began to talk about Fascism, I dare-

say: & I remember thinking, now Clive is reining himself in with L.: being self restrained: which means there's trouble brewing. (I was wrong, as L. told me afterwards.) Julian was now a grown man: I mean, he held his own with Clive & L.: & was cool & independent. I felt he had met many different kinds of people in China. Anyhow, as it was hot, & they talked politics, V[anessa]. & A[ngelica]. & I went out into the Square, & then the others came, & we sat & talked. I remember saying something about Roger's papers, & telling Julian I should leave them to him in my will. He said in his quick way, Better leave them to the British Museum. & I thought, That's because he thinks he may be killed. Of course we all knew that this was our last meeting – all together – before he went. But I had made up my mind to plunge into work, & seeing people, that summer.

* Lottie Hope, who had once been the Woolfs' servant, now worked for Clive Bell at 50 Gordon Square.

I had determined not to think about the risks, because, subconsciously I was sure he would be killed; that is I had a couchant unexpressed certainty, from Thoby's death I think; a legacy of pessimism, which I have decided never to analyse. Then, as we walked towards the gate together, I went with Julian, & said, Won't you have time to write something in Spain? Won't you send it us? (This referred of course to my feeling, a very painful one, that I had treated his essay on Roger too lightly.) And he said, very quickly–he spoke quickly with a suddenness like his movements– "Yes, I'll write something about Spain. And send it you if you like." Do I said, & touched his hand. Then we went up to Clive's room: & then they went: we stood at the door to watch them. Julian was driving Nessa's car. At first it wouldn't start. He sat there at the wheel frowning, looking very magnificent, in his shirt sleeves; with an expression as if he had made up his mind & were determined, though there was this obstacle–the car wouldn't start. Then suddenly it jerked off–& he had his head thrown slightly back, as he drove up the Square with Nessa beside him. Of course I noted it, as it might be our last meeting. What he said was 'Goodbye until this time next year.'

We went in with Clive & drank. And talked about Julian. Clive & L. said that there was no more risk in going to Spain than in driving up & down to Charleston. Clive said that only one man had been hurt by a bomb. And he added, But Julian is very cool, like Cory [Clive's brother] & myself. It's spirited of him to go, he added. I think I said, But it's a worry for Nessa. Then we discussed professions: Clive told us how Picasso had said, As a father, I'm so glad my son does not have one. And he said, he was glad Julian should be a 'character'; he would always have enough money to get bread and butter: it was a good thing he had no profession. He was a person who had no one gift in particular. He did not think he was born to be a writer–No he was a character, like Thoby. For some reason I did not answer, that he was like Thoby. I have always been foolish about that. I did not like any Bell to be like Thoby, partly through snobbishness I suppose; nor do I think that Julian was like Thoby, except in the obvious way that he was young & very fine to look at. I said that Thoby had a natural style, & Julian had not.

There was also the damned literary question. I was always critical of his writing, partly I suspect from the usual generation jealousy; partly from my own enviousness of anyone who can do in writing what I can't do: & again (for I can't analyse out the other strains in a very complex feeling, roused partly by L.; for we envied Nessa I suspect for such a son; and there was L.'s family complex which made him eager, no, on the alert, to criticise her children because he thought I admired them more than his family) I thought him very careless, not 'an artist', too personal in what he wrote, & "all over the place". This is the one thing I regret in our relationship: that I might have encouraged him more as a writer. But again, that's my character: & I'm always forced, in spite of jealousy, to be honest in the end. Still this is my one regret; & I shall always have it; seeing how immensely generous he was to me about what I did-touchingly proud sometimes of my writings. But then I came to the stage 2 years ago of hating 'personality'; desiring anonymity; a complex state which I would one day have discussed with him. Then, I could not sympathise with wishing to be published. I thought it wrong from my new standpoint-a piece of the egomaniac, egocentric mania of the time. (For that reason I would not sign my Janet article). But how could he know why I was so cool about publishing his things? Happily I made L. reconsider his poems, & we published them.

I could be hurt sometimes by his rather caustic teasing, something like Clive's, & I felt it more because I have suffered from Clive's caustic & rather cruel teasing in the past.-Julian had something of the same way of "seeing through one"; but it was less personal, & stronger. That last supper party at Clive's I remember beginning a story about Desmond. It was about the L.S. lecture.* I said "Desmond took it very seriously as a compliment." And I could not remember who had had the L.S. lectureship and said "Didn't David [Cecil] do it?" & then Julian gave his flash of mockery & severity & said Ah, how like you. That's what you said-looking at Clive as though they both joined in suspecting my malice: in which he was that time wrong. But not always. I mean he had claws & could use them. He had feelings about the Bells. He thought I wanted to give pain. He thought me cruel, as Clive thinks me; but he told me, the night I talked to him before he went to China, that he never doubted the warmth of my feelings: that I suffered a great deal: that I had very strong affections.

But our relationship was perfectly secure because it was founded on our passion-not too strong a word for either of us-for Nessa. And it was this passion that made us both reserved when we met this summer.

I was so anxious to do everything to stop him from going that I got him to meet Kingsley Martin once at dinner, & then Stephen Spender, & so never saw him alone-except once, & then only for a short time. I had just come in with the Evening Standard in which The Years was extravagantly praised, much to my surprise. I felt very happy. It was a great relief. And I stood with the paper, hoping L. would come & I could tell him when the bell rang. I went to the top of the stairs, looked down, & saw Julian's great sun hat (he was amazingly careless of dress always-would come here with a tear in his trousers) & I called out in a sepulchral voice "Who is that?" Whereupon he started, & laughed & I let him in. And he said What a voice to hear, or something light: then he came up; it was to ask for Dalton's telephone number. He stood there; I asked him to stay and see Leonard. He hesitated, but seemed to

* The Leslie Stephen Lecture at the University of Cambridge.

make up his mind that he must get on with the business of seeing Dalton. So I went & looked for the number. When I came back he was reading the Standard. I had left it with the review open. But he had turned, I think to the politics. I had half a mind to say, Look how I'm praised. And then thought No, I'm on the top of the wave: & it's not kind to thrust that sort of thing upon people who aren't yet recognised. So I said nothing about it. But I wanted him to stay. And then again I felt, he's afraid I shall try to persuade him not to go. So all I said was, Look here Julian, if you ever want a meal, you've only to ring us up. Yes he said rather doubtingly, as if we might be too busy. So I insisted. We can't see too much of you. And followed him into the hall, & put my arm round him & said You can't think how nice it is having you back. & we half kissed; & he looked pleased & said Do you feel that? And I said yes, & it was as if he asked me to forgive him for all the worry; and then off he stumped, in his great hat and thick coat.

When I was in that horrid state of misery last summer with the proofs of The Years, in such misery that I could only work for 10 minutes & then go & lie down, I wrote him my casual letter about his Roger paper, & he only answered many weeks later to say he had been hurt;* so hadn't written: & then another letter of mine brought back the old family feeling. I was shocked at this, & wrote at once, in time to catch him before he started home, to say don't let us ever quarrel about writing, & I explained & apologised. All the same, for this reason, & because of his summer journey, & also because one always stops writing letters unless one has a regular day, we had one of those lapses in communication which are bound to happen. I thought, when he comes back there'll be time to begin again. I thought he would get some political job & we should see a lot of him.

This lapse perhaps explains why I go on asking myself, without finding an answer, what did he feel about Spain? What made him feel it necessary, knowing as he did how it must torture Nessa, to go? He knew her feeling. We discussed it before he went to China in the most intimate talk I ever had with him. I remember then he said how hard it was for her, now that Roger was dead; & that he was sorry that Quentin was so much at Charleston. He knew that: & yet deliberately inflicted this fearful anxiety on her. What made him do it? I suppose its a fever in the blood of the younger generation which we can't possibly understand. I have never known anyone of my generation have that feeling about a war. We were all C.O.'s in the Great war. And though I understand that this is a 'cause', can be called the cause of liberty & so on, still my natural reaction is to

* Virginia's letter is lost. Julian, in his reply from Wuhan (5 December 1936), says: "I was rather hurt at your not liking my Roger better – which was most unreasonable of me, but I think your letter caught me at the moment when one feels most sensitive about one's work, when its finished past altering and at the same time is still a part of oneself."

fight intellectually: if I were any use, I should write against it: I should evolve some plan for fighting English tyranny. The moment force is used, it becomes meaningless & unreal to me. And I daresay he would soon have lived through the active stage, & have found some other, administrative, work. But that does not explain his determination. . . .

A Note on Sources and References

The notes which follow are intended to direct those who may wish to pursue such matters to the sources I have used. To avoid spattering the main text with distracting numerals, a page number and salient phrase are used to identify the quotation or statement whose origin is here documented.

The principal *published* sources are listed in the Bibliography on p. 282, where abbreviated titles used in the notes are given in full. Page references are given to English editions, and to the first edition of Virginia Woolf's books.

The *unpublished* material to which reference is made is for the greater part contained in three collections (more fully described in the Foreword to Volume I), namely: the Henry W. and Albert A. Berg Collection of English and American Literature of The New York Public Library (Berg); the Charleston Papers in the Library of King's College, Cambridge (CH); and what I have called the Monk's House Papers (MH). These, which formed a part of the estate of the late Leonard Woolf, now belong, thanks to the generosity of Mrs Ian Parsons, to the University of Sussex. In the notes I have identified material from these three repositories by the abbreviations given here in brackets.

In 1955 Leonard Woolf began to assemble copies of Virginia Woolf's letters with the intention of publishing them. The intention was abandoned, but the copies were retained. It is thus that I am familiar with letters whose whereabouts I do not always know. Many remain in private hands; many others have reached the Academic Center of the University of Texas, whose important collection of writers' letters I have unfortunately been unable to visit.

I have also drawn upon various family documents which remain in the possession of the heirs and descendents of Sir Leslie Stephen. The following are referred to by abbreviations: *The Mausoleum Book*, written by Leslie Stephen after the death of his wife Julia in 1895 (MBk); copies of the Stephen children's family newspaper, the *Hyde Park Gate News*, for 1891, 1892 and 1895 (HPGN); and six manuscript memoirs by Vanessa Bell (VB/MS I–VI).

In referring to Virginia Woolf's *Diaries, 1915–1941*, I cite wherever possible the selection published by the Hogarth Press in 1953 under the title *A Writer's Diary* (abbreviated to *AWD*); references to the unpublished portions of the original now in the Berg Collection are prefixed *AWD (Berg)*.

Original documents are transcribed as faithfully as possible, so that errors in spelling and punctuation may be ascribed to the writer, not to the printer.

The following initials are used in place of full names:

CB	Clive Bell	QB	Quentin Bell
DG	Duncan Grant	RF	Roger Fry
EMF	Edward Morgan Forster	SST	Saxon Sydney-Turner
ES	Ethel Smyth	VB	Vanessa (Stephen) Bell
GLS	Giles Lytton Strachey	VD	Violet Dickinson
JMK	John Maynard Keynes	VSW	V. Sackville-West
LW	Leonard Woolf	VW	Virginia (Stephen) Woolf

Hearsay evidence is indicated by the abbreviation *p.i.* followed by the name of my informant.

REFERENCES
Volume I

CHAPTER ONE

Page
1 Imprisonment for debt . . . James Stephen, *Considerations on Imprisonment for Debt* . . ., 1770, passim
2 "want of birth . . ." Leslie Stephen, *Life of Sir James Fitzjames Stephen*, p. 7
2 "What then was to be done?" James Stephen, *Memoirs*, p. 188
3 *War in Disguise* . . . James Stephen, *War in Disguise; or the Fraud of the Neutral Flags*, 1805
5 "Mr Over-Secretary Stephen." Leslie Stephen, *op. cit.*, p. 46
5 "Did you ever know your father . . ." *ibid.*, p. 63
7 "To be weak is to be wretched . . ." *ibid.*, p. 80
8 "He has lost all hope . . ." *p.i. (VW)*
8 "Oh Almighty Lord . . ." *Book of Common Prayer*: for Fair Weather
11 "She and I had our little contentions." *MBk*, p. 17
12 "I got up and found . . ." *MBk*, p. 16
12 "Now Milly has loved me . . ." *MBk*, p. 43
13 "All life seemed a shipwreck . . ." *MBk*, p. 30
13 . . . a permanent loss of faith. *MH/A 6*
13 "I am in love with Julia!" *MBk*, p. 36
14 According to Virginia's cousin . . . H. A. L. Fisher, *An Unfinished Autobiography*, Oxford, 1940, pp. 10–12. See also: E. F. Benson, *As We Were*, 1930, p. 87, and Paul Savile, *Val Prinsep and Royal Academy Painting*, a Mastership Dissertation (Magdalen College, Oxford), 1970
14 The sequel is interesting . . . See E. F. Benson, *As We Were*, 1930, pp. 92–95
16 "she doubled the generosity . . ." VW (quoting Mrs G. F. Watts), introduction to *Victorian Photographs of Famous Men & Fair Women by Julia Margaret Cameron*, Hogarth Press, 1926, p. 3
16 "where only beautiful things . . ." Quoted by Helmut Gernsheim, *Julia Margaret Cameron*, 1948, p. 15
17 her "dear heart, her lamb." *Mrs Jackson to Mrs Leslie Stephen*, passim
18 Mrs Ramsay's relationship with her husband . . . See Mitchell A. Leaska, *Virginia Woolf's Lighthouse*, 1970, chapter 5
18 . . . little tails . . . *p.i. (VB)*

CHAPTER TWO

Page
23 The arrival of Adrian . . . See footnote, p. 116
23 "She reminded me always . . ." *VB/MS I*
24 . . . scratching a distempered wall . . . *p.i. (VB)*

REFERENCES

Page

24 "The Saint" *VB/MS I*; also *MH/A*

24 "purple with rage" *VB/MS I*

25 some indifferent verses . . . Reprinted in F. W. Maitland, *Sir Leslie Stephen*, 1906, p. 318

25 "MY DEAR GODPAPA . . ." *VW to J. R. Lowell*, on a letter from Leslie Stephen, 20 August 1888. (The Houghton Library, Harvard University)

25 "Clementé, dear child . . ." *VB/MS I*

27 Singing was better . . . *VW/VD*, [c. 27 December 1902] (Berg); also *VB/MS I*.

28 "How sweet it was . . ." *HPGN*, 21 March 1892

28 "So the boy turned him lose . . ." *HPGN*, 7 March 1892

29 "Rather clever, I think," *VB/MS I*

29 "Young children should be nipped . . ." *HPGN*, 18 January 1892

29 "Miss Millicent Vaughan . . ." *HPGN*, 14 March 1892

29 ". . . the prince of talkers . . ." *HPGN*, 21 March, 9 May, 7 November 1892

29 "I cannot make up plots . . ." *AWD*, p. 116, 5 October 1927

29 *The Midnight Ride. HPGN*, 25 January, 1 February, 1892

30 ". . . you have jilted me . . ." *HPGN*, 6 June 1892

30 *A Cockney's Farming Experiences. HPGN*, 22 August 1892 *et seq.*

30 "That day . . . is stamped . . ." *HPGN*, 16 May 1892

32 "On Saturday morning . . ." *HPGN*, 12 September 1892

32 Family life at St Ives . . . *VB/RF*, 29 September 1930 (CH)

32 Mr Wolstenholme . . . *MBk*, p. 61

33 Rupert Brooke . . . From Stella Duckworth's *1893 Diary* it is clear that it was in August and September that the Brookes met the Stephens at St Ives, rather than in April 1899 as Christopher Hassall (*Rupert Brooke*, 1964, p. 30) states. The Stephens had in any case left St Ives by 1895. See also: *Mrs Mary Ruth Brooke to VW*, 18 August 1918 (MH)

34 William Fisher . . . *William Wordsworth Fisher* (later Admiral Sir W. W. Fisher) *to Mrs Leslie Stephen*, 5 August [1891]

35 "The felicious family . . ." *HPGN*, 22 August 1892

35 . . . the scene in *The Years* . . . *p.i.* (VB). See VW, *The Years*, p. 29

37 . . . a novel of manners . . . "Extracts from the Diary of Miss Sarah Morgan" in *HPGN*, 14 and 21 January 1895; article beginning "I dreamt one night that I was God . . ." *ibid.*, 11 February 1895

37 a report of the wedding . . . *HPGN*, 21 January 1895

37 "from the tooth of time" *HPGN*, 25 February 1895

37 "For the last fortnight . . ." *HPGN*, 4 March 1895

38 Mrs Jackson had written . . . *Mrs Jackson to VB*, 11 July 1890

38 "Ah, thank Heaven, there is no post . . ." *MH/A 5*

38 . . . crushed and cramped in the womb . . . *AWD* (*Berg*), 3 December 1923

39 "fits of the horrors" *MBk*, p. 68

CHAPTER THREE

Page

40 "Her death . . . was the greatest disaster . . ." *MH/A 6*

40 . . . a panegyric on "My Julia" *MBk*

40 "Oriental gloom" *MH/A 6*

41 . . . "trifles," but also . . . *MBk*, p. 69

REFERENCES

Page
45 in 1896 she did keep a diary . . . It is referred to in the *1897 Diary* (Berg) on 18 January, but has not been preserved
47 "My Julia . . ." *MBk* (addendum), p. 82
47 "he has picked my pocket . . ." *Florence Burke to VW*, 30 April 1928, enclosed with *VW/VB*, 9 May 1928 (Berg)
48 "like the smack of a whip" *MH/A 5*
50 "DENIZENS OF THE KITCHEN . . ." *p.i.* (*VB*)
50 "O Leslie, what a noble boy . . ." *1897 Diary*, 6 January (Berg)
50 "I hope, though I still hope . . ." *Leslie Stephen to Mrs Herbert Fisher*, 14 November 1897
50 "I did some Greek." *1897 Diary*, 3 March (Berg)
51 "Gracious, child, how you gobble" *VW/VSW*, 19 February 1929 (Berg)
51 "Ginia is devouring books . . ." *MBk* (addendum), p. 84
51 Hakluyt's *Voyages* . . . *AWD*, p. 150, 8 December 1929
52 "rather nasty . . ." *Leslie Stephen to Thoby Stephen*, 6 February 1897
53 the "dreadful idea" . . . *1897 Diary*, 7 March (Berg)
53 "Do you think that I may be allowed . . ." *Leslie Stephen to Thoby Stephen*, 27 March 1897; "arrived at father's tailor in Bond St where father ordered himself a whole new suit for the wedding." *1897 Diary*, 29 March (Berg)
53 "about as amusing to me" *Leslie Stephen to Thoby Stephen*, 27 March 1897
54 "third rate actresses . . ." *1897 Diary*, 18 April (Berg)
54 "a good many selfish pangs . . ." *MBk* (addendum), p. 84
55 "Stella was worse . . ." *1897 Diary*, 29 April (Berg)
56 "She . . . irritated me extremely" *1897 Diary*, 12 June (Berg)
56 "unreasonable enough" *1897 Diary*, 4 May (Berg)
56 "This Sunday a most distinct . . ." *1897 Diary*, 9 May (Berg)
57 "I growl at everything . . ." *1897 Diary*, 13 June (Berg)
57 "relentless, thundery sunless heat" *1897 Diary*, 24 June (Berg)
57 "three months of . . . horrible suspense" *VB/MS II*
57 "goodbye" *1897 Diary*, 17 July (Berg)

CHAPTER FOUR

Page
58 "the ghastly mourners" *MH/A 6*
59 "My mother was a saint" H. A. L. Fisher, *An Unfinished Autobiography*, Oxford 1940, p. 15
59 "My dear Virginia . . ." *p.i.* (*VW*)
59 "The Fishers would have made Eden . . ." *VW to Emma Vaughan*, 30 August [1903] (MH)
60 "She talks . . . every minute of the day" *VW to Thoby Stephen*, 5 December 1897 (CH)
60 "the most ungainly creatures . . ." *VB/MS II*
60 . . . ugly and sweated . . . *VW/ES*, 18 May 1931 (Berg)
61 "Madge is here . . ." *p.i.* (*VW*). Also: *AWD* (*Berg*), 2 June 1921
61 "Terrible long dinner . . ." *1897 Diary*, 25/26 September (Berg)
62 "poor boy, . . ." *MH/A 5*
62 "when he was sad, she should be sad; . . ." *MH/A 6*

REFERENCES

Page
62 "Did you hear me call" *MH/A 6*
63 "And you stand there like a block ..." *MH/A 5*
63 "What an aggravating young woman ..." *VB/MS II*
65 "... the edge of this ... [cloud]" *Warboys Diary*, 1 September 1899 (Berg)
66 *VW to Emma Vaughan* (MH)
68 "very white and shrivelled" *VW to Emma Vaughan*, 23 October 1900 (MH)
70 "I don't get anybody to argue ..." *VW to Thoby Stephen*, n.d. [early May 1903] (CH)
72 "So you take their side too" *MH/A 5*
73 (Everyone has forgotten me) *MH/A 5*
74 "Hyde Park Gaters" *Adrian Stephen to VB*, n.d. [April/May 1941] (CH)
74 "Why won't my whiskers grow?" *p.i. (VB)*
74 "Why won't that young man go?" *p.i. (VB)*; alternatively: "Why can't he go? Why can't he go?" *VW, Collected Essays*, 1967, "Leslie Stephen", vol. IV, p. 78
74 "Oh Gibbs, what a bore you are" *MH/A 15*
77 "... the truth of it is, ..." *VW to Emma Vaughan*, 8 August 1901 (MH)
77 "they're not used to young women ..." *MH/A 14*
78 "One day when William Rufus ..." *p.i. (VW)*
79 her drawers fell down ... *VW/VD*, 2 October 1902 (Berg)
79 In an essay written at this time ... "Thoughts upon Social Success" in *HPG Diary*, 15 July 1903 (Berg)
79 "I went to *Two Dances* ..." *VW/VD*, n.d. [?27 December 1902] (Berg)
80 ... a difficult husband ... *VD/VB*, 20 July 1942 (CH)
81 "SHE IS AN AGED GOAT" *p.i. (VB)*
82 "I consider this to be equivalent ..." *MBk* (addendum, 23 April 1902), p. 90
82 "They have, I suppose, explained ..." *Leslie Stephen to Thoby Stephen*, 9 November 1902
82 "her only fault ..." *Leslie Stephen to Mrs Herbert Fisher*, 14 September 1902
82 "We ... showed her to her room ..." *MH/A 26*; see also: *Friendship's Gallery* (Berg)
83 "You remind me ... of Mrs Carlyle." *VW/VD*, 4 May 1903 (Berg)
84 "Ginia ... continues to be good ..." *Leslie Stephen to Mrs Herbert Fisher*, 8 July 1900; also 11 August 1901; also *VW/VD*, [28 January] 1904 (Berg)
85 "The aimiable ladies ..." *Leslie Stephen to Thoby Stephen*, 22 November 1902
85 "Rather too fashionable" *VW/VD*, 4 May 1903 (Berg)
85 to at least one observer ... *p.i. (Desmond MacCarthy)*
85 "I am Henry James." *VD/VB*, 14 May 1942 (CH)
85 "Three mornings I have spent" *VW/VD*, n.d. [?December 1903] (Berg)
85 "This illness" *VW/VD*, 28 November 1903 (Berg)

CHAPTER FIVE
Page
88 "I wonder how we go on ..." *VW/VD* [c. 23] March 1904 (Berg)
88 "to prove to myself ..." *VW/VD*, 10 November 1904 (Berg)
88 "a strange race ..." *VW to Emma Vaughan*, 25 April 1904 (MH)
89 Clive Bell and *his* friend ... *VW/VD*, 7 May 1904 (Berg); also *VB to Margery Snowden*, 3 May 1904 (CH)

REFERENCES

Page

90 "Oh, my Violet . . ." *VW/VD*, 26 September 1904 (Berg)

91 "a poor little red-tape-tied . . ." *VW/VD*, 5 November 1904 (Berg)

92 "She is really quite well . . ." *VB to Madge Vaughan*, 28 October 1904 (CH)

92 "Don't be afraid that I shall quote . . ." *VB to Madge Vaughan*, n.d. [November] 1904 (CH)

93 she sent to *The Guardian* . . . See *VW/VD*, 10, 11, 14 and 21 November 1904 (Berg)

94 "Kitty . . . already screams . . ." *VW/VD*, n.d. [March 1904] (Berg)

95 "there was nothing to be said" *VB/CB*, 29 January 1905 (CH)

96 "with immense pomp" *Thoby Stephen to CB*, n.d. [September 1905] (CH)

96 "I often wonder . . ." *VB to Madge Vaughan*, 25 March [1905] (CH)

97 Leonard Woolf recalled . . . LW, *Sowing*, p. 183

97 That break . . . *SST/LW*, 21 February 1905 (MH)

97 ". . . a great trial;" *VW/VD*, 1 October 1905 (Berg)

98 *Euphrosyne* . . . *Euphrosyne/A Collection of Verse*, published and sold by Elijah Johnson, 30 Trinity Street, Cambridge, 1905

98 . . . a scathing essay . . . *MH/A 13a*; see Appendix C

98 "If you mean wit," I have paraphrased the account given by VW in *MH/A 16*

98 "It filled me with wonder . . ." *MH/A 16*

98 "sort of" *p.i. (VB)*

99 Phyllis and Rosamund . . . *MH/A 23f*

99 George, sweeping in proudly . . . *Adrian Stephen to VB*, n.d. [April/May 1941] (CH)

99 "Oh darling, . . ." *MH/A 16*

99 "Deplorable, deplorable!" *MH/A 16*

100 "I have been splashing about . . ." *VW/VD*, n.d. [16 May 1905] (Berg)

100 "that delightful person . . ." *VB/MS V*

101 ". . . my last Sonata . . ." *SST/CB*, 8 March 1906 (CH)

102 "His friends . . . continued . . ." *MH/A 13c*

103 "like slaves" *p.i. (Desmond MacCarthy)*

103 George noted with approval . . . *George Duckworth to VD*, 23 December 1906

104 Bruce Richmond thought it "admirable" *VW/VD*, 11 March 1905 (Berg)

104 "You will be surprised . . ." *VW/VD*, 30 April 1905 (Berg)

105 "One half of the Committee" *VW/VD*, 19 July 1905 (Berg)

105 "combine amusement and instruction . . ." *VW/VD*, n.d. [c. 3 January 1905] (Berg)

106 "Tomorrow also is my working women" *VW/VD*, n.d. [Summer 1905] (Berg)

106 "the flesh and blood in the shadows" *MH/A 22*; see Appendix B

106 "Then on Wednesdays . . ." *VW/VD*, 9 November 1905 (Berg)

106 "I gave a lecture . . ." *VW/VD*, n.d. [October 1907] (Berg)

107 "a sort of honeymoon . . ." *VW/VD*, 24 August [1906] (Berg)

107 "They had seen Marathon . . ." *MH/A 24b*

109 When they landed at Patras . . . *Adrian Stephen to CB*, 24 October 1906 (CH)

109 a sharp attack of "something or other" *VB to Margery Snowden*, 3 November 1906 (CH)

110 "We are going on well . . ." *VW/VD*, 20 November 1906 (Berg)

110 "Thoby is going on splendidly . . ." *VW/VD*, n.d. [25 November 1906] (Berg)

110 "There will be all Nessa's life . . ." *VW/VD*, 19 December 1906 (Berg)

REFERENCES
CHAPTER SIX

Page

112 . . . her own continuing life . . . *AWD* (*Berg*), 26 December 1929

112 She addressed herself to Lytton . . . *SST/LW*, 4 September and 22 November 1908 (MH); also *GLS/CB*, 18 November 1907 (CH)

112 In a manuscript written at the end of her life . . . *MH/A 5*

114 He was pompous, polished . . . *VW/VD*, 28 and 30 December, 1 and 3 January, 1907 (Berg)

114 "However, I suppose she knows . . ." *Henry James to Mrs W. K. Clifford*, 17 February 1907 (Harvard University, Houghton Library). I am indebted to Professor Leon Edel who called my attention to this letter.

115 "I hate her going away" *VW/VD*, n.d. [6 February 1907] (Berg)

115 "numb and dumb" *VW/VD*, n.d. [?8 February 1907] (Berg)

115 "Beatrice [Thynne] comes round, . . ." *VW/VD*, 15 February 1907 (Berg)

116 "fifteen years younger . . ." *VW/VD*, April 1903 (Berg)

116 the editors of the *News* . . . *HPGN*, 27 June and 1 November 1892

116 unfairly but inevitably . . . *p.i.* (*LW*)

116 The Dwarf . . . *p.i.* (*VB*)

116 he did not believe in G. E. Moore. *p.i.* (*Adrian Stephen*)

117 one witness . . . *p.i.* (*Duncan Grant*)

117 "Virginia . . . must marry." *VW/VD*, n.d. [?29 December] 1906 and 3 January 1907 (Berg)

118 he had a certain eccentric absurdity . . . See E. F. Benson, *As We Were*, 1930, pp. 134–139

119 all her "unpublished works" *VW/VD*, [10 December] 1906 (Berg)

119 she hated "pouring out tea . . ." *VW/VD*, 15 February 1907 (Berg)

119 "a serious interview" *VW/VD*, n.d. [16 March 1907] (Berg)

121 "Country going to the dogs . . ." *VW/VD*, n.d. [?7 July 1907] (Berg)

121 tried to hide from Mrs Humphry Ward *p.i.* (*VW*); but see: DG, "Virginia Woolf" in *Horizon*, 1941, vol. III, no. 18, p. 406

121 "Nessa & Clive live . . ." *VW to Madge Vaughan*, 6 November 1907 (MH)

121 the dog Hans . . . DG, *op. cit.*

122 "Miss Stephen, do you *ever* think?" *p.i.* (*DG*)

122 . . . an account of her father and mother. *MH/A 6*

122 She was also writing . . . *1906–1908 Diary* (Berg)

122 hoping "that old Henry James" . . . *VB/VW*, 14 August 1907 (MH)

122 ". . . we went and had tea . . ." *VW/VD*, [25 August 1907] (Berg)

123 On 27 December, 1907 . . . Minute Book of *The Play Reading Society*

124 "It was a spring evening . . ." *MH/A 16*

125 "I'm going to have a man and a woman . . ." *VW/VD*, n.d. [?November 1903] (Berg)

125 "My only defence . . ." *VW to Madge Vaughan*, n.d. [?June 1906] (MH)

CHAPTER SEVEN

Page

128 she might end by marrying Saxon. *LW/GLS*, n.d. [1 February 1909] (MH)

128 "amazingly beautiful" *DG/GLS*, 7 April 1907 (CH)

REFERENCES

Page

128 found him charming . . . *VB to Margery Snowden,* n.d. [April 1907] (CH)

128 hitching up his trousers . . . *MH/A 16*

128 "That Mr Grant" DG, "Virginia Woolf" in *Horizon,* 1941, vol. III, no. 18, p. 402

129 "I should like Lytton as a brother . . ." *VB/VW,* n.d. [11 August 1908] (MH)

129 Clive . . . suggested that Lytton . . . *CB/VW,* n.d. [12 January 1911] (MH)

130 he lacked . . . magnanimity, *AWD (Berg),* 24 January 1919

130 "Yes they are exquisite . . ." *VW/CB,* n.d. [?9 August 1908]

131 they were tolerant as well as charming . . . Hilton Young (Lord Kennet of the Dene), an unpublished memoir. I am grateful to the present Lord Kennet for allowing me to look at this ms.

132 like an ill-omened cat. *VW/VD,* 13 May 1908 (Berg); see also *VW/GLS, Letters,* p. 13, [28 April 1908]

132 With a sense of desertion . . . *VW/VD,* 13 May 1908 (Berg)

133 "My dear Virginia . . ." *p.i.* (CB)

133 "it will be some time before I can separate . . ." *VW/VD,* [15 October 1907] (Berg)

134 She could, she said, have forgiven . . . *p.i.* (VB)

135 "about the honourable wounds . . ." *CB/VW,* 3 May 1908 (MH)

135 "You brought a tear to my eye . . ." *VW/CB,* n.d. [6 May 1908]

135 "Do you remember" *CB/VW,* 3 May 1908 (MH)

135 "On the top of Rosewall, . . ." *CB/VW,* 7 May 1908 (MH)

136 "Why . . . do you torment me . . ." *VW/CB,* n.d. [6 May 1908]

136 "I wonder what *you* have said . . ." *VB/VW,* 4 May 1908 (MH)

137 "Couldn't you . . . call her Apricot?" *VB/VW,* n.d. [8 August 1908] (MH)

137 "Or Barcelona" *CB/VW,* 23 August 1908 (MH)

137 "write rather well . . ." *VW/VD,* 30 August 1908 (Berg)

137 "I think a great deal . . ." *VW/CB,* n.d. [19 August 1908]

137 a letter to Emma Vaughan . . . *VW to Emma Vaughan,* n.d. [August 1908] (MH)

138 a note book . . . I have been unable to trace the original of this; Leonard Woolf had a copy made from it. It was used during the expedition to Greece in 1906, and brought to Italy in 1908 and 1909

139 . . . screaming at each other, *p.i.* (VW)

139 "Vanessa and Virginia are both . . ." *CB/SST,* 17 September 1908 (CH)

139 "Does it savour of paradox . . ." *SST/CB,* 21 September 1908 (CH)

139 "an admirable man" *VW/VD,* n.d. [4 October 1908] (Berg)

CHAPTER EIGHT

Page

141 "paradise of married peace . . ." *GLS/LW,* 19 February 1909

141 a sexual coward . . . *VW/ES,* 26 June 1930 (Berg)

142 she preserved his letter . . . *Anon to VW,* 30 March [1909] (MH); also *VW/VD,* n.d. [27 March 1909] (Berg)

142 "Life . . . is certainly very exciting" *VW to Madge Vaughan,* 21 March 1909 (MH)

143 landing "as the first cock . . ." *VW/VD,* n.d. [27 March 1909] (Berg)

143 "that unnatural Florentine society" *AWD (Berg),* 21 August 1929

REFERENCES

Page

143 "like a transfixed hare" *Greece/Italy 1906–1909 Notebook* (see note to p. 138)

143 The slightest, the most natural . . . *AWD (Berg)*, 7 December 1917

143 "I was . . . unhappy that summer" *AWD (Berg)*, 21 August 1929

143 "tiresome" in the Bargello *VB/VW*, n.d. [10 May 1909] (MH)

144 "It was rather melancholy . . ." *VB to Margery Snowden*, 10 May 1909 (MH)

144 "We have just got to know . . ." *VW to Madge Vaughan*, n.d. [Early Summer 1909] (MH)

145 "wonderful friends . . ." *et. seq., MH/A 16*

148 "What's the pudding?" *p.i. (VB)*

148 shopping with Adrian . . . *Adrian Stephen to VB*, 9 August 1909 (CH)

150 "We must be a curious sight" *Adrian Stephen to VB*, 18 August 1909 (CH)

150 "There is a great crowd . . ." *VW/VB*, 16 August 1909 (Berg)

150 "It is of no use . . ." *Adrian Stephen to VB*, 18 August 1909 (CH)

150 "The grossness of the Germans . . ." *VW/VB*, n.d. [8 August 1909] (Berg)

150 "Saxon is dormant . . ." *VW/VB*, n.d. [10 August 1909] (Berg)

151 "Saxon is . . . almost sprightly." *VW/VB*, n.d. [19 August 1909] (Berg)

151 ". . . it begins to dawn on me . . ." *SST/CB*, 9 August 1909 (CH)

152 "a bi-sexual bathing dress" *VW/VD*, 21 September 1909 (Berg)

152 "I was most agreeably entertained" *Walter Lamb to CB*, 21 March 1909 (CH)

153 "Now we are back again . . ." *VW/GLS, Letters*, p. 34, [6 October 1909]

153 "a book which one may still buy . . ." *MH/B 21*

154 "expected to be the chef d'oeuvre" *CB/VW*, n.d. [8 November 1909] (MH)

154 "My feeling is that you have impaled . . ." *Reginald Smith to VW*, 10 November 1909 (MH)

155 "Suppose I stayed here . . ." *VW/CB*, 26 December 1909

CHAPTER NINE

Page

157 "like a seedy commercial traveller" Adrian Stephen, *The "Dreadnought" Hoax*, p. 18

157 . . . the author of many practical jokes. See Joseph Hone, "Henry Cole, King of Jokers" in *The Listener*, 4 April 1940

158 she had two days' notice. *Daily Mirror*, 15 February 1910

158 Vanessa was dismayed . . . *VB to Margery Snowden*, 13 February 1910 (CH)

159 "*Entaqui, mahai, kustufani*" Adrian Stephen, *op. cit.*, p. 26

159 "A rum lingo they speak" *p.i. (DG)*; also Adrian Stephen, *op. cit.*, p. 28

159 "Oh Miss Genia, Miss Genia!" *p.i. (VW)*

160 "very good looking . . ." *Daily Mirror*, 14 February 1910

160 a letter from Dorothea . . . *Dorothea Stephen to VW*, 3 March 1910 (Berg)

161 Ever since January 1906 . . . *p.i. (VB)*

161 she could neither do sums . . . *VW to Janet Case*, 1 January 1910 (MH)

161 Miss Rosalind Nash . . . *Rosalind Nash to VW*, 19 January 1910 (MH)

161 ". . . names like Cowgill . . ." *VW/VD*, n.d. [27 February 1910] (Berg)

161 a bloodless, inhuman . . . *VW to Janet Case*, n.d. [?December 1909] (MH)

161 a novel by H. G. Wells . . . *VW/VD*, n.d. [27 February 1910] (Berg)

162 Clive reported . . . *CB/SST*, 2 and 13 April 1910 (CH)

162 ". . . more to mitigate my own lot . . ." *VW/SST*, n.d. [13 June 1910]

REFERENCES

Page
163 "Virginia since early youth . . ." *VB/CB*, 25 June 1910 (CH)
163 "I shall say . . ." *VW/VB*, 24 June 1910 (Berg)
164 "They reverence my gifts, . . ." *VW/VB*, 28 July 1910 (Berg)
164 She "was transformed . . ." CB, *Old Friends*, p. 117
165 "a dark devil" *VW/VB*, 28 July 1910 (Berg)
165 "one cannot help . . ." *VB/VW*, 29 July 1910 (MH)
165 "Oh dear . . ." *VB/VW*, 5 August 1910 (MH)
167 Early in that year . . . *MH/A 16*; *VB/MS VI*
168 imagined a dreadful repetition . . . *VW/VD*, 25 May 1911 (Berg)
168 Roger in command. VW, *Roger Fry: A Biography*, p. 170
170 human nature changed . . . VW, *Mr Bennett and Mrs Brown*, p. 5
170 Vanessa and Virginia . . . *p.i.* (*VB and DG*); also *VB/MS VI*
170 it was whispered that . . . *MH/A 16*
170 "*en France ça aurait* . . ." *p.i.* (*CB*); also *Adrian Stephen to VB*, n.d. [April/May 1941] (CH)
170 "Beloved, It is great devotion . . ." *VW/VB*, n.d. [21 July 1911] (Berg)
172 long and slightly absurd letters. *Walter Lamb to VW*, 23 and 25 July 1911 (MH)
172 Clive, Walter Lamb and Sydney Waterlow . . . *Sydney Waterlow to CB*, 1 August 1911 (CH); *Walter Lamb to VW*, n.d. [August 1911] (MH); *Walter Lamb to CB*, n.d. [end July 1911] (CH)
172 Clive never spoke to him again. *p.i.* (*CB*)
173 in "the heart of young womanhood" *VW/CB*, n.d. [23 January 1911]
173 "Miss Cox is one of the younger . . ." *VW/CB*, n.d. [23 January 1911]
174 she supplied a word . . . Christopher Hassall, *Rupert Brooke*, p. 280; but see the review by VW of "The Collected Poems of Rupert Brooke" in the *Times Literary Supplement*, 8 August 1918
174 If Adrian is to be trusted . . . *Adrian Stephen to CB*, n.d. [c. 25 August 1911] (CH)
174 The visit began badly . . . Hassall, *op. cit.*, p. 281
175 "Oh, its quite alright, . . ." *MH/A 16*; and Marjorie Strachey on *Woman's Hour*, BBC Home Service, 26 April 1967
175 "Julia would not have liked it." *MH/A 16*
176 "Yesterday I finished . . ." *VW/CB*, 18 April 1911
176 "I could not write . . ." *VW/VB*, n.d. [1 June 1911] (Berg)
176 She seems to have had . . . *VW to Sydney Waterlow*, 9 December 1911
177 "Woolf came to tea" *VB/CB*, n.d. [?31 December 1911] (CH)
177 "He is of course very clever . . ." *VB/CB*, 11 October 1911 (CH)
178 "stupid degraded circle . . ." *LW/GLS*, 2 July 1905 (MH)
178 It was on this point . . . *LW/GLS*, 2 July 1905 (MH)
179 even took up painting . . . *LW/VW*, 28 February 1912 (MH); LW's *Diaries*, 1911, 1912 (MH)
179 "Dear Mr Wolf . . ." *VW/LW*, 8 July 1911 (MH)
179 "it was not a cottage . . ." *VW/LW*, 31 August 1911 (MH)
180 "I must see you . . ." *LW/VW* (telegram), 10 January 1912 (MH)
180 "My dear Virginia . . ." *LW/VW*, 11 January 1912 (MH)
181 ". . . I can try & write . . ." *LW/VW*, 12 January 1912 (MH)
181 "There isn't really . . ." *VW/LW*, n.d. [13 January 1912] (MH)
182 ". . . how glad I shall be . . ." *VB/LW*, 13 January 1912 (MH)
182 "coldest day for 40 years;" *VW to Katherine Cox*, 7 February 1912

REFERENCES

Page
182 "a touch of my usual disease . . ." *VW to Katherine Cox*, 7 February 1912
182 "I shall tell you wonderful stories . . ." *VW/LW*, n.d. [5 March 1912] (MH)
184 ". . . I want to see you . . ." *LW/VW*, 29 April 1912 (MH)
185 "What a career . . ." *VW/LW*, 1 May 1912 (MH)
186 "No, I shan't float . . ." *VW to Molly MacCarthy*, n.d. [?March 1912]
187 "I hope you aren't getting too much worried . . ." *VB/VW*, 28 May 1912
(MH)

VOLUME II

CHAPTER ONE

Page
1 Virginia and Leonard are engaged . . . *VB/RF*, 2 June 1919 (CH)
1 "Ha! Ha!" *VW/GLS*, *Letters*, p. 40, 6 June 1912
1 He wrote to her to say . . . *CB/VW*, n.d. [June 1912] (MH)
1 Everyone seemed to be cross . . . *VB/RF*, 2 June 1912 (CH)
2 "An engagement seems . . ." *VB/GLS*, 5 June 1912
2 "My Violet . . ." *VW/VD*, 4 June 1912 (Berg)
2 The case of Madge . . . *p.i.* (*LW*)
3 "A sandwich . . ." *VW to Janet Case*, n.d. [June 1912] (MH)
4 "Work and love . . ." *VW/VD*, n.d. [13 June 1912] (Berg)
4 Saturday, 10 August . . . *VW/VD*, 5 August 1912 (Berg)
4 the official business . . . *VB to Margery Snowden*, 20 August 1912 (CH)
4 a very good way . . . *VW to Janet Case*, n.d. [17 August 1912] (MH)
5 In Barcelona . . . *VB/VW*, 2 September 1912; accounts of the honeymoon
journey also in *VW to Katherine Cox*, 4 September 1912 and *VW/SST*,
17 September 1912
5 "chronically nomadic . . ." *VW to Molly MacCarthy*, 28 September 1912
5 "Why do you think . . ." *VW to Katherine Cox*, 4 September 1912; see
also *DG/VW*, 23 September 1912 (MH)
6 "They seemed very happy . . ." *VB/CB*, 27 December 1912 (CH); see also
CB to Molly MacCarthy, 31 December 1912 (CH)
6 "She dislikes the possessiveness . . ." *VSW*, *Journal of Travel*, 25 September 1928
6 "My Violet, Yesterday . . ." *VW/VD*, 11 October 1912 (Berg)
7 "an abominable race . . ." *VW/VD*, 24 December 1912
7 "a kind of tortured intensity" *LW*, *Beginning Again*, p. 143
8 buying horses and a cow . . . *VW/VD*, 24 December 1912
8 "Virginia has been very nice . . ." *VB/RF*, 24 December 1912 (CH)
8 sisterly bickerings . . . *VB/CB*, n.d. (CH); see also *CB to Molly MacCarthy*,
n.d. [March 1913] (CH)
9 "I wish Woolf didnt irritate . . ." *VB/RF*, 7 January 1913 (CH)
9 "The whole moral significance . . ." Draft of a letter from *LW to Edward
Arnold* in reply to his of 17 February 1914 (MH)
10 economic problems . . . *VW/VD*, 11 April 1913 (Berg)
10 "I expect to have it rejected," *VW/VD*, 11 April 1913 (Berg)
12 "My eyes are bruised," *VW to Katherine Cox*, 16 May 1913

REFERENCES

Page
12 "He seems to have thought . . ." *VB/RF*, 26 July 1913 (CH)
13 A few miserable shaky . . . *VW/LW*, 7 letters, n.d., but postmarks for 26 July and 1, 3, 4, 5 August 1913 (MH)
14 "Virginia" she reported . . . *VB/CB*, 23 August 1913 (CH)
16 Dr Head, nurses, Vanessa . . . I am indebted to Sir Geoffrey Keynes for a description of these events; see also *VB/JMK*, 9 September 1913 (CH); *LW to R. C. Trevelyan*, 13 September 1913 (MH); *Sir George Savage to LW*, 9 September 1913 (MH); also footnote p. 17
17 "Woolfe bicycled over . . ." *CB to Molly MacCarthy*, n.d. [25 September 1913] (CH)
18 "Oh you know very well . . ." *p.i.* (*LW*)
19 a kind of treaty . . . *LW/VW*, 19 June 1914 (MH)
20 This idea filled Leonard . . . *VB/RF*, 2 August 1914 (CH)
20 "It is thought . . ." *VW to Katherine Cox*, 12 August 1914
21 "At one end of the room . . ." *VW to Janet Case*, 10 December 1914 (MH)
22 "Saturday, January 2nd [1915]" *AWD* (Berg)
23 "The Sidney Webbs ask us . . ." *VW to Margaret Llewelyn Davies*, [9 December 1914] (MH)
23 "which everyone . . ." *AWD* (Berg), 27 January 1915
24 "My dear Margaret . . ." *VW to Margaret Llewelyn Davies*, [25 February 1915] (MH)
26 "I saw Woolf yesterday . . ." *VB/RF*, 27 May 1915 (CH)
26 "played out" *Jean Thomas to VD*, 9 April 1915 (Berg)
26 "Ka had been to see Virginia . . ." *VB/RF*, 25 June 1915 (CH)

CHAPTER TWO

Page
28 "Here at last . . ." "Some Press Opinions" printed at the back of *Night and Day*, 1919
28 "That is not a word . . ." *ibid.*
28 One sentence "more or less . . ." *VW to Molly MacCarthy*, 15 December 1914
29 "Your letter still delights me." *VW to Margaret Llewelyn Davies*, n.d. [c. 1 August 1915] (MH)
29 "I think it is about time . . ." *VW/GLS*, *Letters*, p. 53, 22 October 1915
30 "It has vanished . . ." *VW to Katherine Cox*, 19 March [1916]
31 Lady Robert *did* . . . *VW/VB*, 7 June 1916, with enclosure *Lady Robert Cecil to VW*, n.d. (Berg)
32 "My industry . . ." *VW/GLS*, *Letters*, p. 62, 25 July [1916]
32 "I am very much interested . . ." *VW/VB*, 30 July 1916 (Berg)
32 "I wish you'd leave Wissett . . ." *VW/VB*, 4 May 1916 (Berg)
33 "I think the Woolves . . ." *VB/GLS*, 24 October 1916
33 "some pollution theory . . ." *GLS/VB*, 25 October 1916 (CH)
34 "We are not at all anxious . . ." *VW/VB*, 11 September 1916 (Berg)
35 "we have had nothing but brilliancy . . ." *VW to Margaret Llewelyn Davies*, 25 June 1920 (MH)
36 "for we mothers . . ." *VW to Margaret Llewelyn Davies*, 24 January 1917
37 "decidedly an interesting creature . . ." *GLS/VW*, *Letters*, p. 61, 17 July 1916
37 "If," said Virginia . . . *VW/GLS*, *Letters*, p. 62, 25 July 1916

Page
37 "I have had a slight rapprochement . . ." *VW/VB*, 11 February 1917 (Berg)
38 It has been said . . . The original source being, it would appear, Stephen Spender in *World Within World*, 1951, p. 153
38 he increased by speculation . . . E. M. Forster, *Diary*, 10 May 1912
39 "When I said I thought . . ." *VB/MS III*
39 the following account . . . LW, *Diary 1915* (MH)
40 Estimate/Expenditure. LW, *Diary 1916* (MH)
41 "I see that real printing . . ." *VW/VB*, 26 April 1917 (Berg)
41 "It is proposed to issue . . ." A proof of this first production of the Hogarth Press was enclosed with *VW to Margaret Llewelyn Davies*, 7 May 1917 (MH)
42 "all about her new novel . . ." *VB/RF*, [14 April 1917] (CH)
42 ". . . they were the treats . . ." *VW/ES*, 16 October 1930 (Berg)
43 "And then" as Virginia wrote . . . *VW to Margaret Llewelyn Davies*, 9 September 1917 (MH)
43 "I was so much overcome . . ." *VW/VB*, 22 May 1917 (Berg)
44 "She & Virginia . . ." *RF/VB*, 11 June 1917 (CH)
45 Here are three entries . . . *AWD (Berg)*
47 ". . . this sort of writing . . ." *VW Add. Diary*, 7 December 1918. This additional volume covering the period 16 November 1918 to 24 January 1919 was in part copied into the volume for 1919 in the Berg Collection.
48 "an element of unadulterated culture" LW, *Beginning Again*, p. 217
49 Alix said . . . *p.i.* (Mrs James Strachey)
49 "The Bloomsbury hypnotism . . ." *VW/VB*, 17 January 1917 (Berg)
51 "We came back . . ." *AWD (Berg)*, 19 November 1917
53 "This talk . . ." *AWD (Berg)*, 4 January 1918
57 a particularly seductive stable boy . . . *VB/GLS*, 3 and 8 August 1917; *GLS/VB*, 6 August 1917 (CH)
58 "so sweet" Nelly Boxall, *Portrait of Virginia Woolf*, BBC Home Service, 29 August 1956
59 "Whatever you may have said . . ." *VB/VW*, 24 October 1918 (MH)
60 ("as usual") *VW/VB*, 27 October 1917 (Berg)
60 "I just want to put you right . . ." *CB/VB*, 26 October 1918 (CH)
60 "hot water" *AWD (Berg)*, 5 February 1921
60 "Do, for God's sake . . ." *VB/VW*, 21 January 1918 (MH)
61 "The work of government . . ." *AWD (Berg)*, 18 September 1918
61 "Whatever we have done . . ." *AWD (Berg)*, 12 October 1918
61 "We've won the war . . ." *AWD (Berg)*, 15 October 1918

CHAPTER THREE
Page
63 ". . . to be ill at the Lizard . . ." *VW to Katherine Cox*, 5 February [1919]
64 "nothing but the wind . . ." *AWD (Berg)*, 5 March 1919
66 "That would have suited us . . ." *AWD (Berg)*, 3 July 1919
67 "I don't suppose . . ." *ibid.*
69 ". . . a lie in the soul." *The Letters of Katherine Mansfield*, 1928, vol. I, pp. 279, 284 (10 and 13 November 1919). See also: F. A. Lea, *John Middleton Murry*, 1959, p. 68
69 "he could see her . . ." *AWD (Berg)*, 28 November 1919

REFERENCES

Page
69 "We had thought . . ." *Athenaeum*, 26 November 1919
69 ". . . I should need . . ." *AWD* (*Berg*), 18 February 1919
70 "The inscrutable woman . . ." *AWD* (*Berg*), 22 March 1919
70 "a steady discomposing . . ." *AWD* (*Berg*), 31 May 1920
71 "We think we now deserve . . ." *AWD* (*Berg*), 28 December 1919
71 "This is our last . . ." *AWD* (*Berg*), 7 January 1920
72 "It is true I have . . ." *AWD* (*Berg*), 15 November 1919
72 "The day after my birthday . . ." *AWD*, p. 23, 26 January 1920
74 "This made my drive . . ." *AWD* (*Berg*), 8 June 1920
74 "Lay by my side . . ." *Jacob's Room*, p. 107; *Mrs Dalloway*, p. 124
74 "a clubman's view . . ." *AWD* (*Berg*), 2 April 1919
76 "putting his ox's shoulder . . ." *AWD* (*Berg*), 18 October 1920
76 Friday, February 18th [1921] *AWD* (*Berg*)
77 "a mass of corruption . . ." *AWD* (*Berg*), 8 April 1921
77 "and its that . . ." *AWD*, p. 32, 9 April 1921
78 he thought it marvellous. *AWD*, p. 33, 12 April 1921
78 "very complex" *AWD* (*Berg*), 12 December 1921
78 "Carrington grows older . . ." *AWD* (*Berg*), 31 January 1921
79 "Well," Virginia observed . . . *AWD* (*Berg*), 12 December 1920
79 "Oh dear no," *AWD* (*Berg*), 31 January 1921
79 "He was very shrewd . . ." *AWD* (*Berg*), 15 May 1921
79 "put a pistol . . ." LW, *Downhill* . . ., p. 72
80 "You mustn't think . . ." *Carrington, Letters &c*, p. 178
80 "You must not believe . . ." *ibid.*, p. 183
80 "with her love of stirring . . ." Holroyd, *Lytton Strachey*, vol. II, p. 398
80 "He told her that Virginia . . ." *ibid.*, p. 401
80 "So Carrington did . . ." *AWD* (*Berg*), 23 May 1921
81 "I'm not sure . . ." *AWD* (*Berg*), 18 February 1919
83 a chest of drawers . . . *RF/VB*, n.d. [18 May 1921] (CH)
83 "These, this morning . . ." *AWD* (*Berg*), 8 August 1921
84 "had passed the limits . . ." *AWD* (*Berg*), 4 February 1922
85 ". . . I am seeing Clive . . ." *AWD* (*Berg*), 12 March 1922
85 ". . . We talked from 4.30 to 10.15 . . ." *AWD* (*Berg*), 24 March 1922
85 "I hope I shan't . . ." *CB/VB*, 1 March 1922 (CH)
86 "He sang it and chanted it . . ." *AWD* (*Berg*), 23 June 1922
86 prepared a circular . . . Holroyd, *Lytton Strachey*, vol. II, p. 366
86 "After Joyce . . ." *AWD* (*Berg*), 27 September 1922
87 "amazingly well written . . ." *AWD*, p. 47, 26 July 1922
88 "this nervous man . . ." *AWD* (*Berg*), 29 October 1922
88 "You have freed yourself . . ." T. S. *Eliot to VW*, 4 December 1922

CHAPTER FOUR

Page
89 ". . . forging ahead . . ." *AWD* (*Berg*), 3 January 1923
90 "I can foresee . . ." *VW/VB*, 22 December 1922 (Berg)
91 "Mrs Murry's dead!" *AWD* (*Berg*), 16 January 1923
91 "Yet even in this light . . ." *Jacob's Room*, p. 217
91 and it was he . . . *Berta Ruck to QB*, 11 September 1971

REFERENCES

Page

92 "Never allow a Sailor . . ." G. H. W. Rylands, *BBC/TV Omnibus*, 18 January 1970

92 "Leonard thinks himself . . ." *AWD (Berg)*, 7 February 1923

93 "poor dear Tom . . ." *AWD (Berg)*, 19 February 1923

93 "Perhaps because Virginia lacked . . ." Gerald Brenan, *South from Granada*, 1957, chapter 13; see also *VW/VSW*, 15 April 1923 (Berg) and *VW/RF*, 16 April 1923

93 *To Spain.* Reprinted in *The Moment*, 1947

94 "I lie & think . . ." *VW/LW*, 17 April 1922 (MH)

95 "glowing and gleaming . . ." *VW to Jacques Raverat*, 29 November 1924

95 "My boast . . ." *VW/CB*, 9 April 1922

95 "Lady Londonderry . . ." *VW/CB*, 9 April 1930

96 "Leonard thinks less well of me . . ." *AWD (Berg)*, 26 May 1924

96 Virginia was more like . . . *VB to Margery Snowden*, 15 April 1923

97 ". . . her social approach . . ." Ralph Partridge, *Portrait of Virginia Woolf*, BBC Home Service, 29 August 1956

99 "I am a great deal interested . . ." *AWD*, p. 55, 4 June 1923

99 "I took up this book . . ." *AWD*, p. 57, 19 June 1923

100 "sheer weak dribble". *AWD (Berg)*, 6 August 1923

100 "And I meant to record . . ." *AWD (Berg)*, 15 October 1923

101 "back again tomorrow . . ." *AWD (Berg)*, 23 January 1924

102 No. 52 . . . Tavistock Square *p.i.* (*LW*); see also Richard Kennedy, *A Boy at the Hogarth Press*

103 Rylands came to the Hogarth Press . . . G. H. W. Rylands, *BBC/TV Omnibus*, 18 January 1970

103 "Thank God, Angus . . ." G. H. W. Rylands to VW, n.d. [November/ December 1924] (MH)

104 "we are trembling . . ." *Mr Bennett and Mrs Brown*, p. 24

104 "those sleek, smooth novels . . ." *ibid.*, p. 23

105 the "Old Man" . . . *AWD*, p. 68, 17 October 1924

106 "I don't think I shall tell you . . ." *VW to Jacques Raverat*, 4 September 1924

106 His reply . . . *Jacques Raverat to VW*, n.d. [September 1924] (MH)

106 "Certainly" Virginia replied, *VW to Jacques Raverat*, 3 October 1924

107 "I like to please Jacques" *AWD (Berg)*, 22 August 1922

107 "Your letters . . ." *Jacques Raverat to VW*, n.d. [December 1924]

107 "Since I wrote . . ." *AWD*, p. 72, 8 April 1925

107 "all over long ago" *Gwen Raverat to VW*, n.d. [early October 1924]

108 "you'll probably not like Will" *Katherine Cox to VW*, 1 August 1918 (MH)

108 "Never . . . have I felt so much admired" *AWD (Berg)*, 16 May 1925

CHAPTER FIVE

Page

109 "Many scenes . . ." *AWD (Berg)*, 4 September 1927

110 "Woke up perhaps at 3." *AWD (Berg)*, 15 September 1926

111 "Virginia was in . . ." *RF/VB*, 11 May 1926 (CH)

111 "I tremble and shiver . . ." *AWD (Berg)*, 6 May 1926

111 "The Woolves are . . ." *CB/VB*, 19 February 1928 (CH)

111 "Virginia is still . . ." *CB/VB*, 2 March 1928 (CH)

111 "Since February . . ." *AWD (Berg)*, 18 March 1928

Page

111 "... it is not oneself ..." *AWD*, pp. 101–102, 30 September 1926
111 "Monday, Ozzie Dickinson; ..." *AWD (Berg)*, 30 October 1926
112 to "float with the sticks ..." "On Being Ill" in *The Moment*, p. 18
113 "My mornings have all ..." *AWD (Berg)*, 19 July 1925
114 "riding on a flat tyre ..." *AWD*, p. 81, 5 September 1925
115 "amphibious life" *AWD*, p. 82, 13 September 1925
115 "doomed to go to Persia" *AWD (Berg)*, 27 November 1925
115 T. S. Eliot ... deserted ... *AWD (Berg)*, 13 September 1925
116 Mrs Nicolson admired her, *VSW/CB*, 10 November 1922 (CH); see also *AWD (Berg)*, 3 August 1922
116 "the lovely gifted aristocratic ..." *AWD (Berg)*, 22 December 1922
116 "our (Clive and my) Vita" *VW/VB*, 17 September 1925 (Berg)
117 "inviolable (like Virginia)" *VSW/VW*, 14 February [1926?] (MH)
117 "Look on it, ..." Quoted by VW in *VW/VSW*, 4 October 1924 (Berg)
117 "Vita for three days ..." *AWD (Berg)*, 21 December 1925
118 "Vita is now arriving ..." *VW/VB*, 13 June 1926 (Berg)
119 She writes, says Virginia ... *VW to Jacques Raverat*, 26 December 1924
119 "And Vita comes ..." *AWD (Berg)*, 20 May 1926
119 Harold wrote ... *H. Nicolson to VW*, 17 December 1926 (MH)
120 "How beautiful she is" *p.i.* (QB)
120 "Never," she reports ... *AWD (Berg)*, 8 February 1926
120 ... a disastrous evening. *AWD (Berg)*, 27 March 1926; also *VW/VSW*, 29 March 1926 (Berg); and *p.i.* (*LW*)
121 "a good deal lowered ..." *AWD (Berg)*, 24 February 1926
121 "I am going to hand in ..." *AWD (Berg)*, 24 March 1926
122 "Please Ma'am, ..." *AWD (Berg)*, 30 April 1926
122 "I saw this morning ..." *AWD (Berg)*, 12 May 1926
122 ... a tub thumper, ... *AWD (Berg)*, 9 May 1926
122 Robert Bridges ... H. G. Wells. *AWD (Berg)*, 1 and 4 July 1926
123 with Thomas Hardy. *AWD*, p. 89, 25 July 1926
123 "a whole nervous breakdown ..." *AWD*, p. 95, n.d. 1926
123 in a tin hip bath ... Nelly Boxall, *Portrait of Virginia Woolf*, BBC Home Service, 29 August 1956
123 "elderly dowdy fussy ..." *AWD (Berg)*, 28 September 1926
124 "You'll get into trouble ..." *VB/VW*, 5 February 1927 (MH)
125 "a mere popinjay ..." *Mrs St John Hutchinson to VW*, 10 September 1924 (MH)
125 "Madam, we have neither ..." *VW/VB*, 9 April 1927 (Berg)
126 "I don't think I've ever ..." *AWD (Berg)*, 1 May 1927
126 "By the way, ..." *VW/VB*, 8 May 1927 (Berg)
127 *Vita from Virginia* ... B. J. Kirkpatrick, *Bibliography of VW*, A 10; also Benedict Nicolson, *BBC/TV Omnibus*, 18 January 1970
128 "I think I am more incapable ..." *VW/VB*, 11 May 1927 (Berg)
128 "You won't want or expect ..." *RF/VW*, 17 May 1927 (MH)
129 "I meant *nothing* ..." *VW/RF*, 27 May 1927
129 "Only Virginia ..." *CB/VB*, 15 May 1927 (CH)
129 her descriptions of the fauna ... *VW/VSW*, 13 May 1927 (Berg)
129 Seafarers' Educational Society ... *VW/VSW* [?June 1927] (Berg)
129 ... love-letters ... *P. Morrell to VW* [?27 July 1927] (MH); also *AWD (Berg)*, 10 August 1927

REFERENCES

Page

129 after taking their Singer ... *p.i.* (*LW*)
130 ... asked them the time. *p.i.* (*A. Davidson*); also *AWD* (*Berg*), 22 October 1927
131 "Yesterday morning ..." *VW/VSW*, 9 October 1927 (Berg); also *AWD*, pp. 114 and 117, 18 September and 5 October 1927
132 materials which she noted ... *AWD* (*Berg*), 23 January 1927
132 "Don't" he said ... *AWD* (*Berg*), 18 September 1927
132 Maynard and Lydia ... *VW/GLS, Letters*, p. 114, 3 September 1927; also *p.i.* (*QB*)
133 "Lovely little things" E. M. Forster, *Virginia Woolf*, p. 11
133 "I don't think" he said ... *p.i.* (*EMF*)
133 ... when he informed her, *AWD* (*Berg*), 23 January 1924
134 "Your article ..." *EMF/VW*, 13 November 1927
134 "Dear Morgan, ..." *VW/EMF*, 16 November 1927
136 "Often" she declared ... *VW/QB*, 6 May 1928
136 "Clive (who smacked me ...) *AWD* (*Berg*), 17 April 1928; also *AWD* (*Berg*), 21 April 1928
136 a contrite letter ... *CB/VW*, 1 April 1928 (MH); also *VW/CB*, 21 April 1928
136 ... Clive made fun of her hat. *AWD* (*Berg*), 30 June 1926
137 "that he has great fun ..." *p.i.* (*QB*)
137 "a rotten speech" R. Hart-Davis, *Hugh Walpole*, 1952, p. 289
138 "Morgan was here ..." *AWD* (*Berg*), 31 August 1928
139 "I am melancholy ..." *VW/VSW*, n.d. [September 1928] (Berg)
139 "... I was going to thank you ..." *VW to H. Nicolson*, 7 October 1928
139 "The great excitement," wrote Vanessa ... *VB/RF*, 27 October 1928 (CH)
140 "Well there can be no doubt ..." *p.i.* (*QB*)

CHAPTER SIX

Page

141 "The Woolves" Vanessa observed ... *et seq.* *VB/RF*, 19 January 1929 (CH)
143 haul her like a sack *VW/VSW*, [28 January 1929] (Berg)
143 ... the usual symptoms – *VW/VSW*, 7 February 1929 (Berg)
143 "I am writing ..." *VW/QB*, 20 March 1929
143 "Perhaps I ought not ..." *AWD*, p. 141, 28 March 1929
144 "If truth is not ..." *A Room of One's Own*, p. 39
145 "subtle and subterranean glow" *ibid.*, p. 17
145 A mongoose ... *VW/VSW*, 5 April 1929 (Berg); *VW/VB*, 7 April 1929 (Berg)
145 "We met an elephant ..." *p.i.* (*QB*)
146 "She lives" said Clive ... *CB/VB*, 7 July 1929 (CH)
146 "reckoning how many more times ..." *AWD*, p. 141, 4 January 1929
146 "I like printing ..." *VW to Hugh Walpole*, 16 July 1930
146 "What a born melancholic ..." *AWD*, p. 143, 23 June 1929
146 "adders' tails ..." *VW/VSW*, 28 October 1929 (Berg)
146 Ivy Compton-Burnett ... R. Kennedy, *A Boy at the Hogarth Press*, pp. 68, 84; also *VW to E. Sackville-West*, 23 September 1929 (Berg)
147 "a low art ..." *p.i.* (*Mrs Lyn Newman*)
147 "helter skelter random ..." *AWD* (*Berg*), 5 August 1929
148 "... I must think of that book ..." *AWD* (*Berg*), 19 August 1929

Page
148 "And so I might fill . . ." *AWD* (*Berg*), 22 August 1929
149 "If I could stay in bed . . ." *AWD*, p. 153, 16 February 1930
149 "Mr Plomer," she began . . . *p.i.* (*QB*)
149 "I am afraid" . . . *AWD* (*Berg*), 19 August 1929
150 . . . a New Year party ' . . *et seq.* *VW/CB*, 19 January 1930 (CH)
151 "We parted almost . . ." LW, *Downhill* . . ., pp. 122–123
151 "An old woman . . ." *VW/QB*, 14 May 1930
151 "I don't think . . ." *et seq.* C. St John, *Ethel Smyth*, p. 222
152 "how angry . . ." *ibid.*, p. 247
153 "Let me look at you" *AWD* (*Berg*), 20 February 1930
153 "this curious unnatural friendship" *AWD* (*Berg*), 25 August 1930
154 the "elements" . . . *AWD* (*Berg*), 16 June 1930
154 "a very violent summer" *AWD* (*Berg*), 28 August 1930
154 a sprig of white heather . . . *VW to Mrs Wilson*, 12 September 1930
154 "If this don't stop, . . ." *AWD* (*Berg*), 2 September 1930
156 the happiest . . . summer *AWD* (*Berg*), 8 September 1930
156 "I could perhaps . . ." *AWD*, p. 165, 7 January 1931
157 rehearse *The Prison* . . . *AWD*, p. 168, 4 February 1931
157 "Here in the few minutes . . ." *AWD*, p. 169, 7 February 1931
158 "a tight aquiline boy . . ." *AWD* (*Berg*), 7 January 1931
158 "I have finished . . ." *VW/QB*, 11 April 1931
159 "I suppose from your tone . . ." *VW/ES*, 29 June 1931 (Berg)
160 "Yes, this morning . . ." *AWD*, p. 172, 17 July 1931
160 "It is a masterpiece . . ." *AWD*, p. 173, 19 July 1931; also *VW/ES*, 19 July 1931 (Berg)
161 "in a state of rage . . ." *VB/RF*, 20 July 1931 (CH); also *VW/VB*, 23 July 1931 (Berg); *VW/VSW*, 30 July 1931 (Berg); and DG in *BBC/TV Omnibus*, 18 January 1970
161 "My proofs did go . . ." *AWD* (*Berg*), 19 August 1931
161 ". . . it's a London Museum book . . ." *AWD* (*Berg*), 1 September 1931
162 "all about nothing . . ." *AWD* (*Berg*), 15 September 1931
162 "I was delighted . . ." H. Walpole to VW, 4 November 1931
162 "My dear Hugh . . ." *VW to H. Walpole*, 8 November 1931
163 "But Oh the happiness . . ." *AWD* (*Berg*), 16 November 1939
163 "when you're in London . . ." *VW/GLS*, *Letters*, p. 118, 6 December 1931
164 "He is so ill, . . ." *AWD* (*Berg*), 18 January 1932
164 "Much better again" *AWD* (*Berg*), 21 and 22 January 1932

CHAPTER SEVEN

Page
166 "But I do everything wrong." *et seq.* *AWD* (*Berg*), 12 March 1932
167 "Yes, but what can I say . . ." *AWD* (*Berg*), 21 April 1932
167 "It's all likely to end . . ." *VW/VB*, 11 April 1932 (Berg)
168 "so humane, so sympathetic . . ." *VW/ES*, 4 May 1932 (Berg)
168 "We have seen vultures . . ." *VW to Julian Bell*, 5 May 1932
168 "nearer to one of those climaxes . . ." *VW/ES*, 26 May 1932 (Berg)
169 "damnable buggers." *VW/ES*, 29 January 1932 (Berg)
169 "I intend to see them . . ." *AWD* (*Berg*), 24 March 1932

REFERENCES

Page
170 "I don't like old ladies . . ." *AWD (Berg)*, 2 June 1932
170 "I rather think she's through . . ." *ES/VB*, 28 June 1934 (CH)
171 "You are a little like . . ." *ES/VB*, 30 December 1934 (CH)
171 "no sense of glory; . . ." *AWD*, p. 182, 11 July 1932
171 ". . . I'm full of ideas . . ." *VW to G. H. W. Rylands*, 22 November 1931
171 ". . . to take in everything . . ." *AWD*, p. 189, 2 November 1932
174 "I have always been a literary painter . . ." *W. R. Sickert to VW*, n.d.; also *AWD (Berg)*, 17 December 1933
174 she, Virginia, was an angel . . . *VW/QB*, 8 March 1934
174 "the kick screams" *ES/VB*, 23 October 1934 (CH)
175 "Don't you sometimes . . ." *O. Morrell to VW*, 16 October 1934 (MH)
178 "And then," asked Maynard . . . *AWD (Berg)*, 19 April 1934
178 "Our Germany" . . . *AWD*, p. 199, 28 April 1933; also B. Walter, *Themes and Variations*, 1947, p. 289
179 "I am trying to start . . ." *AWD (Berg)*, 27 August 1934
179 "After three days' grind . . ." *AWD*, p. 222, 30 August 1934
179 "I don't think I have ever . . ." *AWD*, p. 223, 2 September 1934
179 "Roger died on Sunday." *AWD (Berg)*, 12 September 1934

CHAPTER EIGHT

Page
180 "They played Bach . . ." *AWD (Berg)*, 15 September 1934
180 "a horrid time" *VW/VSW*, 23 September 1934 (Berg)
181 "So my dear Roger, . . ." *VW/RF*, 18 May 1923 (MH)
181 "I could trace . . ." *VW/RF*, 21 February 1931 (MH)
182 "Have I the indomitable . . ." *AWD*, p. 253, 21 August 1935
182 ". . . she could deal with facts . . ." LW, *The Journey . . .*, p. 43
182 "How to deal with love . . ." *VW/VB*, 8 October 1938 (Berg)
182 "I hope you won't mind . . ." *VB/VW*, 14 October 1938 (MH)
183 Mirsky and Swinnerton . . . D. S. Mirsky, *The Intelligentsia of Great Britain*, 1935; F. Swinnerton, *The Georgian Literary Scene*, 1935
183 *Men without Art* . . . By Wyndham Lewis, 1934, chapter V
184 "tremendous and delightful fun" *AWD*, p. 228, 14 October 1934
184 a letter . . . to *The Spectator*, 2 November 1934. See *The Letters of Wyndham Lewis*, ed. W. K. Rose, 1963, pp. 222–225; and *AWD*, p. 231, 2 November 1934
184 "I don't say it . . ." *AWD*, p. 231, 2 November 1934
187 "like an enormous frog . . ." *p.i.* (QB)
187 her chief reaction was dismay . . . *VW to Julian Bell*, 1 December 1935
188 "Oh my dear Virginia . . ." *EMF/VW*, 6 June 1935
188 "I was pressed . . ." *VW/ES*, 3 August 1936 (Berg)
188 a fainting girl . . . *AWD (Berg)*, 20 March 1936
190 a simple No. *AWD*, p. 249, 19 May 1936
190 "A specimen day" *AWD (Berg)*, 5 November 1935
191 on the steps of the London Library, *AWD*, p. 243, 9 April 1935
192 "that particular vein" *AWD (Berg)*, 6 July 1934; also *AWD*, pp. 298, 299, 240, 241
192 "I think I have . . ." *AWD (Berg)*, 28 March 1935

REFERENCES

Page
193 "I wish for death" *AWD*, p. 250, 5 June 1935
193 "wild retyping" *AWD*, p. 252, 17 July 1935
193 "with the usual pangs" *AWD (Berg)*, 29 August 1935; see also *AWD*, pp. 253, 254, 255, 260, 262, 264, 268
194 "I've had a bad morning . . ." *AWD (Berg)*, 18 December 1935
195 "It's terrible about Virginia" *DG/VB*, 26 April 1936 (CH)
195 ". . . never trust a letter . . ." *VW/ES*, 4 June 1936 (Berg)
196 ". . . at last . . ." *AWD*, p. 268, 11 June 1936
196 "I have to consider . . ." *VW/ES*, 26 August 1936 (Berg)
196 "I think it's extraordinarily . . ." *AWD*, p. 271, 3 November 1936

CHAPTER NINE

Page
197 "I've been on the whole . . ." *AWD (Berg)*
198 *Saturday, February 20th. AWD*, pp. 275–276
198 *Monday, March 1st. AWD (Berg)*
199 *Tuesday March 2nd. AWD (Berg)*
200 *The New York Times* sent . . . *AWD (Berg)*, 28 March 1937
201 ". . . suddenly L. developed . . ." *AWD (Berg)*, 22 October 1937
201 "There were . . . checks and clashes" J. Lehmann, *Whispering Gallery*, p. 328
201 "No one" wrote Virginia *VW to Margaret Llewelyn Davies*, 11 July 1937 (MH)
201 wrote begging him . . . *VW to Julian Bell*, 14 November 1936; see also Stansky and Abrahams, *Journey to the Frontier*, pp. 391–413
202 "there is a kind of grandeur" *VW to W. A. Robson*, 26 July 1937
203 "an unreal state," *VB/VSW*, 2 April 1941; also *VW/VSW*, 1 October 1937 (Berg)
203 "I shall be cheerful . . ." *AWD (Berg)*, 6 August 1937
203 "the only point in the day" *VB/VSW*, 2 April 1941 (Berg)
203 Virginia had helped her . . . *VB/VW*, [4 February 1938] (MH)
203 She had to write to Vita . . . *VSW/VB*, 31 March 1941 (CH)
203 "I couldn't get on . . ." *VB/VW*, [4 February 1938] (MH)
203 "We have the materials . . ." *AWD (Berg)*, 12 October 1937
204 her evident pride . . . *Helen Anrep to VB*, 11 January 1938 (CH)
204 "Vanessa's necrophily" *p.i.* (QB)
205 Maynard Keynes was both angry . . . *p.i.* (QB)
205 long, fluent and forceful . . . *Agnes Smith to VW*, 7 November 1938 (MH)
205 "When the tiger . . ." *AWD (Berg)*, 26 March 1938
205 "Well, here we are in Skye" *VW/VB*, 25 June 1938 (Berg)
206 "fearful niggling drudgery" *AWD (Berg)*, 19 July 1938
207 "They're telling us . . ." *AWD (Berg)*, 28 September 1938
207 "We have peace . . ." *VW/VB*, 1 October 1938 (Berg)
207 "Euston Road School" *VB/VW*, 6 November 1938 (MH)
207 that she lent Helen . . . *Helen Anrep to VB*, 1 November 1938 (CH); also *VB/VW*, 6 November 1938 (MH)
208 "If only I could ever . . ." *Helen Anrep to VB*, 1 November 1938 (CH)
208 deficit which never existed. *p.i.* (Dr Igor Anrep)
208 "We have reached a time . . ." *p.i.* (QB)
209 "Maynard, even Maynard . . ." *AWD (Berg)*, 11 April 1939
209 alert, "screwed up shrunk . . ." *AWD (Berg)*, 29 January 1939

REFERENCES

209 "For the first time for weeks . . ." *AWD* (*Berg*), 12 July 1939
210 "last year's mad voice" *AWD* (*Berg*), 30 August 1939

CHAPTER TEN

Page
211 it was 'they' . . . *AWD* (*Berg*), 3 September 1939
211 "we shall be attended to" *AWD* (*Berg*), 11 September 1939
212 T. S. Eliot wrote . . . *T. S. Eliot to VW*, 12 September 1939
212 "THE WAR BEGINS . . ." *AWD* (*Berg*), 22 October 1939
212 Mrs Sidney Webb . . . *MH/A 20*
213 "an outsider" *AWD*, p. 322, 18 December 1939
214 "Oh it's a queer . . ." *AWD* (*Berg*), 8 February 1940
214 a very severe criticism . . . *AWD*, p. 328, 20 March 1940
214 "It's *him* . . ." *AWD*, p. 328, 20 March 1940
214 "Since Julian died . . ." *VB/VW*, 13 March 1940 (MH)
215 "So my little moment . . ." *AWD*, p. 332, 13 May 1940
215 "I didn't want to be silent" *AWD* (*Berg*), 20 May 1940
216 "Jews were hunted . . ." LW, *The Journey* . . ., p. 14
217 "I can't conceive . . ." *AWD*, p. 337, 22 [actually 27] June 1940
217 "They came very close . . ." *AWD*, p. 342, 16 August 1940
218 . . . heard Vita's voice . . . *VW/VSW* [30 August 1940] (Berg)
218 ". . . what touched . . ." *VW/ES*, 12 September 1940 (Berg)
219 *The Leaning Tower*. Published in *Folios of New Writing*, Autumn 1940; reprinted in *The Moment*, 1947
219 "Our ignorance . . ." *The Niece of an Earl* in *The Common Reader: Second Series*, p. 217
219 "The subject of her writing . . ." R. L. Chambers, *The Novels of VW*, Oliver & Boyd, 1947, p. 1
220 ". . . je me permets . . ." *J. E. Blanche to VW*, 18 September 1938 (MH)
220 He wrote to Virginia . . . *B. Nicolson to VW*, 6 and 19 August 1940 (MH); also *VW to B. Nicolson*, 13 and 24 August 1940
222 *Anon* . . . *MH/B 8a–d*; also *p.i.* (QB)
222 "I wish I were Queen Victoria" *VW/VSW*, 29 November 1940 (Berg)
223 "a life that rings . . ." *AWD*, p. 353, 29 September 1940
224 . . . when Morgan wrote . . . *EMF/VW*, 4 November 1940
224 "a sop" to public opinion. *AWD* (*Berg*), 7 November 1940
224 "and she sat back . . ." Elizabeth Bowen, *BBC/TV Omnibus*, 18 January 1970
225 she would like to write . . . *VW to O. Wilberforce*, n.d. [4 March 1941] (MH)
225 for the next five days . . . *O. Wilberforce to E. Robins*, 27 March 1941; also *ditto*, 28 February, 14, 20 and 28/29 March 1941 (MH)
226 at about 11.30 . . . *The Brighton Argus*, 19 April 1941; also *VB/VSW*, 29 April 1941 (Berg)
226 "the one experience . . ." *AWD* (*Berg*), 23 November 1926

A Short Bibliography

(English editions are published in London, American in New York,
unless otherwise indicated; page references are to English editions)

ANNAN, Noel Gilroy: *Leslie Stephen; his thought and character in relation to his time.*
MacGibbon & Kee, 1951; Cambridge, Mass.: Harvard University Press, 1952

BELL, Clive: *Old Friends: Personal Recollections.* Chatto & Windus, 1956; Harcourt
Brace Jovanovich, 1957

BELL, Julian (and others): *Julian Bell: Essays, Poems and Letters.* Edited by Quentin
Bell. Hogarth Press, 1938

BELL, Quentin: *Bloomsbury.* Weidenfeld & Nicolson, 1968; Basic Books, 1969

CARRINGTON, Dora: *Carrington: Letters and Extracts from her Diaries.* Edited by
David Garnett. Jonathan Cape, 1970

FORSTER, E. M.: *Virginia Woolf.* (The Rede Lecture.) Cambridge University Press,
1942; Harcourt Brace Jovanovich, 1942

FRY, Roger: *Letters of Roger Fry.* Edited by Denys Sutton. Chatto & Windus, 1972

GARNETT, David: *The Golden Echo.* Chatto & Windus, 1953; Harcourt Brace
Jovanovich, 1954

The Flowers of the Forest. Chatto & Windus, 1955; Harcourt Brace Jovanovich,
1956

The Familiar Faces. Chatto & Windus, 1962; Harcourt Brace Jovanovich, 1963

GRANT, Duncan: "Virginia Woolf" in *Horizon*, Volume III, no. 18, June 1941

HARROD, Roy: *The Life of John Maynard Keynes.* Macmillan, 1951; Harcourt
Brace Jovanovich, 1951

HASSALL, Christopher: *Rupert Brooke. A Biography.* Faber, 1964; Harcourt Brace
Jovanovich, 1964

HOLROYD, Michael: *Lytton Strachey. A Critical Biography.* Volume I, *The Unknown
Years.* 1967. Volume II, *The Years of Achievement.* 1968. Heinemann; Holt,
Rinehart & Winston, 1968

JOHNSTONE, J. K.: *The Bloomsbury Group.* Secker & Warburg, 1954; Noonday
Press, 1954

KENNEDY, Richard: *A Boy at the Hogarth Press.* Whittington Press, 1972

KEYNES, John Maynard: *Two Memoirs.* Hart-Davis, 1949; Augustus M. Kelley,
1949

KIRKPATRICK, B. J.: *A Bibliography of Virginia Woolf.* Second Edition, Revised.
Hart-Davis, 1967; Oxford University Press, 1968

LEHMANN, John: *The Whispering Gallery: Autobiography I.* Longmans, 1955; Harcourt Brace Jovanovich, 1955

I am My Brother: Autobiography II. Longmans, 1960

MAITLAND, F. W.: *The Life and Letters of Leslie Stephen.* Duckworth, 1906; Detroit:
Gale Research, 1968

MANSFIELD, Katherine: *Journal of Katherine Mansfield.* Edited by J. Middleton
Murry. Constable, 1927; Alfred A. Knopf, 1927

The Letters of Katherine Mansfield. Edited by J. Middleton Murry. 2 Volumes,
Constable, 1928; Alfred A. Knopf, 1929

MORRELL, Ottoline: *The Early Memoirs of Lady Ottoline Morrell.* Edited by Robert
Gathorne-Hardy. Faber, 1963

BIBLIOGRAPHY

NATHAN, Monique: *Virginia Woolf par elle-même*. Paris, Editions du Seuil, 1956

PIPPETT, Aileen: *The Moth and the Star. A Biography of Virginia Woolf*. Boston: Little, Brown, 1955

SACKVILLE-WEST, V.: *Pepita*. Hogarth Press, 1937; Doubleday, 1937

ST JOHN, Christopher: *Ethel Smyth, A Biography*. Longmans, Green, 1959

SPENDER, Stephen: *World within World*. Hamish Hamilton, 1951; Harcourt Brace Jovanovich, 1951

STANSKY, Peter and ABRAHAMS, William: *Journey to the Frontier. Julian Bell and John Cornford: their lives and the 1930's*. Constable, 1966; Boston: Little, Brown, 1966

STEPHEN, Adrian: *The "Dreadnought" Hoax*. Hogarth Press, 1936

STEPHEN, James: *The Memoirs of James Stephen. Written by Himself for the Use of His Children*. Edited by Merle M. Bevington. Hogarth Press, 1954

STEPHEN, Leslie: *The Life of Sir James Fitzjames Stephen, Bart, K.C.S.I. By his Brother*. Smith, Elder, 1895

STRACHEY, Lytton: *Lytton Strachey by Himself: A Self-Portrait*. Edited by Michael Holroyd. Heinemann, 1971; Holt, Rinehart & Winston, 1971

Letters, see WOOLF, Virginia and STRACHEY, Lytton

WOOLF, Leonard: *The Wise Virgins. A Story of Words, Opinions, and a Few Emotions*. Edward Arnold, 1914

Sowing: An Autobiography of the Years 1880–1904. Hogarth Press, 1960; Harcourt Brace Jovanovich, 1960

Growing: An Autobiography of the Years 1904–1911 Hogarth Press, 1961; Harcourt Brace Jovanovich, 1961

Beginning Again: An Autobiography of the Years 1911–1918. Hogarth Press, 1964; Harcourt Brace Jovanovich, 1964

Downhill all the Way: An Autobiography of the Years 1919–1939. Hogarth Press, 1967; Harcourt Brace Jovanovich, 1967

The Journey not the Arrival Matters: An Autobiography of the Years 1939–1969. Hogarth Press, 1969; Harcourt Brace Jovanovich, 1970

WOOLF, Virginia: for a complete bibliography the reader is referred to B. J. Kirkpatrick, *op. cit.* The following books by Virginia Woolf were all, with the exception of the first and fourth, published by the Hogarth Press in Richmond or London. Harcourt Brace Jovanovich published all but the second, third, seventh, fourteenth and seventeenth in New York, some in different years.

The Voyage Out. Duckworth, 1915

The Mark on the Wall. 1917

Kew Gardens. 1919

Night and Day. Duckworth, 1919

Monday or Tuesday. 1921

Jacob's Room. 1922

Mr Bennett and Mrs Brown. 1924

The Common Reader. 1925

Mrs Dalloway. 1925

To the Lighthouse. 1927

Orlando: A Biography. 1928

A Room of One's Own. 1929

The Waves. 1931

Letter to a Young Poet. 1932

BIBLIOGRAPHY

The Common Reader: Second Series. 1932

Flush: A Biography. 1933

Walter Sickert: a Conversation. 1934

The Years. 1937

Three Guineas. 1938

Roger Fry: A Biography. 1940

Between the Acts. 1941

A Writer's Diary. Being Extracts from the Diary of Virginia Woolf, edited by
Leonard Woolf. 1953

The following selections of essays and stories by Virginia Woolf were published
posthumously by the Hogarth Press and by Harcourt Brace Jovanovich:

The Death of the Moth and Other Essays. 1942

A Haunted House and other Short Stories. 1943

The Moment and Other Essays. 1947

The Captain's Death Bed and Other Essays. 1950

Granite and Rainbow. 1958

Contemporary Writers. 1965

Collected Essays. 4 volumes, 1966-67

WOOLF, Virginia and STRACHEY, Lytton: *Virginia Woolf & Lytton Strachey: Letters.*
Edited by Leonard Woolf and James Strachey. Hogarth Press/Chatto &
Windus, 1956; Harcourt Brace Jovanovich, 1957

INDEX

This is not an exhaustive index. For the sake of brevity I have used the following contractions: 'VB' for Vanessa Bell, 'VW' for Virginia Woolf, 'ref:' for referred to.

Index Volume I

Abyssinia, Emperor and Court of, 158, Appendix E, *passim*

Adult Suffrage Movement, 161, 167

Aeneid, 159n

Aeschylus, 68

Agamemnon, 119

Ajax, 139n

Albert, Prince Consort, 137

Allingham, William (author), 15

Alpine Club, 21

Ambrose, Helen, 136, 207, 209, 210, 211

Antigone, 68

Apostles (Cambridge Society), 7, 102, 120, 183n

Arnold-Forster, Ka (*née* Katherine Cox), described, 173; devotes herself to VW, 183; ref: 171, 174

Asham (Asheham) House his, discovered by VW, 176, 180; house-warming parties 182; ref: 184, 185

Atalanta in Calydon, 123

Athenaeum, The (club), 21

Authoress of the Odyssey, The, 11n

Autocrat of the Breakfast Table, The, 148

Bankes, William (fictional character), 118n

Bargello (Florence), VW tiresome in the, 143

Bath, Lady, 81

Bayreuth, VW visits, 148–51; ref: 101, 172

Beadle, General, Prince of talkers, 29

Bedford, Duchess of (*née* Adeline Somers-Cocks), 14, 20, 85

Bedford Square, 145, 171, 175

Bell, Clive, Thoby's friend at Cambridge, 69, 98; meets VW at Trinity Ball, 76; and in Paris, 89; contributes to *Euphrosyne*, 98; described, 103; marriage 104, 110; VW's varied opinions of, 114, 130, 135; flirtation with VW, 132–3, 136, 139, 142, 143–4, 163, 165, 166, 168, 171; literary confidant of VW, 135, 137, 139–40, 154, Appendix D *passim*; joins in teasing Miss Cole, 146–7; plans to live in France, 154; political activity, 161; concern for VW during her illness, 163, 164; breaks with Lytton Strachey, 166; meets Roger Fry, 167; goes with him to Constantinople, 168; breaks with Walter Lamb, 172; ref: 82, 95, 100, 101, 105 and n, 112, 121, 123, 124, 129n, 130, 132, 139, 146, 147, 155, 162, 166, 168, 172, 176 and n, 177, 179, 182, 187, 205 and n.

— Cory (brother of Clive Bell), 114

— Mrs (*née* Hannah Cory), 113

— Julian Heward, 130, 132, 152, Appendix D, 211

— Vanessa (*née* Stephen), born 22; relationship with Thoby, 22, 23; relationship with VW, 24; education, 27, 28, 50; views on George Duckworth's conduct, 43, 44; and Stella's illness, 57; comforts and falls in love with Jack Hills, 61, 70–1, 72, 81; resists her father's demands, 62–4; unsuccessfully launched in society by George Duckworth, 68, 75–6, 79; daily round, 72–3; friendship with Kitty Maxse, 80, 81; VW resents her happiness, 88–9; care of VW in second breakdown, 89; new ideas about art, 95; desire to be free of her relations, 100,

121; Clive Bell in love with, 104; illness in 1906, 109–10; marries Clive Bell, 110, 114, 115; libertarian views, 113, 124 and n, 129, 146, 170, 176n; on Hilton Young, 131; use of proverbs, 131n; birth of a son, 132; attitude to VW's flirtation with Clive, 134, 136, 142 and n, 144, 166; hopes that VW will marry Lytton Strachey, 142; dismayed by Dreadnought Hoax, 158, 160; political views, 161; rejects VW's accounts of her, 162, 163; care for VW's health, 163, 164–165, 166, 182; meets, travels and falls in love with Roger Fry, 167, 168–9; 'noble and divine', 171; 'a South American forest', 172; reassures George Duckworth, 175; approves of Leonard Woolf, 177, 182; identified as *Helen Ambrose* by Clive, 210; ref: 26, 31, 35, 37n, 40, 46, 48, 49, 52, 53, 54, 65, 66, 70, 75, 84, 91, 92, 95, 96n, 97, 99, 118, 120, 128n, 129n, 131, 137, 139, 142, 143, 146, 147, 150, 152, 154, 163, 167, 170, 176, 177, 179, 184, 187
— William Heward, 113
Bells (family of William Heward Bell), described, 113; ref: 114, 122, 152
— (family of Clive Bell), 122, 123, 133–4, 136, 142, 152, 155, 162, 165, 169, 176n, 182
Bentham, Jeremy, 4, 8, 75
Bentinck, Lord Henry, 145
Bernard (fictional character), 110
Birrell, Francis, 173 n
Blake, William, 94
Bloomsbury (a district), a bad address, 94; Kitty Maxse screams against it, 94–5; ref: 114, 131, 183
— (a group of friends), effects of Thoby's death upon, 113; two centres, 115;

composition in 1908, 123; bawdy, 125, 170; and G. E. Moore, 139; Ottoline's contribution, 145; a party described, 146; plans to end it, 154; Roger Fry joins, 167, 168; Leonard Woolf part of, 180; ref: 100, 105, 173 and n, 177, 179. (*See also* Thursday evenings, Fitzroy Square *and* Gordon Square)
Bognor, its horrors, 52
Booth, Charles 73, 74
Brighton, detested by VW, 54, 59; ref: 31, 142
Broadbent, Dr, 56
Brooke, Justin, 173n
— Richard, 33
— Rupert, VW meets him as a child, 33; bathes naked with him, 174; ref: 171 and n, 173, 174 and n, 179, 183n
Brookfield, Mrs (friend of Thackeray), 62n
Brunswick Square, No 38, collective household at, 175; ref: 171n, 180, 186
Burley, Cambridge Park, Twickenham (a mad house), 164
Burne-Jones, Sir Edward, 15, 17, 30, 59
Buxton, Anthony, in Dreadnought Hoax, 157, 158

Cambridge, aesthetically blind, 103; VW's curiosity about, 112; visit of Sultan of Zanzibar to, 157; ref: 7, 8, 9, 21, 32, 68, 70, 90, 91, 94, 97, 101, 102, 103, 107, 116, 119, 124, 131, 144, 152, 154, 157, 167, 173 and n, 174, 177, 178, 179
—, Mayor of, 157, 160
Cameron, Julia (*née* Pattle), 14, 15, 16, 20
Cannan, Gilbert (author), 145
Carlyle, Thomas, 37, 41
Mrs Carlyle, 41, 83

Carmichael, Augustus (fictional character), model for, 32

Carnarvon, Countess of, 77, 78, 100

Case, Janet, a witness to George's endearments 43n; teaches VW Greek, 68; a confidant, 88; continues to be a friend, 120 and n; enlists VW for suffrage movement, 161; ref: 73, 172

Cat, The (poem by Lytton Strachey), 206n

Cecil, Lord David, 80n

Cecil, Lady Robert, 81, 107

Ceylon, Leonard Woolf departs thither, 101; his feelings about 183; ref: 142n, 171, 176, 177, 178, 180, 183, 186

— the Governor of, 184

Chamberlain, Austen (politician), 73

Churchill, Winston, 145

Clapham Sect, 3, 4, 6

Clifton College, 37, 50, 123, 152

Cole, Horace de Vere (hoaxer), 157, 160

Collegio del Cambio (Perugia), 138

Colonial Office, 4, 5

Colonies, Secretary of State for, 184, 185

Compleat Duty of Man by John Venn, 6

Constantinople, 109, 168

Cook, Ebenezer (art educationalist), 27

Cope's School of Art, 73

Cornford, Frances (poet), 173

Cornhill Magazine, VW writes for, 126; is rejected by, 154; ref: 94, 135

Cornwall, visits to by Stephen family, 30; VW's attachment to, 32; ref: 147, 155, 165

Costelloe, Karin, *see* Stephen, Karin

Costelloe, Ray, *see* Strachey, Ray

Cox, Ka, *see* Arnold-Forster, Katherine

Craye, Miss (fictional character), 68n

Croft, Augusta (*née* Vaughan), 67

Cromer, Lady (*née* Katherine Thynne), 81

Cymbeline, VW's view on, 68-9

Dalloway, Mrs (fictional character), 80 and n, 209, 210

Damien, Father (Belgian missionary), 143

Darwin, Gwen, *see* Raverat, Gwen

Dickie, E. M. O'R., 105n

Dickinson, Violet, described, 82, 83; in Florence with VW, 89; cares for VW in her second breakdown 89-90; joins party in going to Greece, 107; illness on return, 109, 110; Thoby's death concealed from, 110; misgivings concerning Headlam, 118, 118n; objects to Brunswick Square plan, 175; ref: 85, 88, 89, 91, 93, 94 and n, 99, 100, 104, 105, 107, 109, 117, 120, 121n, 122, 135, 137

Dictionary of National Biography, 38, 39

Dodd, Francis (artist) 145 and n

Doucet, Henri (French artist), 170

Dreadnought Hoax, 157-61, Appendix E *passim*

Duckworth (family), 20, 30, 78, 113, 121

— George, incestuous relationship with VW, 42, 43, 43n, 61, 95, 96, 96n; attempts to separate VB from Jack Hills, 70, 71, 72; social ambitions for his half-sisters, 75, 76, 77, 79, 81; courts Lady Flora Russell, 81, 82; marries Lady Margaret Herbert, 96; relationship with Bloomsbury, 95, 96, 98, 99, 121; disapproves of Brunswick Square plan, 175; ref: 13, 22, 26, 32, 53, 54, 57, 70, 73, 75, 87, 93, 100, 103, 109, 115, 118n, 161, 163, 175

— Gerald, disposes of Talland House, 45; in Venice with VW, 88 and n; sets up on his own, 95; ref: 13, 22, 26, 32, 53, 70, 73, 79, 115, 161

— Julia, see Stephen, Julia

— Margaret, Lady (née Herbert), 96, 100

— Sarah ('Aunt Minna'), described, 58, ref: 70, 88, 94, 95

— Stella, see Hills, Stella

Edward VII, lurking in the azaleas, 90

Eliot, George, 126

Etang, Antoine Chevalier de l', 14

Eton College, 32, 35

Euphrosyne, A Collection of Verse, ridiculed by VW, 98, Appendix C passim; name suggested by VB for Rachel Vinrace, 137; ref: 101

Euripides, 68, 73, 152

Farrell, Sophia or Sophy (cook), opinion of VW, 115n; ref: 31, 34, 63, 73, 115, 117, 159

Firle, Sussex, 166, 171, 172

First Post-Impressionist Exhibition, 167

Fisher, family, 30, 31, 59, 158

— Herbert, 58, 62n

— H.A.L. 14, 59, 107

— Florence, see Maitland, Florence

— Mary (née Jackson, 'Aunt Mary'), described, 58-9; critical of VB 72; of VW, 85; comic life of, 93; ref: 16, 50, 70, 75, 76, 95

— William Wordsworth, (Admiral), the Dreadnought Hoax, 158, 160, 215 216, ref: 34

Fitzroy Square, No 29, disreputable, 115; company at 120; lease ends, 175; ref: 117, 128, 131, 145, 152, 159, 166, 176, 180

Florence (Italy), its dark hotels, 88-9; unsatisfactory, 143; ref: 142

Forster, E. M., 171 and n, 177, 214

France, Bells plan to live there, 154; ref: 144

Friday Club, 105 and n

Fritham (New Forest), 68, 70, 82, 84

Frogs, The, 139n

Fry, Roger, meets the Clive Bells, 167, 168; in love with VB, 169; ref: 171, 172 and n, 177, 187

Furse, Charles (painter), 35n, 95 and n, 124

Furse, Katharine (née Symonds), 95 and n

Garnett, David, 173n

Grant, Duncan, friendship with VW, 128-9, 129n; part in Dreadnought Hoax, 157-60, 214-16; ref: 124n, 139, 146, 175, 177, 179, 182

Gibbs, F. W., tedious, 74, 75, ref: 62n

Giggleswick, Yorkshire, 92, 93, 94, 101

Golden Bowl, The, 177

Gordon Square, No 46, described, 94-95; convenient distance from Fitzroy Square, 115; exclusive society at, 121; play reading at, 123; ref: 92, 97, 98, 99, 101, 110, 113, 120, 123 and n, 128, 131, 134, 146, 152, 165, 166, 167, 170, 179

Gosse, Sir Edmund, 39n, 126

Greece, VW and party in, 107-109

Guardian, The (weekly periodical), VW's 1st article, 93 and n; ref: 126, 143 and n

Hakluyt's Voyages, 51

Haldane, R. B. (Liberal statesman), 94

Hambantota District, 178, 179

Hardy, Thomas, 138

Harry Richmond, 138

Hathaway, Anne, 11

Haworth Parsonage, VW article on, 93 and n, 94 and n

Hawthorne, Nathaniel, 51, 57

Hawtrey, R. G. (civil servant), 97, 101

Headlam Walter (Hellenist), flirtation with VW, 118-19; ref: 30, 124, 135

Herbert, Lady Margaret, *see* Duckworth, Margaret

Hilbery, Mrs (fictional character), 11

Hills, Mrs (mother of Jack and Eustace), disliked by VW, 61

— Eustace, 53 and n

Hills, Herbert (Judge, father of Jack and Eustace), 61

— Jack (John Waller), pursuit of Stella, 33, 46, 47, 51; family and character, 45, 46; accepted by Stella, 46, 47; difficulties with Leslie Stephen, 52 and n; marries, 52-3, 54; Stella's illness and death, 55, 56, 57, 61, 64; VB in love with, 70, 71, 72, 81; advises VW on Life of Sir Leslie, 91; to collaborate in writing a play, 125; ref: 36, 43n, 90n, 122

— Mary, Lady (*née* Ashton), 36n, 90n

— Stella (*née* Duckworth), pursued by Jack Hills, 33, 46, 47, 48, 52, 53; by J. K. Stephen, 36 and n; effects of her mother's death, 39, 41-2; wedding of, 53, 54; illness and death, 54, 55, 56, 57, 58; ref: 13, 18, 22, 31, 43, 45, 51, 52n, 63, 64, 75, 81, 115, 117, 118n, 122

Hindhead, Surrey, 45, 46, 109

History of Women (projected work by VW), 51

Holroyd, Michael, 73n

Homer, 131, 159

Hughes, Thomas (author), 15, 62n

Humphry Ward, Mrs, *see* Ward, Mary Augusta

Hunt, Hilary (son of Holman Hunt), 32

— William Holman, 15, 17, 36n, 71, 78

Hyde Park Gate, No 22, described, 22; ref: 35, 36, 46, 51, 58, 60, 62, 64, 74, 85, 87, 95, 96

— No 24, 47, 54

Hyde Park Gate News, described, 28-9;

later numbers 37, 38, 39; its end, 45; ref: 32, 51, 116

Ion, The, 139n

Ives, *see* S[ain]t Ives

Jackson, Dr John, 16

Jackson, Maria (*née* Pattle), wife of the above, character, 17; exhortation to her grandchildren, 38; ref: 16, 20, 28, 30, 32, 34n

— Adeline, *see* Vaughan, Adeline

— Julia, *see* Stephen, Julia

— Mary *see* Fisher, Mary

Jacob's Room, 32, 112, 143n

James, Henry, at Talland House, 32; on VW's friends, 99; reflections on VB's marriage, 114; VW's view of his writing, 122; and of him, 122-3, 122n, 123n; influence on Lytton Strachey and Leonard Woolf, 177, 177n; ref: 50, 57, 85, 103, 151

John, Augustus, 124, 144, 145

— Dorelia, 144

Juvenal, 139n

Kelly, Gerald (painter, later P.R.A.), 89, 103

Kensington, 74, 80, 95, 113

Keynes, Geoffrey, 173n

— John Maynard, accused of indecency, 170; described, 174-5; at 38 Brunswick Square, 175; ref: 124n, 173, 177

Lamb, Henry (painter), 105n, 146

— Nina, 145

— Walter, contributor to *Euphrosyne*, 98, 205 and n; on VW, 152; VW on, 153; sentimental excursion with VW, 170-2; breaks with Clive Bell, 172;

ref: 101, 123, 142 and n, 152, 153, 179, 181
Lapsus Calami, 35
Letter Game, 142 and n
Lettres à une Inconnue, 109
Life and Letters of Leslie Stephen, 27n, 91, 94
Little Holland House, 15 and n
Little Talland House, Firle, described, 166; VW leaves it, 176; ref: 167, 181
Llewelyn Davies, Margaret, 161
— Theodore, 120
London Library, 51
Lowell, James Russell, VW's godfather, 24–5; ref: 9, 32
Lushington, Katherine, *see* Maxse, K.
Lushington Susan, 61, 66, 67, 74
Lytton, Neville (painter), 105n

Macaulay, Lord, 50, 55, 57
MacCarthy, Desmond, his character 101, 102–3; ref: 176, 179
— Mary (Molly), 11n
Macnamara, Mrs, *née* Maria Bayley ('Cousin Mia'), described, 58; ref: 56, 70, 75, 95
Maitland, F. W. (historian), on Leslie Stephen's character, 63; VW assists in *Life* of L. Stephen, 91, ref: 27n, 94 (see also *Life and Letters of Leslie Stephen*)
— Florence (*née* Fisher), 91
Manorbier, Pembroke, VW's affection for, 87 and n; ref: 88, 115, 137, 139
Mayor, Robin, 101
Maxse, Katherine (*née* Lushington), engagement, 33; her tact, 74–5; described, 80; original of Mrs Dalloway, 80n; VB's friend, 81; appalled by Bloomsbury, 95, 99; ref: 54, 85, 100, 113

— Leopold, 33, 80
Melymbrosia (see also: *The Voyage Out*), 125, 135, 162, 176, Appendix D *passim*
Memoir Club, 125n
Memoirs of a Novelist by VW, refused by *Cornhill*, 153
Meredith, George, 30, 32, 138, 151
Merimée, Prosper, 109
Meynell, Alice (poetess), described, 143
Midnight Ride, The, 29
Mill, J. S., 6, 8
Milner, Sibella, *see* Stephen, Sibella
Moore G. E., his disciples, 100; ref: 70, 116, 139, 168, 173, 177, 179
Morley College, VW teaching at, 105, 106, 107, Appendix B *passim*
Morrell, Lady Ottoline, character and appearance 144–5; ref: 142n, 149n
— Philip, 142n, 145, 149n
Morrice, James (painter), 103

Nash, Rosalind, 161
Netherhampton House, Salisbury, 85
Neo-Pagans, 172, 172n, 173, 173n, 174, 174n
Nicolson, the Hon. Mrs Harold (*née* Victoria Sackville-West), 61n
Night and Day, 11n
Norman, Ronald, 74
Norton, Charles Eliot, 9
Norton, H. T. J., joins party going to Constantinople, 168; ref: 146

O'Conor, Roderick (painter), 103
Olivier, Noel, *see* Richards, Noel
—Sir Sydney, 173n

Painswick, Gloucestershire, 58, 61
Pater, Clara (teacher of Greek), identified as *Miss Craye*, 68 and n

Pattle, family, 17, 19
— Adeline (née de l'Etang), 14
— James, myths concerning him, 14
— Julia, see Cameron, Julia
— Maria, see Jackson, Maria
— Sarah, see Prinsep, Sarah
— Virginia, see Somers, Lady
Percival (fictional character), 112
Perugino, 138
Phyllis and Rosamund, 99
Plato, dangers of talking about him, 77; ref: 139n
Post-Impressionist Ball, immodest dresses at, 170
Post-Impressionist Exhibition, 167, 168
Pre-Raphaelites, 80
Principia Ethica, 177 (see also Moore, G. E.)
Prinsep, family, 20, 88
— Sarah (née Pattle), 14, 15
— Thoby, 15

Ramsay, Mrs (fictional character), 18
Raverat, Gwen (née Darwin) 173
— Jacques, 173
Religio Laici, 51
Richards, Dr Noel (née Olivier), 44n
Richmond, Bruce (editor), 104
Ridley, Guy (Dreadnought hoaxer), 157
Ringwood, New Forest, 65
Ritchie, Anne, Lady, (née Thackeray), character, 10, 11; marries, 12; her cruel optimism, 85; ref: 50, 70, 74
— Sir Richmond, cuts VB, 121
Rose (fictional character in The Years), 35
Rose (fictional character in A Society), 160
Ross, Mrs Janet (authoress), 143
Ruskin, John, 15n, 28

Russell, Bertrand, 120, 145
Russell, Lady Flora, 81–2
Rylands, George, 33n

Sackville-West, Vita, see Nicolson, the Hon. Mrs Harold
St Ives, journey thither, 31, 32; abandoned, 45; revisited, 104; ref: 30 34, 36, 66, 91, 132, 166
Sanger, Charles, 120
Savage, Dr George, medical advice to VW, 90; declares she is cured, 94; weak with VW, 165; continued misgivings, 166; ref: 95, 96n, 110, 172
Scenes of Clerical Life, 126
Scott, Sir Walter, 6, 27, 50
Seton, Dr, treats VW in 1st breakdown, 45 and n, 50; treats Stella, 55; and Leslie Stephen, 84
Seton, Sally (fictional character), identified, 61n
Shakespeare, VW's early views on, 68–9; ref: 70, 80, 123
Sheepshanks, Mary, persuades VW to teach at Morley College, 105; condemns her teaching, 106; low opinion of her intellect, 122; ref: 120, 136, 173
Shiel, Dr J., 120n
Shove, Gerald, 173n
Slave Trade, campaign against, 4, 5
Smith, Reginald, rejects contribution by VW, 153, 154
Snowden, Margery (painter), 81, 144
Society, A, story by VW, 160
Somers, Virginia, Countess (née Pattle), 14, 15n, 30
Somers-Cocks, Adeline, see Bedford, Duchess of
— Isabel, see Somerset, Lady Isabel
Somerset, Isabel, Lady Henry Somerset, 14, 15
Sophia, sometimes Sophy, see Farrell

Sophocles, 73

Stephen, family (general), origins, 1; born with little tails, 18–19; ref: 79, 80

— family (other than the Leslie Stephens), 20, 30

Stephen, family (of James Fitzjames), 59, 74, 160

— family (Leslie, Julia and their children), education, 26; manner of life, 30; 'felicious', 35; choice of physicians, 110; ref: 20–1, 22, 30, 31, 35n, 39n, 65, 98, 99, 100, 102

— family (children of Leslie and Julia Stephen), an isolated group? 33; Leonard Woolf dines with, 101; plans for Greece in 1906, 107; ref: 28, 83, 87, 88, 90, 94, 95, 96, 107, 123, 131

— family (girls—the Miss Stephens), seek liberty not licence, 96–7; portrayed by VW, 99; as seen by Desmond MacCarthy, 103; ref: 27, 30, 74, 80, 97, 99, 170

— Adrian Leslie, birth, 22; can't go to the Lighthouse, 32; cramped in the womb? 38–9; Stella's care for, 42, 47; with VW to Spain and Portugal, 104; to Greece, 109; to Fitzroy Square, 114–15; his character, 116; his life with VW, 117; a wife for Lytton? 129; VW tired of living with him, 134, 141; his diary, 145–7; at Bayreuth, 148–9, 150–1; to act, 154, 155; role in Dreadnought Hoax, 157–60, 214, 215; to Brunswick Square, 175; ref: 23, 24, 31, 33n, 34n, 37 and n, 50, 52, 62, 65, 70, 74, 79, 84, 90, 94, 95, 105, 109, 113, 120, 122, 123, 129, 132, 136, 143, 144, 149n, 152, 171, 174, 182, 183

— Caroline Emelia ('Nun' or 'Quaker', her character, 6–7; unfit companion for Leslie, 12; last visit to Leslie, 85; care for VW, 90, 91; VW writes comic life of, 93; death and obituary, 143; ref: 59, 63

— Dorothea (daughter of Fitzjames), described, 60; censures VW, 160

Stephen, Harriet Marian (née Thackeray, 'Minnie'), marries Leslie, 10; death, 11–12; ref: 13

— Harry (son of James Fitzjames), 59, 160

— Herbert (son of James Fitzjames), 59

— James (of Ardenbraught), 1

— James (son of James of Ardenbraught), 1, 2, 19, 20

— James (Master in Chancery), education, 2; guided by God, 3; and Clapham Sect 4; ref: 19

— Sir James (Colonial Under-Secretary), early career, 4; policy, 5; marriage, 6; ref: 9, 19, 20

— Sir James Fitzjames, character and opinions, 7; social and religious views, 8; melancholy end, 36; ref: 5–6, 7, 9, 10, 19, 22

— James Kenneth (author), described, 35; goes mad, 36

— Julia (née Jackson), widow of Herbert Duckworth, 13; engaged to Leslie Stephen, 14; described, 17–18; educates her children, 26; critic of VW's earliest writings, 29; creator of family happiness, 35; illness and death, 37–9; effects of her death, 40–41; attitude to Jack Hills, 46, 47; ref: 20, 21, 28, 31, 32, 34n, 36, 59, 63, 64, 115, 118, 175

— Lady (née Jane Catherine Venn), 5, 6

— Katherine (daughter of Sir James Fitzjames), 59, 97

— Karin (née Costelloe), 173

— Laura (daughter of Leslie), birth, 11;

mental deficiency, 12; ref: 22, 26, 35
— Leslie, education, 7; loss of faith, 8–9; first marriage, 10, 11; widowed, 12; remarries, 14; portrait of Julia, 17–18; educates his children, 26, 27, 27n, 50, 51; financial anxieties, 39n; reactions to Julia's death, 40–41; resents Stella's engagement, 46, 47, 48, 52, 53; reconciled, 54; anger with VB, 62, 63, 64; refuses to intervene in her love affair, 72; his day, 73, 74, 75; accepts K.C.B., 82; has cancer, 82; illness and death, 84, 85, 86; mourned by VW; 87; biography of, 91; ref: 6, 19, 21, 28, 29, 31, 33, 36, 39, 43, 55, 60, 62, 62n, 70, 72, 89, 90, 91, 94, 96, 104, 114, 115, 116, 123, 124, 131
— Lady (née Mary Cunningham wife of Fitzjames, 'Aunt Stephen'), 8, 59, 66, 70
— Minny, see Harriet Marian
— Sibella (née Milner), 1, 2
— Thoby, birth, 18; character as a child, 22, 23, 23n; intellectual influence on VW, 27, 68; contributions to Hyde Park Gate News, 28, 29; at Clifton, 37, 50, at Cambridge, 70; reproves VB, 72; his 'Thursday Evenings, 97–9; his friends 'unsuitable', 100, 101; visit to Greece, illness, death, 109–10; efforts to commemorate, 112; possible influence on Bloomsbury, 113; ref: 24, 26, 31, 33n, 53, 55n, 65, 71, 76, 82, 84, 89, 90, 94, 95, 97, 98, 102, 104, 105, 114, 115, 116, 117, 120, 130
— Vanessa, see Bell, Vanessa
— Virginia, see Woolf, Virginia
— William (son of James Stephen of Ardenbraught), 1, 3
Strachey (family), described, 102; ref: 20

— James, 146, 171 and n, 173n
— Lytton, Thoby's friend, 69; contribution to Euphrosyne, 98; pre-eminent among his friends, 102; his sympathy, 113; he inspires awe, 121; makes Bloomsbury bawdy, 124 and n; character 129–30; VW's feeling for, 131; proposal, 141, 142 and n; VW's continued regard, 144, 186; breaks with Clive Bell, 166; relationship with Leonard Woolf, 177 and n, 178–79; ref: 70, 101, 112, 116, 119, 123, 128, 132, 134, 135, 142 and n, 143, 146, 152, 154, 166, 171, 173, 176, 183, 205 and n
— Marjorie, 166, 173, 179, 182
— Perneel, 105n
— Ray (née Costelloe), 173
Studland, Dorset, 152, 162, 165, 170
Swift, Jonathan, 18n, 101
Swinburne, A. C. (poet), 123, 206
Sydney-Turner, Saxon, Thoby's friends 69; a wit? 98; contributes to Euphrosyne, 98; his manners, 99; his, intelligence and sterility, 101, 102; considered as a lover, 128 and n; bantered, 147; with VW at Bayreuth, 149–51; his character, 151–52; ref: 97, 100, 103, 105n, 112, 113, 121, 123, 130, 132, 134, 136, 139, 142n, 162, 163, 166, 172, 176, 177, 205 and n
Symonds, John Addington, 60
— Katherine, see Furse, Katherine
— Symonds, Margaret, see Vaughan, Madge
Talland House, St Ives, 30, 31, 32, 37, 80, 104, 118

Thackeray, Anne, see Ritchie, Anne
— Harriet Marian, see Stephen, Harriet Marian

Thomas, Jean, care for VW, 164; accused of plotting, 165; to Cornwall with VW, 165; flings telephone from her ear, 172; ref: 166, 182

Thursday Evenings, started at 46 Gordon Square by Thoby, 97, 100, 101; revived by VW, 120; described by Adrian 145, ref: 131, 155 (see also Bloomsbury)

Thynne, Lady Beatrice, 81, 89, 115, 120

Times Literary Supplement, The, VW starts working for, 104; ref: 126, 153

Trachiniae The, 68

Treves, Sir F., recommends operation on Leslie Stephen, gives him six months to live, 84; ref: 86

Trinity College, Cambridge, 69, 97, 103, 152, 177

Two in a Tower, 138

Vaughan, family, 30, 31
— Adeline (née Jackson), 16, 60
— Augusta see Croft, Augusta
— Emma ('Toad'), friendship with VW, 60, 66; ref: 88n, 89, 137
— Halford, 60
— Madge (née Margaret Symonds), her character, VW's passion for, 60, 61; literary correspondance, 125; ref: 66n, 83, 92, 93, 95n, 96, 135
— Margaret ('Marny), her good works, 60; ref: 66, 67, 120
— Millicent, in search of matrimony, 29; marries, 37
— William Wyamar, 60, 92

Venn, Jane Catherine, see Stephen, Jane Catherine

Village in the Jungle, The, 183

Vinrace, Rachel (fictional character), 136, 209, 210

Virgil, 97, 159

Voyage Out, The (see also Melymbrosia) 80, 104, 109n, 125, 126, 136n, 139, 143n, 153, Appendix D passim

Wagner, 149

Ward, Mary Augusta (Mrs Humphry Ward), 74, 88, 121

Warboys, Huntingdonshire, 65, 66

Waterlow, Sydney, amiable, 166; repulsed by VW, 176; view of Bloomsbury, 176n; ref: 123n, 172

Watts, G. F. (painter), 15, 95, 124

Waves The, 32, 110

Wells, H. G., 161

Wolstenholme, Joseph ('The Woolly One'), 32; possible model for Mr Carmichael, 32n

Woolf, Leonard, a strange wild man, 69; first sight, of VW, 97; contributes to Euphrosyne, 98; his silence, 100; dines with Stephens before going to Ceylon, 101; asked to write about Thoby, 112; return from Ceylon, 171 and n, 176-7; discussed by VB, 177; friendship with Lytton Strachey, 177-8; administrative success, 179; in love with VW, 180-4; resigns from Colonial service, 184-6; accepted by VW, 187

— Virginia (née Stephen): I—Life and Opinions: birth, 18; appearance as a baby, 22; temperament, 24; called 'The Goat' 24; severe illness, 25; education, 26, 27; holidays, 30-35; experiences of madness in others, 35-36; her mother's death, 39, 40, 41; George's misconduct, 42, 43n, 44; first breakdown, 44; Stella's engagement and wedding, 48, 52, 53; her appearance in 1897, 51; Stella's illness, nervous condition, 54-5, 56; Stella's death, 57; view of relations,

58, 59; life and hobbies, 60; passion for Madge Vaughan, 60, 61 and n; joins in consoling Jack Hills, 61; witness of family scenes, 63, 64; of VB's love affair, 70–2; daily occupations, 73–5; social miseries with George Duckworth, 76–8, 79; unfortunate telegram, 81; feelings about Kitty Maxse, 81; passion for Violet Dickinson, 83–4; distressed by Sir Leslie's illness and death, 84, 85, 87; in Italy, 88, 89; second breakdown, 89, 90; convalescence, 90–94; first impressions of Thoby's Cambridge friends, 97, 98, Appendix C passim; second impressions, 98–104; to Spain, 104; return to St Ives, 104; teaching at Morley College, 105, 106, 107, Appendix B passim; to Greece, 107, 109; Thoby's death, VB's engagement, VW's conduct, 110–11; effects of Thoby's death, 112–13; feelings concerning VB's marriage, 114; move to Fitzroy Square, 115; life with Adrian, 117; flirtation with Walter Headlam, 118–19 and n; social life, 120–22; Henry James, 122; new freedom of speech, 124, 125; possible husbands, 128–32; flirtation with Clive Bell, 132–37; travel in Italy, 137–39; continues her education, 139; Lytton Strachey makes and withdraws an offer of marriage, 141; the Letter Game, 142; in Florence with Bells, 142, 143; her sad return, 144; proposal by Hilton Young, 144; friendship with Ottoline Morrell, 144, 145; social misbehaviour, 146–147; at Bayreuth, 148–52; plans to live in France, 154; sudden excursion to Cornwall, 155; Dreadnought Hoax, 157–61, Appendix E passim; political views, 161; work for adult suffrage, 161; unwell at Blean, 162–63; in nursing home, 164–65, convalescent, 166; takes Little Talland House, 166; sudden journey to Broussa, 167; friendship with Roger Fry, 168–69; advances by Walter Lamb, 170–72; meets Neo-Pagans, 172–73; friendship with Rupert Brooke, 174; with Maynard Keynes, 174–75; collective establishment at Brunswick Square, 175; leaves Little Talland and takes Asham, 176; declaration of love by Sydney Waterlow, 176; invites Leonard Woolf to stay, 179; he proposes, 180; housewarming at Asham, 182; ten days in a nursing home, 182; hesitations with regard to Leonard Woolf, 184–86; hesitations ended, 187

II—Literary Work: childhood decision to be a writer, 23; family storyteller, 25; Hyde Park Gate News, 28–30; contribution to Tit-Bits, 31; possible origin of To The Lighthouse, 32; later numbers of Hyde Park Gate News, 37; educated by Sir Leslie, 51; early writings, 51; efforts at descriptive prose, 65; epistolary style, 66–7; learning Greek, 68; views on Shakespeare, 68; idea of what she will write, 87; early journals, 93; article on Haworth Parsonage, 93 and n; assists in writing biography of Leslie Stephen, 91, 94; work for The Times Literary Supplement, 104; writes Life of VB, 122; exercises in 1907, 122; beginnings of Melymbrosia, 125; early works discussed with Madge Vaughan, 125–26; on Lytton Strachey's poetry, 130; Clive Bell's belief in her as a writer, 135, Appendix D *passim*; believes she will write rather well, 137; seeks a name for Rachel Vinrace, 137; asks Clive Bell's advice on *Melymbrosia*, 139–40; obituary of C. E. Stephen, 143 and n; *Memoirs of a Novelist* rejected, 153–54; end of *Melymbrosia* in sight, 162, 176

Woolner, Thomas (sculptor), 15, 17

Years, The, 35
Yonge, Charlotte, M., 29
Young, Sir George, 131
Young, Edward Hilton, a desirable *parti*, 131; proposes to VW, 144; ref: 101, 120, 132, 134, 136, 166

Zanzibar, 157, 160

Index Volume II

Abbot, The, 23

Abrahams, William, 255

Aldington, E. G., 86

Alice in Wonderland, 150

America, United States of, projected visit by Woolfs, 125

An Unwritten Novel, 72

Anny, Aunt, *see* Ritchie, Lady

Anon, projected book by VW, 222

Anrep, Helen, at funeral of Roger Fry, 179; relationship to Roger Fry, 179n; "much to remember her for", 180; wants VW to write Fry biography, 182; borrows £150, 207, 208; at Rodmell, 218; ref: 204

Arnold-Forster, Katherine (*née* Cox), at Holford with Woolfs, 15; discovers VW's attempted suicide, 16; reports on her condition, 26; marries, 108; dies, 209; ref: 5, 17n, 18, 20, 22, 63, 65

Art of Fiction, The, 134n

Asham (Asheham) House, honeymoon at, 4; later visits by Woolfs, 8, 12, 17, 19, 29, 30; broken into, 33; its rent, 39; lack of comforts, 55; the Webbs at, 61; loss of, 64, 65, 67, 68; mutilated by Cement Co., 169; ref: 20, 43, 53, 54, 60, 72

Aspects of the Novel, 134

Athenaeum, The, 69

Atlantic Monthly, The, 132

Auden, W. H., 158, 201

Avignon, 4

Bagenal, Barbara (*née* Hiles), at Asham, 33, 34; employed at Hogarth Press, 49; awakes passion in Sydney-Turner, 50; ref: 43, 46, 53, 75

Balzac, Honoré de, 174

Baring, Maurice, 112, 152

Bayreuth, 89

Beaverbrook, Lord, 146

Beecham, Sir Thomas, 170

Beethoven, 130, 157

Beginning Again, 11n

Bell, Angelica, *see* Garnett, Angelica

— Clive, feelings concerning Woolfs' engagement, 1; portrayed in *Wise Virgins*, 9; his view of LW, 10; describes LW's condition, 17; reactions to the war, 20, 31, 51; amours, 23; teasing habits, 55; quarrel with VW, 59, 60; flirtation with VW, 85, 86; game of 'boasts', 95; on Woolfs' morale, 111; admiration for Vita Sackville-West, 119; crisis in his affairs, 124-5; makes fun of VW, 126; thinks *To the Lighthouse* a masterpiece, 129; further quarrel with VW, 136, 137; description of VW, 146; thinks her in a bad way, 147; doesn't like *A Room of One's Own*, 150; ref: 8, 14, 44, 68, 73, 83n, 90, 113, 114, 116, 117n, 174, 177, 179, 182, 189, 255, 256, 257

— Cory (brother of C. Bell), 189, 256

— Julian Heward, early publications, 155; on his generation, 177, 178; advises against Roger Fry biography, 182; to China, 190; killed in Spain, 201-2; ref: 113, 120, 168, 170, 173n, 186, 189n, 209, 214; also Appendix C, 255-9 *passim*. (See also *Julian Bell, Essays, Poems and Letters*, s.v. *Julian*)

Bell, Quentin, 113, 118, 170n, 198, 204n, 258

Bell, Vanessa (*née* Stephen): I—
Relationship to VW as an author:
genesis of *Night and Day*, 32, 42;
woodcuts for *Kew Gardens*, 65; description of the moths, 126, 140;
criticism of *To the Lighthouse*, 127-8;
doubts about *Orlando*, 140; encour-
ages VW to write about Sickert,
173; views on *Roger Fry*, 182, 214

II—*Relationship to LW*: his engagement, 1; jealous of, 8; irritated by,
9; impatient with, 204

III—*General*: at VW's wedding,
4; advice on sex, 5-6; opinion of her
sanity, 8; assists in saving her life, 16;
reticent concerning past madness, 18;
reports on her health, 20, 26; living
with Duncan Grant, 31; blindness
with regard to the nuisance of her
children, 34; on finance, 38-9 and n;
on the 'servant problem', 55, 56, 58,
59, 64; accuses VW of mischief-
making, 59-60; at farewell party at
Asham, 67, 68; VW jealous of, 89,
110, 147; decorates 52 Tavistock
Square, 102; competence when VW
faints, 114; accused of indifference
to VW, 118; does not appreciate Vita
Sackville-West, 119; warns VW,
124; reads her letters aloud, 126;
fear of visitors, 130; negotiates
with Angus Davidson, 130; with
Woolfs in Berlin, 141-3; relations with Ethel Smyth, 153, 170;
entertains George Duckworth, 155;
doesn't like VW's hair style, 158;
tries to get VW to sit for bust,
161; grief at death of Lytton
Strachey, 164; and Roger Fry, 179,
180; blind to her children's faults,
190; death of Julian Bell, 202; an
'emotional wet-blanket', 203; alter-

cation with VW, 218; valedictory
note to, 226; ref: 17, 29, 44, 47, 68,
73, 77n, 83n, 85, 97, 116, 124, 139,
146, 152, 154, 155, 159, 169, 170n,
174, 182, 189 and n, 207, 209, 255,
258

Bells (family of Clive Bell), provide
wedding breakfast, 4; living apart,
31; VW dines with, 46; have four
servants, 56; ref: 37, 49, 149

Bennett, Arnold, 99, 104, 106, 111,
133, 174, 185

Benson, Stella, 113

Bentley, Richard, 98 and n.

Berlin, 141-3

Between the Acts (*Pointz Hall*, *Poynzet
Hall*), 205, 211, 222, 224

Bevin, Ernest, 187

Biron, Sir Chartres, 139

Birrell, Francis, 113

Bismarck, Prince, 189

Blake, William, 149

Blanche, Jacques Emile, on *The Niece
of an Earl*, 220

Bloomsbury (a district), VW removes
from, 7

— (a group of friends), VW remains
in, 3; depicted in *The Wise Virgins*,
9; stunted in the chrysalis, 21; scattered, 22; second-generation, 48; deplorable effect on the young, 49; servants in, 57; and Memoir Club, 83n;
and friendships, 90; its politics, 152;
disapproved of by Ethel Smyth, 159;
Roger Fry's contribution to, 180,
182; last party, 213; responsible for
the war?, 220, 221; ref: 143

Boulanger, Nadia, 197

Bow Street Magistrates' Court, 139

Bowen, Elizabeth, 210, 224

Boxall, Nelly, character, 57, 58;
negotiations with VB, 58-9, 64;

gives and withdraws notice, 121; quarrel with, 147; to leave but reinstated, 150, 154 and n; final departure, 176–7; ref: 36, 84, 111, 192, 193, 221

Brahms, 153, 170n

Brantôme, 159

Brenan, Gerald, on VW, 93

Brett, the Hon. Dorothy, at Garsington, 51 and n, 52, ref: 37

Bridges, Robert, 122

Briscoe, Lily (fictional character), 128

Bristol, 182

Brontë, Emily, 45

Brooke, Rupert, 107

Browning, Elizabeth Barrett, 160, 175

Brunswick Square, No 38, 1, 2, 6, 7, 15, 68

Bussy, Dorothy (*née* Strachey), 113

Cambridge, 9, 103, 104, 182, 224

Cameron, Charles Hay, 189n

— Julia (*née* Pattle), 189n

Cardinal Manning, 19

Carrington, Dora, *see* Partridge, Dora

Carroll, Lewis, 151

Cartwright, Mrs (employee at Hogarth Press), 112, 114n

Case, Janet, friendship with LW, 3; at Asham, 18; her death, 201; ref: 16, 19n, 22, 24

Cassis-sur-mer, 124, 125, 126, 127, 136, 137, 147

Cecil, Lord David, 90, 256

— Lady Gwendolen, 95

— Lord Robert, 197

— Lady Robert, 2, 31

Cézanne, Paul, 183

Chamberlain, Neville, 207, 211

Charleston Farm, rented by VB, 32; inhabitants in 1918, 58; described by VW, 32, 64; on fire, 213n; ref: 34, 35, 43, 59, 65, 66, 110, 114, 130, 149, 155, 198, 203, 210, 217, 224

Chatsworth, 118

Chatto and Windus, 155

Chevalley, Abel, 111

Churchill, Winston, 215

Civilisation, VW's opinion thereof, 137; ref: 126

Clarissa Harlowe, 105

Claik Lectures, 172

Clifford's Inn, Woolfs move to, 7; give up, 17; ref: 16, 21

Colefax, Lady, 95, 111, 113, 161, 213

Coleridge, S. T., 221

Common Reader, The, First Series (*Reading*), begun, 84; '80th systematic beginning', 105; publication, 108; ref: 87, 98, 98n, 100, 101, 112, 123. *Second Series*, 131, 163, 171

Conrad, Joseph, 50

Constantinople, 131

Cornford, Frances, VW's sarcasms concerning, 26; ref: 107

Cornford, John, 254

Cornwall, 19, 21, 37

Costelloe, Karin, *see* Stephen, Karin

Council of Civil Liberties, 36

Cox, Mr, of the London Library, 47

Cox, Katherine, *see* Arnold-Forster, Katherine

Craig, John, 189n

Craig, Maurice, consulted as to whether VW should have children, 8; further consultations, 19; provides LW with medical certificate, 30n

Critic in Judgement, The, 65

Daily Worker, The, 188

Dalingridge Place, Sussex, 16, 17

Dalton, Hugh, 257, 258

Darwin, Gwen, *see* Raverat, Gwen

Davidson, Angus, takes George

Rylands' place at Hogarth Press, 103–104; difficulties and departure, 130–131; ref: 113, 114n

Davies, Margaret Llewelyn, political influence on LW, 3; VW's feelings concerning, 24, 25, 25n; views on Women's Co-operative Guild and venereal disease, 36; ref: 17n, 22, 41, 43, 201

Day Lewis, C., 158, 186, 204n

Death of the Moth, The, 210n

Denham, Ralph (fictional character in *Night and Day*), 3

Diaghilev, 90

Dickens, Charles, 174

Dickinson, G. Lowes, 43, 180

Dickinson, Violet, VW's engagement announced to, 2; her wedding present, 6; tries to lend money to Woolfs, 40; ref: 16n, 26, 38, 68, 127, 175

Doran (American publisher), refuses *Monday or Tuesday*, 77

Dostoevsky, Feodor, 5, 99

Dove's Nest, The, 99

Downhill all the Way, 83n

Dreadnought Hoax, 217

Dryden, John, 132

Duckworth, George, at VW's wedding, 4; blamed for her frigidity, 6; offers use of Dalingridge Place, 16; employs Sophia Farrell, 57; reunion with, 155; death, 177; ref: 2, 170

— Gerald, at VW's wedding, 4; publishes *The Voyage Out*, 10, 11; views on literature, 74; ref: 2, 191

— Margaret, Lady (*née* Herbert), 101n

— Sarah Emily (Aunt Minna), 2

Dunkirk, 215

Economic Consequences of Mr Churchill, The, 114

Eliot, T. S., meets VW, 63; *Poems* published by Hogarth Press, 65; praises *Monday or Tuesday*, 78n; and *Jacob's Room*, 88; Fellowship Fund for, 86 and n, 87; VW would make literary editor of *The Nation*, 93; changes publisher, 115; conversion, 135; on criticism, 173; on the young, 177, 178; ref: 48, 74, 105, 113, 185, 212

Eliot, Vivien, 173

Elizabeth and Essex, 79n, 163

Eminent Victorians, read to VW, 54; publication and success, 54–5; ref: 48

Empire and Commerce in Africa, 74

Empson, William, 111n

English Review, The, 87

Ermyntrude and Esmeralda, 19n

Etchells, Frederick, 4

"Euston Road" School of Drawing and Painting, 207

Everest, Louie, *see* Mayer, Louie

Fabian Society, 12, 23 and n

Farrell, Sophia, 22, 56, 57

Fergusson, Dr, 84

Fête Galante (Ballet), 170–1

Fisher, H. A. L., 61

Fisher, Mary, 2, 4

Flaubert, Gustave, 134

Flush, progress of, 163, 172; taken up again, 171; published, 174; biographical interest of, 175; ref: 42, 160, 186

Forster, E. M., described by VW, 29; on *The Voyage Out*, 28; on *Night and Day*, 68; VW article on, 132–3; feeling for LW, 133; relationship with VW, 133–5; "timid, touching . . . charming," 138; on *Orlando*, 140; on *The Waves*, 162, 163; draws VW into politics, 188; reports ladies found impossible on London Library Committee, 191; discomforts of Monk's House, 213n; invites VW to join London Library Committee, 224; ref: 12, 35, 74, 83n, 86, 105, 111, 113, 129, 155, 185, 188, 204n

Franco, General, 209

Freshwater, 189 and n

Freud, Sigmund, 19n, 103, 209

Frogs, The, 92n

Fry, Margery, in Greece with Woolfs, 167, 168; hesitations concerning a biography, 182; *Roger Fry* approved, 214; ref: 179

— Roger, at wedding, 4; 2nd Post-Impressionist Exhibition, 7; discusses VW's health, 14; on Ottoline and VW, 44; on *To the Lighthouse*, 128–129; as the White Knight, 150; in Greece, 167, 168; his death, 179, 180; VW's flattery of, 181; relationship with Sir W. Rothenstein, 208; LW's lack of sympathy with, 214; ref: 20, 26, 43, 46, 47, 48, 83n, 88, 113, 126, 173, 174, 179n, 190, 192, 255, 258. See also *Roger Fry, a Biography*, and *Roger Fry Memorial Exhibition*, s.v. *Roger Fry*

Frys (sisters of Roger Fry), 182, 207

Galsworthy, John, criticised in *Mr Bennett and Mrs Brown*, 104, 105; ref: 106, 133, 185

Garnett, Angelica (*née* Bell), born, 64; VW makes an allowance to, 160; 21st birthday, 213; ref: 118, 124, 189n, 223, 255

— David (Bunny), to work on the land, 32; breaks into Asham, 33 and n, 34 and n; ref: 31, 35, 58, 185, 204n, 223

— Edward, 10

Garsington Manor, life at, 51, 52; ref: 31, 37n, 44, 99, 122

General Strike, 122

Gerhardi, William, 121

Gertler, Mark, at Garsington, 51 and n; suspected of mischief-making, 59, 60, 60n, 61; death of, 209

Gide, André, 188

Gissing, George, 174

Gloucester, Duke of, 190

Golden Bowl, The, 134

Gordon Square, No 46, 4, 12, 14, 38, 73, 79, 85, 90

— No 50, 137, 177, 255

Gosse, Sir Edmund, 132 and n

— Mrs, 76

Grant, Duncan, at wedding, 4; living with VB, 31; a conscientious objector, 31, 32; decorates 52 Tavistock Square, 102; illness, 124; supposed remarks concerning *To the Lighthouse*, 127; dances with Lydia Keynes, 213; *Anon* to be written for his benefit, 222; ref: 12, 33, 58, 64, 83n, 124, 128, 130, 141, 142, 147, 154, 155, 159, 169, 189n, 195, 206, 208

Greece, Woolfs in, 167–8

Green, Miss, 83

Greene, Sir Nicholas (fictional character), 132n

Hakyluyt, Richard, 47

Hall, Radclyffe, 138

Hambantota, 150

Hambro, Mrs, 206

Ham Spray House, 164, 165

Harcourt, Brace (Publishers), 87

Hardy, Thomas, 45, 108, 123

Haunted House, A, 78

Head, Dr Henry, VW his patient, 16; ref: 14, 138

Heard, Gerald, 188

Hebrides, 129

Heinemann (Publishers), 88

Henderson, Hubert, 138

Herbert, Aubrey, 101 and n

Here and Now, see The Years

Heretics (Society), The, 104

Higher Tregerthen, 65

Hilbery, Katherine (fictional character), 3

Hiles, Barbara, *see* Bagenal, Barbara

Hills, J. W. (Jack,) 2, 39n, 209

— Stella (*née* Duckworth), 39n

Hitler, 178, 186, 191, 194, 209, 212, 213

Hogarth House, Woolfs discover and take it, 21, 23, 25; life at in 1915, 29–30; life at 1916–1918, 35; departure from, 102; ref: 47, 52, 59, 61, 66, 71, 74, 76, 83, 84, 86

Hogarth Letters, The, 171

Hogarth Press, idea of, 23; capital for, 38; beginnings, 41; Publication No 1, 43; Woolfs working in, 49; assistants, 49; offer of *Ulysses* to, 54 and n; publishes T. S. Eliot, Murry and K. Mansfield, 65; Ralph Partridge employed at, 75–6; leaves it, 87, 88; uncomfortable period, 92–3; removed to Tavistock Square, 102; George Rylands employed in, 103; difficulties with Angus Davidson, 130; plan to end it, 131; *Brothers and Sisters* rejected, 146; John Lehmann's connection with, 158, 168, 201, 204; ref: 66, 74, 84, 113, 169, 197

Holford, Somerset, 14, 15

Holroyd, Michael, 218

Hope, Lottie, engaged by Woolfs, 57; differences with, 58, 59, 71; ref: 84, 154n, 255 and n

Hours, The, see Mrs Dalloway

Huddersfield, 205

Humphry Ward, Mrs, *see* Ward, Mary Augusta

Hutchinson, J. St John, 113

— Mary, quarrel concerning, 59–60, 60n; and *The Waste Land*, 86; VW embroiled with, 124, 125; ref: 61, 113

Huxley, Aldous, 51, 162, 185

Hyde Park Gate, No 22, 39

Hyslop, T. B., 8

International Review, The, 75, 83

Interpretation of Dreams, The, 19n

Irvine, Lyn, *see* Newman Lyn

Is Fiction an Art?, 134n

Isherwood, Christopher, 158, 186, 201

Jacob's Room, begun, 73; finished, 84; fair copy made, 87; published, 88; well received, 95; a dead end ? 100; ref: 42, 74, 77, 91, 98, 99, 133, 195

James, Henry, 45, 82, 123, 134

Jebb, R. C., 98 and n

Jessamy Brides, The, see Orlando

Joad, Marjorie, *see* Marshall, Marjorie

Jones, Ernest, 19n

Journey to the Frontier, 255

Joyce, James, 48, 54, 63, 73, 86, 105, 185, 200

Judith Paris, 161, 162

Julian Bell, Essays, Poems and Letters, 204n

Keats, John, 221

Kew Gardens (K.G.), success of, 65, 66; ref: 69, 72, 74, 77n, 133

Keynes, Geoffrey, 7, 16, 113

— Lydia, described, 90; Maynard in love with, 90, 91; with Berta Ruck and VW, 92 and n; marries, 114; her care for Maynard, 201; her last dance, 213; ref: 151

— Maynard, attitude to the war,

31; in love, 91; buys *The Nation!* 92; pamphlet on Mr Churchill, 114 and n; marries, 114; foretells catastrophe, 161; foresees failure of Asham Cement works, 169; on the young, 177-8; likes *The Years*, 200; illness, 201; on *Three Guineas*, 205; unwonted pessimism, 209; ref: 9, 37, 68, 83n, 87, 140, 155, 204n, 221

Keyneses (Maynard and Lydia), 90, 130, 132, 154

King's College, Cambridge, 178

Kitchin, C. H. B., 113

Knole, 132

La Fontaine, Jean de 148

Lamb, Walter, a figure of fun, 22; penchant for royalty, 23

Lansbury, George, 187 and n

Lappin and Lapinova, 208

Lawrence, D. H., only contact with, 65; ref: 50, 105, 151, 162, 185

Leaning Tower, The, 219

Le Grys, Mrs, remembered in *The Years*, 23; ref: 21, 22, 25

Lehmann, John, career in the Hogarth Press, 158, 168, 201, 204; enthusiasm for *The Waves*, 162; ref: 171, 186, 224

Les Rochers, Brittany, 210

Letter to a Young Poet, A, 171

Lewis, Wyndham, on VW, 183, 184; ref: 63, 192

Liverpool University, offers doctorate to VW, 172n

Lloyd, Marie, 77

Loch Ness, Monster of, 206

London Library, 47, 191, 207, 224

London Magazine, The, 86

London Mercury, The, 72

London National Society for Women's Service, 156

Long Barn, Kent, 111, 117

Lopokova, Lydia, *see* Keynes, Lydia

Lubbock, Percy, 134

Lucas, F. L., 90

Lyons' Corner House, 170

Lytton Strachey, a Biography, 218n

Macaulay, Rose, disastrous dinner with, 120-1; ref: 185, 191

MacCarthy, Desmond, resolves to write a novel, 23; his character, 81-3; conversation at Roger Fry's funeral, 180; ref: 43, 59, 83n, 138, 182, 188, 215, 257

— Mary (Molly), 12, 17, 23, 28, 83n

MacColl, Mrs, 47

Mackenzie, Compton, 185

Maitland, Florence, *see* Shove, Florence

Manchester, 77

Manchester University, 172 and n

Mansfield, Katherine, *see* Murry, Katherine

Mark on the Wall, The, 42, 43 and n, 72, 133

Marshall, Marjorie (*née* Thomson, known as Joad), 93, 103, 113

Martin, Kingsley, 170, 192, 206, 211

Martini, Simone, 96

Massingham, H. W., 92

Matisse, Henri, 7

Mauron, Charles, 188, 204n

Maxse, Katherine (Kitty), 87

Mayer, Louie, formerly Everest, 176 and n, 222, 223

Mecklenburgh Square, No 37, 210, 212, 218

Medea, 105

Memoir Club, 83 and n, 217

Men Without Art, 183

Mill House, Tidmarsh, 78

Minna, Aunt, *see* Duckworth, Sarah Emily

Mirrlees, Hope, 113

Mirsky, Prince, 183

Mitford, Miss, 175

Monday or Tuesday, 72, 77 and n, 78 and n, 87, 88

Monk's House, described, 66; sale of, 67; its advantages, 72; bath and hot water installed, 112 and n; journalist at, 200; bombs fall near, 222; ref: 68, 83, 100, 115, 139, 145, 146, 147, 154, 161, 164, 169, 193, 210, 211, 212, 213n

Moor, Leslie, 45

Moore, G. E., 215

Morrell, Julian, see Vinogradoff, Julian

— Lady Ottoline, sees the war as end of civilisation, 20; her brilliant parties, 22; described by VW, 43; her life at Garsington, 51, 52; tries to help T. S. Eliot, 86; advises against the Roger Fry Biography, 182; her death, 209; ref: 9, 12, 34, 99, 113, 175

— Philip, and the war, 31; at Garsington, 51, 52; admiration for VW, 129; ref: 43, 113

Mortimer, Raymond, 90, 113

Moths, The, see Waves, The

Mr Bennett and Mrs Brown, 104, 105, 106, 133, 184, 185

Mrs Dalloway, meditated, 87, 99, 100, 101; finished, 105; sent in proof to Jacques Raverat, 107; ref: 11n, 42, 74, 86, 98, 108, 112, 118, 123, 128

Mrs Dalloway in Bond Street, 87

Munich, 207, 210n

Murphy, Bernadette, 114

Murry, John Middleton, his character, 50; his pamphlet, 65; thinks VW at a dead end, 100; ref: 37n, 51, 69, 70, 74, 100

— Katherine (Katherine Mansfield), wants to meet VW, 36–7; relationship with, 37 and n; to dinner, 45; assessed, 45; cause of dispute between VW and Clive Bell, 59; reviews Night and Day, 69; relationship with VW, 69–71; her death, 91; ref: 41, 43, 46, 47, 48, 51, 65, 74, 99, 116, 117

Myers, Leo, 113

Nation, The, 92, 93, 115, 130

Newman, Lyn, née Irvine, 149

New Renaissance, The (see also Civilisation), 124

New Statesman, The, 212

New Weekly, The, 19n

New York Herald Tribune, 134n

New York Times, 200, 253

Nicolson, Benedict, 220, 221

— Harold, not jealous, 119; in Berlin, 141, 142, 143; leaves Diplomatic Service, 146; ref: 90, 113, 139, 162

— Vita (née V. Sackville-West), on VW's frigidity, 6; character of her relationship with VW, 115–20; at Charleston, 120; returns from Persia, 122; receives dummy copy of To the Lighthouse, 127; as Orlando, 131, 132, 132n; with VW in France, 139; in Berlin, 141, 142, 143; her deplorable friends, 146; on Ethel Smyth, 152; differences with, 163; VW out of love with, 183; critical of Three Guineas, 205; in aerial bombardment, 218; gift of butter, 222; ref: 90, 123n, 129, 154, 155, 175, 216, 226

Nicolsons (Harold and Vita), 116

Niece of an Earl, The, 219, 220

Night and Day, inception, 32; nature, 42; progress, 53; conclusion, 63; Katherine Mansfield on, 69; ref: 3, 47, 68, 70, 72, 133, 171

1917 Club, 45, 46, 48 and n, 50

Noel-Baker, Philip, 113

Norman, Montagu, 178
Northcliffe, Lord, 61
Northumberland, 20–1
Norton, H. T. J., 12
Nostitz, Baroness, 191
Novel Club, The, 83
Novels of E. M. Forster, The, 134n, 135
Noyes, Alfred, 95

Observer, The, 28, 200
Odyssey, The, 98
Old Bedford, The (Music Hall), 77
On Being Despised, see *Three Guineas*
On Being Ill, 115
Onions, Mrs Oliver (Berta Ruck), 91, 92 and n, 113
On Not Knowing Greek, 98, 100, 101
O'Riordan, Mr, 121
Orlando (*The Jessamy Brides*), conceived, 131; sources 132 and n; progress, 136; seen by LW, 138; publication and reception, 139, 140; ref: 42, 118, 136n, 172
Owen, Robert, 25n
Oxford, 51, 90
Oxford, Lady (Mrs Asquith), 224

Pargiter, Elvira (fictional character), 172n, 179
Pargiters, The, see *Years, The*
Paris, fall of, 94, 214, 215, 216
Partridge, Dora (*née* Carrington), burgles Asham, 33 and n; devotion to Lytton, 49–50; at Garsington, 51; transactions leading to marriage of, 79 and n, 80, 81; married life of, 81; despair of, 164, 165; valedictory meeting with, 166–7; death of, 167; ref: 37, 49
— Frances (*née* Marshall), 113
— Ralph, assists in Hogarth Press, 76; mistake over *Monday or Tues-*day, 77; dinner to celebrate *Queen Victoria*, 77; passion for Dora Carrington, 78, 79, 80, 81; leaves Hogarth Press, 87, 88, 93; on VW, 96n, 97–8; ref: 84, 85, 165
Passage to India, A, 133
Pattle, James, 153
Peace at Once, 31n
Peggy (fictional character), 179
Pembroke, Lord and Lady, 216
Penshurst Place, Kent, 216
Persia, 115, 120
Picasso, 7, 255
Pierpont Morgan Library, 41
Pilgrim's Progress, The, 105
Plato, 105
Plomer, William, 149
Pointz Hall, see *Between the Acts*
Polignac, Mme de, 197
Pope, Alexander, 136n
Portraits in Miniature, 163
Post-Impressionist Exhibition (1st), 207
Post-Impressionist Exhibition (2nd), 7
Potsdam, 62, 142
Pound, Ezra, 48, 54, 63
Poyntzet Hall, see *Between the Acts*
Prelude, 48, 49
Priestley, J. B., 185
Prison, The (piece for solo, chorus and orchestra), 157, 158
Pritchard, Mr (of Dollman and Pritchard), 102, 122, 218
Professions for Women, see *Three Guineas*
Proust, Marcel, 48, 138
Psychopathology of Everyday Life, 19n

Queen Victoria, 77, 79

Ramsay, Mr (fictional character), 89
Ramsay, Frank, 90
Raverat, Gwen (*née* Darwin), 107, 113

Raverat, Jacques, 106, 107

Reading, see Common Reader

Rehearsal, The, 113

Rendel, Eleanor, 157

Ricardo, David, 177

Richards, Noel (née Olivier), 64

Richardson, Dorothy, 73

Richmond, Woolfs settle there in 1914, 21; ref: 30, 62, 72, 82, 84, 87, 94, 102

Richmond, Sir Bruce, 47, 54, 84

Ring, of the Niebelungen, 12

Ritchie, Lady (née Anne Thackeray), 2

Robins, Elizabeth, 224

Robson, W. A., 202

Rodmell, 66, 83, 113, 146, 149, 176, 179, 198, 218

— Labour Party, 186

— Women's Institute, 217

Roger Fry, A Biography, inception, 181, 182; problems, 182-3, 183n; notes therefor, 191; beginnings, 194, 204; 'fearful niggling drudgery', 206, 207; discussed with Helen Anrep, 208; first sketch complete, 209; critics, 214; proofs sent off, 215; published, 216; criticised by Benedict Nicolson, 220-1; ref: 205

Roger Fry Memorial Exhibition, 182

Romains, Jules, 191

Room of One's Own, A, style of, 144; in proof, 148; published, 149-50; ref: 153, 156, 204, 221

Rothenstein, Sir William, 208

Rottingdean, 169

Ruck, Berta, see Onions, Mrs Oliver

Rylands, George (Dadie), 90, 103, 113, 131, 171

Sackville-West, Edward, 113, 125, 142

Sackville-West, Victoria, see Nicolson, Vita

St Ives, Cornwall, 19, 37

Salisbury, Lord, 31

Sanger, Daphne, 113

Sargant-Florence, Alix, see Strachey, Alix

Savage, Sir George, 8, 12, 13, 14, 16 and n, 19

Schleicher, General von, 178

Scott, Sir Walter, 212

Scottsboro' Case, 188 and n

Scrutiny, 168

Seafarers' Educational Society, 129

Senhouse, Roger, 166, 167

Sévigné, Mme de, 210n

Sheepshanks, Mary, 35

Shelley, P. B., 109, 221

Sheppard, Sir John, 132

Shove, Fredegond (née Maitland), 29, 29n, 50, 51, 52

— Gerald, 29 and n, 52

Sicily, 125

Sickert, W. R., acts Hamlet, 91; VW writes about him, 173, 174; ref: 182. See also Walter Sickert: a Conversation, s.v. Walter Sickert

Sidney, Sir Philip, 216

Simon, Shena (Lady Simon of Wythenshawe), 172n, 183n, 210

Sissinghurst Castle, Kent, 183, 218

Sitwell, Edith, 113, 148

Skye, Isle of, 205-6

Smith, Agnes, 205

Smith, Logan Pearsall, 74, 88

Smyth, Ethel, described, 151, 152; on VW, 151-2; first meeting with VW, 153; passion for, 154; speech to London National Society for Women's Service, 156; rehearses The Prison, 157; quarrels with VW, 158, 160; her woes and demands, 170; table manners, 170 and n; on Flush, 174; her festival, 176; comforts VW,

184; confidence in victory, 215; ref: 42, 163, 188, 192, 193, 195, 197, 218

Snowden, Margery, 96

Socialism and Co-operation, 75

Sophocles, 101

Spain, 92; see also *To Spain*

Spanish Civil War, 201, 202, 255

Spender, Stephen, 158, 184, 186

Squire, J. C., 46

Stansky, Peter, 255

Stephen, Adrian, shows Clive's letters to Woolfs, 1; relationship with LW, 8; reticence concerning VW's madness, 18; marriage, 31; supplies lethal dose of morphia to Woolfs, 216; ref: 39, 39n, 41, 71, 83n, 90, 113

— Ann, see Synge, Ann

— Caroline Emelia, 39 and n

— Dorothea, 84

— Karin (*née* Costelloe), 31, 71

— Leslie, 25n, 38, 47, 159

— Thoby, 39, 157, 202, 255, 256

Storm Over Asia, 142

Stowe, Harriet Beecher, 221

Strachey, Alix (*née* Sargant-Florence), 49, 50, 80

— James, 50, 164, 166, 167

— Lady (*née* Jane Grant), 60

— Lytton, Woolfs' engagement announced to, 1; LW stays with, 19; sympathy, 19n; attitude to conscription, 30–1; on Woolfs' dislike of neighbours, 33; on Katherine Mansfield, 36–7; Carrington's devotion to, 49–50; on Middleton Murry, 50; at Garsington, 51, 52; wants VW to review *Eminent Victorians*, 54; envied by VW, 55; advances to a stable boy, 57; success of *Queen Victoria*, 77–8; relationship with Ralph Partridge and Carrington, 78,

79 and n, 80; interest in Ralph Partridge's career, 87; *Elizabeth and Essex*, 140; seldom seen by VW, 155; illness and death, 163, 164; idea of a biography of, 165; ref: 9, 12, 19, 29, 31, 43 and n, 68, 83n, 88, 89, 98n, 166, 185. See also *Lytton Strachey, a Biography*, s.v. *Lytton Strachey*

— Marjorie, 23, 70, 91, 213

— Oliver, 12, 165

— Pernel, 43

— Philippa (Pippa), 156, 164, 167

— Rachel (Ray), 12, 29

String Quartette, The, 78 and n

Studien über Hysterie, 20n

Suffield House (*see also* Hogarth House), 21

Swift, Jonathan, 113

Swinnerton, Frank, 50, 183

Sydney-Turner, Saxon, at wedding, 4; passion for Barbara Bagenal, 50; 'never' seen by VW, 155; ref: 22, 46, 83n

Synge, Ann (*née* Stephen), 189n

Tavistock Square, No 52, described, 102–3; shaken by hotel music, 150; to be pulled down, 210; bombed, 218; ref: 115, 120, 130, 146, 176, 208, 210, 253

Tchekhov, Anton, 121

Tennyson, Lord, 189n

Terry, Ellen, 189n

Thomas, Jean, consulted by LW, 8; VW to stay with, 12; views on treatment of VW, 16 and n; VW's mind 'played out', 26

Thomson, Marjorie, see Marshall, Marjorie

Three Guineas (On Being Despised, Professions for Women), idea of, 156; work on, 191, 197, 198; work interrupted, 203; reception, 204, 205, 208; ref: 199, 206, 214

Three Jews, 43

Time and Tide, 200

Times, The (see also *Times Literary Supplement, The*), 77, 82, 209

Times Literary Supplement, The (see also *Times, The*), work for, 41, 47; ref: 45, 48, 54, 66, 183, 199

Todd, Miss, 111

Tolstoy, Count Leo, 134

Tomlin, Stephen, models a head of VW, 160-1; brings news of Carrington's death, 167; death of, 197

To Spain, 93

To the Lighthouse, meditated, 105; rapid progress, 120; Part I finished, 121; *Time Passes* written, 122; finishing, 123, 124; published, 127; reactions to, 128-9; ref: 42, 109, 111, 114, 132, 140, 157, 171, 197

Tree, The (projected work by VW), 163

Trefusis, Violet, 132

Trevelyan, R. C., 35, 53 and n

Trieste, 132

Trollope, Anthony, 134

Twickenham, 12, 13

Two Stories (*Mark on the Wall* and *Three Jews*), 43

Ulysses, 54, 86

Unwritten Novel, An, 42, 72, 73, 77n, 78n

Vaughan, Emma, 2
— Janet, 149
— Madge, 2, 149, 168
— Margaret (Marny), 2, 3
— William Wyamar, 2

Victoria, Queen, 189n, 222 (see also *Queen Victoria*)

Victory, 50

Village in the Jungle, The, 7, 9

Vinogradoff, Julian (*née* Morrell), 113

Vogue, 111

Voyage Out, The, completed and taken to publisher, 7, 10, 11n; appears, 23, 25, 28; ref: 11n, 29, 42, 47, 48, 69, 77, 87, 194, 195

Waley, Arthur, 163

Walpole, Horace, 212

Walpole, Hugh, VW's relationship with, 137-8; on *The Waves*, 162; ref: 138, 161, 185

Walter, Bruno, 178

Walter Sickert: a Conversation, 174 and n

Ward, Mary Augusta (Mrs Humphry Ward), 61

Warmongers, 31n

Warren Smith, Septimus (fictional character), 101, 107

Waste Land, The, 86

Waterlow, Sydney, 22, 23, 43, 83n

Waterlows (Mr and Mrs Sydney Waterlow), 29

Watkins, Ann, 113

Watteau, Antoine, 201

Watts, G. F., 189n

Waves, The, VW at work on, 148; work interrupted, 150; progress, 151; possible source for final passage, 154; final struggles with, 156, 157, 159; read by LW, 160; in proof, 161; Hugh Walpole on, 162; ref: 109, 119, 143, 144, 168, 171, 172, 195

Weaver, Harriet, 54

Webbs (Sidney and Beatrice), enlist LW for political work, 12, 23, 23n; at Asham, 61; a last view of, 212; ref: 76

Wedd, Nathaniel, 182

Wellesley, Lady Dorothy, 197

Well of Loneliness, The, 138, 139

Wells, H. G., criticised in *Mr Bennett and Mrs Brown*, 104, 105; VW's relationship with, 122; ref: 95, 111, 133, 185

Whitman, Walt, 190

Wilberforce, Octavia, 224, 225

Wise Virgins, The, 9 and n

Wissett Lodge, Suffolk, 31, 32, 41

Women's Co-operative Guild, 3, 19, 35, 36, 36n

Woolf family (mother, brothers and sisters of LW), 3, 9, 22, 35

— family (Leonard and Virginia—'Woolfs' or 'Woolves') to Clifford's Inn, 7; consult Savage, 14; at Richmond, 22; settled at Asham, 17; to Cornwall, 19; to Northumberland, 20; attitude to neighbours, 33; plan to buy a press, 38; their economies, 38, 41; keep two servants, 56; take Higher Tregerthen, 65; at Monk's House, 71; experiment with Desmond MacCarthy, 83; *To Spain*, 93; their unity, 94; social life in July 1925, 113; meet the Nicolsons, 116; disastrous meeting with Rose Macaulay, 120–1; to visit America, 125; troubles with Hogarth Press, 130; plan to end Hogarth Press, 131; to Cassis, 136; decide to see few people, 149; intervene to protect a whore, 150–1; to Italy, 126, 189; visit to Carrington, 165–7; plan to leave Rodmell, 170; to Ireland, 177; to France, 200; to Scotland, 205; visit Freud, 209; to Brittany, 210; wartime visits to London, 212; ref: 37n, 51, 87, 153, 176

— Herbert, 46

— Mrs (mother of LW), meets VW, 3; not at wedding, 4; tedious, 155; death of, 209; ref: 38, 46, 161

— Leonard: I—*As a guardian of Virginia Woolf's health*: records of her condition, 12, 13, 14; at Holford, 15; her suicide attempt, 16; his own health suffers, 17, 18, 19; analysis not attempted, 19n; apparent cure, 20, 21; relapse, 24; removal to Hogarth House, 25; VW's antipathy to him in 1915, 26; near to despair, 26; care of VW in 1915/16, 29, 30; role as family dragon, 34–5; restrains VW's generous impulses, 64; opposed to leaving Richmond, 102; promptitude in crisis, 114; regulation of VW's conduct in Berlin, 141, 142, 143; exasperated by her attendance at public meeting, 156; comforts VW when hurt by adverse criticism, 184; restrains her attempts at controversy, 185; conduct in matter of German excursion, 189; misgivings concerning *The Years*, 195; calculated falsehood, 196; diary entries in 1941, 224; consults Dr Wilberforce, 224, 225; dismisses reporter at Monk's House, 253

II—*As a politician*: political formation, 3, 7, 10; renewed activities, 23 and n; work with Margaret Llewelyn Davies, 25; attitude to the war, 30, 46; forms 1917 Club, 48; formation of League of Nations, 61; candidacy, 75, 77; views on General Strike, 122; rebuke to Labour candidate, 163; Labour Party Conference, 187 and n; on Munich Settlement, 207; on the war, 211; joins Local Defence Volunteers, 215

III—*As a publisher*: conception of the Hogarth Press, 23, 38; *Publication*

No 1, 43; work on Hogarth Press, 48; unable to accept *Ulysses*, 54; increasing work on press, 74; Ralph Partridge as assistant, 75, 84; George Rylands, 103; Angus Davidson, 130, 131; *Brothers and Sisters* rejected, 146; Hogarth Press to continue, 158; John Lehmann, 201, 204

IV—*General*: engaged, 1; trials of engagement, 2; return from honeymoon, 5; VW's frigidity, 5–6; work at Grafton Galleries, 7; attitude to 'Bloomsbury', 9–10; relationship with Clive Bell, 10; on neighbours, 32; first meeting with Katherine Mansfield, 37n; finances, 38–41; friendship with Philip Morrell, 43, 52; differences with VW on social life, 46; conduct in air raids, 52–3, 52n; employs Lottie and Nelly, 57; house-hunting, 65, 67; thinks Katherine Mansfield moved by spite, 69; misfortunes, 71; literary editorship of *The Nation*, 92, 93, 121; on VW's mundanities, 96; a late return, 100–1; social life and sciatica, 113; quality of his love for VW, 118; affection for Vita Sackville-West, 119; on VW's snobbery, 120; acquisition of a gramophone 130; friendship of E. M. Forster, 133; on *Orlando*, 138; VW's continuing affection, 139, 203–4; intervention on behalf of whore, 150–1; illness and death of Lytton Strachey, 164, 165; in Greece, 168; as a dog-lover, 175; advocate for Nelly, 176; opinion of *Roger Fry*, 182, 214; illness, 198, 204; impatience with VB, 204; sense of filial duty, 209; with the Webbs, 212; contemplates suicide, 216; thanks for butter, 223; valedictory note to, 226

Woolf, Virginia (*née* Stephen): I—*Descriptions of her person, occupations and character*: described in *The Wise Virgins*, 9; daily life and amusements, 23; at Hogarth House, 30, 35; excursions to London, 47, 48; hardships at Asham, 55–6; domestic compared with VB, 64–5; occupied by Hogarth Press, 74; in 1923–1925, 95–98, 113; habits of speech, 144–6; described by Clive Bell, 146; reviews her 'world', 155; her physical energy, 169; as an animal lover, 175–6; her voice, 200; her gaiety, 209–10, 210n; described by Elizabeth Bowen, 224

II—*Pathography*: sexual frigidity, 5–6; advised not to have children, 7, 8; deterioration in health, 7, 8, 11, 11n, 12–15; attempted suicide, 16; subsequent condition, 17 and n; improvement, 19–22; relapse, 24–7; criticism related to mental stability, 28 and n, 29; danger of visitors, 33, 34; return to normal life, 43; ill in February 1918, 53; again in 1921, 83–4; a mental tremor, 100–1; a state of mind, 109–12; collapse in 1925, 114; *On Being Ill*, 115; *sequelae* of Berlin, 143; reported in a bad way, 147; to lead an invalid life, 163; effect of adverse criticism, 183–5; close to collapse, 195–6, 197–200, 252; contemplates suicide, 216–17; euphoria, 218–224; final breakdown, 224–6; (*et passim*)

III—*Literary work*: end of *The Voyage Out*, 7; keeps a diary, 22; reactions to *The Voyage Out*, 28; *Night and Day*, 32, 42, 53, 63; *Mark on the Wall*, 42, 43; diary renewed, 44–6; sense of a change of style, 72; journalism, 72 and n; vivid experience in London, 73–4; advantage of being one's own publisher, 74; *The Common Reader* and *Mrs Dalloway* written concurrently, 98–100; *Mrs Dalloway*, 101, 105, 107; *The Common Reader*, 105, 108; on biographers, 109; *To the Lighthouse*, 105, 120, 121, 122, 123, 124, 127; reactions to *To the Lighthouse*, 127, 128–9; *The Waves*, 126, 148, 150, 151, 156, 157, 159, 160; *Orlando*, 131, 132 and n, 136, 138; *A Room of One's Own*, 144, 148, 149; *Flush*, 163, 171, 172, 174; attitude to the study of English Literature, 173 and n; *The Years*, 171–2, 176, 179, 182, 185, 189, 191, 194, 195, 196, 198, 199, 200, 201; *Walter Sickert: a Conversation*, 173, 174 and n; *Roger Fry*, 182–3, 183n, 194, 204, 206, 207, 208, 209, 214, 215, 216; *Three Guineas*, 191, 197, 198, 203, 204, 205, 208; *Between the Acts*, 205, 211, 222, 224; unpublished memoirs, 211; *Anon* (unpublished), 222. See also *Anon*, *Between the Acts*, *The Common Reader*, *Mrs Dalloway*, *Flush*, *Jacob's Room*, *Kew Gardens*, *The Mark on the Wall*, *Night and Day*, *Orlando*, *Roger Fry: A Biography*, *A Room of One's Own*, *Walter Sickert: a Conversation*, *Three Guineas*, *To the Lighthouse*, *An Unwritten Novel*, *The Voyage Out*, *The Waves*, *The Years*, etc.)

IV—*Literary friendships*: meeting with Katherine Mansfield, 37 and n; subsequent relationship, 69–71; views on the 'Underworld', 50; on *Ulysses*, 54; relationship to Lytton Strachey, 54–5, 163–4, 165 (see also Partridge); friendship with T. S. Eliot, 63, 86, 135; meets Wells, 122; and Hardy, 123; relationship with E. M. Forster, 132–5, 191; with Hugh Walpole, 137–8; with Ivy Compton Burnett, 146; with John Lehmann, 158. See also *Mr Bennett and Mrs Brown*; Eliot, T. S.; Forster, E. M.; Hogarth Press; Spender, Stephen; Strachey, Lytton; and *Other Personal Relationships*

V—*Other Personal Relationships*: with Leonard Woolf, 1, 4, 5, 9, 94, 139, 204 *et passim*; with Mrs Woolf (her mother-in-law), 3, 4, 155, 209; with Ottoline Morrell, 44, 209; views on 'cropheads', 49; relationship with Nelly Boxall, 58–9, 176; mischief-making and indiscretion, 59–60, 78–80; attitude to Clive Bell, 85, 137; to Lydia and Maynard Keynes, 90; to Berta Ruck, 91–2; to V. Sackville-West, 116–20, 183; to Philip Morrell, 129; to Ethel Smyth, 151–153, 159–60, 170; to Stephen Tomlin, 160–1, 197; to Roger Fry, 179, 180–1; Julian and Vanessa Bell, 201–3, 218; to Janet Case, 201; to Elizabeth Robins, 225. See also Anrep, H; Bell, C.; Bell, J.; Bell, V.; Boxall, N.; Colefax, Lady; Dickinson, V.; Duckworth, G.; Fry, R.; Grant, D.; Keynes, L.; Keynes, M.; MacCarthy, D.; MacCarthy, M.; Nicolson, V.; Smyth, E.; Stephen, A.; and *Literary Friendships*.

VI—*Public affairs*: accompanies LW to industrial areas, 10; on the armistice, 61–2; on the Webbs, 61; the post-war world, 76–7; General Strike, 122; Freedom of Speech, 138;

massacre of June 30, 1936, 178; pacifism, 186; anti-fascist politics, 186-8; in Germany, 189; Munich Crisis, 206-7; outbreak of war, 211; depressed by Webbs, 212; mistrust of patriotic hubris, 215; *The Leaning Tower*, 219-20; controversy with Benedict Nicolson, 220-1

VII—*General*: social trials of her engagement, 2, 3; and wedding, 4; reported to be losing her looks, 10; house-hunting, 21; intervenes on behalf of Duncan Grant with Lady Robert Cecil, 31; hates being burgled, 33 and n; attitude to neighbours, 35; income, 38-41; work in Hogarth Press, 41, 48; life at Garsington, 51-52; conduct in air raids, 53 and n; house-hunting, 65-7; attitude to assistants at Hogarth Press, 75; moment of depression, 89; move to Tavistock Square, 102; discontents, 115; a social disaster, 120-1; confidante of Clive Bell and Mary Hutchinson, 124-5; acquires a motor car, 129; and a gramophone, 130; religious opinions, 136; in Berlin, 141-3; adventure disguised as the March Hare, 151; hair curled, 156; welcomes end of Hogarth Press, 158; £860 in hand, 160 and n; on the young, 177, 178; in Rome, 189-90; guilt concerning nephews, 190; refuses a C.H., 190n; sells share in Hogarth Press, 201; in Skye, 205-6; guarantees Euston Road school, 207; lends Helen Anrep £150, 208; pleasures of country life, 213; thanks for butter, 222-3

Wordsworth, William, 221
Wright, Dr Maurice, 30 and n
Wuthering Heights, 28

Years, The, beginning, 171-2; air-raid scene, 176; beginning of difficulties, 179; a nightmare, 182; apprehensions regarding, 185; development, 189, 191-2, 193-4; VW near to insanity, 195-6; final stages, 198-9; reception, 200, 201, 203; ref: 42, 183, 198, 202, 258

Yegen, Spain, 93
Young, Sir George, 113
— Hilton, 113
Younger, Eve, 189n

Zennor, Cornwall 65
Zululand, 149